www.wadsworth.com

wadsworth.com is the World Wide Web site for Wadsworth and is
your direct source to dozens of online resources.

At wadsworth.com you can find out about supplements, demonstration software, and student resources. You can also send email to
many of our authors and preview new publications and exciting new
technologies.

wadsworth.com
Changing the way the world learns ®

From the Wadsworth Series in Theatre

Plays for the Theatre

Plays for the Theatre

A Drama Anthology

EIGHTH EDITION

Oscar G. Brockett
University of Texas

Robert J. Ball
University of the Incarnate Word

Australia • Canada • Mexico • Singapore • Spain
United Kingdom • United States

THOMSON

WADSWORTH

™

Publisher: Holly J. Allen
Development Editor: Greer Lleuad
Assistant Editor: Shona Burke
Editorial Assistant: Laryssa Polika
Technology Project Manager: Jeanette Wiseman
Marketing Manager: Kimberly Russell
Marketing Assistant: Neena Chandra
Advertising Project Manager: Shemika Britt
Project Manager, Editorial Production: Cathy Linberg
Print/Media Buyer: Kristine Waller
Permissions Editor: Joohee Lee

Production Service: Electronic Publishing Services Inc., NYC
Text Designer: Gopa
Copyeditor: Eileen Smith
Cover Designer: Preston Thomas
Cover Image: © Gerry Goodstein, Angela Vitale in Shelley's *The Cenci* at the Jean Cocteau Repertory Theatre, New York
Compositor: Electronic Publishing Services Inc., NYC
Printer: Maple-Vail Book Manufacturing Group/ Binghampton

Printed in the United States of America
3 4 5 6 7 07 06 05

For more information about our products, contact us at:
Thomson Learning Academic Resource Center
1-800-423-0563
For permission to use material from this text, contact us by:
Phone: 1-800-730-2214   **Fax:** 1-800-730-2215
Web: http://www.thomsonrights.com

Library of Congress Control Number: 2003103232
Student Edition ISBN: 0-534-57786-5

Wadsworth/Thomson Learning
10 Davis Drive
Belmont, CA 94002-3098
USA

Asia
Thomson Learning
5 Shenton Way #01-01
UIC Building
Singapore 068808

Australia
Nelson Thomson Learning
102 Dodds Street
South Melbourne, Victoria 3205
Australia

Canada
Nelson Thomson Learning
1120 Birchmount Road
Toronto, Ontario M1K 5G4
Canada

Europe/Middle East/Africa
Thomson Learning
High Holborn House
50/51 Bedford Row
London WC1R 4LR
United Kingdom

Latin America
Thomson Learning
Seneca, 53
Colonia Polanco
11560 Mexico D.F.
Mexico

Spain
Paraninfo Thomson Learning
Calle/Magallanes, 25
28015 Madrid, Spain

Table of Contents

Preface

he eighth edition of *Plays for the Theatre* is a substantial revision of its predecessor. Whereas the previous edition contained fourteen plays, this edition contains fifteen, including four plays that are new to this collection.

Selecting plays for an anthology is always risky business. For each play chosen, many others, perhaps equally worthy, must be rejected. In choosing plays for inclusion in the present edition, the goal has been to provide a selection of representative, culturally diverse plays from the past and present.

The works included in this anthology are drawn from many periods, ranging from ancient Greece, the Middle Ages, the seventeenth century, the eighteenth century, the late nineteenth century, and the twentieth century. As such they represent a wide range of drama and cultural perspectives.

As in the seventh edition, this collection includes plays by Sophocles, Shakespeare, Molière, Goldoni, Ibsen, O'Neill, Brecht, Williams, and Beckett as well as an anonymous author of a medieval mystery play. The eighth edition provides an even greater variety of world drama and cultural perspectives with its inclusion of a Noh drama—attributed to the Japanese master playwright Zeami—and an African drama by Nobel Prize winner Wole Soyinka. Finally, this edition contains recent American plays chosen for their dramatic power as well as their cultural diversity: these include plays by Latina writer Milcha Sanchez-Scott, Pulitzer Prize–winning African American dramatist August Wilson, and Pulitzer Prize–winning playwright Paula Vogel. Additional diversity is achieved through the inclusion of some plays that touch on homosexuality, although none of the plays is specifically about gay or lesbian themes.

Each of these plays is discussed at some length in a companion book, *The Essential Theatre, Eighth Edition*, also published by Wadsworth/Thomson Learning. This companion volume places each of the plays included in *Plays for the Theatre* within its historical and cultural context. Although each of these books can stand alone, together they provide a greater understanding of the plays than when used separately.

We would like to thank the reviewers who took the time to provide insight and guidance on this project: Kim Axline, Binghamton University, State University of New York; Valerie B. Brugh, Arkansas Tech University; Lyn Dutson, Mesa Community College; Thomas Ellis, California State University, Fresno; Melissa Gibson, California State University, Fresno; Jeffrey Milet, Lehigh University; Jon Pheloung, North Carolina State University; and James Worley, Angelo State University.

We would also like to thank the publishing team at Wadsworth: Holly Allen, publisher; Greer Lleuad, development editor; Shona Burke, assistant editor; Jeanette Wiseman, technology project manager; Kimberly Russell, marketing manager; Neena Chandra, marketing assistant; Shemika Britt, advertising project manager; Cathy Linberg, senior production project manager; and Lake Lloyd, senior production editor at Electronic Publishing Services Inc., NYC.

Oedipus Rex (c. 430 B.C.)

EDIPUS REX was first performed in Athens at the City Dionysia (a major religious and civic festival held annually in honor of Dionysus, the god of wine and fertility) in competition with works by two other playwrights. Each dramatist presented three tragedies and one satyr play each time they competed before the audience of approximately fifteen thousand spectators. Sophocles was awarded first prize for the group of plays that included *Oedipus Rex*, considered by the Greek philosopher Aristotle an ideal example of tragic form.

The most striking feature of Greek tragedy is the alternation of dramatic episodes with choral passages. In Sophocles' day, the tragic chorus included fifteen performers who sang (or recited) and danced the choral passages to musical accompaniment. Other typical features of Greek tragedy are the small number of individualized characters, the restriction of the action to a single place, the tightly unified plot, the serious and philosophic tone, and the poetic language.

The action of *Oedipus Rex* is extremely concentrated: A complete reversal of the protagonist's fortune takes place in a single day. The story follows Oedipus, king of Thebes, as he attempts to discover the murderer of Laïos, the former king, after an oracle declares that the plague now destroying the city will not be lifted until the guilty one is cast out. Oedipus' search gradually uncovers terrible truths about the past and his own origins. The initial suspicion that Oedipus himself may be the slayer of Laïos is rapidly followed by other electrifying moments (among them Iocastê's recognition that she is not only Oedipus' wife but also his mother), and the ultimate outcome: blindness, exile, and anguish for the once-powerful king.

Sophocles is admired particularly for his skillful management of extensive plot materials: He accomplishes the gradual unveiling of mystery after mystery and a steady increase in dramatic tension with the utmost economy of means. Although, like most great plays, *Oedipus Rex* is open to many interpretations, most critics have agreed that a central concern is the uncertainty of fate and humanity's helplessness in the face of destiny.

Sophocles

Oedipus Rex

ENGLISH VERSION BY DUDLEY FITTS AND ROBERT FITZGERALD

Persons Represented

OEDIPUS
A PRIEST
CREON
TEIRESIAS
IOCASTÊ [JOCASTA]
MESSENGER
SHEPHERD OF LAÏOS
SECOND MESSENGER
CHORUS OF THEBAN ELDERS

THE SCENE———*Before the palace of* OEDIPUS, *King of Thebes. A central door and two lateral doors open onto a platform which runs the length of the façade. On the platform, right and left, are altars; and three steps lead down into the "orchestra," or chorus-ground. At the beginning of the action these steps are crowded by suppliants who have brought branches and chaplets of olive leaves and who lie in various attitudes of despair.* OEDIPUS *enters.*

PROLOGUE

OEDIPUS: My children, generations of the living
    In the line of Kadmos, nursed at his ancient hearth:
    Why have you strewn yourselves before these altars
    In supplication, with your boughs and garlands?
    The breath of incense rises from the city
    With a sound of prayer and lamentation.
                         Children,
    I would not have you speak through messengers,
    And therefore I have come myself to hear you—
    I, Oedipus, who bear the famous name.
       [*To a* PRIEST.]
    You, there, since you are eldest in the company,
    Speak for them all, tell me what preys upon you,
    Whether you come in dread, or crave some blessing:
    Tell me, and never doubt that I will help you
    In every way I can; I should be heartless
    Were I not moved to find you suppliant here.
PRIEST: Great Oedipus, O powerful King of Thebes!
    You see how all the ages of our people
    Cling to your altar steps: here are boys

Who can barely stand alone, and here are priests
By weight of age, as I am a priest of God,
And young men chosen from those yet unmarried;
As for the others, all that multitude,
They wait with olive chaplets in the squares,
At the two shrines of Pallas, and where Apollo
Speaks in the glowing embers.
                  Your own eyes,
Must tell you: Thebes is tossed on a murdering sea
And can not lift her head from the death surge.
A rust consumes the buds and fruits of the earth;
The herds are sick; children die unborn,
And labor is vain. The god of plague and pyre
Raids like detestable lightning through the city,
And all the house of Kadmos is laid waste,
All emptied, and all darkened; Death alone
Battens upon the misery of Thebes.

You are not one of the immortal gods, we know;
Yet we have come to you to make our prayer
As to the man surest in mortal ways
And wisest in the ways of God. You saved us
From the Sphinx, that flinty singer, and the tribute
We paid to her so long; yet you were never
Better informed than we, nor could we teach you:
It was some god breathed in you to set us free.

Therefore, O mighty King, we turn to you:
Find us our safety, find us a remedy,
Whether by counsel of the gods or men.
A king of wisdom tested in the past
Can act in a time of troubles, and act well.
Noblest of men, restore
Life to your city! Think how all men call you
Liberator for your triumph long ago;
Ah, when your years of kingship are remembered,
Let them not say *We rose, but later fell—*
Keep the State from going down in the storm!
Once, years ago, with a happy augury,
You brought us fortune; be the same again!
No man questions your power to rule the land:
But rule over men, not over a dead city!
Ships are only hulls, citadels are nothing,
When no life moves in the empty passageways.

OEDIPUS: Poor children! You may be sure I know
All that you longed for in your coming here.
I know that you are deathly sick; and yet,
Sick as you are, not one is as sick as I.
Each of you suffers in himself alone
His anguish, not another's; but my spirit
Groans for the city, for myself, for you.

I was not sleeping, you are not waking me.
No, I have been in tears for a long while
And in my restless thought walked many ways.
In all my search, I found one helpful course,
And that I have taken: I have sent Creon,
Son of Menoikeus, brother of the Queen,
To Delphi, Apollo's place of revelation,
To learn there, if he can,
What act or pledge of mine may save the city.
I have counted the days, and now, this very day,
I am troubled, for he has overstayed his time.
What is he doing? He has been gone too long.
Yet whenever he comes back, I should do ill
To scant whatever duty God reveals.

PRIEST: It is a timely promise. At this instant
    They tell me Creon is here.

OEDIPUS: O Lord Apollo!
    May his news be fair as his face is radiant!

PRIEST: It could not be otherwise: he is crowned with bay,
    The chaplet is thick with berries.

OEDIPUS: We shall soon know;
    He is near enough to hear us now.
        [*Enter* CREON.]
                    O Prince:
    Brother: son of Menoikeus:
    What answer do you bring us from the god?

CREON: A strong one. I can tell you, great afflictions
    Will turn out well, if they are taken well.

OEDIPUS: What was the oracle? These vague words
    Leave me still hanging between hope and fear.

CREON : Is it your pleasure to hear me with all these
    Gathered around us? I am prepared to speak,
    But should we not go in?

OEDIPUS: Let them all hear it.
    It is for them I suffer, more than for myself.

CREON : Then I will tell you what I heard at Delphi.
    In plain words
    The god commands us to expel from the land of Thebes
    An old defilement we are sheltering.
    It is a deathly thing, beyond cure;
    We must not let it feed upon us longer.

OEDIPUS: What defilement? How shall we rid ourselves of it?

CREON : By exile or death, blood for blood. It was
    Murder that brought the plague-wind on the city.

OEDIPUS: Murder of whom? Surely the god has named him?

CREON : My lord: long ago Laïos was our king,
    Before you came to govern us.

OEDIPUS: I know;
    I learned of him from others; I never saw him.

CREON : He was murdered; and Apollo commands us now

      To take revenge upon whoever killed him.
OEDIPUS: Upon whom? Where are they? Where shall we find a clue
      To solve that crime, after so many years?
CREON: Here in this land, he said.
                             If we make enquiry,
      We may touch things that otherwise escape us.
OEDIPUS: Tell me: Was Laïos murdered in his house,
      Or in the fields, or in some foreign country?
CREON: He said he planned to make a pilgrimage.
      He did not come home again.
OEDIPUS: And was there no one,
      No witness, no companion, to tell what happened?
CREON: They were all killed but one, and he got away
      So frightened that he could remember one thing only.
OEDIPUS: What was that one thing? One may be the key
      To everything, if we resolve to use it.
CREON: He said that a band of highwaymen attacked them,
      Outnumbered them, and overwhelmed the King.
OEDIPUS: Strange, that a highwayman should be so daring—
      Unless some faction here bribed him to do it.
CREON: We thought of that. But after Laïos' death
      New troubles arose and he had no avenger.
OEDIPUS: What troubles could prevent your hunting down the killers?
CREON: The riddling Sphinx's song
      Made us deaf to all mysteries but her own.
OEDIPUS: Then once more I must bring what is dark to light.
      It is most fitting that Apollo shows,
      As you do, this compunction for the dead.
      You shall see how I stand by you, as I should,
      To avenge the city and the city's god,
      And not as though it were for some distant friend,
      But for my own sake, to be rid of evil.
      Whoever killed King Laïos might—who knows?—
      Decide at any moment to kill me as well.
      By avenging the murdered king I protect myself.
      Come, then, my children: leave the altar steps,
      Lift up your olive boughs!
                        One of you go
      And summon the people of Kadmos to gather here.
      I will do all that I can; you may tell them that.
           [*Exit a* PAGE.]
      So, with the help of God,
      We shall be saved—or else indeed we are lost.
PRIEST: Let us rise, children. It was for this we came,
      And now the King has promised it himself.
      Phoibos has sent us an oracle; may he descend
      Himself to save us and drive out the plague.
           [*Exeunt* OEDIPUS *and* CREON *into the palace by the central door. The* PRIEST *and the* SUPPLIANTS *disperse R and L. After a short pause the* CHORUS *enters the orchestra.*]

PARODOS

CHORUS: What is God singing in his profound   [STROPHE 1]
    Delphi of gold and shadow?
    What oracle for Thebes, the sunwhipped city?

Fear unjoints me, the roots of my heart tremble.

Now I remember, O Healer, your power, and wonder:
Will you send doom like a sudden cloud, or weave it
Like nightfall of the past?

Speak, speak to us, issue a holy sound:
Dearest to our expectancy: be tender!

Let me pray to Athenê, the immortal daughter of Zeus,

                                     [ANTISTROPHE 1]

And to Artemis her sister
Who keeps her famous throne in the market ring,
And to Apollo, bowman at the far butts of heaven-

O gods, descend! Like three streams leap against
The fires of our grief, the fires of darkness;
Be swift to bring us rest!

As in the old time from the brilliant house
Of air you stepped to save us, come again!

Now our afflictions have no end,   [STROPHE 2]
Now all our stricken host lies down
And no man fights off death with his mind;
The noble plowland bears no grain,
And groaning mothers can not bear—

See, how our lives like birds take wing,
Like sparks that fly when a fire soars,
To the shore of the god of evening.

The plague burns on; it is pitiless,   [ANTISTROPHE 2]
Though pallid children laden with death
Lie unwept in the stony ways,

And old gray women by every path
Flock to the strand about the altars

There to strike their breasts and cry
Worship of Phoibos in wailing prayers:
Be kind, God's golden child!

There are no swords in this attack by fire,   [STROPHE 3]
No shields, but we are ringed with cries.
Send the besieger plunging from our homes

Into the vast sea-room of the Atlantic
Or into the waves that foam eastward of Thrace—

For the day ravages what the night spares—

Destroy our enemy, lord of the thunder!
Let him be riven by lightning from heaven!

Phoibos Apollo, stretch the sun's bowstring,   [ANTISTROPHE 3]
That golden cord, until it sings for us,
Flashing arrows in heaven!
                    Artemis, Huntress,
Race with flaring lights upon our mountains!

O scarlet god, O golden-banded brow,
O Theban Bacchos in a storm of Maenads,
    [*Enter* OEDIPUS, *C.*]
Whirl upon Death, that all the Undying hate.
Come with blinding torches, come in joy!

SCENE I

OEDIPUS: Is this your prayer? It may be answered. Come,
    Listen to me, act as the crisis demands,
    And you shall have relief from all these evils.
    Until now I was a stranger to this tale,
    As I had been a stranger to the crime.
    Could I track down the murderer without a clue?

But now, friends,
As one who became a citizen after the murder,
I make this proclamation to all Thebans:
If any man knows by whose hand Laïos, son of Labdakos,
Met his death, I direct that man to tell me everything,
No matter what he fears for having so long withheld it.
Let it stand as promised that no further trouble
Will come to him, but he may leave the land in safety.

Moreover: If anyone knows the murderer to be foreign,
Let him not keep silent: he shall have his reward from me.
However, if he does conceal it; if any man
Fearing for his friend or for himself disobeys this edict,
Hear what I propose to do:

I solemnly forbid the people of this country,
Where power and throne are mine, ever to receive that man
Or speak to him, no matter who he is, or let him
Join in sacrifice, lustration, or in prayer.
I decree that he be driven from every house,
Being, as he is, corruption itself to us: the Delphic
Voice of Zeus has pronounced this revelation.
Thus I associate myself with the oracle

And take the side of the murdered king.

As for the criminal, I pray to God—
Whether it be a lurking thief, or one of a number—
I pray that that man's life be consumed in evil and wretchedness.
And as for me, this curse applies no less
If it should turn out that the culprit is my guest here,
Sharing my hearth.
           You have heard the penalty.
I lay it on you now to attend to this
For my sake, for Apollo's, for the sick
Sterile city that heaven has abandoned.
Suppose the oracle had given you no command:
Should this defilement go uncleansed for ever?
You should have found the murderer: your king,
A noble king, had been destroyed!
               Now I,
Having the power that he held for me,
Having his bed, begetting children there
Upon his wife, as he would have, had he lived—
Their son would have been my children's brother,
If Laïos had had luck in fatherhood!
(But surely ill luck rushed upon his reign)—
I say I take the son's part, just as though
I were his son, to press the fight for him
And see it won! I'll find the hand that brought
Death to Labdakos' and Polydoros' child,
Heir to Kadmos' and Agenor's line.
And as for those who fail me,
May the gods deny them the fruit of the earth,
Fruit of the womb, and may they rot utterly!
Let them be wretched as we are wretched, and worse!

For you, for loyal Thebans, and for all
who find my actions right, I pray the favor
Of justice, and of all the immortal gods.
CHORAGOS: Since I am under oath, my lord, I swear
    I did not do the murder, I can not name
    The murderer. Might not the oracle
    That has ordained the search tell where to find him?
OEDIPUS: An honest question. But no man in the world
    Can make the gods do more than the gods will.
CHORAGOS: There is one last expedient—
OEDIPUS: Tell me what it is.
    Though it seem slight, you must not hold it back.
CHORAGOS: A lord clairvoyant to the lord Apollo,
    As we all know, is the skilled Teiresias.
    One might learn much about this from him, Oedipus.
OEDIPUS: I am not wasting time:
    Creon spoke of this, and I have sent for him—
    Twice, in fact; it is strange that he is not here.

CHORAGOS: The other matter—that old report—seems useless.
OEDIPUS: Tell me. I am interested in all reports.
CHORAGOS: The King was said to have been killed by highwaymen.
OEDIPUS: I know. But we have no witnesses to that.
CHORAGOS: If the killer can feel a particle of dread,
    Your curse will bring him out of hiding!
OEDIPUS: No.
    The man who dared that act will fear no curse.
        [*Enter the blind seer* TEIRESIAS, *led by a* PAGE.]
CHORAGOS: But there is one man who may detect the criminal.
    This is Teiresias, this is the holy prophet
    In whom, alone of all men, truth was born.
OEDIPUS: Teiresias: seer: student of mysteries,
    Of all that's taught and all that no man tells,
    Secrets of Heaven and secrets of the earth:
    Blind though you are, you know the city lies
    Slick with plague; and from this plague, my lord,
    We find that you alone can guard or save us.

    Possibly you did not hear the messengers?
    Apollo, when we sent to him,
    Sent us back word that this great pestilence
    Would lift, but only if we established clearly
    The identity of those who murdered Laïos.
    They must be killed or exiled.
                         Can you use
    Birdflight or any art of divination
    To purify yourself, and Thebes, and me
    From this contagion? We are in your hands.
    There is no fairer duty
    Than that of helping others in distress.
TEIRESIAS: How dreadful knowledge of the truth can be
    When there's no help in truth! I knew this well,
    But made myself forget. I should not have come.
OEDIPUS: What is troubling you? Why are your eyes so cold?
TEIRESIAS: Let me go home. Bear your own fate, and I'll
    Bear mine. It is better so: trust what I say.
OEDIPUS: What you say is ungracious and unhelpful
    To your native country. Do not refuse to speak.
TEIRESIAS: When it comes to speech, your own is neither temperate
    Nor opportune. I wish to be more prudent.
OEDIPUS: In God's name, we all beg you—
TEIRESIAS: You are all ignorant.
    No; I will never tell you what I know.
    Now it is my misery; then, it would be yours.
OEDIPUS: What! You do know something, and will not tell us?
    You would betray us all and wreck the State?
TEIRESIAS: I do not intend to torture myself, or you.
    Why persist in asking? You will not persuade me.
OEDIPUS: What a wicked old man you are! You'd try a stone's
    Patience! Out with it! Have you no feeling at all?

TEIRESIAS: You call me unfeeling. If you could only see
    The nature of your own feelings…
OEDIPUS: Why,
    Who would not feel as I do? Who could endure
    Your arrogance toward the city?
TEIRESIAS: What does it matter!
    Whether I speak or not, it is bound to come.
OEDIPUS: Then, if "it" is bound to come, you are bound to tell me.
TEIRESIAS: No, I will not go on. Rage as you please.
OEDIPUS: Rage? Why not!
                      And I'll tell you what I think:
    You planned it, you had it done, you all but
    Killed him with your own hands: if you had eyes,
    I'd say the crime was yours, and yours alone.
TEIRESIAS: So? I charge you, then,
    Abide by the proclamation you have made:
    From this day forth
    Never speak again to these men or to me;
    You yourself are the pollution of this country.
OEDIPUS: You dare say that! Can you possibly think you have
    Some way of going free, after such insolence?
TEIRESIAS: I have gone free. It is the truth sustains me.
OEDIPUS: Who taught you shamelessness? It was not your craft.
TEIRESIAS: You did. You made me speak. I did not want to.
OEDIPUS: Speak what? Let me hear it again more clearly.
TEIRESIAS: Was it not clear before? Are you tempting me?
OEDIPUS: I did not understand it. Say it again.
TEIRESIAS: I say that you are the murderer whom you seek.
OEDIPUS: Now twice you have spat out infamy. You'll pay for it!
TEIRESIAS: Would you care for more? Do you wish to be really angry?
OEDIPUS: Say what you will. Whatever you say is worthless.
TEIRESIAS: I say you live in hideous shame with those
    Most dear to you. You can not see the evil.
OEDIPUS: It seems you can go on mouthing like this for ever.
TEIRESIAS: I can, if there is power in truth.
OEDIPUS   There is:
    But not for you, not for you,
    You sightless, witless, senseless, mad old man!
TEIRESIAS: You are the madman. There is no one here
    who will not curse you soon, as you curse me.
OEDIPUS: You child of endless night! You can not hurt me
    Or any other man who sees the sun.
TEIRESIAS: True: it is not from me your fate will come.
    That lies within Apollo's competence.
    As it is his concern.
OEDIPUS: Tell me.
    Are you speaking for Creon, or for yourself?
TEIRESIAS: Creon is no threat. You weave your own doom.
OEDIPUS: Wealth, power, craft of statesmanship!
    Kingly position, everywhere admired!

What savage envy is stored up against these,
If Creon, whom I trusted, Creon my friend,
For this great office which the city once
Put in my hands unsought-if for this power
Creon desires in secret to destroy me!

He has bought this decrepit fortune-teller, this
Collector of dirty pennies, this prophet fraud—
Why, he is no more clairvoyant than I am!
                                        Tell us.
Has your mystic mummery ever approached the truth?
When that hellcat the Sphinx was performing here,
What help were you to these people?
Her magic was not for the first man who came along:
It demanded a real exorcist. Your birds—
What good were they? or the gods, for the matter of that?
But I came by,
Oedipus, the simple man, who knows nothing—
I thought it out for myself, no birds helped me!
And this is the man you think you can destroy,
That you may be close to Creon when he's king!
Well, you and your friend Creon, it seems to me,
Will suffer most. If you were not an old man,
You would have paid already for your plot.
CHORAGOS: We can not see that his words or yours
    Have been spoken except in anger, Oedipus,
    And of anger we have no need. How can God's will
    Be accomplished best? That is what most concerns us.
TEIRESIAS: You are a king. But where argument's concerned
    I am your man, as much a king as you.
    I am not your servant, but Apollo's.
    I have no need of Creon to speak for me.

    Listen to me. You mock my blindness, do you?
    But I say that you, with both your eyes, are blind:
    You can not see the wretchedness of your life,
    Nor in whose house you live, no, nor with whom.
    Who are your father and mother? Can you tell me?
    You do not even know the blind wrongs
    That you have done them, on earth and in the world below.
    But the double lash of your parents' curse will whip you
    Out of this land some day, with only night
    Upon your precious eyes.
    Your cries then—where will they not be heard?
    What fastness of Kithairon will not echo them?
    And that bridal-descant of yours—you'll know it then,
    The song they sang when you came here to Thebes
    And found your misguided berthing.
    All this, and more, that you can not guess at now,
    Will bring you to yourself among your children.

Be angry, then. Curse Creon. Curse my words.
I tell you, no man that walks upon the earth
Shall be rooted out more horribly than you.
OEDIPUS: Am I to bear this from him?—Damnation
Take you! Out of this place! Out of my sight!
TEIRESIAS: I would not have come at all if you had not asked me.
OEDIPUS: Could I have told that you'd talk nonsense, that
You'd come here to make a fool of yourself, and of me?
TEIRESIAS: A fool? Your parents thought me sane enough.
OEDIPUS: My parents again!—Wait: who were my parents?
TEIRESIAS: This day will give you a father, and break your heart.
OEDIPUS: Your infantile riddles! Your damned abracadabra!
TEIRESIAS: You were a great man once at solving riddles.
OEDIPUS: Mock me with that if you like; you will find it true.
TEIRESIAS: It was true enough. It brought about your ruin.
OEDIPUS: But if it saved this town?
TEIRESIAS: [*to the* PAGE] Boy, give me your hand.
OEDIPUS: Yes, boy; lead him away.
　　　—While you are here
We can do nothing. Go; leave us in peace.
TEIRESIAS: I will go when I have said what I have to say.
How can you hurt me? And I tell you again:
The man you have been looking for all this time,
The damned man, the murderer of Laïos,
That man is in Thebes. To your mind he is foreign-born,
But it will soon be shown that he is Theban,
A revelation that will fail to please.
　　　　　　　　　　　　　　A blind man,
Who has his eyes now; a penniless man, who is rich now;
And he will go tapping the strange earth with his staff
To the children with whom he lives now he will be
Brother and father—the very same; to her
Who bore him, son and husband—the very same
Who came to his father's bed, wet with his father's blood.

Enough. Go think that over.
If later you find error in what I have said,
You may say that I have no skill in prophecy.
　　　[*Exit* TEIRESIAS, *led by his* PAGE. OEDIPUS *goes into the palace.*]

ODE I

CHORUS: The Delphic stone of prophecies　　　　　　　　　　　[STROPHE 1]
　　　Remembers ancient regicide
　　　And a still bloody hand.
　　　That killer's hour of flight has come.
　　　He must be stronger than riderless
　　　Coursers of untiring wind,
　　　For the son of Zeus armed with his father's thunder
　　　Leaps in lightning after him;
　　　And the Furies follow him, the sad Furies.

Holy Parnassos' peak of snow   [ANTISTROPHE 1]
Flashes and blinds that secret man,
That all shall hunt him down:
Though he may roam the forest shade
Like a bull wild from pasture
To rage through glooms of stone.
Doom comes down on him; flight will not avail him;
For the world's heart calls him desolate,
And the immortal Furies follow, forever follow.

But now a wilder thing is heard   [STROPHE 2]
From the old man skilled at hearing Fate in the wingbeat of a bird.
Bewildered as a blown bird, my soul hovers and can not find
Foothold in this debate, or any reason or rest of mind.
But no man ever brought—none can bring
Proof of strife between Thebes' royal house,
Labdakos' line, and the son of Polybos;
And never until now has any man brought word
Of Laïos' dark death staining Oedipus the King.

Divine Zeus and Apollo hold   [ANTISTROPHE 2]
Perfect intelligence alone of all tales ever told;
And well though this diviner works, he works in his own night;
No man can judge that rough unknown or trust in second sight,
For wisdom changes hands among the wise.
Shall I believe my great lord criminal
At a raging word that a blind old man let fall?
I saw him, when the carrion woman faced him of old,
Prove his heroic mind! These evil words are lies.

SCENE II

CREON: Men of Thebes:
    I am told that heavy accusations
    Have been brought against me by King Oedipus.

    I am not the kind of man to bear this tamely.

    If in these present difficulties
    He holds me accountable for any harm to him
    Through anything I have said or done—why, then,
    I do not value life in this dishonor.
    It is not as though this rumor touched upon
    Some private indiscretion. The matter is grave.
    The fact is that I am being called disloyal
    To the State, to my fellow citizens, to my friends.
CHORAGOS: He may have spoken in anger, not from his mind.
CREON: But did you not hear him say I was the one
    Who seduced the old prophet into lying?
CHORAGOS: The thing was said; I do not know how seriously.
CREON: But you were watching him! Were his eyes steady?

Did he look like a man in his right mind?

CHORAGOS: I do not know.
　　I can not judge the behavior of great men.
　　But here is the King himself.
　　　　[*Enter* OEDIPUS.]

OEDIPUS: So you dared come back.
　　Why? How brazen of you to come to my house,
　　You murderer!
　　　　　　　Do you think I do not know
　　That you plotted to kill me, plotted to steal my throne?
　　Tell me, in God's name: am I coward, a fool,
　　That you should dream you could accomplish this?
　　A fool who could not see your slippery game?
　　A coward, not to fight back when I saw it?
　　You are the fool, Creon, are you not? hoping
　　Without support or friends to get a throne?
　　Thrones may be won or bought: you could do neither.

CREON: Now listen to me. You have talked; let me talk, too.
　　You can not judge unless you know the facts.

OEDIPUS: You speak well: there is one fact; but I find it hard
　　To learn from the deadliest enemy I have.

CREON: That above all I must dispute with you.

OEDIPUS: That above all I will not hear you deny.

CREON: If you think there is anything good in being stubborn
　　Against all reason, then I say you are wrong.

OEDIPUS: If you think a man can sin against his own kind
　　And not be punished for it, I say you are mad.

CREON: I agree. But tell me: what have I done to you?

OEDIPUS: You advised me to send for that wizard, did you not?

CREON: I did. I should do it again.

OEDIPUS: Very well. Now tell me:
　　How long has it been since Laïos—

CREON: What of Laïos?

OEDIPUS: Since he vanished in that onset by the road?

CREON : It was long ago, a long time.

OEDIPUS: And this prophet,
　　Was he practicing here then?

CREON: He was; and with honor, as now.

OEDIPUS: Did he speak of me at that time?

CREON: He never did:
　　At least, not when I was present.

OEDIPUS: But … the enquiry?
　　I suppose you held one?

CREON: We did, but we learned nothing.

OEDIPUS: Why did the prophet not speak against me then?

CREON: I do not know; and I am the kind of man
　　Who holds his tongue when he has no facts to go on.

OEDIPUS: There's one fact that you know, and you could tell it.

CREON: What fact is that? If I know it, you shall have it.

OEDIPUS: If he were not involved with you, he could not say
　　That it was I who murdered Laïos.

CREON: If he says that, you are the one that knows it!—

But now it is my turn to question you.

OEDIPUS: Put your questions. I am no murderer.

CREON: First, then: You married my sister?

OEDIPUS: I married your sister.

CREON: And you rule the kingdom equally with her?

OEDIPUS: Everything that she wants she has from me.

CREON: And I am the third, equal to both of you?

OEDIPUS: That is why I call you a bad friend.

CREON: No. Reason it out, as I have done.

> Think of this first: Would any sane man prefer
> Power, with all a king's anxieties,
> To that same power and the grace of sleep?
> Certainly not I.
> I have never longed for the king's power—only his rights.
> Would any wise man differ from me in this?
> As matters stand, I have my way in everything
> With your consent, and no responsibilities.
> If I were king, I should be a slave to policy.
>
> How could I desire a scepter more
> Than what is now mine—untroubled influence?
> No, I have not gone mad; I need no honors,
> Except those with the perquisites I have now.
> I am welcome everywhere; every man salutes me,
> And those who want your favor seek my ear,
> Since I know how to manage what they ask.
> Should I exchange this case for that anxiety?
> Besides, no sober mind is treasonable.
> I hate anarchy
> And never would deal with any man who likes it.
>
> Test what I have said. Go to the priestess
> At Delphi; ask if I quoted her correctly.
> And as for this other thing: if I am found
> Guilty of treason with Teiresias,
> Then sentence me to death! You have my word
> It is a sentence I should cast my vote for—
> But not without evidence!
>   You do wrong
> When you take good men for bad, bad men for good.
> A true friend thrown aside—why, life itself
> Is not more precious!
>   In time you will know this well:
> For time, and time alone, will show the just man,
> Though scoundrels are discovered in a day.

CHORAGOS: This is well said, and a prudent man would ponder it.

> Judgments too quickly formed are dangerous.

OEDIPUS: But is he not quick in his duplicity?

> And shall I not be quick to parry him?
> Would you have me stand still, hold my peace, and let
> This man win everything, through my inaction?

CREON: And you want—what is it, then? To banish me?

OEDIPUS: No, not exile. It is your death I want,
    So that all the world may see what treason means.
CREON: You will persist, then? You will not believe me?
OEDIPUS: How can I believe you?
CREON: Then you are a fool.
OEDIPUS: To save myself?
CREON: In justice, think of me.
OEDIPUS: You are evil incarnate.
CREON: But suppose that you are wrong?
OEDIPUS: Still I must rule.
CREON: But not if you rule badly.
OEDIPUS: O city, city!
CREON: It is my city, too!
CHORAGOS: Now, my lords, be still, I see the Queen,
    Iocastê, coming from her palace chambers;
    And it is time she came, for the sake of you both.
    This dreadful quarrel can be resolved through her.
        [*Enter* IOCASTÊ.]
IOCASTÊ: Poor foolish men, what wicked din is this?
    With Thebes sick to death, is it not shameful
    That you should rake some private quarrel up?
        [*To* OEDIPUS:]
    Come into the house.

                  —And you, Creon, go now:
    Let us have no more of this tumult over nothing.
CREON: Nothing? No, sister: what your husband plans for me
    Is one of two great evils: exile or death.
OEDIPUS: He is right.
               Why, woman, I have caught him squarely
    Plotting against my life.
CREON: No! let me die
    Accurst if ever I have wished you harm!
IOCASTÊ: Ah, believe it, Oedipus!
    In the name of the gods, respect this oath of his
    For my sake, for the sake of these people here!   [STROPHE I]

CHORAGOS: Open your mind to her, my lord, Be ruled by her, I beg you!
OEDIPUS: What would you have me do?
CHORAGOS: Respect Creon's word. He has never spoken like a fool,
    And now he has sworn an oath.
OEDIPUS: You know what you ask?
CHORAGOS: I do.
OEDIPUS: Speak on, then.
CHORAGOS: A friend so sworn should not be baited so,
    In blind malice, and without final proof.
OEDIPUS: You are aware, I hope, that what you say
    Means death for me, or exile at the least.
CHORAGOS: No, I swear by Helios, first in Heaven!
    May I die friendless and accurst,
    The worst of deaths, if ever I meant that!

It is the withering fields
  That hurt my sick heart:
Must we bear all these ills,
  And now your bad blood as well?

OEDIPUS: Then let him go. And let me die, if I must,
  Or be driven by him in shame from the land of Thebes.
  It is your unhappiness, and not his talk,
  That touches me.
               As for him—
Wherever he goes, hatred will follow him.

CREON: Ugly in yielding, as you were ugly in rage!
  Natures like yours chiefly torment themselves.

OEDIPUS: Can you not go? Can you not leave me?

CREON: I can.
  You do not know me; but the city knows me,
  And in its eyes, I am just, if not in yours.
    [*Exit* CREON.]

[ANTISTROPHE 1]

CHORAGOS: Lady Iocastê, did you not ask the King to go to his chambers?

IOCASTÊ: First tell me what has happened.

CHORAGOS: There was suspicion without evidence: yet it rankled
  As even false charges will.

IOCASTÊ: On both sides?

CHORAGOS: On both.

IOCASTÊ: But what was said?

CHORAGOS: Oh let it rest, let it be done with!
  Have we not suffered enough?

OEDIPUS: You see to what your decency has brought you:
  You have made difficulties where my heart saw none.

CHORAGOS: Oedipus, it is not once only I have told you—   [ANTISTROPHE 2]
  You must know I should count myself unwise
  To the point of madness, should I now forsake you—
  You, under whose hand,
  In the storm of another time,
    Our dear land sailed out free.
  But now stand fast at the helm!

IOCASTÊ: In God's name, Oedipus, inform your wife as well:
  Why are you so set in this hard anger?

OEDIPUS: I will tell you, for none of these men deserves
  My confidence as you do. It is Creon's work,
  His treachery, his plotting against me.

IOCASTÊ: Go on, if you can make this clear to me.

OEDIPUS: He charges me with the murder of Laïos.

IOCASTÊ: Has he some knowledge? Or does he speak from hearsay?

OEDIPUS: He would not commit himself to such a charge,
  But he has brought in that damnable soothsayer
  To tell his story.

IOCASTÊ: Set your mind at rest.
  If it is a question of soothsayers, I tell you
  That you will find no man whose craft gives knowledge
  Of the unknowable.

Here is my proof.

An oracle was reported to Laïos once
(I will not say from Phoibos himself, but from
His appointed ministers, at any rate)
That his doom would be death at the hands of his own son—
His son, born of his flesh and of mine!

Now, you remember the story: Laïos was killed
By marauding strangers where three highways meet.
But his child had not been three days in this world
Before the King had pierced the baby's ankles
And left him to die on a lonely mountainside.

Thus, Apollo never caused that child
To kill his father, and it was not Laïos' fate
To die at the hands of his son, as he had feared.
This is what prophets and prophecies are worth!
Have no dread of them.
                              It is God himself
Who can show us what he wills, in his own way.

OEDIPUS: How strange a shadowy memory crossed my mind,
    Just now while you were speaking; it chilled my heart.

IOCASTÊ: What do you mean? What memory do you speak of?

OEDIPUS: If I understand you, Laïos was killed
    At a place where three roads meet.

IOCASTÊ: So it was said;
    We have no later story.

OEDIPUS: Where did it happen?

IOCASTÊ: Phokis, it is called: at a place where the Theban Way
    Divides into the roads toward Delphi and Daulia.

OEDIPUS: When?

IOCASTÊ: We had the news not long before you came
    And proved the right to your succession here.

OEDIPUS: Ah, what net has God been weaving for me?

IOCASTÊ: Oedipus! Why does this trouble you?

OEDIPUS: Do not ask me yet.
    First, tell me how Laïos looked, and tell me
    How old he was.

IOCASTÊ: He was tall, his hair just touched
    With white; his form was not unlike your own.

OEDIPUS: I think that I myself may be accurst
    By my own ignorant edict.

IOCASTÊ: You speak strangely.
    It makes me tremble to look at you, my King.

OEDIPUS: I am not sure that the blind man can not see.
    But I should know better if you were to tell me—

IOCASTÊ: Anything—though I dread to hear you ask it.

OEDIPUS: Was the King lightly escorted, or did he ride
    With a large company, as a ruler should?

IOCASTÊ: There were five men with him in all: one was a herald,
    And a single chariot, which he was driving.
OEDIPUS: Alas, that makes it plain enough!

                                      But who—
    Who told you how it happened?
IOCASTÊ: A household servant,
    The only one to escape.
OEDIPUS: And is he still
    A servant of ours?
IOCASTÊ: No; for when he came back at last
    And found you enthroned in the place of the dead king,
    He came to me, touched my hand with his, and begged
    That I would send him away to the frontier district
    Where only the shepherds go—
    As far away from the city as I could send him.
    I granted his prayer; for although the man was a slave,
    He had earned more than this favor at my hands.
OEDIPUS: Can he be called back quickly?
IOCASTÊ: Easily.
    But why?
OEDIPUS: I have taken too much upon myself
    Without enquiry; therefore I wish to consult him.
IOCASTÊ: Then he shall come.

                         But am I not one also
    To whom you might confide these fears of yours?
OEDIPUS: That is your right; it will not be denied you,
    Now least of all; for I have reached a pitch
    Of wild foreboding. Is there anyone
    To whom I should sooner speak?

    Polybos of Corinth is my father.
    My mother is a Dorian: Meropê.
    I grew up chief among the men of Corinth
    Until a strange thing happened—
    Not worth my passion, it may be, but strange.

    At a feast, a drunken man maundering in his cups
    Cries out that I am not my father's son!

    I contained myself that night, though I felt anger
    And a sinking heart. The next day I visited
    My father and mother, and questioned them. They stormed,
    Calling it all the slanderous rant of a fool;
    And this relieved me. Yet the suspicion
    Remained always aching in my mind;
    I know there was talk; I could not rest;
    And finally, saying nothing to my parents,
    I went to the shrine at Delphi.
    The god dismissed my question without reply;
    He spoke of other things.

Some were clear,
Full of wretchedness, dreadful, unbearable:
As, that I should lie with my own mother, breed
Children from whom all men would turn their eyes;
And that I should be my father's murderer.

I heard all this, and fled. And from that day
Corinth to me was only in the stars
Descending in that quarter of the sky,
As I wandered farther and farther on my way
To a land where I should never see the evil
Sung by the oracle. And I came to this country
Where, so you say, King Laïos was killed.

I will tell you all that happened there, my lady.
There were three highways
Coming together at a place I passed;
And there a herald came towards me, and a chariot
Drawn by horses, with a man such as you describe
Seated in it. The groom leading the horses
Forced me off the road at his lord's command;
But as this charioteer lurched over towards me
I struck him in my rage. The old man saw me
And brought his double goad down upon my head
As I came abreast.
                    He was paid back, and more!
Swinging my club in this right hand I knocked him
Out of his car, and he rolled on the ground.
                                        I killed him.
I killed them all.
Now if that stranger and Laïos were—kin,
Where is a man more miserable than I?
More hated by the gods? Citizen and alien alike
Must never shelter me or speak to me—
I must be shunned by all.
                    And I myself
Pronounced this malediction upon myself!
Think of it: I have touched you with these hands,
These hands that killed your husband. What defilement!

Am I all evil, then? It must be so,
Since I must flee from Thebes, yet never again
See my own countrymen, my own country,
For fear of joining my mother in marriage
And killing Polybos, my father.
                              Ah,
If I was created so, born to this fate,
Who could deny the savagery of God?

O holy majesty of heavenly powers!
May I never see that day! Never!
Rather let me vanish from the race of men

Than know the abomination destined me!
CHORAGOS: We, too, my lord, have felt dismay at this.
    But there is hope: you have yet to hear the shepherd.
OEDIPUS: Indeed, I fear no other hope is left me.
IOCASTÊ: What do you hope from him when he comes?
OEDIPUS: This much:
    If his account of the murder tallies with yours,
    Then I am cleared.
IOCASTÊ: What was it that I said
    Of such importance?
OEDIPUS: Why, "marauders," you said,
    Killed the King, according to this man's story.
    If he maintains that still, if there were several,
    Clearly the guilt is not mine: I was alone.
    But if he says one man, singlehanded, did it,
    Then the evidence all points to me.
IOCASTÊ: You may be sure that he said there were several;
    And can he call back that story now? He can not.
    The whole city heard it as plainly as I.
    But suppose he alters some detail of it:
    He can not ever show that Laïos' death
    Fulfilled the oracle: for Apollo said
    My child was doomed to kill him; and my child—
    Poor baby!—it was my child that died first.
    No. From now on, where oracles are concerned,
    I would not waste a second thought on any.
OEDIPUS: You might be right.
                      But come: let someone go
    For the shepherd at once. This matter must be settled.
IOCASTÊ: I will send for him.
    I would not wish to cross you in anything,
    And surely not in this.—Let us go in.
        [*Exeunt into the palace.*]

ODE II

CHORUS: Let me be reverent in the ways of right,   [STROPHE 1]
    Lowly the paths I journey on;
    Let all my words and actions keep
    The laws of the pure universe
    From highest Heaven handed down.
    For Heaven is their bright nurse,
    Those generations of the realms of light;
    Ah, never of mortal kind were they begot,
    Nor are they slaves of memory, lost in sleep;
    Their Father is greater than Time, and ages not.

    The tyrant is a child of Pride   [ANTISTROPHE 1]
    Who drinks from his great sickening cup
    Recklessness and vanity,
    Until from his high crest headlong

He plummets to the dust of hope.
That strong man is not strong.
But let no fair ambition be denied;
May God protect the wrestler for the State
In government, in comely policy,
Who will fear God, and on His ordinance wait.

Haughtiness and the high hand of disdain   [STROPHE 2]
Tempt and outrage God's holy law;
And any mortal who dares hold
No immortal Power in awe
Will be caught up in a net of pain;
The price for which his levity is sold.
Let each man take due earnings, then,
And keep his hands from holy things,
And from blasphemy stand apart—
Else the crackling blast of heaven
Blows on his head, and on his desperate heart;
Though fools will honor impious men,
In their cities no tragic poet sings.
Shall we lose faith in Delphi's obscurities,   [ANTISTROPHE 2]
We who have heard the world's core
Discredited, and the sacred wood
Of Zeus at Elis praised no more?
The deeds and the strange prophecies
Must make a pattern yet to be understood.
Zeus, if indeed you are lord of all,
Throned in light over night and day,
Mirror this in your endless mind:
Our masters call the oracle
Words on the wind, and the Delphic vision blind!
Their hearts no longer know Apollo,
And reverence for the gods has died away.

SCENE III

[*Enter* IOCASTÊ]
IOCASTÊ: Princes of Thebes, it has occurred to me
     To visit the altars of the gods, bearing
     These branches as a suppliant, and this incense.
     Our King is not himself: his noble soul
     Is overwrought with fantasies of dread,
     Else he would consider
     The new prophecies in the light of the old.
     He will listen to any voice that speaks disaster,
     And my advice goes for nothing.

                         To you, then, Apollo,
     Lycean lord, since you are nearest, I turn in prayer.
     Receive these offerings, and grant us deliverance
     From defilement. Our hearts are heavy with fear
     When we see our leader distracted, as helpless sailors

Are terrified by the confusion of their helmsman.
 [*Enter* MESSENGER.]
MESSENGER: Friends, no doubt you can direct me:
 Where shall I find the house of Oedipus,
 Or, better still, where is the King himself?
CHORAGOS: It is this very place, stranger; he is inside.
 This is his wife and mother of his children.
MESSENGER: I wish her happiness in a happy house,
 Blest in all the fulfillment of her marriage.
IOCASTÊ: I wish as much for you: your courtesy
 Deserves a like good fortune. But now, tell me:
 Why have you come? What have you to say to us?
MESSENGER: Good news, my lady, for your house and your husband.
IOCASTÊ: What news? Who sent you here?
MESSENGER: I am from Corinth.
 The news I bring ought to mean joy for you,
 Though it may be you will find some grief in it.
IOCASTÊ: What is it? How can it touch us in both ways?
MESSENGER: The word is that the people of the Isthmus
 Intend to call Oedipus to be their king.
IOCASTÊ But old King Polybos—is he not reigning still?
MESSENGER: No. Death holds him in his sepulchre.
IOCASTÊ: What are you saying? Polybos is dead?
MESSENGER: If I am not telling the truth, may I die myself.
IOCASTÊ: [*to a* MAIDSERVANT] Go in, go quickly; tell this to your master.
 O riddlers of God's will, where are you now!
 This was the man whom Oedipus, long ago,
 Feared so, fled so, in dread of destroying him—
 But it was another fate by which he died.

   [*Enter* OEDIPUS]
OEDIPUS: Dearest Iocastê, why have you sent for me?
IOCASTÊ: Listen to what this man says, and then tell me
 What has become of the solemn prophecies.
OEDIPUS: Who is this man? What is his news for me?
IOCASTÊ: He has come from Corinth to announce your father's death!
OEDIPUS: Is it true, stranger? Tell me in your own words.
MESSENGER: I can not say it more clearly: the King is dead.
OEDIPUS: Was it by treason? Or by an attack of illness?
MESSENGER: A little thing brings old men to their rest.
OEDIPUS: It was sickness, then?
MESSENGER: Yes, and his many years.
OEDIPUS: Ah!
 Why should a man respect the Pythian hearth, or
 Give heed to the birds that jangle above his head?
 They prophesied that I should kill Polybos,
 Kill my own father; but he is dead and buried,
 And I am here—I never touched him, never,
 Unless he died of grief for my departure,
 And thus, in a sense, through me. No. Polybos
 Has packed the oracles off with him underground.
 They are empty words.

IOCASTÊ: Had I not told you so?
OEDIPUS: You had; it was my faint heart that betrayed me.
IOCASTÊ: From now on never think of those things again.
OEDIPUS: And yet—must I not fear my mother's bed?
IOCASTÊ: Why should anyone in this world be afraid,
     Since Fate rules us and nothing can be foreseen?
     A man should live only for the present day.

     Have no more fear of sleeping with your mother:
     How many men, in dreams, have lain with their mothers!
     No reasonable man is troubled by such things.
OEDIPUS: That is true; only—
     If only my mother were not still alive!
     But she is alive. I can not help my dread.
IOCASTÊ: Yet this news of your father's death is wonderful.
OEDIPUS: Wonderful. But I fear the living woman.
MESSENGER: Tell me, who is this woman that you fear?
OEDIPUS: It is Meropê, man; the wife of King Polybos.
MESSENGER: Meropê? Why should you be afraid of her?
OEDIPUS: An oracle of the gods, a dreadful saying.
MESSENGER: Can you tell me about it or are you sworn to silence?
OEDIPUS: I can tell you, and I will.
     Apollo said through his prophet that I was the man
     Who should marry his own mother, shed his father's blood
     With his own hands. And so, for all these years
     I have kept clear of Corinth, and no harm has come—
     Though it would have been sweet to see my parents again.
MESSENGER: And is this the fear that drove you out of Corinth?
OEDIPUS: Would you have me kill my father?
MESSENGER: As for that
     You must be reassured by the news I gave you.
OEDIPUS: If you could reassure me, I would reward you.
MESSENGER: I had that in mind, I will confess: I thought
     I could count on you when you returned to Corinth.
OEDIPUS: No: I will never go near my parents again.
MESSENGER: Ah, son, you still do not know what you are doing—
OEDIPUS: What do you mean? In the name of God tell me!
MESSENGER:—If these are your reasons for not going home.
OEDIPUS: I tell you, I fear the oracle may come true.
MESSENGER: And guilt may come upon you through your parents?
OEDIPUS: That is the dread that is always in my heart.
MESSENGER: Can you not see that all your fears are groundless?
OEDIPUS: How can you say that? They are my parents, surely?
MESSENGER: Polybos was not your father.
OEDIPUS: Not my father?
MESSENGER: No more your father than the man speaking to you.
OEDIPUS: But you are nothing to me!
MESSENGER: Neither was he.
OEDIPUS: Then why did he call me son?
MESSENGER: I will tell you:
     Long ago he had you from my hands, as a gift.
OEDIPUS: Then how could he love me so, if I was not his?

MESSENGER: He had no children, and his heart turned to you.

OEDIPUS: What of you? Did you buy me? Did you find me by chance?

MESSENGER: I came upon you in the crooked pass of Kithairon.

OEDIPUS: And what were you doing there?

MESSENGER: Tending my flocks.

OEDIPUS: A wandering shepherd?

MESSENGER: But your savior, son, that day.

OEDIPUS: From what did you save me?

MESSENGER: Your ankles should tell you that.

OEDIPUS: Ah, stranger, why do you speak of that childhood pain?

MESSENGER: I cut the bonds that tied your ankles together.

OEDIPUS: I have had the mark as long as I can remember.

MESSENGER: That was why you were given the name you bear.

OEDIPUS: God! Was it my father or my mother who did it?
    Tell me!

MESSENGER: I do not know. The man who gave you to me
    Can tell you better than I.

OEDIPUS: It was not you that found me, but another?

MESSENGER: It was another shepherd gave you to me.

OEDIPUS: Who was he? Can you tell me who he was?

MESSENGER: I think he was said to be one of Laïos' people.

OEDIPUS: You mean the Laïos who was king here years ago?

MESSENGER: Yes; King Laïos; and the man was one of his herdsmen.

OEDIPUS: Is he still alive? Can I see him?

MESSENGER: These men here
    Know best about such things.

OEDIPUS: Does anyone here
    Know this shepherd that he is talking about?
    Have you seen him in the fields, or in the town?
    If you have, tell me. It is time things were made plain.

CHORAGOS: I think the man he means is that same shepherd
    You have already asked to see. Iocastê perhaps
    Could tell you something.

OEDIPUS: Do you know anything
    About him, Lady? Is he the man we have summoned?
    Is that the man this shepherd means?

IOCASTÊ: Why think of him?
    Forget this herdsman. Forget it all.
    This talk is a waste of time.

OEDIPUS: How can you say that?
    When the clues to my true birth are in my hands?

IOCASTÊ: For God's love, let us have no more questioning!
    Is your life nothing to you?
    My own is pain enough for me to bear.

OEDIPUS: You need not worry. Suppose my mother a slave,
    And born of slaves: no baseness can touch you.

IOCASTÊ: Listen to me, I beg you: do not do this thing!

OEDIPUS: I will not listen; the truth must be made known.

IOCASTÊ: Everything that I say is for your own good!

OEDIPUS: My own good
    Snaps my patience, then; I want none of it.

IOCASTÊ: You are fatally wrong! May you never learn who you are!

OEDIPUS: Go, one of you, and bring the shepherd here.
  Let us leave this woman to brag of her royal name.
IOCASTÊ: Ah, miserable!
  That is the only word I have for you now.
  That is the only word I can ever have.
    [*Exit into the palace.*]
CHORAGOS: Why has she left us, Oedipus? Why has she gone
  In such a passion of sorrow? I fear this silence:
  Something dreadful may come of it.
OEDIPUS: Let it come!
  However base my birth, I must know about it.
  The Queen, like a woman, is perhaps ashamed
  To think of my low origin. But I
  Am a child of Luck; I can not be dishonored.
  Luck is my mother; the passing months, my brothers,
  Have seen me rich and poor.
                        If this is so,
  How could I wish that I were someone else?
  How could I not be glad to know my birth?

ODE III

CHORUS: If ever the coming time were known   [STROPHE]
  To my heart's pondering,
  Kithairon, now by Heaven I see the torches
  At the festival of the next full moon,
  And see the dance, and hear the choir sing
  A grace to your gentle shade:
  Mountain where Oedipus was found,
  O mountain guard of a noble race!
  May the god who heals us lend his aid,
  And let that glory come to pass
  For our king's cradling-ground.

  Of the nymphs that flower beyond the years,   [ANTISTROPHE I]
  Who bore you, royal child,
  To Pan of the hills or the timberline, Apollo,
  Cold in delight where the upland clears,
  Or Hermês for whom Kyllenê's heights are piled?
  Or flushed as evening cloud,
  Great Dionysos, roamer of mountains,
  He—was it he who found you there,
  And caught you up in his own proud
  Arms from the sweet god-ravisher
  Who laughed by the Muses' fountains?

SCENE IV

OEDIPUS: Sirs: though I do not know the man,
  I think I see him coming, this shepherd we want:
  He is old, like our friend here, and the men

Bringing him seem to be servants of my house.
But you can tell, if you have ever seen him.

[*Enter* SHEPHERD *escorted by servants.*]

CHORAGOS: I know him, he was Laïos' man. You can trust him.

OEDIPUS: Tell me first, you from Corinth: is this the shepherd
    We were discussing?

MESSENGER: This is the very man.

OEDIPUS: [*to* SHEPHERD] Come here. No, look at me. You must answer
    Everything I ask.—You belonged to Laïos?

SHEPHERD: Yes: born his slave, brought up in his house.

OEDIPUS: Tell me: what kind of work did you do for him?

SHEPHERD: I was a shepherd of his, most of my life.

OEDIPUS: Where mainly did you go for pasturage?

SHEPHERD: Sometimes Kithairon, sometimes the hills nearby.

OEDIPUS: Do you remember ever seeing this man out there?

SHEPHERD: What would he be doing there? This man?

OEDIPUS: This man standing here. Have you ever seen him before?

SHEPHERD: No. At least, not to my recollection.

MESSENGER: And that is not strange, my lord. But I'll refresh
    His memory: he must remember when we two
    Spent three whole seasons together, March to September,
    On Kithairon or thereabouts. He had two flocks;
    I had one. Each autumn I'd drive mine home
    And he would go back with his to Laïos' sheepfold.—
    Is this not true, just as I have described it?

SHEPHERD: True, yes; but it was all so long ago.

MESSENGER: Well, then: do you remember, back in those days,
    That you gave me a baby boy to bring up as my own?

SHEPHERD: What if I did? What are you trying to say?

MESSENGER: King Oedipus was once that little child.

SHEPHERD: Damn you, hold your tongue!

OEDIPUS: No more of that!
    It is your tongue needs watching, not this man's.

SHEPHERD: My King, my Master, what is it I have done wrong?

OEDIPUS: You have not answered his question about the boy.

SHEPHERD: He does not know…He is only making trouble…

OEDIPUS: Come, speak plainly, or it will go hard with you.

SHEPHERD: In God's name, do not torture an old man!

OEDIPUS: Come here, one of you; bind his arms behind him.

SHEPHERD: Unhappy king! What more do you wish to learn?

OEDIPUS: Did you give this man the child he speaks of?

SHEPHERD: I did.
    And I would to God I had died that very day.

OEDIPUS: You will die now unless you speak the truth.

SHEPHERD: Yet if I speak the truth, I am worse than dead.

OEDIPUS: Very well; since you insist upon delaying—

SHEPHERD: No! I have told you already that I gave him the boy.

OEDIPUS: Where did you get him? From your house? From somewhere else?

SHEPHERD: Not from mine, no. A man gave him to me.

OEDIPUS: Is that man here? Do you know whose slave he was?

SHEPHERD: For God's love, my King, do not ask me any more!

OEDIPUS: You are a dead man if I have to ask you again.
SHEPHERD: Then... Then the child was from the palace of Laïos.
OEDIPUS: A slave child? or a child of his own line?
SHEPHERD: Ah, I am on the brink of dreadful speech!
OEDIPUS: And I of dreadful hearing. Yet I must hear.
SHEPHERD: If you must be told, then...

                                      They said it was Laïos' child;
    But it is your wife who can tell you about that.
OEDIPUS: My wife!—Did she give it to you?
SHEPHERD: My lord, she did.
OEDIPUS: Do you know why?
SHEPHERD: I was told to get rid of it.
OEDIPUS: An unspeakable mother!
SHEPHERD: There had been prophecies...
OEDIPUS: Tell me.
SHEPHERD: It was said that the boy would kill his own father.
OEDIPUS: Then why did you give him over to this old man?
SHEPHERD: I pitied the baby, my King.
    And I thought that this man would take him far away
    To his own country.
                    He saved him—but for what a fate!
    For if you are what this man says you are,
    No man living is more wretched than Oedipus.
OEDIPUS: Ah God!
    It was true!
           All the prophecies!
                    —Now,
    O, Light, may I look on you for the last time!
    I, Oedipus,
    Oedipus, damned in his birth, in his marriage damned,
    Damned in the blood he shed with his own hand!
      [*He rushes into the palace.*]

ODE IV

CHORUS: Alas for the seed of men.   [STROPHE 1]
    What measure shall I give these generations
    That breathe on the void and are void
    And exist and do not exist?

    Who bears more weight of joy
    Than mass of sunlight shifting in images,
    Or who shall make his thought stay on
    That down time drifts away?

    Your splendor is all fallen.

    O naked brow of wrath and tears,
    O change of Oedipus!
    I who saw your days call no man blest—

Your great days like ghòsts gòne.
That mind was a strong bow.

Deep, how deep you drew it then, hard archer,
At a dim fearful range,
And brought dear glory down!

You overcame the stranger—
The virgin with her hooking lion claws—
And though death sang, stood like a tower
To make pale Thebes take heart.

Fortress against our sorrow!

True king, giver of laws,
Majestic Oedipus!
No prince in Thebes had ever such renown,
No prince won such grace of power.

And now of all men ever known
Most pitiful is this man's story:
His fortunes are most changed, his state
Fallen to a low slave's
Ground under bitter fate.

O Oedipus, most royal one!
The great door that expelled you to the light
Gave at night—ah, gave night to your glory:
As to the father, to the fathering son.

All understood too late.

How could that queen whom Laïos won,
The garden that he harrowed at his height,
Be silent when that act was done?

But all eyes fail before time's eye,
All actions come to justice there.
Though never willed, though far down the deep past,
Your bed, your dread sirings,
Are brought to book at last.
Child by Laïos doomed to die,
Then doomed to lose that fortunate little death,
Would God you never took breath in this air
That with my wailing lips I take to cry:
For I weep the world's outcast.

I was blind, and now I can tell why:
Asleep, for you had given ease of breath
To Thebes, while the false years went by.

ÈXODUS

SECOND MESSENGER: Elders of Thebes, most honored in this land,
    What horrors are yours to see and hear, what weight
    Of sorrow to be endured, if, true to your birth,
    You venerate the line of Labdakos!
    I think neither Istros nor Phasis, those great rivers,
    Could purify this place of the corruption
    It shelters now, or soon must bring to light—
    Evil not done unconsciously, but willed.

    The greatest griefs are those we cause ourselves.
CHORAGOS: Surely, friend, we have grief enough already;
    What new sorrow do you mean?
SECOND MESSENGER: The Queen is dead.
CHORAGOS: Iocastê? Dead? But at whose hand?
SECOND MESSENGER: Her own.
    The full horror of what happened you can not know,
    For you did not see it; but I, who did, will tell you
    As clearly as I can how she met her death.

    When she had left us,
    In passionate silence, passing through the court,
    She ran to her apartment in the house,
    Her hair clutched by the fingers of both hands.
    She closed the doors behind her; then, by that bed
    Where long ago the fatal son was conceived—
    That son who should bring about his father's death—
    We hear her call upon Laïos, dead so many years,
    And heard her wail for the double fruit of her marriage,
    A husband by her husband, children by her child.

    Exactly how she died I do not know:
    For Oedipus burst in moaning and would not let us
    Keep vigil to the end: it was by him
    As he stormed about the room that our eyes were caught.
    From one to another of us he went, begging a sword,
    Cursing the wife who was not his wife, the mother
    Whose womb had carried his own children and himself.
    I do not know: it was none of us aided him,
    But surely one of the gods was in control!
    For with a dreadful cry
    He hurled his weight, as though wrenched out of himself,
    At the twin doors: the bolts gave, and he rushed in.
    And there we saw her hanging, her body swaying
    From the cruel cord she had noosed about her neck.
    A great sob broke from him, heartbreaking to hear,
    As he loosed the rope and lowered her to the ground.

    I would blot out from my mind what happened next!
    For the King ripped from her gown the golden brooches

That were her ornament, and raised them, and lunged them down
Straight into his own eyeballs, crying, "No more,
No more shall you look on the misery about me,
The horrors of my own doing! Too long you have known
The faces of those whom I should never have seen,
Too long been blind to those for whom I was searching!
From this hour, go in darkness!" And as he spoke,
He struck at his eyes—not once, but many times;
And the blood spattered his beard,
Bursting from his ruined sockets like red hail.

So from the unhappiness of two this evil has sprung,
A curse on the man and woman alike. The old
Happiness of the house of Labdakos
Was happiness enough: where is it today?
It is all wailing and ruin, disgrace, death—all
The misery of mankind that has a name—
And it is wholly and for ever theirs.

CHORAGOS: Is he in agony still? Is there no rest for him?

SECOND MESSENGER: He is calling for someone to lead him to the gates
So that all the children of Kadmos may look upon
His father's murderer, his mother's—no,
I can not say it!
              And then he will leave Thebes,
Self-exiled, in order that the curse
Which he himself pronounced may depart from the house.
He is weak, and there is none to lead him,
So terrible is his suffering.
              But you will see:
Look, the doors are opening; in a moment
You will see a thing that would crush a heart of stone.

[*The central door is opened;* OEDIPUS, *blinded, is led in.*]

CHORAGOS: Dreadful indeed for men to see.
Never have my own eyes
Looked on a sight so full of fear.

Oedipus!
What madness came upon you, what daemon
Leaped on your life with heavier
Punishment than a mortal man can bear?
No: I can not even
Look at you, poor ruined one.
And I would speak, question, ponder,
If I were able. No.
You make me shudder.

OEDIPUS : God. God.
Is there a sorrow greater?
Where shall I find harbor in this world?
My voice is hurled far on a dark wind.
What has God done to me?

CHORAGOS : Too terrible to think of, or to see.

OEDIPUS : O cloud of night,   [STROPHE 1]
    Never to be turned away: night coming on,
    I can not tell how: night like a shroud!
    My fair winds brought me here.
                    O God. Again
    The pain of the spikes where I had sight,
    The flooding pain
    Of memory, never to be gouged out.
CHORAGOS: This is not strange.
    You suffer it all twice over, remorse in pain,
    Pain in remorse.
OEDIPUS: Ah dear friend   [ANTISTROPHE 1]
    Are you faithful even yet, you alone?
    Are you still standing near me, will you stay here,
    Patient, to care for the blind?
                  The blind man!
    Yet even blind I know who it is attends me,
    By the voice's tone—
    Though my new darkness hide the comforter.
CHORAGOS: Oh fearful act!
    What god was it drove you to rake black
    Night across your eyes?
OEDIPUS: Apollo. Apollo. Dear   [STROPHE 2]
    Children, the god was Apollo.
    He brought my sick, sick fate upon me.
    But the blinding hand was my own!
    How could I bear to see
    When all my sight was horror everywhere?
CHORAGOS: Everywhere; that is true.
OEDIPUS: And now what is left?
    Images? Love? A greeting even,
    Sweet to the senses? Is there anything?
    Ah, no, friends: lead me away.
    Lead me away from Thebes.
                  Lead the great wreck
    And hell of Oedipus, whom the gods hate.
CHORAGOS: Your fate is clear, you are not blind to that.
    Would God you had never found it out!
OEDIPUS: Death take the man who unbound   [ANTISTROPHE 2]
    My feet on that hillside
    And delivered me from death to life! What life?
    If only I had died,
    This weight of monstrous doom
    Could not have dragged me and my darlings down.
CHORAGOS: I would have wished the same.
OEDIPUS: Oh never to have come here
    With my father's blood upon me! Never
    To have been the man they call his mother's husband!
    Oh accurst! Oh child of evil,
    To have entered that wretched bed—
                  the selfsame one!
    More primal than sin itself, this fell to me.

CHORAGOS: I do not know how I can answer you.
    You were better dead than alive and blind.
OEDIPUS: Do not counsel me any more. This punishment
    That I have laid upon myself is just.
    If I had eyes,
    I do not know how I could bear the sight
    Of my father, when I came to the house of Death,
    Or my mother: for I have sinned against them both
    So vilely that I could not make my peace
    By strangling my own life.
                    Or do you think my children,
    Born as they were born, would be sweet to my eyes?
    Ah never, never! Nor this town with its high walls,
    Nor the holy images of the gods.
                For I,
    Thrice miserable!—Oedipus, noblest of all the line
    Of Kadmos, have condemned myself to enjoy
    These things no more, by my own malediction
    Expelling that man whom the gods declared
    To be a defilement in the house of Laïos.
    After exposing the rankness of my own guilt,
    How could I look men frankly in the eyes?
    No, I swear it,
    If I could have stifled my hearing at its source,
    I would have done it and made all this body
    A tight cell of misery, blank to light and sound:
    So I should have been safe in a dark agony
    Beyond all recollection.
                Ah Kithairon!
    Why did you shelter me? When I was cast upon you,
    Why did I not die? Then I should never
    Have shown the world my execrable birth.

    Ah Polybos! Corinth, city that I believed
    The ancient seat of my ancestors: how fair
    I seemed, your child! And all the while this evil
    Was cancerous within me!
                For I am sick
    In my daily life, sick in my origin.

    O three roads, dark ravine, woodland and way
    Where three roads met: you, drinking my father's blood,
    My own blood, spilled by my own hand: can you remember
    The unspeakable things I did there, and the things
    I went on from there to do?
                O marriage, marriage!
    The act that engendered me, and again the act
    Performed by the son in the same bed—
                      Ah, the net
    Of incest, mingling fathers, brothers, sons,
    With brides, wives, mothers: the last evil
    That can be known by men: no tongue can say

How evil!
        No. For the love of God, conceal me
Somewhere far from Thebes; or kill me; or hurl me
Into the sea, away from men's eyes for ever.

Come, lead me. You need not fear to touch me.
Of all men, I alone can bear this guilt.
        [*Enter* CREON.]
CHORAGOS: We are not the ones to decide; but Creon here
        May fitly judge of what you ask. He only
        Is left to protect the city in your place.
OEDIPUS: Alas, how can I speak to him? What right have I
        To beg his courtesy whom I have deeply wronged?
CREON: I have not come to mock you, Oedipus,
        Or to reproach you either.
                [*To* ATTENDANTS:]—You, standing there:
        If you have lost all respect for man's dignity,
        At least respect the flame of Lord Helios:
        Do not allow this pollution to show itself
        Openly here, an affront to the earth
        And Heaven's rain and the light of day. No, take him
        Into the house as quickly as you can.
        For it is proper
        That only the close kindred see his grief.
OEDIPUS: I pray you in God's name, since your courtesy
        Ignores my dark expectation, visiting
        With mercy this man of all men most execrable:
        Give me what I ask—for your good, not for mine.
CREON: And what is it that you would have me do?
OEDIPUS: Drive me out of this country as quickly as may be
        To a place where no human voice can ever greet me.
CREON: I should have done that before now—only,
        God's will had not been wholly revealed to me.
OEDIPUS: But his command is plain: the parricide
        Must be destroyed. I am that evil man.
CREON: That is the sense of it, yes; but as things are,
        We had best discover clearly what is to be done.
OEDIPUS: You would learn more about a man like me?
CREON: You are ready now to listen to the god.
OEDIPUS: I will listen. But it is to you
        That I must turn for help. I beg you, hear me.
        The woman in there—
        Give her whatever funeral you think proper:
        She is your sister.
                —But let me go, Creon!
        Let me purge my father's Thebes of the pollution
        Of my living here, and go out to the wild hills,
        To Kithairon, that has won such fame with me,
        The tomb my mother and father appointed for me,
        And let me die there, as they willed I should.

And yet I know
Death will not ever come to me through sickness
Or in any natural way: I have been preserved
For some unthinkable fate. But let that be.

As for my sons, you need not care for them.
They are men, they will find some way to live.
But my poor daughters, who have shared my table,
Who never before have been parted from their father—
Take care of them. Creon; do this for me.
And will you let me touch them with my hands
A last time, and let us weep together?
Be kind, my lord.
Great prince, be kind!
                Could I but touch them,
They would be mine again, as when I had my eyes.
      [*Enter* ANTIGONE *and* ISMENE, *attended.*]
Ah, God!
Is it my dearest children I hear weeping?
Has Creon pitied me and sent my daughters?
CREON: Yes, Oedipus: I knew that they were dear to you
    In the old days, and know you must love them still.
OEDIPUS: May God bless you for this—and be a friendlier
    Guardian to you than he has been to me!
    Children, where are you?
    Come quickly to my hands: they are your brother's—
    Hands that have brought your father's once clear eyes
    To this way of seeing—
                Ah dearest ones,
I had neither sight nor knowledge then, your father
By the woman who was the source of his own life!
And I weep for you—having no strength to see you—
I weep for you when I think of the bitterness
That men will visit upon you all your lives.
What homes, what festivals can you attend
Without being forced to depart again in tears?
And when you come to marriageable age,
Where is the man, my daughters, who would dare
Risk the bane that lies on all my children?
Is there any evil wanting? Your father killed
His father; sowed the womb of her who bore him;
Engendered you at the fount of his own existence!
That is what they will say of you
                     Then, whom
Can you ever marry? There are no bridegrooms for you,
And your lives must wither away in sterile dreaming.

O Creon, son of Menoikeus!
You are the only father my daughters have,
Since we, their parents, are both of us gone for ever.

They are your own blood: you will not let them
Fall into beggary and loneliness;
You will keep them from the miseries that are mine!
Take pity on them; see, they are only children,
Friendless except for you. Promise me this,
Great Prince, and give me your hand in token of it.

      [CREON *clasps his right hand.*]

      Children:
I could say much, if you could understand me,
But as it is, I have only this prayer for you:
Live where you can, be as happy as you can—
Happier, please God, than God has made your father!

CREON: Enough. You have wept enough. Now go within.

OEDIPUS: I must; but it is hard.

CREON: Time eases all things.

OEDIPUS: But you must promise—

CREON: Say what you desire.

OEDIPUS: Send me from Thebes!

CREON: God grant that I may!

OEDIPUS: But since God hates me...

CREON: No, he will grant your wish.

OEDIPUS: You promise?

CREON: I can not speak beyond my knowledge.

OEDIPUS: Then lead me in.

CREON: Come now, and leave your children.

OEDIPUS: No! Do not take them from me!

CREON: Think no longer
That you are in command here, but rather think
How, when you were, you served your own destruction.

      [*Exeunt into the house all but the* CHORUS; *the* CHORAGOS *chants directly to the audience.*]

CHORAGOS: Men of Thebes: look upon Oedipus.

This is the king who solved the famous riddle
And towered up, most powerful of men.
No mortal eyes but looked on him with envy,
Yet in the end ruin swept over him.

Let every man in mankind's frailty
Consider his last day; and let none
Presume on his good fortune until he find
Life, at his death, a memory without pain.

Noah and His Sons

(A.D. 1425–1450)

NOAH AND HIS SONS was presented at Wakefield (England), the third of the thirty-two short plays that together dramatized the biblical account of human existence from Creation to the Last Judgment. The entire cycle was presented out of doors during the Corpus Christi festival, a religious celebration of the sacrament of bread and wine (the body and blood of Christ), the union of the human and divine in the person of Christ, and the promise of redemption through His sacrifice.

The central feature of the Corpus Christi festival was a procession (which included representatives from every rank and profession) through the town with the consecrated bread and wine. This procession may have been the inspiration for the staging of the cycle: mounting plays on wagons and performing them at various stops along a processional route. Each play was assigned to a different trade guild that was then responsible for mounting and financing its play. The overall cycle was under the supervision of the town council, and the scripts had to be approved by the church.

Noah and His Sons is one of five plays identified as the work of the "Wakefield Master," works considered far superior to the other plays in the same cycle. *Noah* is noted in part for the variety achieved through the comic bickering of the title character and his wife, an element that locates the action in a world familiar to the medieval audience. The play is short (558 lines), made up of sixty-two nine-line stanzas. The structure of the stanzas suggests a formalized delivery by the performers.

The play is divided into three parts of approximately equal length: the opening expository scene with God and Noah establishing justification for the flood; two scenes of bickering between Noah and his wife; and the scenes showing first the building of the ark and then the time on board. It is clear, entertaining, and didactic.

Noah and His Sons

EDITED BY OSCAR G. BROCKETT

Characters

NOAH
GOD
NOAH'S WIFE
FIRST SON
SECOND SON
THIRD SON
FIRST WIFE
SECOND WIFE
THIRD WIFE

Note: Many obsolete words have been retained so as not to alter unduly the rhyme scheme. The first four lines of each nine-line stanza use both end and midline rhymes; the fifth and ninth lines rhyme, as do lines six through eight. To clarify obsolete words, modern equivalents have been placed in brackets immediately following the words they clarify.

NOAH: Mightful god veray [truly], Maker of all that is,
    Three persons, none say nay, one god in endless bliss,
    Thou made both night and day, beast, fowl, and fish,
    All creatures that live may, wrought thou at thy wish,
      As thou well might;
    The sun, the moon, verament [truly],
    Thou made; the firmament,
    The stars also, full fervent,
      To shine thou made full bright.

    Angels thou made full even, all orders that is,
    To have the bliss in heaven. This did thou more and less,
    Full marvelous to neven [tell]; yet was there unkindness,
    More by folds seven than I can well express;
      For why?
    Of all angels in brightness
    God gave Lucifer most lightness,
    Yet proudly he fled his dais,
      And set him even Him by.

    He thought himself as worthy as Him that him made;

In brightness, in beauty, therefore God did him degrade;
Put him in a low degree soon after, in a brade [minute],
Him and all his menye [minions], where he may be unglad
  For ever.
Shall they never win away,
Hence unto doomsday,
But burn in hell for aye,
  Shall they depart never.

Soon after, that gracious lord in His likeness made man,
That place to be restored, even as he began,
Of the Trinity by accord, Adam and Eve, that woman,
To multiply without discord, in paradise put He them,
  And sayeth to both
Gave in commandment,
On the tree of life to lay no hand;
But yet the false fiend
  Made Him with man wroth,

Enticed man to gluttony, stirred him to sin in pride;
But in paradise securely might no sin abide,
And therefore man full hastily was put out, in that tide [time],
In woe and wretchedness for to be, in pains full cried,
  To know,
First on earth, and then in hell
With fiends for to dwell,
But He his mercy mell [dispenses]
  To those that will Him trow [swear allegiance].

Oil of mercy He has hight [promised], as I have heard said,
To every living wight that would love Him and dread;
But now before His sight every living leyde [person],
Most party day and night, sin in word and deed
  Full bold;
Some in pride, ire, and envy,
Some in covetousness and gluttony,
Some in sloth and lechery,
  And otherwise manifold.

Therefore I dread lest God on us will take vengeance
For sin is now allowed without any repentance;
Six hundred years and odd have I, without distance [dispute],
On earth, as any sod, lived with great grievance
  Always;
And now I wax old,
Sick, sorry, and cold,
As muck upon mold
  I wither away;
But yet will I cry for mercy and call;
Noah thy servant, am I, Lord over all!

Lest me and my fry shall also fall;
Save from villainy and bring to Thy hall
  In heaven;
And keep me from sin,
This world within;
Comely king of mankind,
  I pray Thee, hear my stevyn [voice]!

  [GOD *appears above.*]
GOD: Since I have made all thing that is liffand [living],
  Duke, emperor, and king, with mine own hand,
  For to have their liking by sea and by sand,
  Every man to my bidding should be bound
    Full fervent;
  That made man such a creature,
  Fairest of favor,
  Man must love me par-amour,
    By reason, and repent.

Methought I showed man love when I made him to be
All angels above, like to the Trinity;
And now in great reproof full low lies he,
On earth himself to stuff with sin that displeases me
  Most of all;
Vengeance will I take,
In earth for sin's sake,
My anger thus will I wake,
  Both of great and small.

I repent full sore that ever I made man,
By me he sets no store, and I am his sovereign;
I will destroy, therefore, both beast, man and woman,
All shall perish, less and more; that bargain may they ban [regret],
  That ill has done.
In earth I see right naught
But sin that is unsought [unrepented];
Of those that well has wrought
  Find I almost none.

Therefore shall I undo [destroy] all this middle erd [earth]
With floods that shall flow and run with hideous rerd [noise];
I have good cause thereto: of me no man is afeard,
As I say, shall I do: of vengeance draw my sword,
  And make end
Of all that bears life,
Save Noah and his wife,
For they would never strive
  With me nor me offend.

To him to great win [joy] hastily will I go,
To Noah my servant, ere I blyn [stop] to warn him of his woe.
In earth I see but sin running to and fro,

Among both more and min [less], each the other's foe;
  With all their intent;
They shall I forego [destroy]
With floods that shall flow,
I shall work them woe,
  That will not repent.

     [GOD *descends and comes to* NOAH.]
GOD: Noah, my friend, I thee command, from cares thee dispel,
  A ship I do demand of nail and board full well.
  Thou was e'er a trusty man, to me true as steel,
  To my bidding obedient; friendship shall thou feel
    To mede [in reward].
  Of length thy ship be
  Three hundred cubits, warn I thee,
  Of height even thirty,
    Of fifty also in brede [breadth].

Anoint thy ship with pitch and tar without and also within,
The water out to spar [keep] this is a helpful gyn [means];
Look no man thee mar. Three tiers of chambers begin,
Thou must spend many a spar, this work ere thou win
  To end fully.
Make in thy ship also,
Parlors one or two,
And other houses mo [more],
  For beasts that there must be.

One cubit in height a window shall thou make;
On the side a doore with slyght [skill] beneath shall thou take;
With thee shall no man fight, nor do thee any kind of hate.
When all is done thus right, thy wife, that is thy mate,
  Take in to thee;
Thy sons of good fame,
Shem, Japhet, and Ham,
Take in also them,
  Their wives also three.

For all shall be undone [destroyed] that live on land but ye,
With floods that from above shall fall, and that plentily;
It shall begin full soon to rain incessantly,
After seven days' twill come, and endure days forty,
  Without fail.
Take to thy ship also
Of each kind, beasts two,
Male and female, but no more,
  Ere thou pull up thy sail.

For they may thee avail when all this thing is wrought;
Stuff thy ship with victual, for hunger that ye perish nought;
Of beasts, fowl, and cattle, for them have thou in thought,
For them in my counsel, that some succor be sought,

In haste;
They must have corn and hay,
And other meat alway;
Do now as I thee say,
    In the name of the Holy Ghost.

NOAH: Ah! Benedicite! What art thou that thus
        Tells afore that shall be? Thou art full marvelous!
        Tell me, for charity, thy name so gracious.
GOD: My name is of dignity and also full glorious
        To know.
    I am God most mighty,
    One God in Trinity,
    Made thee and each man to be;
        To love me well thou owe.

NOAH: I thank thee, lord so dear, that would vouch safe
        Thus low to appear to a simple knave;
        Bless us, lord, here, for charity I it crave,
        The better may we steer the ship that we shall have,
        Certain.
GOD: Noah, to thee and thy fry
    My blessing grant I;
    Ye shall wax and multiply,
        And fill the earth again,

        When all these floods are past and fully gone away.
NOAH: Lord, homeward will I haste as fast as that I may;
        My wife will I frast [ask] what she will say, [*Exit* GOD]
        And I am aghast that we get some fray
        Betwixt us both;
    For she is full testy,
    For little oft angry,
    If anything wrong be,
        Soon is she wroth. [*He goes to his wife.*]

        God speed, dear wife, how fare ye?
WIFE: Now, as ever I might thrive, the worst is I see thee;
        Do tell me belife [quickly] where has thou thus long be?
        To death may we drive, or live for thee [for all you care],
        For want indeed.
    When we sweat or swink [labor],
    Thou does what thou think,
    Yet of meat and of drink
        Have we great need.

NOAH: Wife, we are hard stead with tidings new.
WIFE: But thou were worthy be clad in Stafford blue [be beaten blue];
        For thou art always afraid, be it false or true;
        But God knows I am led, and that may I rue,
        For ill;
    For I dare be thy borrow [pledge],
    From even unto morrow,

Thou speaks ever of sorrow;
  God send thee once thy fill!

We women may wary [curse] all ill husbands;
I have one, by Mary, that loosed me of my bands;
If he be troubled I must tarry, how so ever it stands,
With semblance full sorry, wringing both my hands
  For dread.
But yet other while,
With pleasure and with guile,
I shall smite and smile,
  And quit him his mede [give him what he deserves].

NOAH: Well! hold thy tongue ram-skyt, or I shall thee still!
WIFE: By my thrift, if thou smite, I shall turn thee until!
NOAH: We shall assay as tight! Have at thee, Gill!
  Upon the bone shall it bite!
WIFE: Ah, so, marry! thou smitest ill!
  But I suppose
I shall not in thy debt,
Flee from this flett [floor]!
Take thee there a langett [thong]
  To tie up thy hose!

NOAH: A! wilt thou so? Marry, that is mine.
WIFE: Thou shall three for two, I swear by God's pain!
NOAH: And I shall return them though, in faith, ere syne [long].
WIFE: Out upon thee, ho!
NOAH: Thou can both bite and whine,
  with a rerd [noise];
For all if she strike,
Yet fast will she shriek,
In faith I hold none like
  In all middle-earth;

But I will keep charity, for I have work to do.
WIFE: Here shall no man tarry thee. I pray thee go to!
  Full well may we miss thee as ever have I ro [peace];
  To spin will I dress me.
NOAH: Well, farewell, lo!
  But wife,
Pray for me busily,
Till again I come unto thee.
WIFE: Even as thou prays for me,
  As ever might I thrive. [*Exit* WIFE.]

NOAH: I tarry full long from my work, I trow;
  Now my gear will I fang [take] and thitherward draw;
  I may full ill gang [go], the truth for to know,
  But if God help not among, I may sit down daw [melancholy]
  To ken;
Now assay will I
How I can of wrightry [workmanship],

In nomine patris et filii, et spiritus sancti,
  Amen.

To begin of this tree, my bones will I bend,
I trust from the Trinity succor will be sent;
It fares full fair, think me, this work to my hand;
Now blessed be he that this can amend.
  Lo, here the length,
Three hundred cubits evenly,
Of breadth, lo, is it fifty,
The height is even thirty
  Cubits full strength.

Now my gown will I cast, and work in my coat,
Make will I the mast ere I shift one foot,
A! my back, I trow, will burst! This is a sorry note!
It is wonder that I last, such an old dote
  All dulled,
To begin such a work!
My bones are so stark [stiff],
No wonder if they wark [ache],
  For I am full old.

The top and the sail both will I make,
The helm and the castle also will I take;
To drive each single nail will I not forsake;
This gear may never fail, that dare I undertake
  At once.
This is a noble gin [device]
These nails so they run,
Through more and min [less],
  These boards each one;

Window and door, even as he said,
Three chief chambers, they are well made;
Pitch and tar full sure thereupon laid,
This will ever endure, thereof am I paid;
  for why?
It is better wrought
Than I could have thought;
Him that made all of nought
  I thank only.

Now will I hie me and nothing be lither [slow],
My wife and my meneye [family], to bring even hither.
Attend hither tidily wife, and consider,
Hence must us flee, all of us together,
  In haste.
WIFE: Why, sir, what ails you?
  Who is't that assails you?
  To flee it avails you,
    And ye be aghast [afraid].

NOAH: [*seeing his wife spinning*] There is yarn on the reel other, my dame.
WIFE: Tell me that each deal, else get ye blame.
NOAH: He that cares may keill [cool] blessed be his name!
    He has for our seyll [happiness] to shield us from shame,
      And said,
    All this world about
    With floods so stout,
    That shall run on a route,
      Shall be overlaid.

    He said all shall be slain but only we,
    Our sons that are bayn [obedient] and their wives three;
    A ship he bade me ordain, to save us and our fee [property],
    Therefore with all our main, thank we that free
      Healer of bayll [sorrow];
    Hie us fast, go we thither.
WIFE: I know never whither,
    I am dazed and I dither
      For fear of that tale.

NOAH: Be not afeard, have done. Pack up our gear,
    That we be there ere noon without more dere [hindrance].
FIRST SON: It shall be done full soon. Brothers, help to bear.
SECOND SON: Full long shall I not hoyne [delay] to do my share,
    Brother Shem.
THIRD SON: Without any yelp,
    With my might shall I help.
WIFE: Yet for dread of a skelp [blow]
    Help well thy dam.

NOAH : Now are we there as we should be;
    To get in our gear, our cattle and fee,
    In this vessel here, my children free.
WIFE: I was never shut up ere, as now might I be,
    In such an hostel as this,
    In faith I can not find
    Which is before, which is behind.
    But shall we here be confined,
      Noah, as have thou bliss?

NOAH: Dame, as it is skill [reason], here must us abide grace;
    Therefore, wife, with good will come into this place.
WIFE: Sir, for Jack nor for Jill will I turn my face
    Till I have on this hill spun a space
      on my rok [distaff];
    Well were he, might get me,
    Now will I down set me,
    Yet reede [warn] I no man let me [stop me],
      For dread of a knock.

NOAH: Behold from the heaven the cararacts all,
    That are open full even, great and small,

And the planets seven gone from their stall,
These thunders and levyn [lightning] down make fall
  Full stout,
Both halls and bowers,
Castles and towers;
Full sharp are these showers,
  That rain about;

Therefore, wife, have done. Come into ship fast.
WIFE: Yea, Noah, go patch thy shone [shoes] the better will they last.
FIRST WIFE: Good mother, come in soon, for all is overcast,
  Both the sun and the moon.
SECOND WIFE: And many winds blast
  Full sharp.
These floods so thay run,
Therefore, mother, come in.
WIFE: In faith, yet will I spin;
  All in vain ye carp.

THIRD WIFE: If ye like ye may spin, Mother, in the ship.
NOAH: Now is this twice. Come in, dame, on my friendship.
WIFE: Whether I lose or I win, in faith, for thy fellowship
  Care I not a pin. This spindle will I slip
    Upon this hill,
  Ere I stir one foot.
NOAH: Peter! I trow we dote;
  Without any more note
    Come in if ye will.

WIFE: Yea, water nighs so near that I sit not dry;
  Into the ship with a byr [rush] therefore will I hie
  For dread that I drown here.
NOAH: Dame, securely,
  It be bought full dear, ye abode so long by
    Out of the ship.
WIFE: I will not, for thy bidding,
  Go from door to midding [dunghill; do whatever you demand].
NOAH: In faith, and for your long tarrying
  Ye shall taste of the whip.

WIFE : Spare me not, I pray thee, but even as thou think,
  These great words shall not flay me.
NOAH: Abide, dame, and drink,
  For beaten shall thou be, with this staff till thou stink;
  Are the strokes good? say me.
WIFE: What say ye, Wat Wynk?
NOAH: Speak!
  Cry me mercy, I say!
WIFE: Thereto say I nay.
NOAH: Unless thou do, by this day,
  Thy head shall I break.

[*To women in the audience*]

WIFE: Lord, I were at rest and heartily full whole,
Might I once have a mess of widow's coyll [fare];
For thy soul, without jest, should I deal penny doyll [alms],
So would more, no frese [fear], that I see in this sole [place]
   Of wives that are here
For the life they have led
Would their husbands were dead
For, as ever ate I bread,
   So would I our sire were.

[*To men in the audience*]

NOAH: Ye men who have wives whilst they are young,
If you love your lives, chastise their tongue:
Methinks my heart rives, both liver and lung,
To see such strifes, wedmen among;
   But I,
As have I bliss,
Shall chastise this.
WIFE : Yet may you miss,
   Nicholl Neddy!

NOAH: I shall make thee still as stone, beginner of blunder!
I shall beat thee back and bone and break all asunder.
   [*They fight.*]
WIFE: Oh, alas, I am gone! Out upon thee, man's wonder!
NOAH: See how she can groan, and I lie under!
   But, wife,
In this haste let us ho [stop],
For my back is near in two.
WIFE: And I am beat so blue
   That I may not thrive.
   [*They enter the ark.*]

FIRST SON: Ah! why fare ye thus? Father and mother both!
SECOND SON: Ye should not be so spitus [spiteful] standing in such a
   woth [danger].
THIRD SON: These weathers are so hidus [hideous] with many a cold
   coth [disease].
NOAH: We will do as ye bid us. We will no more be wroth,
   Dear bairns!
Now to the helm will I hent [go],
And to my ship tend.
WIFE: I see on the firmament,
   Methinks, the seven stars.

NOAH: This is a great flood, wife, take heed.
WIFE: So me thought, as I stood. We are in great dread;
   These waves are so wode [wild].
NOAH: Help, God, in this need!

As thou art steerman good and best, as I rede [counsel],
  Of all;
Thou rule us in this race,
As thou me promised has.
WIFE: This is a perilous case:
  Help, God, when we call!

NOAH: Wife, attend the steer-tree, and I shall assay
  The deepness of the sea that we bear, if I may.
WIFE: That shall I do full wisely. Now go thy way,
  For upon this flood have we floated many a day,
    With pain.
NOAH: Now the water will I sound
  Ah! it is far to the ground;
  This travail I expound
    Had I to tyne [lose].

Above all hills bedeyn [completely] the water is risen late
Cubits fifteen, but in a higher state
It may not be, I ween, for this well I wate [know],
This forty days has rain been. It will therefore abate
  Full lele [loyal].
This water in haste,
Eft will I test;
Now am I aghast,
  It is waned a great deal.

Now are the weathers ceased and cataracts quit,
Both the most and the least.
WIFE: Methink, by my wit,
  The sun shines in the east. Lo, is not yond it?
  We should have a good feast were these floods flit
    So spytus [malicious].
NOAH: We have been here, all we,
  Three hundred days and fifty.
WIFE: Yea, now wanes the sea;
    Lord, well is us!

NOAH: The third time will I prove [test] what deepness we bear.
WIFE: How long shall thou heave. Lay in thy line there.
NOAH: I may touch with my lufe [hand] the ground even here.
WIFE: Then begins to grufe [grow] to us merry cheer;
    But, husband,
                        What ground may this be?
NOAH: The hills of Armenia.
WIFE: Now blessed be he
    That thus for us ordained!

NOAH: I see tops of hills he [high] many at a sight,
  Nothing to hinder me, the weather is so bright.
WIFE: These are of mercy, tokens full right.
NOAH: Dame, thou counsel me what fowl best might

And cowth [could],
With flight of wing
Bring, without tarrying,
Of mercy some tokening
Either by north or south.

For this is the first day of the tenth moon.
WIFE: The raven, dare I lay, will come again soon;
As fast as thou may cast him forth, have done,
He may happen to day come again ere noon
Without delay.
NOAH: I will cast out also
Doves one or two:
Go your way, go,
God send you some prey!

Now are these fowls flown into separate country;
Pray we fast each one, kneeling on our knee,
To him that is alone worthiest of degree,
That he would send anon our fowls some fee
To glad us.
WIFE: They may not fail of land,
The water is so wanand [waning].
NOAH: Thank we God all weldand [wielding],
That lord that made us.

It is a wondrous thing, me thinks soothly,
They are so long tarrying, the fowls that we
Cast out in the morning.
WIFE: Sir, it may be
They tarry till they bring.
NOAH: The raven is a-hungry
Alway;
He is without any reason,
If he find any carrion,
As peradventure may befon [befall],
He will not away;

The dove is more gentle, her trust I unto,
Like unto the turtle, for she is ay true.
WIFE: Hence but a little. She comes, lew, lew!
She brings in her bill some novels [signs] new;
Behold!
It is of an olive tree
A branch, thinkest me.
NOAH: It is so, perde [par dieu; by our God],
Right so is it called.

Dove, bird full blest, fair might thee befall!
Thou art true for to trust as stone in the wall;
Full well I it wist [knew] thou would come to thy hall.
WIFE: A true token is't we shall be saved all;

For why?
The water, since she come,
Of deepness plumb,
Is fallen a fathom,
    And more hardily [certainly].

FIRST SON: These floods are gone. Father, behold!
SECOND SON: There is left right none, and that be ye bold.
THIRD SON: As still as a stone, our ship is stalled.
NOAH: Upon land here anon that we were, fain I would;
    My childer dear,
    Shem, Japhet, and Ham,
    With glee and with gam [sport],
    Come we all sam [together],
        We will no longer abide here.

WIFE: Here have we been, Noah, long enough,
    With trouble and with teyn [grief], and endured much woe.
NOAH: Behold on this green neither cart nor plough
    Is left, as I ween, neither tree nor bough,
        Nor other thing,
    But all is away;
    Many castles, I say,
    Great towns of array,
        Flit [destroyed] has this flowyng [flood].

WIFE: These floods, not afright, all this world so wide
    Has moved with might, on sea and by side.
NOAH: To death are they dyght [gone], proudest of pride,
    Every wight that ever was spied,
        With sin,
    All are they slain,
    And put unto pain.
WIFE: From thence again
    May they never win.

NOAH: Win? no, I-wis, but He that might has
    Would remember their mys [misery] and admit them to
        grace;
    As He in misfortune is bliss, I pray Him in this space,
    In heaven high with His, to secure us a place,
        That we,
    With His saints in sight,
    And His angels bright,
    May come to His light:
        Amen, for charity.

Hamlet, Prince of Denmark

(c. 1600)

uring the sixteenth century, after religious drama was forbidden, the groups that had financed and staged the cycle plays ceased their support of theatre, disapproving of the professional and commercial role that theatre had been forced to adopt in order to survive. The necessity of attracting a paying audience motivated acting companies to offer a different play each day (though the same play might be repeated at intervals during a season), and thus they created an ongoing demand for new plays. Partially for this reason, the years between 1585 and 1610 produced an exceptional number of outstanding English playwrights. William Shakespeare is universally acknowledged the greatest, and possibly the greatest playwright the world has known.

In addition to being a playwright, Shakespeare was an actor, a shareholder (part owner) both in his acting company and in the theatre in which the company performed. As the company's principal playwright, he wrote an average of two plays each season. Among his thirty-eight surviving plays, *Hamlet* is one of the most admired.

Hamlet, like *Oedipus Rex*, has as its protagonist a man who is charged with punishing the murderer of a king. But Shakespeare uses a much broader canvas than Sophocles does and includes within his drama more facets of his story, more characters, and a wider sweep of time and place. Shakespeare's play develops chronologically and places all important incidents on stage. The only important events that precede the play's opening (Claudius' seduction of his brother's wife and his murder of his brother) are replicated in the play-within-the-play. The rapid shifts in time and place are made possible by theatrical conventions that establish locale and other significant conditions through spoken passages ("spoken decor") that localize as needed the fixed facade against which the action occurred.

Hamlet is thematically rich: the pervasiveness of betrayal (brother of brother, wife of husband, parent of child, friend of friend): the opposing demands made on Hamlet (that he revenge his father's murder and that he adhere to Christian doctrine against murder): the nature of kingship and the need to rule oneself before ruling others: and several other themes. Shakespeare's dramatic poetry is generally conceded to be the finest in the English language. The basic medium is blank verse, which allows the flexibility of ordinary speech while elevating it through imagery and rhythm.

Because of its compelling story, powerful characters, and great poetry, *Hamlet* is one of the world's finest achievements in drama. Although it embodies many ideas typical of its time, it transcends the limitations of a particular era. It continues to move spectators in the theatre as it has since its first presentation around 1600.

WILLIAM SHAKESPEARE

Hamlet, Prince of Denmark

Dramatis Personae

CLAUDIUS, *King of Denmark*
HAMLET, *son to the former and nephew to the present king*
POLONIUS, *Lord Chamberlain*
HORATIO, *friend to Hamlet*
LAERTES, *son to Polonius*
VOLTEMAND ⎫
CORNELIUS
ROSENCRANTZ
GUILDENSTERN ⎬ *courtiers*
OSRIC
A GENTLEMAN ⎭
A PRIEST
MARCELLUS ⎫
BERNARDO ⎬ *officers*
FRANCISCO, *a soldier*
REYNALDO, *servant to Polonius*
PLAYERS
TWO CLOWNS, *grave diggers*
FORTINBRAS, *prince of Norway*
A NORWEGIAN CAPTAIN
ENGLISH AMBASSADORS
GERTRUDE, *queen of Denmark, and mother of Hamlet*
OPHELIA, *daughter to Polonius*
GHOST *of Hamlet's father*
LORDS, LADIES, OFFICERS, SOLDIERS, SAILORS, MESSENGERS,
    AND ATTENDANTS

SCENE————*Denmark.*

ACT I

SCENE I————*Elsinore. The guard-platform of the Castle.*

[FRANCISCO *at his post. Enter to him* BERNARDO.]
BERNARDO: Who's there?
FRANCISCO: Nay, answer me. Stand and unfold* yourself.

---

*indicates a note identified by line number. The textual reference is given in bold type, its clarification in roman type.
1,i, 2 **unfold** identify

BERNARDO: Long live the king!

FRANCISCO: Bernardo?

BERNARDO: He.

FRANCISCO: You come most carefully upon your hour. 5

BERNARDO: 'Tis now struck twelve; get thee to bed, Francisco.

FRANCISCO: For this relief much thanks. 'Tis bitter cold,
>And I am sick at heart.

BERNARDO: Have you had quiet guard? 10

FRANCESO: Not a mouse stirring.

BERNARDO: Well; good night.
>If you do meet Horatio and Marcellus,
>The rivals* of my watch, bid them make haste.
>>[*Enter* HORATIO *and* MARCELLUS.]

FRANCISCO: I think I hear them. Stand, ho! Who is there? 15

HORATIO: Friends to this ground.

MARCELLUS: And liegemen to the Dane.*

FRANCISCO: Give you good night.

MARCELLUS: O, farewell, honest soldier!
>Who hath reliev'd you? 20

FRANCISCO: Bernardo hath my place.
>Give you good night. [*Exit.*]

MARCELLUS: Holla, Bernardo!

BERNARDO: Say—
>What, is Horatio there? 25

HORATIO: A piece of him.

BERNARDO: Welcome, Horatio; welcome, good Marcellus.

HORATIO: What, has this thing appear'd again to-night?

BERNARDO: I have seen nothing.

MARCELLUS: Horatio says 'tis but our fantasy, 30
>And will not let belief take hold of him
>Touching this dreaded sight, twice seen of us;
>Therefore I have entreated him along
>With us to watch the minutes of this night,
>That, if again this apparition come, 35
>He may approve* our eyes and speak to it.

HORATIO: Tush, tush, 'twill not appear.

BERNARDO: Sit down awhile,
>And let us once again assail your ears,
>That are so fortified against our story, 40
>What we have two nights seen.

HORATIO: Well, sit we down,
>And let us hear Bernardo speak of this.

---

14 **rivals** companions
17 **liegemen to the Dane** loyal subjects to the king of Denmark
36 **approve** confirm

BERNARDO: Last night of all,
 When yond same star that's westward from the pole   45
 Had made his course t' illume that part of heaven
 Where now it burns, Marcellus and myself,
 The bell then beating one—
  [*Enter* GHOST.]
MARCELLUS: Peace, break thee off; look where it comes again.
BERNARDO: In the same figure, like the King that's dead.   50
MARCELLUS: Thou art a scholar; speak to it, Horatio.
BERNARDO: Looks 'a not like the King? Mark it, Horatio.
HORATIO: Most like. It harrows me with fear and wonder.
BERNARDO: It would be spoke to.
MARCELLUS: Question it, Horatio.   55
HORATIO: What art thou that usurp'st this time of night
 Together with that fair and warlike form
 In which the majesty of buried Denmark*
 Did sometimes march? By heaven I charge thee, speak!
MARCELLUS: It is offended.   60
BERNARDO: See, it stalks away.
HORATIO: Stay! speak, speak! I charge thee, speak!
  [*Exit* GHOST.]
MARCELLUS: 'Tis gone, and will not answer.
BERNARDO: How now, Horatio! You tremble and look pale.
 Is not this something more than fantasy?   65
 What think you on't?
HORATIO: Before my God, I might not this believe
 Without the sensible and true avouch*
 Of mine own eyes.
MARCELLUS: Is it not like the King?   70
HORATIO: As thou art to thyself:
 Such was the very armour he had on
 When he the ambitious Norway* combated;
 So frown'd he once when, in an angry parle,*
 He smote the sledded Polacks* on the ice.   75
 'Tis strange.
MARCELLUS: Thus twice before, and jump* at this dead hour,
 With martial stalk hath he gone by our watch.
HORATIO: In what particular thought to work I know not;
 But, in the gross and scope* of mine opinion,   80
 This bodes some strange eruption to our state.
MARCELLUS: Good now, sit down, and tell me, he that knows,
 Why this same strict and most observant watch

---

58 **buried Denmark** buried king of Denmark
68 **avouch** proof
73 **Norway** king of Norway
74 **parle** parley
75 **sledded Polacks** Poles on sleds
77 **jump** just
80 **gross and scope** general drift

So nightly toils the subject* of the land;
And why such daily cast of brazen cannon, 85
And foreign mart* for implements of war;
Why such impress* of shipwrights, whose sore task
Does not divide the Sunday from the week;
What might be toward,* that this sweaty haste
Doth make the night joint-labourer with the day: 90
Who is't that can inform me?
HORATIO: That can I;
At least, the whisper goes so. Our last King,
Whose image even but now appear'd to us,
Was, as you know, by Fortinbras of Norway, 95
Thereto prick'd on by a most emulate pride,
Dar'd to the combat; in which our valiant Hamlet—
For so this side of our known world esteem'd him—
Did slay this Fortinbras; who, by a seal'd compact,
Well ratified by law and heraldry,* 100
Did forfeit, with his life, all those his lands
Which he stood seiz'd of,* to the conqueror;
Against the which a moiety competent*
Was gaged* by our King; which had return'd
To the inheritance of Fortinbras, 105
Had he been vanquisher; as, by the same comart*
And carriage of the article design'd,*
His fell to Hamlet. Now, sir, young Fortinbras,
Of unimproved* mettle hot and full,
Hath in the skirts* of Norway, here and there, 110
Shark'd up a list of lawless resolutes,*
For food and diet, to some enterprise
That hath a stomach in't,* which is no other,
As it doth well appear unto our state,
But to recover of us, by strong hand 115
And terms compulsatory, those foresaid lands
So by his father lost; and this, I take it,
Is the main motive of our preparations,
The source of this our watch, and the chief head*

---

84 **nightly toils the subject** citizens work by night (as well as by day)
86 **mart** trade
87 **impress** forced service
89 **toward** in preparation
100 **law and heraldry** heraldic law
102 **seiz'd of** in possession of
103 **moiety competent** like portion
104 **gaged** pledged
106 **comart** agreement
107 **carriage of the article design'd** provisions of the pact
109 **unimproved** unproved
110 **skirts** borders, outskirts
111 **Shark'd up a list of lawless resolutes** enlisted a force of desperate men
113 **hath a stomach in't** requires courage
119 **chief head** principal reason

Of this post-haste and romage* in the land.   120
BERNARDO: I think it be no other but e'en so.
    Well may it sort,* that this portentous figure
    Comes armed through our watch; so like the King
    That was and is the question of these wars.
HORATIO: A mote it is to trouble the mind's eye.   125
    In the most high and palmy state of Rome,
    A little ere the mightiest Julius fell,
    The graves stood tenantless, and the sheeted dead
    Did squeak and gibber in the Roman streets;
    As, stars with trains of fire, and dews of blood,   130
    Disasters* in the sun; and the moist star*
    Upon whose influence Neptune's empire* stands
    Was sick almost to doomsday with eclipse;
    And even the like precurse* of fear'd events,
    As harbingers preceding still the fates   135
    And prologue to the omen coming on,
    Have heaven and earth together demonstrated
    Unto our climatures* and countrymen.
        [*Reenter* GHOST.]
    But, soft, behold! Lo, where it comes again!
    I'll cross it,* though it blast me. Stay, illusion.   140
        [GHOST *spreads its arms.*]
    If thou hast any sound or use of voice,
    Speak to me.
    If there be any good thing to be done,
    That may to thee do ease and grace to me,
    Speak to me.   145
    If thou art privy to thy country's fate,
    Which happily* foreknowing may avoid,
    O, speak!
    Or if thou hast uphoarded in thy life
    Extorted treasure in the womb of earth,   150
    For which, they say, you spirits oft walk in death,
        [*The cock crows.*]
    Speak of it. Stay, and speak. Stop it, Marcellus.
MARCELLUS: Shall I strike at it with my partisan?*
HORATIO: Do, if it will not stand.
BERNARDO: 'Tis here!   155
HORATIO: 'Tis here!

---

120 **romage** bustling activity
122 **sort** turn out
131 **Disasters** threatening signs
131 **moist star** the moon
132 **Neptune's empire** the ocean (the Roman god Neptune's domain)
134 **precurse** foreshadowing
138 **climatures** regions
140 **cross it** cross its path
147 **happily** haply, perhaps
153 **partisan** pike (weapon)

MARCELLUS: 'Tis gone!   [*Exit* GHOST.]
    We do it wrong, being so majestical,
    To offer it the show of violence;
    For it is, as the air, invulnerable,   160
    And our vain blows malicious mockery.
BERNARDO: It was about to speak, when the cock crew.
HORATIO: And then it started like a guilty thing
    Upon a fearful summons. I have heard
    The cock, that is the trumpet to the morn,   165
    Doth with his lofty and shrill-sounding throat
    Awake the god of day; and at his warning,
    Whether in sea or fire, in earth or air,
    Th' extravagant and erring* spirit hies
    To his confine; and of the truth herein   170
    This present object made probation.*
MARCELLUS: It faded on the crowing of the cock.
    Some say that ever 'gainst* that season comes
    Wherein our Saviour's birth is celebrated,
    This bird of dawning singeth all night long;   175
    And then, they say, no spirit dare stir abroad,
    The nights are wholesome, then no planets strike,*
    No fairy takes, nor witch hath power to charm,
    So hallowed and so gracious is that time.
HORATIO: So have I heard, and do in part believe it.   180
    But look, the morn, in russet mantle clad,
    Walks o'er the dew of yon high eastward hill.
    Break we our watch up; and, by my advice,
    Let us impart what we have seen to-night
    Unto young Hamlet; for, upon my life,   185
    This spirit, dumb to us, will speak to him.
    Do you consent we shall acquaint him with it,
    As needful in our loves, fitting our duty?
MARCELLUS: Let's do't, I pray; and I this morning know
    Where we shall find him most convenient.   190
                                                [*Exeunt.*]

SCENE II————*Elsinore. The Castle.*

[*Flourish.* *Enter* CLAUDIUS KING OF DENMARK, GERTRUDE THE QUEEN, *and*
COUNCILLORS, *including* POLONIUS, *his son* LAERTES, VOLTEMAND, CORNELIUS,
and HAMLET.]
KING: Though yet of Hamlet our dear brother's death
    The memory be green; and that it us befitted
    To bear our hearts in grief, and our whole kingdom
    To be contracted in one brow of woe;

---

169 **extravagant and erring** wandering outside its proper realm
171 **made probation** gives proof
173 **ever 'gainst** just before
177 **strike** exert evil influence
I,ii (stage direction) **Flourish** trumpet fanfare

Yet so far hath discretion fought with nature   5
That we with wisest sorrow think on him,
Together with remembrance of ourselves.
Therefore our sometime sister,* now our queen,
Th' imperial jointress* to this warlike state,
Have we, as 'twere with a defeated joy,   10
With an auspicious and a dropping eye,
With mirth in funeral, and with dirge in marriage,
In equal scale weighing delight and dole,
Taken to wife; nor have we herein barr'd
Your better wisdoms, which have freely gone   15
With this affair along. For all, our thanks.
Now follows that you know: young Fortinbras,
Holding a weak supposal of our worth,
Or thinking by our late dear brother's death
Our state to be disjoint and out of frame,*   20
Co-leagued with this dream of his advantage*—
He hath not fail'd to pester us with message
Importing the surrender of those lands
Lost by his father, with all bands of law,
To our most valiant brother. So much for him.   25
Now for ourself, and for this time of meeting,
Thus much the business is: we have here writ
To Norway, uncle of young Fortinbras—
Who, impotent and bed-rid, scarcely hears
Of this his nephew's purpose—to suppress   30
His further gait* herein, in that the levies,
The lists, and full proportions,* are all made
Out of his subject;* and we here dispatch
You, good Cornelius, and you, Voltemand,
For bearers of this greeting to old Norway;   35
Giving to you no further personal power
To business with the King more than the scope
Of these dilated articles* allow.
Farewell; and let your haste commend your duty.

CORNELIUS: ⎫
VOLTEMAND: ⎬   In that and in all things will we show our duty.   40

KING: We doubt it nothing; heartily farewell.
            [*Exeunt* VOLTEMAND *and* CORNELIUS.]
And now, Laertes, what's the news with you?
You told us of some suit; what is't, Laertes?
You cannot speak of reason to the Dane

---

8 **our sometime sister** my former sister-in-law
9 **jointress** joint ruler
20 **frame** order
21 **advantage** superior power
31 **gait** proceeding
32 **proportions** war supplies
33 **Out of his subject** out of the Norwegian king's subjects
38 **dilated articles** detailed documents

And lose your voice.* What wouldst thou beg, Laertes,   45
That shall not be my offer, not thy asking?
The head is not more native* to the heart,
The hand more instrumental to the mouth,
Than is the throne of Denmark to thy father.
What wouldst thou have, Laertes?   50
LAERTES: My dread lord,
    Your leave and favour to return to France;
    From whence though willingly I came to Denmark
    To show my duty in your coronation,
    Yet now, I must confess, that duty done,   55
    My thoughts and wishes bend again toward France,
    And bow them to your gracious leave and pardon.
KING: Have you your father's leave? What says Polonius?
POLONIUS: 'A hath, my lord, wrung from me my slow leave
    By laboursome petition; and at last   60
    Upon his will I seal'd my hard consent.*
    I do beseech you, give him leave to go.
KING: Take thy fair hour, Laertes; time be thine,
    And thy best graces spend it at thy will!
    But now, my cousin* Hamlet, and my son—   65
HAMLET: [*aside*] A little more than kin, and less than kind.
KING: How is it that the clouds* still hang on you?
HAMLET: Not so, my Lord; I am too much in the sun.
QUEEN: Good Hamlet, cast thy nighted colour off,
    And let thine eye look like a friend on Denmark.   70
    Do not for ever with thy vailed lids*
    Seek for thy noble father in the dust.
    Thou know'st 'tis common—all that lives must die,
    Passing through nature to eternity.
HAMLET: Ay, madam, it is common.   75
QUEEN: If it be,
    Why seems it so particular with thee?
HAMLET: Seems, madam! Nay, it is; I know not seems.
    'Tis not alone my inky cloak, good mother,
    Nor customary suits of solemn black,   80
    Nor windy suspiration* of forc'd breath,
    No, nor the fruitful river in the eye,
    Nor the dejected haviour of the visage,
    Together with all forms, moods, shapes of grief,
    That can denote me truly. These, indeed, seem;   85
    For they are actions that a man might play;
    But I have that within which passes show—

---

45 **lose your voice** waste your breath
47 **native** related
61 **hard consent** reluctantly gave consent
65 **cousin** kinsman
67 **clouds** grief; mourning dress
71 **vailed lids** lowered eyes
81 **windy suspiration** heavy sighs

These but the trappings and the suits of woe.
KING: 'Tis sweet and commendable in your nature, Hamlet,
  To give these mourning duties to your father; 90
  But you must know your father lost a father;
  That father lost, lost his; and the survivor bound,
  In filial obligation, for some term
  To do obsequious* sorrow. But to persever
  In obstinate condolement* is a course 95
  Of impious stubbornness; 'tis unmanly grief;
  It shows a will most incorrect to heaven,
  A heart unfortified, a mind impatient,
  An understanding simple and unschool'd;
  For what we know must be, and is as common 100
  As any the most vulgar thing to sense,
  Why should we in our peevish opposition
  Take it to heart? Fie! 'tis a fault to heaven,
  A fault against the dead, a fault to nature,
  To reason most absurd; whose common theme 105
  Is death of fathers, and who still hath cried,
  From the first corse* till he that died to-day,
  'This must be so.' We pray you throw to earth
  This unprevailing* woe, and think of us
  As of a father; for let the world take note 110
  You are the most immediate to our throne;
  And with no less nobility of love
  Than that which dearest father bears his son
  Do I impart toward you. For your intent
  In going back to school in Wittenberg, 115
  It is most retrograde* to our desire;
  And we beseech you bend you* to remain
  Here, in the cheer and comfort of our eye,
  Our chiefest courtier, cousin, and our son.
QUEEN: Let not thy mother lose her prayers, Hamlet: 120
  I pray thee stay with us; go not to Wittenberg.
HAMLET: I shall in all my best obey you, madam.
KING: Why, 'tis a loving and a fair reply.
  Be as ourself in Denmark. Madam, come;
  This gentle and unforc'd accord of Hamlet 125
  Sits smiling to my heart; in grace whereof,
  No jocund health that Denmark drinks to-day
  But the great cannon to the clouds shall tell
  And the King's rouse* the heaven shall bruit* again,

94 **obsequious** funereal
95 **condolement** mourning
107 **corse** corpse
109 **unprevailing** unavailing
116 **retrograde** contrary
117 **bend you** agree
129 **rouse** drinking, carousing
129 **bruit** noisily announce

Re-speaking earthly thunder. Come away.   130
    [*Flourish. Exeunt all but* HAMLET.]
HAMLET: O, that this too too solid flesh would melt,
    Thaw, and resolve itself into a dew!
    Or that the Everlasting had not fix'd
    His canon* 'gainst self-slaughter! O God! God!
    How weary, stale, flat, and unprofitable,   135
    Seem to me all the uses of this world!
    Fie on't! Ah, fie! 'tis an unweeded garden,
    That grows to seed; things rank and gross in nature
    Possess it merely.* That it should come to this!
    But two months dead! Nay, not so much, not two.   140
    So excellent a king that was to this
    Hyperion* to a satyr, so loving to my mother,
    That he might not beteem* the winds of heaven
    Visit her face too roughly. Heaven and earth!
    Must I remember? Why, she would hang on him   145
    As if increase of appetite had grown
    By what it fed on; and yet, within a month—
    Let me not think on't. Frailty, thy name is woman!—
    A little month, or ere those shoes were old
    With which she followed my poor father's body,   150
    Like Niobe,* all tears—why she, even she—
    O God! a beast that wants discourse of reason*
    Would have mourn'd longer—married with my uncle,
    My father's brother; but no more like my father
    Than I to Hercules. Within a month,   155
    Ere yet the salt of most unrighteous tears
    Had left the flushing in her galled eyes,
    She married. O, most wicked speed, to post*
    With such dexterity to incestuous* sheets!
    It is not, nor it cannot come to good.   160
    But break, my heart, for I must hold my tongue.
    [*Enter* HORATIO, MARCELLUS, *and* BERNARDO.]
HORATIO: Hail to your lordship!
HAMLET: I am glad to see you well.
    Horatio—or I do forget myself.
HORATIO: The same, my lord, and your poor servant ever.   165
HAMLET: Sir, my good friend. I'll change* that name with you.
    And what make you from Wittenberg, Horatio?
    Marcellus?
MARCELLUS: My good lord!

134 **canon** law
139 **merely** completely
142 **Hyperion** the sun god noted for beauty
143 **beteem** permit
151 **Niobe** mother in Greek mythology who wept without stopping for the death of her children
152 **wants discourse of reason** lacks reasoning power
158 **post** hasten
159 **incestuous** incestuous because the church considered a sister-in-law equivalent to being a sister
166 **change** exchange

HAMLET: I am very glad to see you. [*to* BERNARDO] Good even, sir.—   170
    But what, in faith, make you from Wittenberg?
HORATIO: A truant disposition, good my lord.
HAMLET: I would not hear your enemy say so;
    Nor shall you do my ear that violence,
    To make it truster* of your own report.   175
    Against yourself. I know you are no truant.
    But what is your affair in Elsinore?
    We'll teach you to drink deep ere you depart.
HORATIO: My lord, I came to see your father's funeral.
HAMLET: I prithee do not mock me, fellow-student;   180
    I think it was to see my mother's wedding.
HORATIO: Indeed, my lord, it followed hard upon.
HAMLET: Thrift, thrift, Horatio! The funeral bak'd-meats
    Did coldly furnish forth the marriage tables.
    Would I had met my dearest* foe in heaven   185
    Or ever I had seen that day, Horatio!
    My father—methinks I see my father.
HORATIO: Where, my lord?
HAMLET: In my mind's eye, Horatio.
HORATIO: I saw him once; 'a was a goodly king.   190
HAMLET: 'A* was a man, take him for all in all,
    I shall not look upon his like again.
HORATIO: My lord, I think I saw him yesternight.
HAMLET: Saw who?
HORATIO: My lord, the King your father.   195
HAMLET: The King my father!
HORATIO: Season your admiration* for a while
    With an attent ear, till I may deliver,
    Upon the witness of these gentlemen,
    This marvel to you.   200
HAMLET: For God's love, let me hear.
HORATIO: Two nights together had these gentlemen,
    Marcellus and Bernardo, on their watch,
    In the dead waste and middle of the night,
    Been thus encount'red. A figure like your father,   205
    Armed at point exactly, cap-a-pe,*
    Appears before them, and with solemn march
    Goes slow and stately by them; thrice he walk'd
    By their oppress'd and fear-surprised eyes,
    Within his truncheon's length,* whilst they, distill'd*   210
    Almost to jelly with the act of fear,

---

175 **truster** believer
185 **dearest** most hated
191 **'A** he
197 **Season your admiration** control your wonder
206 **cap-a-pe** head to foot
210 **truncheon's length** space of a short club
210 **distill'd** reduced

Stand dumb and speak not to him. This to me
In dreadful* secrecy impart they did;
And I with them the third night kept the watch;
Where, as they had delivered, both in time, 215
Form of the thing, each word made true and good,
The apparition comes. I knew your father;
These hands are not more like.

HAMLET: But where was this?

MARCELLUS: My lord, upon the platform where we watch. 220

HAMLET: Did you not speak to it?

HORATIO: My lord, I did;
But answer made it none; yet once methought
It lifted up its head and did address
Itself to motion, like as it would speak; 225
But even then the morning cock crew loud,
And at the sound it shrunk in haste away
And vanish'd from our sight.

HAMLET: 'Tis very strange.

HORATIO: As I do live, my honour'd lord, 'tis true; 230
And we did think it writ down in our duty
To let you know of it.

HAMLET: Indeed, indeed, sirs, but this troubles me.
Hold you the watch to-night?

ALL: We do, my lord. 235

HAMLET: Arm'd, say you?

ALL: Arm'd, my lord.

HAMLET: From top to toe?

ALL: My lord, from head to foot.

HAMLET: Then saw you not his face? 240

HORATIO: O yes, my lord; he wore his beaver* up.

HAMLET: What, look'd he frowningly?

HORATIO: A countenance more in sorrow than in anger.

HAMLET: Pale or red?

HORATIO: Nay, very pale. 245

HAMLET: And fix'd his eyes upon you?

HORATIO: Most constantly.

HAMLET: I would I had been there.

HORATIO: It would have much amaz'd you.

HAMLET: Very like, very like. Stay'd it long?

HORATIO: While one with moderate haste might tell* a hundred. 250

BOTH: Longer, longer.

HORATIO: Not when I saw't.

HAMLET: His beard was grizzl'd*—no?

HORATIO: It was, as I have seen it in his life,
A sable silver'd.* 255

---

213 **dreadful** terrified
241 **beaver** visor, face guard
251 **tell** count
253 **grizzl'd** gray
255 **sable silver'd** black mixed with gray

HAMLET: I will watch to-night;
   Perchance 'twill walk again.
HORATIO: I warr'nt it will.
HAMLET: If it assume my noble father's person.   260
   I'll speak to it, though hell itself should gape
   And bid me hold my peace, I pray you all,
   If you have hitherto conceal'd this sight,
   Let it be tenable* in your silence still;
   And whatsoever else shall hap to-night,   265
   Give it an understanding, but no tongue;
   I will requite your loves. So, fare you well—
   Upon the platform, 'twixt eleven and twelve,
   I'll visit you.
ALL: Our duty to your honour.   270
HAMLET: Your loves, as mine to you; farewell.
   [*Exeunt all but* HAMLET.]
   My father's spirit in arms! All is not well.
   I doubt* some foul play. Would the night were come!
   Till then sit still, my soul. Foul deeds will rise,
   Though all the earth o'erwhelm them, to men's eyes.   [*Exit.*] 275

SCENE III————*Elsinore. The house of* POLONIUS.

   [*Enter* LAERTES *and* OPHELIA *his* sister.]
LAERTES: My necessaries are embark'd. Farewell.
   And, sister, as the winds give benefit
   And convoy* is assistant, do not sleep,
   But let me hear from you.
OPHELIA: Do you doubt that?   5
LAERTES: For Hamlet, and the trifling of his favour,
   Hold it a fashion and a toy* in blood,
   A violet in the youth of primy* nature,
   Forward* not permanent, sweet not lasting,
   The perfume and suppliance* of a minute;   10
   No more.
OPHELIA: No more but so?
LAERTES: Think it no more;
   For nature crescent* does not grow alone
   In thews* and bulk, but as this temple* waxes,   15
   The inward service of the mind and soul
   Grows wide withal. Perhaps he loves you now,

---

264 **tenable** held
273 **doubt** suspect
I,iii,3 **convoy** conveyance
7 **toy** idle fancy
8 **primy** youthful, springlike
9 **Forward** premature
10 **suppliance** diversion
14 **crescent** increasing
15 **thews** sinews
15 **temple** the body

And now no soil nor cautel* doth besmirch
The virtue of his will; but you must fear,
His greatness weigh'd,* his will is not his own;   20
For he himself is subject to his birth:
He may not, as unvalued* persons do,
Carve for himself; for on his choice depends
The sanity and health of this whole state;
And therefore must his choice be circumscrib'd   25
Unto the voice and yielding of that body
Whereof he is the head. Then if he says he loves you,
It fits your wisdom so far to believe it
As he in his particular act and place
May give his saying deed; which is no further   30
Than the main voice of Denmark goes withal.
Then weigh what loss your honour may sustain,
If with too credent* ear you list his songs,
Or lose your heart, or your chaste treasure open
To his unmast'red importunity.   35
Fear it, Ophelia, fear it, my dear sister;
And keep you in the rear of your affection,
Out of the shot and danger of desire.
The chariest maid is prodigal enough
If she unmask her beauty to the moon.   40
Virtue itself scapes not calumnious strokes;
The canker* galls the infants of the spring
Too oft before their buttons* be disclos'd;
And in the morn and liquid dew of youth
Contagious blastments are most imminent.   45
Be wary, then; best safety lies in fear:
Youth to itself rebels, though none else near.
OPHELIA: I shall the effect of this good lesson keep
As watchman to my heart. But, good my brother,
Do not, as some ungracious* pastors do,   50
Show me the steep and thorny way to heaven,
Whiles, like a puff'd and reckless libertine,
Himself the primrose path of dalliance treads
And recks not his own rede.*
LAERTES: O, fear me not!   55
    [*Enter* POLONIUS.]
I stay too long. But here my father comes.
A double blessing is a double grace;
Occasion smiles upon a second leave.
POLONIUS: Yet here, Laertes! Aboard, aboard, for shame!

---

18 **cautel** deceit
20 **greatness weigh'd** high rank considered
22 **unvalued** of low rank
33 **credent** credulous
42 **canker** worm
43 **buttons** buds
50 **ungracious** without themselves being in God's grace
54 **recks not his own rede** doesn't heed his own advice

The wind sits in the shoulder of your sail,   60
And you are stay'd for. There—my blessing with thee!
And these few precepts in thy memory
Look thou character.* Give thy thoughts no tongue,
Nor any unproportion'd* thought his act.
Be thou familiar, but by no means vulgar.   65
Those friends thou hast, and their adoption tried,
Grapple them to thy soul with hoops of steel;
But do not dull thy palm with entertainment
Of each new-hatch'd, unfledg'd comrade. Beware
Of entrance to a quarrel; but, being in,   70
Bear't that th' opposed may beware of thee.
Give every man thy ear, but few thy voice;
Take each man's censure, but reserve thy judgment.
Costly thy habit as thy purse can buy,
But not express'd in fancy; rich, not gaudy;   75
For the apparel oft proclaims the man;
And they in France of the best rank and station
Are of a most select and generous choice in that.
Neither a borrower nor a lender be;
For loan oft loses both itself and friend,   80
And borrowing dulls the edge of husbandry.*
This above all—to thine own self be true,
And it must follow, as the night the day,
Thou canst not then be false to any man.
Farewell; my blessing season* this in thee!   85
LAERTES: Most humbly do I take my leave, my lord.
POLONIUS: The time invites you; go, your servants tend.*
LAERTES: Farewell, Ophelia; and remember well
    What I have said to you.
OPHELIA: 'Tis in my memory lock'd,   90
    And you yourself shall keep the key of it.
LAERTES: Farewell.
POLONIUS: What is't, Ophelia, he hath said to you?
OPHELIA: So please you, something touching the Lord Hamlet.
POLONIUS: Marry,* well bethought!   95
    'Tis told me he hath very oft of late
    Given private time to you; and you yourself
    Have of your audience been most free and bounteous.
    If it be so—as so 'tis put on me,
    And that in way of caution—I must tell you   100
    You do not understand yourself so clearly
    As it behooves my daughter and your honour.

---

63 **character** inscribe
64 **unproportion'd** unconsidered
81 **husbandry** thrift
85 **season** make fruitful
87 **tend** await
95 **Marry** By the Virgin Mary

What is between you? Give me up the truth.

OPHELIA: He hath, my lord, of late made many tenders
    Of his affection to me. 105

POLONIUS: Affection! Pooh! You speak like a green girl,
    Unsifted* in such perilous circumstance.
    Do you believe his tenders, as you call them?

OPHELIA: I do not know, my lord, what I should think.

POLONIUS: Marry, I will teach you: think yourself a baby 110
    That you have ta'en these tenders for true pay
    Which are not sterling. Tender yourself more dearly;
    Or—not to crack the wind of the poor phrase,
    Running it thus—you'll tender me a fool.*

OPHELIA: My lord, he hath importun'd me with love 115
    In honourable fashion.

POLONIUS: Ay, fashion you may call it; go to, go to.

OPHELIA: And hath given countenance to his speech, my lord,
    With almost all the holy vows of heaven.

POLONIUS: Ay, springes to catch woodcocks!* I do know, 120
    When the blood burns, how prodigal the soul
    Lends the tongue vows. These blazes, daughter,
    Giving more light than heat—extinct in both,
    Even in their promise, as it is a-making—
    You must not take for fire. From this time 125
    Be something scanter of your maiden presence;
    Set your entreatments* at a higher rate
    Than a command to parle. For Lord Hamlet,
    Believe so much in him, that he is young,
    And with a larger tether may he walk 130
    Than may be given you. In few, Ophelia,
    Do not believe his vows; for they are brokers,*
    Not of that dye* which their investments* show,
    But mere implorators* of unholy suits,
    Breathing like sanctified and pious bonds,* 135
    The better to beguile. This is for all—
    I would not, in plain terms, from this time forth
    Have you so slander* any moment leisure
    As to give words or walk with the Lord Hamlet.
    Look to't, I charge you. Come your ways. 140

OPHELIA: I shall obey, my lord.   [*Exeunt.*]

---

107 **Unsifted** untried
114 **tender me a fool** present me with a baby
120 **springes to catch woodcocks** snares to catch unwary birds
127 **entreatments** conversations
132 **brokers** procurers
133 **dye** kind
133 **investments** outer garments
134 **implorators** solicitors
135 **bonds** pledges
138 **slander** disgrace

SCENE IV————*Elsinore. The guard-platform of the Castle.*

[*Enter* HAMLET, HORATIO, *and* MARCELLUS.]
HAMLET: The air bites shrewdly;* it is very cold.
HORATIO: It is a nipping and an eager* air.
HAMLET: What hour now?
HORATIO: I think it lacks of twelve.
MARCELLUS: No, it is struck.   5
HORATIO: Indeed? I heard it not. It then draws near the season
    Wherein the spirit held his wont to walk.
       [*A flourish of trumpets, and two pieces go off.*]
    What does this mean, my lord?
HAMLET: The King doth wake* to-night and takes his rouse,*
    Keeps wassail, and the swagg'ring up-spring* reels,   10
    And, as he drains his draughts of Rhenish* down,
    The kettledrum and trumpet thus bray out
    The triumph of his pledge.*
HORATIO: Is it a custom?
HAMLET: Ay, marry, is't;   15
    But to my mind, though I am native here
    And to the manner born, it is a custom
    More honour'd in the breach than the observance.
    This heavy-headed revel east and west
    Makes us traduc'd and tax'd of* other nations;   20
    They clepe* us drunkards, and with swinish phrase
    Soil our addition,* and, indeed, it takes
    From our achievements, though perform'd at height,
    The pith and marrow of our attribute.*
    So, oft it chances in particular men   25
    That, for some vicious mole* of nature in them,
    As in their birth, wherein they are not guilty,
    Since nature cannot choose his origin;
    By the o'ergrowth of some complexion,*
    Oft breaking down the pales* and forts of reason;   30
    Or by some habit that too much o'er-leavens*
    The form of plausive* manners—that these men,

I,iv,1 **shrewdly** bitterly
2 **eager** sharp
9 **wake** revel
9 **rouse** carouses
10 **up-spring** dance
11 **Rhenish** Rhine wine
13 **The triumph of his pledge** drinking a glass of wine in one draught
20 **tax'd of** accused by
21 **clepe** call
22 **addition** honor
24 **attribute** reputation
26 **mole** blemish
29 **complexion** natural disposition
30 **pales** walls
31 **o'er-leavens** overdoes, corrupts
32 **plausive** pleasing

Carrying, I say, the stamp of one defect,
Being nature's livery or fortune's star,*
His virtues else, be they as pure as grace,   35
As infinite as man may undergo,
Shall in the general censure* take corruption
From that particular fault. The dram of eale
Doth all the noble substance of a doubt
To his own scandal.   40
      [*Enter* GHOST.]
HORATIO: Look, my lord, it comes.
HAMLET: Angels and ministers of grace defend us!
  Be thou a spirit of health* or goblin damn'd,
  Bring with thee airs from heaven or blasts from hell,
  Be thy intents wicked or charitable,   45
  Thou com'st in such a questionable* shape
  That I will speak to thee. I'll call thee Hamlet,
  King, father, royal Dane. O, answer me!
  Let me not burst in ignorance, but tell
  Why thy canoniz'd* bones, hearsed in death,   50
  Have burst their cerements;* why the sepulchre
  Wherein we saw thee quietly enurn'd
  Have op'd his ponderous and marble jaws
  To cast thee up again. What may this mean
  That thou, dead corse, again in complete steel   55
  Revisits thus the glimpses of the moon,
  Making night hideous, and we fools of nature
  So horridly to shake our disposition*
  With thoughts beyond the reaches of our souls?
  Say, why is this? wherefore? What should we do?   60
      [GHOST *beckons* HAMLET.]
HORATIO: It beckons you to go away with it,
  As if some impartment* did desire
  To you alone.
MARCELLUS: Look with what courteous action
  It waves you to a more removed ground.   65
  But do not go with it.
HORATIO: No, by no means.
HAMLET: It will not speak; then I will follow it.
HORATIO: Do not, my lord.
HAMLET: Why, what should be the fear?   70
  I do not set my life at a pin's fee;
  And for my soul, what can it do to that,

---

³⁴ **nature's livery or fortune's star** determined by nature or by the stars
³⁷ **general censure** popular judgment
⁴³ **spirit of health** good spirit
⁴⁶ **questionable** of dubious identity
⁵⁰ **canoniz'd** buried according to church rules
⁵¹ **cerements** burial garments
⁵⁸ **shake our disposition** unsettle our minds
⁶² **impartment** message to impart

Being a thing immortal as itself?
It waves me forth again; I'll follow it.
HORATIO: What if it tempt you toward the flood, my lord,   75
   Or to the dreadful summit of the cliff
   That beetles* o'er his base into the sea,
   And there assume some other horrible form,
   Which might deprive your sovereignty of reason
   And draw you into madness? Think of it: 80
   The very place puts toys* of desperation,
   Without more motive, into every brain
   That looks so many fathoms to the sea
   And hears it roar beneath.
HAMLET: It waves me still.   85
   Go on; I'll follow thee.
MARCELLUS: You shall not go, my lord.
HAMLET: Hold off your hands.
HORATIO: Be rul'd; you shall not go.
HAMLET: My fate cries out,   90
   And makes each petty arture* in this body
   As hardy as the Nemean lion's nerve.* [GHOST *beckons.*]
   Still am I call'd. Unhand me, gentlemen.
   By heaven, I'll make a ghost of him that lets* me.
   I say, away! Go on; I'll follow thee.   95
   [*Exeunt* GHOST *and* HAMLET.]
HORATIO: He waxes desperate with imagination.
MARCELLUS: Let's follow; 'tis not fit thus to obey him.
HORATIO: Have after. To what issue will this come?
MARCELLUS: Something is rotten in the state of Denmark.
HORATIO: Heaven will direct it.   100
MARCELLUS: Nay, let's follow him.   [*Exeunt.*]

SCENE V———*Elsinore. The Battlements of the Castle.*

[*Enter* GHOST *and* HAMLET.]
HAMLET: Whither wilt thou lead me? Speak. I'll go no further.
GHOST: Mark me.
HAMLET: I will.
GHOST: My hour is almost come,
   When I to sulph'rous and tormenting flames   5
   Must render up myself.
HAMLET: Alas, poor ghost!
GHOST: Pity me not, but lend thy serious hearing
   To what I shall unfold.
HAMLET: Speak; I am bound to hear.   10
GHOST: So art thou to revenge, when thou shalt hear.
HAMLET: What?
GHOST: I am thy father's spirit,

77 **beetles** juts out
81 **toys** notions
91 **arture** artery
92 **Nemean lion's nerve** sinews of the mythical lion slain by Heracles
94 **lets** hinders

Doom'd for a certain term to walk the night,
And for the day confin'd to fast in fires, 15
Till the foul crimes done in my days of nature
Are burnt and purg'd away. But that I am forbid
To tell the secrets of my prison-house,
I could a tale unfold whose lightest word
Would harrow up thy soul, freeze thy young blood, 20
Make thy two eyes, like stars, start from their spheres,
Thy knotted and combined locks to part,
And each particular hair to stand an end,
Like quills upon the fretful porpentine.*
But this eternal blazon* must not be 25
To ears of flesh and blood. List, list, O, list!
If thou didst ever thy dear father love—
HAMLET: O God!
GHOST: Revenge his foul and most unnatural murder.
HAMLET: Murder! 30
GHOST: Murder most foul, as in the best it is;
But this most foul, strange, and unnatural.
HAMLET: Haste me to know't, that I, with wings as swift
As meditation or the thoughts of love,
May sweep to my revenge. 35
GHOST: I find thee apt;
And duller shouldst thou be than the fat weed
That roots itself in ease on Lethe wharf,*
Wouldst thou not stir in this. Now, Hamlet, hear:
'Tis given out that, sleeping in my orchard, 40
A serpent stung me; so the whole ear of Denmark
Is by a forged process* of my death
Rankly abus'd; but know, thou noble youth,
The serpent that did sting thy father's life
Now wears his crown. 45
HAMLET: O my prophetic soul!
My uncle!
GHOST: Ay, that incestuous, that adulterate* beast,
With witchcraft of his wits, with traitorous gifts—
O wicked wit and gifts that have the power 50
So to seduce—won to his shameful lust
The will of my most seeming virtuous queen.
O Hamlet, what a falling off was there,
From me, whose love was of that dignity
That it went hand in hand even with the vow 55
I made to her in marriage; and to decline
Upon a wretch whose natural gifts were poor
To those of mine!
But virtue, as it never will be moved,
Though lewdness court it in a shape of heaven, 60

---

24 **fretful porpentine** fearful porcupine
25 **eternal blazon** revelation about eternity
38 **Lethe wharf** bank of the river of forgetfulness in Hades
42 **forged process** false account
48 **adulterate** adulterous

So lust, though to a radiant angel link'd,
Will sate itself in a celestial bed
And prey on garbage.
But soft! methinks I scent the morning air.
Brief let me be. Sleeping within my orchard,   65
My custom always of the afternoon,
Upon my secure* hour thy uncle stole,
With juice of cursed hebona* in a vial,
And in the porches of my ears did pour
The leperous distilment; whose effect   70
Holds such an enmity with blood of man
That swift as quicksilver it courses through
The natural gates and alleys of the body;
And with a sudden vigour it doth posset*
And curd, like eager* droppings into milk,   75
The thin and wholesome blood. So did it mine;
And a most instant tetter* bark'd about,
Most lazar-like,* with vile and loathsome crust,
All my smooth body.
Thus was I, sleeping, by a brother's hand   80
Of life, of crown, of queen, at once dispatch'd;
Cut off even in the blossoms of my sin,
Unhous'led, disappointed, unanel'd;*
No reck'ning made, but sent to my account
With all my imperfections on my head   85
O, horrible! O, horrible! most horrible!
If thou hast nature in thee, bear it not;
Let not the royal bed of Denmark be
A couch for luxury* and damned incest.
But howsoever thou pursuest this act,   90
Taint not thy mind, nor let thy soul contrive
Against thy mother aught; leave her to heaven,
And to those thorns that in her bosom lodge
To prick and sting her. Fare thee well at once.
The glowworm shows the matin* to be near,   95
And gins to pale his uneffectual fire.
Adieu, adieu, adieu! Remember me.   [*Exit.*]
HAMLET: O all you host of heaven! O earth! What else?
And shall I couple hell? O, fie! Hold, hold, my heart;
And you, my sinews, grow not instant old,   100
But bear me stiffly up. Remember thee!

67 **secure** unsuspecting
68 **hebona** poisonous plant
74 **posset** curdle
75 **eager** acid
77 **tetter** inflammation of the skin
78 **lazar-like** leperlike
83 **Unhous'led, disappointed, unanel'd** without the sacrament of communion, unabsolved of sin, without extreme unction
89 **luxury** lust
95 **matin** morning

Ay, thou poor ghost, whiles memory holds a seat
In this distracted globe.* Remember thee!
Yea, from the table* of my memory
I'll wipe away all trivial fond* records,   105
All saws* of books, all forms, all pressures* past,
That youth and observation copied there,
And thy commandment all alone shall live
Within the book and volume of my brain,
Unmix'd with baser matter. Yes, by heaven!   110
O most pernicious woman!
O villain, villain, smiling, damned villain!
My tables—meet it is I set it down
That one may smile, and smile, and be a villain;
At least I am sure it may be so in Denmark. [*writing*]   115
So, uncle, there you are. Now to my word:
It is 'Adieu, adieu! Remember me.'
I have sworn't.
HORATIO: *within*] My lord, my lord!
      [*Enter* HORATIO *and* MARCELLUS.]
MARCELLUS: Lord Hamlet!   120
HORATIO: Heavens secure him!
HAMLET: So be it!
MARCELLUS: Illo, ho, ho,* my lord!
HAMLET: Hillo, ho, ho, boy! Come, bird, come.
MARCELLUS: How is't, my noble lord?   125
HORATIO: What news, my lord?
HAMLET: O, wonderful!
HORATIO: Good my lord, tell it.
HAMLET: No; you will reveal it.
HORATIO: Not I, my lord, by heaven!   130
MARCELLUS: Nor I, my lord.
HAMLET: How say you, then; would heart of man once think it?
    But you'll be secret?
BOTH: Ay, by heaven, my lord!
HAMLET: There's never a villain dwelling in all Denmark   135
    But he's an arrant knave.
HORATIO: There needs no ghost, my lord, come from the grave
    To tell us this.
HAMLET: Why, right; you are in the right;
    And so, without more circumstance* at all,   140
    I hold it fit that we shake hands and part;
    You, as your business and desire shall point you—
    For every man hath business and desire,

103 **globe** head
104 **table** tablet
105 **fond** foolish
106 **saws** maxims
106 **pressures** impressions
123 **Illo, ho, ho** falconer's call to his hawk
140 **circumstance** details

Such as it is; and for my own poor part,
Look you, I will go pray.   145
HORATIO: These are but wild and whirling words, my lord.
HAMLET: I am sorry they offend you, heartily;
Yes, faith, heartily.
HORATIO: There's no offence, my lord.
HAMLET: Yes, by Saint Patrick, but there is, Horatio,   150
And much offence, too. Touching this vision here—
It is an honest ghost,* that let me tell you.
For your desire to know what is between us,
O'ermaster't as you may. And now, good friends,
As you are friends, scholars, and soldiers,   155
Give me one poor request.
HORATIO: What is't, my lord? We will.
HAMLET: Never make known what you have seen to-night.
BOTH: My lord, we will not.
HAMLET: Nay, but swear't.   160
HORATIO: In faith,
My lord, not I.
MARCELLUS: Nor I, my lord, in faith.
HAMLET: Upon my sword.
MARCELLUS: We have sworn, my lord, already.   165
HAMLET: Indeed, upon my sword, indeed.
GHOST: [*cries under the stage*] Swear.
HAMLET: Ha, ha, boy! say'st thou so? Art thou there, true-penny?*
Come on. You hear this fellow in the cellarage:
Consent to swear.   170
HORATIO: Propose the oath, my lord.
HAMLET: Never to speak of this that you have seen,
Swear by my sword.
GHOST: [*beneath*] Swear.
HAMLET: Hic et ubique?* Then we'll shift our ground.   175
Come hither, gentlemen,
And lay your hands again upon my sword.
Swear by my sword
Never to speak of this that you have heard.
GHOST: [*beneath*] Swear, by his sword.   180
HAMLET: Well said, old mole! Canst work i' th' earth so fast?
A worthy pioneer!* Once more remove, good friends.
HORATIO: O day and night, but this is wondrous strange!
HAMLET: And therefore as a stranger give it welcome.
There are more things in heaven and earth, Horatio,   185
Than are dreamt of in your philosophy.
But come.
Here, as before, never, so help you mercy,

---

152 **honest ghost** true ghost of his father rather than a demon
168 **true-penny** honest fellow
175 **Hic et ubique** here and everywhere
182 **pioneer** miner

How strange or odd soe'er I bear myself—
As I perchance hereafter shall think meet   190
To put an antic disposition* on—
That you, at such times, seeing me, never shall,
With arms encumb'red* thus, or this head-shake,
Or by pronouncing of some doubtful phrase,
As 'Well, well, we know' or 'We could, an if we would'   195
Or, 'If we list to speak' or 'There be, an if they might'
Or such ambiguous giving out, to note
That you know aught of me—this do swear,
So grace and mercy at your most need help you.
GHOST: [*beneath*] Swear.   200
HAMLET: Rest, rest, perturbed spirit! So, gentlemen,
With all my love I do commend me* to you;
And what so poor a man as Hamlet is
May do t'express his love and friending to you,
God willing, shall not lack. Let us go in together;   205
And still your fingers on your lips, I pray.
The time is out of joint. O cursed spite,
That ever I was born to set it right!
Nay, come, let's go together.   [*Exeunt.*]

ACT II

SCENE I———*Elsinore. The house of POLONIUS.*

[*Enter* POLONIUS *and* REYNALDO.]
POLONIUS: Give him this money and these notes, Reynaldo.
REYNALDO: I will, my lord.
POLONIUS: You shall do marvellous wisely, good Reynaldo,
Before you visit him, to make inquire
Of his behaviour.   5
REYNALDO: My lord, I did intend it.
POLONIUS: Marry, well said; very well said. Look you, sir,
Enquire me first what Danskers* are in Paris;
And how, and who, what means, and where they keep,*
What company, at what expense; and finding   10
By this encompassment and drift of question
That they do know my son, come you more nearer
Than your particular demands will touch it.
Take you, as 'twere, some distant knowledge of him;
As thus: 'I know his father and his friends,   15
And in part him.' Do you mark this, Reynaldo?
REYNALDO: Ay, very well, my lord.

---

191 **antic disposition** strange behavior
193 **encumb'red** folded
202 **commend me** entrust myself
II,i,8 **Danskers** Danes
9 **keep** dwell

POLONIUS: 'And in part him—but' you may say 'not well;
　　But if't be he I mean, he's very wild;
　　Addicted so and so'; and there put on him
　　What forgeries you please; marry, none so rank　　　　　　　20
　　As may dishonour him; take heed of that;
　　But, sir, such wanton, wild, and usual slips
　　As are companions noted and most known
　　To youth and liberty.　　　　　　　　　　　　　　　　25
REYNALDO: As gaming, my lord.
POLONIUS: Ay, or drinking, fencing, swearing, quarrelling.
　　Drabbing*—you may go so far.
REYNALDO: My lord, that would dishonour him.
POLONIUS: Faith, no; as you may season it in the charge.　　　30
　　You must not put another scandal on him,
　　That he is open to incontinency;
　　That's not my meaning. But breathe his faults so quaintly*
　　That they may seem the taints of liberty;
　　The flash and outbreak of a fiery mind,　　　　　　　　35
　　A savageness in unreclaimed blood,
　　Of general assault.*
REYNALDO: But, my good lord—
POLONIUS: Wherefore should you do this?
REYNALDO: Ay, my lord,　　　　　　　　　　　　　　　40
　　I would know that.
POLONIUS: Marry, sir, here's my drift,
　　And I believe it is a fetch of warrant: *
　　You laying these slight sullies on my son,
　　As 'twere a thing a little soil'd wi' th' working,　　　　　45
　　Mark you,
　　Your party in converse, him you would sound,
　　Having ever seen in the prenominate crimes*
　　The youth you breathe of guilty, be assur'd
　　He closes with you in this consequence—*　　　　　　　50
　　'Good sir' or so, or 'friend' or 'gentleman'
　　According to the phrase or the addition*
　　Of man and country.
REYNALDO: Very good, my lord.
POLONIUS: And then, sir, does 'a* this—'a does—What was　　55
　　I about to say? By the mass, I was about to say something;
　　Where did I leave?
REYNALDO: At 'closes in the consequence,' at 'friend or so' and 'gentleman.'
POLONIUS: At 'closes in the consequence'—ay, marry,

---

28 **Drabbing** womanizing
33 **quaintly** ingeniously
37 **Of general assault** common to all men
43 **fetch of warrant** justifiable device
48 **Having . . . crimes** if he has ever seen the aforementioned crimes
50 **He closes . . . this consequence** agrees with you
52 **addition** title
55 **'a** he

He closes thus: 'I know the gentleman; 60
I saw him yesterday, or t'other day,
Or then, or then; with such, or such; and, as you say,
There was 'a gaming; there o'ertook in's rouse;
There falling out at tennis'; or perchance
'I saw him enter such a house of sale,' 65
Videlicet,* a brothel, or so forth. See you now
Your bait of falsehood take this carp of truth;
And thus do we of wisdom and of reach,
With windlasses and with assays of bias,*
By indirections find directions out; 70
So, by my former lecture and advice,
Shall you my son. You have me, have you not?
REYNALDO: My lord, I have.
POLONIUS: God buy ye; fare ye well.
REYNALDO: Good my lord! 75
POLONIUS: Observe his inclination in yourself.*
REYNALDO: I shall, my lord.
POLONIUS: And let him ply his music.
REYNALDO: Well, my lord.
POLONIUS: Farewell! [*Exit* REYNALDO.] 80
        [*Enter* OPHELIA.]
    How now, Ophelia! What's the matter?
OPHELIA: O my lord, my lord, I have been so affrighted!
POLONIUS: With what, i' th' name of God?
OPHELIA: My lord, as I was sewing in my closet,*
    Lord Hamlet, with his doublet all unbrac'd,* 85
    No hat upon his head, his stockings fouled,
    Ungart'red and down-gyved* to his ankle;
    Pale as his shirt, his knees knocking each other,
    And with a look so piteous in purport
    As if he had been loosed out of hell 90
    To speak of horrors—he comes before me.
POLONIUS: Mad for thy love?
OPHELIA: My lord, I do not know,
    But truly I do fear it.
POLONIUS: What said he? 95
OPHELIA: He took me by the wrist, and held me hard;
    Then goes he to the length of all his arm,
    And, with his other hand thus o'er his brow,
    He falls to such a perusal of my face
    As 'a would draw it. Long stay'd he so. 100
    At last, a little shaking of mine arm,

---

66 **Videlicet** namely
69 **windlasses . . . bias** indirect means
76 **in yourself** for yourself
84 **closet** private room
85 **doublet all unbrac'd jacket** entirely unlaced/open
87 **down-gyved** hanging down

And thrice his head thus waving up and down,
He rais'd a sigh so piteous and profound
As it did seem to shatter all his bulk
And end his being. That done, he lets me go,   105
And, with his head over his shoulder turn'd,
He seem'd to find his way without his eyes;
For out adoors he went without their help
And to the last bended their light on me.
POLONIUS: Come, go with me. I will go seek the King.   110
    This is the very ecstasy* of love,
    Whose violent property fordoes* itself,
    And leads the will to desperate undertakings
    As oft as any passion under heaven
    That does afflict our natures. I am sorry—   115
    What, have you given him any hard words of late?
OPHELIA: No, my good lord; but, as you did command,
    I did repel his letters, and denied
    His access to me.
POLONIUS: That hath made him mad.   120
    I am sorry that with better heed and judgment
    I had not quoted* him. I fear'd he did but trifle,
    And meant to wreck thee; but beshrew my jealousy!*
    By heaven, it is as proper to our age
    To cast beyond ourselves in our opinions   125
    As it is common for the younger sort
    To lack discretion. Come, go we to the King.
    This must be known; which, being kept close, might move
    More grief to hide than hate to utter love.*
    Come.   [*Exeunt.*] 130

SCENE II———*Elsinore. The Castle.*

[*Flourish. Enter* KING, QUEEN, ROSENCRANTZ, GUILDENSTERN, *and attendants.*]
KING: Welcome, dear Rosencrantz and Guildenstern!
    Moreover that we much did long to see you,
    The need we have to use you did provoke
    Our hasty sending. Something have you heard
    Of Hamlet's transformation; so I call it,   5
    Sith* nor th' exterior nor the inward man
    Resembles that it was. What it should be,
    More than his father's death, that thus hath put him
    So much from th' understanding of himself,
    I cannot deem of. I entreat you both   10

---

111 **ecstasy** madness
112 **property fordoes** quality destroys
122 **quoted** noted
123 **beshrew my jealousy** curse on my suspicions
127–29 **Come, go . . . utter love** telling the king may anger him, but not telling him might anger him more
II,i,6 **Sith** since

That, being of so* young days brought up with him,
And sith so neighboured to his youth and haviour,
That you vouchsafe your rest* here in our court
Some little time; so by your companies
To draw him on to pleasures, and to gather, 15
So much as from occasion you may glean,
Whether aught to us unknown afflicts him thus
That, open'd,* lies within our remedy.

QUEEN: Good gentlemen, he hath much talk'd of you;
And sure I am two men there is not living 20
To whom he more adheres. If it will please you
To show us so much gentry* and good will
As to expend your time with us awhile
For the supply and profit of our hope,
Your visitation shall receive such thanks 25
As fits a king's remembrance.

ROSENCRANTZ: Both your Majesties
Might, by the sovereign power you have of us,
Put your dread pleasures more into command
Than to entreaty. 30

GUILDENSTERN: But we both obey,
And here give up ourselves, in the full bent,*
To lay our service freely at your feet,
To be commanded.

KING: Thanks, Rosencrantz and gentle Guildenstern. 35

QUEEN: Thanks, Guildenstern and gentle Rosencrantz.
And I beseech you instantly to visit
My too much changed son. Go, some of you,
And bring these gentlemen where Hamlet is.

GUILDENSTERN: Heavens make our presence and our practices 40
Pleasant and helpful to him!

QUEEN: Aye amen! [*Exeunt* ROSENCRANTZ, GUILDENSTERN, *and some attendants.*]
            [*Enter* POLONIUS.]

POLONIUS: Th' ambassadors from Norway, my good lord,
Are joyfully return'd.

KING: Thou still hast been the father of good news. 45

POLONIUS: Have I, my lord? I assure you, my good liege,
I hold my duty, as I hold my soul,
Both to my God and to my gracious King;
And I do think—or else this brain of mine
Hunts not the trail of policy so sure 50
As it hath us'd to do—that I have found
The very cause of Hamlet's lunacy.

KING: O, speak of that; that do I long to hear.

---

11 **of so** from such
13 **vouchsafe your rest** consent to remain
18 **open'd** revealed
22 **gentry** courtesy
32 **in the full bent** entirely

POLONIUS: Give first admittance to th' ambassadors;
　　My news shall be the fruit to that great feast.　　　　　　55
KING: Thyself do grace to them, and bring them in.
　　　　[*Exit* POLONIUS.]
　　He tells me, my dear Gertrude, he hath found
　　The head and source of all your son's distemper.
QUEEN: I doubt it is no other but the main,
　　His father's death and our o'erhasty marriage.　　　　　　60
KING: Well, we shall sift him.
　　　　[*Reenter* POLONIUS, *with* VOLTEMAND *and* CORNELIUS.]
　　Welcome, my good friends!
　　Say, Voltemand, what from our brother Norway?
VOLTEMAND: Most fair return of greetings and desires.
　　Upon our first,* he sent out to suppress　　　　　　　　65
　　His nephew's levies; which to him appear'd
　　To be a preparation 'gainst the Polack;
　　But, better look'd into, he truly found
　　It was against your Highness. Whereat griev'd,
　　That so his sickness, age, and impotence,　　　　　　　　70
　　Was falsely borne in hand,* sends out arrests
　　On Fortinbras; which he, in brief, obeys;
　　Receives rebuke from Norway; and, in fine,
　　Makes vow before his uncle never more
　　To give th' assay of arms against your Majesty.　　　　　75
　　Whereon old Norway, overcome with joy,
　　Gives him threescore thousand crowns in annual fee,
　　And his commission to employ those soldiers,
　　So levied as before, against the Polack;
　　With an entreaty, herein further shown, [*gives a paper*]　　80
　　That it might please you to give quiet pass
　　Through your dominions for this enterprise,
　　On such regards of safety and allowance
　　As therein are set down.
KING: It likes us well;　　　　　　　　　　　　　　　　85
　　And at our more considered time we'll read,
　　Answer, and think upon this business.
　　Meantime we thank you for your well-took labour.
　　Go to your rest; at night we'll feast together.
　　Most welcome home!　　　　　[*Exeunt* AMBASSADORS *and attendants.*]　90
POLONIUS: This business is well ended.
　　My liege, and madam, to expostulate
　　What majesty should be, what duty is,
　　Why day is day, night night, and time is time,
　　Were nothing, but to waste night, day, and time.　　　　　95
　　Therefore, since brevity is the soul of wit,
　　And tediousness the limbs and outward flourishes,
　　I will be brief. Your noble son is mad.

---

65 **first** first meeting
71 **falsely borne in hand** deceived

Mad call I it; for, to define true madness,
What is't but to be nothing else but mad?   100
But let that go.
QUEEN: More matter with less art.
POLONIUS: Madam, I swear I use no art at all.
That he's mad, 'tis true: 'tis true 'is pity;
And pity 'is 'tis true. A foolish figure!   105
But farewell it, for I will use no art.
Mad let us grant him, then; and now remains
That we find out the cause of this effect;
Or rather say the cause of this defect,
For this effect defective comes by cause.   110
Thus it remains, and the remainder thus.
Perpend.*
I have a daughter—have while she is mine—
Who in her duty and obedience, mark,
Hath given me this. Now gather, and surmise. [*reads*]   115
   '*To the celestial, and my soul's idol, the most beautified Ophelia.*' That's an ill
     phrase, a vile phrase; 'beautified' is a vile phrase. But you shall hear.
     Thus: [*reads*]
   '*In her excellent white bosom, these, &c.*'
QUEEN: Came this from Hamlet to her?   120
POLONIUS: Good madam, stay awhile; I will be faithful. [*reads*]
     '*Doubt thou the stars are fire;*
       Doubt that the sun doth move;
   Doubt* truth to be a liar;
       But never doubt I love.   125
   '*O dear Ophelia, I am ill at these numbers.* I have not art to reckon my groans;*
     but that I love thee best, O most best, believe it. Adieu.
                 '*Thine evermore, most dear lady, whilst*
                       this machine is to him,
                          Hamlet.'   130

This, in obedience, hath my daughter shown me;
And more above,* hath his solicitings,
As they fell out by time, by means, and place,
All given to mine ear.
KING: But how hath she   135
Receiv'd his love?
POLONIUS: What do you think of me?
KING: As of a man faithful and honourable.
POLONIUS: I would fain prove so. But what might you think,
When I had seen this hot love on the wing,   140
As I perceiv'd it, I must tell you that,
Before my daughter told me—what might you,
Or my dear Majesty your Queen here think,

---

112 **Perpend** consider carefully
124 **Doubt** suspect
126 **ill at these numbers** unskilled at versifying
132 **above** besides

If I had play'd the desk or table-book;*
Or given my heart a winking,* mute and dumb; 145
Or look'd upon this love with idle sight—
What might you think? No, I went round to work,
And my young mistress thus I did bespeak:
'Lord Hamlet is a prince out of thy star;
This must not be.' And then I prescripts gave her, 150
That she should lock herself from his resort,
Admit no messengers, receive no tokens.
Which done, she took the fruits of my advice;
And he repelled, a short tale to make,
Fell into a sadness, then into a fast, 155
Thence to a watch,* thence into a weakness,
Thence to a lightness,* and, by this declension,
Into the madness wherein now he raves
And all we mourn for.
KING: Do you think 'tis this? 160
QUEEN: It may be, very like.
POLONIUS: Hath there been such a time—I would fain know that—
That I have positively said ''Tis so,'
When it prov'd otherwise?
KING: Not that I know. 165
POLONIUS: Take this from this,* if this be otherwise.
If circumstances lead me, I will find
Where truth is hid, though it were hid indeed
Within the centre.*
KING: How may we try it further? 170
POLONIUS: You may know sometimes he walks four hours together,
Here in the lobby.
QUEEN: So he does, indeed.
POLONIUS: At such a time I'll loose my daughter to him.
Be you and I behind an arras* then; 175
Mark the encounter: if he love her not,
And be not from his reason fall'n thereon,
Let me be no assistant for a state,
But keep a farm and carters.
KING: We will try it. 180
[*Enter* HAMLET, *reading on a book.*]
QUEEN: But look where sadly the poor wretch comes reading.
POLONIUS: Away, I do beseech you, both away:
I'll board him presently.* O, give me leave.
[*Exeunt* KING *and* QUEEN.]

---

[144] **play'd the desk or table-book** been a passive receiver of secrets
[145] **winking** closed my eyes
[156] **watch** wakefulness
[157] **lightness** mental derangement
[166] **this from this** (indicating by pointing) head from body
[169] **centre** center of the earth
[175] **arras** tapestry
[183] **board him presently** accost him at once

How does my good Lord Hamlet? 185

HAMLET: Well, God-a-mercy.

POLONIUS: Do you know me, my lord?

HAMLET: Excellent well; you are a fishmonger.*

POLONIUS: Not I, my lord.

HAMLET: Then I would you were so honest a man. 190

POLONIUS: Honest, my lord!

HAMLET: Ay, sir; to be honest, as this world goes, is to be one man pick'd out of ten thousand.

POLONIUS: That's very true, my lord.

HAMLET: For if the sun breed maggots in a dead dog, being a good kissing carrion—Have you a daughter? 195

POLONIUS: I have, my lord.

HAMLET: Let her not walk i' th' sun. Conception* is a blessing. But as your daughter may conceive—friend, look to't.

POLONIUS: How say you by that? [*aside*] Still harping on my daughter. Yet he knew me not at first; 'a said I was a fishmonger. 'A is far gone, far gone. And truly in 200 my youth I suff'red much extremity for love. Very near this. I'll speak to him again.—What do you read, my lord?

HAMLET: Words, words, words.

POLONIUS: What is the matter, my lord?

HAMLET: Between who? 205

POLONIUS: I mean, the matter that you read, my lord.

HAMLET: Slanders, sir; for the satirical rogue says here that old men have grey beards; that their faces are wrinkled; their eyes purging thick amber and plum-tree gum; and that they have a plentiful lack of wit, together with most weak hams—all which, sir, though I most powerfully and potently be- 210 lieve, yet I hold it not honesty to have it thus set down; for you yourself, sir, shall grow old as I am, if, like a crab, you could go backward.

POLONIUS: [*aside*] Though this be madness, yet there is method in't.—Will you walk out of the air, my lord?

HAMLET: Into my grave? 215

POLONIUS: Indeed, that's out of the air. [*aside*] How pregnant sometimes his replies are! a happiness that often madness hits on, which reason and sanity could not so prosperously be delivered of. I will leave him, and suddenly contrive the means of meeting between him and my daughter.—My lord. I will take my leave of you. 220

HAMLET: You cannot, sir, take from me anything that I will more willingly part withal—except my life, except my life, except my life.

[*Enter* ROSENCRANTZ *and* GUILDENSTERN.]

POLONIUS: Fare you well, my lord.

HAMLET: These tedious old fools!

POLONIUS: You go to seek the Lord Hamlet; there he is. 225

ROSENCRANTZ: [*to* POLONIUS] God save you, sir!

[*Exit* POLONIUS.]

GUILDENSTERN: My honour'd lord!

ROSENCRANTZ: My most dear lord!

---

187 **fishmonger** dealer in fish (slang for procurer)
197 **Conception** understanding; becoming pregnant

HAMLET: My excellent good friends! How dost thou, Guildenstern? Ah, Rosencrantz! Good lads, how do you both?   230

ROSENCRANTZ: As the indifferent* children of the earth.

GUILDENSTERN: Happy in that we are not over-happy;
On fortune's cap we are not the very button.

HAMLET: Nor the soles of her shoe?

ROSENCRANTZ: Neither, my lord.   235

HAMLET: Then you live about her waist, or in the middle of her favours?

GUILDENSTERN: Faith, her privates we.

HAMLET: In the secret parts of Fortune? O, most true; she is a strumpet. What
news?

ROSENCRANTZ: None, my lord, but that the world's grown honest.   240

HAMLET: Then is doomsday near. But your news is not true. Let me question more
in particular. What have you, my good friends, deserved at the hands of
Fortune, that she sends you to prison hither?

GUILDENSTERN: Prison, my lord!

HAMLET: Denmark's a prison.   245

ROSENCRANTZ: Then is the world one.

HAMLET: A goodly one; in which there are many confines, wards, and dungeons,
Denmark being one o' th' worst.

ROSENCRANTZ: We think not so, my lord.

HAMLET: Why, then, 'tis none to you; for there is nothing either good or bad, but   250
thinking makes it so. To me it is a prison.

ROSENCRANTZ: Why, then your ambition makes it one; 'tis too narrow for your
mind.

HAMLET: O God, I could be bounded in a nutshell and count myself a king of
infinite space, were it not that I have bad dreams.   255

GUILDENSTERN: Which dreams indeed are ambition; for the very substance of the
ambitious is merely the shadow of a dream.

HAMLET: A dream itself is but a shadow.

ROSENCRANTZ: Truly, and I hold ambition of so airy and light a quality that it is
but a shadow's shadow.   260

HAMLET: Then are our beggars bodies, and our monarchs and oustretch'd heroes
the beggars' shadows. Shall we to th' court? for, by my fay,* I cannot reason.

BOTH: We'll wait upon you.

HAMLET: No such matter. I will not sort you with the rest of my servants; for, to
speak to you like an honest man, I am most dreadfully attended. But, in the   265
beaten way of friendship, what make you at Elsinore?

ROSENCRANTZ: To visit you, my lord; no other occasion.

HAMLET: Beggar that I am, I am even poor in thanks; but I thank you; and sure,
dear friends, my thanks are too dear a half-penny.* Were you not sent for?
Is it your own inclining? It is a free visitation? Come, come, deal justly with   270
me. Come, come; nay, speak.

GUILDENSTERN: What should we say, my lord?

HAMLET: Why, any thing. But to th' purpose: you were sent for; and there is a

---

231 **indifferent** ordinary
262 **fay** faith
269 **too dear a half-penny** not worth a half-penny

kind of confession in your looks, which your modesties have not craft enough to colour; I know the good King and Queen have sent for you. 275

ROSENCRANTZ: To what end, my lord?

HAMLET: That you must teach me. But let me conjure you by the rights of our fellowship, by the consonancy of our youth, by the obligation of our ever-preserved love, and by what more dear a better proposer can charge you withal, be even and direct with me, whether you were sent for or no? 280

ROSENCRANTZ: [*aside to* GUILDENSTERN] What say you?

HAMLET: [*aside*] Nay, then, I have an eye of you.—If you love me, hold not off.

GUILDENSTERN: My lord, we were sent for.

HAMLET: I will tell you why; so shall my anticipation prevent your discovery,* and your secrecy to the King and Queen moult no feather. I have of late— 285 but wherefore I know not—lost all my mirth, forgone all custom of exercises; and indeed it goes so heavily with my disposition that this goodly frame, the earth, seems to me a sterile promontory; this most excellent canopy the air, look you, this brave o'er-hanging firmament, this majestical roof fretted* with golden fire—why, it appeareth no other thing to me than 290 a foul and pestilent congregation of vapours. What a piece of work is man! How noble in reason! how infinite in faculties! in form and moving, how express* and admirable! in action, how like an angel! in apprehension, how like a god! the beauty of the world! the paragon of animals! And yet, to me, what is this quintessence of dust? Man delights not me—no, nor woman 295 neither, though by your smiling you seem to say so.

ROSENCRANTZ: My lord, there was no such stuff in my thoughts.

HAMLET: Why did ye laugh, then, when I said 'Man delights not me'?

ROSENCRANTZ: To think, my lord, if you delight not in man, what lenten entertainment the players shall receive from you. We coted* them on the way; 300 and hither are they coming to offer you service.

HAMLET: He that plays the king shall be welcome—his Majesty shall have tribute on me; the adventurous knight shall use his foil and target;* the lover shall not sigh gratis; the humorous man shall end his part in peace; the clown shall make those laugh whose lungs are tickle o' th' sere;* and the lady 305 shall say her mind freely, or the blank verse shall halt* for't. What players are they?

ROSENCRANTZ: Even those you were wont to take such delight in—the tragedians of the city.

HAMLET: How chances it they travel? Their residence, both in reputation and 310 profit, was better both ways.

ROSENCRANTZ: I think their inhibition* comes by the means of the late innovation.*

---

284 **prevent your discovery** forestall your disclosure
289 **fretted** adorned
292 **express** exact
300 **coted** overtook
303 **target** shield
305 **tickle o' th' sere** on a hair trigger
306 **halt** limp
312 **inhibition** hindrance
312 **innovation** probably a reference to the boys' theatre companies that were at this time offering serious competition to the adult companies

HAMLET: Do they hold the same estimation they did when I was in the city? Are they so followed? 315

ROSENCRANTZ: No, indeed, are they not.

HAMLET: How comes it? Do they grow rusty?

ROSENCRANTZ: Nay, their endeavour keeps in the wonted pace; but there is, sir, an eyrie* of children, little eyases that cry out on the top of question,* and are most tyrannically clapp'd* for't. These are now the fashion, and so be- 320 rattle the common stages*—so they call them—that many wearing rapiers are afraid of goose quills* and dare scarce come thither.

HAMLET: What, are they children? Who maintains 'em? How are they escoted?* Will they pursue the quality* no longer than they can sing? Will they not say afterwards, if they should grow themselves to common players—as it is 325 most like, if their means are no better—their writers do them wrong to make them exclaim against their own succession?*

ROSENCRANTZ: Faith, there has been much to-do on both sides; and the nation holds it no sin to tarre* them to controversy. There was for a while no money bid for argument,* unless the poet and the player went to cuffs in 330 the question.

HAMLET: Is't possible?

GUILDENSTERN: O, there has been much throwing about of brains.

HAMLET: Do the boys carry it away?

ROSENCRANTZ: Ay, that they do, my lord—Hercules and his load,* too. 335

HAMLET: It is not very strange; for my uncle is King of Denmark, and those that would make mows at him while my father lived give twenty, forty, fifty, a hundred ducats apiece for his picture in little. 'Sblood, there is something in this more than natural, if philosophy could find it out.

    [*a flourish*]

GUILDENSTERN: There are the players. 340

HAMLET: Gentlemen, you are welcome to Elsinore. Your hands, come then; th' appurtenance of welcome is fashion and ceremony. Let me comply* with you in this garb;* lest my extent* to the players, which, I tell you, must show fairly outwards, should more appear like entertainments than yours. You are welcome. But my uncle-father and aunt-mother are deceived. 345

GUILDENSTERN: In what, my dear lord?

HAMLET: I am but mad north-north-west; when the wind is southerly I know a hawk from a handsaw.

    [*Reenter* POLONIUS.]

---

³¹⁹ **eyrie** nest
³¹⁹ **little eyases . . . question** young hawks that cry shrilly above others in a debate
³²⁰ **tyrannically clapp'd** violently applauded
³²⁰⁻²¹ **berattle the common stages** put down the public theatres
³²² **goose quills** pens (of those who satirize the public theatres and their audiences)
³²³ **escoted** financially supported
³²⁴ **quality** profession of acting
³²⁷ **succession** future profession
³²⁹ **tarre** incite
³³⁰ **argument** for a playscript
³³⁵ **Hercules and his load** reference to the Globe Theatre, whose sign showed Hercules carrying the globe on his shoulders
³⁴² **comply** be courteous
³⁴³ **garb** outward show
³⁴³ **extent** behavior

POLONIUS: Well be with you, gentlemen!

HAMLET: Hark you, Guildenstern, and you, too—at each ear a hearer: that great   350
baby you see there is not yet out of his swaddling clouts.

ROSENCRANTZ: Happily* he is the second time come to them; for they say an old
man is twice a child.

HAMLET: I will prophesy he comes to tell me of the players; mark it. You say
right, sir: a Monday morning; 'twas then indeed.   355

POLONIUS: My lord, I have news to tell you.

HAMLET: My lord, I have news to tell you. When Roscius was an actor in
Rome—

POLONIUS: The actors are come hither, my lord.

HAMLET: Buzz, buzz!   360

POLONIUS: Upon my honour—

HAMLET: They came each actor on his ass—

POLONIUS: The best actors in the world, either for tragedy, comedy, history,
pastoral, pastoral-comical, historical-pastoral, tragical-historical, tragical-
comical-historical-pastoral, scene individable, or poem unlimited. Seneca   365
cannot be too heavy nor Plautus too light. For the law of writ and the liberty,* these are the only men.

HAMLET: O Jephthah, judge of Israel, what a treasure hadst thou!

POLONIUS: What a treasure had he, my lord?

HAMLET: Why—   370

> 'One fair daughter, and no more,
> The which he loved passing well.'

POLONIUS: [*aside*] Still on my daughter.

HAMLET: Am I not i' th' right, old Jephthah?

POLONIUS: If you call me Jephthah, my lord, I have a daughter that I love pass-   375
ing well.

HAMLET: Nay, that follows not.

POLONIUS: What follows then, my lord?

HAMLET: Why—

> 'As by lot, God wot'   380

and then, you know,

> 'It came to pass, as most like it was.'

The first row of the pious chanson* will show you more; for look where my
abridgement* comes.

[*Enter the* PLAYERS.]

You are welcome, masters; welcome all.—I am glad to see thee well.—   385
Welcome, good friends.—O, my old friend! Why thy face is valanc'd* since
I saw thee last; com'st thou to beard me in Denmark?—What, my young
lady* and mistress! By'r lady, your ladyship is nearer to heaven than when I
saw you last by the altitude of a chopine.* Pray God, your voice, like a piece
of uncurrent gold, be not crack'd within the ring.*—Masters, you are all   390

---

352 **Happily** perhaps
366–67 **law of writ and the liberty** sticking to the text and improvising
383 **first row of the pious chanson** first stanza of a religious song
384 **abridgement** interruption
386 **valanc'd** furnished with a beard
387–88 **young lady** boy who played female roles
389 **chopine** thick-soled shoe
390 **crack'd within the ring** comparing a boy's breaking voice with a cracked coin (which it was illegal to use)

welcome. We'll e'en to't like French falconers, fly at anything we see. We'll have a speech straight. Come, give us a taste of your quality; come, a passionate speech.

FIRST PLAYER: What speech, my good lord?

HAMLET: I heard thee speak me a speech once, but it was never acted; or, if it was, not above once; for the play, I remember, pleas'd not the million; 'twas caviary to the general.* But it was—as I received it, and others whose judgments in such matters cried in the top of mine*—an excellent play, well digested in the scenes, set down with as much modesty as cunning.* I remember one said there were no sallets* in the lines to make the matter savoury, nor no matter in the phrase that might indict the author of affectation; but call'd it an honest method, as wholesome as sweet, and by very much more handsome than fine.* One speech in it I chiefly lov'd; 'twas Aeneas' tale to Dido; and thereabout of it especially where he speaks of Priam's slaughter. If it live in your memory, begin at this line—let me see: 405

'*The rugged Pyrrhus, like th' Hyrcanian beast,*'*

'Tis not so; it begins with Pyrrhus.

'*The rugged Pyrrhus, he whose sable* arms,*
Black as his purpose, did the night resemble
When he lay couched in the ominous horse,*   410
Hath now this dread and black complexion smear'd
With heraldry more dismal; head to foot
Now is he total gules, horridly trick'd*
With blood of fathers, mothers, daughters, sons,
Bak'd and impasted* with the parching streets,   415
That lend a tyrannous and damned light
To their lord's murder. Roasted in wrath and fire,
And thus o'er-sized* with coagulate gore,
With eyes like carbuncles, the hellish Pyrrhus
Old grandsire Priam seeks.'   420

So proceed you.

POLONIUS: Fore God, my lord, well spoken, with good accent and good discretion.

FIRST PLAYER: '*Anon he finds him*
Striking too short at Greeks; his antique sword,
Rebellious to his arm, lies where it falls,   425
Repugnant to command. Unequal match'd,
Pyrrhus at Priam drives, in rage strikes wide;
But with the whiff and wind of his fell sword
Th' unnerved father falls. Then senseless Ilium,*

395

400

---

397 **caviary to the general** too rich for the common audience
398 **top of mine** agreed with or exceeded mine
399 **modesty as cunning** restraint as cleverness
400 **sallets** salads (spicy jests)
403 **more handsome than fine** well proportioned rather than ornamented
406 **Hyrcanian beast** tiger
408 **sable** black
410 **ominous horse** the wooden horse used in taking Troy
413 **total gules, horridly trick'd** entirely red, horridly adorned
415 **impasted** encrusted
418 **o'er-sized** smeared over
429 **Ilium** Troy

Seeming to feel this blow, with flaming top   430
Stoops to his base,* and with a hideous crash
Takes prisoner Pyrrhus' ear. For, lo! his sword,
Which was declining on the milky head
Of reverend Priam, seem'd i' th' air to stick.
So, as a painted tyrant, Pyrrhus stood   435
And, like a neutral to his will and matter,
Did nothing.
But as we often see, against* some storm,
A silence in the heavens, the rack* stand still,
The bold winds speechless, and the orb below   440
As hush as death, anon the dreadful thunder
Doth rend the region; so, after Pyrrhus' pause,
A roused vengeance sets him new a-work;
And never did the Cyclops' hammers fall
On Mars' armour, forg'd for proof eterne,*   445
With less remorse than Pyrrhus' bleeding sword
Now falls on Priam.
Out, out, thou strumpet, Fortune! All you gods,
In general synod,* take away her power;
Break all the spokes and fellies* from her wheel,   450
And bowl the round nave* down the hill of heaven,
As low as to the fiends.'

POLONIUS: This is too long.

HAMLET: It shall to the barber's, with your beard. Prithee say on. He's for a jig,
or a tale of bawdry, or he sleeps. Say on; come to Hecuba.   455

FIRST PLAYER: *'But who, ah, who had seen the mobled* queen—'*

HAMLET: 'The mobled queen'?

POLONIUS: That's good; 'mobled queen' is good.

FIRST PLAYER: *'Run barefoot up and down, threat'ning the flames*
With bisson rheum,* a clout* upon that head   450
Where late the diadem stood, and for a robe,
About her lank and all o'er-teemed loins,*
A blanket, in the alarm of fear caught up—
Who this had seen, with tongue in venom steep'd,
'Gainst Fortune's state would treason have pronounc'd.   465
But if the gods themselves did see her then,
When she saw Pyrrhus make malicious sport
In mincing with his sword her husband's limbs,

---

431 **Stoops to his base** collapses
438 **against** before
439 **rack** clouds
445 **proof eterne** to last forever
449 **synod** council
450 **fellies** rims
451 **nav**e hub
456 **mobled** muffled
460 **bisson rheum** blinding tears
460 **clout** rag
462 **o'er-teemed loins** exhausted with childbearing

> *The instant burst of clamour that she made—*
> *Unless things mortal move them not at all—* 470
> *Would have made milch* the burning eyes of heaven,*
> *And passion in the gods.'*

POLONIUS: Look whe'er* he has not turn'd his colour, and has tears in 's eyes. Prithee no more.

HAMLET: 'Tis well; I'll have thee speak out the rest of this soon.—Good my lord, 475 will you see the players well bestowed? Do you hear: let them be well used; for they are the abstract and brief chronicles of the time; after your death you were better have a bad epitaph than their ill report while you live.

POLONIUS: My lord, I will use them according to their desert.

HAMLET: God's bodkins, man, much better. Use every man after his desert, and 480 who shall 'scape whipping? Use them after your own honour and dignity; the less they deserve, the more merit is in your bounty. Take them in.

POLONIUS: Come, sirs.

HAMLET: Follow him, friends. We'll hear a play to-morrow. Dost thou hear me, old friend; can you play 'The Murder of Gonzago'? 485

FIRST PLAYER: Ay, my lord.

HAMLET: We'll ha't to-morrow night. You could, for a need, study a speech of some dozen or sixteen lines which I would set down and insert in't, could you not?

FIRST PLAYER: Ay, my lord. 490

HAMLET: Very well. Follow that lord; and look you mock him not. [*Exeunt* POLONIUS *and* PLAYERS.] My good friends, I'll leave you till night. You are welcome to Elsinore.

ROSENCRANTZ: Good my lord!

> [*Exeunt* ROSENCRANTZ *and* GUILDENSTERN.]

HAMLET: Ay, so God buy to you! Now I am alone. 495
> O, what a rogue and peasant slave am I!
> Is it not monstrous that this player here,
> But in a fiction, in a dream of passion,
> Could force his soul so to his own conceit*
> That from her working all his visage wann'd; 500
> Tears in his eyes, distraction in's aspect,
> A broken voice, and his whole function* suiting
> With forms* to his conceit? And all for nothing!
> For Hecuba!
> What's Hecuba to him or he to Hecuba, 505
> That he should weep for her? What would he do,
> Had he the motive and the cue for passion
> That I have? He would drown the stage with tears,
> And cleave the general ear with horrid speech;
> Make mad the guilty, and appal the free,* 510
> Confound the ignorant, and amaze indeed

---

471 **milch** moist
473 **whe'er** whether
499 **conceit** imagination
502 **function** action
503 **forms** bodily expressions
510 **appal the free** terrify the guiltless

The very faculties of eyes and ears.
Yet I,
A dull and muddy-mettl'd* rascal, peak,
Like John-a-dreams,* unpregnant of* my cause, 515
And can say nothing; no, not for a king
Upon whose property and most dear life
A damn'd defeat was made. Am I a coward?
Who calls me villain, breaks my pate across,
Plucks off my beard and blows it in my face, 520
Tweaks me by the nose, gives me the lie i' th' throat
As deep as to the lungs? Who does me this?
Ha!
'Swounds, I should take it; for it cannot be
But I am pigeon-liver'd* and lack gall 525
To make oppression bitter, or ere this
I should 'a fatted all the region kites*
With this slave's offal. Bloody, bawdy villain!
Remorseless, treacherous, lecherous, kindless* villain!
O, vengeance! 530
Why, what an ass am I! This is most brave,
That I, the son of a dear father murder'd,
Prompted to my revenge by heaven and hell,
Must, like a whore, unpack my heart with words,
And fall a-cursing like a very drab,* 535
A scullion!* Fie upon't! foh!
About,* my brains. Hum—I have heard
That guilty creatures, sitting at a play,
Have by the very cunning of the scene
Been struck so to the soul that presently* 540
They have proclaim'd their malefactions;
For murder, though it have no tongue, will speak
With most miraculous organ. I'll have these players
Play something like the murder of my father
Before mine uncle. I'll observe his looks; 545
I'll tent* him to the quick. If 'a do blench,*
I know my course. The spirit that I have seen
May be a devil; and the devil hath power
T'assume a pleasing shape; yea and perhaps
Out of my weakness and my melancholy, 550

514 **muddy-mettl'd** weak spirited
514-15 **peak, Like John-a-dreams** mope like a dreamer
515 **unpregnant of** unmoved by
525 **pigeon-liver'd** a coward
527 **kites** scavenger birds
529 **kindless** unnatural
535 **drab** prostitute
536 **scullion** kitchen servant
537 **About** to work
540 **presently** immediately
546 **tent** probe
546 **blench** blanch

As he is very potent with such spirits,
Abuses me to damn me. I'll have grounds
More relative* than this. The play's the thing
Wherein I'll catch the conscience of the King.   [*Exit.*]

ACT III

SCENE I——*Elsinore. The Castle.*

[*Enter* KING, QUEEN, POLONIUS, OPHELIA, ROSENCRANTZ, *and* GUILDENSTERN.]
KING: And can you by no drift of conference*
    Get from him why he puts on this confusion,
    Grating so harshly all his days of quiet
    With turbulent and dangerous lunacy?
ROSENCRANTZ: He does confess he feels himself distracted,   5
    But from what cause 'a will by no means speak.
GUILDENSTERN: Nor do we find him forward to be sounded;*
    But, with a crafty madness, keeps aloof
    When we would bring him on to some confession
    Of his true state.   10
QUEEN: Did he receive you well?
ROSENCRANTZ: Most like a gentleman.
GUILDENSTERN: But with much forcing of his disposition.*
ROSENCRANTZ: Niggard of question; but of our demands
    Most free in his reply.   15
QUEEN: Did you assay* him
    To any pastime?
ROSENCRANTZ: Madam, it so fell out that certain players
    We o'er-raught* on the way. Of these we told him;
    And there did seem in him a kind of joy   20
    To hear of it. They are here about the court,
    And, as I think, they have already order
    This night to play before him.
POLONIUS: 'Tis most true;
    And he beseech'd me to entreat your Majesties   25
    To hear and see the matter.
KING: With all my heart; and it doth much content me
    To hear him so inclin'd.
    Good gentlemen, give him a further edge,
    And drive his purpose into these delights.   30
ROSENCRANTZ: We shall, my lord.
        [*Exeunt* ROSENCRANTZ *and* GUILDENSTERN.]
KING: Sweet Gertrude, leave us, too;

---

553   **relative** certain
III,i,1   **conference** conversation
7   **forward to be sounded** willing to be questioned
13   **forcing of his disposition** effort
16   **assay** tempt
19   **o'er-raught** overtook

For we have closely* sent for Hamlet hither,
That he, as 'twere by accident, may here
Affront* Ophelia.　　　　　　　　　　　　　　　　　　　　35
Her father and myself—lawful espials*—
Will so bestow ourselves that, seeing unseen,
We may of their encounter frankly judge,
And gather by him, as he is behav'd,
If't be th' affliction of his love or no　　　　　　　　　40
That thus he suffers for.
QUEEN: I shall obey you;
　　And for your part, Ophelia, I do wish
　　That your good beauties be the happy cause
　　Of Hamlet's wildness; so shall I hope your virtues　　45
　　Will bring him to his wonted way again,
　　To both your honours.
OPHELIA: Madam, I wish it may.　　　　　　　　[*Exit* QUEEN.]
POLONIUS: Ophelia, walk you here.—Gracious, so please you,
　　We will bestow ourselves.—Read on this book;　　50
　　That show of such an exercise may colour*
　　Your loneliness.—We are oft to blame in this:
　　'Tis too much prov'd, that with devotion's visage
　　And pious action we do sugar o'er
　　The devil himself.　　　　　　　　　　　　　　　　55
KING: [*aside*] O, 'tis too true!
　　How smart a lash that speech doth give my conscience!
　　The harlot's cheek, beautied with plast'ring art,
　　Is not more ugly to the thing that helps it
　　Than is my deed to my most painted word.　　　　60
　　O heavy burden!
POLONIUS: I hear him coming; let's withdraw, my lord.
　　　　[*Exeunt* KING *and* POLONIUS.]
　　　　[*Enter* HAMLET.]
HAMLET: To be, or not to be—that is the question;
　　Whether 'tis nobler in the mind to suffer
　　The slings and arrows of outrageous fortune,　　65
　　Or to take arms against a sea of troubles,
　　And by opposing end them? To die, to sleep—
　　No more; and by a sleep to say we end
　　The heart-ache and the thousand natural shocks
　　That flesh is heir to. 'Tis a consummation　　　70
　　Devoutly to be wish'd. To die, to sleep;
　　To sleep, perchance to dream. Ay, there's the rub;*
　　For in that sleep of death what dreams may come,
　　When we have shuffled off this mortal coil,*

---

33 **closely** secretly
35 **Affront** meet face to face
36 **espials** observers
51 **colour** give an excuse for
72 **rub** impediment
74 **shuffled off this mortal coil** separated body from soul

Must give us pause. There's the respect*   75
That makes calamity of so long life;
For who would bear the whips and scorns of time,
Th' oppressor's wrong, the proud man's contumely,
The pangs of despis'd love, the law's delay,
The insolence of office, and the spurns   80
That patient merit of th' unworthy takes,
When he himself might his quietus* make
With a bare bodkin?* Who would these fardels* bear,
To grunt and sweat under a weary life,
But that the dread of something after death—   85
The undiscover'd country, from whose bourn*
No traveller returns—puzzles the will,
And makes us rather bear those ills we have
Than fly to others that we know not of?
Thus conscience does make cowards of us all;   90
And thus the native hue of resolution
Is sicklied o'er with the pale cast* of thought,
And enterprises of great pitch and moment,
With this regard, their currents turn awry
And lose the name of action.—Soft you now!   95
The fair Ophelia.—Nymph, in thy orisons*
Be all my sins rememb'red.
OPHELIA: Good my lord,
    How does your honour for this many a day?
HAMLET: I humbly thank you; well, well, well.   100
OPHELIA: My lord, I have remembrance of yours
    That I have longed to re-deliver.
    I pray you now receive them.
HAMLET: No, not I;
    I never gave you aught.   105
OPHELIA: My honour'd lord, you know right well you did,
    And with them words of so sweet breath compos'd
    As made the things more rich; their perfume lost,
    Take these again; for to the noble mind
    Rich gifts wax poor when givers prove unkind.   110
    There, my lord.
HAMLET: Ha, Ha! Are you honest?*
OPHELIA: My lord?
HAMLET: Are you fair?
OPHELIA: What means your lordship?   115
HAMLET: That if you be honest and fair, your honesty should admit no discourse
    to your beauty.

---

75 **respect** consideration
82 **quietus** end
83 **bodkin** dagger
83 **fardels** burdens
86 **bourn** region
92 **cast** color
96 **orisons** prayers
112 **Are you honest?** are you modest; chaste; truthful

OPHELIA: Could beauty, my lord, have better commerce than with honesty?

HAMLET: Ay, truly; for the power of beauty will sooner transform honesty from what it is to a bawd* than the force of honesty can translate beauty into his likeness. This was sometime a paradox, but now the time gives it proof. I did love you once. 120

OPHELIA: Indeed, my lord, you made me believe so.

HAMLET: You should not have believ'd me; for virtue cannot so inoculate our old stock but we shall relish of it.* I loved you not. 125

OPHELIA: I was the more deceived.

HAMLET: Get thee to a nunnery. Why wouldst thou be a breeder of sinners? I am myself indifferent honest,* but yet I could accuse me of such things that it were better my mother had not borne me: I am very proud, revengeful, ambitious; with more offences at my beck than I have thoughts to put them in, 130 imagination to give them shape, or time to act them in. What should such fellows as I do crawling between earth and heaven? We are arrant knaves, all; believe none of us. Go thy ways to a nunnery. Where's your father?

OPHELIA: At home, my lord.

HAMLET: Let the doors be shut upon him, that he may play the fool nowhere but 135 in's own house. Farewell.

OPHELIA: O, help him, you sweet heavens!

HAMLET: If thou dost marry, I'll give thee this plague for thy dowry: be thou as chaste as ice, as pure as snow, thou shalt not escape calumny. Get thee to a nunnery, go, farewell. Or, if thou wilt needs marry, marry a fool; for wise 140 men know well enough what monsters* you make of them. To a nunnery go; and quickly, too. Farewell.

OPHELIA: O heavenly powers, restore him!

HAMLET: I have heard of your paintings, too, well enough; God hath given you one face, and you make yourselves another. You jig and amble, and you lisp, 145 and nickname God's creatures, and make your wantonness your ignorance.* Go to, I'll no more on't; it hath made me mad. I say we will have no more marriage: those that are married already, all but one, shall live; the rest shall keep as they are. To a nunnery, go.
    [*Exit.*]

OPHELIA: O, what a noble mind is here o'erthrown! 150
    The courtier's, soldier's, scholar's, eye, tongue, sword;
    Th' expectancy and rose* of the fair state,
    The glass of fashion and the mould of form,*
    Th' observ'd of all observers—quite, quite down!
    And I, of ladies most deject and wretched, 155
    That suck'd the honey of his music vows,
    Now see that noble and most sovereign reason,
    Like sweet bells jangled, out of time and harsh;
    That unmatch'd form and feature of blown* youth

---

120 **bawd** procurer
124-25 **virtue cannot . . . relish of it** virtue cannot shield us from still desiring sinful pleasures
128 **indifferent honest** modestly virtuous
141 **monsters** cuckolds
146 **make your wantonness your ignorance** excuse your wantonness by pretending ignorance
152 **expectancy and rose** hope
153 **mould of form** pattern of excellent behavior
159 **blown** blooming

Blasted with ecstasy.* O, woe is me   160
T' have seen what I have seen, see what I see!
    [*Reenter* KING *and* POLONIUS.]

KING: Love! His affections do not that way tend;
    Nor what he spake, though it lack'd form a little,
    Was not like madness. There's something in his soul
    O'er which his melancholy sits on brood;   165
    And I do doubt* the hatch and the disclose
    Will be some danger; which to prevent
    I have in quick determination
    Thus set it down: he shall with speed to England
    For the demand of our neglected tribute.   170
    Haply the seas and countries different,
    With variable objects, shall expel
    This something-settled matter in his heart
    Whereon his brains still beating puts him thus
    From fashion of himself. What think you on't?   175
POLONIUS: It shall do well. But yet do I believe
    The origin and commencement of his grief
    Sprung from neglected love. How now, Ophelia!
    You need not tell us what Lord Hamlet said;
    We heard it all. My lord, do as you please;   180
    But if you hold it fit, after the play
    Let his queen mother all alone entreat him
    To show his grief. Let her be round* with him;
    And I'll be placed, so please you, in the ear
    Of all their conference. If she find him not,*   185
    To England send him; or confine him where
    Your wisdom best shall think.
KING: It shall be so:
    Madness in great ones must not unwatch'd go.
    [*Exeunt.*]

SCENE II————*Elsinore. The Castle.*

[*Enter* HAMLET *and three of the* PLAYERS.]

HAMLET: Speak the speech, I pray you, as I pronounc'd it to you, trippingly on
the tongue; but if you mouth it, as many of our players do, I had as lief the
towncrier spoke my lines. Nor do not saw the air too much with your hand,
thus, but use all gently; for in the very torrent, tempest, and, as I may say,
whirlwind of your passion, you must acquire and beget a temperance that   5
may give it smoothness. O, it offends me to the soul to hear a robustious
periwig-pated* fellow tear a passion to tatters, to very rags, to split the ears
of the groundlings,* who, for the most part, are capable of nothing* but

---

¹⁶⁰ **ecstasy** madness
¹⁶⁶ **doubt** fear
¹⁸³ **round** blunt
¹⁸⁵ **find him not** doesn't find out what is bothering him
^{III,ii,7} **periwig-pated** wig-wearing
⁸ **groundlings** spectators who stood in the space surrounding the stage; presumably the poorest and least-educated spectators
⁸ **are capable of nothing** understand nothing

inexplicable dumb shows* and noise. I would have such a fellow whipp'd for
o'erdoing Termagant; it out-herods Herod.* Pray you avoid it.   10

FIRST PLAYER: I warrant your honour.

HAMLET: Be not too tame neither, but let your own discretion be your tutor. Suit
the action to the word, the word to the action; with this special observance,
that you o'erstep not the modesty of nature; for anything so o'erdone is
from* the purpose of playing, whose end, both at the first and now, was and   15
is to hold, as 'twere, the mirror up to nature; to show virtue her own feature,
scorn her own image, and the very age and body of the time his form and
pressure.* Now, this overdone or come tardy off, though it makes the un-
skilful laugh, cannot but make the judicious grieve; the censure of the which
one must, in your allowance, o'erweigh a whole theatre of others. O, there   20
be players that I have seen play—and heard others praise, and that highly—
not to speak it profanely, that, neither having th' accent of Christians,
nor the gait of Christian, pagan, nor man, have so strutted and bellowed that I
have thought some of Nature's journeymen* had made men, and not made
them well, they imitated humanity so abominably.   25

FIRST PLAYER: I hope we have reform'd that indifferently* with us, sir.

HAMLET: O, reform it altogether. And let those that play your clowns speak no
more than is set down for them; for there be of them that will themselves
laugh, to set on some quantity of barren spectators to laugh, too, though in
the meantime some necessary question of the play be then to be considered.   25
That's villainous, and shows a most pitiful ambition in the fool that uses it.
Go, make you ready.

    [*Exeunt* PLAYERS.]

    [*Enter* POLONIUS, ROSENCRANTZ, *and* GUILDENSTERN.]

    How now, my lord! Will the King hear this piece of work?

POLONIUS: And the Queen, too, and that presently.

HAMLET: Bid the players make haste.   [*Exit* POLONIUS.] 35
    Will you two help to hasten them?

ROSENCRANTZ: Ay, my lord.   [*Exeunt they two.*]

HAMLET: What, ho, Horatio!

    [*Enter* HORATIO.]

HORATIO: Here, sweet lord, at your service.

HAMLET: Horatio, thou art e'en as just a man   40
    As e'er my conversation cop'd withal.*

HORATIO: O my dear lord!

HAMLET: Nay, do not think I flatter;
    For what advancement may I hope from thee,
    That no revenue hast but thy good spirits   45
    To feed and clothe thee? Why should the poor be flatter'd?
    No, let the candied* tongue lick absurd pomp,
    And crook the pregnant hinges of the knee*

---

9 **dumb shows** silent miming (used, as later in this scene, as prologues to plays)
10 **Termagant . . . Herod** exaggeratedly overacted roles in medieval mystery plays
15 **from** contrary to
18 **pressure** image
24 **journeymen** workers not yet masters of their craft
26 **indifferently** mostly
41 **cop'd withal** met with
47 **candied** sugared, flattering
48 **pregnant hinges of the knee** quick to curtsy and kneel

Where thrift* may follow fawning. Dost thou hear?
Since my dear soul was mistress of her choice   50
And could of men distinguish her election,
S'hath seal'd thee* for herself; for thou hast been
As one, in suff'ring all, that suffers nothing;
A man that Fortune's buffets and rewards
Hast ta'en with equal thanks; and blest are those   55
Whose blood* and judgment are so well commingled
That they are not a pipe for Fortune's finger
To sound what stop she please. Give me that man
That is not passion's slave, and I will wear him
In my heart's core, ay, in my heart of heart,   60
As I do thee. Something too much of this.
There is a play to-night before the King;
One scene of it comes near the circumstance
Which I have told thee of my father's death.
I prithee, when thou seest that act afoot,   65
Even with the very comment* of thy soul
Observe my uncle. If his occulted* guilt
Do not itself unkennel in one speech,
It is a damned ghost that we have seen,
And my imaginations are as foul   70
As Vulcan's stithy.*Give him heedful note;
For I mine eyes will rivet to his face;
And, after, we will both our judgments join
In censure of his seeming.*
HORATIO: Well, my lord.   75
    If 'a steal aught the whilst this play is playing,
    And 'scape detecting, I will pay the theft.
        [*Enter trumpets and kettledrums. Danish march. Sound a flourish. Enter* KING,
        QUEEN, POLONIUS, OPHELIA, ROSENCRANTZ, GUILDENSTERN, *and other* LORDS
        attendant, with the guard carrying torches.]
HAMLET: They are coming to the play; I must be idle.*
    Get you a place.
KING: How fares our cousin Hamlet?   80
HAMLET: Excellent, i' faith; of the chameleon's dish.* I eat the air promise-
    cramm'd; you cannot feed capons so.
KING: I have nothing with this answer, Hamlet; these words are not mine.
HAMLET: No, nor mine now. [*to* POLONIUS] My lord, you play'd once in th' uni-
    versity, you say?   85
POLONIUS: That did I, my lord, and was accounted a good actor.

---

⁴⁹ **thrift** profit
⁵² **S'hath seal'd thee** my soul has chosen you
⁵⁶ **blood** feelings
⁶⁶ **very comment** deepest wisdom
⁶⁷ **occulted** hidden
⁷¹ **Vulcan's stithy** forge of the Greek god
⁷⁴ **censure of his seeming** judgment on his response
⁷⁸ **be idle** play the fool
⁸¹ **chameleon's dish** air on which chameleons were thought to live

HAMLET: What did you enact?

POLONIUS: I did enact Julius Caesar; I was kill'd i' th' Capitol; Brutus kill'd me.

HAMLET: It was a brute part of him to kill so capital a calf there. Be the players ready? 90

ROSENCRANTZ: Ay, my lord; they stay upon your patience.

QUEEN: Come hither, my dear Hamlet, sit by me.

HAMLET: No, good mother; here's metal more attractive.*

POLONIUS: [*to the* KING] O, ho! do you mark that?

HAMLET: Lady, shall I lie in your lap? [*lying down at* OPHELIA'S *feet*] 95

OPHELIA: No, my lord.

HAMLET: I mean, my head upon your lap?

OPHELIA: Ay, my lord.

HAMLET: Do you think I meant country matters?*

OPHELIA: I think nothing, my lord. 100

HAMLET: That's a fair thought to lie between maids' legs.

OPHELIA: What is, my lord?

HAMLET: Nothing.

OPHELIA: You are merry, my lord.

HAMLET: Who, I? 105

OPHELIA: Ay, my lord.

HAMLET: O God, your only jig-maker!* What should a man do but be merry? For look you how cheerfully my mother looks, and my father died within's two hours.

OPHELIA: Nay, 'tis twice two months, my lord. 110

HAMLET: So long? Nay then, let the devil wear black, for I'll have a suit of sables. O heavens! die two months ago, and not forgotten yet? Then there's hope a great man's memory may outlive his life half a year; but, by'r lady, 'a must build churches, then; or else shall 'a suffer not thinking on, with the hobby-horse,* whose epitaph is 'For O, for O, the hobby-horse is forgot!' 115

[*The trumpet sounds. Hautboys play. The Dumb Show enters.*]

[*Enter a* KING *and a* QUEEN, *very lovingly; the* QUEEN *embracing him and he her. She kneels, and makes a show of protestation unto him. He takes her up, and declines his head upon her neck. He lies him down upon a bank of flowers; she, seeing him asleep, leaves him. Anon comes in a* FELLOW, *takes off his crown, kisses it, pours poison in the sleeper's ears, and leaves him. The* QUEEN *returns; finds the* KING *dead, and makes passionate action. The* POISONER, *with some two or three* MUTES, *comes in again, seeming to condole with her. The dead body is carried away. The* POISONER *woos the* QUEEN *with gifts: she seems harsh awhile, but in the end accepts his love. Exeunt.*]

OPHELIA: What means this, my lord?

HAMLET: Marry, this is miching mallecho;* it means mischief.

OPHELIA: Belike this show imports the argument* of the play.

[*Enter* PROLOGUE.]

93 **attractive** magnetic
99 **country matters** a sexual innuendo
107 **jig-maker** composer of songs and dances (jigs were often performed as afterpieces in the theatre, and often by the fool)
114 **hobby-horse** mock horse worn by a performer in mummers plays
117 **miching mallecho** sneaky mischief
118 **argument** plot

HAMLET: We shall know by this fellow: the players cannot keep counsel; they'll   120
    tell all.

OPHELIA: Will 'a tell us what this show meant?

HAMLET: Ay, or any show that you show him. Be not you asham'd to show, he'll
    not shame to tell you what it means.

OPHELIA: You are naught, you are naught.* I'll mark the play.

PROLOGUE: *For us, and for our tragedy,*   125
    Here stooping to your clemency,
    We beg your hearing patiently.
        [*Exit.*]

HAMLET: Is this a prologue, or the posy of a ring?*

OPHELIA: 'Tis brief, my lord.

HAMLET: As woman's love.   130
        [*Enter the* PLAYER KING *and* QUEEN.]

PLAYER KING: *Full thirty times hath Phoebus' cart* gone round*
    Neptune's salt wash and Tellus's* orbed ground,*
    And thirty dozen moons with borrowed sheen
    About the world have times twelve thirties been,
    Since love our hearts and Hymen did our hands*   135
    Unite comutual in most sacred bands.

PLAYER QUEEN: *So many journeys may the sun and moon*
    Make us again count o'er ere love be done!
    But, woe is me, you are so sick of late,
    So far from cheer and from your former state,   140
    That I distrust you. Yet, though I distrust,*
    Discomfort you, my lord, it nothing must;
    For women fear too much even as they love,
    And women's fear and love hold quantity,
    In neither aught, or in extremity.   145
    Now, what my love is, proof hath made you know;
    And as my love is siz'd, my fear is so.
    Where love is great, the littlest doubts are fear;
    Where little fears grow great, great love grows there.

PLAYER KING: *Faith, I must leave thee, love, and shortly, too:*   150
    My operant powers their functions leave to do;*
    And thou shalt live in this fair world behind,
    Honour'd, belov'd; and haply one as kind
    For husband shalt thou—

PLAYER QUEEN: *O, confound the rest!*   155
    Such love must needs be treason in my breast.
    In second husband let me be accurst!
    None wed the second but who kill'd the first.

---

124 **naught** naughty
128 **posy of a ring** sentiment inscribed in a ring
131 **Phoebus' cart** the sun god's chariot
132 **Neptune's salt wash** the sea
132 **Tellus** Roman goddess of the Earth
135 **Hymen** god of marriage
141 **distrust** am anxious about
151 **operant** active

HAMLET: That's wormwood, wormwood.*

PLAYER QUEEN: *The instances*that second marriage move**   160
    Are base respects of thrift, but none of love.*
    A second time I kill my husband dead,
    When second husband kisses me in bed.

PLAYER KING: *I do believe you think what now you speak;*
    But what we do determine oft we break.   165
    Purpose is but the slave to memory,
    *Of violent birth, but poor validity;**
    Which now, the fruit unripe, sticks on the tree;
    But fall unshaken when they mellow be.
    Most necessary 'tis that we forget   170
    To pay ourselves what to ourselves is debt.
    What to ourselves in passion we propose,
    The passion ending, doth the purpose lose,
    The violence of either grief or joy
    Their own enactures with themselves destroy.*   175
    Where joy most revels grief doth most lament;
    Grief joys, joy grieves, on slender accident.
    This world is not for aye; nor 'tis not strange
    That even our loves should with our fortunes change;
    For 'tis a question left us yet to prove,   180
    Whether love lead fortune or else fortune love.
    The great man down, you mark his favourite flies;
    The poor advanc'd makes friends of enemies.
    And hitherto doth love on fortune tend;
    For who not needs shall never lack a friend,   185
    And who in want a hollow friend doth try,
    Directly seasons him his enemy.*
    But, orderly to end where I begun,
    Our wills and fates do so contrary run
    That our devices still are overthrown;   190
    Our thoughts are ours, their ends none of our own.
    So think thou wilt no second husband wed;
    But die thy thoughts when thy first lord is dead.

PLAYER QUEEN: *Nor earth to me give food, nor heaven light,*
    Sport and repose lock from me day and night,   195
    To desperation turn my trust and hope,
    An anchor's cheer in prison be my scope,*
    Each opposite that blanks the face of joy*
    Meet what I would have well, and it destroy,
    Both here and hence pursue my lasting strife,   200
    If, once a widow, ever I be wife!

---

159 **wormwood** a bitter herb
160 **instances** motives
160 **move** induce
161 **base respects of thrift** considerations of profit
167 **validity** strength
175 **enactures** acts
187 **seasons** ripens him into
197 **anchor's** anchorite, hermit
198 **opposite that blanks** adverse thing that makes the face blanch

HAMLET: If she should break it now!

PLAYER KING: *'Tis deeply sworn. Sweet, leave me here awhile;*
  My spirits grow dull, and fain I would beguile
  The tedious day with sleep.   [*Sleeps.*] 205

PLAYER QUEEN: *Sleep rock thy brain,*
  And never come mischance between us twain!

HAMLET: Madam, how like you this play?

QUEEN: The lady doth protest too much, methinks.

HAMLET: O, but she'll keep her word.   210

KING: Have you heard the argument?* Is there no offence in't?

HAMLET: No, no; they do but jest, poison in jest; no offence i' th' world.

KING: What do you call the play?

HAMLET: 'The Mouse-trap.' Marry, how? Tropically.* This play is the image of a murder done in Vienna: Gonzago is the duke's name; his wife, Baptista. You shall see anon. 'Tis a knavish piece of work; but what of that? Your Majesty, and we that have free* souls, it touches us not. Let the galled jade* wince, our withers are unwrung.
  [*Enter* LUCIANUS.]
  This is one Lucianus, nephew to the King.

OPHELIA: You are as good as a chorus, my lord.   220

HAMLET: I could interpret* between you and your love, if I could see the puppets dallying.

OPHELIA: You are keen, my lord, you are keen.

HAMLET: It would cost you a groaning to take off mine edge.*

OPHELIA: Still better, and worse.   225

HAMLET: So you mis-take* your husbands.—Begin, murderer; pox, leave thy damnable faces and begin. Come; the croaking raven doth bellow for revenge.

LUCIANUS: *Thoughts black, hands apt, drugs fit, and time agreeing;*
  Confederate season, else no creature seeing;*   230
  Thou mixture rank, of midnight weeds collected,
  With Hecate's ban thrice blasted, thrice infected.*
  *Thy natural magic and dire property**
  On wholesome life usurps immediately.
  [*Pours the poison in his ears.*]

HAMLET: 'A poisons him i' th' garden for his estate. His name's Gonzago. The   235
story is extant, and written in very choice Italian. You shall see anon how the murderer gets the love of Gonzago's wife.

OPHELIA: The King rises.

HAMLET: What, frighted with false fire!*

211 **argument** plot
214 **Tropically** figuratively
217 **free** souls free of guilt
217 **galled jade** chafed horse
221 **interpret** explain like a puppet master if he could see the puppets playing wantonly
224 **cost . . . edge** a sexual reference
226 **mis-take** err in taking
230 **Confederate season** the opportunity offered me
232 **Hecate's ban** the goddess of sorcery's curse
233 **property** nature
239 **false fire** blank firing of a gun

QUEEN: How fares my lord?   240
POLONIUS: Give o'er the play.
KING: Give me some light. Away!
POLONIUS: Lights, lights, lights!
       [*Exeunt all but* HAMLET *and* HORATIO.]
HAMLET: Why, let the strucken deer go weep,
    The hart ungalled play;   245
    For some must watch, while some must sleep;
    Thus runs the world away.
    Would not this, sir, and a forest of feathers*—if the rest of my fortunes turn
    Turk* with me—with two Provincial roses on my raz'd shoes,* get me a fel-
    lowship in a cry of players,* sir?   250
HORATIO: Half a share.
HAMLET: A whole one, I.
    For thou dost know, O Damon dear,
    This realm dismantled was
    Of Jove himself; and now reigns here   255
    A very, very—peacock.
HORATIO: You might have rhym'd.
HAMLET: O good Horatio, I'll take the ghost's word for a thousand pound. Didst
    perceive?
HORATIO: Very well, my lord.   260
HAMLET: Upon the talk of the poisoning.
HORATIO: I did very well note him.
HAMLET: Ah, ha! Come, some music. Come, the recorders.
    For if the King like not the comedy,
    Why, then, belike he likes it not, perdy.*   265
    Come, some music.
       [*Reenter* ROSENCRANTZ *and* GUILDENSTERN.]
GUILDENSTERN: Good my lord, vouchsafe me a word with you.
HAMLET: Sir, a whole history.
GUILDENSTERN: The King, sir—
HAMLET: Ay, sir, what of him?   270
GUILDENSTERN: Is, in his retirement, marvellous distemp'red.
HAMLET: With drink, sir?
GUILDENSTERN: No, my lord, rather with choler.*
HAMLET: Your wisdom should show itself more richer to signify this to his doc-
    tor; for for me to put him to his purgation would perhaps plunge him into   275
    far more choler.
GUILDENSTERN: Good my lord, put your discourse into some frame,* and start
    not so wildly from my affair.
HAMLET: I am tame, sir. Pronounce.
GUILDENSTERN: The Queen, your mother, in most great affliction of spirit, hath   280
    sent me to you.

---

248 **forest of feathers** costume with feathers
248–49 **turn Turk** go badly
249 **raz'd shoes** shoes ornamented with slashes
250 **cry of players** company of actors
265 **perdy** by God (par dieu)
273 **choler** anger
277 **frame** order, control

HAMLET: You are welcome.

GUILDENSTERN: Nay, good my lord, this courtesy is not of the right breed. If it shall please you to make me a wholesome answer, I will do your mother's commandment; if not, your pardon and my return shall be the end of my business. 285

HAMLET: Sir, I cannot.

ROSENCRANTZ: What, my lord?

HAMLET: Make you a wholesome* answer, my wit's diseas'd. But, sir, such answer as I can make, you shall command: or rather, as you say, my mother. There- 290 fore no more, but to the matter: my mother, you say—

ROSENCRANTZ: Then thus she says: your behaviour hath struck her into amazement and admiration.*

HAMLET: O wonderful son, that can so stonish a mother! But is there no sequel at the heels of this mother's admiration? Impart. 295

ROSENCRANTZ: She desires to speak with you in her closet ere you go to bed.

HAMLET: We shall obey, were she ten times our mother. Have you any further trade with us?

ROSENCRANTZ: My lord, you once did love me.

HAMLET: And do still, by these pickers and stealers.* 300

ROSENCRANTZ: Good my lord, what is your cause of distemper? You do surely bar the door upon your own liberty, if you deny your griefs to your friend.

HAMLET: Sir, I lack advancement.*

ROSENCRANTZ: How can that be, when you have the voice of the King himself for your succession in Denmark? 305

HAMLET: Ay, sir, but 'While the grass grows'—the proverb* is something musty.
  [*Reenter the* PLAYERS, *with recorders.*]
  O, the recorders! Let me see one. To withdraw* with you—why do you go about to recover the wind of me,* as if you would drive me into a toil?*

GUILDENSTERN: O my lord, if my duty be too bold, my love is too unmannerly.*

HAMLET: I do not well understand that. Will you play upon this pipe? 310

GUILDENSTERN: My lord, I cannot.

HAMLET: I pray you.

GUILDENSTERN: Believe me, I cannot.

HAMLET: I do beseech you.

GUILDENSTERN: I know no touch of it, my lord. 315

HAMLET: It is as easy as lying: govern these ventages* with your fingers and thumb, give it breath with your mouth, and it will discourse most eloquent music. Look you, these are the stops.

GUILDENSTERN: But these cannot I command to any utterance of harmony; I have not the skill. 320

HAMLET: Why, look you now, how unworthy a thing you make of me! You would

---

289 **wholesome** sane
293 **admiration** wonder
300 **pickers and stealers** hands
303 **advancement** promotion
306 **proverb** (the rest of the proverb is "the horse starveth")
307 **withdraw** speak privately
308 **recover the wind of me** get on the windward side of me
308 **toil** snare
309 **duty . . . unmannerly** if I have seemed rude it is because my love for you leads me beyond good manners
316 **ventages** vents, stops on a musical instrument

play upon me; you would seem to know my stops; you would pluck out the
heart of my mystery; you would sound me from my lowest note to the top of
my compass;* and there is much music, excellent voice, in this little organ,*
yet cannot you make it speak. 'Sblood, do you think I am easier to be play'd   325
on than a pipe? Call me what instrument you will, though you can fret me,
yet you cannot play upon me.
      [*Reenter* POLONIUS.]
God bless you, sir!

POLONIUS: My lord, the Queen would speak with you, and presently.

HAMLET: Do you see yonder cloud that's almost in shape of a camel?   330

POLONIUS: By th' mass, and 'tis like a camel indeed.

HAMLET: Methinks it is like a weasel.

POLONIUS: It is back'd like a weasel.

HAMLET: Or like a whale?

POLONIUS: Very like a whale.   335

HAMLET: Then I will come to my mother by and by. [*aside*] They fool me to the
    top of my bent.*—I will come by and by.

POLONIUS: I will say so.   [*Exit* POLONIUS.]

HAMLET: 'By and by' is easily said. Leave me, friends.
      [*Exeunt all but* HAMLET.]
    'Tis now the very witching time of night,   340
    When churchyards yawn, and hell itself breathes out
    Contagion to this world. Now could I drink hot blood,
    And do such bitter business as the day
    Would quake to look on. Soft! now to my mother.
    O heart, lose not thy nature; let not ever   345
    The soul of Nero* enter this firm bosom.
    Let me be cruel, not unnatural:
    I will speak daggers to her, but use none.
    My tongue and soul in this be hypocrites—
    How in my words somever she be shent,*   350
    To give them seals* never, my soul, consent!
      [*Exit.*]

SCENE III————Elsinore. The Castle.

[*Enter* KING, ROSENCRANTZ, *and* GUILDENSTERN.]

KING: I like him not; nor stands it safe with us
    To let his madness range. Therefore prepare you;
    I your commission will forthwith dispatch,
    And he to England shall along with you.
    The terms* of our estate may not endure   5
    Hazard so near's as doth hourly grow
    Out of his brows.

---

324 **compass** range
324 **organ** the recorder
336-37 **fool me . . . my bent** they force me to play the fool to the fullest
346 **Nero** Roman emperor who killed his mother
350 **shent** rebuked
351 **give them seals** confirm them with deeds
III,iii,5 **terms** conditions

GUILDENSTERN: We will ourselves provide.
　　　Most holy and religious fear it is
　　　To keep those many many bodies safe　　　　　　　　　10
　　　That live and feed upon your Majesty.
ROSENCRANTZ: The single and peculiar* life is bound
　　　With all the strength and armour of the mind
　　　To keep itself from noyance;* but much more
　　　That spirit upon whose weal depends and rests　　　　15
　　　The lives of many. The cease of majesty
　　　Dies not alone, but like a gulf* doth draw
　　　What's near it with it. It is a massy wheel,
　　　Fix'd on the summit of the highest mount,
　　　To whose huge spokes ten thousand lesser things　　　20
　　　Are mortis'd and adjoin'd; which when it falls,
　　　Each small annexment, petty consequence,
　　　Attends the boist'rous ruin. Never alone
　　　Did the king sigh, but with a general groan.
KING: Arm* you, I pray you, to this speedy voyage;　　　　25
　　　For we will fetters put about this fear,
　　　Which now goes too free-footed.
ROSENCRANTZ: We will haste us.
　　　　　[*Exeunt* ROSENCRANTZ *and* GUILDENSTERN.]
　　　　　[*Enter* POLONIUS.]
POLONIUS: My lord, he's going to his mother's closet.
　　　Behind the arras I'll convey myself　　　　　　　　　30
　　　To hear the process.* I'll warrant she'll tax him home;*
　　　And, as you said, and wisely was it said,
　　　'Tis meet that some more audience than a mother,
　　　Since nature makes them partial, should o'erhear
　　　The speech, of vantage.* Fare you well, my liege.　　　35
　　　I'll call upon you ere you go to bed,
　　　And tell you what I know.
KING: Thanks, dear my lord.　　　　　　　　[*Exit* POLONIUS.]
　　　O, my offence is rank, it smells to heaven;
　　　It hath the primal eldest curse* upon't—　　　　　　40
　　　A brother's murder! Pray can I not,
　　　Though inclination be as sharp as will.
　　　My stronger guilt defeats my strong intent,
　　　And, like a man to double business bound,
　　　I stand in pause where I shall first begin,　　　　　　45
　　　And both neglect. What if this cursed hand
　　　Were thicker than itself with brother's blood,

---

¹² **peculiar** private
¹⁴ **noyance** injury
¹⁷ **gulf** whirlpool
²⁵ **Arm** prepare
³¹ **process** proceedings
³¹ **tax him home** rebuke him sharply
³⁵ **of vantage** from some advantageous place
⁴⁰ **primal eldest curse** oldest curse (Cain's murder of his brother Abel)

Is there not rain enough in the sweet heavens
To wash it white as snow? Whereto serves mercy
But to confront the visage of offence?   50
And what's in prayer but this twofold force,
To be forestalled ere we come to fall,
Or pardon'd being down? Then I'll look up;
My fault is past. But, O, what form of prayer
Can serve my turn? 'Forgive me my foul murder'!   55
That cannot be; since I am still possess'd
Of those effects* for which I did the murder—
My crown, mine own ambition, and my queen.
May one be pardon'd and retain th' offence?
In the corrupted currents of this world   60
Offence's gilded hand may shove by justice;
And oft 'tis seen the wicked prize itself
Buys out the law. But 'tis not so above:
There is no shuffling;* there the action lies
In his true nature; and we ourselves compell'd,   65
Even to the teeth and forehead of our faults,
To give in evidence. What then? What rests?*
Try what repentance can. What can it not?
Yet what can it when one cannot repent?
O wretched state! O bosom black as death!   70
O limed* soul, that, struggling to be free,
Art more engag'd!* Help, angels. Make assay:
Bow, stubborn knees; and, heart, with strings of steel,
Be soft as sinews of the new-born babe.
All may be well.   [*He kneels.*]   75
      [*Enter* HAMLET.]
HAMLET: Now might I do it pat, now 'a is a-praying;
And now I'll do't—and so 'a goes to heaven,
And so am I reveng'd. That would be scann'd.*
A villain kills my father; and for that,
I, his sole son, do this same villain send   80
To heaven.
Why, this is hire and salary, not revenge.
'A took my father grossly, full of bread,*
With all his crimes broad blown, as flush* as May;
And how his audit* stands who knows save heaven?   85
But in our circumstance and course of thought
'Tis heavy with him; and am I then reveng'd

---

57 **effects** things gained
64 **shuffling** trickery
67 **rests** remains
71 **limed** trapped (birds were caught by liming tree limbs with a sticky substance)
72 **engag'd** entrapped
78 **would be scann'd** needs to be thought about
83 **full of bread** worldly gratifications
84 **crimes . . . flush** sins in full bloom as flowers in May
85 **audit** account

To take him in the purging of his soul,
When he is fit and season'd for his passage?
No.   90
Up, sword, and know thou a more horrid hent.
When he is drunk asleep, or in his rage;
Or in th' incestuous pleasure of his bed;
At game, a-swearing, or about some act
That has no relish of salvation in't—   95
Then trip him, that his heels my kick at heaven,
And that his soul may be as damn'd and black
As hell, whereto it goes. My mother stays.
This physic* but prolongs thy sickly days.   [*Exit.*]
KING: [*rising*] My words fly up, my thoughts remain below.   100
Words without thoughts never to heaven go.   [*Exit.*]

SCENE IV———*The* QUEEN's *closet.*

[*Enter* QUEEN *and* POLONIUS.]
POLONIUS: 'A will come straight. Look you lay home* to him;
Tell him his pranks have been too broad* to bear with,
And that your Grace hath screen'd and stood between
Much heat and him. I'll silence me even here.
Pray you be round with him.   5
HAMLET: [*within*] Mother, mother, mother!
QUEEN: I'll warrant you. Fear me not.
Withdraw, I hear him coming.
          [POLONIUS *goes behind the arras.*]
          [*Enter* HAMLET.]
HAMLET: Now, mother, what's the matter?
QUEEN: Hamlet, thou hast thy father much offended.   10
HAMLET: Mother, you have my father much offended.
QUEEN: Come, come, you answer with an idle* tongue.
HAMLET: Go, go, you question with a wicked tongue.
QUEEN: Why, how now, Hamlet!
HAMLET: What's the matter now?   15
QUEEN: Have you forgot me?
HAMLET: No, by the rood,* not so:
You are the Queen, your husband's brother's wife;
And—would it were not so!—you are my mother.
QUEEN: Nay then, I'll set those to you that can speak.   20
HAMLET: Come, come, and sit you down; you shall not budge.
You go not till I set you up a glass*
Where you may see the inmost part of you.
QUEEN: What wilt thou do? Thou wilt not murder me?
Help, help, ho!   25

---

⁹⁹ **physic** (to Claudius) this medicine (prayer)
III,iv,1 **lay home** rebuke him sharply
² **broad** unrestrained
¹² **idle** foolish
¹⁷ **rood** cross
²² **glass** mirror

POLONIUS: [*behind*] What, ho! help, help, help!

HAMLET: [*draws*] How now! a rat?
　　　Dead, for a ducat, dead!
　　　　[*kills* POLONIUS *with a pass through the arras*]

POLONIUS: [*behind*] O, I am slain!

QUEEN: O me, what hast thou done?　　　　　　　　　　　30

HAMLET: Nay, I know not:
　　　Is it the King?

QUEEN: O, what a rash and bloody deed is this!

HAMLET: A bloody deed!—almost as bad, good mother,
　　　As kill a king and marry with his brother.　　　　　35

QUEEN: As kill a king!

HAMLET: Ay, lady, it was my word. [*parting the arras*]
　　　Thou wretched, rash, intruding fool, farewell!
　　　I took thee for thy better. Take thy fortune;
　　　Thou find'st to be too busy is some danger.　　　　40
　　　Leave wringing of your hands. Peace; sit you down,
　　　And let me wring your heart; for so I shall,
　　　If it be made of penetrable stuff;
　　　If damned custom have not braz'd* it so
　　　That it be proof and bulwark against sense.*　　　　45

QUEEN: What have I done that thou dar'st wag thy tongue
　　　In noise so rude against me?

HAMLET: Such an act
　　　That blurs the grace and blush of modesty;
　　　Calls virtue hypocrite; takes off the rose　　　　　50
　　　From the fair forehead of an innocent love,
　　　And sets a blister there,* makes marriage-vows
　　　As false as dicers' oaths. O, such a deed
　　　As from the body of contraction* plucks
　　　The very soul, and sweet religion makes　　　　　55
　　　A rhapsody* of words. Heaven's face does glow
　　　O'er this solidity and compound mass
　　　With heated visage, as against the doom—
　　　Is thought-sick at the act.

QUEEN: Ay me, what act,　　　　　　　　　　　　　60
　　　That roars so loud and thunders in the index?*

HAMLET: Look here upon this picture and on this,
　　　The counterfeit presentment* of two brothers.
　　　See what a grace was seated on this brow;
　　　Hyperion's curls; the front* of Jove himself;　　　65
　　　An eye like Mars, to threaten and command;
　　　A station* like the herald Mercury

---

⁴⁴ **braz'd** hardened
⁴⁵ **proof . . . sense** armored against feeling
⁵² **sets a blister** brands (as a harlot)
⁵⁴ **contraction** marriage contract
⁵⁶ **rhapsody** senseless string
⁶¹ **index** prologue
⁶³ **counterfeit presentment** represented image
⁶⁵ **front** forehead
⁶⁷ **station** bearing

New lighted on a heaven-kissing hill—
A combination and a form indeed
Where every god did seem to set his seal, 70
To give the world assurance of a man.
This was your husband. Look you now what follows:
Here is your husband, like a mildew'd ear
Blasting his wholesome brother. Have you eyes?
Could you on this fair mountain leave to feed, 75
And batten* on this moor? Ha! have you eyes?
You cannot call it love; for at your age
The heyday in the blood is tame, it's humble,
And waits upon the judgment; and what judgment
Would step from this to this? Sense, sure, you have, 80
Else could you not have motion; but sure that sense
Is apoplex'd;* for madness would not err,
Nor sense to ecstasy* was ne'er so thrall'd
But it reserv'd some quantity of choice
To serve in such a difference. What devil was't 85
That thus hath cozen'd you at hoodman-blind?*
Eyes without feeling, feeling without sight.
Ears without hands or eyes, smelling sans* all,
Or but a sickly part of one true sense
Could not so mope.* O shame! where is thy blush? 90
Rebellious hell,
If thou canst mutine in a matron's bones,
To flaming youth let virtue be as wax
And melt in her own fire; proclaim no shame
When the compulsive ardour gives the charge, 95
Since frost itself as actively doth burn,
And reason panders will.*
QUEEN: O Hamlet, speak no more!
Thou turn'st my eyes into my very soul;
And there I see such black and grained spots 100
As will not leave their tinct.*
HAMLET: Nay, but to live
In the rank sweat of an enseamed* bed,
Stew'd in corruption, honeying and making love
Over the nasty sty! 105
QUEEN: O, speak to me no more!
These words like daggers enter in my ears;
No more, sweet Hamlet.

---

76 **batten** feed gluttonously
82 **apoplex'd** paralyzed
83 **ecstasy** madness
86 **hoodman-blind** cheated you at blindman's buff
88 **sans** without
90 **so mope** be so stupid
97 **reason panders will** reason acts as a panderer for desire
101 **tinct** color
103 **enseamed** rumpled

HAMLET: A murderer and a villain!
    A slave that is not twentieth part the tithe* 110
    Of your precedent lord; a vice* of kings;
    A cutpurse of the empire and the rule,
    That from a shelf the precious diadem stole
    And put it in his pocket!
QUEEN: No more! 115
        [*Enter* GHOST.]
HAMLET: A king of shreds and patches—
    Save me, and hover o'er me with your wings,
    You heavenly guards! What would your gracious figure?
QUEEN: Alas, he's mad!
HAMLET: Do you not come your tardy son to chide, 120
    That, laps'd in time and passion, lets go by
    Th' important acting of your dread command?
    O, say!
GHOST: Do not forget; this visitation
    Is but to whet thy almost blunted purpose. 125
    But look, amazement on thy mother sits.
    O, step between her and her fighting soul!
    Conceit* in weakest bodies strongest works.
    Speak to her, Hamlet.
HAMLET: How is it with you, lady? 130
QUEEN: Alas, how is't with you,
    That you do bend your eye on vacancy,
    And with th' incorporal* air do hold discourse?
    Forth at your eyes and spirits wildly peep;
    And, as the sleeping soldiers in th' alarm, 135
    Your bedded* hairs like life in excrements*
    Start up and stand an end. O gentle son,
    Upon the heat and flame of thy distemper
    Sprinkle cool patience! Whereon do you look?
HAMLET: On him, on him! Look you how pale he glares. 140
    His form and cause conjoin'd, preaching to stones,
    Would make them capable.*—Do not look upon me,
    Lest with this piteous action you convert
    My stern effects;* then what I have to do
    Will want true colour—tears perchance for blood. 145
QUEEN: To whom do you speak this?
HAMLET: Do you see nothing there?
QUEEN: Nothing at all; yet all that is I see.
HAMLET: Nor did you nothing hear?

---

110 **tithe** tenth part
111 **vice** wicked character in medieval plays
128 **Conceit** imagination
133 **incorporal** empty, bodiless
136 **bedded** flat-lying
136 **excrements** outgrowths
142 **capable** receptive
143–44 **convert my stern effects** divert my serious purpose

QUEEN: No, nothing but ourselves. 150
HAMLET: Why, look you there. Look how it steals away.
    My father, in his habit* as he liv'd!
    Look where he goes even now out at the portal.
        [*Exit* GHOST.]
QUEEN: This is the very coinage of your brain.
    This bodiless creation ecstasy 155
    Is very cunning in.
HAMLET: Ecstasy!
    My pulse as yours doth temperately keep time.
    And makes as healthful music. It is not madness
    That I have utt'red. Bring me to the test, 160
    And I the matter will re-word which madness
    Would gambol* from. Mother, for love of grace,
    Lay not that flattering unction* to your soul,
    That not your trespass but my madness speaks:
    It will but skin and film the ulcerous place, 165
    Whiles rank corruption, mining* all within,
    Infects unseen. Confess yourself to heaven;
    Repent what's past; avoid what is to come;
    And do not spread the compost on the weeds,
    To make them ranker. Forgive me this my virtue; 170
    For in the fatness of these pursy* times
    Virtue itself of vice must pardon beg,
    Yea, curb* and woo for leave to do him good.
QUEEN: O Hamlet, thou hast cleft my heart in twain.
HAMLET: O, throw away the worser part of it, 175
    And live the purer with the other half.
    Good night—but go not to my uncle's bed;
    Assume a virtue, if you have it not.
    That monster custom, who all sense doth eat,
    Of habits devil, is angel yet in this, 180
    That to the use* of actions fair and good
    He likewise gives a frock or livery
    That aptly is put on. Refrain to-night;
    And that shall lend a kind of easiness
    To the next abstinence; the next more easy; 185
    For use almost can change the stamp of nature,
    And either curb the devil, or throw him out,
    With wondrous potency. Once more, good night;
    And when you are desirous to be blest,
    I'll blessing beg of you. For this same lord 190
    I do repent; but Heaven hath pleas'd it so,

---

152 **habit** garment
162 **gambol** start away
163 **unction** ointment
166 **mining** undermining
171 **pursy** bloated
173 **curb** bow low
181 **use** practice

To punish me with this, and this with me,
That I must be their scourge and minister.
I will bestow him, and will answer well
The death I gave him. So, again, good night.   195
I must be cruel only to be kind;
Thus bad begins and worse remains behind.
One word more, good lady.

QUEEN: What shall I do?

HAMLET: Not this, by no means, that I bid you do: 200
Let the bloat King tempt you again to bed;
Pinch wanton on your cheek; call you his mouse;
And let him, for a pair of reechy* kisses,
Or paddling in your neck with his damn'd fingers,
Make you to ravel all this matter out,   205
That I essentially am not in madness,
But mad in craft. 'Twere good you let him know;
For who that's but a queen, fair, sober, wise,
Would from a paddock,* from a bat, a gib,*
Such dear concernings hide? Who would do so?   210
No, in despite of sense and secrecy,
Unpeg the basket on the house's top,
Let the birds fly, and, like the famous ape,
To try conclusions,* in the basket creep
And break your own neck down.   215

QUEEN: Be thou assur'd, if words be made of breath
And breath of life, I have no life to breathe
What thou hast said to me.

HAMLET: I must to England; you know that?

QUEEN: Alack,   220
I had forgot. 'Tis so concluded on.

HAMLET: There's letters seal'd; and my two school-fellows,
Whom I will trust as I will adders fang'd—
They bear the mandate;* they must sweep my way
And marshal me to knavery. Let it work;   225
For 'tis the sport to have the engineer
Hoist with his own petar;* and't shall go hard
But I will delve one yard below their mines
And blow them at the moon, O, 'tis most sweet
When in one line two crafts* directly meet.   230
This man shall set me packing.
I'll lug the guts into the neighbour room.
Mother, good night. Indeed, this counsellor
Is now most still, most secret, and most grave,

---

203 **reechy** foul
209 **paddock** toad
209 **gib** tomcat
214 **try conclusions** make experiments
224 **mandate** command
227 **petar** bomb
230 **crafts** intrigues

Who was in life a foolish prating knave.   235
Come, sir, to draw toward an end with you.
Good night, mother.
    [*Exeunt severally;* HAMLET *tugging in* POLONIUS.]

ACT IV

SCENE I———*Elsinore. The Castle.*

    [*Enter* KING, QUEEN, ROSENCRANTZ, *and* GUILDENSTERN.]
KING: There's matter in these sighs, these profound heaves,
    You must translate; 'tis fit we understand them.
    Where is your son?
QUEEN: Bestow this place on us a little while.
    [*Exeunt* ROSENCRANTZ *and* GUILDENSTERN.]
    Ah, mine own lord, what have I seen to-night!   5
KING: What, Gertrude? How does Hamlet?
QUEEN: Mad as the sea and wind, when both contend
    Which is the mightier. In his lawless fit,
    Behind the arras hearing something stir,
    Whips out his rapier, cries 'A rat, a rat!'   10
    And in this brainish apprehension* kills
    The unseen good old man.
KING: O heavy deed!
    It had been so with us had we been there.
    His liberty is full of threats to all—   15
    To you yourself, to us, to every one.
    Alas, how shall this bloody deed be answer'd?
    It will be laid to us, whose providence*
    Should have kept short, restrain'd, and out of haunt,*
    This mad young man. But so much was our love,   20
    We would not understand what was most fit;
    But, like the owner of a foul disease,
    To keep it from divulging, let it feed
    Even on the pith of life. Where is he gone?
QUEEN: To draw apart the body he hath kill'd;   25
    O'er whom his very madness, like some ore
    Among a mineral of metals base,*
    Shows itself pure: 'a weeps for what is done.
KING: O Gertrude, come away!
    The sun no sooner shall the mountains touch   30
    But we will ship him hence; and this vile deed
    We must with all our majesty and skill
    Both countenance and excuse. Ho Guildenstern!
    [*Reenter* ROSENCRANTZ *and* GUILDENSTERN.]
    Friends, both go join you with some further aid:

IV,i,11 **brainish apprehension** mad imagination
18 **providence** foresight
19 **out of haunt** away from association with others
26–27 **ore . . . base** like gold among baser metals

Hamlet in madness hath Polonius slain,   35
And from his mother's closet hath he dragg'd him;
Go seek him out; speak fair, and bring the body
Into the chapel. I pray you haste in this.
   [*Exeunt* ROSENCRANTZ *and* GUILDENSTERN.]
Come, Gertrude, we'll call up our wisest friends
And let them know both what we mean to do   40
And what's untimely done; so haply slander—
Whose whisper o'er the world's diameter,
As level as the cannon to his blank,*
Transports his pois'ned shot—may miss our name,
And hit the woundless* air. O, come away!   45
My soul is full of discord and dismay.   [*Exeunt.*]

SCENE II————*Elsinore. The Castle.*

   [*Enter* HAMLET.]
HAMLET: Safely stow'd.
GENTLEMEN: [*within*] Hamlet! Lord Hamlet!
HAMLET: But soft! What noise? Who calls on Hamlet? O, here they come!
   [*Enter* ROSENCRANTZ *and* GUILDENSTERN.]
ROSENCRANTZ: What have you done, my lord, with the dead body?
HAMLET: Compounded it with dust, whereto 'tis kin.   5
ROSENCRANTZ: Tell us where 'tis, that we may take it thence. And bear it to the chapel.
HAMLET: Do not believe it.
ROSENCRANTZ: Believe what?
HAMLET: That I can keep your counsel, and not mine own. Besides, to be de-   10
   manded of* a sponge—what replication* should be made by the son of a
   king?
ROSENCRANTZ: Take you me for a sponge, my lord?
HAMLET: Ay, sir; that soaks up the King's countenance,* his rewards, his author-
   ities. But such officers do the King best service in the end: he keeps them like an   15
   ape an apple in the corner of his jaw; first mouth'd to be last swallowed;
   when he needs what you have glean'd, it is but squeezing you and, sponge,
   you shall be dry again.
ROSENCRANTZ: I understand you not, my lord.
HAMLET: I am glad of it; a knavish speech sleeps in a foolish ear.   20
ROSENCRANTZ: My lord, you must tell us where the body is, and go with us to
   the King.
HAMLET: The body is with the King, but the King is not with the body. The King
   is a thing—
GUILDENSTERN: A thing, my lord!   25
HAMLET: Of nothing. Bring me to him. Hide fox, and all after.*   [*Exeunt.*]

---

43 **blank** white center of a target
45 **woundless** invulnerable
IV,ii,10–11 **demanded of** questioned by
11 **replication** reply
14 **countenance** favor
26 **Hide fox, and all after** call in game (as in hide-and-seek)

SCENE III————*Elsinore. The Castle.*

[*Enter* KING, *attended.*]

KING: I have sent to seek him, and to find the body.
How dangerous is it that this man goes loose!
Yet must not we put the strong law on him:
He's lov'd of the distracted* multitude,
Who like not in their judgment but their eyes;   5
And where 'tis so, th' offender's scourge is weigh'd,
But never the offence. To bear* all smooth and even,
This sudden sending him away must seem
Deliberate pause.* Diseases desperate grown
By desperate appliance are reliev'd,   10
Or not at all.
            [*Enter* ROSENCRANTZ.]
How now! what hath befall'n?
ROSENCRANTZ: Where the dead body is bestow'd, my lord,
We cannot get from him.
KING: But where is he?   15
ROSENCRANTZ: Without, my lord; guarded, to know your pleasure.
KING: Bring him before us.
ROSENCRANTZ: Ho, Guildenstern! bring in the lord.
            [*Enter* HAMLET *and* GUILDENSTERN.]
KING: Now, Hamlet, where's Polonius?
HAMLET: At supper.   20
KING: At supper! Where?
HAMLET: Not where he eats, but where 'a is eaten; a certain convocation of
    politic* worms are e'en at him. Your worm is your only emperor for diet: we
    fat all creatures else to fat us, and we fat ourselves for maggots; your fat king
    and your lean beggar is but variable service*—two dishes, but to one table. 25
    That's the end.
KING: Alas, alas!
HAMLET: A man may fish with the worm that hath eat of a king, and eat of the fish
    that hath fed of that worm.
KING: What dost thou mean by this?   30
HAMLET: Nothing but to show you how a king may go a progress through the
    guts of a beggar.
KING: Where is Polonius?
HAMLET: In heaven; send thither to see; if your messenger find him not there,
    seek him i' th' other place yourself. But if, indeed, you find him not within 35
    this month, you shall nose him as you go up the stairs into the lobby.
KING: [*to attendants*] Go seek him there.
HAMLET: 'A will stay till you come.   [*Exeunt attendants.*]
KING: Hamlet, this deed, for thine especial safety—

IV,iii,4 **distracted** confused
7 **bear** carry out
9 **pause** planning
23 **politic** statesmanlike
25 **variable service** different courses

Which we do tender,* as we dearly grieve   40
For that which thou hast done—must send thee hence
With fiery quickness. Therefore prepare thyself;
The bark is ready, and the wind at help,
Th' associates tend,* and everything is bent
For England.   45
HAMLET: For England!
KING: Ay, Hamlet.
HAMLET: Good!
KING: So is it, if thou knew'st our purposes.
HAMLET: I see a cherub that sees them. But, come; for England! Farewell, dear   50
    mother.
KING: Thy loving father, Hamlet.
HAMLET: My mother: father and mother is man and wife; man and wife is one flesh; and
    so, my mother. Come, for England.   [*Exit.*]
KING: Follow him at foot;* tempt him with speed aboard;   55
    Delay it not; I'll have him hence to-night.
    Away! for everything is seal'd and done
    That else leans* on th' affair. Pray you make haste.
        [*Exeunt all but the* KING.]
    And, England, if my love thou hold'st at aught—
    As my great power thereof may give thee sense,   60
    Since yet thy cicatrice* looks raw and red
    After the Danish sword, and thy free awe*
    Pays homage to us—thou mayst not coldly set
    Our sovereign process;* which imports at full,
    By letters congruing to that effect,   65
    The present* death of Hamlet. Do it, England:
    For like the hectic* in my blood he rages,
    And thou must cure me. Till I know 'tis done,
    Howe'er my haps,* my joys were ne'er begun.   [*Exit.*]

SCENE IV———*A plain in Denmark.*

[*Enter* FORTINBRAS *with his army over the stage.*]
FORTINBRAS: Go, Captain, from me greet the Danish king.
    Tell him that by his license Fortinbras
    Craves the conveyance of a promis'd march
    Over his kingdom. You know the rendezvous.

40 **tender** hold dear
44 **tend** wait
55 **at foot** closely
58 **leans** depends
61 **cicatrice** scar
62 **free awe** uncompelled submission
63-64 **coldly set our sovereign process** disregard our royal command
66 **present** immediate
67 **hectic** fever
69 **haps** fortunes

If that his Majesty would aught with us,   5
    We shall express our duty in his eye;*
    And let him know so.
CAPTAIN: I will do't, my lord.
FORTINBRAS: Go softly* on.   *[Exeunt all but the* CAPTAIN.]
    [*Enter* HAMLET, ROSENCRANTZ, GUILDENSTERN, *and others.*]
HAMLET: Good sir, whose powers are these?   10
CAPTAIN: They are of Norway, sir.
HAMLET: How purpos'd, sir, I pray you?
CAPTAIN: Against some part of Poland.
HAMLET: Who commands them, sir?
CAPTAIN: The nephew to old Norway, Fortinbras.   15
HAMLET: Goes it against the main* of Poland, sir,
    Or for some frontier?
CAPTAIN: Truly to speak, and with no addition,
    We go to gain a little patch of ground
    That hath in it no profit but the name.   20
    To pay five ducats, five, I would not farm it;
    Nor will it yield to Norway or the Pole
    A ranker* rate should it be sold in fee.*
HAMLET: Why, then the Polack never will defend it.
CAPTAIN: Yes, it is already garrison'd.   25
HAMLET: Two thousand souls and twenty thousand ducats
    Will not debate* the question of this straw.
    This is th' imposthume* of much wealth and peace,
    That inward breaks, and shows no cause without
    Why the man dies. I humbly thank you, sir.   30
CAPTAIN: God buy you, sir.
ROSENCRANTZ: Will't please you go, my lord?
HAMLET: I'll be with you straight. Go a little before.
    [*Exeunt all but* HAMLET.]
    How all occasions do inform against me,
    And spur my dull revenge! What is a man,   35
    If his chief good and market* of his time
    Be but to sleep and feed? A beast, no more!
    Sure he that made us with such large discourse,*
    Looking before and after, gave us not
    That capability and godlike reason   40
    To fust* in us unus'd. Now, whether it be
    Bestial oblivion, or some craven scruple
    Of thinking too precisely on th' event—

IV,iv,6 **in his eye** in his presence
⁹ **softly** slowly
¹⁶ **main** main part
²³ **ranker** higher
²³ **in fee** outright
²⁷ **debate** settle
²⁸ **imposthume** ulcer
³⁶ **market** profit
³⁸ **discourse** understanding
⁴¹ **fust** grow moldy

A thought which, quarter'd, hath but one part wisdom
And ever three parts coward—I do not know   45
Why yet I live to say 'This thing's to do,'
Sith I have cause, and will, and strength, and means,
To do't. Examples gross* as earth exhort me:
Witness this army, of such mass and charge,*
Led by a delicate and tender prince,   50
Whose spirit, with divine ambition puff'd,
Makes mouths at the invisible event,*
Exposing what is mortal and unsure
To all that fortune, death, and danger dare,
Even for an egg-shell. Rightly to be great   55
Is not to stir without great argument,*
But greatly* to find quarrel in a straw,
When honour's at the stake. How stand I, then,
That have a father kill'd, a mother stain'd,
Excitements* of my reason and my blood,   60
And let all sleep, while to my shame I see
The imminent death of twenty thousand men
That, for a fantasy and trick of fame,
Go to their graves like beds, fight for a plot
Whereon the numbers cannot try the cause,   65
Which is not tomb enough and continent*
To hide the slain? O, from this time forth,
My thoughts be bloody, or be nothing worth!   [*Exit.*]

SCENE V———*Elsinore. The Castle.*

[*Enter* QUEEN, HORATIO, *and a* GENTLEMAN.]
QUEEN: I will not speak with her.
GENTLEMAN: She is importunate, indeed distract.
    Her mood will needs be pitied.
QUEEN: What would she have?
GENTLEMAN: She speaks much of her father; says she hears   5
    There's tricks i' th' world, and hems, and beats her heart;
    Spurns enviously at straws;* speaks things in doubt,*
    That carry but half sense. Her speech is nothing,
    Yet the unshaped use of it doth move
    The hearers to collection;* they yawn* at it,   10

---

⁴⁸ **gross** large
⁴⁹ **charge** expense
⁵² **Makes mouths . . . event** scorns the outcome
⁵⁶ **argument** reason
⁵⁷ **greatly** nobly
⁶⁰ **Excitements** incentives
⁶⁶ **continent** container
IV,v,7 **Spurns . . . straws** objects to insignificant matters
⁷ **in doubt** uncertainly
¹⁰ **collection** gather and listen
¹⁰ **yawn** gape

And botch the words up fit to their own thoughts;
Which, as her winks and nods and gestures yield them,
Indeed would make one think there might be thought,
Though nothing sure, yet much unhappily.

HORATIO: 'Twere good she were spoken with; for she may strew   15
Dangerous conjectures in ill-breeding minds.

QUEEN: Let her come in.   [*Exit* GENTLEMAN.]
[*aside*] To my sick soul, as sin's true nature is,
Each toy seems prologue to some great amiss.*
So full of artless jealousy* is guilt,   20
It spills* itself in fearing to be spilt.
[*Enter* OPHELIA *distracted.*]

OPHELIA: Where is the beauteous Majesty of Denmark?

QUEEN: How now, Ophelia!

OPHELIA: [*sings*]

> How should I your true love know
> From another one?   25
> By his cockle hat and staff,
> And his sandal shoon.*

QUEEN: Alas, sweet lady, what imports this song?

OPHELIA: Say you? Nay, pray you, mark.   [*sings*]

> He is dead and gone, lady,   30
> He is dead and gone;
> At his head a grass-green turf,
> At his heels a stone.

O, ho!

QUEEN: Nay, but, Ophelia—   35

OPHELIA: Pray you, mark.   [*sings*]

> White his shroud as the mountain snow—
[*Enter* KING.]

QUEEN: Alas, look here, my lord.

OPHELIA: Larded* with sweet flowers;
> Which bewept to the grave did not go   40
> With true-love showers.

KING: How do you, pretty lady?

OPHELIA: Well, God dild* you! They say the owl was a baker's daughter. Lord,
we know that we are, but know not what we may be. God be at your table!

KING: Conceit* upon her father.   45

OPHELIA: Pray let's have no words of this; but when they ask you what it means,
say you this: [*sings*]

> To-morrow is Saint Valentine's day,,
> All in the morning betime,

---

19 **amiss** misfortune
20 **artless jealousy** crude suspicion
21 **spills** destroys
27 **shoon** shoes
39 **Larded** decorated
43 **dild** reward
45 **Conceit** brooding

And I a maid at your window,　　　　　　　50
To be your Valentine.
Then up he rose, and donn'd his clothes,
And dupp'd* the chamber-door;
Let in the maid, that out a maid
Never departed more.　　　　　　　　　55

KING: Pretty Ophelia!

OPHELIA: Indeed, la, without an oath, I'll make an end on't.   [*sings*]

By Gis* and by Saint Charity,
Alack, and fie for shame!
Young men will do't, if they come to't;　　60
By Cock, they are to blame.
Quoth she 'Before you tumbled me,
You promis'd me to wed.'

He answers:

'So would I 'a done, by yonder sun,　　　65
An thou hadst not come to my bed.'

KING: How long hath she been thus?

OPHELIA: I hope all will be well. We must be patient; but I cannot choose but weep to think they would lay him i' th' cold ground. My brother shall know of it; and so I thank you for your good counsel. Come, my coach! Good   70
night, ladies; good night, sweet ladies, good night, good night.
　　　[*Exit.*]

KING: Follow her close; give her good watch, I pray you.
　　　[*Exeunt* HORATIO *and* GENTLEMAN.]
　　O, this is the poison of deep grief; it springs
　　All from her father's death. And now behold—
　　O Gertrude, Gertrude!　　　　　　　　　　　　　75
　　When sorrows come, they come not single spies,
　　But in battalions! First, her father slain;
　　Next, your son gone, and he most violent author
　　Of his own just remove; the people muddied,*
　　Thick and unwholesome in their thoughts and whispers　　80
　　For good Polonius' death; and we have done but greenly*
　　In hugger-mugger* to inter him; poor Ophelia
　　Divided from herself and her fair judgment,
　　Without the which we are pictures, or mere beasts;
　　Last, and as much containing as all these,　　　　　　85
　　Her brother is in secret come from France;
　　Feeds on his wonder,* keeps himself in clouds,
　　And wants not buzzers* to infect his ear
　　With pestilent speeches of his father's death;

---

53 **dupp'd** opened
58 **Gis** Jesus
79 **muddied** confused
81 **greenly** foolishly
82 **hugger-mugger** secret haste
87 **wonder** suspicion
88 **buzzers** tale bearers

Wherein necessity, of matter beggar'd,*   90
Will nothing stick* our person to arraign
In ear and ear. O my dear Gertrude, this,
Like to a murd'ring piece,* in many places
Gives me superfluous death.   *[a noise within]*
QUEEN: Alack, what noise is this?   95
KING: Attend!
   [*Enter a* GENTLEMAN.]
 Where are my Switzers!* Let them guard the door.
 What is the matter?
GENTLEMAN: Save yourself, my lord:
 The ocean, overpeering of his list,*   100
 Eats not the flats with more impetuous haste
 Than young Laertes, in a riotous head,*
 O'erbears your officers. The rabble call him lord;
 And, as the world were now but to begin,
 Antiquity forgot, custom not known,   105
 The ratifiers and props of every word,
 They cry 'Choose we; Laertes shall be king.'
 Caps, hands, and tongues, applaud it to the clouds,
 'Laertes shall be king, Laertes king.'
QUEEN: How cheerfully on the false trail they cry!
   [*noise within*]   110
 O, this is counter, you false Danish dogs!
KING: The doors are broke.[*Enter* LAERTES, *with others, in arms.*]
LAERTES: Where is this king?—Sirs, stand you all without.
ALL: No, let's come in.
LAERTES: I pray you give me leave.   115
ALL: We will, we will.
   [*Exeunt.*]
LAERTES: I thank you. Keep the door.—O thou vile king,
 Give me my father!
QUEEN: Calmly, good Laertes.
LAERTES: That drop of blood that's calm proclaims me bastard; 120
 Cries cuckold to my father; brands the harlot
 Even here, between the chaste unsmirched brow
 Of my true mother.
KING: What is the cause, Laertes,
 That thy rebellion looks so giant-like?   125
 Let him go, Gertrude; do not fear our person:
 There's such divinity doth hedge a king
 That treason can but peep to what it would,
 Acts little of his will. Tell me, Laertes,
 Why thou art thus incens'd. Let him go, Gertrude. 130
 Speak, man.

---

90 **beggar'd** lacking facts
91 **Will nothing stick** will not hesitate
93 **murd'ring piece** cannon
97 **Switzers** Swiss guards
100 **list** shore
102 **in a riotous head** with a rebellious mob

LAERTES: Where is my father?
KING: Dead.
QUEEN: But not by him.
KING: Let him demand his fill.   135
LAERTES: How came he dead? I'll not be juggled with.
    To hell, allegiance! Vows, to the blackest devil!
    Conscience and grace, to the profoundest pit!
    I dare damnation. To this point I stand,
    That both the worlds I give to negligence,*   140
    Let come what comes; only I'll be reveng'd
    Most thoroughly for my father.
KING: Who shall stay you?
LAERTES: My will, not all the world's.
    And for my means, I'll husband them* so well   145
    They shall go far with little.
KING: Good Laertes,
    If you desire to know the certainty
    Of your dear father, is't writ in your revenge
    That, swoopstake,* you will draw both friend and foe,   150
    Winner and loser?
LAERTES: None but his enemies.
KING: Will you know them, then?
LAERTES: To his good friends thus wide I'll ope my arms
    And, like the kind life-rend'ring pelican,   155
    Repast* them with my blood.
KING: Why, now you speak
    Like a good child and a true gentleman.
    That I am guiltless of your father's death,
    And am most sensibly in grief for it,   160
    It shall as level to your judgment 'pear
    As day does to your eye.   [*A noise within:* 'Let her come in.']
LAERTES: How now! What noise is that?
    [*Reenter* OPHELIA]
    O, heat dry up my brains! tears seven times salt
    Burn out the sense and virtue* of mine eye!   165
    By heaven, thy madness shall be paid with weight
    Till our scale turn the beam.* O rose of May!
    Dear maid, kind sister, sweet Ophelia!
    O heavens! is't possible a young maid's wits
    Should be as mortal as an old man's life?   170
    Nature is fine* in love; and where 'tis fine
    It sends some precious instance* of itself
    After the thing it loves.

---

140 **both the worlds . . . negligence** I care not what may happen to me in this world or the next
145 **husband them** use them economically
150 **swoopstake** in a full sweep
155–56 **pelican, repast** (pelicans were thought to use their own blood to feed their young)
165 **virtue** power
167 **scale turn the beam** weigh down the balance of a scale
171 **fine** refined
172 **instance** sample

OPHELIA: [*sings*]

> They bore him barefac'd on the bier;
> Hey non nonny, nonny, hey nonny;
> And in his grave rain'd many a tear—

    Fare you well, my dove!

LAERTES: Hadst thou thy wits, and didst persuade revenge,
    It could not move thus.

OPHELIA: You must sing 'A-down, a-down,' an you call him a-down-a. O, how the
    wheel becomes it! It is the false steward, that stole his master's daughter.

LAERTES: This nothing's more than matter.*

OPHELIA: There's rosemary, that's for remembrance; pray you, love, remember.
    And there is pansies, that's for thoughts.

LAERTES: A document* in madness—thoughts and remembrance fitted.

OPHELIA: There's fennel for you, and columbines. There's rue for you; and here's
    some for me. We may call it herb of grace a Sundays. O, you must wear your
    rue with a difference. There's a daisy. I would give you some violets, but they
    wither'd all when my father died. They say 'a made a good end.
    [*sings*] For bonny sweet Robin is all my joy.

LAERTES: Thought and affliction, passion, hell itself,
    She turns to favour* and to prettiness.

OPHELIA: [*sings*]

> And will 'a not come again
> And will 'a not come again?
> No, no, he is dead,
> Go to thy death-bed,
> He never will come again.
>
> His beard was as white as snow,
> All flaxen was his poll;*
> He is gone, he is gone,
> And we cast away moan:
> God-a-mercy on his soul!

    And of all Christian souls, I pray God. God buy you.
    [*Exit.*]

LAERTES: Do you see this, O God?

KING: Laertes, I must commune with your grief,
    Or you deny me right. Go but apart,
    Make choice of whom your wisest friends you will,
    And they shall hear and judge 'twixt you and me.
    If by direct or by collateral* hand
    They find us touch'd,* we will our kingdom give,
    Our crown, our life, and all that we call ours,
    To you in satisfaction; but if not,
    Be you content to lend your patience to us,
    And we shall jointly labour with your soul
    To give it due content.

175

180

185

190

195

200

205

210

215

---

182 **nothing's . . . matter** this nonsense contains more meaning than does a statement of great matter
185 **document** lesson
192 **favour** to beauty
199 **flaxen was his poll** his hair was white
209 **collateral** indirect
210 **touch'd** implicated

LAERTES: Let this be so.
　　His means of death, his obscure funeral—
　　No trophy, sword, nor hatchment,* o'er his bones,　　　　　　　　220
　　No noble rite nor formal ostentation*—
　　Cry to be heard, as 'twere from heaven to earth,
　　That I must call't in question.
KING: So you shall;
　　And where th' offence is, let the great axe fall.　　　　　　　　225
　　I pray you go with me.　　　　　　　　　　　　　*[Exeunt.]*

SCENE VI———*Elsinore. The Castle.*

[*Enter* HORATIO *with an* ATTENDANT.]
HORATIO: What are they that would speak with me?
ATTENDANT: Sea-faring men, sir; they say they have letters for you.
HORATIO: Let them come in.　　　　　　　　　　*[Exit* ATTENDANT.]
　　I do not know from what part of the world
　　I should be greeted, if not from Lord Hamlet.　　　　　　　　5
　　　　[*Enter* SAILORS.]
SAILOR: God bless you, sir.
HORATIO: Let Him bless thee, too.
SAILOR: 'A shall, sir, an't please Him. There's a letter for you, sir; it came from
　　th'ambassador that was bound for England—if your name be Horatio, as I
　　am let to know it is.　　　　　　　　　　　　　　　　　　10
HORATIO: [*reads*] 'Horatio, when thou shalt have overlook'd* this, give these
　　fellows some means to the King: they have letters for him. Ere we were two
　　days old at sea, a pirate of very warlike appointment gave us chase. Finding
　　ourselves too slow of sail, we put on a compelled valour; and in the grapple
　　I boarded them. On the instant they got clear of our ship; so I alone became　　15
　　their prisoner. They have dealt with me like thieves of mercy; but they knew
　　what they did; I am to do a good turn for them. Let the King have the letters
　　I have sent; and repair thou to me with as much speed as thou wouldest fly
　　death. I have words to speak in thine ear will make thee dumb; yet are they
　　much too light for the bore of the matter. These good fellows will bring thee　　20
　　where I am. Rosencrantz and Guildenstern hold their course for England; of
　　them I have much to tell thee. Farewell.
　　　　　　　He that thou knowest thine, Hamlet.'
　　Come, I will give you way for these your letters,
　　And do't the speedier that you may direct me　　　　　　　　25
　　To him from whom you brought them.　　　　　　　*[Exeunt.]*

SCENE VII———*Elsinore. The Castle.*

[*Enter* KING *and* LAERTES.]
KING: Now must your conscience my acquittance seal,
　　And you must put me in your heart for friend,
　　Sith you have heard, and with a knowing ear,

---

218 **hatchment** stone bearing coat of arms
219 **ostentation** ceremony
IV,vi,11 **overlook'd** read

That he which hath your noble father slain
Pursu'd my life.   5
LAERTES: It well appears. But tell me
   Why you proceeded not against these feats,
   So crimeful and so capital* in nature,
   As by your safety, wisdom, all things else,
   You mainly were stirr'd up.   10
KING: O, for two special reasons,
   Which may to you, perhaps, seem much unsinew'd,*
   But yet to me th' are strong. The Queen his mother
   Lives almost by his looks; and for myself,
   My virtue or my plague, be it either which—   15
   She is so conjunctive* to my life and soul
   That, as the star moves not but in his sphere,
   I could not but by her. The other motive,
   Why to a public count I might not go,
   Is the great love the general gender* bear him;   20
   Who, dipping all his faults in their affection,
   Work like the spring that turneth wood to stone,
   Convert his gyves* to graces; so that my arrows,
   Too slightly timber'd* for so loud a wind,
   Would have reverted to my bow again,   25
   But not where I have aim'd them.
LAERTES: And so have I a noble father lost;
   A sister driven into desp'rate terms,
   Whose worth, if praises may go back again,
   Stood challenger on mount of all the age   30
   For her perfections. But my revenge will come.
KING: Break not your sleeps for that. You must not think
   That we are made of stuff so flat and dull
   That we can let our beard be shook with danger,
   And think it pastime. You shortly shall hear more   35
   I lov'd your father, and we love our self;
   And that, I hope, will teach you to imagine—
      [*Enter a* MESSENGER *with letters.*]
   How now! What news?
MESSENGER: Letters, my lord, from Hamlet:
   These to your Majesty; this to the Queen.   40
KING: From Hamlet! Who brought them?
MESSENGER: Sailors, my lord, they say; I saw them not.
   They were given me by Claudio; he receiv'd them
   Of him that brought them.
KING: Laertes, you shall hear them.   45
   Leave us   [*Exit* MESSENGER.]

IV,vii,8 **capital** deserving death
12 **unsinew'd** weak
16 **conjunctive** closely united
20 **general gender** common people
23 **gyves** fetters
24 **timber'd** shafted

[*reads*] 'High and Mighty. You shall know I am set naked* on your kingdom.
To-morrow shall I beg leave to see your kingly eyes; when I shall, first asking
your pardon thereunto, recount the occasion of my sudden and more
strange return. 50

Hamlet.'

What should this mean? Are all the rest come back?
Or is it some abuse,* and no such thing?

LAERTES: Know you the hand? 55

KING: 'Tis Hamlet's character. 'Naked'!
And in a postscript here, he says 'alone.'
Can you devise* me?

LAERTES: I am lost in it, my lord. But let him come;
It warms the very sickness in my heart
That I shall live and tell him to his teeth 60
'Thus didest thou.'

KING: If it be so, Laertes—
As how should it be so, how otherwise?—
Will you be rul'd by me?

LAERTES: Ay, my lord; 65
So you will not o'errule me to a peace.

KING: To thine own peace. If he be now return'd,
As checking at* his voyage, and that he means
No more to undertake it, I will work him
To an exploit now ripe in my device, 70
Under the which he shall not choose but fall;
And for his death, no wind of blame shall breathe;
But even his mother shall uncharge the practice
And call it accident.

LAERTES: My lord, I will be rul'd 75
The rather, if you could devise it so
That I might be the organ.

KING: It falls right.
You have been talk'd of since your travel much,
And that in Hamlet's hearing, for a quality 80
Wherein they say you shine. Your sum of parts
Did not together pluck such envy from him
As did that one; and that, in my regard,
Of the unworthiest siege.*

LAERTES: What part is that, my lord? 85

KING: A very riband in the cap of youth,
Yet needful, too; for youth no less becomes
The light and careless livery that it wears
Than settled age his sables and his weeds,*

---

⁴⁷ **naked** destitute
⁵³ **abuse** deception
⁵⁷ **devise** advise
⁶⁸ **checking at** abandoning
⁸⁴ **siege** rank
⁸⁹ **weeds** sober attire

Importing health and graveness. Two months since   90
Here was a gentleman of Normandy—
I have seen myself, and serv'd against, the French,
And they can well on horseback; but this gallant
Had witchcraft in't; he grew into his seat,
And to such wondrous doing brought his horse,   95
As had he been incorps'd and demi-natur'd
With the brave beast. So far he topp'd my thought,
That I, in forgery* of shapes and tricks,
Come short of what he did.
LAERTES: A Norman was't?   100
KING: A Norman.
LAERTES: Upon my life, Lamord.
KING: The very same.
LAERTES: I know him well. He is the brooch* indeed
And gem of all the nation.   105
KING: He made confession* of you;
And gave you such a masterly report
For art and exercise in your defence,
And for your rapier most especial,
That he cried out 'twould be a sight indeed   110
If one could match you. The scrimers* of their nation
He swore had neither motion, guard, nor eye,
If you oppos'd them. Sir, this report of his
Did Hamlet so envenom with his envy
That he could nothing do but wish and beg   115
Your sudden coming o'er, to play with you.
Now out of this—
LAERTES: What out of this, my lord?
KING: Laertes, was your father dear to you?
Or are you like the painting of a sorrow,   120
A face without a heart?
LAERTES: Why ask you this?
KING: Not that I think you did not love your father;
But that I know love is begun by time,
And that I see, in passages of proof,*   125
Time qualifies* the spark and fire of it.
There lives within the very flame of love
A kind of wick or snuff that will abate it;
And nothing is at a like goodness still;
For goodness, growing to a pleurisy,*   130
Dies in his own too much. That we would do,

⁹⁸ **forgery** invention
¹⁰⁴ **brooch** ornament
¹⁰⁶ **confession** report
¹¹¹ **scrimers** fencers
¹²⁵ **passages of proof** proved cases
¹²⁶ **qualifies** diminishes
¹³⁰ **pleurisy** excess

We should do when we would; for this 'would' changes,
And hath abatements and delays as many
As there are tongues, are hands, are accidents;
And then this 'should' is like a spendthrift's sigh   135
That hurts by easing. But to the quick* of th' ulcer:
Hamlet comes back; what would you undertake
To show yourself in deed your father's son
More than in words?
LAERTES: To cut his throat i' th' church.   140
KING: No place, indeed, should murder sanctuarize;*
Revenge should have no bounds. But, good Laertes,
Will you do this? Keep close within your chamber.
Hamlet return'd shall know you are come home.
We'll put on those shall praise your excellence,   145
And set a double varnish on the fame
The Frenchman gave you; bring you, in fine,* together,
And wager on your heads. He, being remiss,
Most generous, and free from all contriving,
Will not peruse the foils; so that with ease   150
Or with a little shuffling, you may choose
A sword unbated,* and, in a pass of practice,*
Requite him for your father.
LAERTES: I will do't;
And for that purpose I'll anoint my sword.   155
I bought an unction of a mountebank,
So mortal that but dip a knife in it,
Where it draws blood no cataplasm* so rare,
Collected from all simples* that have virtue
Under the moon, can save the thing from death   160
That is but scratch'd withal. I'll touch my point
With this contagion, that, if I gall him slightly,
It may be death.
KING: Let's further think of this;
Weigh what convenience both of time and means   165
May fit us to our shape.* If this should fail,
And that our drift look through* our bad performance,
'Twere better not assay'd, therefore this project
Should have a back or second, that might hold
If this did blast in proof.* Soft! let me see.   170
We'll make a solemn wager on your cunnings—

---

136 **quick** sensitive part
141 **sanctuarize** protect
147 **in fine** finally
152 **unbated** not blunted
152 **pass of practice** treacherous thrust
158 **cataplasm** poultice
159 **simples** medicinal herbs
166 **shape** role
167 **drift look through** purpose show through
170 **blast in proof** fail in performance

I ha't.
When in your motion you are hot and dry—
As make your bouts more violent to that end—
And that he calls for drink, I'll have preferr'd him   175
A chalice for the nonce,* whereon but sipping,
If he by chance escape your venom'd stuck,*
Our purpose may hold there. But stay; what noise?
        [*Enter* QUEEN.]
QUEEN: One woe doth tread upon another's heel,
    So fast they follow. Your sister's drown'd, Laertes.   180
LAERTES: Drown'd? O, where?
QUEEN: There is a willow grows aslant the brook
    That shows his hoar* leaves in the glassy stream;
    Therewith fantastic garlands did she make
    Of crowflowers, nettles, daisies, and long purples   185
    That liberal* shepherds give a grosser name,
    But our cold maids do dead men's fingers call them.
    There, on the pendent boughs her coronet weeds
    Clamb'ring to hang, an envious sliver broke;
    When down her weedy trophies and herself   190
    Feel in the weeping brook. Her clothes spread wide
    And, mermaid-like, awhile they bore her up;
    Which time she chanted snatches of old lauds,*
    As one incapable* of her own distress,
    Or like a creature native and indued*   195
    Unto that element; but long it could not be
    Till that her garments, heavy with their drink,
    Pull'd the poor wretch from her melodious lay
    To muddy death.
LAERTES: Alas, then she is drown'd!   200
QUEEN: Drown'd, drown'd.
LAERTES: Too much of water hast thou, poor Ophelia,
    And therefore I forbid my tears; but yet
    It is our trick,* nature her custom holds,
    Let shame say what it will. When these are gone,   205
    The woman* will be out. Adieu, my lord.
    I have a speech o' fire that fain would blaze
    But that this folly douts it.   [*Exit.*]
KING: Let's follow, Gertrude.
    How much I had to do to calm his rage!   210
    Now fear I this will give it start again;
    Therefore let's follow.   [*Exeunt.*]

---

176 **nonce** occasion
177 **stuck** thrust
183 **hoar** silver gray
186 **liberal** coarse-mouthed
193 **lauds** hymns
194 **incapable** unaware
195 **indued** in harmony with
204 **trick** way
206 **woman** womanly part

ACT V

SCENE I——*Elsinore. A churchyard.*

[*Enter two* CLOWNS *with spades and picks.*]

FIRST CLOWN: Is she to be buried in Christian burial when she wilfully seeks her
own salvation?

SECOND CLOWN: I tell thee she is; therefore make her grave straight.* The
crowner* hath sat on her, and finds it Christian burial.

FIRST CLOWN: How can that be, unless she drown'd herself in her own defence? 5

SECOND CLOWN: Why, 'tis found so.

FIRST CLOWN: It must be 'se offendendo';* it cannot be else. For here lies the
point: if I drown myself wittingly, it argues an act; and an act hath three
branches—it is to act, to do, to perform; argal,* she drown'd herself
wittingly. 10

SECOND CLOWN: Nay, but hear you, Goodman Delver.

FIRST CLOWN: Give me leave. Here lies the water; good. Here stands the man;
good. If the man go to this water and drown himself, it is, will he, nill he,
he goes—mark you that; but if the water come to him and drown him, he
drowns not himself. Argal, he that is not guilty of his own death shortens 15
not his own life.

SECOND CLOWN: But is this law?

FIRST CLOWN: Ay, marry is't; crowner's quest* law.

SECOND CLOWN: Will you ha' the truth an't? If this had not been a gentlewoman,
she should have been buried out a Christian burial. 20

FIRST CLOWN: Why, there thou say'st; and the more pity that great folk should
have count'nance* in this world to drown or hang themselves more than
their even Christen.* Come, my spade. There is no ancient gentlemen but
gard'ners, ditchers, and grave-makers; they hold up* Adam's profession.

SECOND CLOWN: Was he a gentleman? 25

FIRST CLOWN: 'A was the first that ever bore arms.*

SECOND CLOWN: Why, he had none.

FIRST CLOWN: What, art a heathen? How dost thou understand the Scripture?
The Scripture says Adam digg'd. Could he dig without arms? I'll put another question to thee. If thou answerest me not to the purpose, confess
thyself—

SECOND CLOWN: Go to.

FIRST CLOWN: What is he that builds stronger than either the mason, the shipwright, or the carpenter?

SECOND CLOWN: The gallows-maker; for that frame outlives a thousand tenants. 35

FIRST CLOWN: I like thy wit well; in good faith the gallows does well; but how
does it well? It does well to those that do ill. Now thou dost ill to say the

---

V.i,3 **straight** straight way

4 **crowner** coroner

7 **se offendendo** false latin, instead of "se defendendo" meaning "in self-defense"

9 **argal** false Latin for "ergo" ("therefore")

18 **crowner's quest** coroner's inquest

22 **count'nance** privilege

23 **even Christen** fellow Christian

24 **hold up** keep up

26 **bore arms** had a coat of arms

gallows is built stronger than the church; argal, the gallows may do well to thee. To't again, come.

SECOND CLOWN: Who builds stronger than a mason, a shipwright, or a carpenter?   40

FIRST CLOWN: Ay, tell me that, and unyoke.*

SECOND CLOWN: Marry, now I can tell.

FIRST CLOWN: To't.

SECOND CLOWN: Mass, I cannot tell.

>   [*Enter* HAMLET *and* HORATIO, *afar off.*]

FIRST CLOWN: Cudgel thy brains no more about it, for your dull ass will not   45
mend his pace with beating, and when you are ask'd this question next, say 'a grave-maker': the house he makes lasts till doomsday. Go, get thee to Yaughan; fetch me a stoup* of liquor.   [*Exit* SECOND CLOWN.]

>   [*digs and sings*]

> In youth, when I did love, did love
> Methought it was very sweet,   50
> To contract-o-the time for-a my behove,*
> O, methought there-a-was nothing-a meet.

HAMLET: Has this fellow no feeling of his business, that 'a sings in grave-making?

HORATIO: Custom hath made it in him a property of easiness.*

HAMLET: 'Tis e'en so; the hand of little employment hath the daintier sense.   55

FIRST CLOWN: [*sings*]

> But age, with his stealing steps,
> Hath clawed me in his clutch,
> And hath shipped me intil the land,
> As if I had never been such.

>   [*throws up a skull*]

HAMLET: That skull had a tongue in it, and could sing once. How the knave jowls*   60
it to the ground, as if 'twere Cain's jawbone, that did the first murder! This might be the pate of a politician, which this ass now o'erreaches; one that would circumvent God, might it not?

HORATIO: It might, my lord.

HAMLET: Or of a courtier; which could say 'Good morrow, sweet lord! How dost   65
thou, sweet lord?' This might be my Lord Such-a-one, that praised my Lord Such-a-one's horse, when 'a meant to beg it—might it not?

HORATIO: Ay, my lord.

HAMLET: Why, e'en so; and now my Lady Worm's, chapless,* and knock'd about the mazard* with a sexton's spade. Here's fine revolution, an we had the   70
trick to see't. Did these bones cost no more the breeding but to play at log-gats* with them? Mine ache to think on't.

FIRST CLOWN: [*sings*]

> A pick-axe and a spade, a spade
> For and a shrouding sheet:

---

41 **unyoke** quit work for the day
48 **stoup** tankard
51 **behove** advantage
54 **Custom . . . easiness** constant practice has made it easy
60 **jowls** hurls
69 **chapless** missing the lower jaw
70 **mazard** head
71 **loggats** a game involving throwing at objects

> *O, a pit of clay for to be made*   75
> *For such a guest is meet.*

[*throws up another skull*]

HAMLET: There's another. Why may not that be the skull of a lawyer? Where be his quiddities* now, his quillets,* his cases, his tenures,* and his tricks? Why does he suffer this rude knave now to knock him about the sconce* with a dirty shovel, and will not tell him of his action of battery? Hum! This fellow   80 might be in's time a great buyer of land, with his statutes, his recognizances, his fines,* his double vouchers, his recoveries. Is this the fine* of his fines, and the recovery of his recoveries, to have his fine pate full of fine dirt? Will his vouchers vouch him no more of his purchases, and double ones, too, than the length and breadth of a pair of indentures?* The very conveyances of his   85 lands will scarcely lie in this box; and must th' inheritor himself have no more, ha?

HORATIO: Not a jot more, my lord.

HAMLET: Is not parchment made of sheep-skins?

HORATIO: Ay, my lord, and of calves' skins, too.   90

HAMLET: They are sheep and calves which seek out assurance in that. I will speak to this fellow. Whose grave's this, sirrah?

FIRST CLOWN: Mine, sir.   [*sings*]

> *O, a pit of clay for to be made*
> *For such a guest is meet.*

HAMLET: I think it be thine indeed, for thou liest in't.

FIRST CLOWN: You lie out on't, sir, and therefore 'tis not yours. For my part, I do not lie in't, yet it is mine.

HAMLET: Thou dost lie in't, to be in't and say it is thine; 'tis for the dead, not for the quick; therefore thou liest.   100

FIRST CLOWN: 'Tis a quick lie, sir; 'twill away again from me to you.

HAMLET: What man dost thou dig it for?

FIRST CLOWN: For no man, sir.

HAMLET: What woman, then?

FIRST CLOWN: For none neither.   105

HAMLET: Who is to be buried in't?

FIRST CLOWN: One that was a woman, sir; but, rest her soul, she's dead.

HAMLET: How absolute* the knave is! We must speak by the card,* or equivocation will undo us. By the Lord, Horatio, this three years I have took note of it: the age is grown so picked* that the toe of the peasant comes so near the   110 heel of the courtier, he galls his kibe.* How long hast thou been a gravemaker?

FIRST CLOWN: Of all the days i' th' year, I came to't that day that our last King Hamlet overcame Fortinbras.

HAMLET: How long is that since?   115

FIRST CLOWN: Cannot you tell that? Every fool can tell that: it was that very day

---

78 **quiddities, quillets, tenures** legal terms
79 **sconce** head
82–83 **fines, fine** play on words for documents, death, and so on
85 **indentures** contracts
108 **absolute** positive, certain
108 **card** exactly
110 **picked** refined
111 **kibe** sore on the heel

that young Hamlet was born—he that is mad, and sent into England.

HAMLET: Ay, marry, why was he sent into England?

FIRST CLOWN: Why, because 'a was mad: 'a shall recover his wits there; or, if 'a do not, 'tis no great matter there.   120

HAMLET: Why?

FIRST CLOWN: 'Twill not be seen in him there: there the men are as mad as he.

HAMLET: How came he mad?

FIRST CLOWN: Very strangely, they say.

HAMLET: How strangely?   125

FIRST CLOWN: Faith, e'en with losing his wits.

HAMLET: Upon what ground?

FIRST CLOWN: Why, here in Denmark. I have been sexton here, man and boy, thirty years.

HAMLET: How long will a man lie i' th' earth ere he rot?   130

FIRST CLOWN: Faith, if 'a be not rotten before 'a die—as we have many pocky corses* now-a-days that will scarce hold the laying in—'a will last you some eight year or nine year. A tanner will last you nine year.

HAMLET: Why he more than another?

FIRST CLOWN: Why, sir, his hide is so tann'd with his trade that 'a will keep out   135 water a great while; and your water is a sore decayer of your whoreson dead body. Here's a skull now; this skull has lien you i' th' earth three and twenty years.

HAMLET: Whose was it?

FIRST CLOWN: A whoreson mad fellow's it was. Whose do you think it was?   140

HAMLET: Nay, I know not.

FIRST CLOWN: A pestilence on him for a mad rogue! 'A poured a flagon of Rhenish on my head once. This same skull, sir, was, sir, Yorick's skull, the King's jester.

HAMLET: This?   145

FIRST CLOWN: E'en that.

HAMLET: Let me see. [*takes the skull*] Alas, poor Yorick! I knew him, Horatio: a fellow of infinite jest, of most excellent fancy; he hath borne me on his back a thousand times. And now how abhorred in my imagination it is! My gorge rises at it. Here hung those lips that I have kiss'd I know not how oft. Where be your gibes now, your gambols, your songs, your flashes of merriment that were wont to set the table on a roar? Not one now to mock your own grinning—quite chap-fall'n?* Now get you to my lady's chamber, and tell her, let her paint an inch thick, to this favour* she must come; make her laugh at that. Prithee, Horatio, tell me one thing.   155

HORATIO: What's that, my lord?

HAMLET: Dost thou think Alexander look'd o' this fashion i' th' earth?

HORATIO: E'en so.

HAMLET: And smelt so? Pah   [*throws down the skull*]

HORATIO: E'en so, my lord.   160

HAMLET: To what base uses we may return, Horatio! Why may not imagination trace the noble dust of Alexander till 'a find it stopping a bung-hole?

---

131 **pocky corses** corpses of those with syphilis
153 **chap-fall'n** jawless (down in the mouth)
154 **favour** appearance, condition

HORATIO: 'Twere to consider too curiously* to consider so.

HAMLET: No, faith, not a jot; but to follow him thither with modesty enough, and likelihood to lead it, as thus: Alexander died, Alexander was buried, Alexan- 165
der returneth to dust; the dust is earth; of earth we make loam, and why of that loam whereto he was converted might they not stop a beer-barrel?

> Imperious Caesar, dead and turn'd to clay,
> Might stop a hole to keep the wind away.
> O, that that earth which kept the world in awe 170
> Should patch a wall t' expel the winter's flaw!*

But soft! but soft! awhile. Here comes the King.

[*Enter the* KING, QUEEN, LAERTES, *in funeral procession after the coffin, with* PRIEST *and* LORDS *attendant.*]

The Queen, the courtiers. Who is this they follow?
And with such maimed* rites? This doth betoken
The corse they follow did with desperate hand 175
Fordo it own life. 'Twas of some estate.*
Couch* we awhile and mark.   [*retiring with* HORATIO]

LAERTES: What ceremony else?

HAMLET: That is Laertes, a very noble youth. Mark.

LAERTES: What ceremony else? 180

PRIEST: Her obsequies have been so far enlarg'd
As we have warrantise. Her death was doubtful;
And, but that great command o'ersways the order,
She should in ground unsanctified have lodg'd
Till the last trumpet; for charitable prayers, 185
Shards, flints, and pebbles, should be thrown on her;
Yet here she is allow'd her virgin crants,*
Her maiden strewments, and the bringing home
Of bell and burial.

LAERTES: Must there no more be done? 190

PRIEST: No more be done.
We should profane the service of the dead
To sing sage requiem and such rest to her
As to peace-parted souls.

LAERTES: Lay her i' th' earth; 195
And from her fair and unpolluted flesh
May violets spring! I tell thee, churlish priest,
A minist'ring angel shall my sister be
When thou liest howling.

HAMLET: What, the fair Ophelia! 200

QUEEN: Sweets to the sweet; farewell! [*scattering flowers*]
I hop'd thou shouldst have been my Hamlet's wife;
I thought thy bride-bed to have deck'd, sweet maid,
And not have strew'd thy grave.

---

163 **curiously** minutely
171 **flaw** gust
174 **maimed** curtailed
176 **estate** high rank
177 **Couch** hide
187 **crants** garlands

LAERTES: O, treble woe   205
    Fall ten times treble on that cursed head
    Whose wicked deed thy most ingenious sense*
    Depriv'd thee of! Hold off the earth awhile,
    Till I have caught her once more in mine arms.
       [leaps into the grave]
    Now pile your dust upon the quick and dead,   210
    Till of this flat a mountain you have made
    T' o'er-top old Pelion or the skyish head
    Of blue Olympus.
HAMLET: *[advancing]* What is he whose grief
    Bears such an emphasis, whose phrase of sorrow   215
    Conjures the wand'ring stars, and makes them stand
    Like wonder-wounded hearers? This is I,
    Hamlet, the Dane.   *[leaps into the grave]*
LAERTES: The devil take thy soul! *[grappling with him]*
HAMLET: Thou pray'st not well.   220
    I prithee take thy fingers from my throat;
    For, though I am not splenitive* and rash,
    Yet have I in me something dangerous,
    Which let thy wiseness fear. Hold off thy hand.
KING: Pluck them asunder.   225
QUEEN: Hamlet! Hamlet!
ALL: Gentlemen!
HORATIO: Good my lord, be quiet.
    [The attendants part them, and they come out of the grave.]
HAMLET: Why, I will fight with him upon this theme
    Until my eyelids will no longer wag.   230
QUEEN: O my son, what theme?
HAMLET: I lov'd Ophelia: forty thousand brothers
    Could not, with all their quantity of love
    Make up my sum. What wilt thou do for her?
KING: O, he is mad, Laertes.   235
QUEEN: For love of God, forbear him.
HAMLET: 'Swounds, show me what th'owt do:
    Woo't weep, woo't fight, woo't fast, woo't tear thyself,
    Woo't drink up eisel,* eat a crocodile?
    I'll do't. Dost come here to whine?   240
    To outface me with leaping in her grave?
    Be buried quick with her, and so will I;
    And, if thou prate of mountains, let them throw
    Millions of acres on us, till our ground,
    Singeing his pate against the burning zone,*   245
    Make Ossa like a wart! Nay, an thou'lt mouth,
    I'll rant as well as thou.

[207] **ingenious sense** finely endowed mind
[222] **splenitive** fiery spirited
[239] **eisel** vinegar
[245] **burning zone** the sun

QUEEN: This is mere madness;
    And thus awhile the fit will work on him;
    Anon, as patient as the female dove   250
    When that her golden couplets are disclos'd*
    His silence will sit drooping.
HAMLET: Hear you, sir:
    What is the reason that you use me thus?
    I lov'd you ever. But it is no matter.   255
    Let Hercules himself do what he may,
    The cat will mew, and dog will have his day.   [*Exit.*]
KING: I pray thee, good Horatio, wait upon him.
        [*Exit* HORATIO.]
    [*to* LAERTES] Strengthen your patience in our last night's speech;
    We'll put the matter to the present push.*—   260
    Good Gertrude, set some watch over your son.—
    This grave shall have a living* monument.
    An hour of quiet shortly shall we see;
    Till then in patience our proceeding be.   [*Exeunt.*]

SCENE II————*Elsinore. The Castle.*

[*Enter* HAMLET *and* HORATIO.]
HAMLET: So much for this, sir; now shall you see the other.
    You do remember all the circumstance?
HORATIO: Remember it, my lord!
HAMLET: Sir, in my heart there was a kind of fighting
    That would not let me sleep. Methought I lay   5
    Worse than the mutines in the bilboes.* Rashly,
    And prais'd be rashness for it—let us know,
    Our indiscretion sometime serves us well,
    When our deep plots do pall,* and that should learn us
    There's a divinity that shapes our ends,   10
    Rough-hew them how we will.
HORATIO: That is most certain.
HAMLET: Up from my cabin,
    My sea-gown scarf'd about me, in the dark
    Grop'd to find out them; had my desire;   15
    Finger'd* their packet, and in fine withdrew
    To mine own room again, making so bold,
    My fears forgetting manners, to unseal
    Their grand commission; where I found, Horatio,
    Ah, royal knavery! an exact command,   20

---

251 **golden couplets are disclos'd** doves were thought to lay only two eggs; here the reference is to young, just-hatched doves
260 **present push** immediate test
262 **living** lasting
V.ii,6 **mutines in the bilboes** mutineers in chains
9 **pall** fail
16 **Finger'd** stole

Larded* with many several sorts of reasons,
Importing Denmark's health and England's, too,
With, ho! such bugs and goblins in my life*—
That, on the supervise,* no leisure bated,*
No, not to stay the grinding of the axe,   25
My head should be struck off.
HORATIO: Is't possible?
HAMLET: Here's the commission; read it at more leisure.
But wilt thou hear now how I did proceed?
HORATIO: I beseech you.   30
HAMLET: Being thus benetted round with villainies—
Ere I could make a prologue to my brains,
They had begun the play—I sat me down;
Devis'd a new commission; wrote it fair.
I once did hold it, as our statists* do,   35
A baseness to write fair,* and labour'd much
How to forget that learning; but sir, now
It did me yeoman's service. Wilt thou know
Th' effect* of what I wrote?
HORATIO: Ay, good my lord.   40
HAMLET: An earnest conjuration from the King,
As England was his faithful tributary,
As love between them like the palm might flourish,
As peace should still her wheaten garland wear
And stand a comma* tween their amities,   45
And many such like as's of great charge,
That, on the view and knowing of these contents,
Without debatement further more or less,
He should those bearers put to sudden death,
Not shriving-time* allow'd.   50
HORATIO: How was this seal'd?
HAMLET: Why, even in that was heaven ordinant.*
I had my father's signet in my purse,
Which was the model of that Danish seal;
Folded the writ up in the form of th' other;   55
Subscrib'd it, gave't th' impression, plac'd it safely,
The changeling never known. Now, the next day
Was our sea-fight; and what to this was sequent
Thou knowest already.
HORATIO: So Guildenstern and Rosencrantz go to't.   60

21 **Larded** enriched
23 **bugs . . . my life** imagined terrors if were allowed to live
24 **supervise** reading
24 **leisure bated** delay allowed
35 **statists** statesmen
36 **fair** clearly
39 **effect** purport
45 **comma** link
50 **shriving-time** time to be absolved of sin
52 **ordinant** on my side

HAMLET: Why, man, they did make love to this employment;
    They are not near my conscience; their defeat
    Does by their own insinuation* grow:
    'Tis dangerous when the baser nature comes
    Between the pass and fell* incensed points   65
    Of mighty opposites.
HORATIO: Why, what a king is this!
HAMLET: Does it not, think thee, stand me now upon*—
    He that hath kill'd my king and whor'd my mother,
    Popp'd in between th' election* and my hopes;   70
    Thrown out his angle for my proper life,*
    And with such coz'nage*—is't not perfect conscience
    To quit* him with this arm? And is't not to be damn'd
    To let this canker of our nature come
    In further evil?   75
HORATIO: It must be shortly known to him from England
    What is the issue of the business there.
HAMLET: It will be short; the interim is mine.
    And a man's life's no more than to say 'one.'
    But I am very sorry, good Horatio,   80
    That to Laertes I forgot myself;
    For by the image of my cause I see
    The portraiture of his. I'll court his favours.
    But sure the bravery of his grief did put me
    Into a tow'ring passion.   85
HORATIO: Peace; who comes here?
        [*Enter young* OSRIC.]
OSRIC: Your lordship is right welcome back to Denmark.
HAMLET: I humbly thank you, sir. [*aside to* HORATIO] Dost know this water-fly?
HORATIO: [*aside to* HAMLET] No, my good lord.
HAMLET: [*aside to* HORATIO] Thy state is the more gracious; for 'tis a vice to   90
    know him. He hath much land, and fertile. Let a beast be lord of beasts, and
    his crib shall stand at the king's mess!* 'Tis a chough,* but, as I say,
    spacious* in the possession of dirt.
OSRIC: Sweet lord, if your lordship were at leisure, I should impart a thing to you
    from his Majesty.   95
HAMLET: I will receive it, sir, with all diligence of spirit. Put your bonnet to his
    right use, 'tis for the head.
OSRIC: I thank your lordship; it is very hot.
HAMLET: No, believe me, 'tis very cold; the wind is northerly.

---

63 **insinuation** meddling
65 **pass and fell** thrust and cruel
68 **stand me now upon** became incumbent on me
70 **election** selection to be king
71 **angle for my proper life** tried to end my own life
72 **coz'nage** trickery
73 **quit** pay back
92 **mess** table
92 **chough** chatterer
93 **spacious** well off

OSRIC: It is indifferent cold, my lord, indeed.   100
HAMLET: But yet methinks it is very sultry and hot for my complexion.*
OSRIC: Exceedingly, my lord; it is very sultry, as 'twere—I cannot tell how. But,
    my lord, his Majesty bade me signify to you that 'a has laid a great wager
    on your head. Sir, this is the matter—
HAMLET: I beseech you, remember.   105
                [HAMLET *moves him to put on his hat.*]
OSRIC: Nay, good my lord; for my ease, in good faith. Sir, here is newly come to
    court Laertes; believe me, an absolute gentleman, full of most excellent dif-
    ferences,* of very soft society and great showing. Indeed, to speak feelingly
    of him, he is the card* or calendar of gentry, for you shall find in him the
    continent* of what part a gentleman would see.   110
HAMLET: Sir, his definement* suffers no perdition* in you; though, I know, to di-
    vide him inventorially would dozy* th' arithmetic of memory, and yet but
    yaw neither in respect of his quick sail. But, in the verity of extolment, I take
    him to be a soul of great article, and his infusion of such dearth and rareness,
    as to make true diction of him, his semblable is his mirror, and who else   115
    would trace him, his umbrage, nothing more.
OSRIC: Your lordship speaks most infallibly of him.
HAMLET: The concernancy,* sir? Why do we wrap the gentleman in our more
    rawer breath?
OSRIC: Sir?   120
HORATIO: [*aside to* HAMLET] Is't not possible to understand in another tongue?
    You will to't, sir, really.
HAMLET: What imports the nomination of this gentleman?
OSRIC: Of Laertes?
HORATIO: [*aside*] His purse is empty already; all's golden words are spent.   125
HAMLET: Of him, sir.
OSRIC : I know you are not ignorant—
HAMLET: I would you did, sir; yet, in faith, if you did, it would not much ap-
    prove* me. Well, sir.
OSRIC: You are not ignorant of what excellence Laertes is—   130
HAMLET: I dare not confess that, lest I should compare with him in excellence;
    but to know a man well were to know himself.
OSRIC: I mean, sir, for his weapon; but in the imputation* laid on him by them,
    in his meed* he's unfellowed.
HAMLET: What's his weapon?   135
OSRIC : Rapier and dagger.
HAMLET: That's two of his weapons—but well.

---

¹⁰¹ **complexion** temperament
¹⁰⁷ **differences** distinguishing characteristics
¹⁰⁹ **card** model
¹¹⁰ **continent** summary
¹¹¹ **definement** description
¹¹¹ **perdition** loss (this entire speech mocks Osric's use of overblown language)
¹¹² **dozy** dizzy
¹¹⁸ **concernancy** meaning
¹²⁸ **approve** commend
¹³³ **imputation** reputation
¹³⁴ **meed** merit

OSRIC: The King, sir, hath wager'd him with six Barbary horses; against the which he has impon'd,* as I take it, six French rapiers and poniards, with their assigns,* as girdle, hangers, and so—three of the carriages, in faith, are   140
very dear to fancy, very responsive to the hilts, most delicate carriages, and of very liberal conceit.

HAMLET: What call you the carriages?

HORATIO: [*aside to* HAMLET] I knew you must be edified by the margent* ere you had done.   145

OSRIC: The carriages, sir, are the hangers.

HAMLET: The phrase would be more germane to the matter if we could carry a cannon by our sides. I would it might be hangers till then. But on: six Barbary horses against six French swords, their assigns, and three liberal conceited carriages; that's the French bet against the Danish. Why is this all   150
impon'd, as you call it?

OSRIC: The King, sir, hath laid, sir, that in a dozen passes between yourself and him he shall not exceed you three hits; he hath laid on twelve for nine, and it would come to immediate trial if your lordship would vouchsafe the answer.

HAMLET: How if I answer no?   155

OSRIC: I mean, my lord, the opposition of your person in trial.

HAMLET: Sir, I will walk here in the hall. If it please his Majesty, it is the breathing time of day* with me; let the foils be brought, the gentlemen willing, and the King hold his purpose, I will win for him an I can; if not, I will gain nothing but my shame and the odd hits.   160

OSRIC: Shall I redeliver you e'en so?

HAMLET: To this effect, sir, after what flourish your nature will.

OSRIC: I commend my duty to your lordship.

HAMLET: Yours, yours. [*Exit* OSRIC.] He does well to commend it himself; there are no tongues else for's turn.   165

HORATIO: This lapwing runs away with the shell on his head.

HAMLET: 'A did comply, sir, with his dug before 'a suck'd it.* Thus has he, and many more of the same bevy, that I know the drossy age dotes on, only got the tune of the time and outward habit of encounter*—a kind of yesty* collection, which carries them through and through the most fann'd and win-   170
nowed opinions; and do but blow them to their trial, the bubbles are out.*

[*Enter a* LORD.]

LORD: My lord, his Majesty commended him to you by young Osric, who brings back to him that you attend him in the hall. He sends to know if your pleasure hold to play with Laertes, or that you will take longer time.

HAMLET: I am constant to my purposes; they follow the king's pleasure: if his fit-   175
ness speaks, mine is ready now—or whensoever, provided I be so able as now.

---

139 **impon'd** wagered
140 **assigns** accompaniments
144 **margent** exaggerated terminology
157–158 **breathing time of day** time when I do my exercises
167 **'A did comply . . . suck'd it** He was ceremoniously polite to his mother's breast before he sucked it
169 **habit of encounter** superficial way of talking to people
169 **yesty** frothy
171 **blow them . . . bubbles are out** question them and they are at a loss

LORD: The King and Queen and all are coming down.

HAMLET: In happy time.

LORD: The Queen desires you to use some gentle entertainment* to Laertes be-   180
fore you fall to play.

HAMLET: She well instructs me.   [*Exit* LORD.]

HORATIO: You will lose this wager, my lord.

HAMLET: I do not think so; since he went into France I have been in continual
practice. I shall win at the odds. But thou wouldst not think how ill all's   185
here about my heart; but it is no matter.

HORATIO: Nay, good my lord—

HAMLET: It is but foolery; but it is such a kind of gaingiving* as would perhaps
trouble a woman.

HORATIO: If your mind dislike anything, obey it. I will forestall their repair hither,   190
and say you are not fit.

HAMLET: Not a whit, we defy augury: there is a special providence in the fall of
a sparrow. If it be now, 'tis not to come; if it be not to come, it will be now;
if it be not now, yet it will come—the readiness is all. Since no man owes of
aught he leaves, what is't to leave betimes?* Let be.   195

[*A table prepared. Trumpets, drums, and officers with cushions, foils, and daggers.*
Enter KING, QUEEN, LAERTES, *and all the state.*]

KING: Come, Hamlet, come, and take this hand from me.

[*The* KING *puts* LAERTES' *hand into* HAMLET's.]

HAMLET: Give me your pardon, sir. I have done you wrong;
But pardon't, as you are a gentleman.
This presence* knows,
And you must needs have heard how I am punish'd   200
With a sore distraction. What I have done
That might your nature, honour, and exception,*
Roughly awake, I here proclaim was madness.
Was't Hamlet wrong'd Laertes? Never Hamlet.
If Hamlet from himself be ta'en away,   205
And when he's not himself does wrong Laertes,
Then Hamlet does it not, Hamlet denies it.
Who does it, then? His madness. If't be so,
Hamlet is of the faction* that is wrong'd;
His madness is poor Hamlet's enemy.   210
Sir, in this audience,
Let my disclaiming from a purpos'd evil
Free me so far in your most generous thoughts
That I have shot my arrow o'er the house
And hurt my brother.   215

LAERTES: I am satisfied in nature,
Whose motive in this case should stir me most

180 **gentle entertainment** be courteous
188 **gaingiving** misgiving
195 **betimes** early
199 **presence** assembly
202 **exception** disapproval
209 **faction** group

To my revenge; but in my terms of honour
I stand aloof, and will no reconcilement
Till by some elder masters of known honour   220
I have a voice and precedent of peace
To keep my name ungor'd—but till that time
I do receive your offer'd love like love,
And will not wrong it.
HAMLET: I embrace it freely;   225
   And will this brother's wager frankly play.
   Give us the foils. Come on.
LAERTES: Come, one for me.
HAMLET: I'll be your foil, Laertes; in mine ignorance
   Your skill shall, like a star i' th' darkest night,   230
   Stick fiery off* indeed.
LAERTES: You mock me, sir.
HAMLET: No, by this hand.
KING: Give them the foils, young Osric. Cousin Hamlet,
   You know the wager?   235
HAMLET: Very well, my lord;
   Your Grace has laid the odds a' th' weaker side.
KING: I do not fear it: I have seen you both;
   But since he's better'd,* we have therefore odds.
LAERTES: This is too heavy; let me see another.   240
HAMLET: This likes me well. These foils have all a length?
   [*They prepare to play.*]
OSRIC : Ay, my good lord.
KING: Set me the stoups of wine upon that table.
   If Hamlet give the first or second hit,
   Or quit in answer of the third exchange,   245
   Let all the battlements their ordnance fire;
   The King shall drink to Hamlet's better breath,
   And in the cup an union* shall he throw,
   Richer than that which four successive kings
   In Denmark's crown have worn. Give me the cups;   250
   And let the kettle* to the trumpet speak,
   The trumpet to the cannoneer without,
   The cannons to the heavens, the heaven to earth,
   'Now the King drinks to Hamlet.' Come, begin—
   And you, the judges, bear a wary eye.   255
HAMLET: Come on, sir.
LAERTES: Come, my lord.   [*They play.*]
HAMLET: One.
LAERTES: No.
HAMLET: Judgment?   260

231 **stick fiery off** stand out brilliantly
239 **better'd** improved
248 **union** pearl
251 **kettle** kettledrum

OSRIC : A hit, a very palpable hit.
LAERTES: Well, again.
KING: Stay, give me drink. Hamlet, this pearl is thine;
   Here's to thy health. [*drum, trumpets, and shot*] Give him the cup.
HAMLET: I'll play this bout first; set it by awhile.   265
   Come. [*They play.*] Another hit; what say you?
LAERTES: A touch, a touch, I do confess't.
KING: Our son shall win.
QUEEN: He's fat,* and scant of breath.
   Here, Hamlet, take my napkin, rub thy brows.   270
   The Queen carouses to thy fortune, Hamlet.
HAMLET: Good madam!
KING: Gertrude, do not drink.
QUEEN: I will, my lord; I pray you pardon me.
KING: [*aside*] It is the poison'd cup; it is too late.   275
HAMLET: I dare not drink yet, madam; by and by.
QUEEN: Come, let me wipe thy face.
LAERTES: My lord, I'll hit him now.
KING: I do not think't.
LAERTES: [*aside*] And yet it is almost against my conscience.   280
HAMLET: Come, for the third. Laertes, you do but dally;
   I pray you pass with your best violence;
   I am afeard you make a wanton* of me.
LAERTES: Say you so? Come on.   [*They play.*]
OSRIC: Nothing, neither way.   285
LAERTES: Have at you now!
     [LAERTES *wounds* HAMLET; *then, in scuffling, they change rapiers, and* HAMLET
     wounds LAERTES.]
KING: Part them; they are incens'd.
HAMLET: Nay, come again.   [*The* QUEEN *falls.*]
OSRIC: Look to the Queen there, ho!
HORATIO: They bleed on both sides. How is it, my lord?   290
OSRIC: How is't, Laertes?
LAERTES: Why, as a woodcock, to mine own springe,* Osric;
   I am justly kill'd with mine own treachery.
HAMLET: How does the Queen?
KING: She swoons to see them bleed.   295
QUEEN: No, no, the drink, the drink! O my dear Hamlet!
   The drink, the drink! I am poison'd.   [*dies*]
HAMLET: O, villainy! Ho! let the door be lock'd.
   Treachery! Seek it out.   [LAERTES *falls.*]
LAERTES: It is here, Hamlet. Hamlet, thou art slain;   300
   No med'cine in the world can do thee good;
   In thee there is not half an hour's life;
   The treacherous instrument is in thy hand,
   Unbated and envenom'd. The foul practice*

---

269 **fat** sweaty
283 **wanton** spoiled child
292 **springe** snare
304 **foul practice** deception

Hath turn'd itself on me; lo, here I lie,   305
Never to rise again. Thy mother's poison'd.
I can no more. The King, the King's to blame.
HAMLET: The point envenom'd, too!   *[stabs the KING]*
Then, venom, to thy work.
ALL: Treason! treason!   310
KING: O, yet defend me, friends; I am but hurt.
HAMLET: Here, thou incestuous, murd'rous, damned Dane,
Drink off this potion. Is thy union here?
Follow my mother.   *[KING dies.]*
LAERTES: He is justly serv'd: 315
It is a poison temper'd* by himself.
Exchange forgiveness with me, noble Hamlet.
Mine and my father's death come not upon thee,
Nor thine on me!   *[dies]*
HAMLET: Heaven make thee free of it! I follow thee.   320
I am dead, Horatio. Wretched Queen, adieu!
You that look pale and tremble at this chance,
That are but mutes or audience to this act,
Had I but time, as this fell sergeant Death
Is strict in his arrest, O, I could tell you—   325
But let it be. Horatio, I am dead:
Thou livest; report me and my cause aright
To the unsatisfied.
HORATIO: Never believe it.
I am more an antique Roman* than a Dane;   330
Here's yet some liquor left.
HAMLET: As th'art a man,
Give me the cup. Let go. By heaven, I'll ha't.
O good Horatio, what a wounded name,
Things standing thus unknown, shall live behind me!   335
If thou didst ever hold me in thy heart,
Absent thee from felicity awhile,
And in this harsh world draw thy breath in pain,
To tell my story. *[march afar off, and shot within]* What warlike noise
is this?
OSRIC: Young Fortinbras, with conquest come from Poland,   340
To th'ambassadors of England gives
This warlike volley.
HAMLET: O, I die, Horatio!
The potent poison quite o'er-crows* my spirit.
I cannot live to hear the news from England,   345
But I do prophesy th' election lights
On Fortinbras; he has my dying voice.
So tell him, with th' occurrents,* more and less,
Which have solicited*—the rest is silence.   *[dies]*

316 **temper'd** mixed
330 **antique Roman** given to suicide
344 **o'er-crows** overpowers
348 **occurrents** occurrences
349 **solicited** incited

HORATIO: Now cracks a noble heart. Good night, sweet prince,   350
    And flights of angels sing thee to thy rest!   [*march within*]
    Why does the drum come hither?
      [*Enter* FORTINBRAS *and* ENGLISH AMBASSADORS, *with drum, colours,*
      and attendants.]
FORTINBRAS: Where is this sight?
HORATIO: What is it you would see?
    If aught of woe or wonder, cease your search.
FORTINBRAS: This quarry* cries on havoc.* O proud death,   355
    What feast is toward* in thine eternal cell
    That thou so many princes at a shot
    So bloodily hast struck?
FIRSY AMBASSADOR: The sight is dismal;
    And our affairs from England come too late: 360
    The ears are senseless that should give us hearing
    To tell him his commandment is fulfill'd
    That Rosencrantz and Guildenstern are dead.
    Where should we have our thanks?
HORATIO: Not from his* mouth,   365
    Had it th' ability of life to thank you:
    He never gave commandment for their death.
    But since, so jump* upon this bloody question,
    You from the Polack wars, and you from England,
    And here arrived, give order that these bodies   370
    High on a stage* be placed to the view;
    And let me speak to th' yet unknowing world
    How these things came about. So shall you hear
    Of carnal, bloody, and unnatural acts;
    Of accidental judgments, casual* slaughters;   375
    Of deaths put on by cunning and forc'd cause;
    And, in this upshot, purposes mistook
    Fall'n on th' inventors' heads—all this can I
    Truly deliver.
FORTINBRAS: Let us haste to hear it,   380
    And call the noblest to the audience.
    For me, with sorrow I embrace my fortune;
    I have some rights of memory* in this kingdom,
    Which now to claim my vantage doth invite me.
HORATIO: Of that I shall have also cause to speak,   385
    And from his mouth whose voice will draw on more.*
    But let this same be presently perform'd,
    Even while men's minds are wild, lest more mischance

---

355 **quarry** heap of slain bodies
355 **cries on havoc** proclaims general slaughter
356 **toward** in preparation
365 **his** Claudius'
368 **jump** precisely
371 **stage** platform
375 **casual** unplanned
383 **rights of memory** past claims
386 **voice will draw on more** vote will influence others
389 **On** on top of earlier

On* plots and errors happen.

FORTINBRAS: Let four captains 390
Bear Hamlet like a soldier to the stage;
For he was likely, had he been put on,
To have prov'd most royal; and for his passage*
The soldier's music and the rite of war
Speak loudly for him. 395
Take up the bodies. Such a sight as this
Becomes the field, but here shows much amiss.
Go, bid the soldiers shoot.

> [*Exeunt marching. A peal of ordnance shot off.*]

393 **passage** death

The Servant of Two Masters (1745)

ommedia dell'arte was one of the most popular of all theatrical forms between 1575 and 1775. Originally, a commedia script was merely a scenario that outlined the situation, complications, and outcome. In performance, the actors improvised the dialogue and fleshed out the action. The plots were most often comic, revolving around love affairs, comic misunderstandings, and deliberate deceptions. The actors also developed a number of surefire bits of comic business (*lazzi*) that could be brought in as the actors saw fit.

Commedia scripts utilized a number of stock characters. There were usually two pairs of young lovers. Unlike the other roles, these did not make use of masks, and they dressed in the latest fashions. They were usually the children of other stock characters, most often Pantalone (a Venetian merchant) and Dottore (a doctor or lawyer who loved to show off his spurious learning). These latter characters had fixed costumes and masks. The most varied of the commedia types were the servants (*zanni*), of whom the most popular was Arlecchino (Harlequin), a character with a mixture of cunning and simplemindedness who was usually at the center of every intrigue and mix-up. His mask was black, and his costume was made of diamond-shaped red, green, and blue-patterned cloth. Sometimes the character was called by other names; in *The Servant of Two Masters*, he is called Truffaldino. Among the other servants, a rather coarse, somewhat bawdy maid figured prominently. In *The Servant of Two Masters*, she is called Smeraldina.

By the 1730s, commedia had lost much of its vitality, in part because it had become repetitious and predictable. Carlo Goldoni, a Venetian playwright, sought to revive it by reforming some of its conventions. He convinced some companies to let him write out all the dialogue but to leave room for improvisation. *The Servant of Two Masters* is among the most successful plays of this type. Through it, we can recapture much of the flavor and spirit of commedia, even though the element of improvisation has been greatly reduced.

The Servant of Two Masters incorporates the stock characters of commedia. There are two pairs of lovers (Clarice and Silvio; Beatrice and Florindo), two masters (Pantalone and Dottore), and three servants (Truffaldino, Smeraldina, and Brighella, although Brighella has been transformed into an innkeeper). By far the most important character is Truffaldino, for, though the story revolves around the lovers, it is Truffaldino's simplemindedness that creates most of the difficulties and his cleverness that resolves them. He is also offered several opportunities to improvise *lazzi*.

Goldoni is a master of plot development. Everything is set up carefully in the opening scenes, although much of the subsequent action is dependent on coincidence, especially that Beatrice (disguised as her brother) and Florindo (her lover) take up residence in the same inn and each hires Truffaldino as a servant.

In *The Servant of Two Masters*, Goldoni is concerned primarily with providing entertainment for a popular audience and with reworking the conventions of a long-familiar form. That he succeeded is indicated by the continuing popularity of the play.

The Servant of Two Masters by Carlo Goldoni; translated and edited by Edward J. Dent. © 1928 and 1952. Reprinted with the permission of Cambridge University Press.

CARLO GOLDONI

The Servant of Two Masters

ENGLISH VERSION BY EDWARD J. DENT

Characters

PANTALONE DEI BISOGNOSI, *a Venetian merchant*
CLARICE, *his daughter*
DR. LOMBARDI
SILVIO, *his son*
BEATRICE RASPONI, *a lady of Turin, disguised as her brother* FEDERICO RASPONI
FLORINDO ARETUSI, *of Turin, lover of* BEATRICE
BRIGHELLLA, *an innkeeper*
SMERALDINA, *maidservant of* CLARICE
TRUFFALDINO, *servant first to* BEATRICE, *and afterward to* FLORINDO
FIRST WAITER
SECOND WAITER
FIRST PORTER
SECOND PORTER

The scene is laid in Venice. The action takes place within a single day.

ACT I

SCENE I———*A Room in the House of* PANTALONE.

SILVIO:[*offering his hand to* CLARICE] Here is my hand, and with it I give you my whole heart.

PANTALONE: [*to* CLARICE] Come, come, not so shy, give him your hand too. Then you will be betrothed, and very soon you will be married.

CLARICE: Dear Silvio, here is my hand. I promise to be your wife.

SILVIO: And I promise to be your husband.
[*They take hands.*]

DR. LOMBARDI: Well done. Now that is settled, and there's no going back on it.

SMERALDINA: [*aside*] There's luck for you! And me just bursting to get married!

PANTALONE: [*to* BRIGHELLLA *and* SMERALDINA] You two shall be witnesses of this betrothal of my daughter Clarice to Signor Silvio, the worthy son of our good Dr. Lombardi!

BRIGHELLLA: [*to* PANTALONE] We will, sir, and I thank you for the honor.

PANTALONE: Look you, I was witness at your wedding, and now you are a witness to my daughter's. I have asked no great company of friends and relations, for the doctor too is a man of my sort. We will have dinner together; we will enjoy ourselves and nobody shall disturb us.

[*to* CLARICE *and* SILVIO]

What say you, children, does that suit you?

SILVIO: I desire nothing better than to be near my beloved bride.

SMERALDINA: [*aside*] Yes, that's the best of all foods.

DR. LOMBARDI: My son is no lover of vanities. He is an honest lad; he loves your daughter and thinks of nothing else.

PANTALONE: Truly we may say that this marriage was made in Heaven, for had it not been for the death of Federigo Rasponi, my correspondent at Turin, you know, I had promised my daughter to him.

[*to* SILVIO]

I could not then have given her to my dear son-in-law.

SILVIO: I can call myself fortunate indeed, sir; I know not if Signora Clarice will say the same.

CLARICE: You wrong me, dear Silvio. You should know if I love you. I should have married Signor Rasponi in obedience to my father; but my heart has always been yours.

DR. LOMBARDI: 'Tis true indeed, the will of Heaven is wrought in unexpected ways.

[*to* PANTALONE]

Pray, sir, how did Federigo Rasponi come to die?

PANTALONE: Poor wretch, I hardly know. He was killed one night on account of some affair about his sister. Someone ran a sword through him and that was the end of him.

BRIGHELLLA: Did that happen at Turin, sir?

PANTALONE: At Turin.

BRIGHELLLA: Alas, poor gentleman! I am indeed sorry to hear it.

PANTALONE: [*to* BRIGHELLLA] Did you know Signor Federigo Rasponi?

BRIGHELLLA: Indeed and I did, sir. I was three years at Turin. I knew his sister too—a fine high-spirited young woman—dressed like a man and rode a-horseback; and he loved her more than anyone in the world. Lord! Who'd ha' thought it?

PANTALONE: Well, misfortune waits for all of us. But come, let us talk no more of sad things. Do you know what I have in mind, good master Brighella? I know you love to show your skill in the kitchen. Now, I would have you make us a few dishes of your best.

BRIGHELLLA: 'Tis a pleasure to serve you, sir. Though I say it that shouldn't, customers are always well contented at my house. They say there's no place where they eat as they do there. You shall taste something fine, sir.

PANTALONE: Good, good. Let's have something with plenty of gravy that we can sop the bread in.

[*a knock at the door*]

Oh! Someone is knocking. Smeraldina, see who it is.

SMERALDINA: Yes, sir.

[*goes to door*]

CLARICE: [*wishing to retire*] Sir, may I beg your leave?

PANTALONE: Wait; we are all coming. Let us hear who is there.

SMERALDINA: [*coming back*] Sir, there is a gentleman's servant below who desires to give you a message. He would tell me nothing. He says he would speak to the master.

PANTALONE: Tell him to come up. We'll hear what he has to say.
SMERALDINA: I'll fetch him, sir.
> [*Exit.*]
CLARICE: May I not go, sir?
PANTALONE: Whither then, madam?
CLARICE: I know not—to my own room—
PANTALONE: No, madam, no; you stay here.
> [*aside to* DR. LOMBARDI]
> These lovebirds can't be left alone just yet for a while.
DR. LOMBARDI: [*aside to* PANTALONE] Prudence above all things!
> [SMERALDINA *brings in* TRUFFALDINO.]
TRUFFALDINO: My most humble duty to the ladies and gentlemen. And a very fine company too, to be sure! Very fine, indeed!
PANTALONE: Who are you, my good friend? And what is your business?
TRUFFALDINO: [*to* PANTALONE, *pointing to* CLARICE] Who is this fair gentlewoman?
PANTALONE: That is my daughter.
TRUFFALDINO: Delighted to hear it.
SMERALDINA: [*to* TRUFFALDINO] What's more, she is going to be married.
TRUFFALDINO: I'm sorry to hear it. And who are you?
SMERALDINA: I am her maid, sir.
TRUFFALDINO: I congratulate her.
PANTALONE: Come, sir, have done with ceremony. What do you want with me? Who are you? Who sends you hither?
TRUFFALDINO: Patience, patience, my good sir, take it easy. Three questions at once is too much for a poor man.
PANTALONE: [*aside to* DR. LOMBARDI] I think the man's a fool.
DR. LOMBARDI: [*aside to* PANTALONE] I think he's playing the fool.
TRUFFALDINO: [*to* SMERALDINA] Is it you that are going to be married?
SMERALDINA: [*sighs*] No, sir.
PANTALONE: Will you tell me who you are, or will you go about your business?
TRUFFALDINO: If you only want to know who I am, I'll tell you in two words. I am the servant of my master.
> [*turns to* SMERALDINA]
> To go back to what I was saying—
PANTALONE: But who is your master?
TRUFFALDINO: [*to* PANTALONE] He is a gentleman who desires the honor of paying his respects to you.
> [*to* SMERALDINA]
> We must have a talk about this marriage.
PANTALONE: Who is this gentleman, I say? What is his name?
TRUFFALDINO: Oh, that's a long story. Si'or Federigo Rasponi of Turin, that's my master, and he sends his compliments, and he has come to see you, and he's down below, and he sends me to say that he would like to come up and he's waiting for an answer. Anything else, or will that do?
> [*All look surprised.*]
> [*to* SMERALDINA, *as before*]
> Let's begin again.
PANTALONE: Come here and talk to me. What the devil do you mean?
TRUFFALDINO: And if you want to know who I am, I am Truffaldin' Battocchio from Bergamo.

PANTALONE: I don't care who *you* are. Tell me again, who is this master of yours? I fear I did not understand you rightly.

TRUFFALDINO: Poor old gentleman! He must be hard of hearing. My master is Si'or Federigo Rasponi of Turin.

PANTALONE: Away! You must be mad. Signor Federigo Rasponi of Turin is dead.

TRUFFALDINO: Dead?

PANTALONE: To be sure he's dead, worse luck for him.

TRUFFALDINO: [*aside*] The devil! My master dead? Why, I left him alive downstairs!
> [*to* PANTALONE]
> You really mean he is dead?

PANTALONE: I tell you for an absolute certainty, he is dead.

DR. LOMBARDI: 'Tis the honest truth; he is dead; we can have no doubt about it.

TRUFFALDINO: [*aside*] Alas, my poor master! He must have met with an accident.
> [*to* PANTALONE *as if retiring*]
> Your very humble servant, sir.

PANTALONE: Can I do nothing more for you?

TRUFFALDINO: If he's dead, there's nothing more to do.
> [*aside*]
> But I'm going to see if it's true or not.
> [*Exit.*]

PANTALONE: What are we to make of this fellow? Is he knave or fool?

DR. LOMBARDI: I really don't know. Probably a little of both.

BRIGHELLLA: I should say he was just a zany. He comes from Bergamo; I can't think he is a knave.

SMERALDINA: He's not such a fool, neither.
> [*aside*]
> I like that little dark fellow.

PANTALONE: But what is this nightmare about Signor Federigo?

CLARICE: If 'tis true indeed that he is here, it would be the worst of news for me.

PANTALONE: What nonsense! Did not you see the letters yourself?

SILVIO: If he *is* alive and here after all, he has come too late.
> [*reenter* TRUFFALDINO.]

TRUFFALDINO: Gentlemen, I am surprised at you. Is that the way to treat a poor man? Is that the way you deceive strangers? Is that the behavior of a gentleman? I shall insist upon satisfaction.

PANTALONE: [*to* DR. LOMBARDI] We must be careful, the man's mad.
> [*to* TRUFFALDINO]
> What's the matter? What have they done to you?

TRUFFALDINO: To go and tell me that Si'or Federigo Rasponi was dead!

PANTALONE: Well, what then?

TRUFFALDINO: What then? Well, he's here, safe and sound, in good health and spirits, and he desires to pay his respects to you, with your kind permission.

PANTALONE: Signor Federigo?

TRUFFALDINO: Si'or Federigo.

PANTALONE: Rasponi?

TRUFFALDINO: Rasponi.

PANTALONE: Of Turin?

TRUFFALDINO: Of Turin.

PANTALONE: Be off to Bedlam, my lad; that's the place for you.

TRUFFALDINO: The Devil take *you* there, sir! You'll make me swear like a Turk. I tell you he's here, in the house, in the next room, bad luck to you.

PANTALONE: If you say any more I'll break your head.

DR. LOMBARDI: No, no, Signor Pantalone; I tell you what to do. Tell him to bring in this person whom he thinks to be Federigo Rasponi.

PANTALONE: Well, bring in this man that is risen from the dead.

TRUFFALDINO: He may have been dead and risen from the dead, for all I know. That's no affair of mine. But he's alive now, sure enough, and you shall see him with your own eyes. I'll go and tell him to come.

> [*angrily to* PANTALONE]

And 'tis time you learned how to behave properly to strangers, to gentlemen of my position, to honorable citizens of Bergamo.

> [*to* SMERALDINA]

Young woman, we will have some talk together when you will.

> [*Exit.*]

CLARICE: Silvio, I am all of a tremble.

SILVIO: Have no fear; whatever happens, you shall be mine.

DR. LOMBARDI: Now we shall discover the truth.

PANTALONE: Some rogue, I dare say, come to tell me a string of lies.

BRIGHELLLA: Sir, as I told you just now, I knew Signor Federigo; we shall see if it be he.

SMERALDINA: [*aside*] That little dark fellow doesn't look like a liar. I wonder, now, if—

> [*curtsy to* PANTALONE]

By your good leave, sir.

> [*Exit.*]

> [*Enter* BEATRICE, *dressed as a man.*]

BEATRICE: Signor Pantalone, that courtesy which I have so much admired in your correspondence is but ill matched in the treatment which I have received from you in person. I send my servant to pay you my respects, and you keep me standing in the street for half an hour before you condescend to allow me to enter.

PANTALONE: [*nervously*] I ask your pardon. But, sir, who are you?

BEATRICE: Your obedient servant, sir, Federigo Rasponi of Turin.

> [*All look bewildered.*]

PANTALONE: Extraordinary!

BRIGHELLLA: [*aside*] What does this mean? This is not Federigo, this is his sister Beatrice.

PANTALONE: I rejoice to see you, sir, alive and in health, after the bad news which we had received.

> [*aside to* DR. LOMBARDI]

I tell you, I am not convinced yet.

BEATRICE: I know; 'twas reported that I was killed in a duel. Heaven be praised, I was but wounded; and no sooner was I restored to health than I set out for Venice, according to our previous arrangement.

PANTALONE: I don't know what to say. You have the appearance of an honest man, sir, but I have sure and certain evidence that Signor Federigo is dead, and you will understand that if you cannot give us proof of the contrary—

BEATRICE: Your doubt is most natural; I recognize that I must give you proof of my identity. Here are four letters from correspondents of yours whom you know personally; one of them is from the manager of our bank. You will recognize the signatures and you will satisfy yourself as to who I am.

> [*gives four letters to* PANTALONE, *who reads them to himself*]

CLARICE: Ah, Silvio, we are lost.

SILVIO: I will lose my life before I lose you.

BEATRICE: [*noticing* BRIGHELLLA, *aside*] Heavens! Brighella! How the devil does he come to be here? If he betrays me—
> [*aloud to* BRIGHELLLA]

Friend, I think I know you.

BRIGHELLLA: Indeed yes, sir; do you not remember Brighella Cavicchio at Turin?

BEATRICE: Ah yes, now I recognize you.
> [*goes up to him*]

And what are you doing in Venice, my good fellow?
> [*aside to* BRIGHELLLA]

For the love of heaven do not betray me.

BRIGHELLLA: [*aside to* BEATRICE] Trust me.
> [*aloud*]

I keep an inn, sir, at your service.

BEATRICE: The very thing for me; as I have the pleasure of your acquaintance, I shall come to lodge at your inn.

BRIGHELLLA: You do me honor, sir.
> [*aside*]

Running contraband, I'll be bound.

PANTALONE: I have read the letters. Certainly they present Signor Federigo Rasponi to me, and if you present them, I am bound to believe that you are—the person named therein.

BEATRICE: If you are still in doubt, here is Master Brighella; he knows me, he can assure you as to who I am.

BRIGHELLLA: Of course, sir, I am happy to assure you.

PANTALONE: Well, if that be so, and my good friend Brighella confirms the testimony of the letters, then, dear Signor Federigo, I am delighted to see you and I ask your pardon for having doubted your word.

CLARICE: Then, sir, this gentleman is indeed Signor Federigo Rasponi?

PANTALONE: But of course he is.

CLARICE: [*aside to* SILVIO] Oh misery, what will happen to us?

SILVIO: [*aside to* CLARICE] Don't be frightened; you are mine and I will protect you.

PANTALONE: [*aside to* DR. LOMBARDI] What do you say to it, Doctor? He has come just in the nick of time.

DR. LOMBARDI: *Accidit in puncto, quod non contingit in anno.*

BEATRICE: [*pointing to* CLARICE] Signor Panatlone, who is that young lady?

PANTALONE: That is my daughter Clarice.

BEATRICE: The one who was promised in marriage to me?

PANTALONE: Precisely, sir; that is she.
> [*aside*]

Now I am in a pretty mess.

BEATRICE: [*to* CLARICE] Madam, permit me to have the honor.

CLARICE: [*stiffly*] Your most humble servant, sir.

BEATRICE: [*to* PANTALONE] She receives me somewhat coldly.

PANTALONE: You must forgive her, she is shy by nature.

BEATRICE: [*to* PANTALONE, *pointing at* SILVIO] And this gentleman is a relative of yours?

PANTALONE: Yes, sir; he is a nephew of mine.

SILVIO: [*to* BEATRICE] No, sir, I am not his nephew at all; I am the promised husband of Signora Clarice.

DR. LOMBARDI: [*aside to* SILVIO] Well said, my boy! Don't lose your chance! Stand up for your rights, but do nothing rash.

BEATRICE: What? You the promised husband of Signora Clarice? Was she not promised to me?

PANTALONE: There, there, I'll explain the whole matter. My dear Signor Federigo, I fully believed that the story of your accident was true, that you were dead, in fact, and so I had promised my daughter to Signor Silvio; but there is not the least harm done. You have arrived at last, just in time. Clarice is yours, if you will have her, and I am here to keep my word. Signor Silvio, I don't know what to say; you can see the position yourself. You remember what I said to you; and you will have no cause to bear me ill-will.

SILVIO: But Signor Federigo will never consent to take a bride who has given her hand to another.

BEATRICE: Oh, I am not so fastidious. I will take her in spite of that.
    [*aside*]
I mean to have some fun out of this.

DR. LOMBARDI: [*sarcastically*] There's a fine fashionable husband! I like him.

BEATRICE: I hope Signora Clarice will not refuse me her hand.

SILVIO: Sir, you have arrived too late. Signora Clarice is to be my wife, and you need have no hope that I will yield her to you. If Signor Pantalone does me wrong, I will be avenged upon him; and whoever presumes to desire Clarice will have to fight for her against this sword.

DR. LOMBARDI: [*aside*] That's a fine boy, by the Lord!

BEATRICE: [*aside*] Thank you, but I don't mean to die just yet.

DR. LOMBARDI: Sir, I must beg to inform you that you are too late. Signora Clarice is to marry my son. The law, the law, sir, is clear on the point. *Prior in tempore, potior in jure.*
    [*Exeunt* DR. LOMBARDI *and* SILVIO.]

BEATRICE: [*to* CLARICE] And you, madam bride, do you say nothing?

CLARICE: I say—I say—I'd sooner marry the hangman.
    [*Exit.*]

PANTALONE: What, you minx! What did you say?
    [*starts to run after her*]

BEATRICE: Stay, Signor Pantalone; I am sorry for her. It is not the moment for severity. In course of time I hope I may deserve her favor. Meanwhile let us go into our accounts together, for, as you know, that is one of the two reasons that have brought me to Venice.

PANTALONE: Everything is in order for your inspection. You shall see the books; your money is ready for you, and we will make up the account whenever you like.

BEATRICE: I will call on you at some more convenient time. Now, if you will allow me, I will go with Brighella to settle some little business which I have to do.

PANTALONE: You shall do as you please, and if you have need of anything, I am at your service.

BEATRICE: Well, if you could give me a little money, I should be greatly obliged; I did not bring any with me, for fear of being robbed on the way.

PANTALONE: I am delighted to serve you; but the cashier is not here just now. The moment he comes I will send the money to your lodgings. Are you not staying at my friend Brighella's?

BEATRICE: Yes, I lie there. But I will send my servant; he is entirely honest. You can trust him with anything.

PANTALONE: Very well. I will carry out your wishes, and if you may be pleased to take pot luck with me, I am yours to command.

BEATRICE: For today I thank you. Another day I shall be happy to wait upon you.

PANTALONE: Then I shall expect you.

> [*Enter* SMERALDINA.]

SMERALDINA: [*to* PANTALONE] Sir, you are asked for.

PANTALONE: Who is it?

SMERALDINA: I couldn't say, sir.

PANTALONE: I will come directly. Sir, I beg you to excuse me. Brighella, you are at home here; be good enough to attend Signor Federigo.

BEATRICE: Pray do not put yourself about for me, sir.

PANTALONE: I must go. Farewell, sir.

> [*aside*]

I don't want to have trouble in my house.

> [*Exit with* SMERALDINA.]

BRIGHELLLA: May I ask, Signora Beatrice—?

BEATRICE: Hush, for the love of Heaven, don't betray me. My poor brother is dead. 'Twas thought Florindo Aretusi killed him in a duel. You remember, Florindo loved me, and my brother would not have it. They fought, Federigo fell, and Florindo fled from justice. I heard he was making for Venice, so I put on my brother's clothes and followed him. Thanks to the letters of credit, which are my brother's, and thanks still more to you, Signor Pantalone takes me for Federigo. We are to make up our accounts; I shall draw the money, and then I shall be able to help Florindo too, if he has need of it. Be my friend, dear Brighella, help me, please! You shall be generously rewarded.

BRIGHELLLA: That's all very well, but I don't want to be responsible for Signor Pantalone paying you out money in good faith and then finding himself made a fool of.

BEATRICE: Made a fool of? If my brother is dead, am I not his heir?

BRIGHELLLA: Very true. Then why not say so?

BEATRICE: If I do that, I can do nothing. Pantalone will begin by treating me as if he were my guardian; then they will all worry me and say my conduct is unbecoming and all that sort of thing. I want my liberty. Help me to it. 'Twill not last long.

BRIGHELLLA: Well, well, you were always one for having your own way. Trust me, and I'll do my best for you.

BEATRICE: Thank you. And now let us go to your inn.

BRIGHELLLA: Where is your servant?

BEATRICE: I told him to wait for me in the street.

BRIGHELLLA: Wherever did you get hold of that idiot? He cannot even speak plain.

BEATRICE: I picked him up on the journey. He seems a fool at times; but he isn't really a fool and I can rely on his loyalty.

BRIGHELLLA: Yes, loyalty's a fine thing. Well, I am at your service. To think what love will make people do!

BEATRICE: Oh, this is nothing. Love makes people do far worse things than this.

BRIGHELLLA: Well, here's a good beginning. If you go on that way, Lord knows what may come of it!

> [*Exeunt* BEATRICE *and* BRIGHELLLA.]

SCENE II———*A Street with* BRIGHELLA'S *Inn.*

TRUFFALDINO: I'm sick of waiting; I can hold out no longer. With this master of mine there's not enough to eat, and the less there is the more I want it. The town clock struck twelve half an hour ago, and my belly struck two hours ago at least. If I only knew where we were going to lodge! With my other masters the first thing they did, as soon as they came to a town, was to go to a tavern. This gentleman—Lord no! He leaves his trunks in the boat at the landing stage, goes off to pay visits, and forgets all about his poor servant. When they say we ought to serve our masters with love, they ought to tell the masters to have a little charity toward their servants.

Here's an inn. I've half a mind to go in and see if I could find something to tickle my teeth; but what if my master comes to look for me? His own fault; he ought to know better. I'll go in—but now I come to think of it, there's another little difficulty that I hadn't remembered; I haven't a penny. Oh poor Truffaldin'! Rather than be a servant, devil take me, I'd—what indeed? By the grace of Heaven there's nothing I can do.

[*Enter* FLORINDO *in traveling dress with a* PORTER *carrying a trunk on his shoulder.*]

PORTER: I tell you, sir, I can go no farther; the weight's enough to kill me.

FLORINDO: Here is the sign of an inn. Can't you carry it these few steps?

PORTER: Help! The trunk is falling.

FLORINDO: I told you you could not carry it; you're too weak; you have no strength at all.

[FLORINDO *rearranges the trunk on the* PORTER'S *shoulder.*]

TRUFFALDINO: Here's a chance for sixpence.

[*to* FLORINDO]

Sir, can I do anything for you?

FLORINDO: My good man, be so good as to carry this trunk into the inn there.

TRUFFALDINO: Yes, sir, let me take it, sir. See how I do it.

[*to the* PORTER]

You be off!

[TRUFFALDINO *puts his shoulder under the trunk and takes it by himself, knocking the* PORTER *down at the same time.*]

FLORINDO: Well done!

TRUFFALDINO: It weighs nothing. A mere trifle.

[*goes into the inn with the* trunk]

FLORINDO: [*to* PORTER] There! You see how it's done.

PORTER: I can do no more. I work as a porter for my misfortune, but I am the son of a respectable person.

FLORINDO: What did your father do?

PORTER: My father? He skinned lambs in the town.

FLORINDO: The fellow's mad.

[*to* PORTER]

That will do.

[*going towards the inn*]

PORTER: Please your honor—

FLORINDO: What do you want?

PORTER: The money for the porterage.

FLORINDO: How much am I to give you for ten yards? There's the landing stage!

[*pointing off*]

PORTER: I didn't count them. I want my pay.

[*holds out his hand*]

FLORINDO: There's twopence.

[*gives money*]

PORTER: I want my pay.

[*still holding out his hand*]

FLORINDO: Lord, what obstinacy! Here's twopence more.

[*gives money*]

PORTER: I want my pay.

FLORINDO: [*kicks him*] Go and be hanged!

PORTER: Thank you, sir, that's enough.

[*Exit.*]

FLORINDO: There's a humorous fellow! He was positively waiting for me to kick him. Well, let us go and see what the inn is like—

[*Reenter* TRUFFALDINO.]

TRUFFALDINO: Sir, everything is ready for you.

FLORINDO: What lodging is there here?

TRUFFALDINO: 'Tis a very good place, sir. Good beds, fine looking glasses, and a grand kitchen with a smell to it that is very comforting. I have talked with the waiter. You will be served like a king.

FLORINDO: What's your trade?

TRUFFALDINO: Servant.

FLORINDO: Are you a Venetian?

TRUFFALDINO: Not from Venice, but of the State. I'm from Bergamo, at your service.

FLORINDO: Have you a master now?

TRUFFALDINO: At the moment—to tell the truth, I have not.

FLORINDO: You are without a master?

TRUFFALDINO: You see me, sir. I am without a master.

[*aside*]

My master is not here, so I tell no lies.

FLORINDO: Will you come and be my servant?

TRUFFALDINO: Why not?

[*aside*]

If his terms are better.

FLORINDO: At any rate, for as long as I stay in Venice.

TRUFFALDINO: Very good, sir. How much will you give me?

FLORINDO: How much do you want?

TRUFFALDINO: I'll tell you: another master I had, who is here no more, he gave me a shilling a day and all found.

FLORINDO: Good, I will give you as much.

TRUFFALDINO: You must give me a little more than that.

FLORINDO: How much more do you want?

TRUFFALDINO: A halfpenny a day for a snuff.

FLORINDO: Oh, I'll give you that and welcome.

TRUFFALDINO: If that's so, I'm your man, sir.

FLORINDO: But I should like to know a little more about you.

TRUFFALDINO: If you want to know all about me, you go to Bergamo; anyone there will tell you who I am.

FLORINDO: Have you nobody in Venice who knows you?

TRUFFALDINO: I only arrived this morning, sir.

FLORINDO: Well, well, I take you for an honest man. I will give you a trial.

TRUFFALDINO: You give me a trial and you shall see.

FLORINDO: First of all, I am anxious to know if there are letters at the Post for me. Here is half a crown; go to the Turin Post and ask if there are letters for Florindo Aretusi; if there are, take them and bring them at once. I shall wait for you.

TRUFFALDINO: Meanwhile you will order dinner, sir?

FLORINDO: Yes, well said! I will order it.

[*aside*]

He is a wag, I like him. I'll give him a trial.

[FLORINDO *goes into the inn.*]

TRUFFALDINO: A halfpenny more a day, that's fifteen pence a month. 'Tis not true that the other gentleman gave me a shilling; he gives me six pennies. Maybe six pennies make a shilling, but I'm not quite sure. And this gentleman from Turin is nowhere to be seen. He's mad. He's a young fellow without a beard and without any sense neither. He may go about his business; I shall go to the Post for my new gentleman.

[*As he is going,* BEATRICE *enters with* BRIGHELLLA *and meets him.*]

BEATRICE: That's a nice way to behave! Is that the way you wait for me?

TRUFFALDINO: Here I am, sir. I am still waiting for you.

BEATRICE: And how do you come to be waiting for me here, and not in the street where I told you? 'Tis a mere accident that I have found you.

TRUFFALDINO: I went for a bit of a walk to take away my appetite.

BEATRICE: Well, go at once to the landing stage; fetch my trunk and take it to the inn of Master Brighella.

BRIGHELLLA: There's my inn, you cannot mistake it.

BEATRICE: Very well, then, make haste, and I will wait for you.

TRUFFALDINO: The devil! In *that* inn?

BEATRICE: Here, you will go at the same time to the Turin Post and ask if there are any letters for me. You may ask if there are letters for Federigo Rasponi and also for Beatrice Rasponi. That's my sister. Some friends of hers might perhaps write to her; so be sure to see if there are letters either for her or for me.

TRUFFALDINO: [*aside*] What *am* I to do? Here's a pretty kettle of fish!

BRIGHELLLA: [*to* BEATRICE] Why do you expect letters in your real name if you left home secretly?

BEATRICE: I told the steward to write to me; and I don't know which name he may use. I'll tell you more later.

[*to* TRUFFALDINO]

Make haste, be off with you to the Post and the landing stage. Fetch the letters and have the trunk brought to the inn; I shall be there.

[*Exit* BEATRICE *into the inn.*]

TRUFFALDINO: Are you the landlord?

BRIGHELLLA: Yes, I am. You behave properly and you need have no fear, I will do you well.

[*Exit* BRIGHELLLA *into the inn.*]

TRUFFALDINO: There's luck! There are many that look in vain for a master, and I have found two. What the devil am I to do? I cannot wait upon them both. No? Why not? Wouldn't it be a fine thing to wait upon both of them, earn two men's wages and eat and drink for two? 'Twould be a fine thing indeed, if neither of them found out. And if they did? What then? No matter! If one sends me away, I stay with the other. I swear I'll try it. If it last but a day, I'll try it. Whatever happens I shall have done a fine thing. Here goes. Let's go to the Post for both of 'em.

[*Enter* SILVIO *and meets* TRUFFALDINO.]

SILVIO: [*aside*] That is the servant of Federigo Rasponi.

[*To* TRUFFALDINO.]

My good man.

TRUFFALDINO: Sir?

SILVIO: Where is your master?

TRUFFALDINO: My master? He's in that inn there.

SILVIO: Go at once and tell your master that I wish to speak to him; if he be a man of honor let him come down; I wait for him.

TRUFFALDINO: My dear sir—

SILVIO: [*angrily*] Go at once.

TRUFFALDINO: But I must tell you, my master—

SILVIO: Don't answer me; or, by Heaven, I'll—

TRUFFALDINO: But which do you want?

SILVIO: At once, I say, or I'll beat you.

TRUFFALDINO: [*aside*] Well, I don't know—I'll send the first I can find.

[*Exit* TRUFFALDINO *into the inn.*]

SILVIO: No, I will never suffer the presence of a rival. Federigo may have got off once with his life, but he shall not always have the same fortune. Either he shall renounce all claims to Clarice, or he shall give me the satisfaction of a gentleman. Here are some more people coming out of the inn. I don't want to be disturbed.

[*retires to the opposite side*]

[*Enter* TRUFFALDINO *with* FLORINDO.]

TRUFFALDINO: [*points out* SILVIO *to* FLORINDO] There's the fire-eating gentleman, sir.

FLORINDO: I do not know him. What does he want with me?

TRUFFALDINO: I don't know. I go to fetch the letters, with your good leave, sir.

[*aside*]

I don't want any more trouble.

[*Exit.*]

SILVIO: [*aside*] Federigo does not come?

FLORINDO: [*aside*] I must find out what the truth is.

[*to* SILVIO]

Sir, are you the gentleman who inquired for me?

SILVIO: I, sir? I have not even the honor of your acquaintance.

FLORINDO: But that servant who has just gone told me that with a loud and threatening voice you made bold to challenge me.

SILVIO: He misunderstood. I said I wished to speak to his master.

FLORINDO: Very well, I am his master.

SILVIO: You his master?

FLORINDO: Certainly. He is in my service.

SILVIO: Then I ask your pardon. Either your servant is exactly like another whom I saw this morning, or he waits on another person.

FLORINDO: You may set your mind at rest; he waits on me.

SILVIO: If that be so, I ask your pardon again.

FLORINDO: No harm done. Mistakes often occur.

SILVIO: Are you a stranger here, sir?

FLORINDO: From Turin, sir, at your service.

SILVIO: The man whom I would have provoked was from Turin.

FLORINDO: Then perhaps I may know him; if he has given you offence, I shall gladly assist you to obtain just satisfaction.

SILVIO: Do you know one Federigo Rasponi?

FLORINDO: Ah! I knew him only too well.

SILVIO: He makes claim, on the strength of her father's word, to the lady who this morning swore to be my wife.

FLORINDO: My good friend, Federigo Rasponi cannot take your wife away from you. He is dead.

SILVIO: Yes, we all believed that he was dead; but this morning to my disgust he arrived in Venice safe and sound.

FLORINDO: Sir, you petrify me.

SILVIO: No wonder! I was petrified myself.

FLORINDO: I assure you Federigo Rasponi is dead.

SILVIO: I assure you that Federigo Rasponi is alive.

FLORINDO: Take care you are not deceived.

SILVIO: Signor Pantalone dei Bisognosi, the young lady's father, has made all possible inquiries to assure himself and is in possession of incontestable proofs that he is here in person.

FLORINDO: [*aside*] Then he was not killed in the duel, as everybody believed!

SILVIO: Either he or I must renounce claim to the love of Clarice or to life.

FLORINDO: [*aside*] Federigo here?

SILVIO: I am surprised that you have not seen him. He was to lodge at this very inn.

FLORINDO: I have not seen him. They told me that there was no one else at all staying there.

SILVIO: He must have changed his mind. Forgive me, sir, if I have troubled you. If you see him, tell him that for his own welfare he must abandon the idea of this marriage. Silvio Lombardi is my name; I am your most obedient servant, sir.

FLORINDO: I shall be greatly pleased to have the honor of your friendship.

[*aside*]

I am confounded.

SILVIO: May I beg to know your name, sir?

FLORINDO: [*aside*] I must not discover myself.

[*to* SILVIO]

Your servant, sir, Orazio Ardenti.

SILVIO: Signor Orazio, I am yours to command.

[*Exit* SILVIO.]

FLORINDO: I was told he died on the spot. Yet I fled so hurriedly when accused of the crime that I had no chance of finding out the truth. Then, since he is not dead, it will be better for me to go back to Turin and console my beloved Beatrice, who is perhaps in suffering and sorrow for my absence.

[*Enter* TRUFFALDINO, *with another* PORTER *who carries* BEATRICE'S *trunk.* TRUFFALDINO *comes forward a few steps, sees* FLORINDO *and, fearing to be seen himself, makes the* PORTER *retire.*]

TRUFFALDINO: Come along. This way—The devil! There's my other master. Go back, friend, and wait for me at that corner.

[*Exit* PORTER.]

FLORINDO: [*continuing to himself*] Yes, without delay. I will go back to Turin.

TRUFFALDINO: Here I am, sir.

FLORINDO: Truffaldino, will you come to Turin with me?

TRUFFALDINO: When?

FLORINDO: Now; at once.

TRUFFALDINO: Before dinner?

FLORINDO: No, we will have dinner, and then we will go.

TRUFFALDINO: Very good, sir. I'll think it over at dinner.

FLORINDO: Have you been to the Post?

TRUFFALDINO: Yes, sir.

FLORINDO: Have you found my letters?

TRUFFALDINO: I have, sir.

FLORINDO: Where are they?

TRUFFALDINO: I will give you them.

[*Takes three letters out of his pocket. Aside.*]

The devil! I have mixed up one master's letters with the other's. How shall I find out which are his? I cannot read.

FLORINDO: Come, give me my letters.

TRUFFALDINO: Directly, sir.

[*aside*]

Here's a muddle.

[*to* FLORINDO]

I must tell you, sir; these three letters are not all for your honor. I met another servant, who knows me; we were in service together in Bergamo; I told him I was going to the Post, and he asked me to see whether there was anything for *his* master. I think there was one letter, but I don't know which of them it was.

FLORINDO: Let me see; I will take mine and give you the other back.

TRUFFALDINO: There, sir; I only wanted to do my friend a good turn.

FLORINDO: [*aside*] What is this? A letter addressed to Beatrice Rasponi? To Beatrice Rasponi at Venice?

TRUFFALDINO: Did you find the one that belongs to my mate?

FLORINDO: Who is this mate of yours who asked you to do this for him?

TRUFFALDINO: He is a servant—his name is Pasqual'—

FLORINDO: Whom does he wait upon?

TRUFFALDINO: I do not know, sir.

FLORINDO: But if he told you to fetch his master's letters, he must have told you his name.

TRUFFALDINO: Of course he did.

[*aside*]

The muddle's getting thicker.

FLORINDO: Well, what name did he tell you?

TRUFFALDINO: I don't remember.

FLORINDO: What?

TRUFFALDINO: He wrote it down on a bit of paper.

FLORINDO: And where is the paper?

TRUFFALDINO: I left it at the Post.

FLORINDO: [*aside*] Confusion! What does this mean?

TRUFFALDINO: [*aside*] I am learning my part as I go along.

FLORINDO: Where does this fellow Pasquale live?

TRUFFALDINO: Indeed, sir, I haven't the slightest idea.

FLORINDO: How will you be able to give him the letter?

TRUFFALDINO: He said he would meet me in the Piazza.

FLORINDO: [*aside*] I don't know what to make of it.

TRUFFALDINO: [*aside*] If I get through this business clean 'twill be a miracle.

[*to* FLORINDO]

Pray give me the letter, sir, and I shall find him somewhere.

FLORINDO: No; I mean to open this letter.

TRUFFALDINO: Oh, sir, do not do that, sir. Besides, you know how wrong it is to open letters.

FLORINDO: I care not; this letter interests me too much. It is addressed to a person on whom I have a certain claim. I can open it without scruple.

[*opens letter*]

TRUFFALDINO: As you will, sir.

[*aside*]

He has opened it.

FLORINDO: [*reads*] "Madam, your departure from this city has given rise to much talk, and all understand that you have gone to join Signor Florindo. The Court of Justice has discovered that you have fled in man's dress and intends to have you arrested. I have not sent this letter by the courier from Turin to Venice, so as not to reveal the place whither you were bound, but I have sent it to a friend at Genoa to be forwarded to Venice. If I have any more news to tell you, I will not fail to send it by the same means. Your most humble servant, Antonio."

TRUFFALDINO: That's a nice way to behave! Reading other people's letters!

FLORINDO: [*aside*] What is all this? Beatrice has left home? In man's dress? To join me? Indeed she loves me. Heaven grant I may find her in Venice.

      [*to* TRUFFALDINO]

Here, my good Truffaldino, go and do all you can to find Pasquale; find out from him who his master is, and if he be man or woman. Find out where he lodges, and if you can, bring him here to me, and both he and you shall be handsomely rewarded.

TRUFFALDINO: Give me the letter; I will try to find him.

FLORINDO: There it is. I count upon you. This matter is of infinite importance to me.

TRUFFALDINO: But am I to give him the letter open like this?

FLORINDO: Tell him it was a mistake, an accident. Don't make difficulties.

TRUFFALDINO: And are you going to Turin now?

FLORINDO: No, not for the present. Lose no time. Go and find Pasquale.

      [*aside*]

Beatrice in Venice, Federigo in Venice! If her brother finds her, unhappy woman! I will do all I can to discover her first.

      [*Exit toward the town.*]

TRUFFALDINO: Upon my word, I hope he is not going away. I want to see how my two jobs will work out. I'm on my mettle. This letter, now, which I have to take to my other master—I don't like to have to give it to him opened. I must try to fold it again.

      [*tries various awkward folds*]

And now it must be sealed. If I only knew how to do it! I have seen my grand-mother sometimes seal letters with chewed bread. I'll try it.

      [*takes a piece of bread out of his pocket*]

It's a pity to waste this little piece of bread, but still something must be done.

      [*chews a little bread to seal the letter and accidentally swallows it*]

The devil! It has gone down. I must chew another bit.

      [*same business*]

No good, nature rebels. I'll try once more.

      [*chews again; would like to swallow the bread, but restrains himself and with great difficulty removes the bread from his mouth*]

Ah, here it is; I'll seal the letter.

      [*seals the letter with the bread*]

I think that looks quite well. I'm always a great man for doing things cleanly. Lord! I had forgotten the porter.

      [*calls off*]

Friend, come hither; take the trunk on your shoulder.

      [*Reenter* PORTER.]

PORTER: Here I am; where am I to carry it?

TRUFFALDINO: Take it into that inn; I am coming directly.

      [BEATRICE *comes out of the inn.*]

BEATRICE: Is this my trunk?

TRUFFALDINO: Yes, sir.

BEATRICE: [*to* PORTER] Carry it into my room.

PORTER: Which is your room?

BEATRICE: Ask the waiter.

PORTER: There's one and threepence to pay.

BEATRICE: Go on, I will pay you.

PORTER: Please be quick about it.

BEATRICE: Don't bother me.

PORTER: I've half a mind to throw the trunk down in the middle of the street.

[*goes into the inn*]

TRUFFALDINO: Great folk for politeness, these porters!

BEATRICE: Have you been to the Post?

TRUFFALDINO: Yes, sir.

BEATRICE: Any letters for me?

TRUFFALDINO: One for your sister.

BEATRICE: Good; where is it?

TRUFFALDINO: Here.

[*gives letter*]

BEATRICE: This letter has been opened.

TRUFFALDINO: Opened? No! Impossible!

BEATRICE: Yes, opened, and then sealed with bread.

TRUFFALDINO: I can't think how that can have happened.

BEATRICE: You cannot think, eh? Rascal, who has opened this letter? I must know.

TRUFFALDINO: Sir, I'll tell you, I'll confess the truth. We are all liable to make mistakes.
At the Post there was a letter for me; I can't read very much, and by mistake, instead
of opening my letter, I opened yours. I ask your pardon—

BEATRICE: If that was all, there's no great harm done.

TRUFFALDINO: 'Tis true, on the word of a poor man.

BEATRICE: Have you read this letter? Do you know what is in it?

TRUFFALDINO: Not a word. I can't read the handwriting.

BEATRICE: Has anyone else seen it?

TRUFFALDINO: [*with an air of great indignation*] Oh!

BEATRICE: Take care now—

TRUFFALDINO: [*same business*] Sir!

BEATRICE: [*aside*] I hope he is not deceiving me.

[*reads to herself*]

TRUFFALDINO: That's all put straight.

BEATRICE: [*aside*] Antonio is a faithful servant and I am obliged to him.

[*to* TRUFFALDINO]

Listen; I have some business to do close by. You go into the inn, open the trunk—
here are my keys—and unpack my things. When I come back, we will have dinner.

[*aside*]

I have seen nothing of Signor Pantalone, and I am anxious to have my money.

[*Exit.*]

TRUFFALDINO: Come, that all went well; it couldn't have gone better. I'm a great fellow;
I think a deal more of myself than I did before.

[*Enter* PANTALONE.]

PANTALONE: Tell me, my good man, is your master in the house?

TRUFFALDINO: No, sir, he is not there.

PANTALONE: Do you know where he may be?

TRUFFALDINO: Not that neither.

PANTALONE: Is he coming home to dinner?

TRUFFALDINO: Yes, I should think so.

PANTALONE: Here, as soon as he comes home give him this purse with these hundred guineas. I cannot stay, I have business. Good day to you.

[*Exit* PANTALONE.]

TRUFFALDINO: And a good day to you, sir! He never told me to which of my masters I was to give it.

[*Enter* FLORINDO.]

FLORINDO: Well, did you find Pasquale?

TRUFFALDINO: No sir, I did not find Pasqual', but I found a gentleman who gave me a purse with a hundred guineas in it.

FLORINDO: A hundred guineas? What for?

TRUFFALDINO: Tell me truly, sir, were you expecting money from anyone?

FLORINDO: Yes; I had presented a letter of credit to a merchant.

TRUFFALDINO: Then this money will be for you.

FLORINDO: What did he say when he gave it to you?

TRUFFALDINO: He told me to give it to my master.

FLORINDO: Then of course it is mine. Am I not your master? What doubt could you have?

TRUFFALDINO: [*aside*] Yes, but what about t'other one?

FLORINDO: And you do not know who gave you the money?

TRUFFALDINO: No, sir; I think I have seen his face somewhere, but I don't remember exactly.

FLORINDO: It will have been the merchant to whom I had a letter.

TRUFFALDINO: Yes, of course, sir.

FLORINDO: You won't forget Pasquale.

TRUFFALDINO: I'll find him after dinner.

FLORINDO: Then let us go and order our meal.

[*goes into the inn*]

TRUFFALDINO: We will. Lucky I made no mistake this time. I've given the purse to the right one.

[*goes into the inn*]

SCENE III———*A Room in the House of* PANTALONE.

PANTALONE: That's the long and short of it; Signor Federigo is to be your husband. I have given my word and I am not to be cozened.

CLARICE: You have my obedience, sir; but I beseech you, this is tyranny.

PANTALONE: When Signor Federigo first asked for your hand, I told you; you never replied that you did not wish to marry him. You should have spoken then; now it is too late.

CLARICE: My fear of you, sir, and my respect, made me dumb.

PANTALONE: Then your fear and respect should do the same now.

CLARICE: Indeed I cannot marry him, sir.

PANTALONE: No? And why not?

CLARICE: Nothing shall induce me to marry Federigo.

PANTALONE: You dislike him so much?

CLARICE: He is odious in my eyes.

PANTALONE: And supposing I were to show you how you might begin to like him a little?

CLARICE: What do you mean, sir?

PANTALONE: Put Signor Silvio out of your mind, and you will soon like Federigo well enough.

CLARICE: Silvio is too firmly stamped upon my heart; and your own approval, sir, has rooted him there the more securely.

PANTALONE: [*aside*] In some ways I am sorry for her.
>[*to* CLARICE]
You have got to make a virtue of necessity.

CLARICE: My heart is not capable of so great an effort.

PANTALONE: Come, come; you shall!
>[*Enter* SMERALDINA.]

SMERALDINA: Sir, Signor Federigo is here and desires to speak with you.

PANTALONE: Tell him to come in; I am at his service.

CLARICE: [*weeping*] Alas! What torture!

SMERALDINA: What is it, madam? You are weeping? Truly you do wrong. Have you not noticed how handsome Signor Federigo is? If I had such luck, I would not cry; no, I would laugh with the whole of my mouth.
>[*Exit* SMERALDINA.]

PANTALONE: There, there, my child; you must not be seen crying.

CLARICE: But if I feel my heart bursting!
>[*Enter* BEATRICE *in man's dress.*]

BEATRICE: My respects to Signor Pantalone.

PANTALONE: Your servant, sir. Did you receive a purse with a hundred guineas in it?

BEATRICE: No.

PANTALONE: But I gave it to your servant just now. You told me he was a trustworthy man.

BEATRICE: Yes, indeed; there is no danger. I did not see him. He will give me the money when I come home again.
>[*aside to* PANTALONE]
What ails Signora Clarice that she is weeping?

PANTALONE: [*aside to* BEATRICE] Dear Signor Federigo, you must have pity on her. The news of your death was the cause of this trouble. I hope it will pass away in time.

BEATRICE: [*to* PANTALONE] Do me a kindness, Signor Pantalone, and leave me alone with her a moment, to see if I cannot obtain a kind word from her.

PANTALONE: With pleasure, sir. I will go, and come back again.
>[*to* CLARICE]
My child, stay here, I will be back directly. You must entertain your promised husband awhile.
>[*softly to* CLARICE]
Now, be careful.
>[*Exit* PANTALONE.]

BEATRICE: Signora Clarice, I beg you—

CLARICE: Stand away, and do not dare to importune me.

BEATRICE: So severe with him who is your destined husband?

CLARICE: They may drag me by force to the altar, but you will have only my hand, never my heart.

BEATRICE: You disdain me, but I hope to appease you.

CLARICE: I shall abhor you to all eternity.

BEATRICE: But if you knew me, you would not say so.

CLARICE: I know you well enough as the destroyer of my happiness.

BEATRICE: But I can find a way to comfort you.

CLARICE: You deceive yourself; there is no one who can comfort me but Silvio.

BEATRICE: 'Tis true, I cannot give you the same comfort as your Silvio might, but I can at least contribute to your happiness.

CLARICE: I think it is quite enough, sir, that although I speak to you as harshly as I can, you should continue to torture me.

BEATRICE: [*aside*] Poor girl! I can't bear to see her suffer.

CLARICE: [*aside*] I'm so angry, I don't care how rude I am.

BEATRICE: Signora Clarice, I have a secret to tell you.

CLARICE: I make no promise to keep it; you had better not tell it me.

BEATRICE: Your severity deprives me of the means to make you happy.

CLARICE: You can never make me anything but miserable.

BEATRICE: You are wrong, and to convince you I will speak plainly. You have no desire for me; I have no use for you. You have promised your hand to another, I to another have already pledged my heart.

CLARICE: Oh! Now you begin to please me.

BEATRICE: Did I not tell you that I knew how to comfort you?

CLARICE: Ah, I feared you would deceive me.

BEATRICE: Nay, madam, I speak in all sincerity; and if you promise me that discretion which you refused me just now, I will confide to you a secret, which will ensure your peace of mind.

CLARICE: I vow I will observe the strictest silence.

BEATRICE: I am not Federigo Rasponi, but his sister Beatrice.

CLARICE: What! I am amazed. You a woman?

BEATRICE: I am indeed. Imagine my feelings when I claimed you as my bride!

CLARICE: And what news have you of your brother?

BEATRICE: He died indeed by the sword. A lover of mine was thought to have killed him, and 'tis he whom I am seeking now in these clothes. I beseech you by all the holy laws of friendship and of love not to betray me.

CLARICE: Won't you let me tell Silvio?

BEATRICE: No; on the contrary I forbid you absolutely.

CLARICE: Well, I will say nothing.

BEATRICE: Remember I count upon you.

CLARICE: You have my promise. I will be silent.

BEATRICE: Now, I hope, you will treat me more kindly.

CLARICE: I will be your friend indeed; and if I can be of service to you, dispose of me.

BEATRICE: I too swear eternal friendship to you. Give me your hand.

CLARICE: I don't quite like to—

BEATRICE: Are you afraid I am not a woman after all? I will give you proof positive.

CLARICE: It all seems just like a dream.

BEATRICE: Yes. 'Tis a strange business.

CLARICE: 'Tis indeed fantastic.

BEATRICE: Come, I must be going. Let us embrace in sign of honest friendship and loyalty.

CLARICE: There! I doubt you no longer.

    [*Enter* PANTALONE.]

PANTALONE: Well done, well done; I congratulate you.

    [*to* CLARICE]

My child, you have been very quick in adapting yourself.

BEATRICE: Did I not tell you, Signor Pantalone, that I should win her round?

PANTALONE: Magnificent! You have done more in four minutes than I should have done in four years.

CLARICE: [*aside*] Now I am in a worse tangle than ever.

PANTALONE: [*to* CLARICE] Then we will have the wedding at once.

CLARICE: Pray do not be in too much haste, sir.

PANTALONE: What? Holding hands on the sly and kissing, and then in no haste about it? No, no, I don't want you to get yourself into trouble. You shall be married tomorrow.

BEATRICE: Signor Pantalone, 'twill be necessary first of all to arrange the settlement and to go into our accounts.

PANTALONE: We will do all that. These things can be done in a couple of hours.

CLARICE: Sir, I beseech you—

PANTALONE: Madam, I am going straight away to say a word to Signor Silvio.

CLARICE: For the love of Heaven do not anger him.

PANTALONE: What, what? Do you want two husbands?

CLARICE: Not exactly—but—

PANTALONE: But me no buts. 'Tis all settled. Your servant, sir.
    [going]

BEATRICE: *[to* PANTALONE*]* Listen, sir—

PANTALONE: You are husband and wife.
    [going]

CLARICE: Had you not better—

PANTALONE: We will talk about it this evening.
    [Exit.]

CLARICE: Oh, Signora Beatrice, 'tis worse than it was before!

ACT II

SCENE I———*The Courtyard of* PANTALONE'S *House.*

SILVIO: Sir, I entreat you to leave me alone.

DR. LOMBARDI: Stay, answer me.

SILVIO: I am beside myself.

DR. LOMBARDI: What are you doing in the courtyard of Signor Pantalone?

SILVIO: I intend either that he should keep his word that he has given me, or that he should render me account for this intolerable insult.

DR. LOMBARDI: But you cannot do this in Pantalone's own house. You are a fool to let yourself be so transported with anger.

SILVIO: A man who behaves so abominably deserves no consideration.

DR. LOMBARDI: True; but that is no reason why you should be so rash. Leave him to me, my dear boy, leave him to me; let me talk to him; maybe I can bring him to reason and make him see where his duty lies. Go away somewhere and wait for me; leave this courtyard; do not let us make a scene. I will wait for Signor Pantalone.

SILVIO: But sir, I—

DR. LOMBARDI: But, sir, I will have you obey me.

SILVIO: I obey you, sir. I will go. Speak to him. I wait for you at the apothecary's. But if Signor Pantalone persists, he will have to settle with me.
    [Exit SILVIO.*]*

DR. LOMBARDI: Poor dear boy, I feel truly sorry for him. Signor Pantalone ought never to have led him on so far before he was quite certain that man from Turin was dead. I must see him quietly; I must not let my temper get the better of me.
    [Enter PANTALONE.*]*

PANTALONE: *[aside]* What is the doctor doing in my house?

DR. LOMBARDI: Oh, Signor Pantalone, your servant.

PANTALONE: Your servant, Doctor. I was just going to look for you and your son.

DR. LOMBARDI: Indeed? Good! I suppose you were coming to give us your assurance that Signora Clarice is to be Silvio's wife.

PANTALONE: *[much embarrassed]* Well, the fact is, I was coming to tell you—

DR. LOMBARDI: No, no; there is no need for explanations. You have my sympathy in a very awkward situation. But we are old friends and we will let bygones be bygones.

PANTALONE : [*still hesitating*] Yes, of course, in view of the promise made to Signor Federigo—

DR. LOMBARDI: He took you by surprise, and you had no time for reflection; you did not think of the affront you were giving to our family.

PANTALONE : You can hardly talk of an affront, when a previous contract—

DR. LOMBARDI: I know what you are going to say. It seemed at first sight out of the question that your promise to the Turin gentleman could be repudiated, because it was a formal contract. But that was a contract merely between you and him; whereas ours is confirmed by the girl herself.

PANTALONE : Very true, but—

DR. LOMBARDI: And as you know, in matrimonial cases, *consensus, et non concubitus, facit virum.*

PANTALONE : I am no Latin scholar; but I must tell you—

DR. LOMBARDI: And girls must not be sacrificed.

PANTALONE : Have you anything more to say?

DR. LOMBARDI: I have nothing more to say.

PANTALONE : Have you finished?

DR. LOMBARDI: I have finished.

PANTALONE : May I speak?

DR. LOMBARDI: You may.

PANTALONE : My dear Doctor, with all your learning—

DR. LOMBARDI: As regards the dowry, we can easily arrange matters. A little more or a little less, I will make no difficulties.

PANTALONE : I must begin all over again. Will you allow me to speak?

DR. LOMBARDI: With pleasure.

PANTALONE : I must tell you; I have the greatest respect for your legal learning, but in this case it does not apply.

DR. LOMBARDI: And you mean to tell me that this other marriage is to take place?

PANTALONE : For my part I have given my word and I cannot go back upon it. My daughter is content; what impediment can there be? I was just coming to look for you or Signor Silvio, to tell you this. I am extremely sorry, but I see no help for it.

DR. LOMBARDI: I am not surprised at your daughter's behavior. But I am surprised at yours, sir, at your treating me in this disgraceful way. If you were not perfectly certain about the death of Signor Federigo, you had no business to enter into an engagement with my son; and having entered into an engagement with him, you are bound to maintain that engagement whatever it may cost you. The news of Federigo's death was quite sufficient to justify, even to Federigo, your new intention; he could have no right to reproach you, still less to demand compensation. The marriage which was contracted this morning between Signora Clarice and my son *coram testibus* cannot be dissolved by a mere word given by you to another party. If I were to listen to my son I should insist upon the annulment of the new contract and compel your daughter to marry him; but I should be ashamed to receive into my house so disreputable a daughter-in-law, the daughter of a man who breaks his word as you do. Signor Pantalone, you have done me an injury, you have done an injury to the house of Lombardi. The time will come when you will have to pay for it; yes, sir, the time will come—*omnia tempus habent.*

[*Exit* DOCTOR.]

PANTALONE: You may go to the devil for all I care. I don't care a fig, I'm not afraid of you. The Rasponis are worth a hundred of the Lombardis. An only son, and as rich as he is—you won't find that every day. It has got to be.

[*Enter* SILVIO.]

SILVIO: [*aside*] 'Tis all very fine for my father to talk. Let him keep his temper who can.

PANTALONE: [*seeing* SILVIO, *aside*] Here comes the other.

SILVIO: [*rudely*] Your servant, sir.

PANTALONE: Yours to command, sir.

[*aside*]

He is boiling.

SILVIO: I have just heard something from my father; am I to believe that it is true?

PANTALONE: If your father said it, it must certainly be true.

SILVIO: Then the marriage is settled between Signora Clarice and Signor Federigo?

PANTALONE: Yes, sir, settled and concluded.

SILVIO: I am amazed that you should have the face to tell me so. You are a man of no reputation; you are no gentleman.

PANTALONE: What is all this? Is that the way you speak to a man of my age?

SILVIO: I don't care how old you are; I have a mind to run you straight through the body.

PANTALONE: I am not a frog, sir, to be spitted. Do you come into my own house to make all this turmoil?

SILVIO: Come outside then.

PANTALONE: I am surprised at you, sir.

SILVIO: Come on, if you are a man of honor.

PANTALONE: I am accustomed to be treated with respect.

SILVIO: You are a low fellow, a coward, and a villain.

PANTALONE: You are a most impertinent young puppy.

SILVIO: I swear to Heaven—

[*lays his hand to his sword*]

PANTALONE: Help! Murder!

[*draws a pistol*]

[*Enter* BEATRICE *with a drawn sword.*]

BEATRICE: [*to* PANTALONE] I am here to defend you.

PANTALONE: My dear son-in-law, I am much obliged to you.

SILVIO: [*to* BEATRICE] You are the very man I want to fight.

BEATRICE: [*aside*] I am in for it now.

SILVIO: [*to* BEATRICE] Come on, sir.

PANTALONE: [*frightened*] My dear son-in-law—

BEATRICE: It is not the first time that I have been in danger.

[*to* SILVIO]

I am not afraid of you.

[*presents sword*]

PANTALONE: Help! Help!

[PANTALONE *runs toward the street.* BEATRICE *and* SILVIO *fight.* SILVIO *falls and drops his sword.* BEATRICE *holds her point to his heart.*]

CLARICE: [*to* BEATRICE] Stop, stop!

BEATRICE: Fair Clarice, at your request I grant Silvio his life, and in consideration of my mercy, I beg you to remember your oath.

[*Exit* BEATRICE.]

CLARICE: Dear Silvio, are you hurt?

SILVIO: Dear Silvio! Faithless deceiver! Dear Silvio! To a lover disdained, to a betrayed husband!

CLARICE: No, Silvio, I do not deserve your reproaches. I love you, I adore you, I am indeed faithful.

SILVIO: Oh, lying jade! Faithful to me, forsooth! You call that fidelity, to plight your troth to another?

CLARICE: I never did so, nor will I ever. I will die rather than desert you.

SILVIO: I heard just now that you have given your oath.

CLARICE: My oath does not bind me to marry him.

SILVIO: Then what did you swear?

CLARICE: Dear Silvio, have mercy on me; I cannot tell you.

SILVIO: Why not?

CLARICE: Because I am sworn to silence.

SILVIO: That proves your guilt.

CLARICE: No, I am innocent.

SILVIO: Innocent people have no secrets.

CLARICE: Indeed I should be guilty if I spoke.

SILVIO: And to whom have you sworn this silence?

CLARICE: To Federigo.

SILVIO: And you will observe it so jealously?

CLARICE: I will observe it, rather than be a perjuress.

SILVIO: And you tell me you do not love him? He's a fool that believes you. I do not believe you, cruel, deceiver! Begone from my sight!

CLARICE: If I did not love you, I should not have run hither in all haste to save your life.

SILVIO: Then I loathe my life, if I must owe it to one so ungrateful.

CLARICE: I love you with all my heart.

SILVIO: I abhor you with all my soul.

CLARICE: I will die, if you are not to be appeased.

SILVIO: I would sooner see you dead than unfaithful.

CLARICE: Then you shall have that satisfaction.
[*Picks up his sword.*]

SILVIO: Yes, that sword should avenge my wrongs.

CLARICE: Are you so cruel to your Clarice?

SILVIO: 'Twas you that taught me cruelty.

CLARICE: Then you desire my death?

SILVIO: I know not what I desire.

CLARICE: I do.
[*points the sword at her breast*]
[*Enter* SMERALDINA.]

SMERALDINA: Stop, stop! What on earth are you doing?
[*takes the sword away from* CLARICE.]
And you, you dog, you would have let her die?
[*to* SILVIO]
Have you the heart of a tiger, of a hyena, of a devil? Look at you, you're a pretty little fellow, that expects ladies to disembowel themselves for you! You are much too kind to him, madam. He doesn't want you any more, I suppose? The man that doesn't want you doesn't deserve you. Let this murderer go to the devil; and you come along with me. There's no shortage of men; I'll promise to find you a dozen before evening.
[*She throws down the sword.* SILVIO *picks it up.*]

CLARICE: [*weeping*] Ungrateful! Can it be that my death should cost you not a single sigh? But I shall die, and die of grief. I *shall* die, and you will be content. But one day you will know that I am innocent, and then, when it is too late, you will be sorry you did not believe me; you will weep for my misfortune and for your own barbarous cruelty.
　　[*Exit* CLARICE.]
SMERALDINA: Here's something I really don't understand. Here's a girl on the point of killing herself, and you sit there looking on, just as if you were at a play.
SILVIO: Nonsense, woman! Do you suppose she really meant to kill herself?
SMERALDINA: How should I know? I know that if I had not arrived in time, she would have been gone, poor thing.
SILVIO: The point was nowhere near her heart.
SMERALDINA: Did you ever hear such a lie? It was just ready to pierce her.
SILVIO: You women always invent things.
SMERALDINA: We should indeed, if we were like you. It's as the old saw says; we get the kicks and you the halfpence. They say women are unfaithful, but men are committing infidelities all day long. People talk about the women, and they never say a word about the men. We get all the blame, and you are allowed to do as you please. Do you know why? Because 'tis the men who have made the laws. If the women had made them, things would be just the other way. If I were a queen, I'd make every man who was unfaithful carry a branch of a tree in his hand, and I know all the towns would look like forests.
　　[*Exit* SMERALDINA.]
SILVIO: Clarice faithless! Clarice a traitress! Her pretense at suicide was a trick to deceive me, to move my compassion. But though fate made me fall before my rival, I will never give up the thought of revenge. That wretch shall die, and my ungrateful Clarice shall see her lover wallowing in his own gore.
　　[*Exit* SILVIO.]

SCENE II———*A Room in* BRIGHELLA'S *Inn with a door at each side and two doors at the back, facing the audience.*

TRUFFALDINO: Just my luck! Two masters and neither of them comes home to dinner. 'Tis two o'clock, and not one to be seen. Sure enough they will both come at the same time, and I shall be in a mess; I shall not be able to wait on both together, and the whole thing will be found out. Hush, here comes one. All the better.
　　[*Enter* FLORINDO.]
FLORINDO: Well, did you find that fellow Pasquale?
TRUFFALDINO: Didn't we say, sir, that I was to look for him after dinner?
FLORINDO: I am impatient to see him.
TRUFFALDINO: You should have come back to dinner a little sooner.
FLORINDO: [*aside*] I can find no way of making certain whether Beatrice is here.
TRUFFALDINO: You told me to go and order dinner, and then you go out. The dinner will have been spoiled.
FLORINDO: I don't want to eat anything.
　　[*aside*]
　　I shall go to the Post; I must go myself; then perhaps I shall find out something.
TRUFFALDINO: You know, sir, at Venice you must eat; if you do not, you will fall sick.
FLORINDO: I must go out; I have important business. If I come back to dinner, well and good; if not, I shall eat in the evening. You can get yourself some food, if you like.
TRUFFALDINO: Very good, sir; just as you please, sir; you're the master.

FLORINDO: This money is heavy; here, put it in my trunk. There is the key.

> [*gives* TRUFFALDINO *the purse and his keys*]

TRUFFALDINO: Certainly, sir; I'll bring the key back at once.

FLORINDO: No, no, you can give it me later. I can't stop. If I do not come back to dinner come to the Piazza; I can't rest till you have found Pasquale.

> [*Exit* FLORINDO.]

TRUFFALDINO: Well, anyway, he said I could get myself some food; we are agreed about that. If he won't eat his dinner, he can leave it. My complexion was not made for fasting. I'll just put away this purse, and then—

> [*Enter* BEATRICE.]

BEATRICE: Oh, Truffaldino!

TRUFFALDINO: [*aside*] The devil!

BEATRICE: Did Signor Pantalone dei Bisognosi give you a purse of a hundred guineas?

TRUFFALDINO: Yes, indeed he did.

BEATRICE: Then why did you not give it to me?

TRUFFALDINO: Was it meant for your honor?

BEATRICE: Was it meant for me? What did he say when he gave you the purse?

TRUFFALDINO: He told me I was to give it to my master.

BEATRICE: Well, and who is your master?

TRUFFALDINO: Your honor.

BEATRICE: Then why do you ask if the purse is mine?

TRUFFALDINO: Then it will be yours.

BEATRICE: Where is it?

TRUFFALDINO: Here, sir.

> [*gives* BEATRICE *the purse*]

BEATRICE: Is the money all there?

TRUFFALDINO: I never touched it, sir.

BEATRICE: [*aside*] I shall count it.

TRUFFALDINO: [*aside*] I made a mistake over the purse; but that puts it straight. I wonder what the other gentleman will say? Oh well, if the money wasn't his, he'll say nothing at all.

BEATRICE: Is the landlord in?

TRUFFALDINO: Yes, sir.

BEATRICE: Tell him I shall have a friend to dinner with me, and he must get it ready as soon as he can.

TRUFFALDINO: What do you want for dinner, sir? How many dishes?

BEATRICE: Oh, Signor Pantalone dei Bisognosi is not a man who expects a great deal. Tell him to give us five or six dishes; something good.

TRUFFALDINO: You leave it all to me, sir?

BEATRICE: Yes, you order it; do the best you can. I am going to fetch the gentleman; he is not far off; see that all is ready by the time we come back.

> [*going*]

TRUFFALDINO: You shall see how they serve you here.

BEATRICE: Look! Take this paper; put it in my trunk. Be careful with it; 'tis a bill of exchange for four thousand crowns.

TRUFFALDINO: Be sure of it, sir, I'll put it away at once.

BEATRICE: See that everything is ready.

> [*aside*]

Poor old Signor Pantalone—I gave him a terrible fright! I must cheer him up a little.

[*Exit* BEATRICE.]

TRUFFALDINO: Now's the time to do myself proud. 'Tis the first time this master of mine has told me to order him a dinner. I'll show him I am a man of good taste. I'll just put away this paper and then—no, I'll put it away afterward; I must not waste time. Ho there! Is nobody at home?

[*calling into the inn*]

Call Master Brighella, tell him I want to talk to him.

[*returning*]

Now with a really good dinner 'tis not the having such and such dishes, but the way it is served. A properly laid table is worth more than a mountain of dishes.

[*Enter* BRIGHELLLA.]

BRIGHELLLA: What is it, Si'or Truffaldin'? What can I do for you?

TRUFFALDINO: My master has got a gentleman to dine with him. He wants a good dinner, and that quickly. Have you got enough in the kitchen?

BRIGHELLLA: I always have plenty of everything. In half an hour I can put on any sort of dinner you like.

TRUFFALDINO: Very well, then. Tell me what you can give us.

BRIGHELLLA: For two persons, we will have two courses of four dishes each; will that do?

TRUFFALDINO: He said five or six dishes—better say six or eight. That will do. What will you give us?

BRIGHELLLA: For the first course, I shall give you soup, fried, boiled, and a fricandeau.

TRUFFALDINO: Three of the dishes I know, but I do not know the last.

BRIGHELLLA: 'Tis a French dish—a ragout—very tasty indeed.

TRUFFALDINO: Very well, that will do for the first course; now the second.

BRIGHELLLA: For the second course the roast, the salad, a meat pie—and a trifle.

TRUFFALDINO: [*indignant*] What's that? A trifle? My master and his guest are gentlemen of substance; they won't be satisfied with a mere trifle. A trifle indeed!

BRIGHELLLA: You don't understand. I said

[*impressively*]

a trifle! That's an English dish, a pudding, my very own speciality; there's not another man in Venice knows how to make it!

TRUFFALDINO: [*nonchalantly*] Oh well, I dare say it will do. But how are you going to arrange the table?

BRIGHELLLA: Oh, that's easy enough. The waiter will see to that.

TRUFFALDINO: No, my good friend, laying the table is a very important matter; that's the first thing about a dinner, to have the table properly laid.

BRIGHELLLA: Well, you might put the soup here, the fried there, there the boiled and here the fricandeau.

[*makes an imaginary arrangement*]

TRUFFALDINO: I don't like that. Don't you put something in the middle?

BRIGHELLLA: Then we should want five dishes.

TRUFFALDINO: Good, then let us have five.

BRIGHELLLA: We can put the gravy in the middle.

TRUFFALDINO: No, no, friend, you know nothing about laying a table; you can't put the gravy in the middle; soup always goes in the middle.

BRIGHELLLA: Then the meat on one side, and the gravy on the other.

TRUFFALDINO: Lord, lord, that won't do at all. You innkeepers may know how to cook, but you have no idea of butlering. Now I'll show you.

[*kneels down on one knee and points to the floor*]

Suppose this is the table. Now you look how we arrange the five dishes. Like this:

here in the middle the soup.

[*He tears off a piece of the bill of exchange and puts in on the floor to represent a dish.*]

Now the boiled meat.

[*same business*]

Here we put the fried opposite,

[*same business*]

here the gravy and here that—what-d'ye-call-it. There now! Won't that look fine?

BRIGHELLLA: H'm, 'twill do; but you have put the gravy too far away from the meat.

TRUFFALDINO: Very well, we must see if we can't put it a little nearer.

[*Enter* BEATRICE *and* PANTALONE.]

BEATRICE: What are you doing on your knees?

TRUFFALDINO: [*stands up*] I was just planning how to have the table laid.

BEATRICE: What is that paper?

TRUFFALDINO: [*aside*] The devil! The letter that he gave me!

BEATRICE: That is my bill of exchange.

TRUFFALDINO: I am very sorry, sir; I will stick it together again.

BEATRICE: You rascal! Is that the way you look after my things? Things of such value too! You deserve a good thrashing. What say you, Signor Pantalone? Did you ever see such a piece of folly?

PANTALONE: To tell the truth, I cannot help laughing. 'Twould be a serious matter if it could not be mended, but I will write you out another and then all will be in order.

BEATRICE: But just think if the bill had been made out not here but in some place a long way off!

[*to* TRUFFALDINO]

You ignorant fool!

TRUFFALDINO: This has all come about because Brighella doesn't know how to lay a table.

BRIGHELLLA: He finds fault with everything I do.

TRUFFALDINO: I am a man that knows his business.

BEATRICE: [*to* TRUFFALDINO] Go away.

TRUFFALDINO: Things must be done properly.

BEATRICE: Be off, I tell you.

TRUFFALDINO: In the matter of pantry work I won't give way to the first butler in the land.

[*Exit* TRUFFALDINO.]

BRIGHELLLA: I don't understand that fellow; sometimes he is a knave and sometimes a fool.

BEATRICE: This tomfoolery is all put on. Well, is dinner ready?

BRIGHELLLA: If you will have five dishes to each course, 'twill take a little time.

PANTALONE: What's this about courses of five dishes? We'll take pot luck—a risotto, a couple of other dishes, and I shall be most obliged to you. My tastes are simple.

BEATRICE: [*to* BRIGHELLLA] You hear that? That will do nicely.

BRIGHELLLA: Very good, sir; but will you please to tell me if there might be anything you would particularly fancy?

PANTALONE: I should like some rissoles if you have them; my teeth are not very good nowadays.

BEATRICE: You hear? Rissoles.

BRIGHELLLA: Very good, sir. If you will sit down here for a moment, gentlemen, dinner will be ready directly.

BEATRICE: Tell Truffaldino to come and wait on us.

BRIGHELLLA: I'll tell him, sir.

[*Exit* BRIGHELLLA.]

BEATRICE: Signor Pantalone, I fear you will indeed have to be content with pot luck.

PANTALONE: My dear sir, I am overcome with all the attention you show me; in fact you are doing for me what I ought to be doing for you. But, you see, I have that girl of mine at home, and until everything is finally settled it would not be proper for you to be together. So I accept your kind hospitality to raise my spirits a little; indeed I still feel quite upset. Had it not been for you, that young scoundrel would have done for me.

BEATRICE: I am glad that I arrived in time.

> [WAITERS *enter from the kitchen and carry glasses, wine, bread, etc., into the room where* BEATRICE *and* PANTALONE *are to dine.*]

PANTALONE: They are very quick about their business here.

BEATRICE: Brighella is a smart fellow. He was servant to a great nobleman at Turin, and still wears his livery.

PANTALONE: There's a very good tavern on the other side of the Grand Canal opposite the Rialto where you can eat very well; I have often been there with various good friends of mine, very sound men, too; I often think of that place. They had some wonderful Burgundy wine there to—'twas a wine for the gods.

BEATRICE: There's nothing one enjoys more than good wine in good company.

PANTALONE: Good company! Ah, if you had known them! That was good company! Good honest fellows, with many a good story to tell. God bless them. Seven or eight of them there were, and there wasn't the like of them in all the world.

> [*The* WAITERS *come out of the room and return to the kitchen.*]

BEATRICE: You often had a merry time with these gentlemen, eh?

PANTALONE: And I hope I may live to have many more.

> [*Enter* TRUFFALDINO *carrying the soup tureen.*]

TRUFFALDINO: [*to* BEATRICE] Dinner is ready for you in that room, sir.

BEATRICE: Go and put the soup on the table.

TRUFFALDINO: [*makes a bow*] After you, sir.

PANTALONE: A queer fellow, that servant of yours.

> [*goes in*]

BEATRICE: [*to* TRUFFALDINO] I want less wit and more attention.

> [*goes in*]

TRUFFALDINO: Call that a dinner! One dish at a time! They have money to spend, but they get nothing good for it. I wonder if this soup is worth eating; I'll try it.

> [*takes a spoon out of his pocket and tastes the soup*]

I always carry my weapons about me. Not bad; it might be worse.

> [*goes into room with soup*]
> [*Enter* FIRST WAITER *with a dish.*]

FIRST WAITER: When is that man coming to take the dishes?

TRUFFALDINO: [*reentering*] Here I am, friend. What have you got for me?

FIRST WAITER: Here's the boiled meat. There's another dish to follow.

> [*Exit* FIRST WAITER.]

TRUFFALDINO: Mutton? Or veal? Mutton, I think. Let's taste it.

> [*tastes*]

No, 'tis neither mutton nor veal; 'tis lamb, and very good, too.

> [*goes toward* BEATRICE'S *room*]
> [*Enter* FLORINDO.]

FLORINDO: Where are you going?

TRUFFALDINO: [*aside*] Oh dear, oh dear!

FLORINDO: What are you doing with that dish?

TRUFFALDINO: I was just putting it on the table, sir.

FLORINDO: For whom?

TRUFFALDINO: For you, sir.

FLORINDO: Why do you serve dinner before I come in?

TRUFFALDINO: I saw you from the window.

    [*aside*]

I must find some excuse.

FLORINDO: And you begin with boiled meat instead of soup?

TRUFFALDINO: You must know, sir, at Venice soup is always taken last.

FLORINDO: I have other habits. I want my soup. Take that back to the kitchen.

TRUFFALDINO: Yes, sir, as you wish, sir.

FLORINDO: Make haste; afterward I want to have a nap.

TRUFFALDINO: Yes, sir.

    [*makes as if going to the kitchen*]

FLORINDO: [*aside*] Shall I never find Beatrice again?

    [FLORINDO *goes into the other room. As soon as he is in,* TRUFFALDINO *quickly takes the dish in to* BEATRICE. *Enter* FIRST WAITER *with another dish.* FLORINDO *calls from his room.*]

FLORINDO: Truffaldino! Truffaldino! Am I always to be kept waiting?

TRUFFALDINO: [*coming out of* BEATRICE'S *room*] Coming, sir.

    [*to* FIRST WAITER]

Quick, go and lay the table in that other room; the other gentleman has arrived; bring the soup at once.

FIRST WAITER: Directly.

    [*Exit* FIRST WAITER.]

TRUFFALDINO: What may this dish be? This must be the "fricandeau."

    [*tastes it*]

That's good, upon my word.

    [*takes it in to* BEATRICE]

    [WAITERS *enter and carry glasses, wine, bread, etc., into* FLORINDO'S *room.*]

TRUFFALDINO: [*to* WAITERS] Good lads, that's right.

    [*aside*]

They're as lively as kittens. Well, if I can manage to wait at table on two masters at once, 'twill be a great accomplishment indeed.

    [*The* WAITERS *come back out of* FLORINDO'S *room and go toward the kitchen.*]

TRUFFALDINO: Hurry up, lads, the soup!

FIRST WAITER: You look after your own table; we'll take care of this one.

    [*Exeunt* WAITERS.]

TRUFFALDINO: I want to look after both, if I can.

    [*Reenter* FIRST WAITER *with* FLORINDO'S *soup.*]

TRUFFALDINO: Here, give me that; I'll take it. Go and get the stuff for the other room.

    [*takes soup from* FIRST WAITER *and carries it into* FLORINDO'S *room*]

FIRST WAITER: That's a strange fellow. He wants to wait on everyone. Let him. They will have to give me my tip all the same.

    [TRUFFALDINO *comes out of* FLORINDO'S *room.*]

BEATRICE: [*calling from her room*] Truffaldino!

FIRST WAITER: [*to* TRUFFALDINO] Your master's calling.

TRUFFALDINO: Coming, sir.

    [*goes into* BEATRICE'S *room*]

    [SECOND WAITER *brings the boiled meat for* FLORINDO. TRUFFALDINO *brings the dirty plates out of* BEATRICE'S *room.*]

TRUFFALDINO: Here, give it to me.

[*Exit* SECOND WAITER.]

FLORINDO: [*calls*] Truffaldino!

TRUFFALDINO: [*wishes to take the meat from* WAITER] Give it to me.

FIRST WAITER: No, I'm taking this.

TRUFFALDINO: Didn't you hear him call for me?

[*Takes meat from him and carries it in to* FLORINDO.]

FIRST WAITER: Well, that's fine! He wants to do everything.

[SECOND WAITER *brings in a dish of rissoles, gives it to the* FIRST WAITER *and exit.*]

I would take this in myself, but I don't want to have words with that fellow.

[*Reenter* TRUFFALDINO *from* FLORINDO'S *room with dirty plates.*]

Here, master Jack-of-all-trades; take these rissoles to your master.

TRUFFALDINO: [*takes dish*] Rissoles?

FIRST WAITER: Yes, the rissoles he ordered.

[*Exit* FIRST WAITER.]

TRUFFALDINO: Oh, fine! Now which table are these to go to? I wonder which the devil of my two masters can have ordered them? If I go to the kitchen and ask, they'll begin to suspect; if I make a mistake and carry them to the one who didn't order them, then the other will ask for them and I shall be found out. I know what I'll do; I'll divide them on two plates, take half to each, and then I shall see who ordered them.

[*takes plates and divides the rissoles*]

That's four and that's four. There's one over. Who's to have that? We mustn't cause ill-feeling; I'll eat that one myself.

[*eats it*]

Now. We'll take the rissoles to this gentleman.

[TRUFFALDINO *puts one plate of rissoles on the floor and takes the other in to* BEATRICE. FIRST WAITER *enters with an English pudding* (*trifle*).]

FIRST WAITER: Truffaldino!

TRUFFALDINO: [*comes out of* BEATRICE'S *room*] Coming!

FIRST WAITER: Take this pudding—

TRUFFALDINO: Wait a moment, I'm coming.

[*Takes the other dish of rissoles and is going to* FLORINDO'S *room.*]

FIRST WAITER: That's not right, the rissoles belong there.

TRUFFALDINO: I know they do, sir; I have carried them there; and my master sends these four as a courtesy to this gentleman.

[*Goes into* FLORINDO'S *room.*]

FIRST WAITER: I see, they know each other—friends, you might say? They might as well have dined together.

TRUFFALDINO: [*reentering*] What's this affair?

FIRST WAITER: That's an English pudding.

TRUFFALDINO: Who is it for?

FIRST WAITER: For your master.

[*Exit* FIRST WAITER.]

TRUFFALDINO: What the devil is this "pudding"? It smells delicious, and looks like polenta. Oh! If it is polenta, that would be good indeed. I'll taste it.

[*brings a fork out of his pocket and tries the pudding*]

It's not polenta, but it's very much like it.

[*eats*]

Much better than polenta.

[*goes on eating*]

BEATRICE: [*calling*] Truffaldino!

TRUFFALDINO: [*with mouth full*] Coming, sir.

FLORINDO: [*calling*] Truffaldino!

TRUFFALDINO: [*with mouth full*] Coming, sir.

[*to himself*]

Oh what wonderful stuff! Just another mouthful and then I'll go.

[*goes on eating*]

[BEATRICE *comes out of her room, sees* TRUFFALDINO *eating, kicks him, and says:*]

BEATRICE: You come and wait on me.

[*She goes back to her room.*]

Truffaldino!

TRUFFALDINO: Coming!

[TRUFFALDINO *puts the pudding on the floor and goes into* BEATRICE'S *room.* FLORINDO *comes out of his.*]

FLORINDO: [*calling*] Truffaldino! Where the devil is he?

[TRUFFALDINO *comes out of* BEATRICE'S *room.*]

TRUFFALDINO: Here, sir.

[*seeing* FLORINDO]

FLORINDO: What are you doing? Where have you been?

TRUFFALDINO: I just went to fetch the next course, sir.

FLORINDO: Is there anything more to eat?

TRUFFALDINO: I'll go and see.

FLORINDO: Make haste, I tell you, because I want to have a nap afterward.

[*goes back into his room*]

TRUFFALDINO: Very good, sir.

[*calling*]

Waiter, is there anything more to come?

[*aside*]

I'll put this pudding aside for myself.

[*hides it*]

[*Enter* FIRST WAITER *with dish.*]

FIRST WAITER: Here's the roast.

TRUFFALDINO: [*takes the roast*] Quick, the dessert!

FIRST WAITER: Lord, what a fluster! In a minute.

[*Exit* FIRST WAITER.]

TRUFFALDINO: I'll take the roast to this gentleman.

[*takes it to* FLORINDO]

[*Reenter* FIRST WAITER.]

FIRST WAITER: [*with plate of fruit*] Here's the dessert; where are you?

TRUFFALDINO: [*reentering from* FLORINDO'S *room*] Here.

FIRST WAITER: [*gives him the fruit*] There. Anything more?

TRUFFALDINO: Wait.

[*takes the dessert to* BEATRICE]

FIRST WAITER: He jumps about here and there like the devil himself.

TRUFFALDINO: [*reentering*] That will do. Nobody wants any more.

FIRST WAITER: I'm glad to hear it.

TRUFFALDINO: And now lay the table for me.

FIRST WAITER: In a moment.

[*Exit* FIRST WAITER.]

TRUFFALDINO: Now for my pudding! Hurrah! I've got through it all, they are all content, they want nothing more, they've had a very good dinner. I have waited at table on two masters at once, and neither of 'em knew anything about the other. But if I have waited for two, now I am going to eat for four.

SCENE III———*A Street with* BRIGHELLA'S *Inn.*

[*Enter* SMERALDINA.]

SMERALDINA: A very proper sort of young lady my mistress is! To send me all alone with a letter to a tavern, a young girl like me! Waiting on a woman in love is a sad business. This young lady of mine does a thousand crazy things, and what I cannot understand is this—if she is so much in love with Signor Silvio as to be ready to disembowel herself for him, why does she send letters to another gentleman? One for summer and one for winter, I suppose! Well, there it is!

I am not going inside that tavern. I'll call; somebody will come out. Hey there! Anyone at home?

[FIRST WAITER *comes out of the inn.*]

FIRST WAITER: Now, young woman, what do you want?

SMERALDINA: [*aside*] I feel thoroughly ashamed.

[*to* WAITER]

Tell me—a certain Signor Federigo Rasponi lodges here, does he not?

FIRST WAITER: Yes, indeed. He has just this moment finished dinner.

SMERALDINA: I have something to say to him.

FIRST WAITER: A message? You can come inside.

SMERALDINA: And what sort of a girl do you take me for? I am the waiting maid of the lady he is to marry.

FIRST WAITER: [*more politely*] Well then, pray step this way.

SMERALDINA: Oh, but I don't like to go in there.

FIRST WAITER: Do you expect me to bring him out into the street for you? That would not be at all the right thing; more especially as he has Signor Pantalone dei Bisognosi with him.

SMERALDINA: What, my master? Worse and worse! I'll not come in.

FIRST WAITER: I can send his servant, if you like.

SMERALDINA: The little dark man?

FIRST WAITER: Exactly so.

SMERALDINA: Yes, do send him.

FIRST WAITER: [*aside*] I understand. She fancies the little dark man, and is ashamed to come inside. She is not ashamed to be seen with him in the middle of the street.

[*goes in*]

SMERALDINA: If the master sees me, whatever shall I say? I'll tell him I came to look for him; that will do nicely. I'm never short of an answer.

[*Enter* TRUFFALDINO *with a glass, a napkin, and a bottle in his hand.*]

TRUFFALDINO: Who sent for me?

SMERALDINA: I did, sir. I ask pardon if I have troubled you.

TRUFFALDINO: Not a bit of it. I am here to receive your commands.

SMERALDINA: I fear I must have taken you from your dinner.

TRUFFALDINO: I was having dinner, but I can go back to it.

SMERALDINA: I am truly sorry.

TRUFFALDINO: I am delighted. The fact is, I have had my bellyful, and your bright eyes are just the right thing to make me digest it.

SMERALDINA: [*aside*] Very gallant!

TRUFFALDINO: I'll just set down this bottle, and then I'm with you, my dear.

SMERALDINA: [*aside*] He called me "my dear"!

[*to* TRUFFALDINO]

My mistress sends this letter to Signor Federigo Rasponi; I do not like to come into the tavern, so I thought I might put you to this trouble, as you are his man.

TRUFFALDINO: I'll take it with pleasure; but first, you must know that I have a message for you.

SMERALDINA: From whom?

TRUFFALDINO: From a very honest man. Tell me, are you acquainted with one Truffaldin' Battocchio?

SMERALDINA: I think I have heard him spoken of, but I am not sure.

[*aside*]

It must be himself.

TRUFFALDINO: He's a good-looking man; short, thickset, with plenty of wit to his talk. Understands butlering too—

SMERALDINA: I don't know him from Adam.

TRUFFALDINO: Yes, you do; and what's more, he's in love with you.

SMERALDINA: Oh! You are making fun of me.

TRUFFALDINO: And if he could only have just a little hope that his affections were returned, he would make himself known.

SMERALDINA: Well, sir, if I were to see him, and he took my fancy, it might possibly be that I should return his affection.

TRUFFALDINO: Shall I show him to you?

SMERALDINA: I should like to see him.

TRUFFALDINO: Just a moment.

[*goes into the inn*]

SMERALDINA: Then 'tis not he.

[TRUFFALDINO *comes out of the inn, makes low bows to* SMERALDINA, *passes close to her, sighs, and goes back into the inn.*]

SMERALDINA: I do not understand this play-acting.

TRUFFALDINO: [*reentering*] Did you see him?

SMERALDINA: See whom?

TRUFFALDINO: The man who is in love with your beauty.

SMERALDINA: I saw no one but you.

TRUFFALDINO: [*sighs*] Well!

SMERALDINA: It is you, then, who profess to be in love with me?

TRUFFALDINO: It is.

[*sighs*]

SMERALDINA: Why did you not say so before?

TRUFFALDINO: Because I am rather shy.

SMERALDINA: [*aside*] He would make a stone fall in love with him.

TRUFFALDINO: Well, and what do you say?

SMERALDINA: I say—

TRUFFALDINO: Come, tell me.

SMERALDINA: Oh—I am rather shy too.

TRUFFALDINO: Then if we were joined up, 'twould be a marriage of two people who are rather shy.

SMERALDINA: I must say, you are just my fancy.

TRUFFALDINO: Are you a maid?

SMERALDINA: Need you ask?

TRUFFALDINO: I suppose that means "certainly not."

SMERALDINA: On the contrary, it means "certainly I am."

TRUFFALDINO: I am a bachelor too.

SMERALDINA: I could have been married fifty times, but I never found the man I really fancied.

TRUFFALDINO: Do you think there is any hope for me?

SMERALDINA: Well—to tell the truth—really—I must say—there's a—something about you—No, I won't say another word.

TRUFFALDINO: If somebody wanted to marry you, what would he have to do?

SMERALDINA: I have neither father nor mother. He would have to speak to my master, or to my mistress.

TRUFFALDINO: And if I speak to them, what will they say?

SMERALDINA: They will say, that if I am content—

TRUFFALDINO: And what will you say?

SMERALDINA: I shall say—that if they are content too—

TRUFFALDINO: That will do. We shall all be content. Give me the letter and when I bring you back the answer, we will have a talk.

SMERALDINA: Here's the letter.

TRUFFALDINO: Do you know what is in it?

SMERALDINA: No—if you only knew how curious I am to know!

TRUFFALDINO: I hope it is not a disdainful letter, or I shall get my face spoiled.

SMERALDINA: Who knows? It can't be a love letter.

TRUFFALDINO: I don't want to get into trouble. If I don't know what is in the letter, I am not going to take it.

SMERALDINA: We could open it—but how are we to seal it again?

TRUFFALDINO: Leave it to me; sealing letters is just my job. No one will ever know anything.

SMERALDINA: Then let us open it.

TRUFFALDINO: Can you read?

SMERALDINA: A little. But you can read quite well, I'm sure.

TRUFFALDINO: Yes, I too can read just a little.

SMERALDINA: Then let us hear.

TRUFFALDINO: We must open it cleanly.

      [*tears off a piece*]

SMERALDINA: Oh! What have you done?

TRUFFALDINO: Nothing. I've a secret way to mend it. Here it is, open.

SMERALDINA: Quick, read it.

TRUFFALDINO: *You* read it. You will know your young lady's handwriting better than I do.

SMERALDINA: [*looking at the letter*] Really, I can't make out a word.

TRUFFALDINO: [*same business*] Nor I neither.

SMERALDINA: Then what was the good of opening it?

TRUFFALDINO: [*takes the letter*] Wait; let me think; I can make out some of it.

SMERALDINA: Oh I know some of the letters too.

TRUFFALDINO: Let us try one by one. Isn't that an M?

SMERALDINA: No! That's an R!

TRUFFALDINO: Between R and M there is very little difference.

SMERALDINA: *Ri, ri, o.* No, no: keep quiet; I think it *is* an M—*Mi, mi, o—mio*!

TRUFFALDINO: It's not *mio*, it's *mia*.

SMERALDINA: But it is, there's the hook—

TRUFFALDINO: That proves it is *mia*.
  [BEATRICE *comes out of the inn with* PANTALONE.]
PANTALONE: [*to* SMERALDINA] What are you doing here?
SMERALDINA: [*frightened*] Nothing sir; I came to look for you.
PANTALONE: [*to* SMERALDINA] What do you want with me?
SMERALDINA: The mistress wants you, sir.
BEATRICE: [*to* TRUFFALDINO] What is this paper?
TRUFFALDINO: [*frightened*] Nothing, just a bit of paper—
BEATRICE: Let me see.
TRUFFALDINO: [*gives paper, trembling*] Yes, sir.
BEATRICE: What? This is a letter addressed to me. Villain, will you open all my letters?
TRUFFALDINO: I know nothing about it, sir—
BEATRICE: Look, Signor Pantalone, here is a letter from Signora Clarice, in which she tells
  me of Silvio's insane jealousy—and this rascal has the impudence to open it!
PANTALONE: [*to* SMERALDINA] And you helped him to do so?
SMERALDINA: I know nothing about it, sir.
BEATRICE: Who opened this letter?
TRUFFALDINO: Not I.
SMERALDINA: Nor I.
PANTALONE: Well, who brought it?
SMERALDINA: Truffaldino brought it to his master.
TRUFFALDINO: And Smeraldina brought it to Truffaldino.
SMERALDINA: [*aside*] Sneak! I don't like you any more.
PANTALONE: You meddlesome little hussy, so you are the cause of all this trouble, are you?
  I've a good mind to smack your face.
SMERALDINA: I've never had my face smacked by any man; I'm surprised at you.
PANTALONE: [*coming near her*] Is that the way you answer me?
SMERALDINA: You won't catch me. You're too rheumatic; you can't run.
  [*Exit running.*]
PANTALONE: You saucy minx, I'll show you if I can run; I'll catch you.
  [*runs after her*]
TRUFFALDINO: [*aside*] If I only knew how to get out of this!
BEATRICE: [*looking at the letter, aside*] Poor Clarice! She is in despair over Silvio's jealousy;
  'twill be best for me to discover myself and set her mind at rest.
TRUFFALDINO: [*tries to steal away quietly*] I don't think he is looking. I'll try to get away.
BEATRICE: Where are you off to?
TRUFFALDINO: Nowhere.
  [*stops*]
BEATRICE: Why did you open this letter?
TRUFFALDINO: It was Smeraldina; I had nothing to do with it.
BEATRICE: Smeraldina, forsooth! You did it, you rascal. One and one make two. That's the
  second letter of mine you have opened today. Come here.
TRUFFALDINO: [*approaching timidly*] Oh, for mercy's sake, sir—
BEATRICE: Come here, I say.
TRUFFALDINO: [*same business*] Oh, for the love of Heaven—
  [BEATRICE *takes the stick which* TRUFFALDINO *has at his flank (i.e., Harlequin's
  wooden sword or baton) and beats him well, she standing with her back to the
  inn.* FLORINDO *appears at the window and sees the beating.*]
FLORINDO: What's this? Beating my servant?
  [*leaves window*]

TRUFFALDINO: Stop, stop, sir, for pity's sake.

BEATRICE: Take that, rascal, and learn to open my letters.

> [*throws stick on the ground, and exit to street*]

TRUFFALDINO: [*after* BEATRICE *has gone*] My blood! My body! Is that the way to treat a man of my sort? Beat a man like me? If a servant is no good, you can send him away, but you don't beat him.

> [FLORINDO *comes out, unseen by* TRUFFALDINO.]

FLORINDO: What's that?

TRUFFALDINO: [*seeing* FLORINDO] Oh! I said people had no business to beat other people's servants like that. This is an insult to my master.

> [*looking toward direction of* BEATRICE'S *exit*]

FLORINDO: Yes, 'tis an affront put upon *me*. Who was it gave you a thrashing?

TRUFFALDINO: I couldn't say, sir; I do not know him.

FLORINDO: Why did he thrash you?

TRUFFALDINO: Because I—I spat on his shoe.

FLORINDO: And you let yourself be beaten like that? Did nothing? Made no attempt to defend yourself? And you expose your master to insult, with perhaps serious consequences? Ass! Poltroon!

> [*picks up the stick*]

Since you enjoy being thrashed, I'll give you your pleasure, I'll thrash you myself as well.

> [*thrashes him and exit into inn*]

TRUFFALDINO: Well, there's no mistake about my being the servant of two masters. They have both paid me my wages.

> [*Exit into the inn.*]

ACT III

SCENE I———*A Room in* BRIGHELLA'S *inn.*

TRUFFALDINO: I don't care that for my beating! I have eaten well, I've dined well, and this evening I shall sup still better; and as long as I can serve two masters, there's this at least, that I draw double wages.

> And now what's to be done? Master number one is out of doors, master number two is fast asleep; why, it's just the moment to give those clothes an airing—take them out of the trunks and see if there's anything wants doing. Here are the keys. This room will do nicely. I'll get the trunks out and make a proper job of it. I must have someone to help me though.
>
> [*calls*]
>
> Waiter!
>
> [*Enter* WAITERS.]

FIRST WAITER: What do you want?

TRUFFALDINO: I want you to lend a hand to bring some trunks out of those rooms, to give the clothes an airing.

FIRST WAITER: [*to* SECOND WAITER] Go and help him.

TRUFFALDINO: [*to* SECOND WAITER] Come along, and I'll give you a good handful of what my masters gave me.

> [TRUFFALDINO *and* SECOND WAITER *go into* BEATRICE'S *room.*]

FIRST WAITER: He looks like a rare good servant—quick, ready, and most attentive; but I'll warrant he has his faults somewhere. I've been a servant myself and I know the ropes. Nobody does anything just for love. Whatever they do, either they are robbing their masters or they are throwing dust in their eyes.

[TRUFFALDINO *comes out of the room with the* SECOND WAITER *carrying a trunk.*]

TRUFFALDINO: Gently! Let's put it down here.

[*They put the trunk in the middle of the room.*]

Now let's fetch the other. But quietly, for my master is in there asleep.

[TRUFFALDINO *and* SECOND WAITER *go into* FLORINDO'S *room.*]

FIRST WAITER: Either he's a real first-rate fellow, or he's a real knave; I never saw anybody wait on two gentlemen at once like that. I shall just keep my eyes open; maybe, under the pretense of waiting on two gentlemen at once, he means to rob them both.

[TRUFFALDINO *and* SECOND WAITER *reenter with the other trunk.*]

TRUFFALDINO: And we'll put this one here.

[*They put it down a little way off from the other.*]

[*to* SECOND WAITER]

There! You can run along now, if you like. I don't want anything more.

FIRST WAITER: [*to* SECOND WAITER] Go on; off with you to the kitchen.

[Exit SECOND WAITER.]

[*to* TRUFFALDINO]

Can I help you?

TRUFFALDINO: No, thank you; I can do my work myself.

FIRST WAITER: I must say, you are a giant for work; it's a marvel to me how you get through it all.

[*Exit* FIRST WAITER.]

TRUFFALDINO: Now I'm going to do my work properly, in peace and quiet, with no one to worry me.

[*takes a key out of his pocket*]

Now which key is this, I wonder? Which trunk does it fit? Let's try.

[*opens one trunk*]

I guessed right at once. I'm the cleverest man on earth. And this other will open t'other trunk.

[*takes out second key and opens second trunk*]

Now they are both open. Let's take everything out.

[*He takes all the clothes out of both trunks and puts them on the table. In each trunk there must be a black suit, books and papers, and anything else ad lib.*]

I'll just see if there is anything in the pockets. You never know, sometimes they leave biscuits or sweets in them.

[*searches the pockets of* BEATRICE'S *suit and finds a portrait*]

My word, what a pretty picture! There's a handsome man! Who can it be? A queer thing, I seem to know him, but yet I can't remember. He is just the least little bit like my other master; but no, *he* never wears clothes like that, nor that wig neither.

[FLORINDO *calls from his room.*]

FLORINDO: Truffaldino!

TRUFFALDINO: Oh, plague take him! He was woken up. If the devil tempts him to come out and he sees this other trunk, he'll want to know—quick, quick—I'll lock it up and say I don't know whose it is.

[*begins putting clothes in again*]

FLORINDO: [*calling*] Truffaldino!

TRUFFALDINO: Coming, sir!

[*aside*]

I must put these things away first. But I can't remember which trunk this coat came from, nor these papers neither.

FLORINDO: [*calling*] Come here, I say; or must I fetch a stick to you?

TRUFFALDINO: In a minute, sir.

> [*aside*]

Quick, before he comes! I'll put all straight when he goes out.

> [*Stuffs the things into the trunks anyhow and locks them.* FLORINDO *comes out in a dressing gown.*]

FLORINDO: What the devil are you doing?

TRUFFALDINO: Pray, sir, didn't you tell me to give your clothes an airing? I was just about to do it here.

FLORINDO: And this other trunk, whose is that?

TRUFFALDINO: I couldn't say, sir; 'twill belong to some other gentleman.

FLORINDO: Give me my black coat.

TRUFFALDINO: Very good, sir.

> [*Opens* FLORINDO'S *trunk and gives him the black suit.* FLORINDO *takes off his dressing gown with* TRUFFALDINO'S *help and puts on the black coat, then puts his hand into the pockets and finds the portrait.*]

FLORINDO: [*much surprised*] What is this?

TRUFFALDINO: [*aside*] Oh Lord, I've made a mistake. I ought to have put it into the other gentleman's pocket. 'Tis the color made me go wrong.

FLORINDO: [*aside*] Heavens! There can be no mistake. This is my own portrait; the one I gave to my beloved Beatrice.

> [*to* TRUFFALDINO]

Tell me, how ever did this portrait come to be in the pocket of my coat? It wasn't there before.

TRUFFALDINO: [*aside*] Now what's the answer to that? I don't know. Let me think—

FLORINDO: Come on, out with it, answer me. How did this portrait come to be in my pocket?

TRUFFALDINO: Sir, be kind and forgive me for taking a liberty. The portrait belongs to me, and I hid it there for safety, for fear I might lose it.

FLORINDO: How did you come by this portrait?

TRUFFALDINO: My master left it to me.

FLORINDO: Left it to you?

TRUFFALDINO: Yes, sir; I had a master who died, and he left me a few trifles which I sold, all except this portrait, sir.

FLORINDO: Great heavens! And how long is it since this master of yours died?

TRUFFALDINO: 'Twill be just about a week ago, sir.

> [*aside*]

I say the first thing that comes into my head.

FLORINDO: What was your master's name?

TRUFFALDINO: I do not know, sir; he lived incognito.

FLORINDO: Incognito? How long were you in his service?

TRUFFALDINO: Only a short time, sir; ten or twelve days.

FLORINDO: [*aside*] Heavens! More and more do I fear that it was Beatrice. She escaped in man's dress; she concealed her name—Oh, wretched me, if it be true!

TRUFFALDINO: [*aside*] As he believes it all, I may as well go on with the fairy tale.

FLORINDO: [*despairingly*] Tell me, was your master young?

TRUFFALDINO: Yes, sir, quite a young gentleman.

FLORINDO: Without a beard?

TRUFFALDINO: Without a beard, sir.

FLORINDO: [*aside, with a sigh*] 'Twas she, doubtless.

TRUFFALDINO: [*aside*] I hope I'm not in for another thrashing.

FLORINDO: At least, you know where your late master came from?

TRUFFALDINO: I did know, sir, but I can't now call it to mind.

FLORINDO: Was it from Turin?

TRUFFALDINO: Turin it was, sir.

FLORINDO: [*aside*] Every word he speaks is a sword thrust in my heart.

> [*to* TRUFFALDINO]

Tell me again, this young gentleman from Turin, is he really dead?

TRUFFALDINO: He is dead indeed, sir.

FLORINDO: Of what did he die?

TRUFFALDINO: He met with an accident, and that was the end of him.

> [*aside*]

That seems to be the best way out.

FLORINDO: Where was he buried?

TRUFFALDINO: [*aside*] I wasn't ready for that one.

> [*to* FLORINDO]

He wasn't buried, sir.

FLORINDO: What!

TRUFFALDINO: No, sir, another servant from the same place got permission to have him put into a coffin and sent home, sir.

FLORINDO: And was it, by any chance, the same servant who got you to fetch his letters for him from the Post this morning?

TRUFFALDINO: Exactly so, sir; it was Pasqual'.

FLORINDO: [*aside*] Then all hope is lost. Beatrice is dead. Unhappy Beatrice! The discomforts of the journey and the tortures of her heart must have killed her. Oh! I can no longer endure the agony of my grief!

> [*Exit into his room.*]

TRUFFALDINO: That portrait has touched him in the guts. He must have known the gentleman. Well, I had better take the trunks back to the rooms again, or I shall be in for more trouble of the same sort. Oh dear! Here comes my other master.

> [*Enter* BEATRICE *and* PANTALONE.]

BEATRICE: I assure you, Signor Pantalone, the last consignment of mirrors and wax candles has been put down twice over.

PANTALONE: Maybe my young men have made a mistake. We will go through the books again, and then we shall find out exactly how things stand.

BEATRICE: I too have a list copied from my own books. We will compare them. Perhaps that may decide the point either in your favor or mine. Truffaldino!

TRUFFALDINO: Here, sir.

BEATRICE: Have you the key of my trunk?

TRUFFALDINO: Yes, sir; here it is.

BEATRICE: Why have you brought my trunk in here?

TRUFFALDINO: To air your clothes, sir.

BEATRICE: Have you aired them?

TRUFFALDINO: I have, sir.

BEATRICE: Open the trunk and give me—Whose is that other trunk?

TRUFFALDINO: It belongs to another gentleman who has just come.

BEATRICE: Give me the memorandum book which you will find there.

TRUFFALDINO: Yes, sir.

> [*aside*]

The Lord help me this time!

[*opens trunk and looks for the book*]

PANTALONE: As I say, they may have made a mistake; of course, if there is a mistake, you will not have to pay.

BEATRICE: We may find that all is in order; we shall see.

TRUFFALDINO: Is this the book, sir?

[*holding out a book to* BEATRICE]

BEATRICE: I expect so.

[*takes the book without looking carefully and opens it*]

No, this is not it—Whose is this book?

TRUFFALDINO: [*aside*] I've done it now!

BEATRICE: [*aside*] These are two letters which I wrote to Florindo. Alas, these notes, these accounts belong to him. I tremble, I am in a cold sweat, I know not where I am.

PANTALONE: What ails you, Signor Federigo? Are you unwell?

BEATRICE: 'Tis nothing.

[*aside* to TRUFFALDINO]

Truffaldino, how did this book come to be in my trunk? It is not mine.

TRUFFALDINO: I hardly know, sir—

BEATRICE: Come, out with it—tell me the truth.

TRUFFALDINO: I ask your pardon for the liberty I took, sir, putting the book into your trunk. It belongs to me, and I put it there for safety.

[*aside*]

That was a good enough story for the other gentleman, I hope 'twill do for this one too.

BEATRICE: The book is your own, you say, and yet you gave it to me instead of mine, without noticing?

TRUFFALDINO: [*aside*] He's much too clever.

[*to* BEATRICE]

I'll tell you, sir; I have only had the book a very short time, so I did not recognize it at once.

BEATRICE: And how came you by this book?

TRUFFALDINO: I was in service with a gentleman at Venice, and he died and left the book to me.

BEATRICE: How long ago?

TRUFFALDINO: I don't remember exactly—ten or twelve days.

BEATRICE: How can that be, when I met you at Verona?

TRUFFALDINO: I had just come away from Venice on account of my poor master's death.

BEATRICE: [*aside*] Alas for me!

[*to* TRUFFALDINO]

Your master—was his name—Florindo?

TRUFFALDINO: Yes, sir; Florindo.

BEATRICE: And his family name Aretusi?

TRUFFALDINO: That was it, sir; Aretusi.

BEATRICE: And you are sure he is dead?

TRUFFALDINO: As sure as I stand here.

BEATRICE: Of what did he die? Where was he buried?

TRUFFALDINO: He tumbled into the canal and was drowned and never seen again.

BEATRICE: Oh, wretched that I am! Florindo is dead, my beloved is dead; my one and only hope is dead. All is lost. Love's stratagems are fruitless! I leave my home, I leave my relatives, I dress as a man, I confront danger, I hazard my very life, all for

Florindo—and Florindo is dead. Unhappy Beatrice! Was the loss of my brother so little to me that Fate must make me lose my lover as well? Oh! Grief overwhelms me, I can no longer bear the light of day. My adored one, my beloved, I will follow you to the tomb.

    [*Exits into her room raving.*]

PANTALONE: [*who has listened to her speech with astonishment*] Truffaldino!

TRUFFALDINO: Si'or Pantalon'?

PANTALONE: A woman!

TRUFFALDINO: A female!

PANTALONE: Most extraordinary!

TRUFFALDINO: Who'd have thought it?

PANTALONE: I'm struck all of a heap.

TRUFFALDINO: You might knock me down with a feather.

PANTALONE: I shall go straight home and tell my daughter.

    [*Exit.*]

TRUFFALDINO: It seems I am not the servant of two masters but of a master and a mistress.

    [*Exit.*]

SCENE II———A Street.

[*Enter* DR. LOMBARDI *meeting* PANTALONE.]

DR. LOMBARDI: [*aside*] This doddering old villain Pantalone sticks in my gizzard. The more I think about him, the more I abominate him.

PANTALONE: [*cheerfully*] Good day, my dear Doctor, your servant.

DR. LOMBARDI: I am surprised that you have the effrontery to address me.

PANTALONE: I have news for you. Do you know—

DR. LOMBARDI: You are going to tell me that the marriage has already been performed? I care not a fig if it has.

PANTALONE: The whole story is untrue. Let me speak, plague take you.

DR. LOMBARDI: Speak on then, pox on you.

PANTALONE: [*aside*] I should like to give him a good doctoring with my fists.

    [*to* DR. LOMBARDI]

My daughter shall marry your son whenever you please.

DR. LOMBARDI: I am vastly obliged to you. Pray do not put yourself to inconvenience. My son is not prepared to stomach that, sir. You may give her to the Turin gentleman.

PANTALONE: If you knew who the Turin gentleman is, you would say differently.

DR. LOMBARDI: He may be who he will. Your daughter has been seen with him, *et hoc sufficit*.

PANTALONE: But 'tis not true that he is—

DR. LOMBARDI: I will not hear another word.

PANTALONE: If you won't hear me, 'twill be the worse for you.

DR. LOMBARDI: We shall see for whom it will be the worse.

PANTALONE: My daughter is a girl of unblemished reputation, and—

DR. LOMBARDI: The devil take you.

PANTALONE: The devil take you, sir.

DR. LOMBARDI: You disreputable old villain!

    [*Exit* DR. LOMBARDI.]

PANTALONE: Damn you! He is more like a beast than a man. Why, how could I ever tell him that the man was a woman? Not a bit of it, he wouldn't let me speak. But here comes that young lout of a son of his; now I shall be in for more impertinence.

    [*Enter* SILVIO.]

SILVIO: [*aside*] There is Pantalone. I should like to run a sword through his paunch.

PANTALONE: Signor Silvio, if you will give me leave, I should like to give you a piece of good news, if you will condescend to allow me to speak, and not behave like that windmill of a father of yours.

SILVIO: What have you to say to me? Pray speak, sir.

PANTALONE: You must know, sir, that the marriage of my daughter to Signor Federigo has come to nothing.

SILVIO: Indeed? Do not deceive me.

PANTALONE: 'Tis true indeed, and if you are still of your former mind, my daughter is ready to give you her hand.

SILVIO: Oh, heavens! You bring me back from death to life.

PANTALONE: [*aside*] Well, well, he is not quite such a bear as his father.

SILVIO: But heavens! How can I clasp to my bosom her who has for so long been the bride of another?

PANTALONE: To cut a long story short, Federigo Rasponi has turned into Beatrice his sister.

SILVIO: What? I do not understand you.

PANTALONE: Then you are very thickheaded. The person whom we thought to be Federigo has been discovered to be Beatrice.

SILVIO: Dressed as a man?

PANTALONE: Dressed as a man.

SILVIO: At last I understand.

PANTALONE: About time you did.

SILVIO: How did it happen? Tell me.

PANTALONE: Let us go to my house. My daughter knows nothing of it. I need only tell the story once to satisfy you both.

SILVIO: I will come, sir; and I must humbly beg your forgiveness, for having allowed myself to be transported by passion—

PANTALONE: 'Twas a mere nothing; I appreciate your feelings. I know what love is. Now, my dear boy, come along with me.
[*going*]

SILVIO: [*aside*] Who is happier than I am? What heart could be more contended?
[*Exit with* PANTALONE.]

SCENE III———*A Room in* BRIGHELLA'S *Inn.*

[BEATRICE *and* FLORINDO *come out of their rooms simultaneously; each holds a sword or dagger and is on the point of committing suicide.* BRIGHELLLA *is restraining* BEATRICE *and the* FIRST WAITER *restraining* FLORINDO. *They all come forward in such a way that* BEATRICE *and* FLORINDO *are unaware of each other's presence.*]

BRIGHELLLA: [*seizing* BEATRICE'S *hand*] Stop, stop!

BEATRICE: [*trying to break loose*] For pity's sake, let me go.

FIRST WAITER: [*holding* FLORINDO] This is madness.

FLORINDO: [*breaks away from* WAITER] Go to the devil.

BEATRICE: [*breaking away from* BRIGHELLLA] You shall not hinder me.
[*Both come forward, determined to kill themselves, they see each other, recognize each other, and stand dazed.*]

FLORINDO: What do I see?

BEATRICE: Florindo!

FLORINDO: Beatrice!

BEATRICE: Are you alive?

FLORINDO: Are you too living?

BEATRICE: Oh, destiny!

FLORINDO: Oh, my adored one!

> [*They drop their weapons and embrace.*]

BRIGHELLLA: [*jokingly to the* WAITER] You had better mop up the blood; we don't want a mess here.

> [*Exit* BRIGHELLLA.]

FIRST WAITER: [*aside*] Anyway I'll pick up the weapons and I shall not give them back again.

> [*picks up the daggers and exits*]

FLORINDO: What brought you to attempt such an act of madness?

BEATRICE: The false news of your death.

FLORINDO: Who told you that I was dead?

BEATRICE: My servant.

FLORINDO: And mine gave me to believe that you were dead; and I too, carried away by the same agony of grief, intended to take my life.

BEATRICE: It was this book caused me to believe the story.

FLORINDO: That book was in my trunk. How came it into your hands? Ah, now I know. By the same means, no doubt, as the portrait I found in my coat pocket. Here it is. The one I gave you in Turin.

BEATRICE: Those rascally servants of ours—Heaven only knows what they have been up to.

FLORINDO: Where are they, I wonder?

BEATRICE: Nowhere to be seen.

FLORINDO: Let us find them and confront them.

> [*calling*]

Ho there! Is nobody there?

> [*Enter* BRIGHELLLA.]

BRIGHELLLA: Did you call, sir?

FLORINDO: Where are our servants?

BRIGHELLLA: I don't know, sir. Shall I send to look for them?

FLORINDO: Find them at once if you can and send them to us here.

BRIGHELLLA: For myself I only know one of them; I will ask the waiters, they will know them both. I congratulate you, sir, and madam, on having made such a satisfactory end of yourselves; if you want to get yourselves buried, you must try some other establishment; that's more than we can undertake. Your servant, madam and sir.

> [*Exit* BRIGHELLLA.]

FLORINDO: Then you too are lodged in this inn?

BEATRICE: I arrived this morning.

FLORINDO: I too this morning. And yet we never saw each other.

BEATRICE: Fate has been pleased to torment us a little.

FLORINDO: Tell me: your brother Federigo—is he dead?

BEATRICE: Have you any doubt? He died on the spot.

FLORINDO: I was told he was alive and here in Venice.

BEATRICE: It was I who traveled in his name and in these clothes to follow—

FLORINDO: To follow me—I know, my dearest; I read it in a letter from your servant in Turin.

BEATRICE: How came it into your hands?

FLORINDO: My servant gave it me by mistake and seeing it was addressed to you, I could not help opening it.

BEATRICE: I suppose a lover's curiosity is always legitimate.

FLORINDO: But where are these servants of ours? Ah!

> [*Sees* TRUFFALDINO *approaching.*]

Here is one.

BEATRICE: He looks like the worse knave of the two.

FLORINDO: I think you are not far wrong.

> [*Enter* TRUFFALDINO *brought in by force by* BRIGHELLLA *and the* FIRST WAITER.]

FLORINDO: Come here, come here, don't be frightened.

BEATRICE: We shall do you no harm.

TRUFFALDINO: [*aside*] H'm, I still remember the thrashing.

BRIGHELLLA: We have found this one; if we can find the other, we will bring him.

FLORINDO: Yes, we must have them both here together.

BRIGHELLLA: [*aside to* WAITER] Do you know the other?

FIRST WAITER: [*to* BRIGHELLLA] Not I.

BRIGHELLLA: We'll ask in the kitchen. Someone there will know him.

FIRST WAITER: If he had been there, I should have known him too.

> [*Exeunt* FIRST WAITER *and* BRIGHELLLA.]

FLORINDO: [*to* TRUFFALDINO] Come, now, tell us what happened about that changing of the portrait and the book, and why you and that other rascal conspired to drive us distracted.

TRUFFALDINO : [*signs to both with his finger to keep silence*] Hush!

> [*to* FLORINDO]

Pray, sir, a word with you in private.

> [*to* BEATRICE *just as he turns to speak to* FLORINDO]

I will tell you everything directly.

> [*to* FLORINDO]

You must know, sir, I am not to blame for anything that has happened; it's all Pasqual's fault, the servant of that lady there.

> [*cautiously pointing at* BEATRICE]

It was he mixed up the things, and put into one trunk what belonged to the other, without my knowledge. The poor man begged and prayed me to take the blame, for fear his master should send him away, and as I am a kindhearted fellow that would let himself be drawn and quartered for his friends, I made up all these stories to see if I could help him. I never dreamed it was a portrait of you or that you would be so much upset at hearing of the death of the owner. Now I have told you the whole truth, sir, as an honest man and a faithful servant.

BEATRICE: [*aside*] 'Tis a very long story he is telling. I am curious to know what the mystery is about.

FLORINDO: [*aside to* TRUFFALDINO] Then the man who got you to fetch that letter from the Post was the servant of Signora Beatrice?

TRUFFALDINO: [*aside to* FLORINDO] Yes, sir, that was Pasqual'.

FLORINDO: Then why conceal from me a fact I so urgently desired to know?

TRUFFALDINO: He begged me not to tell anyone, sir.

FLORINDO: Who?

TRUFFALDINO: Pasqual'.

FLORINDO: Why didn't you obey your master?

TRUFFALDINO: For the love of Pasqual'.

FLORINDO: You and Pasquale deserve a sound thrashing together.

TRUFFALDINO: [*aside to himself*] In that case I should get both.

BEATRICE: Have you not yet finished this long cross-examination?

FLORINDO: This fellow has been telling me—

TRUFFALDINO: [aside to FLORINDO] For the love of Heaven, your honor, do not say it was Pasqual'. I'd rather you told the lady it was me. You can give me a beating if you like, but don't, don't let any trouble come to Pasqual'.

FLORINDO: [aside to TRUFFALDINO] Are you so devoted a friend to Pasquale?

TRUFFALDINO: I love him as if he were my very own self. Now I am going to the lady, and I am going to tell her that it was all my fault; she may scold me as she pleases and do what she will to me, but I will protect Pasqual'.

[TRUFFALDINO moves toward BEATRICE.]

FLORINDO: [aside] Well, he's certainly a very loyal and affectionate character.

TRUFFALDINO: [to BEATRICE] Here I am, madam.

BEATRICE: [aside to TRUFFALDINO] What is all this long story you've been telling Signor Florindo?

TRUFFALDINO: [aside to BEATRICE] You must know, madam, that that gentleman has a servant called Pasqual'; he is the most arrant noddy in the world; it was he made all that mess of things; but because the poor man was afraid his master would send him away, I made up all the story about the book and the master who was dead and drowned, and all the rest of it. And just now I've been telling Si'or Florindo that I was the cause of it all.

BEATRICE: But why accuse yourself of faults which you have never committed?

TRUFFALDINO: Madam, 'tis all for the love I bear Pasqual'.

FLORINDO: [aside] This seems a very long business.

TRUFFALDINO: [to BEATRICE as before] Dear madam, I beg of you, don't get him into trouble.

BEATRICE: Whom?

TRUFFALDINO: Pasqual'.

BEATRICE: Pasquale and you are a pretty pair of rascals.

TRUFFALDINO: [aside to himself] I fear I'm the only one.

FLORINDO: Come. That's enough. Signora Beatrice, our servants certainly deserve to be punished; but in consideration of our own great happiness, we surely may forgive what is past.

BEATRICE: True; but your servant—

TRUFFALDINO: [aside to BEATRICE] For the love of Heaven don't mention Pasqual'.

BEATRICE: [to FLORINDO] Well, I must go and call upon Signor Pantalone dei Bisognosi; will you accompany me?

FLORINDO: I would do so with pleasure, but I have to wait here and see my banker. I will come later, if you are in haste.

BEATRICE: I am; I must go at once. I shall expect you at Signor Pantalone's; and shall stay there till you come.

FLORINDO: I don't know where he lives.

TRUFFALDINO: I know, sir, I'll show you the way.

BEATRICE: Very well, and now I must go to my room and tidy myself up.

TRUFFALDINO: [aside to BEATRICE] Very good, madam; I am at your service directly.

BEATRICE: Dear Florindo! What torments have I not endured for love of you!

[BEATRICE goes into her room.]

FLORINDO: Mine have been no less.

TRUFFALDINO: Sir, Pasqual' is not here, and Si'ora Beatrice has no one to help her dress; will you give me leave to wait upon her instead of Pasqual'?

FLORINDO: Yes, by all means. Wait upon her with diligence; I am delighted.

TRUFFALDINO: [*aside*] For invention, for promptness and for intrigue I will challenge the attorney general.

[TRUFFALDINO *goes into* BEATRICE'S *room.*]

FLORINDO: What strange things have happened in the course of this one day! Tears, lamentations, and anguish, and then at last consolation and happiness. From tears to laughter is a happy step, which makes us forget our agonies, but when we pass from pleasure to pain the change is even yet more acutely perceptible.

[*Reenter* BEATRICE *followed by* TRUFFALDINO.]

BEATRICE: Here I am, have I not been quick?

FLORINDO: When will you change these clothes?

BEATRICE: Do I not look well in them?

FLORINDO: I long to see you in a woman's dress. Your beauties ought not to be so completely disguised.

BEATRICE: Well, I shall expect you at Signor Pantalone's; make Truffaldino show you the way.

FLORINDO: I must wait for the banker; if he does not come soon another time will do.

BEATRICE: Show me your love in your anxiety to attend me.

[*about to go*]

TRUFFALDINO: [*aside to* BEATRICE] Do you wish me to stay and wait upon this gentleman?

BEATRICE: Yes, you will show him the way to Signor Pantalone's.

TRUFFALDINO: Yes, madam, certainly, as Pasqual' is not here.

BEATRICE: Wait upon him, I shall be pleased indeed.

[*aside to herself*]

I love him more than my very self.

[*Exit* BEATRICE.]

TRUFFALDINO: The fellow's nowhere to be seen. His master wants to dress, and he goes out on his own and is nowhere to be found.

FLORINDO: Of whom are you speaking?

TRUFFALDINO: Of Pasqual'. I love him, he is a good friend of mine, but he's a lazy dog. Now I am a servant worth two.

FLORINDO: Come and dress my wig. The banker will be here directly.

TRUFFALDINO: Please your honor, I hear your honor has to go to Si'or Pantalon's.

FLORINDO: Yes, what then?

TRUFFALDINO: I want to ask a favor of you.

FLORINDO: Well, you deserve it after all you have done.

TRUFFALDINO: If there has been any trouble, you know, sir, 'tis all the fault of Pasqual'.

FLORINDO: But where on earth is this cursed Pasquale? Can't one see him?

TRUFFALDINO: He'll come, the knave. And so, sir, I want to ask you this favor.

FLORINDO: What do you want?

TRUFFALDINO: You see, sir, I'm in love too.

FLORINDO: In love?

TRUFFALDINO: Yes, sir, and my young woman is maidservant to Si'or Pantalon'; and it would be very kind if your honor—

FLORINDO: How do I come into it?

TRUFFALDINO: I won't say, sir, that you come into it; but I being your servant, you might say a word for me to Si'or Pantalon'.

FLORINDO: We must see first whether the girl wants you.

TRUFFALDINO: The girl wants me, no mistake. All I want is a word to Si'or Pantalon'; I beg you, sir, of your charity.

FLORINDO: Certainly, I will speak for you, but how can you keep a wife?

TRUFFALDINO: I shall do what I can. I shall ask for help from Pasqual'.

FLORINDO: You had better ask help from someone with more sense.

> [FLORINDO *goes into his room.*]

TRUFFALDINO: Well, if I don't show sense this time, I shall never show it again.

> [TRUFFALDINO *follows* FLORINDO *into his room.*]

SCENE IV———*A Room in the House of* PANTALONE.

PANTALONE: Come, Clarice, pull yourself together. You see that Signor Silvio has repented and asks your foreigveness. If he acted foolishly, it was all for love of you; I have forgiven him his extravagances, you ought to forgive him too.

SILVIO: Measure my agony by your own, Signora Clarice, and rest assured that I most truly love you, since 'twas the fear of losing you that rendered me distracted. Heaven desires our happiness; do not be ungrateful for the blessings of Providence. Do not let the idea of revenge spoil the most beautiful day of your life.

DR. LOMBARDI: I join my prayers to those of my son; Signora Clarice, my dear daughter-in-law, have pity on the poor young man; he nearly went out of his mind.

SMERALDINA: Come, dear madam, what would you? Men are all cruel to us, some more, some less. They demand the most absolute fidelity, and on the least shadow of suspicion they bully us, ill-treat us and are like to murder us. Well, you have got to marry one or another of them some day, so I say to you as one says to sick people—since you have got to take your nasty medicine, take it.

PANTALONE: There, do you hear that? Smeraldina calls matrimony medicine. You must not think it is poison.

> [*aside to* DR. LOMBARDI]

We must try to cheer her up.

DR. LOMBARDI: Certainly, 'tis not poison, nor even nasty medicine. Matrimony is a lollipop, a jujube, a lozenge!

SILVIO: But dear Clarice, won't you say a word? I know I deserve to be punished by you, but, of your mercy, punish me with hard words rather than with silence. Behold me at your feet; have pity upon me.

CLARICE: [*to* SILVIO *with a sigh*] Cruel!

PANTALONE: [*aside to* DR. LOMBARDI] You heard that little sigh? A good sign.

DR. LOMBARDI: [*aside to* SILVIO] Strike while the iron is hot.

SMERALDINA: [*aside*] A sigh is like lightning; it promises rainfall.

SILVIO: If I could think that you desired my blood to avenge my supposed cruelty, I give it you with all my heart. But, oh God! instead of the blood of my veins, accept, I beg you, that which gushes from my eyes.

> [*weeps*]

PANTALONE: Bravo! Bravo! Well said!

DR. LOMBARDI: Capital! Capital!

CLARICE: [*sighing as before, but more tenderly*] Cruel!

DR. LOMBARDI: [*aside to* PANTALONE] She's done to a turn.

PANTALONE: Here, come up with you.

> [*He raises* SILVIO, *takes him by the hand.*]

Stand over there.

> [*takes* CLARICE'S *hand*]

And you come here too, madam. Now, join your hands together again; and make peace. So no more tears, be happy, no more nonsense and Heaven bless you both.

DR. LOMBARDI: There; 'tis done.

SMERALDINA: 'Tis done, 'tis done.

SILVIO: [*holding* CLARICE'S *hand*] Oh, Signora Clarice, for pity's sake

CLARICE: Ungrateful!

SILVIO: Dearest!

CLARICE: Inhuman!

SILVIO: Beloved!

CLARICE: Monster!

SILVIO: Angel!

CLARICE: [*sighs*] Ah!

PANTALONE: [*aside*] Going, going—

SILVIO: Forgive me, for the love of Heaven.

CLARICE: [*sighs*] I forgive you.

PANTALONE: [*aside*] Gone!

DR. LOMBARDI: Come, Silvio, she has forgiven you.

SMERALDINA: The patient is ready; give her her medicine.

[*Enter* BRIGHELLLA.]

BRIGHELLLA: By your leave, sir, may I come in?

PANTALONE: Pray come in, good friend Brighella. 'Twas you, was it not, that told me all these pretty stories, who assured me that that party was Signor Federigo—eh?

BRIGHELLLA: My dear sir, who would not have been deceived? They were twin brother and sister, as like as two peas. In those clothes I would have wagered my head that it was he.

PANTALONE: Enough. That's all done with. What is the news?

BRIGHELLLA: Signora Beatrice is here, and desires to pay her respects.

PANTALONE: Let her come in; she is most welcome.

CLARICE: Poor Signora Beatrice, I am happy to think that her troubles are over.

SILVIO: You are sorry for her?

CLARICE: I am indeed.

SILVIO: And for me?

CLARICE: Oh, cruel!

PANTALONE: [*aside to* DR. LOMBARDI] You hear these loving words?

DR. LOMBARDI: [*aside to* PANTALONE] Ah, my son has a way with him.

PANTALONE: My daughter, poor dear child, has a very good heart.

SMERALDINA: Yes, they will both of them do their duty by each other.

[*Enter* BEATRICE.]

BEATRICE: Ladies and gentlemen, I come to ask your pardon and forgiveness, that you should on my account have been put to inconvenience—

CLARICE: No, no, my dear; come to me.

[*embraces her*]

SILVIO: [*annoyed at the embrace*] How now?

BEATRICE: [*to* SILVIO] What! May she not even embrace a woman?

SILVIO: [*aside*] 'Tis those clothes again.

PANTALONE: Well, well, Signora Beatrice, I must say, for a young woman of your age you have a wonderful courage.

DR. LOMBARDI: [*to* BEATRICE] Too much spirit, madam.

BEATRICE: Love makes one do great things.

PANTALONE: And you have found your young gentleman at last? So I hear.

BEATRICE: Yes, Heaven has made us happy.

DR. LOMBARDI: A nice reputation you have made yourself!

BEATRICE: Sir, you have no business in my affairs.

SILVIO: [*to* DR. LOMBARDI] Sir, I beg you, let everyone do as they will; do not be so put out about it. Now that I am happy, I want all the world to be happy too. Is anyone else going to be married? Let them all get married!

SMERALDINA: [*to* SILVIO] What about me, sir?

SILVIO: Whom are you going to marry?

SMERALDINA: The first man that comes along, sir.

SILVIO: Find him then, here am I.

CLARICE: [*to* SILVIO] You? What for?

SILVIO: To give her a wedding present.

CLARICE: That is no affair of yours.

SMERALDINA: [*aside*] She's afraid everybody will eat him. She likes the taste of him, I see.
[*Enter* TRUFFALDINO.]

TRUFFALDINO: My respects to the company.

BEATRICE: [*to* TRUFFALDINO] Where is Signor Florindo?

TRUFFALDINO: He is here and would like to come in, by your leave.

BEATRICE: Signor Pantalone, will you give Signor Florindo leave?

PANTALONE: Is that your young gentleman?

BEATRICE: He is going to marry me.

PANTALONE: I shall be pleased to meet him.

BEATRICE: [*to* TRUFFALDINO] Show him in.

TRUFFALDINO: [*aside to* SMERALDINA] Young woman, my respects to you.

SMERALDINA: [*aside to* TRUFFALDINO] Pleased to see you, my little darkie.

TRUFFALDINO: We will have to talk.

SMERALDINA: What about?

TRUFFALDINO: [*makes as though giving her a wedding ring*] Are you willing?

SMERALDINA: Why not?

TRUFFALDINO: We'll have a talk.
[*Exit* TRUFFALDINO.]

SMERALDINA: [*to* CLARICE] Madam, with the company's leave, I want a favor of you.

CLARICE: [*going aside to listen to* SMERALDINA] What is it?

SMERALDINA: [*to* CLARICE] I too am a poor young girl that would like to settle myself; there's the servant of Signora Beatrice who wants to marry me; now if you would say a kind word to his mistress, and get her to allow him to take me to wife, I should be the happiest girl in the world.

CLARICE: Dear Smeraldina, with all the pleasure in life; as soon as I can speak freely to Beatrice, I will certainly do so.

PANTALONE: [*to* CLARICE] What is all this whispering about?

CLARICE: Nothing, sir. She had something to say to me.

SILVIO: [*to* CLARICE] May I not know?

CLARICE: How inquisitive they all are! And then they talk about us women!
[*Enter* FLORINDO *shown in by* TRUFFALDINO.]

FLORINDO: Your most humble servant, ladies and gentlemen.
[*All bow and curtsy.*]
[*to* PANTALONE]
Are you the master of the house, sir?

PANTALONE: Yours to command, sir.

FLORINDO: Allow me, sir, to have the honor of waiting upon you this evening; I present myself by command of the Signora Beatrice, whose adventures will be known to you, and mine too.

PANTALONE: I am happy to know you, sir, and to see you here; I congratulate you most heartily on your good fortune.

FLORINDO: Signora Beatrice is to be my wife, and if you will not disdain to do us the honor, I hope you will give away the bride.

PANTALONE: Whatever has to be done, let it be done at once. Give her your hand.

FLORINDO: Signora Beatrice, I am willing.

BEATRICE: Here is my hand, Signor Florindo.

SMERALDINA: [*aside*] *They* don't want pressing.

PANTALONE: Afterward we will settle up our accounts. You will put yours in order; then we will settle ours.

CLARICE: [*to* BEATRICE] Dear friend, I congratulate you.

BEATRICE: [*to* CLARICE] And I you, with all my heart.

SILVIO: [*to* FLORINDO] Sir, do you know me again?

FLORINDO: [*to* SILVIO] Indeed I do, sir; you would have provoked me to a duel.

SILVIO: 'Twas to my own disaster. Here is the adversary
        [*pointing to* BEATRICE]
    who disarmed me and very nearly killed me.

BEATRICE: And gave you your life too, you might say.

SILVIO: 'Tis true.

CLARICE: At my entreaty.

SILVIO: That is very true.

PANTALONE: Everything is in order; everything is settled.

TRUFFALDINO: The best is yet to come, ladies and gentlemen.

PANTALONE: What is yet to come?

TRUFFALDINO: [*to* FLORINDO, *taking him apart*] With your good leave, sir, one word.

FLORINDO: What do you want?

TRUFFALDINO: You remember what you promised me, sir?

FLORINDO: What did I promise? I do not recollect.

TRUFFALDINO: To ask Si'or Pantalon' for Smeraldina as my wife.

FLORINDO: Of course, now I remember; I will do so at once.

TRUFFALDINO: [*aside*] I, too, poor man, want to put myself right with the world.

FLORINDO: Signor Pantalone, although this is the first occasion on which I have had the honor of knowing you, I make bold to desire a favor of you.

PANTALONE: You may command me, sir; I will serve you the best of my powers.

FLORINDO: My manservant desires to marry your maid; have you any objection to giving your consent?

SMERALDINA: [*aside*] Wonderful! Here's another who wants to marry me! Who the devil can he be? I wish I knew him.

PANTALONE: For my part I am agreed.
        [*to* SMERALDINA]
    What say you, girl?

SMERALDINA: If I thought he would make a good husband—

PANTALONE: Is he a good honest man, this servant of yours?

FLORINDO: For the short time he has been with me he has certainly proved himself trusty, and he seems to be intelligent.

CLARICE: Signor Florindo, you have anticipated me in something that *I* ought to have done. I was to propose the marriage of my maid with the manservant of Signora Beatrice. You have asked for her for *your* servant, I can say no more.

FLORINDO: No, no; since you so earnestly desire this, I withdraw altogether and leave you completely free.

CLARICE: Indeed, sir, I could never permit myself to have my own wishes preferred to yours. Besides, I must admit that I am not fully authorized. Pray continue in your proposal.

FLORINDO: You say so out of courtesy, madam. Signor Pantalone, I withdraw all that I have said. I will not say another word on behalf of my servant; on the contrary, I am absolutely opposed to his marrying her.

CLARICE: If *your* man is not to marry her, no more shall the other man. We must be fair on both sides.

TRUFFALDINO: [*aside*] Here's a state of things! They pay each other compliments, and meanwhile I am left without a wife at all.

SMERALDINA: [*aside*] It looks as if I should have neither one nor the other.

PANTALONE: Come, we *must* settle it somehow; this poor girl wants to get married, let us give her either to the one or the other.

FLORINDO: Not to *my* man. Nothing shall induce me to do Signora Clarice an injustice.

CLARICE: Nor will I ever tolerate an injustice to Signor Florindo.

TRUFFALDINO: Sir, madam, I can settle the matter myself.
> [*with his usual air of great ingenuity*]
Si'or Florindo, did you not ask the hand of Smeraldina for your servant?

FLORINDO: I did; did you not hear me?

TRUFFALDINO: And you, Si'ora Clarice, did you not intend Smeraldina to marry the servant of Si'ora Beatrice?

CLARICE: Most certainly I was to do so.

TRUFFALDINO: Good; then if that is so, give me your hand, Smeraldina.

PANTALONE: And pray what right have *you* to ask for her hand?

TRUFFALDINO: Because I am the servant of Si'or Florindo and of Si'ora Beatrice too.

FLORINDO: What?

BEATRICE: What do you say?

TRUFFALDINO: Pray be calm. Si'or Florindo, who asked you to ask Si'or Pantalon' for Smeraldina?

FLORINDO: You did.

TRUFFALDINO: And you, Si'ora Clarice, whom had you in mind as the intended husband of Smeraldina?

CLARICE: Yourself.

TRUFFALDINO: *Ergo*, Smeraldina is mine.

FLORINDO: Signora Beatrice, where is your servant?

BEATRICE: Why, here! Truffaldino, of course.

FLORINDO: Truffaldino? He is *my* servant!

BEATRICE: Is not yours called Pasquale?

FLORINDO: Pasquale? I thought Pasquale was *yours!w*

BEATRICE: [*to* TRUFFALDINO] How do you explain this?
> [TRUFFALDINO *makes silent gestures asking for forgiveness.*]

FLORINDO: You rascal!

BEATRICE: You knave!

FLORINDO: So you waited on two masters at once?

TRUFFALDINO: Yes, sir, I did; that was the very trick. I took on the job without thinking; just to see what I could do. It did not last long, 'tis true; but at any rate I can boast that nobody would ever have found me out, if I had not given myself away for love of this girl here. I have done a hard day's work, and I dare say I had my shortcomings, but I hope that in consideration of the fun of the thing, all these ladies and gentlemen will forgive me.

MOLIÈRE (JEAN-BAPTISTE POQUELIN, 1622–1673)

Tartuffe (1664, 1667, 1669)

While English drama of Shakespeare's time owed much to medieval conventions, French dramatists after the 1630s looked back to Greece and Rome for their standards. This conscious imitation of the classics gave rise to a set of literary standards summed up in the term *neoclassicism*. These included the unities of time, place, and action; strict distinction between tragedy and comedy, with no intermingling of the two; the use of universalized character types; and the demand that drama teach moral lessons. Many of the plays written in compliance with these demands now seem lifeless, but the tragedies of Racine and the comedies of Molière, written in France during the last half of the seventeenth century, reached a peak of artistry in the neoclassical mode. Unlike plays of earlier eras, these were written for the proscenium arch stage and for perspective settings composed of wings, drops, and borders.

Molière is one of the most skillful and inventive comic dramatists of all times, and *Tartuffe* is one of his most admired plays. Within the restricted frame of one room, one day, and one main story, using a limited number of characters and little physical action, Molière creates an excellent comedy of character. The action of *Tartuffe*, divided into five acts, develops through five stages: the demonstration of Tartuffe's complete hold over Orgon; the unmasking of Tartuffe; Tartuffe's attempted revenge; the foiling of Tartuffe's plan; and the happy resolution. Molière has been criticized for delaying Tartuffe's first appearance until the third act, but he makes skillful use of this delay by having all the other characters establish his hypocrisy and Orgon's gullibility in trusting Tartuffe. The resolution, in which Tartuffe is suddenly discovered to be a notorious criminal, has also been criticized as overly contrived, but it is emotionally satisfying because it punishes Tartuffe and reestablishes the norm.

In *Tartuffe* Molière uses the verse form that by that time had become standard in French tragedy—the alexandrine (twelve-syllable lines, with each pair of adjacent lines rhyming). Richard Wilbur's translation, used here, is generally considered one of the finest now available both for its accuracy and for its rendition of Molière's verse.

When *Tartuffe* was written in 1664, it was immediately denounced as an attack on religious piety. The controversy was so intense that Louis XIV forbade the play's production. Molière rewrote it in 1667, only to have it banned once more. Finally, in 1669 he was able to gain permission for its production. It has remained in the repertory continuously since that time. It is still performed more often than any other play by Molière.

MOLIÈRE

Tartuffe

TRANSLATED INTO ENGLISH VERSE BY RICHARD WILBUR

Characters

MME. PERNELLE, *Orgon's mother*
ORGON, *Elmire's husband*
ELMIRE, *Orgon's wife*
DAMIS, *Orgon's son, Elmire's stepson*
MARIANE, *Orgon's daughter, Elmire's stepdaughter, in love with Valère*
VALÈRE, *in love with Mariane*
CLÉANTE, *Orgon's brother-in-law*
TARTUFFE, *a hypocrite*
DORINE, *Mariane's lady's-maid*
M. LOYAL, *a bailiff*
A POLICE OFFICER
FLIPOTE, *Mme. Pernelle's maid*

The scene throughout: ORGON'S *house in Paris*

ACT I

SCENE I

MADAME PERNELLE: Come, come, Flipote; it's time I left this place.
ELMIRE: I can't keep up, you walk at such a pace.
MADAME PERNELLE: Don't trouble, child; no need to show me out.
　　It's not your manners I'm concerned about.
ELMIRE: We merely pay you the respect we owe.
　　But, Mother, why this hurry? Must you go?
MADAME PERNELLE: I must. This house appals me. No one in it
　　Will pay attention for a single minute.

Children, I take my leave much vexed in spirit.
I offer good advice, but you won't hear it.
You all break in and chatter on and on.
It's like a madhouse with the keeper gone.

DORINE: If . . .

MADAME PERNELLE: Girl, you talk too much, and I'm afraid
You're far too saucy for a lady's-maid.
You push in everywhere and have your say.

DAMIS: But . . .

MADAME PERNELLE: You, boy, grow more foolish every day.
To think my grandson should be such a dunce!
I've said a hundred times, if I've said it once,
That if you keep the course on which you've started,
You'll leave your worthy father broken-hearted.

MARIANE: I think . . .

MADAME PERNELLE: And you, his sister, seem so pure,
So shy, so innocent, and so demure.
But you know what they say about still waters.
I pity parents with secretive daughters.

ELMIRE: Now, Mother . . .

MADAME PERNELLE: And as for you, child, let me add
That your behavior is extremely bad,
And a poor example for these children, too.
Their dear, dead mother did far better than you.
You're much too free with money, and I'm distressed
To see you so elaborately dressed.
When it's one's husband that one aims to please,
One has no need of costly fripperies.

CLÉANTE: Oh, Madam, really . . .

MADAME PERNELLE: You are her brother, Sir,
And I respect and love you; yet if I were
My son, this lady's good and pious spouse,
I wouldn't make you welcome in my house.
You're full of worldly counsels which, I fear,
Aren't suitable for decent folk to hear.
I've spoken bluntly, Sir; but it behooves us
Not to mince words when righteous fervor moves us.

DAMIS: Your man Tartuffe is full of holy speeches . . .

MADAME PERNELLE: And practices precisely what he preaches.
He's a fine man, and should be listened to.
I will not hear him mocked by fools like you.

DAMIS: Good God! Do you expect me to submit
To the tyranny of that carping hypocrite?
Must we forgo all joys and satisfactions
Because that bigot censures all our actions?

DORINE: To hear him talk—and he talks all the time—
There's nothing one can do that's not a crime.
He rails at everything, your dear Tartuffe.

MADAME PERNELLE: Whatever he reproves deserves reproof.
    He's out to save your souls, and all of you
    Must love him, as my son would have you do.
DAMIS: Ah no, Grandmother, I could never take
    To such a rascal, even for my father's sake.
    That's how I feel, and I shall not dissemble.
    His every action makes me seethe and tremble
    With helpless anger, and I have no doubt
    That he and I will shortly have it out.
DORINE: Surely it is a shame and a disgrace
    To see this man usurp the master's place—
    To see this beggar who, when first he came,
    Had not a shoe or shoestring to his name
    So far forget himself that he behaves
    As if the house were his, and we his slaves.
MADAME PERNELLE: Well, mark my words, your souls would fare far better
    If you obeyed his precepts to the letter.
DORINE: You see him as a saint. I'm far less awed;
    In fact, I see right through him. He's a fraud.
MADAME PERNELLE: Nonsense!
DORINE: His man Laurent's the same, or worse;
    I'd not trust either with a penny purse.
MADAME PERNELLE: I can't say what his servant's morals may be;
    His own great goodness I can guarantee.
    You all regard him with distaste and fear
    Because he tells you what you're loath to hear,
    Condemns your sins, points out your moral flaws,
    And humbly strives to further Heaven's cause.
DORINE: If sin is all that bothers him, why is it
    He's so upset when folk drop in to visit?
    Is Heaven so outraged by a social call
    That he must prophesy against us all?
    I'll tell you what I think: if you ask me,
    He's jealous of my mistress' company.
MADAME PERNELLE: Rubbish! [*to* ELMIRE] He's not alone, child, in complaining
    Of all of your promiscuous entertaining.
    Why, the whole neighborhood's upset, I know,
    By all these carriages that come and go,
    With crowds of guests parading in and out
    And noisy servants loitering about.
    In all of this, I'm sure there's nothing vicious;
    But why give people cause to be suspicious?
CLÉANTE: They need no cause, they'll talk in any case.
    Madam, this world would be a joyless place
    If, fearing what malicious tongues might say,
    We locked our doors and turned our friends away.
    And even if one did so dreary a thing,
    D'you think those tongues would cease their chattering?
    One can't fight slander; it's a losing battle;

Let us instead ignore their tittle-tattle.
Let's strive to live by conscience's clear decrees,
And let the gossips gossip as they please.
DORINE: If there is talk against us, I know the source:
It's Daphne and her little husband, of course.
Those who have greatest cause for guilt and shame
Are quickest to besmirch a neighbor's name.
When there's a chance for libel, they never miss it;
When something can be made to seem illicit
They're off at once to spread the joyous news,
Adding to fact what fantasies they choose.
By talking up their neighbor's indiscretions
They seek to camouflage their own transgressions,
Hoping that others' innocent affairs
Will lend a hue of innocence to theirs,
Or that their own black guilt will come to seem
Part of a general shady color-scheme.
MADAME PERNELLE: All that is quite irrelevant. I doubt
That anyone's more virtuous and devout
Than dear Orante; and I'm informed that she
Condemns your mode of life most vehemently.
DORINE: Oh, yes, she's strict, devout, and has no taint
Of worldliness; in short, she seems a saint.
But it was time which taught her that disguise;
She's thus because she can't be otherwise.
So long as her attractions could enthrall,
She flounced and flirted and enjoyed it all,
But now that they're no longer what they were
She quits a world which fast is quitting her,
And wears a veil of virtue to conceal
Her bankrupt beauty and her lost appeal.
That's what becomes of old coquettes today:
Distressed when all their lovers fall away,
They see no recourse but to play the prude,
And so confer a style on solitude.
Thereafter, they're severe with everyone,
Condemning all our actions, pardoning none,
And claiming to be pure, austere, and zealous
When, if the truth were known, they're merely jealous,
And cannot bear to see another know
The pleasures time has forced them to forgo.
MADAME PERNELLE: [*initially to* ELMIRE] That sort of talk is what you like to hear;
Therefore you'd have us all keep still, my dear,
While Madam rattles on the livelong day.
Nevertheless, I mean to have my say.
I tell you that you're blest to have Tartuffe
Dwelling, as my son's guest, beneath this roof;
That Heaven has sent him to forestall its wrath
By leading you, once more, to the true path;

That all he reprehends is reprehensible,
And that you'd better heed him, and be sensible.
These visits, balls, and parties in which you revel
Are nothing but inventions of the Devil.
One never hears a word that's edifying:
Nothing but chaff and foolishness and lying,
As well as vicious gossip in which one's neighbor
Is cut to bits with épée, foil, and saber.
People of sense are driven half-insane
At such affairs, where noise and folly reign
And reputations perish thick and fast.
As a wise preacher said on Sunday last,
Parties are Towers of Babylon, because
The guests all babble on with never a pause;
And then he told a story which, I think . . .
[*to* CLÉANTE] I heard that laugh, Sir, and I saw that wink!
Go find your silly friends and laugh some more!
Enough; I'm going; don't show me to the door.
I leave this household much dismayed and vexed;
I cannot say when I shall see you next.
[*slapping* FLIPOTE] Wake up, don't stand there gaping into space!
I'll slap some sense into that stupid face.
Move, move, you slut.

> [*All except* CLÉANTE *and* DORINE *exit.*]

SCENE II

CLÉANTE: I think I'll stay behind;
 I want no further pieces of her mind.
 How that old lady . . .
DORINE: Oh, what wouldn't she say
 If she could hear you speak of her that way!
 She'd thank you for the *lady*, but I'm sure
 She'd find the *old* a little premature.
CLÉANTE: My, what a scene she made, and what a din!
 And how this man Tartuffe has taken her in!
DORINE: Yes, but her son is even worse deceived;
 His folly must be seen to be believed.
 In the late troubles, he played an able part
 And served his king with wise and loyal heart,
 But he's quite lost his senses since he fell
 Beneath Tartuffe's infatuating spell.
 He calls him brother, and loves him as his life,
 Preferring him to mother, child, or wife.
 In him and him alone will he confide;
 He's made him his confessor and his guide;
 He pets and pampers him with love more tender
 Than any pretty mistress could engender,
 Gives him the place of honor when they dine,
 Delights to see him gorging like a swine,
 Stuffs him with dainties till his guts distend,
 And when he belches, cries "God bless you, friend!"

In short, he's mad; he worships him; he dotes;
His deeds he marvels at, his words he quotes;
Thinking each act a miracle, each word
Oracular as those that Moses heard.
Tartuffe, much pleased to find so easy a victim,
Has in a hundred ways beguiled and tricked him,
Milked him of money, and with his permission
Established here a sort of Inquisition.
Even Laurent, his lackey, dares to give
Us arrogant advice on how to live;
He sermonizes us in thundering tones
And confiscates our ribbons and colognes.
Last week he tore a kerchief into pieces
Because he found it pressed in a *Life of Jesus:*
He said it was a sin to juxtapose
Unholy vanities and holy prose.

SCENE III

ELMIRE: [*to* CLÉANTE] You did well not to follow; she stood in the door
    And said *verbatim* all she'd said before.
    I saw my husband coming. I think I'd best
    Go upstairs now, and take a little rest.
CLÉANTE: I'll wait and greet him here; then I must go.
    I've really only time to say hello.
DAMIS: Sound him about my sister's wedding, please.
    I think Tartuffe's against it, and that he's
    Been urging Father to withdraw his blessing.
    As you well know, I'd find that most distressing.
    Unless my sister and Valère can marry,
    My hopes to wed *his* sister will miscarry,
    And I'm determined . . .
DORINE: He's coming.

SCENE IV

ORGON: Ah, Brother, good-day.
CLÉANTE: Well, welcome back. I'm sorry I can't stay.
    How was the country? Blooming, I trust, and green?
ORGON: Excuse me, Brother; just one moment.
    [*to* DORINE] Dorine . . .
    [*to* CLÉANTE] To put my mind at rest, I always learn
    The household news the moment I return.
    [*to* DORINE] Has all been well, these two days I've been gone?
    How are the family? What's been going on?
DORINE: Your wife, two days ago, had a bad fever,
    And a fierce headache which refused to leave her.
ORGON: Ah. And Tartuffe?
DORINE: Tartuffe? Why, he's round and red,
    Bursting with health, and excellently fed.
ORGON: Poor fellow!

DORINE: That night, the mistress was unable
  To take a single bite at the dinner-table.
  Her headache-pains, she said, were simply hellish.
ORGON: Ah. And Tartuffe?
DORINE: He ate his meal with relish,
  And zealously devoured in her presence
  A leg of mutton and a brace of pheasants.
ORGON: Poor fellow!
DORINE: Well, the pains continued strong,
  And so she tossed and tossed the whole night long,
  Now icy-cold, now burning like a flame.
  We sat beside her bed till morning came.
ORGON: Ah. And Tartuffe?
DORINE: Why, having eaten, he rose
  And sought his room, already in a doze,
  Got into his warm bed, and snored away
  In perfect peace until the break of day.
ORGON: Poor fellow!
DORINE: After much ado, we talked her
  Into dispatching someone for the doctor.
  He bled her, and the fever quickly fell.
ORGON: Ah. And Tartuffe?
DORINE: He bore it very well.
  To keep his cheerfulness at any cost,
  And make up for the blood *Madame* had lost,
  He drank, at lunch, four beakers full of port.
ORGON: Poor fellow!
DORINE: Both are doing well, in short.
  I'll go and tell *Madame* that you've expressed
  Keen sympathy and anxious interest.

SCENE V

CLÉANTE: That girl was laughing in your face, and though
  I've no wish to offend you, even so
  I'm bound to say that she had some excuse.
  How can you possibly be such a goose?
  Are you so dazed by this man's hocus-pocus
  That all the world, save him, is out of focus?
  You've given him clothing, shelter, food, and care;
  Why must you also . . .
ORGON: Brother, stop right there.
  You do not know the man of whom you speak.
CLÉANTE: I grant you that. But my judgment's not so weak
  That I can't tell, by his effect on others . . .
ORGON: Ah, when you meet him, you two will be like brothers!
  There's been no loftier soul since time began.
  He is a man who . . . a man who . . . an excellent man.
  To keep his precepts is to be reborn,
  And view this dunghill of a world with scorn.

Yes, thanks to him I'm a changed man indeed.
Under his tutelage my soul's been freed
From earthly loves, and every human tie:
My mother, children, brother, and wife could die,
And I'd not feel a single moment's pain.
CLÉANTE: That's a fine sentiment, Brother; most humane.
ORGON: Oh, had you seen Tartuffe as I first knew him,
Your heart, like mine, would have surrendered to him.
He used to come into our church each day
And humbly kneel nearby, and start to pray.
He'd draw the eyes of everybody there
By the deep fervor of his heartfelt prayer;
He'd sigh and weep, and sometimes with a sound
Of rapture he would bend and kiss the ground;
And when I rose to go, he'd run before
To offer me holy-water at the door.
His serving-man, no less devout than he,
Informed me of his master's poverty;
I gave him gifts, but in his humbleness
He'd beg me every time to give him less.
"Oh, that's too much," he'd cry, "too much by twice!
I don't deserve it. The half, Sir, would suffice."
And when I wouldn't take it back, he'd share
Half of it with the poor, right then and there.
At length, Heaven prompted me to take him in
To dwell with us, and free our souls from sin.
He guides our lives, and to protect my honor
Stays by my wife, and keeps an eye upon her;
He tells me whom she sees, and all she does,
And seems more jealous than I ever was!
And how austere he is! Why, he can detect
A mortal sin where you would least suspect;
In smallest trifles, he's extremely strict.
Last week, his conscience was severely pricked
Because, while praying, he had caught a flea
And killed it, so he felt, too wrathfully.
CLÉANTE: Good God, man! Have you lost your common sense—
Or is this all some joke at my expense?
How can you stand there and in all sobriety . . .
ORGON: Brother, your language savors of impiety.
Too much free-thinking's made your faith unsteady,
And as I've warned you many times already,
'Twill get you into trouble before you're through.
CLÉANTE: So I've been told before by dupes like you:
Being blind, you'd have all others blind as well;
The clear-eyed man you call an infidel,
And he who sees through humbug and pretense
Is charged, by you, with want of reverence.
Spare me your warnings, Brother; I have no fear
Of speaking out, for you and Heaven to hear,

Against affected zeal and pious knavery.
There's true and false in piety, as in bravery,
And just as those whose courage shines the most
In battle, are the least inclined to boast,
So those whose hearts are truly pure and lowly
Don't make a flashy show of being holy.
There's a vast difference, so it seems to me,
Between true piety and hypocrisy:
How do you fail to see it, may I ask?
Is not a face quite different from a mask?
Cannot sincerity and cunning art,
Reality and semblance, be told apart?
Are scarecrows just like men, and do you hold
That a false coin is just as good as gold?
Ah, Brother, man's a strangely fashioned creature
Who seldom is content to follow Nature,
But recklessly pursues his inclination
Beyond the narrow bounds of moderation,
And often, by transgressing Reason's laws,
Perverts a lofty aim or noble cause.
A passing observation, but it applies.
ORGON: I see, dear Brother, that you're profoundly wise;
    You harbor all the insight of the age.
    You are our one clear mind, our only sage,
    The era's oracle, its Cato, too,
    And all mankind are fools compared to you.
CLÉANTE: Brother, I don't pretend to be a sage,
    Nor have I all the wisdom of the age.
    There's just one insight I would dare to claim:
    I know that true and false are not the same;
    And just as there is nothing I more revere
    Than a soul whose faith is steadfast and sincere,
    Nothing that I more cherish and admire
    Than honest zeal and true religious fire,
    So there is nothing that I find more base
    Than specious piety's dishonest face
    Than these bold mountebanks, these histrios
    Whose impious mummeries and hollow shows
    Exploit our love of Heaven, and make a jest
    Of all that men think holiest and best;
    These calculating souls who offer prayers
    Not to their Maker, but as public wares,
    And seek to buy respect and reputation
    With lifted eyes and sighs of exaltation;
    These charlatans, I say, whose pilgrim souls
    Proceed, by way of Heaven, toward earthly goals,
    Who weep and pray and swindle and extort,
    Who preach the monkish life, but haunt the court,
    Who make their zeal the partner of their vice—
    Such men are vengeful, sly, and cold as ice,

And when there is an enemy to defame
They cloak their spite in fair religion's name,
Their private spleen and malice being made
To seem a high and virtuous crusade,
Until, to mankind's reverent applause,
They crucify their foe in Heaven's cause.
Such knaves are all too common; yet, for the wise,
True piety isn't hard to recognize,
And happily, these present times provide us
With bright examples to instruct and guide us.
Consider Ariston and Périandre;
Look at Oronte, Alcidamas, Clitandre;
Their virtue is acknowledged; who could doubt it?
But you won't hear them beat the drum about it.
They're never ostentatious, never vain,
And their religion's moderate and humane;
It's not their way to criticize and chide:
They think censoriousness a mark of pride,
And therefore, letting others preach and rave,
They show, by deeds, how Christians should behave.
They think no evil of their fellow man,
But judge of him kindly as they can.
They don't intrigue and wangle and conspire;
To lead a good life is their one desire;
The sinner wakes no rancorous hate in them;
It is the sin alone which they condemn;
Nor do they try to show a fiercer zeal
For Heaven's cause than Heaven itself could feel.
These men I honor, these men I advocate
As models for us all to emulate.
Your man is not their sort at all, I fear:
And, while your praise of him is quite sincere,
I think that you've been dreadfully deluded.

ORGON: Now then, dear Brother, is your speech concluded?

CLÉANTE: Why, yes.

ORGON: Your servant, Sir. [*He turns to go.*]

CLÉANTE: No, Brother; wait.
There's one more matter. You agreed of late
That young Valère might have your daughter's hand.

ORGON: I did.

CLÉANTE: And set the date, I understand.

ORGON: Quite so.

CLÉANTE: You've now postponed it; is that true?

ORGON: No doubt.

CLÉANTE: The match no longer pleases you?

ORGON: Who knows?

CLÉANTE: D'you mean to go back on your word?

ORGON: I won't say that.

CLÉANTE: Has anything occurred
Which might entitle you to break your pledge?

ORGON: Perhaps.

CLÉANTE: Why must you hem and haw, and hedge?
   The boy asked me to sound you in this affair . . .

ORGON: It's been a pleasure.

CLÉANTE: But what shall I tell Valère?

ORGON: Whatever you like.

CLÉANTE: But what have you decided?
   What are your plans?

ORGON: I plan, Sir, to be guided
   By Heaven's will.

CLÉANTE: Come, Brother, don't talk rot.
   You've given Valère your word; will you keep it, or not?

ORGON: Good day.

CLÉANTE: This looks like poor Valère's undoing;
   I'll go and warn him that there's trouble brewing.

ACT II

SCENE I

ORGON: Mariane.

MARIANE: Yes, Father?

ORGON: A word with you; come here.

MARIANE: What are you looking for?

ORGON: [*peering into a small closet*] Eavesdroppers, dear.
   I'm making sure we shan't be overheard.
   Someone in there could catch our every word.
   Ah, good, we're safe. Now, Mariane, my child,
   You're a sweet girl who's tractable and mild,
   Whom I hold dear, and think most highly of.

MARIANE: I'm deeply grateful, Father, for your love.

ORGON: That's well said, Daughter; and you can repay me
   If, in all things, you'll cheerfully obey me.

MARIANE: To please you, Sir, is what delights me best.

ORGON: Good, good. Now, what d'you think of Tartuffe, our guest?

MARIANE: I, Sir?

ORGON: Yes. Weigh your answer; think it through.

MARIANE: Oh, dear. I'll say whatever you wish me to.

ORGON: That's wisely said, my Daughter. Say of him, then,
   That he's the very worthiest of men,
   And that you're fond of him, and would rejoice
   In being his wife, if that should be my choice.
   Well?

MARIANE: What?

ORGON: What's that?

MARIANE: I . . .

ORGON: Well?

MARIANE: Forgive me, pray.

ORGON: Did you not hear me?

MARIANE: Of *whom*, Sir, must I say

That I am fond of him, and would rejoice
In being his wife, if that should be your choice?
ORGON: Why, of Tartuffe.
MARIANE: But, Father, that's false, you know.
Why would you have me say what isn't so?
ORGON: Because I am resolved it shall be true.
That it's my wish should be enough for you.
MARIANE: You can't mean, Father . . .
ORGON: Yes, Tartuffe shall be
Allied by marriage to this family,
And he's to be your husband, is that clear?
It's a father's privilege . . .

SCENE II

ORGON: [*to* DORINE] What are you doing in here?
Is curiosity so fierce a passion
With you, that you must eavesdrop in this fashion?
DORINE: There's lately been a rumor going about—
Based on some hunch or chance remark, no doubt—
That you mean Mariane to wed Tartuffe.
I've laughed it off, of course, as just a spoof.
ORGON: You find it so incredible?
DORINE: Yes, I do.
I won't accept that story, even from you.
ORGON: Well, you'll believe it when the thing is done.
DORINE: Yes, yes, of course. Go on and have your fun.
ORGON: I've never been more serious in my life.
DORINE: Ha!
ORGON: Daughter, I mean it; you're to be his wife.
DORINE: No, don't believe your father; it's all a hoax.
ORGON: See here, young woman . . .
DORINE: Come, Sir, no more jokes;
You can't fool us.
ORGON: How dare you talk that way?
DORINE: All right, then: we believe you, sad to say.
But how a man like you, who looks so wise
And wears a moustache of such splendid size,
Can be so foolish as to . . .
ORGON: Silence, please!
My girl, you take too many liberties.
I'm master here, as you must not forget.
DORINE: Do let's discuss this calmly; don't be upset.
You can't be serious, Sir, about this plan.
What should that bigot want with Mariane?
Praying and fasting ought to keep him busy.
And then, in terms of wealth and rank, what is he?
Why should a man of property like you
Pick out a beggar son-in-law?
ORGON: That will do.

Speak of his poverty with reverence.
His is pure and saintly indigence
Which far transcends all worldly pride and pelf.
He lost his fortune, as he says himself,
Because he cared for Heaven alone, and so
Was careless of his interests here below.
I mean to get him out of his present straits
And help him to recover his estates—
Which, in his part of the world, have no small fame.
Poor though he is, he's a gentleman just the same.

DORINE: Yes, so he tells us; and, Sir, it seems to me
    Such pride goes very ill with piety.
    A man whose spirit spurns this dungy earth
    Ought not to brag of lands and noble birth;
    Such worldly arrogance will hardly square
    With meek devotion and the life of prayer.
    . . . But this approach, I see, has drawn a blank;
    Let's speak, then, of his person, not his rank.
    Doesn't it seem to you a trifle grim
    To give a girl like her to a man like him?
    When two are so ill-suited, can't you see
    What the sad consequence is bound to be?
    A young girl's virtue is imperilled, Sir,
    When such a marriage is imposed on her;
    For if one's bridegroom isn't to one's taste,
    It's hardly an inducement to be chaste,
    And many a man with horns upon his brow
    Has made his wife the thing that she is now.
    It's hard to be a faithful wife, in short,
    To certain husbands of a certain sort,
    And he who gives his daughter to a man she hates
    Must answer for her sins at Heaven's gates.
    Think, Sir, before you play so risky a role.

ORGON: This servant-girl presumes to save my soul!

DORINE: You would do well to ponder what I've said.

ORGON: Daughter, we'll disregard this dunderhead.
    Just trust your father's judgment. Oh, I'm aware
    That I once promised you to young Valère;
    But now I hear he gambles, which greatly shocks me;
    What's more, I've doubts about his orthodoxy.
    His visits to church, I note, are very few.

DORINE: Would you have him go at the same hours as you,
    And kneel nearby, to be sure of being seen?

ORGON: I can dispense with such remarks, Dorine.
    [*to* MARIANE]
    Tartuffe, however, is sure of Heaven's blessing,
    And that's the only treasure worth possessing.
    This match will bring you joys beyond all measure;
    Your cup will overflow with every pleasure;

You two will interchange your faithful loves
Like two sweet cherubs, or two turtle-doves.
No harsh word shall be heard, no frown be seen,
And he shall make you happy as a queen.
DORINE: And she'll make him a cuckold, just wait and see.
ORGON: What language!
DORINE: Oh, he's a man of destiny;
He's *made* for horns, and what the stars demand
Your daughter's virtue surely can't withstand.
ORGON: Don't interrupt me further. Why can't you learn
That certain things are none of your concern?
DORINE: It's for your own sake that I interfere.
[*She repeatedly interrupts* ORGON *just as he is turning to speak to his daughter.*]
ORGON: Most kind of you. Now, hold your tongue, d'you hear?
DORINE: If I didn't love you . . .
ORGON: Spare me your affection.
DORINE: I'll love you, Sir, in spite of your objection.
ORGON: Blast!
DORINE: I can't bear, Sir, for your honor's sake,
To let you make this ludicrous mistake.
ORGON: You mean to go on talking?
DORINE: If I didn't protest
This sinful marriage, my conscience couldn't rest.
ORGON: If you don't hold your tongue, you little shrew . . .
DORINE: What, lost your temper? A pious man like you?
ORGON: Yes! Yes! You talk and talk. I'm maddened by it.
Once and for all, I tell you to be quiet.
DORINE: Well, I'll be quiet. But I'll be thinking hard.
ORGON: Think all you like, but you had better guard
That saucy tongue of yours, or I'll . . . [*turning back to* MARIANE] Now, child,
I've weighed this matter fully.
DORINE: [*aside*] It drives me wild
That I can't speak.
[ORGON *turns his head, and she is silent.*]
ORGON: Tartuffe is no young dandy,
But, still, his person . . .
DORINE: [*aside*] Is as sweet as candy.
ORGON: Is such that, even if you shouldn't care
For his other merits . . .
[*He turns and stands facing* DORINE, *arms crossed.*]
DORINE: [*aside*] They'll make a lovely pair.
If I were she, no man would marry me
Against my inclination, and go scot-free.
He'd learn, before the wedding-day was over,
How readily a wife can find a lover.
ORGON: [*to* DORINE] It seems you treat my orders as a joke.
DORINE: Why, what's the matter? 'Twas not to you I spoke.
ORGON: What *were* you doing?
DORINE: Talking to myself, that's all.

ORGON: Ah! [*aside*] One more bit of impudence and gall,
    And I shall give her a good slap in the face.
        [*He puts himself in position to slap her,* DORINE, *whenever he glances at her,
        stands immobile and silent.*]
    Daughter, you shall accept, and with good grace,
    The husband I've selected . . . Your wedding-day . . .
    [*to* DORINE] Why don't you talk to yourself?
DORINE: I've nothing to say.
ORGON: Come, just one word.
DORINE: No thank you, Sir. I pass.
ORGON: Come, speak; I'm waiting.
DORINE: I'd not be such an ass.
ORGON: [*turning to* MARIANE] In short, dear Daughter, I mean to be obeyed,
    And you must bow to the sound choice I've made.
DORINE: [*moving away*] I'd not wed such a monster, even in jest.
        [ORGON *attempts to slap her, but misses.*]
ORGON: Daughter, that maid of yours is a thorough pest;
    She makes me sinfully annoyed and nettled.
    I can't speak further; my nerves are too unsettled.
    She's so upset me by her insolent talk,
    I'll calm myself by going for a walk.

SCENE III

DORINE: [*returning*] Well, have you lost your tongue, girl? Must I play
    Your part, and say the lines you ought to say?
    Faced with a fate so hideous and absurd,
    Can you not utter one dissenting word?
MARIANE: What good would it do? A father's power is great.
DORINE: Resist him now, or it will be too late.
MARIANE: But . . .
DORINE: Tell him one cannot love at a father's whim;
    That you shall marry for yourself, not him;
    That since it's you who are to be the bride,
    It's you, not he, who must be satisfied;
    And that if his Tartuffe is so sublime,
    He's free to marry him at any time.
MARIANE: I've bowed so long to Father's strict control,
    I couldn't oppose him now, to save my soul.
DORINE: Come, come, Mariane. Do listen to reason, won't you?
    Valère has asked your hand. Do you love him, or don't you?
MARIANE: Oh, how unjust of you! What can you mean
    By asking such a question, dear Dorine?
    You know the depth of my affection for him;
    I've told you a hundred times how I adore him.
DORINE: I don't believe in everything I hear;
    Who knows if your professions were sincere?
MARIANE: They were, Dorine, and you do me wrong to doubt it;
    Heaven knows that I've been all too frank about it.
DORINE: You love him, then?

MARIANE: Oh, more than I can express.

DORINE: And he, I take it, cares for you no less?

MARIANE: I think so.

DORINE: And you both, with equal fire,
    Burn to be married?

MARIANE: That is our one desire.

DORINE: What of Tartuffe, then? What of your father's plan?

MARIANE: I'll kill myself, if I'm forced to wed that man.

DORINE: I hadn't thought of that recourse. How splendid!
    Just die, and all your troubles will be ended!
    A fine solution. Oh, it maddens me
    To hear you talk in that self-pitying key.

MARIANE: Dorine, how harsh you are! It's most unfair.
    You have no sympathy for my despair.

DORINE: I've none at all for people who talk drivel
    And, faced with difficulties, whine and snivel.

MARIANE: No doubt I'm timid, but it would be wrong . . .

DORINE: True love requires a heart that's firm and strong.

MARIANE: I'm strong in my affection for Valère,
    But coping with my father is his affair.

DORINE: But if your father's brain has grown so cracked
    Over his dear Tartuffe that he can retract
    His blessing, though your wedding-day was named,
    It's surely not Valère who's to be blamed.

MARIANE: If I defied my father, as you suggest,
    Would it not seem unmaidenly, at best?
    Shall I defend my love at the expense
    Of brazenness and disobedience?
    Shall I parade my heart's desires, and flaunt . . .

DORINE: No, I ask nothing of you. Clearly you want
    To be Madame Tartuffe, and I feel bound
    Not to oppose a wish so very sound.
    What right have I to criticize the match?
    Indeed, my dear, the man's a brilliant catch.
    Monsieur Tartuffe! Now, there's a man of weight!
    Yes, yes, Monsieur Tartuffe, I'm bound to state,
    Is quite a person; that's not to be denied;
    'Twill be no little thing to be his bride.
    The world already rings with his renown;
    He's a great noble—in his native town;
    His ears are red, he has a pink complexion,
    And all in all, he'll suit you to perfection.

MARIANE: Dear God!

DORINE: Oh, how triumphant you will feel
    At having caught a husband so ideal!

MARIANE: Oh, do stop teasing, and use your cleverness
    To get me out of this appalling mess.
    Advise me, and I'll do whatever you say.

DORINE: Ah no, a dutiful daughter must obey
    Her father, even if he weds her to an ape.

You've a bright future; why struggle to escape?
Tartuffe will take you back where his family lives,
To a small town aswarm with relatives—
Uncles and cousins whom you'll be charmed to meet.
You'll be received at once by the elite,
Calling upon the bailiff's wife, no less—
Even, perhaps, upon the mayoress,
Who'll sit you down in the *best* kitchen chair.
Then, once a year, you'll dance at the village fair
To the drone of bagpipes—two of them, in fact—
And see a puppet-show, or an animal act.
Your husband . . .

MARIANE: Oh, you turn my blood to ice!
    Stop torturing me, and give me your advice.
DORINE: [*threatening to go*] Your servant, Madam.
MARIANE: Dorine, I beg of you . . .
DORINE: No, you deserve it; this marriage must go through.
MARIANE: Dorine!
DORINE: No.
MARIANE: Not Tartuffe! You know I think him . . .
DORINE: Tartuffe's your cup of tea, and you shall drink him.
MARIANE: I've always told you everything, and relied . . .
DORINE: No. You deserve to be tartuffified.
MARIANE: Well, since you mock me and refuse to care,
    I'll henceforth seek my solace in despair:
    Despair shall be my counsellor and friend,
    And help me bring my sorrows to an end.
        [*She starts to leave.*]
DORINE: There now, come back; my anger has subsided.
    You do deserve some pity, I've decided.
MARIANE: Dorine, if Father makes me undergo
    This dreadful martyrdom, I'll die, I know.
DORINE: Don't fret; it won't be difficult to discover
    Some plan of action . . . But here's Valère, your lover.

SCENE IV

VALÈRE: Madam, I've just received some wondrous news
    Regarding which I'd like to hear your views.
MARIANE: What news?
VALÈRE: You're marrying Tartuffe.
MARIANE: I find
    That Father does have such a match in mind.
VALÈRE: Your father, Madam . . .
MARIANE: . . . has just this minute said
    That it's Tartuffe he wishes me to wed.
VALÈRE: Can he be serious?
MARIANE: Oh, indeed he can;
    He's clearly set his heart upon the plan.

VALÈRE: And what position do you propose to take,
    Madam?
MARIANE: Why—I don't know.
VALÈRE: For heaven's sake—
    You don't know?
MARIANE: No.
VALÈRE: Well, well!
MARIANE: Advise me, do.
VALÈRE: Marry the man. That's my advice to you.
MARIANE: That's your advice?
VALÈRE: Yes.
MARIANE: Truly?
VALÈRE: Oh, absolutely.
    You couldn't choose more wisely, more astutely.
MARIANE: Thanks for this counsel; I'll follow it, of course.
VALÈRE: Do, do; I'm sure 'twill cost you no remorse.
MARIANE: To give it didn't cause your heart to break.
VALÈRE: I gave it, Madam, only for your sake.
MARIANE: And it's for your sake that I take it, Sir.
DORINE: [*withdrawing to the rear of the stage*]
    Let's see which fool will prove the stubborner.
VALÈRE: So! I am nothing to you, and it was flat
    Deception when you . . .
MARIANE: Please, enough of that.
    You've told me plainly that I should agree
    To wed the man my father's chosen for me,
    And since you've deigned to counsel me so wisely,
    I promise, Sir, to do as you advise me.
VALÈRE: Ah, no 'twas not by me that you were swayed.
    No, your decision was already made;
    Though now, to save appearances, you protest
    That you're betraying me at my behest.
MARIANE: Just as you say.
VALÈRE: Quite so. And I now see
    That you were never truly in love with me.
MARIANE: Alas, you're free to think so if you choose.
VALÈRE: I choose to think so, and here's a bit of news:
    You've spurned my hand, but I know where to turn
    For kinder treatment, as you shall quickly learn.
MARIANE: I'm sure you do. Your noble qualities
    Inspire affection . . .
VALÈRE: Forget my qualities, please.
    They don't inspire you overmuch, I find.
    But there's another lady I have in mind
    Whose sweet and generous nature will not scorn
    To compensate me for the loss I've borne.
MARIANE: I'm no great loss, and I'm sure that you'll transfer
    Your heart quite painlessly from me to her.
VALÈRE: I'll do my best to take it in my stride.

The pain I feel at being cast aside
Time and forgetfulness may put an end to.
Or if I can't forget, I shall pretend to.
No self-respecting person is expected
To go on loving once he's been rejected.

MARIANE: Now, that's fine, high-minded sentiment.

VALÈRE: One to which any sane man would assent.
Would you prefer it if I pined away
In hopeless passion till my dying day?
Am I to yield you to a rival's arms
And not console myself with other charms?

MARIANE: Go then: console yourself; don't hesitate.
I wish you to; indeed, I cannot wait.

VALÈRE: You wish me to?

MARIANE: Yes.

VALÈRE: That's the final straw.
Madam, farewell. Your wish shall be my law.
[*He starts to leave, and then returns: this repeatedly.*]

MARIANE: Splendid.

VALÈRE: [*coming back again*] This breach, remember, is of your making;
It's you who've driven me to the step I'm taking.

MARIANE: Of course.

VALÈRE: [*coming back again*] Remember, too, that I am merely
Following your example.

MARIANE: I see that clearly.

VALÈRE: Enough. I'll go and do your bidding, then.

MARIANE: Good.

VALÈRE: [*coming back again*] You shall never see my face again.

MARIANE: Excellent.

VALÈRE: [*walking to the door, then turning about*] Yes?

MARIANE: What?

VALÈRE: What's that? What did you say?

MARIANE: Nothing. You're dreaming.

VALÈRE: Ah. Well, I'm on my way.
Farewell, *Madame.*
[*He moves slowly away.*]

MARIANE: Farewell.

DORINE: [*to* MARIANE] If you ask me,
Both of you are as mad as mad can be.
Do stop this nonsense, now. I've only let you
Squabble so long to see where it would get you.
Whoa there, Monsieur Valère!
[*She goes and seizes* VALÈRE *by the arm; he makes a great show of resistance.*]

VALÈRE: What's this, Dorine?

DORINE: Come here.

VALÈRE: No, no, my heart's too full of spleen.
Don't hold me back; her wish must be obeyed.

DORINE: Stop!

VALÈRE: It's too late now; my decision's made.

DORINE: Oh, pooh!

MARIANE: [*aside*] He hates the sight of me, that's plain.
    I'll go, and so deliver him from pain.
DORINE: [*leaving* VALÈRE, *running after* MARIANE] And now *you* run away!
    Come back.
MARIANE: No, no.
    Nothing you say will keep me here. Let go!
VALÈRE: [*aside*] She cannot bear my presence, I perceive.
    To spare her further torment, I shall leave.
DORINE: [*leaving* MARIANE, *running after* VALÈRE] Again! You'll not escape, Sir; don't you
    try it.
    Come here, you two. Stop fussing, and be quiet.
        [*She takes* VALÈRE *by the hand, then* MARIANE, *and draws them together.*]
VALÈRE: [*to* DORINE] What do you want of me?
MARIANE: [*to* DORINE] What is the point of this?
DORINE: We're going to have a little armistice.
    [*to* VALÈRE] Now, weren't you silly to get so overheated?
VALÈRE: Didn't you see how badly I was treated?
DORINE: [*to* MARIANE] Aren't you a simpleton, to have lost your head?
MARIANE: Didn't you hear the hateful things he said?
DORINE: [*to* VALÈRE] You're both great fools. Her sole desire, Valère,
    Is to be yours in marriage. To that I'll swear.
    [*to* MARIANE] He loves you only, and he wants no wife
    But you, Mariane. On that I'll stake my life.
MARIANE: [*to* VALÈRE] Then why you advised me so, I cannot see.
VALÈRE: [*to* MARIANE] On such a question, why ask advice of *me?*
DORINE: Oh, you're impossible. Give me your hands, you two.
        [*to* VALÈRE] Yours first.
VALÈRE: [*giving* DORINE *his hand*] But why?
DORINE: [*to* MARIANE] And now a hand from you.
MARIANE: [*also giving* DORINE *her hand*] What are you doing?
DORINE: There: a perfect fit.
    You suit each other better than you'll admit.
        [VALÈRE *and* MARIANE *hold hands for some time without looking at each other.*]
VALÈRE: [*turning toward* MARIANE] Ah, come, don't be so haughty. Give a man
    A look of kindness, won't you, Mariane?
        [MARIANE *Turns toward* VALÈRE *and smiles.*]
DORINE: I'll tell you, lovers are completely mad!
VALÈRE: [*to* MARIANE] Now come, confess that you were very bad
    To hurt my feelings as you did just now.
    I have a just complaint, you must allow.
MARIANE: *You* must allow that you were most unpleasant . . .
DORINE: Let's table that discussion for the present;
    Your father has a plan which must be stopped.
MARIANE: Advise us, then; what means must we adopt?
DORINE: We'll use all manner of means, and all at once.
    [*to* MARIANE] Your father's addled; he's acting like a dunce.
    Therefore you'd better humor the old fossil.
    Pretend to yield to him, be sweet and docile,
    And then postpone, as often as necessary,
    The day on which you have agreed to marry.

You'll thus gain time, and time will turn the trick.
Sometimes, for instance, you'll be taken sick,
And that will seem good reason for delay;
Or some bad omen will make you change the day—
You'll dream of muddy water, or you'll pass
A dead man's hearse, or break a looking-glass
If all else fails, no man can marry you
Unless you take his ring and say "I do."
But now, let's separate. If they should find
Us talking here, our plot might be divined.
[*to* VALÈRE] Go to your friends, and tell them what's occurred,
And have them urge her father to keep his word.
Meanwhile, we'll stir her brother into action,
And get Elmire, as well, to join our faction.
Good-bye.

VALÈRE: [*to* MARIANE] Though each of us will do his best,
It's your true heart on which my hopes shall rest.

MARIANE: [*to* VALÈRE] Regardless of what Father may decide,
None but Valère shall claim me as his bride.

VALÈRE: Oh, how those words content me! Come what will . . .

DORINE: Oh, lovers, lovers! Their tongues are never still.
Be off, now.

VALÈRE: [*turning to go, then turning back*] One last word . . .

DORINE: No time to chat:
You leave by this door; and *you* leave by that.
[DORINE *pushes them, by the shoulders, toward opposing doors.*]

ACT III

SCENE I

DAMIS: May lightning strike me even as I speak,
May all men call me cowardly and weak,
If any fear or scruple holds me back
From settling things, at once, with that great quack!

DORINE: Now, don't give way to violent emotion.
Your father's merely talked about this notion,
And words and deeds are far from being one.
Much that is talked about is left undone.

DAMIS: No, I must stop that scoundrel's machinations;
I'll go and tell him off; I'm out of patience.

DORINE: Do calm down and be practical. I had rather
My mistress dealt with him—and with your father.
She has some influence with Tartuffe, I've noted.
He hangs upon her words, seems most devoted,
And may, indeed, be smitten by her charm.
Pray Heaven it's true! 'Twould do our cause no harm.
She sent for him, just now, to sound him out
On this affair you're so incensed about;
She'll find out where he stands, and tell him, too

What dreadful strife and trouble will ensue
If he lends countenance to your father's plan.
I couldn't get in to see him, but his man
Says that he's almost finished with his prayers.
Go, now. I'll catch him when he comes downstairs.

DAMIS: I want to hear this conference, and I will.

DORINE: No, they must be alone.

DAMIS: Oh, I'll keep still.

DORINE: Not you. I know your temper. You'd start a brawl,
And shout and stamp your foot and spoil it all.
Go on.

DAMIS: I won't; I have a perfect right . . .

DORINE: Lord, you're a nuisance! He's coming; get out of sight.

    [DAMIS *conceals himself in a closet at the rear of the stage.*]

SCENE II

TARTUFFE: [*observing* DORINE, *and calling to his manservant offstage*] Hang up my hair-
shirt, put my scourge in place,
And pray, Laurent, for Heaven's perpetual grace.
I'm going to the prison now, to share
My last few coins with the poor wretches there.

DORINE: [*aside*] Dear God, what affectation! What a fake!

TARTUFFE: You wished to see me?

DORINE: Yes . . .

TARTUFFE: [*taking a handkerchief from his pocket*] For mercy's sake,
Please take this handkerchief, before you speak.

DORINE: What?

TARTUFFE: Cover that bosom, girl. The flesh is weak,
And unclean thoughts are difficult to control.
Such sights as that can undermine the soul.

DORINE: Your soul, it seems, has very poor defenses,
And flesh makes quite an impact on your senses.
It's strange that you're so easily excited;
My own desires are not so soon ignited,
And if I saw you naked as a beast,
Not all your hide would tempt me in the least.

TARTUFFE: Girl, speak more modestly; unless you do,
I shall be forced to take my leave of you.

DORINE: Oh, no, it's I who must be on my way;
I've just one little message to convey.
Madame is coming down, and begs you, Sir,
To wait and have a word or two with her.

TARTUFFE: Gladly.

DORINE: [*aside*] *That* had a softening effect!
I think my guess about him was correct.

TARTUFFE: Will she be long?

DORINE: No: that's her step I hear.
Ah, here she is, and I shall disappear.

SCENE III

TARTUFFE: May heaven, whose infinite goodness we adore,
    Preserve your body and soul forevermore,
    And bless your days, and answer thus the plea
    Of one who is its humblest votary.
ELMIRE: I thank you for that pious wish. But please,
    Do take a chair and let's be more at ease.
        [*They sit down.*]
TARTUFFE: I trust that you are once more well and strong?
ELMIRE: Oh, yes: the fever didn't last for long.
TARTUFFE: My prayers are too unworthy, I am sure,
    To have gained from Heaven this most gracious cure;
    But lately, Madam, my every supplication
    Has had for object your recuperation.
ELMIRE: You shouldn't have troubled so. I don't deserve it.
TARTUFFE: Your health is priceless, Madam, and to preserve it
    I'd gladly give my own, in all sincerity.
ELMIRE: Sir, you outdo us all in Christian charity.
    You've been most kind. I count myself your debtor.
TARTUFFE: 'Twas nothing, Madam. I long to serve you better.
ELMIRE: There's a private matter I'm anxious to discuss.
    I'm glad there's no one here to hinder us.
TARTUFFE: I, too, am glad; it floods my heart with bliss
    To find myself alone with you like this.
    For just this chance I've prayed with all my power—
    But prayed in vain, until this happy hour.
ELMIRE: This won't take long, Sir, and I hope you'll be
    Entirely frank and unconstrained with me.
TARTUFFE: Indeed, there's nothing I had rather do
    Than bare my inmost heart and soul to you.
    First, let me say that what remarks I've made
    About the constant visits you are paid
    Were prompted not by any mean emotion,
    But rather by a pure and deep devotion,
    A fervent zeal . . .
ELMIRE: No need for explanation.
    Your sole concern, I'm sure, was my salvation.
TARTUFFE: [*taking* ELMIRE'S *hand and pressing her fingertips*] Quite so; and such great fervor do I feel . . .
ELMIRE: Ooh! Please! You're pinching!
TARTUFFE: 'Twas from excess of zeal.
    I never meant to cause you pain, I swear.
    I'd rather . . . [*He places his hand on* ELMIRE'S *knee.*]
ELMIRE: What can your hand be doing there?
TARTUFFE: Feeling your gown; what soft, fine-woven stuff!
ELMIRE: Please, I'm extremely ticklish. That's enough.
        [*She draws her chair away;* TARTUFFE *pulls his after her.*]
TARTUFFE: [*fondling the lace collar of her gown*] My, my, what lovely lacework on your
  dress!

The workmanship's miraculous, no less.
I've not seen anything to equal it.
ELMIRE: Yes, quite. But let's talk business for a bit.
They say my husband means to break his word
And give his daughter to you, Sir. Had you heard?
TARTUFFE: He did once mention it. But I confess
I dream of quite a different happiness.
It's elsewhere, Madam, that my eyes discern
The promise of that bliss for which I yearn.
ELMIRE: I see: you care for nothing here below.
TARTUFFE: Ah, well—my heart's not made of stone, you know.
ELMIRE: All your desires mount heavenward, I'm sure,
In scorn of all that's earthly and impure.
TARTUFFE: A love of heavenly beauty does not preclude
A proper love for earthly pulchritude;
Our senses are quite rightly captivated
By perfect works our Maker has created.
Some glory clings to all that Heaven has made;
In you, all Heaven's marvels are displayed.
On that fair face, such beauties have been lavished,
The eyes are dazzled and the heart is ravished;
How could I look on you, O flawless creature,
And not adore the Author of all Nature,
Feeling a love both passionate and pure
For you, this triumph of self-portraiture?
At first, I trembled lest that love should be
A subtle snare that Hell had laid for me;
I vowed to flee the sight of you, eschewing
A rapture that might prove my soul's undoing;
But soon, fair being, I became aware
That my deep passion could be made to square
With rectitude, and with my bounden duty.
I thereupon surrendered to your beauty.
It is, I know, presumptuous on my part
To bring you this poor offering of my heart,
And it is not my merit, Heaven knows,
But your compassion on which my hopes repose.
You are my peace, my solace, my salvation;
On you depends my bliss—or desolation;
I bide your judgment and, as you think best,
I shall be either miserable or blest.
ELMIRE: Your declaration is most gallant, Sir,
But don't you think it's out of character?
You'd have done better to restrain your passion
And think before you spoke in such a fashion.
It ill becomes a pious man like you . . .
TARTUFFE: I may be pious, but I'm human, too:
With your celestial charms before his eyes,
A man has not the power to be wise.
I know such words sound strangely, coming from me,

But I'm no angel, nor was meant to be,
And if you blame my passion, you must needs
Reproach as well the charms on which it feeds.
Your loveliness I had no sooner seen
Than you became my soul's unrivalled queen;
Before your seraph glance, divinely sweet,
My heart's defenses crumbled in defeat,
And nothing fasting, prayer, or tears might do
Could stay my spirit from adoring you.
My eyes, my sighs have told you in the past
What now my lips make bold to say at last,
And if, in your great goodness, you will deign
To look upon your slave, and ease his pain—
If, in compassion for my soul's distress,
You'll stoop to comfort my unworthiness,
I'll raise to you, in thanks for that sweet manna,
An endless hymn, an infinite hosanna.
With me, of course, there need be no anxiety,
No fear of scandal or of notoriety.
These young court gallants, whom all the ladies fancy,
Are vain in speech, in action rash and chancy;
When they succeed in love, the world soon knows it;
No favor's granted them but they disclose it
And by the looseness of their tongues profane
The very altar where their hearts have lain.
Men of my sort, however, love discreetly,
And one may trust our reticence completely.
My keen concern for my good name insures
The absolute security of yours;
In short, I offer you, my dear Elmire,
Love without scandal, pleasure without fear.

ELMIRE: I've heard your well-turned speeches to the end,
And what you urge I clearly apprehend.
Aren't you afraid that I may take a notion
To tell my husband of your warm devotion,
And that, supposing he were duly told,
His feelings toward you might grow rather cold?

TARTUFFE: I know, dear lady, that your exceeding charity
Will lead your heart to pardon my temerity;
That you'll excuse my violent affection
As human weakness, human imperfection;
And that—O fairest!—you will bear in mind
That I'm but flesh and blood, and am not blind.

ELMIRE: Some women might do otherwise, perhaps,
But I shall be discreet about your lapse;
I'll tell my husband nothing of what's occurred
If, in return, you'll give your solemn word
To advocate as forcefully as you can

The marriage of Valère and Mariane,
Renouncing all desire to dispossess
Another of his rightful happiness,
And . . .

SCENE IV

DAMIS: [*emerging from the closet where he has been hiding*] No! We'll not hush up this vile affair;
I heard it all inside that closet there,
Where Heaven, in order to confound the pride
Of this great rascal, prompted me to hide.
Ah, now I have my long-awaited chance
To punish his deceit and arrogance,
And give my father clear and shocking proof
Of the black character of his dear Tartuffe.

ELMIRE: Ah no, Damis; I'll be content if he
Will study to deserve my leniency.
I've promised silence—don't make me break my word;
To make a scandal would be too absurd.
Good wives laugh off such trifles, and forget them;
Why should they tell their husbands, and upset them?

DAMIS: You have your reasons for taking such a course,
And I have reasons, too, of equal force.
To spare him now would be insanely wrong.
I've swallowed my just wrath for far too long
And watched this insolent bigot bringing strife
And bitterness into our family life.
Too long he's meddled in my father's affairs,
Thwarting my marriage-hopes, and poor Valère's.
It's high time that my father was undeceived,
And now I've proof that can't be disbelieved—
Proof that was furnished me by Heaven above.
It's too good not to take advantage of.
This is my chance, and I deserve to lose it
If, for one moment, I hesitate to use it.

ELMIRE: Damis . . .

DAMIS: No, I must do what I think right.
Madam, my heart is bursting with delight,
And, say whatever you will, I'll not consent
To lose the sweet revenge on which I'm bent.
I'll settle matters without more ado;
And here, most opportunely, is my cue.

SCENE V

DAMIS: Father, I'm glad you've joined us. Let us advise you
Of some fresh news which doubtless will surprise you.

You've just now been repaid with interest
For all your loving-kindness to our guest.
He's proved his warm and grateful feelings toward you;
It's with a pair of horns he would reward you.
Yes, I surprised him with your wife, and heard
His whole adulterous offer, every word.
She, with her all-too-gentle disposition,
Would not have told you of his proposition;
But I shall not make terms with brazen lechery,
And feel that not to tell you would be treachery.

ELMIRE: And I hold that one's husband's peace of mind
    Should not be spoilt by tattle of this kind.
    One's honor doesn't require it: to be proficient
    In keeping men at bay is quite sufficient.
    These are my sentiments, and I wish, Damis,
    That you had heeded me and held your peace. [*Exit.*]

SCENE VI

ORGON: Can it be true, this dreadful thing I hear?
TARTUFFE: Yes, Brother, I'm a wicked man, I fear:
    A wretched sinner, all depraved and twisted,
    The greatest villain that has ever existed.
    My life's one heap of crimes, which grows each minute;
    There's naught but foulness and corruption in it;
    And I perceive that Heaven, outraged by me,
    Has chosen this occasion to mortify me.
    Charge me with any deed you wish to name;
    I'll not defend myself, but take the blame.
    Believe what you are told, and drive Tartuffe
    Like some base criminal from beneath your roof;
    Yes, drive me hence, and with a parting curse:
    I shan't protest, for I deserve far worse.
ORGON: [*to* DAMIS] Ah, you deceitful boy, how dare you try
    To stain his purity with so foul a lie?
DAMIS: What! are you taken in by such a bluff?
    Did you not hear . . . ?
ORGON: Enough, you rogue, enough!
TARTUFFE: Ah. Brother, let him speak: you're being unjust.
    Believe his story; the boy deserves your trust.
    Why, after all, should you have faith in me?
    How can you know what I might do, or be?
    Is it on my good actions that you base
    Your favor? Do you trust my pious face?
    Ah, no, don't be deceived by hollow shows;
    I'm far, alas, from being what men suppose;
    Though the world takes me for a man of worth,
    I'm truly the most worthless man on Earth.

[*to* DAMIS] Yes, my dear son, speak out now: call me the chief
Of sinners, a wretch, a murderer, a thief;
Load me with all the names men most abhor;
I'll not complain; I've earned them all, and more;
I'll kneel here while you pour them on my head
As a just punishment for the life I've led.

ORGON: [*to* TARTUFFE] This is too much, dear Brother. [*to* DAMIS] Have you no heart?

DAMIS: Are you so hoodwinked by this rascal's art . . . ?

ORGON: Be still, you monster. [*to* TARTUFFE] Brother, I pray you, rise.
[*to* DAMIS] Villain!

DAMIS: But . . .

ORGON: Silence!

DAMIS: Can't you realize . . . ?

ORGON: Just one word more, and I'll tear you limb from limb.

TARTUFFE: In God's name, Brother, don't be harsh with him.
I'd rather far be tortured at the stake
Than see him bear one scratch for my poor sake.

ORGON: [*to* DAMIS] Ingrate!

TARTUFFE: If I must beg you, on bended knee,
To pardon him . . .

ORGON: [*falling to his knees, addressing* TARTUFFE] Such goodness cannot be!
[*to* DAMIS] Now, *there's* true charity!

DAMIS: What, you . . . ?

ORGON: Villain, be still!
I know your motives; I know you wish him ill:
Yes, all of you—wife, children, servants, all—
Conspire against him and desire his fall,
Employing every shameful trick you can
To alienate me from this saintly man.
Ah, but the more you seek to drive him away,
The more I'll do to keep him. Without delay,
I'll spite this household and confound its pride
By giving him my daughter as his bride.

DAMIS: You're going to force her to accept his hand?

ORGON: Yes, and this very night, d'you understand?
I shall defy you all, and make it clear
That I'm the one who gives the orders here.
Come, wretch, kneel down and clasp his blessed feet,
And ask his pardon for your black deceit.

DAMIS: I ask that swindler's pardon? Why, I'd rather . . .

ORGON: So! You insult him, and defy your father!
A stick! A stick! [*to* TARTUFFE] No, no—release me, do.
[*to* DAMIS] Out of my house this minute! Be off with you,
And never dare set foot in it again.

DAMIS: Well, I shall go, but . . .

ORGON: Well, go quickly, then.
I disinherit you; an empty purse
Is all you'll get from me—except my curse!

SCENE VII

ORGON: How he blasphemed your goodness! What a son!

TARTUFFE: Forgive him, Lord, as I've already done.
[*to* ORGON] You can't know how it hurts when someone tries
To blacken me in my dear Brother's eyes.

ORGON: Ahh!

TARTUFFE: The mere thought of such ingratitude
Plunges my soul into so dark a mood . . .
Such horror grips my heart . . . I gasp for breath,
And cannot speak, and feel myself near death.

ORGON: [*He runs, in tears, to the door through which he has just driven his son.*]
You blackguard! Why did I spare you? Why did I not
Break you in little pieces on the spot?
Compose yourself, and don't be hurt, dear friend.

TARTUFFE: These scenes, these dreadful quarrels, have got to end.
I've much upset your household, and I perceive
That the best thing will be for me to leave.

ORGON: What are you saying!

TARTUFFE: They're all against me here;
They'd have you think me false and insincere.

ORGON: Ah, what of that? Have I ceased believing in you?

TARTUFFE: Their adverse talk will certainly continue,
And charges which you now repudiate
You may find credible at a later date.

ORGON: No, Brother, never.

TARTUFFE: Brother, a wife can sway
Her husband's mind in many a subtle way.

ORGON: No, no.

TARTUFFE: To leave at once is the solution;
Thus only can I end their persecution.

ORGON: No, no, I'll not allow it; you shall remain.

TARTUFFE: Ah, well; 'twill mean much martyrdom and pain,
But if you wish it . . .

ORGON: Ah!

TARTUFFE: Enough; so be it.
But one thing must be settled, as I see it.
For your dear honor, and for our friendship's sake,
There's one precaution I feel bound to take.
I shall avoid your wife, and keep away . . .

ORGON: No, you shall not, whatever they may say.
It pleases me to vex them, and for spite
I'd have them see you with her day and night.
What's more, I'm going to drive them to despair
By making you my only son and heir;
This very day, I'll give to you alone
Clear deed and title to everything I own.
A dear, good friend and son-in-law-to-be
Is more than wife, or child, or kin to me.

Will you accept my offer, dearest son?
TARTUFFE: In all things, let the will of Heaven be done.
ORGON: Poor fellow! Come, we'll go draw up the deed.
      Then let them burst with disappointed greed!

ACT IV

SCENE I

CLÉANTE: Yes, all the town's discussing it, and truly,
      Their comments do not flatter you unduly.
      I'm glad we've met, Sir, and I'll give my view
      Of this sad matter in a word or two.
      As for who's guilty, that I shan't discuss;
      Let's say it was Damis who caused the fuss;
      Assuming, then, that you have been ill-used
      By young Damis, and groundlessly accused,
      Ought not a Christian to forgive, and ought
      He not to stifle every vengeful thought?
      Should you stand by and watch a father make
      His only son an exile for your sake?
      Again I tell you frankly, be advised:
      The whole town, high and low, is scandalized;
      This quarrel must be mended, and my advice is
      Not to push matters to a further crisis.
      No, sacrifice your wrath to God above,
      And help Damis regain his father's love.
TARTUFFE: Alas, for my part I should take great joy
      In doing so. I've nothing against the boy.
      I pardon all, I harbor no resentment;
      To serve him would afford me much contentment.
      But Heaven's interest will not have it so:
      If he comes back, then I shall have to go.
      After his conduct—so extreme, so vicious—
      Our further intercourse would look suspicious.
      God knows what people would think! Why, they'd describe
      My goodness to him as a sort of bribe;
      They'd say that out of guilt I made pretense
      Of loving-kindness and benevolence—
      That, fearing my accuser's tongue, I strove
      To buy his silence with a show of love.
CLÉANTE: Your reasoning is badly warped and stretched,
      And these excuses, Sir, are most farfetched.
      Why put yourself in charge of Heaven's cause?
      Does Heaven need our help to enforce its laws?
      Leave vengeance to the Lord, Sir; while we live,
      Our duty's not to punish, but forgive;
      And what the Lord commands, we should obey

Without regard to what the world may say.
What! Shall the fear of being misunderstood
Prevent our doing what is right and good?
No, no; let's simply do what Heaven ordains,
And let no other thoughts perplex our brains.

TARTUFFE: Again, Sir, let me say that I've forgiven
Damis, and thus obeyed the laws of Heaven;
But I am not commanded by the Bible
To live with one who smears my name with libel.

CLÉANTE: Were you commanded, Sir, to indulge the whim
Of poor Orgon, and to encourage him
In suddenly transferring to your name
A large estate to which you have no claim?

TARTUFFE: 'Twould never occur to those who know me best
To think I acted from self-interest.
The treasures of this world I quite despise;
Their specious glitter does not charm my eyes;
And if I have resigned myself to taking
The gift which my dear Brother insists on making,
I do so only, as he well understands,
Lest so much wealth fall into wicked hands,
Lest those to whom it might descend in time
Turn it to purposes of sin and crime,
And not, as I shall do, make use of it
For Heaven's glory and mankind's benefit.

CLÉANTE: Forget these trumped-up fears. Your argument
Is one the rightful heir might well resent;
It *is* a moral burden to inherit
Such wealth, but give Damis a chance to bear it.
And would it not be worse to be accused
Of swindling, than to see that wealth misused?
I'm shocked that you allowed Orgon to broach
This matter, and that you feel no self-reproach;
Does true religion teach that lawful heirs
May freely be deprived of what is theirs?
And if the Lord has told you in your heart
That you and young Damis must dwell apart,
Would it not be the decent thing to beat
A generous and honorable retreat,
Rather than let the son of the house be sent,
For your convenience, into banishment?
Sir, if you wish to prove the honesty
Of your intentions . . .

TARTUFFE: Sir, it is half-past three.
I've certain pious duties to attend to,
And hope my prompt departure won't offend you.

CLÉANTE: [*alone*] Damn.

SCENE II

DORINE: Stay, Sir, and help Mariane, for Heaven's sake!
 She's suffering so, I fear her heart will break.
 Her father's plan to marry her off tonight
 Has put the poor child in a desperate plight.
 I hear him coming. Let's stand together, now,
 And see if we can't change his mind, somehow,
 About this match we all deplore and fear.

SCENE III

ORGON: Hah! Glad to find you all assembled here.
 [*to* MARIANE] This contract, child, contains your happiness,
 And what it says I think your heart can guess.
MARIANE: [*falling to her knees*] Sir, by that Heaven which sees me here distressed,
 And by whatever else can move your breast,
 Do not employ a father's power, I pray you,
 To crush my heart and force it to obey you,
 Nor by your harsh commands oppress me so
 That I'll begrudge the duty which I owe—
 And do not so embitter and enslave me
 That I shall hate the very life you gave me.
 If my sweet hopes must perish, if you refuse
 To give me to the one I've dared to choose,
 Spare me at least—I beg you, I implore—
 The pain of wedding one whom I abhor;
 And do not, by a heartless use of force,
 Drive me to contemplate some desperate course.
ORGON: [*feeling himself touched by her*] Be firm, my soul. No human weakness, now.
MARIANE: I don't resent your love for him. Allow
 Your heart free rein, Sir; give him your property,
 And if that's not enough, take mine from me;
 He's welcome to my money; take it, do,
 But don't, I pray, include my person, too.
 Spare me, I beg you; and let me end the tale
 Of my sad days behind a convent veil.
ORGON: A convent! Hah! When crossed in their amours,
 All lovesick girls have the same thought as yours.
 Get up! The more you loathe the man, and dread him,
 The more ennobling it will be to wed him.
 Marry Tartuffe, and mortify your flesh!
 Enough; don't start that whimpering afresh.
DORINE: But why . . . ?
ORGON: Be still, there. Speak when you're spoken to.
 Not one more bit of impudence out of you.
CLÉANTE: If I may offer a word of counsel here . . .

ORGON: Brother, in counseling you have no peer;
  All your advice is forceful, sound, and clever;
  I don't propose to follow it, however.
ELMIRE: [*to* ORGON] I am amazed, and don't know what to say;
  Your blindness simply takes my breath away.
  You are indeed bewitched, to take no warning
  From our account of what occurred this morning.
ORGON: Madam, I know a few plain facts and one
  Is that you're partial to my rascal son;
  Hence, when he sought to make Tartuffe the victim
  Of a base lie, you dared not contradict him.
  Ah, but you underplayed your part, my pet;
  You should have looked more angry, more upset.
ELMIRE: When men make overtures, must we reply
  With righteous anger and a battle-cry?
  Must we turn back their amorous advances
  With sharp reproaches and with fiery glances?
  Myself, I find such offers merely amusing,
  And make no scenes and fusses in refusing;
  My taste is for good-natured rectitude,
  And I dislike the savage sort of prude
  Who guards her virtue with her teeth and claws,
  And tears men's eyes out for the slightest cause:
  The Lord preserve me from such honor as that,
  Which bites and scratches like an alley-cat!
  I've found that a polite and cool rebuff
  Discourages a lover quite enough.
ORGON: I know the facts, and I shall not be shaken.
ELMIRE: I marvel at your power to be mistaken.
  Would it, I wonder, carry weight with you
  If I could *show* you that our tale was true?
ORGON: Show me?
ELMIRE: Yes.
ORGON: Rot.
ELMIRE: Come, what if I found a way
  To make you see the facts as plain as day?
ORGON: Nonsense.
ELMIRE: Do answer me; don't be absurd.
  I'm not now asking you to trust our word.
  Suppose that from some hiding-place in here
  You learned the whole sad truth by eye and ear—
  What would you say of your good friend, after that?
ORGON: Why, I'd say . . . nothing, by Jehoshaphat!
  It can't be true.
ELMIRE: You've been too long deceived,
  And I'm quite tired of being disbelieved.
  Come now: let's put my statements to the test,
  And you shall see the truth made manifest.
ORGON: I'll take that challenge. Now do your uttermost.
  We'll see how you make good your empty boast.
ELMIRE: [*to* DORINE] Send him to me.

DORINE: He's crafty; it may be hard
    To catch the cunning scoundrel off his guard.
ELMIRE: No, amorous men are gullible. Their conceit
    So blinds them that they're never hard to cheat.
    Have him come down. [*to* CLÉANTE *and* MARIANE] Please leave us, for a bit.
                           [DORINE, CLÉANTE, *and* MARIANE *exit.*]

SCENE IV

ELMIRE: Pull up this table, and get under it.
ORGON: What?
ELMIRE: It's essential that you be well-hidden.
ORGON: Why there?
ELMIRE: Oh, Heavens! Just do as you are bidden.
    I have my plans; we'll soon see how they fare.
    Under the table, now; and once you're there,
    Take care that you are neither seen nor heard.
ORGON: Well, I'll indulge you, since I gave my word
    To see you through this infantile charade.
ELMIRE: Once it is over, you'll be glad we played.
        [*to her husband, who is now under the table*]
    I'm going to act quite strangely, now, and you
    Must not be shocked at anything I do.
    Whatever I may say, you must excuse
    As part of that deceit I'm forced to use.
    I shall employ sweet speeches in the task
    Of making that impostor drop his mask;
    I'll give encouragement to his bold desires,
    And furnish fuel to his amorous fires.
    Since it's for your sake, and for his destruction,
    That I shall seem to yield to his seduction,
    I'll gladly stop whenever you decide
    That all your doubts are fully satisfied.
    I'll count on you, as soon as you have seen
    What sort of man he is, to intervene,
    And not expose me to his odious lust
    One moment longer than you feel you must.
    Remember: you're to save me from my plight
    Whenever . . . He's coming! Hush! Keep out of sight!

SCENE V

TARTUFFE: You wish to have a word with me, I'm told.
ELMIRE: Yes. I've a little secret to unfold.
    Before I speak, however, it would be wise
    To close that door, and look for spies.
        [TARTUFFE *goes to the door, closes it, and returns.*]
    The very last thing that must happen now
    Is a repetition of this morning's row.
    I've never been so badly caught off guard.

Oh, how I feared for you! You saw how hard
I tried to make that troublesome Damis
Control his dreadful temper, and hold his peace.
In my confusion, I didn't have the sense
Simply to contradict his evidence;
But as it happened, that was for the best,
And all has worked out in our interest.
This storm has only bettered your position;
My husband doesn't have the least suspicion,
And now, in mockery of those who do,
He bids me be continually with you.
And that is why, quite fearless of reproof,
I now can be alone with my Tartuffe,
And why my heart—perhaps too quick to yield—
Feels free to let its passion be revealed.

TARTUFFE: Madam, your words confuse me. Not long ago,
You spoke in quite a different style, you know.

ELMIRE: Ah, Sir, if that refusal made you smart,
It's little that you know of woman's heart,
Or what that heart is trying to convey
When it resists in such a feeble way!
Always, at first, our modesty prevents
The frank avowal of tender sentiments;
However high the passion which inflames us,
Still, to confess its power somehow shames us.
Thus we reluct, at first, yet in a tone
Which tells you that our heart is overthrown,
That what our lips deny, our pulse confesses,
And that, in time, all noes will turn to yesses.
I fear my words are all too frank and free,
And a poor proof of woman's modesty;
But since I'm started, tell me, if you will—
Would I have tried to make Damis be still,
Would I have listened, calm and unoffended,
Until your lengthy offer of love was ended,
And be so very mild in my reaction,
Had your sweet words not given me satisfaction?
And when I tried to force you to undo
The marriage-plans my husband has in view,
What did my urgent pleading signify
If not that I admired you, and that I
Deplored the thought that someone else might own
Part of a heart I wished for mine alone?

TARTUFFE: Madam, no happiness is so complete
As when, from lips we love, come words so sweet;
Their nectar floods my every sense, and drains
In honeyed rivulets through all my veins.
To please you is my joy, my only goal;
Your love is the restorer of my soul;
And yet I must beg leave, now, to confess

Some lingering doubts as to my happiness.
Might this not be a trick? Might not the catch
Be that you wish me to break off the match
With Mariane, and so have feigned to love me?
I shan't quite trust your fond opinion of me
Until the feelings you've expressed so sweetly
Are demonstrated somewhat more concretely,
And you have shown, by certain kind concessions,
That I may put my faith in your professions.

ELMIRE: [*She coughs, to warn her husband.*] Why be in such a hurry? Must my heart
Exhaust its bounty at the very start?
To make that sweet admission cost me dear,
But you'll not be content, it would appear,
Unless my store of favors is disbursed
To the last farthing, and at the very first.

TARTUFFE: The less we merit, the less we dare to hope,
And with our doubts, mere words can never cope.
We trust no promised bliss till we receive it;
Not till a joy is ours can we believe it.
I, who so little merit your esteem,
Can't credit this fulfillment of my dream,
And shan't believe it, Madam, until I savor
Some palpable assurance of your favor.

ELMIRE: My, how tyrannical your love can be,
And how it flusters and perplexes me!
How furiously you take one's heart in hand,
And make your every wish a fierce command!
Come, must you hound and harry me to death?
Will you not give me time to catch my breath?
Can it be right to press me with such force,
Give me no quarter, show me no remorse,
And take advantage, by your stern insistence,
Of the fond feelings which weaken my resistance?

TARTUFFE: Well, if you look with favor upon my love,
Why, then, begrudge me some clear proof thereof?

ELMIRE: But how can I consent without offense
To Heaven, toward which you feel such reverence?

TARTUFFE: If Heaven is all that holds you back, don't worry.
I can remove that hindrance in a hurry.
Nothing of that sort need obstruct our path.

ELMIRE: Must one not be afraid of Heaven's wrath?

TARTUFFE: Madam, forget such fears, and be my pupil,
And I shall teach you how to conquer scruple.
Some joys, it's true, are wrong in Heaven's eyes;
Yet Heaven is not averse to compromise;
There is a science, lately formulated,
Whereby one's conscience may be liberated,
And any wrongful act you care to mention
May be redeemed by purity of intention.
I'll teach you, Madam, the secrets of that science;

Meanwhile, just place on me your full reliance.
Assuage my keen desires, and feel no dread:
The sin, if any, shall be on my head.
    [ELMIRE *coughs, this time more loudly.*]
You've a bad cough.
ELMIRE: Yes, yes. It's bad indeed.
TARTUFFE: [*producing a little paper bag*] A bit of licorice may be what you need.
ELMIRE: No, I've a stubborn cold, it seems. I'm sure it
    Will take much more than licorice to cure it.
TARTUFFE: How aggravating.
ELMIRE: Oh, more than I can say.
TARTUFFE: If you're still troubled, think of things this way:
    No one shall know our joys, save us alone,
    And there's no evil till the act is known;
    It's scandal, Madam, which makes it an offense,
    And it's no sin to sin in confidence.
ELMIRE: [*having coughed once more*] Well, clearly I must do as you require,
    And yield to your importunate desire.
    It is apparent, now, that nothing less
    Will satisfy you, and so I acquiesce.
    To go so far is much against my will;
    I'm vexed that it should come to this; but still,
    Since you are so determined on it, since you
    Will not allow mere language to convince you,
    And since you ask for concrete evidence, I
    See nothing for it, now, but to comply.
    If this is sinful, if I'm wrong to do it,
    So much the worse for him who drove me to it.
    The fault can surely not be charged to me.
TARTUFFE: Madam, the fault is mine, if fault there be,
    And . . .
ELMIRE: Open the door a little, and peek out;
    I wouldn't want my husband poking about.
TARTUFFE: Why worry about the man? Each day he grows
    More gullible; one can lead him by the nose.
    To find us here would fill him with delight,
    And if he saw the worst, he'd doubt his sight.
ELMIRE: Nevertheless, do step out for a minute
    Into the hall, and see that no one's in it.

                                                    [TARTUFFE *exits.*]

SCENE VI

ORGON: [*coming out from under the table*] That man's a perfect monster, I must admit!
    I'm simply stunned. I can't get over it.
ELMIRE: What, coming out so soon? How premature!
    Get back in hiding, and wait until you're sure.
    Stay till the end, and be convinced completely;
    We mustn't stop till things are proved concretely.
ORGON: Hell never harbored anything so vicious!

ELMIRE: Tut, don't be hasty. Try to be judicious.
    Wait, and be certain that there's no mistake.
    No jumping to conclusions, for Heaven's sake!
       [*She places* ORGON *behind her, as* TARTUFFE *reenters.*]

SCENE VII

TARTUFFE: [*not seeing* ORGON] Madam, all things have worked out to perfection;
    I've given the neighboring rooms a full inspection;
    No one's about; and now I may at last . . .
ORGON: [*intercepting him*] Hold on, my passionate fellow, not so fast!
    I should advise a little more restraint.
    Well, so you thought you'd fool me, my dear saint!
    How soon you wearied of the saintly life—
    Wedding my daughter, and coveting my wife!
    I've long suspected you, and had a feeling
    That soon I'd catch you at your double-dealing.
    Just now, you've given me evidence galore;
    It's quite enough; I have no wish for more.
ELMIRE: [*to* TARTUFFE] I'm sorry to have treated you so slyly,
    But circumstances forced me to be wily.
TARTUFFE: Brother, you can't think . . .
ORGON: No more talk from you;
    Just leave this household, without more ado.
TARTUFFE: What I intended . . .
ORGON: That seems fairly clear.
    Spare me your falsehoods and get out of here.
TARTUFFE: No, I'm the master, and you're the one to go!
    This house belongs to me, I'll have you know,
    And I shall show you that you can't hurt *me*
    By this contemptible conspiracy,
    That those who cross me know not what they do,
    And that I've means to expose and punish you,
    Avenge offended Heaven, and make you grieve
    That ever you dared order me to leave.
       [TARTUFFE *exits.*]

SCENE VIII

ELMIRE: What was the point of all that angry chatter?
ORGON: Dear God, I'm worried. This is no laughing matter.
ELMIRE: How so?
ORGON: I fear I understood his drift.
    I'm much disturbed about that deed of gift.
ELMIRE: You gave him . . . ?
ORGON: Yes, it's all been drawn and signed.
    But one thing more is weighing on my mind.
ELMIRE: What's that?
ORGON: I'll tell you; but first let's see if there's
    A certain strong-box in his room upstairs.

ACT V

SCENE I

CLÉANTE: Where are you going so fast?
ORGON: God knows!
CLÉANTE: Then wait;
    Let's have a conference, and deliberate
    On how this situation's to be met.
ORGON: That strong-box has me utterly upset;
    This is the worst of many, many shocks.
CLÉANTE: Is there some fearful mystery in that box?
ORGON: My poor friend Argas brought that box to me
    With his own hands, in utmost secrecy;
    'Twas on the very morning of his flight.
    It's full of papers which, if they came to light,
    Would ruin him—or such is my impression.
CLÉANTE: Then why did you let it out of your possession?
ORGON: Those papers vexed my conscience, and it seemed best
    To ask the counsel of my pious guest.
    The cunning scoundrel got me to agree
    To leave the strong-box in his custody,
    So that, in case of an investigation,
    I could employ a slight equivocation
    And swear I didn't have it, and thereby,
    At no expense to conscience, tell a lie.
CLÉANTE: It looks to me as if you're out on a limb.
    Trusting him with that box, and offering him
    That deed of gift, were actions of a kind
    Which scarcely indicate a prudent mind.
    With two such weapons, he has the upper hand,
    And since you're vulnerable, as matters stand,
    You erred once more in bringing him to bay.
    You should have acted in some subtler way.
ORGON: Just think of it: behind that fervent face,
    A heart so wicked, and a soul so base!
    I took him in, a hungry beggar, and then . . .
    Enough, by God! I'm through with pious men:
    Henceforth I'll hate the whole false brotherhood,
    And persecute them worse than Satan could.
CLÉANTE: Ah, there you go—extravagant as ever!
    Why can you not be rational? You never
    Manage to take the middle course, it seems,
    But jump, instead, between absurd extremes.
    You've recognized your recent grave mistake
    In falling victim to a pious fake;
    Now, to correct that error, must you embrace
    An even greater error in its place,
    And judge our worthy neighbors as a whole
    By what you've learned of one corrupted soul?

Come, just because one rascal made you swallow
A show of zeal which turned out to be hollow,
Shall you conclude that all men are deceivers,
And that, today, there are no true believers?
Let atheists make that foolish inference;
Learn to distinguish virtue from pretense,
Be cautious in bestowing admiration,
And cultivate a sober moderation.
Don't humor fraud, but also don't asperse
True piety; the latter fault is worse,
And it is best to err, if err one must,
As you have done, upon the side of trust.

SCENE II

DAMIS: Father, I hear that scoundrel's uttered threats
    Against you; that he pridefully forgets
    How, in his need, he was befriended by you,
    And means to use your gifts to crucify you.
ORGON: It's true, my boy. I'm too distressed for tears.
DAMIS: Leave it to me, Sir; let me trim his ears.
    Faced with such insolence, we must not waver.
    I shall rejoice in doing you the favor
    Of cutting short his life, and your distress.
CLÉANTE: What a display of young hotheadedness!
    Do learn to moderate your fits of rage.
    In this just kingdom, this enlightened age,
    One does not settle things by violence.

SCENE III

MADAME PERNELLE: [*entering with* ELMIRE *and* MARIANE]
    I hear strange tales of very strange events.
ORGON: Yes, strange events which these two eyes beheld.
    The man's ingratitude is unparalleled.
    I save a wretched pauper from starvation,
    House him, and treat him like a blood relation,
    Shower him every day with my largesse,
    Give him my daughter, and all that I possess;
    And meanwhile the unconscionable knave
    Tries to induce my wife to misbehave;
    And not content with such extreme rascality,
    Now threatens me with my own liberality,
    And aims, by taking base advantage of
    The gifts I gave him out of Christian love,
    To drive me from my house, a ruined man,
    And make me end a pauper, as he began.
DORINE: Poor fellow!
MADAME PERNELLE: No, my son, I'll never bring
    Myself to think him guilty of such thing.

ORGON: How's that?

MADAME PERNELLE: The righteous always were maligned.

ORGON: Speak clearly, Mother. Say what's on your mind.

MADAME PERNELLE: I mean that I can smell a rat, my dear.
　　You know how everybody hates him, here.

ORGON: That has no bearing on the case at all.

MADAME PERNELLE: I told you a hundred times, when you were small,
　　That virtue in this world is hated ever;
　　Malicious men may die, but malice never.

ORGON: No doubt that's true, but how does it apply?

MADAME PERNELLE: They've turned you against him by a clever lie.

ORGON: I've told you, I was there and saw it done.

MADAME PERNELLE: Ah, slanderers will stop at nothing, Son.

ORGON: Mother, I'll lose my temper . . . For the last time,
　　I tell you I was witness to the crime.

MADAME PERNELLE: The tongues of spite are busy night and noon,
　　And to their venom no man is immune.

ORGON: You're talking nonsense. Can't you realize
　　I saw it; saw it; saw it with my eyes?
　　Saw, do you understand me? Must I shout it
　　Into your ears before you'll cease to doubt it?

MADAME PERNELLE: Appearances can deceive, my son. Dear me,
　　We cannot always judge by what we see.

ORGON: Drat! Drat!

MADAME PERNELLE: One often interprets things awry;
　　Good can seem evil to a suspicious eye.

ORGON: Was I to see his pawing at Elmire
　　As an act of charity?

MADAME PERNELLE: Till his guilt is clear
　　A man deserves the benefit of the doubt.
　　You should have waited, to see how things turned out.

ORGON: Great God in Heaven, what more proof did I need?
　　Was I to sit there, watching, until he'd . . .
　　You drive me to the brink of impropriety.

MADAME PERNELLE: No, no, a man of such surpassing piety
　　Could not do such a thing. You cannot shake me.
　　I don't believe it, and you shall not make me.

ORGON: You vex me so that, if you weren't my mother,
　　I'd say to you . . . some dreadful thing or other.

DORINE: It's your turn now, Sir, not to be listened to;
　　You'd not trust us, and now she won't trust you.

CLÉANTE: My friends, we're wasting time which should be spent
　　In facing up to our predicament.
　　I fear that scoundrel's threats weren't made in sport.

DAMIS: Do you think he'd have the nerve to go to court?

ELMIRE: I'm sure he won't: they'd find it all too crude
　　A case of swindling and ingratitude.

CLÉANTE: Don't be too sure. He won't be at a loss
　　To give his claims a high and righteous gloss;
　　And clever rogues with far less valid cause

Have trapped their victims in a web of laws.
I say again that to antagonize
A man so strongly armed was most unwise.
ORGON: I know it; but the man's appalling cheek
Outraged me so, I couldn't control my pique.
CLÉANTE: I wish to Heaven that we could devise
Some truce between you, or some compromise.
ELMIRE: If I had known what cards he held, I'd not
Have roused his anger by my little plot.
ORGON: [*to* DORINE, *as* M. LOYAL *enters*] What is that fellow looking for? Who is he?
Go talk to him—and tell him that I'm busy.

SCENE IV

MONSIEUR LOYAL: Good day, dear sister. Kindly let me see
Your master.
DORINE: He's involved with company,
And cannot be disturbed just now, I fear.
MONSIEUR LOYAL: I hate to intrude; but what has brought me here
Will not disturb your master, in any event.
Indeed, my news will make him most content.
DORINE: Your name?
MONSIEUR LOYAL: Just say that I bring greetings from
Monsieur Tartuffe, on whose behalf I've come.
DORINE: [*to* ORGON] Sir, he's a very gracious man, and bears
A message from Tartuffe, which, he declares,
Will make you most content.
CLÉANTE: Upon my word,
I think this man had best be seen, and heard.
ORGON: Perhaps he has some settlement to suggest.
How shall I treat him? What manner would be best?
CLÉANTE: Control your anger, and if he should mention
Some fair adjustment, give him your full attention.
MONSIEUR LOYAL: Good health to you, good Sir. May Heaven confound
Your enemies, and may your joys abound.
ORGON: [*aside, to* CLÉANTE] A gentle salutation: it confirms
My guess that he is here to offer terms.
MONSIEUR LOYAL: I've always held your family most dear;
I served your father, Sir, for many a year.
ORGON: Sir, I must ask your pardon; to my shame,
I cannot now recall your face or name.
MONSIEUR LOYAL: Loyal's my name; I come from Normandy,
And I'm a bailiff, in all modesty.
For forty years, praise God, it's been my boast
To serve with honor in that vital post,
And I am here, Sir, if you will permit
The liberty, to serve you with this writ . . .
ORGON: To—*what?*
MONSIEUR LOYAL: Now, please, Sir, let us have no friction:
It's nothing but an order of eviction.

You are to move your goods and family out
And make way for new occupants, without
Deferment or delay, and give the keys . . .
ORGON: I? Leave this house?
MONSIEUR LOYAL: Why yes, Sir, if you please.
This house, Sir, from the cellar to the roof,
Belongs now to the good Monsieur Tartuffe,
And he is lord and master of your estate
By virtue of a deed of present date,
Drawn in due form, with clearest legal phrasing . . .
DAMIS: Your insolence is utterly amazing!
MONSIEUR LOYAL: Young man, my business here is not with you,
But with your wise and temperate father, who,
Like every worthy citizen, stands in awe
Of justice, and would never obstruct the law.
ORGON: But . . .
MONSIEUR LOYAL: Not for a million, Sir, would you rebel
Against authority; I know that well.
You'll not make trouble, Sir, or interfere
With the execution of my duties here.
DAMIS: Someone may execute a smart tattoo
On that black jacket of yours, before you're through.
MONSIEUR LOYAL: Sir, bid your son be silent. I'd much regret
Having to mention such a nasty threat
Of violence, in writing my report.
DORINE: [*aside*] This man Loyal's a most disloyal sort!
MONSIEUR LOYAL: I love all men of upright character,
And when I agreed to serve these papers, Sir,
It was your feelings that I had in mind.
I couldn't bear to see the case assigned
To someone else, who might esteem you less
And so subject you to unpleasantness.
ORGON: What's more unpleasant than telling a man to leave
His house and home?
MONSIEUR LOYAL: You'd like a short reprieve?
If you desire it, Sir, I shall not press you,
But wait until tomorrow to dispossess you.
Splendid. I'll come and spend the night here, then,
Most quietly, with half a score of men.
For form's sake, you might bring me, just before
You go to bed, the keys to the front door.
My men, I promise, will be on their best
Behavior, and will not disturb your rest.
But bright and early, Sir, you must be quick
And move out all your furniture, every stick:
The men I've chosen are both young and strong,
And with their help it shouldn't take you long.
In short, I'll make things pleasant and convenient,
And since I'm being so extremely lenient,
Please show me, Sir, a like consideration,

And give me your entire cooperation.
ORGON: [*aside*] I may be all but bankrupt, but I vow
      I'd give a hundred louis, here and now,
      Just for the pleasure of landing one good clout
      Right on the end of that complacent snout.
CLÉANTE: Careful; don't make things worse.
DAMIS: My bootsole itches
      To give that beggar a good kick in the breeches.
DORINE: Monsieur Loyal, I'd love to hear the whack
      Of a stout stick across your fine broad back.
MONSIEUR LOYAL: Take care: a woman, too, may go to jail if
      She uses threatening language to a bailiff.
CLÉANTE: Enough, enough, Sir. This must not go on.
      Give me that paper, please, and then begone.
MONSIEUR LOYAL: Well, *au revoir*. God give you all good cheer!
ORGON: May God confound you, and him who sent you here!

SCENE V

ORGON: Now, Mother, was I right or not? This writ
      Should change your notion of Tartuffe a bit.
      Do you perceive his villainy at last?
MADAME PERNELLE: I'm thunderstruck. I'm utterly aghast.
DORINE: Oh, come, be fair. You mustn't take offense
      At this new proof of his benevolence.
      He's acting out of selfless love, I know.
      Material things enslave the soul, and so
      He kindly has arranged your liberation
      From all that might endanger your salvation.
ORGON: Will you not ever hold your tongue, you dunce?
CLÉANTE: Come, you must take some action, and at once.
ELMIRE: Go tell the world of the low trick he's tried.
      The deed of gift is surely nullified
      By such behavior, and public rage will not
      Permit the wretch to carry out his plot.

SCENE VI

VALÈRE: Sir, though I hate to bring you more bad news,
      Such is the danger that I cannot choose.
      A friend who is extremely close to me
      And knows my interest in your family
      Has, for my sake, presumed to violate
      The secrecy that's due to things of state,
      And sends me word that you are in a plight
      From which your salvation lies in flight.
      That scoundrel who's imposed upon you so
      Denounced you to the King an hour ago
      And, as supporting evidence, displayed
      The strong-box of a certain renegade

Whose secret papers, so he testified,
You had disloyally agreed to hide.
I don't know just what charges may be pressed,
But there's a warrant out for your arrest;
Tartuffe has been instructed, furthermore,
To guide the arresting officer to your door.
CLÉANTE: He's clearly done this to facilitate
His seizure of your house and your estate.
ORGON: That man, I must say, is a vicious beast!
VALÈRE: Quick, Sir; you mustn't tarry in the least.
My carriage is outside, to take you hence;
This thousand louis should cover all expense.
Let's lose no time, or you shall be undone;
The sole defense, in this case, is to run.
I shall go with you all the way, and place you
In a safe refuge to which they'll never trace you.
ORGON: Alas, dear boy, I wish that I could show you
My gratitude for everything I owe you.
But now is not the time; I pray the Lord
That I may live to give you your reward.
Farewell, my dears; be careful . . .
CLÉANTE: Brother, hurry.
We shall take care of things; you needn't worry.

SCENE VII

TARTUFFE: Gently, Sir, gently; stay right where you are.
No need for haste; your lodging isn't far.
You're off to prison, by order of the Prince.
ORGON: This is the crowning blow, you wretch; and since
It means my total ruin and defeat,
Your villainy is now at last complete.
TARTUFFE: You needn't try to provoke me; it's no use.
Those who serve Heaven must expect abuse.
CLÉANTE: You are indeed most patient, sweet, and blameless.
DORINE: How he exploits the name of Heaven! It's shameless.
TARTUFFE: Your taunts and mockeries are all for naught;
To do my duty is my only thought.
MARIANE: Your love of duty is most meritorious,
And what you've done is little short of glorious.
TARTUFFE: All deeds are glorious, Madam, which obey
The sovereign Prince who sent me here today.
ORGON: I rescued you when you were destitute;
Have you forgotten that, you thankless brute?
TARTUFFE: No, no, I well remember everything;
But my first duty is to serve my King.
That obligation is so paramount
That other claims, beside it, do not count;
And for it I would sacrifice my wife,
My family, my friend, or my life.

ELMIRE: Hypocrite!

DORINE: All that we most revere, he uses
    To cloak his plots and camouflage his ruses.

CLÉANTE: If it is true that you are animated
    By pure and loyal zeal, as you have stated,
    Why was this zeal not roused until you'd sought
    To make Orgon a cuckold, and been caught?
    Why weren't you moved to give your evidence
    Until your outraged host had driven you hence?
    I shan't say that the gift of all his treasure
    Ought to have damped your zeal in any measure;
    But if he is a traitor, as you declare,
    How could you condescend to be his heir?

TARTUFFE: [*to the* OFFICER] Sir, spare me all this clamor; it's growing shrill.
    Please carry out your orders, if you will.

OFFICER: Yes, I've delayed too long, Sir. Thank you kindly.
    You're just the proper person to remind me.
    Come, you are off to join the other boarders
    In the King's prison, according to his orders.

TARTUFFE: Who? I, Sir?

OFFICER: Yes.

TARTUFFE: To prison? This can't be true!

OFFICER: I owe an explanation, but not to you.
    [*to* ORGON] Sir, all is well; rest easy, and be grateful.
    We serve a Prince to whom all sham is hateful,
    A Prince who sees into our inmost hearts,
    And can't be fooled by any trickster's arts.
    His royal soul, though generous and human,
    Views all things with discernment and acumen;
    His sovereign reason is not lightly swayed,
    And all his judgments are discreetly weighed.
    He honors righteous men of every kind,
    And yet his zeal for virtue is not blind,
    Nor does his love of piety numb his wits
    And make him tolerant of hypocrites.
    'Twas hardly likely that this man could cozen
    A King who's foiled such liars by the dozen.
    With one keen glance, the King perceived the whole
    Perverseness and corruption of his soul,
    And thus high Heaven's justice was displayed:
    Betraying you, the rogue stood self-betrayed.
    The King soon recognized Tartuffe as one
    Notorious by another name, who'd done
    So many vicious crimes that one could fill
    Ten volumes with them, and be writing still.
    But to be brief: our sovereign was appalled
    By this man's treachery toward you, which he called
    The last, worst villainy of a vile career,
    And bade me follow the impostor here
    To see how gross his impudence could be,

And force him to restore your property.
Your private papers, by the King's command,
I hereby seize and give into your hand.
The King, by royal order, invalidates
The deed which gave this rascal your estates,
And pardons, furthermore, your grave offense
In harboring an exile's documents.
By these decrees, our Prince rewards you for
Your loyal deeds in the late civil war,
And shows how heartfelt is his satisfaction
In recompensing any worthy action,
How much he prizes merit, and how he makes
More of men's virtues than of their mistakes.

DORINE: Heaven be praised!

MADAME PERNELLE: I breathe again, at last.

ELMIRE: We're safe.

MARIANE: I can't believe the danger's past.

ORGON: [*to* TARTUFFE] Well, traitor, now you see . . .

CLÉANTE: Ah, Brother, please,
Let's not descend to such indignities.
Leave the poor wretch to his unhappy fate,
And don't say anything to aggravate
His present woes; but rather hope that he
Will soon embrace an honest piety,
And mend his ways, and by a true repentance
Move our just King to moderate his sentence.
Meanwhile, go kneel before your sovereign's throne
And thank him for the mercies he has shown.

ORGON: Well said: let's go at once and, gladly kneeling,
Express the gratitude which all are feeling.
Then, when that first great duty has been done,
We'll turn with pleasure to a second one,
And give Valère, whose love has proven so true,
The wedded happiness which is his due.

A Doll's House (1879)

bsen's early plays (beginning in 1850) were poetic dramas about Norwegian legend or history. In the 1870s, Ibsen deliberately abandoned his earlier approach to write prose plays about contemporary life. *A Doll's House* and *Ghosts* made Ibsen the most controversial playwright in Europe, for the former was thought to attack the institution of marriage and the family, and the latter brought the taboo subject of venereal disease to the stage. Ibsen's prose plays were thought to epitomize realism, a new movement then under way. Subsequently, his prose works were said to have initiated the modern drama.

Undergirding *A Doll's House* is the basic assumption that hereditary and environmental forces determine character and action. What each character is and does is explained by information about background, upbringing, and experience. During the course of the action, we learn enough about all the characters to understand how they have arrived at where they are. Ibsen could have made his play melodramatic by depicting Krogstad as villain and Nora as persecuted heroine. Instead, all of the characters strive for what they consider right. Thus instead of a type, each character appears to be a complex, fallible human being.

A Doll's House is usually read today as a play about the status of women in the late nineteenth century. It pleases Torvald to think of Nora as incapable of making decisions, even about what she should wear to a party. The play also shows that women were legally reduced to the state of childhood (or doll) because a wife was required to have her husband's consent in almost all matters, whereas her husband could act wholly independently, even disposing of property originally hers without her consent or knowledge. At the end of the play, Nora's alienation is not only from her husband but also from society in general. She chooses to leave her husband and children because, finding herself in disagreement with both law and public opinion and not yet certain of her own convictions, she does not believe herself ready to meet her responsibilities as a wife and mother. It was this ending that made the play so controversial, for it challenged the status quo.

A Doll's House could serve as a model of cause-to-effect dramatic structure. The first act sets up masterfully and with seeming naturalness all of the conditions out of which the subsequent action grows logically and seemingly inexorably.

Henrik Ibsen

A Doll's House

TRANSLATED BY WILLIAM ARCHER (WITH EMENDATIONS BY OSCAR G. BROCKETT)

Characters

TORVALD HELMER
NORA, *his wife*
DOCTOR RANK
MRS. LINDE
NILS KROGSTAD
THE HELMERS' THREE YOUNG CHILDREN
ANNE, *their nurse*
A HOUSEMAID
A PORTER

The action of the play takes place in the Helmers' house.

ACT I

SCENE———*A room furnished comfortably and tastefully but not extravagantly. At the back, a door to the right leads to the entrance-hall, another to the left leads to* HELMER's *study. Between the doors stands a piano. In the middle of the left-hand wall is a door, and beyond it a window. Near the window are a round table, armchairs, and a small sofa. In the right-hand wall, at the farther end, another door; and on the same side, nearer the footlights, a stove, two easy chairs, and a rocking chair; between the stove and the door, a small table. Engravings on the walls; a cabinet with china and other small objects; a small book-case with well-bound books. The floors are carpeted, and a fire burns in the stove. It is winter.*

A bell rings in the hall; shortly afterwards the door is heard to open. Enter NORA, *humming a tune and in high spirits. She is in out-door dress and carries a number of parcels; these she lays on the table to the right. She leaves the outer door open after her, and through it is seen a* PORTER *who is carrying a Christmas tree and a basket, which he gives to the* MAID, *who has opened the door.*

NORA: Hide the Christmas tree carefully, Helen. Be sure the children don't see it till this evening, when it is trimmed [*to the* PORTER *taking out her purse*] How much?
PORTER: A half-crown.
NORA: There's a crown. No, keep the change. [*The* PORTER *thanks her, and goes out.* NORA *shuts the door. She is laughing to herself, as she takes off her hat and coat. She takes a packet of macaroons from her pocket and eats one or two; then goes cautiously to her husband's door and listens*] Yes, he is in. [*Still humming, she goes to the table on the right.*]
HELMER: [*calls out from his room*] Is that my little lark twittering out there?
NORA: [*busy opening some of the parcels*] Yes, it is!

HELMER: Is it my little squirrel bustling about?

NORA: Yes!

HELMER: When did my squirrel come home?

NORA: Just now. [*puts the bag of macaroons into her pocket and wipes her mouth*] Come in here, Torvald, and see what I have bought.

HELMER: Don't disturb me. [*A little later he opens the door and looks into the room, pen in hand*] Bought, did you say? All these things? Has my little spendthrift been wasting money again?

NORA: Yes, but, Torvald, this year we really can let ourselves go a little. This is the first Christmas that we have not needed to economize.

HELMER: Still, you know, we can't spend money recklessly.

NORA: Yes, Torvald, we may be a wee bit more reckless now, mayn't we? Just a tiny wee bit! You are going to have a big salary and earn lots and lots of money.

HELMER: Yes, after the New Year; but then it will be a whole quarter before the salary is due.

NORA: Pooh! We can borrow till then.

HELMER: Nora! [*goes up to her and takes her playfully by the ear*] The same little featherhead! Suppose, now, that I borrowed one thousand crowns to-day, and you spent it all in the Christmas week, and then on New Year's Eve a roof tile fell on my head and killed me, and—

NORA: [*putting her hands over his mouth*] Oh! don't say such horrid things.

HELMER: Still, suppose that happened—what then?

NORA: If that were to happen, I don't suppose I should care whether I owed money or not.

HELMER: Yes, but what about the people who had lent it?

NORA: They? Who would care about them? I wouldn't know who they were.

HELMER: How like a woman! But seriously, Nora, you know what I think about that. No debt, no borrowing. There can be no freedom or beauty about a home that depends on borrowing and debt. We two have kept bravely on the straight road so far, and we will go on the same way for the short time left.

NORA: [*moving towards the stove*] As you please, Torvald.

HELMER: [*following her*] Come, come, my little skylark must not droop her wings. What is this! Is my little squirrel sulking? [*taking out his purse*] Nora, what do you think I've got here?

NORA: [*turning round quickly*] Money!

HELMER: There you are. [*gives her some money*] Do you think I don't know what a lot is needed for housekeeping at Christmas-time?

NORA: [*counting*] One-two-three! Thank you, thank you, Torvald; that will keep me going for a long time.

HELMER: Indeed it must.

NORA: Yes, yes, it will. But come here and let me show you what I have bought. And all so cheap! Look, here is a new suit for Ivar, and a sword; and a horse and trumpet for Bob; and a doll and a doll's bed for Emmy—they are very plain, but anyway she'll soon break them. And here are dress materials and handkerchiefs for the maids; old Anne ought really to have something better.

HELMER: And what is in this parcel?

NORA: [*crying out*] No, no! You mustn't see that till this evening.

HELMER: Very well. But now tell me, you extravagant little person, what would you like for yourself?

NORA: For myself? Oh, I'm sure I don't want anything.

HELMER: Yes, but you must. Tell me something reasonable that you would particularly like to have.

NORA: No, I really can't think of anything—unless, Torvald—

HELMER: Well?

NORA: [*playing with his coat buttons, and without raising her eyes to his*] if you really want to give me something, you might—you might—

HELMER: Well, out with it!

NORA: [*speaking quickly*] You might give me money, Torvald. Only just as much as you can afford; and then one of these days I will buy something with it.

HELMER: But, Nora—

NORA: Oh, do! dear Torvald; please, please do! Then I will wrap it up in beautiful gold paper and hang it on the Christmas tree. Wouldn't that be fun?

HELMER: What are little people called that are always wasting money?

NORA: Spendthrifts—I know. Let's do what you suggest, Torvald, and then I shall have time to think what I need most. That is a very sensible plan, isn't it?

HELMER: [*smiling*] Indeed it is—that is to say, if you were really to save out of the money I give you, and then really buy something for yourself. But if you spend it all on the housekeeping and any number of unnecessary things, then I merely have to pay up again.

NORA: Oh but, Torvald—

HELMER: You can't deny it, my dear little Nora. [*puts his arm around her waist*] It's a sweet little spendthrift, but she uses up a lot of money. One would hardly believe how expensive such little persons are!

NORA: It's a shame to say that. I do really save all I can.

HELMER: [*laughing*] That's very true—all you can. But you can't save anything!

NORA: [*smiling quietly and happily*] You haven't any idea how many expenses we skylarks and squirrels have, Torvald.

HELMER: You are an odd little soul. Very like your father. You always find some new way of wheedling money out of me, and, as soon as you have got it, it seems to melt in your hands. You never know where it has gone. Still, one must take you as you are. It is in the blood; for indeed it is true that you can inherit these things, Nora.

NORA: Ah, I wish I had inherited many of papa's qualities.

HELMER: And I would not wish you to be anything but just what you are, my sweet little skylark. But, do you know, it strikes me that you are looking rather—what shall I say—rather guilty to-day?

NORA: Do I?

HELMER: You do, really. Look straight at me.

NORA: [*looks at him*] Well?

HELMER: [*wagging his finger at her*] Hasn't Miss Sweet-Tooth been breaking rules in town to-day?

NORA: No; what makes you think that?

HELMER: Hasn't she paid a visit to the pastry shop?

NORA: No, I assure you, Torvald—

HELMER: Not been nibbling sweets?

NORA: No, certainly not.

HELMER: Not even taken a bite at a macaroon or two?

NORA: No, Torvald, I assure you really—

HELMER: There, there, of course I was only joking.

NORA: [*going to the table on the right*] I wouldn't think of going against your wishes.

HELMER: No, I am sure of that; besides, you gave me your word— [*going up to her*] Keep your little Christmas secrets to yourself, my darling. They will all be revealed to-night when the Christmas tree is lit, no doubt.

NORA: Did you remember to invite Doctor Rank?

HELMER: No. But there is no need; he will come to dinner with us as he always does. However, I will ask him when he comes in this morning. I have ordered some good wine. Nora, you can't think how I am looking forward to this evening.

NORA: So am I! And how the children will enjoy themselves, Torvald!

HELMER: It is splendid to feel that one has a secure job and a big enough income. It's delightful to think of, isn't it?

NORA: It's wonderful.

HELMER: Do you remember last Christmas? For a full three weeks beforehand you shut yourself up every evening till long after midnight, making ornaments for the Christmas tree and all the other fine things that were to be a surprise to us. It was the dullest three weeks I ever spent!

NORA: I didn't find it dull.

HELMER: [*smiling*] But there was precious little to show for it, Nora.

NORA: Oh, you shouldn't tease me about that again. How could I help the cat's getting in and tearing everything to pieces?

HELMER: Of course you couldn't, poor little girl. You had the best of intentions to please us all, and that's the main thing. But it is a good thing that our hard times are over.

NORA: Yes, it is really wonderful.

HELMER: This time I needn't be all alone and bored and you needn't ruin your dear eyes and your pretty little hands—

NORA: [*clapping her hands*] No, Torvald, I don't have to any longer, do I! It's wonderful to hear you say so! [*taking his arm*] Now I will tell you how I have been thinking we ought to arrange things, Torvald. As soon as Christmas is over— [*A bell rings in the hall.*] There's the doorbell. [*She tidies the room a little.*] There's someone at the door. What a nuisance!

HELMER: If it is a caller, remember I am not at home.

MAID: [*in the doorway*] A lady to see you, ma'am—a stranger.

NORA: Ask her to come in.

MAID: [*to* HELMER] The doctor came at the same time, sir.

HELMER: Did he go straight into my study?

MAID: Yes, sir.

> [HELMER *goes into his room. The* MAID *ushers in* MRS. LINDE, *who is in travelling clothes and shuts the door.*]

MRS. LINDE: [*in a dejected and timid voice*] How do you do, Nora?

NORA: [*doubtfully*] How do you do—

MRS. LINDE: You don't recognise me, I suppose.

NORA: No, I'm afraid—yes, to be sure, I seem to—[*suddenly*] Yes! Christine! Is it really you?

MRS. LINDE: Yes, it is I.

NORA: Christine! To think of my not recognising you! And yet how could I— [*in a gentle voice*] How you've changed, Christine!

MRS. LINDE: Yes, I have indeed. In nine, ten long years—

NORA: Is it so long since we met? I suppose it is. The last eight years have been a happy time for me, I can tell you. And so now you have come into town, and have taken this long journey in winter—that was brave of you.

MRS. LINDE: I arrived by boat this morning.

NORA: To have some fun at Christmas-time, of course. How delightful! We will have such fun together! But take off your things. You are not cold, I hope. [*helps her*] Now we will sit down by the stove, and be comfortable. No, take this armchair; I will sit here in the rocking chair. [*takes her hands*] Now you look like your old self again; it was only the first moment—You are a little paler, Christine, and perhaps a little thinner.

MRS. LINDE: And much, much older, Nora.

NORA: Perhaps a little older; very, very little; certainly not much. [*stops suddenly and speaks seriously*] What a thoughtless creature I am, chattering away like this. My poor, dear Christine, do forgive me.

MRS. LINDE: What do you mean, Nora?

NORA: [*gently*] Poor Christine, you are a widow.

MRS. LINDE: Yes; it is three years ago now.

NORA: Yes, I know; I saw it in the papers. I assure you, Christine, I meant to write to you at the time, but I always put it off and something always prevented me.

MRS. LINDE: I quite understand, dear.

NORA: It was very bad of me, Christine. Poor thing, how you must have suffered. And he left you nothing?

MRS. LINDE: No.

NORA: And no children?

MRS. LINDE: No.

NORA: Nothing at all, then?

MRS. LINDE: Not even sorrow or grief to live upon.

NORA: [*looking incredulously at her*] But, Christine, is that possible?

MRS. LINDE: [*smiles sadly and strokes her hair*] It sometimes happens, Nora.

NORA: So you are quite alone. How dreadfully sad that must be. I have three lovely children. You can't see them just now, for they are out with their nurse. But now you must tell me everything.

MRS. LINDE: No, no; I want to hear about you.

NORA: No, you must begin. I mustn't be selfish to-day; to-day I must only think of your affairs. But there is one thing I must tell you. Have you heard about our great piece of good luck?

MRS. LINDE: No, what is it?

NORA: Just imagine, my husband has been made manager of the Bank!

MRS. LINDE: Your husband? What good luck!

NORA: Yes, tremendous! A lawyer's profession is such an uncertain thing, especially if he won't undertake unsavoury cases; and naturally Torvald has never been willing to do that, and I quite agree with him. You may imagine how pleased we are! He'll begin his job in the Bank at the New Year, and then he'll have a big salary and lots of commissions. For the future we can live quite differently—we can do just as we like. I feel so relieved and so happy, Christine! It will be splendid to have heaps of money and not need to have any anxiety, won't it?

MRS. LINDE: Yes, anyhow I think it would be delightful to have what one needs.

NORA: No, not only what one needs, but heaps and heaps of money.

MRS. LINDE: [*smiling*] Nora, Nora, haven't you learnt sense yet? In our schooldays you were a great spendthrift.

NORA: [*laughing*] Yes, that is what Torvald says now. [*wags her finger at her*] But "Nora, Nora" isn't so silly as you think. We have not been in a position for me to waste money. We have both had to work.

MRS. LINDE: You, too!

NORA: Yes; odds and ends, needlework, crochetings, embroidery, and that kind of thing. [*dropping her voice*] And other things as well. You know Torvald left his office when we were married? There was no prospect of promotion there, and he had to try and earn more than before. But during the first year he overworked himself dreadfully. You see, he had to make money every way he could, and he worked early and late; but he couldn't stand it, and fell dreadfully ill, and the doctors said it was necessary for him to go south.

MRS. LINDE: You spent a whole year in Italy, didn't you?

NORA: Yes. It was no easy matter to get away, I can tell you. It was just after Ivar was born; but naturally we had to go. It was a wonderfully beautiful trip and it saved Torvald's life. But it cost a tremendous lot of money, Christine.

MRS. LINDE: So I should think.

NORA: It cost about forty-eight hundred crowns. That's a lot, isn't it?

MRS. LINDE: Yes, and in emergencies like that it is lucky to have the money.

NORA: We got the money from papa.

MRS. LINDE: Oh, I see. It was just about that time that he died, wasn't it?

NORA: Yes; and just think of it, I couldn't go and nurse him. I was expecting little Ivar's birth every day and I had my poor sick Torvald to look after. My dear, kind father—I never saw him again, Christine. That was the saddest time I have known since our marriage.

MRS. LINDE: I know how fond you were of him. And then you went off to Italy?

NORA: Yes; you see, we had money then, and the doctors insisted on our going, so we started a month later.

MRS. LINDE: And your husband came back quite well?

NORA: As sound as a bell!

MRS. LINDE: But—the doctor?

NORA: What doctor?

MRS. LINDE: I thought your maid said the gentleman who arrived here just as I did, was the doctor?

NORA: Yes, that was Doctor Rank, but he doesn't come here professionally. He is our closest friend, and comes in at least once every day. No, Torvald has not had an hour's illness since then, and our children are strong and healthy and so am I. [*jumps up and claps her hands*] Christine! Christine! it's good to be alive and happy! But how horrid of me; I am talking of nothing but my own affairs. [*sits on a stool near her, and rests her arms on her knees*] You mustn't be angry with me. Tell me, is it really true that you did not love your husband? Why did you marry him?

MRS. LINDE: My mother was alive then, and was bedridden and helpless, and I had to provide for my two younger brothers; so I didn't think I was justified in refusing his offer.

NORA: No, perhaps you were quite right. He was rich at that time, then?

MRS. LINDE: I believe he was quite well off. But his business was a precarious one; and, when he died, it all went to pieces and there was nothing left.

NORA: And then?—

MRS. LINDE: Well, I had to turn my hand to anything I could find—first a small shop, then a small school, and so on. The last three years have seemed like one long working-day, with no rest. Now it is at an end, Nora. My poor mother needs me no more, for she is gone; and the boys don't need me either; they have got jobs and can shift for themselves.

NORA: What a relief you must feel—

MRS. LINDE: No, indeed; I only feel my life unspeakably empty. No one to live for any more. [*gets up restlessly*] That was why I could not stand the life in my little backwater any longer. I hope it may be easier here to find something which will busy me and occupy my thoughts. If only I could have the good luck to get some regular work—office work of some kind—

NORA: But, Christine, that is so frightfully tiring, and you look tired out now. You had far better go away to some watering-place.

MRS. LINDE: [*walking to the window*] I have no father to give me money for a journey, Nora.

NORA: [*rising*] Oh, don't be angry with me.

MRS. LINDE: [*going up to her*] It is you that mustn't be angry with me, dear. The worst of a position like mine is that it makes one so bitter. No one to work for, and yet obliged to be always on the look-out for chances. One must live, and so one becomes selfish. When you told me of the happy turn your fortunes have taken—you will hardly believe it—I was delighted not so much on your account as on my own.

NORA: How do you mean?—Oh, I understand. You mean that perhaps Torvald could get you something to do.

MRS. LINDE: Yes, that was what I was thinking of.

NORA: He must, Christine. Just leave it to me; I will broach the subject very cleverly—I will think of something that will please him very much. It will make me so happy to be of some use to you.

MRS. LINDE: How kind you are, Nora, to be so anxious to help me! It is doubly kind in you, for you know so little of the burdens and troubles of life.

NORA: I—? I know so little of them?

MRS. LINDE: [*smiling*] My dear! Small household cares and that sort of thing! You are a child, Nora.

NORA: [*tosses her head and crosses the stage*] You ought not to be so superior.

MRS. LINDE: No!

NORA: You are just like the others. They all think that I am incapable of anything really serious—

MRS. LINDE: Come, come—

NORA: —that I have gone through nothing in this world of cares.

MRS. LINDE: But, my dear Nora, you have just told me all your troubles.

NORA: Pooh!—Those were trifles. [*lowering her voice*] I have not told you the important thing.

MRS. LINDE: The important thing! What do you mean?

NORA: You look down on me, Christine—but you shouldn't. You are proud, aren't you, of having worked so hard and so long for your mother?

MRS. LINDE: Indeed, I don't look down on any one. But it is true that I am proud and glad to think that I was privileged to make the end of my mother's life almost free from care.

NORA: And you are proud to think of what you have done for your brothers.

MRS. LINDE: I think I have the right to be.

NORA: I think so, too. But now, listen to this; I, too, have something to be proud and glad of.

MRS. LINDE: I have no doubt you have. But what do you refer to?

NORA: Speak low. Suppose Torvald were to hear! He mustn't on any account—no one in the world must know, Christine, except you.

MRS. LINDE: But what is it?

NORA: Come here. [*pulls her down on the sofa beside her*] Now I'll show you that I also have something to be proud and glad of. It was I who saved Torvald's life.

MRS. LINDE: "Saved"? How?

NORA: I told you about our trip to Italy. Torvald would never have recovered if he had not gone there—

MRS. LINDE: Yes, but your father gave you the necessary funds.

NORA: [*smiling*] Yes, that is what Torvald and all the others think, but—

MRS. LINDE: But—

NORA: Papa didn't give us a crown. It was I who procured the money.

MRS. LINDE: You? All that large sum?

NORA: Forty-eight hundred crowns. What do you think of that?

MRS. LINDE: But, Nora, how could you possibly do it? Did you win a prize in the Lottery?

NORA: [*contemptuously*] In the Lottery? There would have been no credit in that.

MRS. LINDE: But where did you get it then?

NORA: [*humming and smiling with an air of mystery*] Hm, hm! Aha!

MRS. LINDE: Because you couldn't have borrowed it.

NORA: Couldn't I? Why not?

MRS. LINDE: No, a wife cannot borrow without her husband's consent.

NORA: [*tossing her head*] Oh, if it's a wife who has any head for business—a wife who has the wit to be a little bit clever—

MRS. LINDE: I don't understand it at all, Nora.

NORA: There is no need you should. I never said I had borrowed the money. I may have got it some other way. [*lies back on the sofa*] Perhaps I got it from some admirer. When you're as attractive as I am—

MRS. LINDE: You're mad.

NORA: Now, you know you're full of curiosity, Christine.

MRS. LINDE: Listen to me, Nora dear. Haven't you been a little bit foolish?

NORA: [*sits up straight*] Is it foolish to save your husband's life?

MRS. LINDE: It seems to me foolish without his knowledge, to—

NORA: But it was absolutely necessary that he not know! My goodness, can't you understand that? It was necessary he should have no idea what a dangerous condition he was in. It was to me that the doctors came and said that his life was in danger, and that the only thing to save him was to live in the south. Do you suppose I didn't try, first of all, to get what I wanted as if it were for myself? I told him how much I should love to travel abroad like other young wives; I tried tears and entreaties with him; I told him that he ought to remember the condition I was in, and that he ought to be kind and indulgent to me; I even hinted that he might raise a loan. That nearly made him angry, Christine. He said I was thoughtless, and that it was his duty as my husband not to indulge me in my whims and caprices—as I believe he called them. Very well, I thought, you must be saved—and that was how I came to devise a way out of the difficulty—

MRS. LINDE: And did your husband never find out from your father that the money hadn't come from him?

NORA: No, never. Papa died just at that time. I had meant to let him into the secret and beg him never to reveal it. But he was so ill then—unfortunately there was no need to tell him.

MRS. LINDE: And since then have you never told your secret to your husband?

NORA: Good Heavens, no! How could you think that? A man who has such strong opinions about these things! And besides, how painful and humiliating it would be for Torvald, with his male pride, to know that he owed me anything! It would upset our relationship altogether; our beautiful happy home would no longer be the same.

MRS. LINDE: Do you mean never to tell him about it?

NORA: [*meditatively, and with a half smile*] Yes—some day, perhaps, after many years, when I'm no longer as attractive as I am now. Don't laugh at me! I mean, of course, when Torvald is no longer as devoted to me as he is now; when my dancing and dressing-up and reciting have palled on him; then it may be a good thing to have something in reserve—[*breaking off*] What nonsense! That time will never come. Now, what do you think of my great secret, Christine? Do you still think I am of no use? I can tell you, too, that this affair has caused me a lot of worry. It has been by no means easy for me to meet my payments punctually. I may tell you that there is something that is called, in business, quarterly interest, and another thing called payment in installments, and it is always so dreadfully difficult to manage them. I have had to save a little here and there, where I could, you understand. I have not been able to put aside much from my housekeeping money, for Torvald must have a good table. I couldn't let my children be shabbily dressed; I have felt obliged to use up all he gave me for them, the sweet little darlings!

MRS. LINDE: So it has all had to come out of your own expenses, poor Nora?

NORA: Of course. Besides, I was the one responsible for it. Whenever Torvald has given me money for new dresses and such things, I have never spent more than half of it; I have always bought the simplest and cheapest things. Thank Heaven, any clothes look good on me, and so Torvald has never noticed it. But it was often very hard on me, Christine—because it is delightful to be really well dressed, isn't it?

MRS. LINDE: Quite so.

NORA: Well, then I have found other ways of earning money. Last winter I was lucky enough to get a lot of copying to do; so I locked myself up and sat writing every evening until quite late at night. Many a time I was desperately tired; but all the same it was a tremendous pleasure to sit there working and earning money. It was like being a man.

MRS. LINDE: How much have you been able to pay off in that way?

NORA: I can't tell you exactly. You see, it is very difficult to keep an account of a business matter of that kind. I only know that I have paid every penny that I could scrape together. Many a time I was at my wits' end. [*smiles*] Then I used to sit here and imagine that a rich old gentleman had fallen in love with me—

MRS. LINDE: What! Who was it?

NORA: —that he had died; and that when his will was opened it contained, written in big letters, the instruction: "The lovely Mrs. Nora Helmer is to have all I possess paid over to her at once in cash."

MRS. LINDE: But, my dear Nora—who could the man be!

NORA: Good gracious, can't you understand? There was no old gentleman at all; it was only something that I used to sit here and imagine, when I couldn't think of any way of getting money. But it's all the same now; the tiresome old person can stay where he is, as far as I am concerned; I don't care about him or his will, either, for I am free from care now. [*jumps up*] My goodness, it's delightful to think of, Christine! Free from care! To be able to be free from care, quite free from care; to be able to play and romp with the children; to be able to keep the house beautifully and have everything just as Torvald likes it! And, think of it, soon the spring will come and the big blue sky! Perhaps we shall be able to take a little trip—perhaps I shall see the sea again! Oh, it's a wonderful thing to be alive and be happy. [*a bell is heard in the hall*]

MRS. LINDE: [*rising*] There's the doorbell; perhaps I had better go.

NORA: No, don't go; no one will come in here; it is sure to be for Torvald.

SERVANT: [*at the hall door*] Excuse me, ma'am—there is a gentleman to see the master, and as the doctor is with him—

NORA: Who is it?

KROGSTAD: [*at the door*] It is I, Mrs. Helmer. [MRS. LINDE *starts, trembles, and turns to the window.*]

NORA: [*takes a step towards him, and speaks in a strained, low voice*] You? What is it? What do you want to see my husband about?

KROGSTAD: Bank business—in a way. I have a small post in the Bank, and I hear your husband is to be our chief now—

NORA: Then it is—

KROGSTAD: Nothing but dry business matters, Mrs. Helmer; absolutely nothing else.

NORA: Be so good to go into the study, then. [*She bows indifferently to him and shuts the door into the hall; then comes back and makes up the fire in the stove.*]

MRS. LINDE: Nora—who was that man?

NORA: A lawyer named Krogstad.

MRS. LINDE: Then it really was he.

NORA: Do you know the man?

MRS. LINDE: I used to—many years ago. At one time he was a solicitor's clerk in our town.

NORA: Yes, he was.

MRS. LINDE: He is greatly altered.

NORA: He made a very unhappy marriage.

MRS. LINDE: He is a widower now isn't he?

NORA: With several children. There now, it's burning. [*shuts the door of the stove and moves the rocking chair aside*]

MRS. LINDE: They say he carried on various kinds of business.

NORA: Really! Perhaps he does; I don't know anything about it. But don't let's think of business: it is so boring.

DOCTOR RANK: [*comes out of* HELMER's *study. Before he shuts the door he calls to him.*] No, my dear fellow, I won't disturb you; I would rather go in to your wife for a little while. [*shuts the door and sees* MRS. LINDE] I beg your pardon; I'm afraid I'm disturbing you, too.

NORA: No, not at all. [*introducing him*] Doctor Rank, Mrs. Linde.

RANK: I have often heard Mrs. Linde's name mentioned here. I think I passed you on the stairs when I arrived, Mrs. Linde?

MRS. LINDE: Yes, I go up very slowly; I can't manage stairs well.

RANK: Ah! Some slight internal weakness?

MRS. LINDE: No, the fact is I have been overworking myself.

RANK: Nothing more than that? Then I suppose you have come to town to amuse yourself with our entertainments?

MRS. LINDE: I have come to look for work.

RANK: Is that a good cure for overwork?

MRS. LINDE: One must live, Doctor Rank.

RANK: Yes, the general opinion seems to be that it's necessary.

NORA: Look here, Doctor Rank—you know you want to live.

RANK: Certainly. However wretched I may feel, I want to prolong the agony as long as possible. All my patients are like that. And so are those who are morally sick—one of them, and a bad case, too, is at this very moment with Helmer—

MRS. LINDE: [*sadly*]. Ah!

NORA: Whom do you mean?

RANK: A lawyer, Krogstad, a fellow you don't know at all. He suffers from a diseased moral character, Mrs. Helmer; but even he began talking about it being highly important that he should live.

NORA: Did he? What did he want to speak to Torvald about?

RANK: I have no idea; I only heard that it was something about the Bank.

NORA: I didn't know this—what's his name—Krogstad had anything to do with the Bank.

RANK: Yes, he has some sort of appointment there. [*to* MRS. LINDE] I don't know whether you find also in your part of the world that there are certain people who go zealously sniffing about to smell out moral corruption, and, as soon as they have found some, put the person concerned into some lucrative position where they can keep their eye on him. Healthy natures are left out in the cold.

MRS. LINDE: Still I think the sick are those who most need taking care of.

RANK: [*shrugging his shoulders*] Yes, there you are. That is the sentiment that is turning Society into a hospital.

> [NORA, *who has been absorbed in her thoughts, breaks out into smothered laughter and claps her hands.*]

RANK: Why do you laugh at that? Have you any notion what Society really is?

NORA: What do I care about tiresome Society? I am laughing at something quite different, something extremely amusing. Tell me, Doctor Rank, are all the people who are employed in the Bank dependent on Torvald now?

RANK: Is that what you find so extremely amusing?

NORA: [*smiling and humming*] That's my affair! [*walking about the room*] It's perfectly glorious to think that we have—that Torvald has so much power over so many people. [*takes the packet from her pocket*] Doctor Rank, what do you say to a macaroon?

MRS. LINDE: What, macaroons? I thought they were forbidden here.

NORA: Yes, but these are some Christine gave me.

MRS. LINDE: What! I?

NORA: Oh, well, don't be alarmed! You couldn't know that Torvald had forbidden them. I must tell you that he's afraid they will spoil my teeth. But—once in a while—That's so, isn't it, Doctor Rank? Here [*puts a macaroon into his mouth*] you must have one, too, Christine. And I shall have one, just a little one—or at most two. [*walking about*] I am tremendously happy. There is just one thing in the world now that I should dearly love to do.

RANK: Well, what is that?

NORA: It's something I should dearly love to say so Torvald could hear me.

RANK: Well, why can't you say it?

NORA: No, I daren't; it's so shocking.

MRS. LINDE: Shocking?

RANK: Well, I should not advise you to say it. Still, with us you might. What is it you would so much like to say so Torvald could hear?

NORA: I should just love to say—Well, I'm damned!

RANK: Are you mad?

MRS. LINDE: Nora, dear—!

RANK: Say it, here he is!

NORA: [*hiding the packet*] Hush! Hush! Hush! [HELMER *comes out of his room, with his coat over his arm and his hat in his hand.*]

NORA: Well, Torvald dear, have you got rid of him?

HELMER: Yes, he's gone.

NORA: Let me introduce you—this is Christine, who has come to town.

HELMER: Christine—? Excuse me, but I don't know—

NORA: Mrs. Linde, dear; Christine Linde.

HELMER: Of course. A school friend of my wife, I presume?

MRS. LINDE: Yes, we've known each other since then.

NORA: And just think, she's taken a long journey in order to see you.

HELMER: What do you mean?

MRS. LINDE: No, really I—

NORA: Christine is tremendously clever at office work and she's frightfully anxious to work under some clever man, so as to improve—

HELMER: Very sensible, Mrs. Linde.

NORA: And when she heard you had been appointed manager of the Bank—the news was telegraphed, you know—she travelled here as quick as she could, Torvald, I'm sure you will be able to do something for Christine, for my sake, won't you?

HELMER: Well, it is not altogether impossible. I presume you are a widow, Mrs. Linde?

MRS. LINDE: Yes.

HELMER: And have had some experience of office work?

MRS. LINDE: Yes, a fair amount.

HELMER: Ah! well, it's very likely I may be able to find something for you.

NORA: [*clapping her hands*] What did I tell you? What did I tell you?

HELMER: You have just come at a fortunate moment, Mrs. Linde.

MRS. LINDE: How am I to thank you?

HELMER: There's no need. [*puts on his coat*] But to-day you must excuse me—

RANK: Wait a minute, I'll come with you. [*brings his fur coat from the hall and warms it at the fire*]

NORA: Don't be long away, Torvald dear.

HELMER: About an hour, not more.

NORA: Are you going, too, Christine?

MRS. LINDE: [*putting on her cloak*] Yes, I must go and look for a room.

HELMER: Oh, well then, we can walk together.

NORA: [*helping her*] What a pity it is we are so short of space here; I am afraid it is impossible for us—

MRS. LINDE: Please don't think of it! Good-bye, Nora dear, and many thanks.

NORA: Good-bye for the present. Of course you will come back this evening. And you, too, Doctor Rank. What do you say? If you are well enough? Oh, you must be! Wrap yourself up well. [*They go to the door all talking together. Children's voices are heard on the staircase.*]

NORA: There they are. There they are! [*She runs to open the door. The* NURSE *comes in with the children.*] Come in! Come in! [*stoops and kisses them*] Oh, you sweet blessings! Look at them, Christine! Aren't they darlings?

RANK: Don't let's stand here in the draught.

HELMER: Come along, Mrs. Linde; the place will only be bearable for a mother now! [RANK, HELMER, *and* MRS. LINDE *go downstairs. The* NURSE *comes forward with the children;* NORA *shuts the hall door.*]

NORA: How fresh and well you look! Such red cheeks!—like apples and roses. [*The children all talk at once while she speaks to them.*] Have you had great fun? That's splendid! What, you pulled both Emmy and Bob along on the sled?—both at once?—that *was* good. You are a clever boy, Ivar. Let me take her for a little, Anne. My sweet little baby doll! [*takes the baby from the* MAID *and dances it up and down*] Yes, yes, mother will dance with Bob, too. What! Have you been snowballing? I wish I had been there, too! No, no, I will take their things off, Anne; please let me do it, it's such fun. Go in now, you look half frozen. There's some hot coffee for you on the stove.

[*The* NURSE *goes into the room on the left.* NORA *takes off the children's things and throws them about, while they all talk to her at once.*]

NORA: Really! Did a big dog run after you? But it didn't bite you? No, dogs don't bite nice little dolly children. You mustn't look at the parcels, Ivar. What are they? Ah, I daresay you would like to know. No, no—it's something nasty! Come, let us have a game! What shall we play? Hide-and-Seek? Yes, we'll play Hide-and-Seek. Bob shall hide first. Must I hide? Very well, I'll hide first. [*She and the children laugh and shout, and romp in and out of the room; at last* NORA *hides under the table, the children rush in and look for her, but do not see her; they hear her smothered laughter, run to the table, lift up the cloth and find her. Shouts of laughter. She crawls forward and pretends to frighten them. Fresh laughter. Meanwhile there has been a knock at the hall door, but none of them has noticed it. The door is half opened, and* KROGSTAD *appears. He waits a little; the game goes on.*]

KROGSTAD: Excuse me, Mrs. Helmer.

NORA: [*with a stifled cry, turns round and gets up on to her knees*] Ah! What do you want?

KROGSTAD: Excuse me, the outer door was ajar; I suppose someone forgot to shut it.

NORA: [*rising*] My husband is out, Mr. Krogstad.

KROGSTAD: I know that.

NORA: What do you want here, then?

KROGSTAD: A word with you.

NORA: With me?—[*to the children, gently*] Go in to nurse. What? No, the strange man won't do mother any harm. When he's gone we will have another game. [*She takes the children into the room on the left, and shuts the door after them.*] You want to speak to me?

KROGSTAD: Yes, I do.

NORA: To-day? It is not the first of the month yet.

KROGSTAD: No, it is Christmas Eve, and it will depend on yourself what sort of a Christmas you will spend.

NORA: What do you want? To-day it is absolutely impossible for me—

KROGSTAD: We won't talk about that till later on. This is something different. I presume you can give me a moment?

NORA: Yes—yes, I can—although—

KROGSTAD: Good. I was in Olsen's Restaurant and saw your husband going down the street—

NORA: Yes?

KROGSTAD: With a lady.

NORA: What then?

KROGSTAD: May I make so bold as to ask if it was a Mrs. Linde?

NORA: It was.

KROGSTAD: Just arrived in town?

NORA: Yes, to-day.

KROGSTAD: She's a great friend of yours, isn't she?

NORA: She is. But I don't see—

KROGSTAD: I knew her, too, once upon a time.

NORA: I'm aware of that.

KROGSTAD: Are you? So you know all about it; I thought as much. Then I can ask you, without beating about the bush—is Mrs. Linde to have an appointment in the Bank?

NORA: What right have you to question me, Mr. Krogstad?—You, one of my husband's subordinates! But since you ask, you shall know. Yes, Mrs. Linde *is* to have an appointment. And it was I who pleaded her cause, Mr. Krogstad, let me tell you that.

KROGSTAD: I was right in what I thought, then.

NORA: [*walking up and down*] Sometimes one has a tiny little bit of influence, I should hope. Because one is a woman, it doesn't necessarily follow that—. When anyone is in a subordinate position, Mr. Krogstad, they should really be careful to avoid offending anyone who—who—

KROGSTAD: Who has influence?

NORA: Exactly.

KROGSTAD: [*changing his tone*] Mrs. Helmer, you will be so good as to use your influence on my behalf.

NORA: What? What do you mean?

KROGSTAD: You will be so kind as to see that I am allowed to keep my subordinate position in the Bank.

NORA: What do you mean by that? Who proposes to take your post away from you?

KROGSTAD: Oh, there is no necessity to keep up the pretence of ignorance. I can quite understand that your friend is not very anxious to expose herself to the chance of rubbing shoulders with me; and I quite understand, too, whom I have to thank for being discharged.

NORA: But I assure you—

KROGSTAD: Very likely; but, to come to the point, the time has come when I should advise you to use your influence to prevent that.

NORA: But, Mr. Krogstad, I *have* no influence.

KROGSTAD: Haven't you? I thought you said yourself just now—

NORA: Naturally I didn't mean you to put that construction on it. I! What should make you think I have any influence of that kind with my husband?

KROGSTAD: Oh, I have known your husband from our student days. I don't suppose he's any more unassailable than other husbands.

NORA: If you speak slightingly of my husband, I shall turn you out of the house.

KROGSTAD: You are bold, Mrs. Helmer.

NORA: I'm not afraid of you any longer. As soon as the New Year comes, I shall in a very short time be free of the whole thing.

KROGSTAD: [*controlling himself*] Listen to me, Mrs. Helmer. If necessary, I am prepared to fight for my small post in the Bank as if I were fighting for my life.

NORA: So it seems.

KROGSTAD: It's not only for the sake of the money; indeed, that weighs least with me in the matter. There's another reason—well, I may as well tell you. My position is this. I daresay you know, like everybody else, that once, many years ago, I was guilty of an indiscretion.

NORA: I think I've heard something of the kind.

KROGSTAD: The matter never came into court; but every way seemed to be closed to me after that. So I took to the business that you know of. I had to do something; and, honestly, I don't think I've been one of the worst. But now I must cut myself free from all that. My sons are growing up; for their sake I must try and win back as much respect as I can in the town. This post in the Bank was like the first step up for me—and now your husband is going to kick me downstairs again into the mud.

NORA: But you must believe me, Mr. Krogstad; it's not in my power to help you at all.

KROGSTAD: Then it's because you haven't the will; but I have means to compel you.

NORA: You don't mean that you will tell my husband that I owe you money?

KROGSTAD: Hm!—Suppose I were to tell him?

NORA: It would be shameful of you. [*sobbing*] To think of his learning my secret, which has been my joy and pride, in such an ugly, clumsy way—that he should learn it from you! And it would put me in a horribly disagreeable position—

KROGSTAD: Only disagreeable?

NORA: [*impetuously*] Well, do it, then!—and it will be the worse for you. My husband will see for himself what a blackguard you are, and you certainly won't keep your post then.

KROGSTAD: I asked you if it was only a disagreeable scene at home that you were afraid of?

NORA: If my husband does get to know of it, of course he will at once pay you what is still owing, and we shall have nothing more to do with you.

KROGSTAD: [*coming a step nearer*] Listen to me, Mrs. Helmer. Either you have a very bad memory or you know very little of business. I shall be obliged to remind you of a few details.

NORA: What do you mean?

KROGSTAD: When your husband was ill, you came to me to borrow forty-eight hundred crowns.

NORA: I didn't know any one else to go to.

KROGSTAD: I promised to get you that amount—

NORA: Yes, and you did so.

KROGSTAD: I promised to get you that amount, on certain conditions. Your mind was so taken up with your husband's illness, and were so anxious to get the money for your journey, that you seem to have paid no attention to the conditions of our bargain. Therefore it will not be amiss if I remind you of them. Now, I promised to get the money on the security of a bond which I drew up.

NORA: Yes, and which I signed.

KROGSTAD: Good. But below your signature there were a few lines constituting your father a surety for the money; those lines your father should have signed.

NORA: Should? He did sign them.

KROGSTAD: I had left the date blank; that is to say your father should himself have inserted the date on which he signed the paper. Do you remember that?

NORA: Yes, I think I remember—

KROGSTAD: Then I gave you the bond to send by post to your father. Is that not so?

NORA: Yes.

KROGSTAD: And you naturally did so at once, because five or six days afterwards you brought me the bond with your father's signature. And then I gave you the money.

NORA: Well, haven't I been paying it off regularly?

KROGSTAD: Fairly so, yes. But—to come back to the matter in hand—that must have been a very trying time for you, Mrs. Helmer?

NORA: It was, indeed.

KROGSTAD: Your father was very ill, wasn't he?

NORA: He was very near his end.

KROGSTAD: And died soon afterwards?

NORA: Yes.

KROGSTAD: Tell me, Mrs. Helmer, can you by any chance remember what day your father died?—on what day of the month, I mean.

NORA: Papa died on the 29th of September.

KROGSTAD: That is correct; I have ascertained it for myself. And, as that is so, there is a discrepancy [*taking a paper from his pocket*] which I cannot account for.

NORA: What discrepancy? I don't know—

KROGSTAD: The discrepancy consists, Mrs. Helmer, in the fact that your father signed this bond three days after his death.

NORA: What do you mean? I don't understand—

KROGSTAD: Your father died on the 29th of September. But, look here; your father has dated his signature the 2nd of October. It is a discrepancy, isn't it? [NORA *is silent.*] Can you explain it to me? [NORA *is still silent.*] It is a remarkable thing, too, that the words "2nd of October," as well as the year, are not written in your father's handwriting but in one that I think I know. Well, of course it can be explained; your father may have forgotten to date his signature, and someone else may have dated it before they knew of his death. There is no harm in that. It all depends on the signature of the name; and *that* is genuine, I suppose, Mrs. Helmer? It was your father himself who signed his name here?

NORA: [*after a short pause, throws her head up and looks defiantly at him*] No, it was not. It was I that wrote papa's name.

KROGSTAD: Are you aware that is a dangerous confession?

NORA: In what way? You'll have your money soon.

KROGSTAD: Let me ask you a question; why did you not send the paper to your father?

NORA: It was impossible; papa was so ill. If I'd asked him for his signature, I should have had to tell him what the money was to be used for; and when he was so ill himself I couldn't tell him that my husband's life was in danger—it was impossible.

KROGSTAD: It would have been better for you if you had given up your trip abroad.

NORA: No, that was impossible. That trip was to save my husband's life; I couldn't give that up.

KROGSTAD: But did it never occur to you that you were committing a fraud on me?

NORA: I couldn't take that into account; I didn't trouble myself about you at all. I couldn't bear you, because you put so many heartless difficulties in my way, although you knew what a dangerous condition my husband was in.

KROGSTAD: Mrs. Helmer, you evidently do not realize clearly what it is that you have been guilty of. But I can assure you that my one false step, which lost me all my reputation, was nothing more or nothing worse than what you have done.

NORA: You? Do you ask me to believe that you were brave enough to run a risk to save your wife's life?

KROGSTAD: The law cares nothing about motives.

NORA: Then it must be a very foolish law.

KROGSTAD: Foolish or not, it is the law by which you will be judged, if I produce this paper in court.

NORA: I don't believe it. Is a daughter not to be allowed to spare her dying father anxiety and care? Is a wife not to be allowed to save her husband's life? I don't know much about law; but I am certain that there must be laws permitting such things as that. Have you no knowledge of such laws—you who are a lawyer? You must be a very poor lawyer, Mr. Krogstad.

KROGSTAD: Maybe. But matters of business—such business as you and I have had together—do you think I don't understand that? Very well. Do as you please. But let me tell you this—if I lose my position a second time, you shall lose yours with me. [*He bows, and goes out through the hall.*]

NORA: [*appears buried in thought for a short time, then tosses her head*] Nonsense! Trying to frighten me like that!—I am not so silly as he thinks. [*begins to busy herself putting the children's things in order*] And yet—? No, it's impossible! I did it for love's sake.

THE CHILDREN: [*in the doorway on the left*] Mother, the stranger has gone out through the gate.

NORA: Yes, dears, I know. But, don't tell anyone about the stranger. Do you hear? Not even papa.

CHILDREN: No, mother; but will you come and play again?

NORA: No, no—not now.

CHILDREN: But, mother, you promised.

NORA: Yes, but I can't now. Go in; I have such a lot to do. Go in, my sweet little darlings. [*She gets them into the room by degrees and shuts the door on them; then sits down on the sofa, takes up a piece of needlework and sews a few stitches, but soon stops.*] No! [*throws down the work, gets up, goes to the hall door and calls out*] Helen! bring the tree in. [*goes to the table on the left, opens a drawer, and stops again*] No, no! it is quite impossible!

MAID: [*coming in with the tree*] Where shall I put it, ma'am?

NORA: Here, in the middle of the floor.

MAID: Shall I get you anything else?

NORA: No, thank you. I have all I want.

[*Exit* MAID.]

NORA: [*begins dressing the tree*] A candle here—and flowers here—. The horrible man! It's all nonsense—there's nothing wrong. The tree shall be splendid! I'll do everything I can think of to please you, Torvald!—I'll sing for you, dance for you—[HELMER *comes in with some papers under his arm.*] Oh! are you back already?

HELMER: Yes. Has anyone been here?

NORA: Here? No.

HELMER: That's strange. I saw Krogstad going out of the gate.

NORA: Did you? Oh yes, I forgot, Krogstad was here for a moment.

HELMER: Nora, I can see from your manner that he has been here begging you to say a good word for him.

NORA: Yes.

HELMER: And you were to appear to do it of your own accord; you were to conceal from me the fact of his having been here; didn't he beg that of you, too?

NORA: Yes, Torvald, but—

HELMER: Nora, Nora, and you would be a party to that sort of thing? To have any talk with a man like that, and give him any sort of promise? And to tell me a lie into the bargain?

NORA: A lie—?

HELMER: Didn't you tell me no one had been here? [*shakes his finger at her*] My little song-bird must never do that again. A song-bird must have a clean beak to chirp with—no false notes! [*puts his arm round her waist*] That's so, isn't it? Yes, I'm sure it is. [*lets her go*] We will say no more about it. [*sits down by the stove*] How warm and snug it is here! [*turns over his papers*]

NORA: [*after a short pause, during which she busies herself with the Christmas tree*] Torvald!

HELMER: Yes.

NORA: I am looking forward tremendously to the fancy dress ball at the Stenborgs' the day after to-morrow.

HELMER: And I'm tremendously curious to see what you're going to surprise me with.

NORA: It was very silly of me to want to do that.

HELMER: What do you mean?

NORA: I can't hit upon anything that will do; everything I think of seems so silly and insignificant.

HELMER: Does my little Nora acknowledge that at last?

NORA: [*standing behind his chair with her arms on the back of it*] Are you very busy, Torvald?

HELMER: Well—

NORA: What are all those papers?

HELMER: Bank business.

NORA: Already?

HELMER: I have got authority from the retiring manager to undertake the necessary changes in the staff and in the reorganization of the work; and I must make use of the Christmas week for that, so as to have everything in order for the new year.

NORA: Then that was why this poor Krogstad—

HELMER: Hm!

NORA: [*leans against the back of his chair and strokes his hair*] If you hadn't been so busy I should have asked you a tremendously big favour, Torvald.

HELMER: What's that? Tell me.

NORA: There is no one has such good taste as you. And I do so want to look nice at the costume ball. Torvald, couldn't you take me in hand and decide what I shall go as, and what sort of a dress I shall wear?

HELMER: Aha! So my obstinate little woman is obliged to get someone to come to her rescue?

NORA: Yes, Torvald, I can't get along at all without your help.

HELMER: Very well, I'll think it over, we shall manage to hit on something.

NORA: That is nice of you. [*goes to the Christmas tree. A short pause.*] How pretty the red flowers look—. But, tell me, was it really something very bad that this Krogstad was guilty of?

HELMER: He forged someone's name. Have you any idea what that means?

NORA: Isn't it possible that he was driven to do it by necessity?

HELMER: Yes; or, as in so many cases, by imprudence. I am not so heartless as to condemn a man altogether because of a single false step of that kind.

NORA: No, you wouldn't, would you, Torvald?

HELMER: Many a man has been able to retrieve his character, if he has openly confessed his fault and taken his punishment.

NORA: Punishment—?

HELMER: But Krogstad did nothing of that sort; he got himself out of it by a cunning trick, and that is why he has gone under altogether.

NORA: But do you think it would—?

HELMER: Just think how a guilty man like that has to lie and play the hypocrite with everyone, how he has to wear a mask in the presence of those near and dear to him, even before his own wife and children. And about the children—that's the most terrible part of it all, Nora.

NORA: How?

HELMER: Because such an atmosphere of lies infects and poisons the whole life of a home. Each breath the children take in such a house is full of the germs of evil.

NORA: [*coming nearer him*] Are you sure of that?

HELMER: My dear, I have often seen it in the course of my life as a lawyer. Almost everyone who has gone to the bad early in life has had a deceitful mother.

NORA: Why do you only say—mother?

HELMER: It seems most commonly to be the mother's influence, though naturally a bad father's would have the same result. Every lawyer is familiar with the fact. This Krogstad, now, has been persistently poisoning his own children with lies and dissimulation; that's why I say he has lost all moral character. [*holds out his hands to her*] That's why my sweet little Nora must promise me not to plead his cause. Give me your hand on it. Come, come, what's this? Give me your hand. There now, that's settled. I assure you it would be quite impossible for me to work with him; I literally feel physically ill when I am in the company of such people.

NORA: [*takes her hand out of his and goes to the opposite side of the Christmas tree*] How hot it is in here; and I have such a lot to do.

HELMER: [*getting up and putting his papers in order*] Yes, and I must try and read through some of these before dinner; and I must think about your costume, too. And it's just possible I may have something ready in gold paper to hang up on the tree. [*puts his hand on her head*] My precious little singing-bird! [*He goes into his room and shuts the door after him.*]

NORA: [*after a pause, whispers*] No, no—it isn't true. It's impossible; it must be impossible.
[*The* NURSE *opens the door on the left.*]

NURSE: The little ones are begging so hard to be allowed to come in to mamma.

NORA: No, no, no! Don't let them come in to me! You stay with them, Anne.

NURSE: Very well, ma'am. [*shuts the door*]

NORA: [*pale with terror*] Deprave my little children? Poison my home? [*A short pause. Then she tosses her head.*] It's not true. It can't possibly be true.

ACT II

THE SAME SCENE————*The Christmas tree is in the corner by the piano, stripped of its orna-ments and with burnt-down candle-ends on its disheveled branches.* NORA's *cloak and hat are lying on the sofa. She is alone in the room, walking about uneasily. She stops by the sofa and takes up her cloak.*

NORA: [*drops the cloak*] Someone is coming now! [*goes to the door and listens*] No—it's no one. Of course, no one will come to-day, Christmas Day—nor to-morrow, either. But, perhaps—[*opens the door and looks out*] No, nothing in the mail box; it's quite empty. [*comes forward*] What rubbish! Of course he can't be in earnest about it. Such a thing couldn't happen; it's impossible—I have three little children.

  [*Enter the* NURSE *from the room on the left, carrying a big cardboard box.*]

NURSE: At last I've found the box with the fancy dress.

NORA: Thanks; put it on the table.

NURSE: [*doing so*] But it's very much in want of mending.

NORA: I should like to tear it into a hundred thousand pieces.

NURSE: What an idea! It can easily be put in order—just a little patience.

NORA: Yes, I'll go and get Mrs. Linde to come and help me with it.

NURSE: What, out again? In this horrible weather? You'll catch cold, ma'am, and make yourself ill.

NORA: Well, worse than that might happen. How are the children?

NURSE: The poor little souls are playing with their Christmas presents, but—

NORA: Do they ask much for me?

NURSE: You see, they're so accustomed to have their mamma with them.

NORA: Yes, but nurse, I shan't be able to be so much with them now as I was before.

NURSE: Oh well, young children easily get accustomed to anything.

NORA: Do you think so? Do you think they would forget their mother if she went away altogether?

NURSE: Good heavens!—went away altogether?

NORA: Nurse, I want you to tell me something I have often wondered about—how could you have the heart to put your own child out among strangers?

NURSE: I was obliged to, if I wanted to be little Nora's nurse.

NORA: Yes, but how could you be willing to do it?

NURSE: What, when I was going to get such a good place by it? A poor girl who has got into trouble should be glad to. Besides, that wicked man didn't do a single thing for me.

NORA: But I suppose your daughter has quite forgotten you.

NURSE: No, indeed she hasn't. She wrote to me when she was confirmed, and when she was married.

NORA: [*putting her arms around her neck*] Dear old Anne, you were a good mother to me when I was little.

NURSE: Little Nora, poor dear, had no other mother but me.

NORA: And if my little ones had no other mother, I'm sure you would—. What nonsense I'm talking! [*opens the box*] Go in to them. Now I must—. You will see to-morrow how charming I'll look.

NURSE: I'm sure there will be no one at the ball so charming as you, ma'am. [*goes into the room on the left*]

NORA: [*begins to unpack the box, but soon pushes it away from her*] If only I dared go out. If only no one would come. If only I could be sure nothing would happen here in the meantime. Stuff and nonsense! No one will come. Only I mustn't think about it. I'll brush my muff. What lovely, lovely gloves! Out of my thoughts, out of my thoughts! One, two, three, four, five, six—[*screams*] Ah! there is someone coming—.[*makes a movement towards the door, but stands irresolute*]

[*Enter* MRS. LINDE *from the hall, where she has taken off her cloak and hat.*]

NORA: Oh, it's you, Christine. There is no one else out there, is there? How good of you to come!

MRS. LINDE: I heard you were up asking for me.

NORA: Yes, I was passing by. As a matter of fact, it's something you could help me with. Let us sit down here on the sofa. Look here. To-morrow evening there is to be a costume ball at the Stenborgs', who live above us; and Torvald wants me to go as a Neapolitan fisher-girl, and dance the Tarantella that I learned on Capri.

MRS. LINDE: I see; you're going to perform a character.

NORA: Yes, Torvald wants me to. Look, here's the dress; Torvald had it made for me there, but now it's all so torn, and I haven't any idea—.

MRS. LINDE: We'll easily put that right. It's only some of the trimming come unsewn here and there. Needle and thread? Now then, that's all we need.

NORA: It *is* nice of you.

MRS. LINDE: [*sewing*] So you're going to be dressed up to-morrow, Nora. I'll tell you what— I'll come in for a moment and see you in your fine feathers. But I have completely forgotten to thank you for a delightful evening yesterday.

NORA: [*gets up, and crosses the stage*] Well, I don't think yesterday was as pleasant as usual. You ought to have come to town a little earlier, Christine. Certainly Torvald does understand how to make a house attractive.

MRS. LINDE: And so do you, it seems to me; you are not your father's daughter for nothing. But tell me, is Doctor Rank always as depressed as he was yesterday?

NORA: No; yesterday it was very noticeable. I must tell you that he suffers from a very dangerous disease. He has tuberculosis of the spine, poor creature. His father was a horrible man who committed all sorts of excesses; and that's why his son was sickly from childhood, do you understand?

MRS. LINDE: [*dropping her sewing*] But my dearest Nora, how do you know anything about such things?

NORA: [*walking about*] Pooh! When you have three children, you get visits now and then from—from married women, who know something of medical matters, and they talk about one thing and another.

MRS. LINDE: [*goes on sewing. A short silence*] Does Doctor Rank come here every day?

NORA: Every day regularly. He's Torvald's best friend, and a great friend of mine, too. He's just like one of the family.

MRS. LINDE: But tell me this—is he perfectly sincere? I mean, isn't he the kind of man that is very anxious to make himself agreeable?

NORA: Not in the least. What makes you think that?

MRS. LINDE: When you introduced him to me yesterday, he declared he had often heard my name mentioned in this house; but afterwards I noticed that your husband hadn't the slightest idea who I was. So how could Doctor Rank—?

NORA: That's quite right, Christine. Torvald is so absurdly fond of me that he wants me absolutely to himself, as he says. At first he used to seem almost jealous if I mentioned any of my friends back home, so naturally I gave up doing so. But I often talk about such things with Doctor Rank, because he likes hearing about them.

MRS. LINDE: Listen to me, Nora. You are still very like a child in many things, and I'm older than you in many ways and have a little more experience. Let me tell you this—you ought to make an end of it with Doctor Rank.

NORA: What ought I to make an end of?

MRS. LINDE: Of two things, I think. Yesterday you talked some nonsense about a rich admirer who was to leave you money—

NORA: An admirer who doesn't exist, unfortunately! But what then?

MRS. LINDE: Is Doctor Rank well off?

NORA: Yes, he is.

MRS. LINDE: And has no one to provide for?

NORA: No, no one; but—

MRS. LINDE: And comes here every day?

NORA: Yes, I told you so.

MRS. LINDE: But how can this well-bred man be so tactless?

NORA: I don't understand you at all.

MRS. LINDE: Don't pretend, Nora. Do you suppose I don't guess who lent you the forty-eight hundred crowns?

NORA: Are you out of your senses? How can you think of such a thing! A friend of ours, who comes here every day! Do you realize what a horribly painful position that would be?

MRS. LINDE: Then it really isn't he?

NORA: No certainly not. It would never have entered my head for a moment. Besides, he had no money to lend then; he came into his money afterwards.

MRS. LINDE: Well, I think that was lucky for you, my dear Nora.

NORA: No, it would never have come into my head to ask Doctor Rank. Although I am quite sure that if I had asked him—

MRS. LINDE: But of course you won't.

NORA: Of course not. I have no reason to think it could possibly be necessary. But I'm quite sure that if I told Doctor Rank—

MRS. LINDE: Behind your husband's back?

NORA: I must make an end of it with the other one, and that will be behind his back, too. I must make an end of it with him.

MRS. LINDE: Yes, that's what I told you yesterday, but—

NORA: [*walking up and down*] A man can put a thing like that straight much easier than a woman—

MRS. LINDE: One's husband, yes.

NORA: Nonsense! [*standing still*] When you pay off a debt you get your bond back, don't you?

MRS. LINDE: Yes, as a matter of course.

NORA: And can tear it into a hundred thousand pieces, and burn it—the nasty dirty paper!

MRS. LINDE: [*looks hard at her, lays down her sewing and gets up slowly*] Nora, you are keeping something from me.

NORA: Do I look as if I were?

MRS. LINDE: Something has happened to you since yesterday morning. Nora, what is it?

NORA: [*going nearer to her*] Christine! [*listens*] Hush! There's Torvald come home. Do you mind going in to the children for the present? Torvald can't bear to see dressmaking going on. Let Anne help you.

MRS. LINDE: [*gathering some of the things together*] Certainly—but I'm not leaving till we've had it out with one another. [*She goes into the room on the left, as* HELMER *comes in from the hall.*]

NORA: [*going up to* HELMER] I have wanted you so much, Torvald dear.

HELMER: Was that the dressmaker?

NORA: No, it was Christine; she is helping me to put my costume in order. You will see I shall look quite smart.

HELMER: Wasn't that a happy thought of mine, now?

NORA: Splendid! But don't you think it's nice of me, too, to do as you wish?

HELMER: Nice?—because you do as your husband wishes? Well, well, you little rogue, I'm sure you did not mean it in that way. But I'm not going to disturb you; you will want to be trying on your costume, I expect.

NORA: I suppose you're going to work.

HELMER: Yes. [*shows her a bundle of papers*] Look at that. I have just been to the Bank. [*turns to go into his room*]

NORA: Torvald.

HELMER: Yes.

NORA: If your little squirrel were to ask you something very, very prettily—?

HELMER: What then?

NORA: Would you do it?

HELMER: I should like to hear what it is, first.

NORA: Your squirrel would run about and do all her tricks if you would be nice, and do what she wants.

HELMER: Speak plainly.

NORA: Your skylark would chirp about in every room, with her song rising and falling—

HELMER: Well, my skylark does that anyhow.

NORA: I'd be a fairy and dance for you in the moonlight, Torvald.

HELMER: Nora—you surely don't mean that request you made of me this morning?

NORA: [*going near him*] Yes, Torvald, I beg you so earnestly—

HELMER: Have you really the nerve to bring up that question again?

NORA: Yes, dear, you *must* do as I ask; you *must* let Krogstad keep his post in the Bank.

HELMER: My dear Nora, it is his post that I have arranged for Mrs. Linde to have.

NORA: Yes, you've been awfully kind about that; but you could just as well dismiss some other clerk instead of Krogstad.

HELMER: This is simply incredible obstinacy! Because you chose to give him a thoughtless promise that you would speak for him, I am expected to—

NORA: That isn't the reason, Torvald. It is for your own sake. This fellow writes in the most scurrilous newspapers; you've told me so yourself. He can do you an unspeakable amount of harm. I am frightened to death of him—

HELMER: Ah, I understand; it is recollections of the past that scare you.

NORA: What do you mean?

HELMER: Naturally you are thinking of your father.

NORA: Yes—yes, of course. Just recall in your mind what these malicious creatures wrote in the papers about papa, and how horribly they slandered him. I believe they would have procured his dismissal if the Department had not sent you over to inquire into it, and if you had not been so kindly disposed and helpful to him.

HELMER: My little Nora, there is an important difference between your father and me. Your father's reputation as a public official was not above suspicion. Mine is, and I hope it will continue to be so, as long as I hold my office.

NORA: You never can tell what mischief these men may contrive. We ought to be so well off, so snug and happy here in our peaceful home, and have no cares—you and I and the children, Torvald! That's why I beg you so earnestly—

HELMER: And it's just by interceding for him that you make it impossible for me to keep him. It's already known at the Bank that I mean to dismiss Krogstad. Is it to get about now that the new manager has changed his mind at his wife's bidding—

NORA: And what if it did?

HELMER: Of course!—if only this obstinate little person can get her way! Do you suppose I'm going to make myself ridiculous before my entire staff, to let people think that I am a man to be swayed by all sorts of outside influence? I should very soon feel the consequences of that, I can tell you! And besides, there is something that makes it quite impossible for me to have Krogstad in the Bank as long as I am manager.

NORA: Whatever is that?

HELMER: His moral failings I might perhaps have overlooked, if necessary—

NORA: Yes, you could—couldn't you?

HELMER: And I hear he is a good worker, too. But I knew him when we were boys. It was one of those rash friendships that so often prove an embarrassment later in life. I may as well tell you plainly, we were once on first-name terms with one another. But this tactless fellow lays no restraint on himself when other people are present. On the contrary, he thinks it gives him the right to adopt a familiar tone with me, and every minute it is "I say, Helmer, old fellow!" and that sort of thing. It's extremely painful for me. He would make my position in the Bank intolerable.

NORA: Torvald, I don't believe you mean that.

HELMER: Don't you? Why not?

NORA: Because it is such a petty way of looking at things.

HELMER: What are you saying? Petty? Do you think I'm petty?

NORA: No, just the opposite, dear—it's exactly for that reason.

HELMER: It's the same thing. You say my point of view is petty, so I must be so, too. Petty. Very well—I must put an end to this. [*goes to the hall door and calls*] Helen!

NORA: What are you going to do?

HELMER: [*looking among his papers*] Settle it. [*Enter* MAID.] Look here; take this letter and go downstairs with it at once. Find a messenger and tell him to deliver it, and be quick. The address is on it, and here is the money.

MAID: Very well, sir. [*exit with the letter*]

HELMER: [*putting his papers together*] Now then, little Miss Obstinate.

NORA: [*breathless*] Torvald—what was that letter?

HELMER: Krogstad's dismissal.

NORA: Call her back, Torvald! There is still time. Oh Torvald, call her back! Do it for my sake—for your own sake—for the children's sake! Do you hear me, Torvald? Call her back! You don't know what that letter can bring upon us.

HELMER: It's too late.

NORA: Yes, it's too late.

HELMER: My dear Nora, I can forgive the anxiety you are in, although really it is an insult to me. It is, indeed. Isn't it an insult to think that I should be afraid of a starving journalist's vengeance? But I forgive you nevertheless, because it's such eloquent witness to your great love for me. [*takes her in his arms*] And that's as it should be, my own darling Nora. Come what will, you may be sure I'll have both courage and strength if they be needed. You'll see I am man enough to take everything upon myself.

NORA: [*in a horror-stricken voice*] What do you mean by that?

HELMER: Everything, I say

NORA: [*recovering herself*] You'll never have to do that.

HELMER: That's right. Well, we'll share it, Nora, as man and wife should. That's how it should be. [*caressing her*] Are you happy now? There, there!—not these frightened dove's eyes! The whole thing is only the wildest fantasy—Now, you must go and play through the Tarantella and practice with your tambourine. I'll go into the inner office and shut the door, and I'll hear nothing, you can make as much noise as you please. [*turns back at the door*] And when Rank comes, tell him where he can find me. [*nods to her, takes his papers and goes into his room and shuts the door after him*]

NORA: [*bewildered with anxiety, stands as if rooted to the spot, and whispers*] He was capable of doing it. He will do it. He will do it in spite of everything—No, not that! Never,

never! Anything rather than that! Oh, for some help, some way out of it! [*the door-bell rings*] Doctor Rank! Anything rather than that—anything, whatever it is! [*She puts her hands over her face, pulls herself together, goes to the door and opens it.* RANK *is standing without, hanging up his coat. During the following dialogue it begins to grow dark.*]

NORA: Good-day, Doctor Rank. I knew your ring. But you mustn't go into Torvald now; I think he is busy with something.

RANK: And you?

NORA: [*brings him in and shuts the door after him*] Oh, you know very well I always have time for you.

RANK: Thank you. I shall make use of as much of it as I can.

NORA: What do you mean by that? As much of it as you can?

RANK: Well, does that alarm you?

NORA: It was such a strange way of putting it. Is anything likely to happen?

RANK: Nothing but what I've long been prepared for. But I certainly didn't expect it to happen so soon.

NORA: [*gripping him by the arm*] What have you found out? Doctor Rank, you must tell me.

RANK: [*sitting down by the stove*] It's all up with me. And it can't be helped.

NORA: [*with a sigh of relief*] Is it about yourself?

RANK: Who else? It's no use lying to one's self. I am the most wretched of all my patients, Mrs. Helmer. Lately I've been taking stock of my internal economy. Bankrupt! Probably within a month I shall lie rotting in the churchyard.

NORA: What an ugly thing to say!

RANK: The thing itself is cursedly ugly, and the worst of it is that I'll have to face so much more that is ugly before that. I'll only make one more examination of myself; when I have done that, I'll know pretty certainly when the horrors of dissolution will begin. There's something I want to tell you. Helmer's sensitivity makes him disgusted at everything that is ugly; I won't have him in my sickroom.

NORA: Oh, but, Doctor Rank—

RANK: I won't have him there. Not on any account. I bar my door to him. As soon as I'm quite certain that the worst has come, I'll send you my card with a black cross on it, and then you will know that the loathsome end has begun.

NORA: You are quite absurd to-day. And I wanted you so much to be in a really good humour.

RANK: With death stalking beside me?—To have to pay this penalty for another man's sin! Is there any justice in that? And in every single family, in one way or another, some such inexorable retribution is being exacted—

NORA: [*putting her hands over her ears*] Rubbish! Do talk of something cheerful.

RANK: Oh, it's a mere laughing matter, the whole thing. My poor innocent spine has to suffer for my father's youthful amusements.

NORA: [*sitting at the table on the left*] I suppose you mean that he was too partial to asparagus and paté de foie gras, don't you?

RANK: Yes, and to truffles.

NORA: Truffles, yes. And oysters, too, I suppose?

RANK: Oysters, of course, that goes without saying.

NORA: And heaps of port and champagne. It is sad that all these nice things should take their revenge on our bones.

RANK: Especially that they should revenge themselves on the unlucky bones of those who have not had the satisfaction of enjoying them.

NORA: Yes, that's the saddest part of it all.

RANK: [*with a searching look at her*] Hm!—

NORA: [*after a short pause*] Why did you smile?

RANK: No, it was you that laughed.

NORA: No, it was you that smiled, Doctor Rank!

RANK: [*rising*] You're a bigger tease than I thought.

NORA: I'm in a silly mood to-day.

RANK: So it seems.

NORA: [*putting her hands on his shoulders*] Dear, dear Doctor Rank, death mustn't take you away from Torvald and me.

RANK: It's a loss you would easily recover from. Those who are gone are soon forgotten.

NORA: [*looking at him anxiously*] Do you believe that?

RANK: People form new ties, and then—

NORA: Who will form new ties?

RANK: Both you and Helmer, when I'm gone. You yourself are already on the high road to it, I think. What did Mrs. Linde want here last night?

NORA: Oho!—you don't mean to say you're jealous of poor Christine?

RANK: Yes, I am. She'll be my successor in this house. When I'm done for, this woman will—

NORA: Hush! don't speak so loud. She's in that room.

RANK: To-day again. There, you see.

NORA: She's only come to sew my costume for me. Bless my soul, how unreasonable you are! [*sits down on the sofa*] Be nice now, Doctor Rank, and to-morrow you will see how beautifully I shall dance, and you can imagine I'm doing it all for you—and for Torvald, too, of course. [*takes various things out of the box*] Doctor Rank, come and sit down here, and I'll show you something.

RANK: [*sitting down*] What is it?

NORA: Just look at those!

RANK: Silk stockings.

NORA: Flesh-coloured. Aren't they lovely? It is so dark here now, but to-morrow—. No, no, no! you must only look at the feet. Oh well, you may have leave to look at the legs, too.

RANK: Hm!—

NORA: Why are you looking so critical? Don't you think they will fit me?

RANK: I have no means of forming an opinion about that.

NORA: [*looks at him for a moment*] For shame! [*hits him lightly on the ear with the stockings*] That's to punish you. [*folds them up again*]

RANK: And what other nice things am I to be allowed to see?

NORA: Not a single thing more, for being so naughty. [*She looks among the things, humming to herself.*]

RANK: [*after a short silence*] When I'm sitting here, talking to you as intimately as this, I can't imagine for a moment what would have become of me if I had never come into this house.

NORA: [*smiling*] I believe you do feel thoroughly at home with us.

RANK: [*in a lower voice, looking straight in front of him*] And to be obliged to leave it all—

NORA: Nonsense, you're not going to leave it.

RANK: [*as before*] And not be able to leave behind one the slightest token of one's gratitude, scarcely even a fleeting regret—nothing but an empty place which the first comer can fill as well as any other.

NORA: And if I asked you now for a—? No!

RANK: For what?

NORA: For a big proof of your friendship—

RANK: Yes, yes!

NORA: I mean a tremendously big favour—

RANK: Would you really make me so happy for once?

NORA: Ah, but you don't know what it is yet.

RANK: No—but tell me.

NORA: I really can't, Doctor Rank. It's something out of all reason; it means advice, and help, and a favour—

RANK: The bigger the better. I can't conceive what it is you mean. Do tell me. Haven't I your confidence?

NORA: More than anyone else. I know you are my truest and best friend, and so I'll tell you what it is. Well, Doctor Rank, it's something you must help me to prevent. You know how devotedly, how inexpressibly deeply Torvald loves me; he would never for a moment hesitate to give his life for me.

RANK: [*leaning towards her*] Nora—do you think he is the only one—?

NORA: [*with a slight start*] The only one—?

RANK: The only one who would gladly give his life for your sake.

NORA: [*sadly*] Is that it?

RANK: I was determined you should know it before I went away, and there'll never be a better opportunity than this. Now you know it, Nora. And now you know, too, that you can trust me as you would trust no one else.

NORA: [*rises, deliberately and quietly*] Let me pass.

RANK: [*makes room for her to pass him, but sits still*] Nora!

NORA: [*at the hall door*] Helen, bring in the lamp. [*goes over to the stove*] Dear Doctor Rank, that was really horrid of you.

RANK: To have loved you as much as anyone else does? Was that horrid?

NORA: No, but to go and tell me so. There was really no need—

RANK: What do you mean? Did you know—? [MAID *enters with lamp, puts it down on the table, and goes out.*] Nora—Mrs. Helmer—tell me, had you any idea of this?

NORA: Oh, how do I know whether I had or whether I hadn't? I really can't tell you—To think you could be so clumsy, Doctor Rank! We were getting on so nicely.

RANK: Well, at all events you know now that you can command me, body and soul. So won't you speak out?

NORA: [*looking at him*] After what happened?

RANK: I beg you to let me know what it is.

NORA: I can't tell you anything now.

RANK: Yes, yes. You mustn't punish me in that way. Let me have permission to do for you whatever a man may do.

NORA: You can do nothing for me now. Besides, I really don't need any help at all. You will find the whole thing is merely fancy on my part. It really is so—of course it is! [*Sits down in the rocking chair, and looks at him with a smile.*] You are a nice man, Doctor Rank!—don't you feel ashamed of yourself, now the lamp has come!

RANK: Not a bit. But perhaps I had better go—for ever?

NORA: No, indeed, you shall not. Of course you must come here just as before. You know very well Torvald can't do without you.

RANK: Yes, but you?

NORA: Oh I'm always tremendously pleased when you come.

RANK: It's just that, that put me on the wrong track. You are a riddle to me. I've often thought that you'd almost as soon be in my company as in Helmer's.

NORA: Yes—you see there are some people one loves best, and others whom one would almost always rather have as companions.

RANK: Yes, there is something in that.

NORA: When I was at home, of course I loved papa best. But I always thought it tremendous fun if I could steal down into the maids' room, because they never moralised at all, and talked to each other about such entertaining things.

RANK: I see—it is their place I have taken.

NORA: [*jumping up and going to him*] Oh, dear, nice Doctor Rank, I never meant that at all. But surely you can understand that being with Torvald is a little like being with papa— [*Enter* MAID *from the hall.*]

MAID: If you please, ma'am. [*whispers and hands her a card*]

NORA: [*glancing at the card*] Oh! [*puts it in her pocket*]

RANK: Is there anything wrong?

NORA: No, no, not in the least. It's only something—it's my new dress—

RANK: What? Your dress is lying there.

NORA: Oh, yes, that one; but this is another. I ordered it. Torvald mustn't know about it—

RANK: Oho! Then that was the great secret.

NORA: Of course. Just go in to him; he is sitting in the inner room. Keep him as long as—

RANK: Make your mind easy; I won't let him escape. [*goes into* HELMER's *room*]

NORA: [*to the* MAID] And he's waiting in the kitchen?

MAID: Yes; he came up the back stairs.

NORA: But didn't you tell him no one was in?

MAID: Yes, but it was no good.

NORA: He won't go away?

MAID: No; he says he won't until he has seen you, ma'am.

NORA: Well, let him come in—but quietly. Helen, you mustn't say anything about it to anyone. It's a surprise for my husband.

MAID: Yes, ma'am, I quite understand. [*exit*]

NORA: This dreadful thing is going to happen! It will happen in spite of me! No, no, no, it can't happen—it shan't happen! [*She bolts the door of* HELMER's *room. The* MAID *opens the hall door for* KROGSTAD *and shuts it after him. He is wearing a fur coat, high boots, and a fur cap.*]

NORA: [*advancing towards him*] Speak low—my husband is at home.

KROGSTAD: No matter about that!

NORA: What do you want of me?

KROGSTAD: An explanation.

NORA: Make haste then. What is it?

KROGSTAD: You know, I suppose, that I've got my dismissal.

NORA: I couldn't prevent it, Mr. Krogstad. I fought as hard as I could on your side, but it was no good.

KROGSTAD: Does your husband love you so little, then? He knows what I can expose you to, and yet he ventures—

NORA: How can you suppose that he has any knowledge of the sort?

KROGSTAD: I didn't suppose so at all. It would not be the least like our dear Torvald Helmer to show so much courage—

NORA: Mr. Krogstad, a little respect for my husband, please.

KROGSTAD: Certainly—all the respect he deserves. But since you have kept the matter so carefully to yourself, I make bold to suppose that you have a little clearer idea, than you had yesterday, of what it actually is that you have done?

NORA: More than you could ever teach me.

KROGSTAD: Yes, bad lawyer that I am.

NORA: What is it you want of me?

KROGSTAD: Only to see how you were, Mrs. Helmer. I have been thinking about you all day long. A mere cashier, hackwriter, a—well, a man like me—even he has a little of what is called feeling, you know.

NORA: Show it, then; think of my little children.

KROGSTAD: Have you and your husband thought of mine? But never mind about that. I only wanted to tell you that you need not take this matter too seriously. In the first place there will be no accusation made on my part.

NORA: No, of course not; I was sure of that.

KROGSTAD: The whole thing can be arranged amicably; there is no reason why anyone should know anything about it. It will remain a secret between us three.

NORA: My husband must never get to know anything about it.

KROGSTAD: How will you be able to prevent it? Am I to understand that you can pay the balance that's owing?

NORA: No, not just at present.

KROGSTAD: Or perhaps that you have some means of raising the money soon?

NORA: None that I mean to make use of.

KROGSTAD: Well, in any case, it would've been of no use to you now. If you stood there with ever so much money in your hand, I would never part with your bond.

NORA: Tell me what purpose you mean to put it to.

KROGSTAD: I shall only preserve it—keep it in my possession. No one who is not concerned in the matter shall have the slightest hint of it. So that if the thought of it has driven you to any desperate resolution—

NORA: It has.

KROGSTAD: If you had it in your mind to run away from your home—

NORA: I had.

KROGSTAD: Or even something worse—

NORA: How could you know that?

KROGSTAD: Give up the idea.

NORA: How did you know I had thought of *that*?

KROGSTAD: Most of us think of that at first. I did, too—but I hadn't the courage.

NORA: [*faintly*] No more had I.

KROGSTAD: [*in a tone of relief*] No, that's it, isn't it—you hadn't the courage, either?

NORA: No, I haven't—I haven't.

KROGSTAD: Besides, it would have been a great piece of folly. Once the first storm at home is over—. I have a letter for your husband in my pocket.

NORA: Telling him everything?

KROGSTAD: In as lenient a manner as I possibly could.

NORA: [*quickly*] He mustn't get that letter. Tear it up. I will find some means of getting money.

KROGSTAD: Excuse me, Mrs. Helmer, but I think I told you just now—

NORA: I am not speaking of what I owe you. Tell me what sum you are asking my husband for, and I will get the money.

KROGSTAD: I am not asking your husband for a penny.

NORA: What do you want, then?

KROGSTAD: I will tell you. I want to rehabilitate myself, Mrs. Helmer; I want to get on; and in that your husband must help me. For the last year and a half I have not had a hand in anything dishonourable, and all that time I have been struggling in most restricted circumstances. I was content to work my way up step by step. Now I'm turned out, and I'm not going to be satisfied with merely being taken into favour again. I want to get on, I tell you. I want to get into the Bank again, in a higher position. Your husband must make a place for me—

NORA: That he will never do!

KROGSTAD: He will; I know him; he dare not protest. And as soon as I'm in there again with him, then you will see! Within a year I shall be the manager's right hand. It will be Nils Krogstad and not Torvald Helmer who manages the Bank.

NORA: That's a thing you will never see!

KROGSTAD: Do you mean that you will—?

NORA: I have courage enough for it now.

KROGSTAD: Oh, you can't frighten me. A fine, spoilt lady like you—

NORA: You'll see, you'll see.

KROGSTAD: Under the ice, perhaps? Down into the cold, coal-black water? And then, in the spring, to float up to the surface, all horrible and unrecognisable, with your hair fallen out—

NORA: You can't frighten me.

KROGSTAD: Nor you me. People don't do such things, Mrs. Helmer. Besides, what use would it be? I should have him completely in my power all the same.

NORA: Afterwards? When I am no longer—

KROGSTAD: Have you forgotten that it is I who have the keeping of your reputation? [*Nora stands speechlessly looking at him.*] Well, now, I've warned you. Don't do anything foolish. When Helmer has received my letter, I shall expect a message from him. And be sure you remember that it's your husband himself who has forced me into such ways as this again. I'll never forgive him for that. Good-bye, Mrs. Helmer. [*exit through the hall*]

NORA: [*goes to the hall door, opens it slightly and listens*] He's going. He's not putting the letter in the box. Oh no, no! that's impossible! [*opens the door by degrees*] What's that? He's standing outside. He's not going downstairs. Is he hesitating? Can he—? [*A letter drops into the box; then* KROGSTAD's *footsteps are heard, till they die away as he goes downstairs.* NORA *utters a stifled cry, and runs across the room to the table by the sofa. A short pause.*]

NORA: In the mail box. [*steals across to the hall door*] There it lies—Torvald, Torvald, there is no hope for us now!

[MRS. LINDE *comes in from the room on the left, carrying the dress.*]

MRS. LINDE: There, I can't see anything more to mend now. Would you like to try it on—?

NORA: [*in a hoarse whisper*] Christine, come here.

MRS. LINDE: [*throwing the dress down on the sofa*] What's the matter with you? You look so upset.

NORA: Come here. Do you see that letter? There, look—you can see it through the glass in the box.

MRS. LINDE: Yes, I see it.

NORA: That letter is from Krogstad.

MRS. LINDE: Nora—it was Krogstad who lent you the money!

NORA: Yes, and now Torvald will know all about it.

MRS. LINDE: Believe me, Nora, that's the best thing for both of you.

NORA: You don't know all. I forged a name.

MRS. LINDE: Good heavens—!

NORA: I only want to say this to you, Christine—you must be my witness.

MRS. LINDE: Your witness? What do you mean? What am I to—?

NORA: If I should go out of my mind—and it might easily happen—

MRS. LINDE: Nora!

NORA: Or if anything else should happen to me—anything, for instance, that might prevent my being here—

MRS. LINDE: Nora! Nora! You're quite out of your mind.

NORA: And if it should happen that there were someone who wanted to take all the responsibility, all the blame, you understand—

MRS. LINDE: Yes, yes—but how can you suppose—?

NORA: Then you must be my witness, that it's not true, Christine. I'm not out of my mind at all. I'm in my right senses now, and I tell you no one else has known anything about it; I, and I alone, did the whole thing. Remember that.

MRS. LINDE: I will, indeed. But I don't understand all this.

NORA: How should you understand it? A miracle is going to happen.

MRS. LINDE: A miracle?

NORA: Yes, a miracle.—But it's so terrible, Christine; it *mustn't* happen, not for all the world.

MRS. LINDE: I will go at once and see Krogstad.

NORA: Don't go to him; he will do you some harm.

MRS. LINDE: There was a time when he would gladly do anything for my sake.

NORA: He?

MRS. LINDE: Where does he live?

NORA: How should I know—? Yes [*feeling in her pocket*] here is his card. But the letter, the letter—!

HELMER: [*calls from his room, knocking at the door*] Nora!

NORA: [*cries out anxiously*] Oh, what's that? What do you want?

HELMER: Don't be so frightened. We are not coming in; you have locked the door. Are you trying on your dress?

NORA: Yes, that's it. I look so nice, Torvald.

MRS. LINDE: [*who has read the card*] I see he lives at the corner here.

NORA: Yes, but it's no use. It's hopeless. The letter is lying there in the box.

MRS. LINDE: And your husband keeps the key?

NORA: Yes, always.

MRS. LINDE: Krogstad must ask for his letter back unread, he must find some pretence—

NORA: But it's just at this time that Torvald generally—

MRS. LINDE: You must delay him. Go in to him in the meantime. I'll come back as soon as I can. [*She goes out hurriedly through the hall door.*]

NORA: [*goes to* HELMER's *door, opens it and peeps in*] Torvald!

HELMER: [*from the inner room*] Well? May I venture at last to come into my own room again? Come along, Rank, now you'll see—[*halting in the doorway*] But what is this?

NORA: What is what, dear?

HELMER: Rank led me to expect a splendid transformation.

RANK: [*in the doorway*] I understood so, but evidently I was mistaken.

NORA: Yes, nobody is to have the chance of admiring me in my costume until to-morrow.

HELMER: But, my dear Nora, you look so worn out. Have you been practising too much?

NORA: No, I have not practised at all.

HELMER: But you will need to—

NORA: Yes, indeed I shall, Torvald. But I can't get on a bit without you to help me; I have absolutely forgotten the whole thing.

HELMER: Oh, we'll soon work it up again.

NORA: Yes, help me, Torvald. Promise that you will! I'm so nervous about it—all the people. You must give yourself up to me entirely this evening. Not the tiniest bit of business—you mustn't even take a pen in your hand. Will you promise, Torvald dear?

HELMER: I promise: This evening I'll be wholly and absolutely at your service, you helpless little thing. But, first of all I'll just—[*goes towards the hall door*]

NORA: What are you going to do there?

HELMER: Only see if any letters have come.

NORA: No, no! Don't do that, Torvald!

HELMER: Why not?

NORA: Torvald, please don't. There is nothing there.

HELMER: Well, let me look. [*Turns to go to the letterbox.* NORA, *at the piano, plays the first bars of the Tarantella.* HELMER *stops in the doorway.*] Aha!

NORA: I can't dance to-morrow if I don't practise with you.

HELMER: [*going up to her*] Are you really so afraid of it, dear?

NORA: Yes, so dreadfully afraid of it. Let me practise at once; there is time now, before we go to dinner. Sit down and play for me, Torvald dear; coach me, and correct me as you play.

HELMER: With great pleasure, if you wish me to. [*sits down at the piano*]

NORA: [*Takes out of the box a tambourine and a long variegated shawl. She hastily drapes the shawl round her. Then she springs to the front of the stage and calls out.*] Now play for me! I'm going to dance!

[HELMER *plays and* NORA *dances.* RANK *stands by the piano behind* HELMER, *and looks on.*]

HELMER: [*as he plays*] Slower, slower!

NORA: I can't do it any other way.

HELMER: Not so violently, Nora!

NORA: This is the way.

HELMER: [*stops playing*] No, no—that's not a bit right.

NORA: [*laughing and swinging the tambourine*] Didn't I tell you so?

RANK: Let me play for her.

HELMER: [*getting up*] Yes, do. I can correct her better then.

[RANK *sits down at the piano and plays.* NORA *dances more and more wildly.* HELMER *has taken up a position beside the stove, and during her dance gives her frequent instructions. She does not seem to hear him; her hair comes down and falls over her shoulders; she pays no attention to it, but goes on dancing. Enter* MRS. LINDE.]

MRS. LINDE: [*standing as if spellbound in the doorway*] Oh!—

NORA: [*as she dances*] Such fun, Christine!

HELMER: My dear darling Nora, you are dancing as if your life depended on it.

NORA: So it does.

HELMER: Stop, Rank; this is sheer madness. Stop, I tell you! [RANK *stops playing, and* NORA *suddenly stands still.* HELMER *goes up to her.*] I could never have believed it. You have forgotten everything I taught you.

NORA: [*throwing away the tambourine*] There, you see.

HELMER: You'll want a lot of coaching.

NORA: Yes, you see how much I need it. You must coach me up to the last minute. Promise me that, Torvald!

HELMER: You can depend on me.

NORA: You must not think of anything but me, either to-day or to-morrow; you mustn't open a single letter—not even open the mail box—

HELMER: Ah, you're still afraid of that fellow—

NORA: Yes, indeed I am.

HELMER: Nora, I tell from your looks that there is a letter from him lying there.

NORA: I don't know; I think there is; but you must not read anything of that kind now. Nothing horrid must come between us till this is all over.

RANK: [*whispers to* HELMER] You mustn't contradict her.

HELMER: [*taking her in his arms*] The child shall have her way. But to-morrow night, after you've danced—

NORA: Then you will be free. [*The* MAID *appears in the doorway to the right.*]

MAID: Dinner is served, ma'am.

NORA: We will have champagne, Helen.

MAID: Very good, ma'am. [*exit*]

HELMER: Hullo!—are we going to have a banquet?

NORA: Yes, a champagne banquet till the small hours. [*calls out*] And a few macaroons, Helen—lots, just for once!

HELMER: Come, come, don't be so wild and nervous. Be my own little skylark.

NORA: Yes, dear, I will. But go in now and you, too, Doctor Rank. Christine, you must help me to do up my hair.

RANK: [*whispers to* HELMER *as they go out*] I suppose there's nothing—she is not expecting anything?

HELMER: Far from it, my dear fellow; it is simply nothing more than this childish nervousness I was telling you of. [*They go into the right-hand room.*]

NORA: Well!

MRS. LINDE: Gone out of town.

NORA: I could tell from your face.

MRS. LINDE: He's coming home to-morrow evening. I wrote a note for him.

NORA: You should have let it alone; you must prevent nothing. After all, it is splendid to be waiting for a wonderful thing to happen.

MRS. LINDE: What is it that you are waiting for?

NORA: Oh, you wouldn't understand. Go in to them, I will come in a moment. [MRS. LINDE *goes into the dining room.* NORA *stands still for a little while, as if to compose herself. Then she looks at her watch.*] Five o'clock. Seven hours till midnight; and then twenty-four hours till the next midnight. Then the Tarantella will be over. Twenty-four and seven? Thirty-one hours to live.

HELMER: [*from the doorway on the right*] Where's my little skylark?

NORA: [*going to him with her arms outstretched*] Here she is!

ACT III

THE SAME SCENE——The table has been placed in the middle of the stage, with chairs round it. A lamp is burning on the table. The door into the hall stands open. Dance music is heard in the room above. MRS. LINDE *is sitting at the table idly turning over the leaves of a book she tries to read, but does not seem able to collect her thoughts. Every now and then she listens intently for a sound at the outer door.*

MRS. LINDE: [*looking at her watch*] Not yet—and the time is nearly up. If only he doesn't—. [*listens again*] Ah, there he is. [*Goes into the hall and opens the outer door carefully. Light footsteps are heard on the stairs. She whispers.*] Come in. There's no one here.

KROGSTAD: [*in the doorway*] I found a note from you at home. What does this mean?

MRS. LINDE: It's absolutely necessary that I have a talk with you.

KROGSTAD: Really! And is it absolutely necessary that it should be here?

MRS. LINDE: It's impossible where I live; there's no private entrance to my rooms. Come in; we're quite alone. The maid's asleep and the Helmers are at the dance upstairs.

KROGSTAD: [*coming into the room*] Are the Helmers really at a dance to-night?

MRS. LINDE: Yes, why not?

KROGSTAD: Certainly—why not?

MRS. LINDE: Now, Nils, let's have a talk.

KROGSTAD: Can we two have anything to talk about.

MRS. LINDE: We have a great deal to talk about.

KROGSTAD: I shouldn't have thought so.

MRS. LINDE: No, you have never properly understood me.

KROGSTAD: Was there anything else to understand except what was obvious to all the world—a heartless woman jilts a man when a better catch turns up.

MRS. LINDE: Do you believe I'm as absolutely heartless as all that? And do you believe that I did it with a light heart?

KROGSTAD: Didn't you?

MRS. LINDE: Nils, did you really think that?

KROGSTAD: If it were as you say, why did you write to me as you did at that time?

MRS. LINDE: I could do nothing else. As I had to break with you, it was my duty also to put an end to all that you felt for me.

KROGSTAD: [*wringing his hands*] So that was it. And all this—only for the sake of money!

MRS. LINDE: You must not forget that I had a helpless mother and two little brothers. We couldn't wait for you, Nils; your prospects seemed hopeless then.

KROGSTAD: That may be so, but you had no right to throw me over for any one else's sake.

MRS. LINDE: Indeed I don't know. Many a time did I ask myself if I had the right to do it.

KROGSTAD: [*more gently*] When I lost you, it was as if all the solid ground went from under my feet. Look at me now—I'm a shipwrecked man clinging to a bit of wreckage.

MRS. LINDE: But help may be near.

KROGSTAD: It *was* near; but then you came and stood in my way.

MRS. LINDE: Unintentionally, Nils. It was only to-day that I learned it was your place I was going to take in the Bank.

KROGSTAD: I believe you, if you say so. But now that you know it, are you not going to give it up to me?

MRS. LINDE: No, because that would not benefit you in the least.

KROGSTAD: Oh, benefit, benefit—I would have done it whether or no.

MRS. LINDE: I have learned to act prudently. Life, and hard, bitter necessity have taught me that.

KROGSTAD: And life has taught me not to believe in fine speeches.

MRS. LINDE: Then life has taught you something very reasonable. But deeds you must believe in?

KROGSTAD: What do you mean by that?

MRS. LINDE: You said you were like a shipwrecked man clinging to some wreckage.

KROGSTAD: I had good reason to say so.

MRS. LINDE: Well, I am like a shipwrecked woman clinging to some wreckage—no one to mourn for, no one to care for.

KROGSTAD: It was your own choice.

MRS. LINDE: There was no other choice—then.

KROGSTAD: Well, what now?

MRS. LINDE: Nils, how would it be if we two shipwrecked people could join forces?

KROGSTAD: What are you saying?

MRS. LINDE: Two on the same piece of wreckage would stand a better chance than each on their own.

KROGSTAD: Christine!

MRS. LINDE: What do you suppose brought me to town?

KROGSTAD: Do you mean that you gave me a thought?

MRS. LINDE: I couldn't endure life without work. All my life, as long as I can remember, I have worked, and it's been my greatest and only pleasure. But now I'm quite alone in the world—my life is so dreadfully empty and I feel so forsaken. There is not the least pleasure in working for one's self. Nils, give me someone and something to work for.

KROGSTAD: I don't trust that. It's nothing but a woman's overstrained sense of generosity that prompts you to make such an offer of yourself.

MRS. LINDE: Have you ever noticed anything of the sort in me?

KROGSTAD: Could you really do it? Tell me—do you know all about my past life?

MRS. LINDE: Yes.

KROGSTAD: And do you know what they think of me here?

MRS. LINDE: You seemed to me to imply that with me you might have been quite another man.

KROGSTAD: I'm certain of it.

MRS. LINDE: Is it too late now?

KROGSTAD: Christine, are you saying this deliberately? Yes, I'm sure you are. I see it in your face. Have you really the courage, then—?

MRS. LINDE: I want to be a mother to someone, and your children need a mother. We two need each other. Nils, I have faith in your real character—I can dare anything together with you.

KROGSTAD: [*grasps her hand*] Thanks, thanks, Christine! Now I shall find a way to clear myself in the eyes of the world. Ah, but I forgot—

MRS. LINDE: [*listening*] Hush! The Tarantella! Go, go!

KROGSTAD: Why? What is it?

MRS. LINDE: Do you hear them up there? When that is over, we may expect them back.

KROGSTAD: Yes, yes—I will go. But it's all no use. Of course you're not aware what steps I've taken in the matter of the Helmers.

MRS. LINDE: Yes, I know all about that.

KROGSTAD: And in spite of that have you the courage to—?

MRS. LINDE: I understand very well to what lengths a man like you might be driven by despair.

KROGSTAD: If I could only undo what I've done!

MRS. LINDE: You cannot. Your letter is lying in the mail box now.

KROGSTAD: Are you sure of that?

MRS. LINDE: Quite sure, but—

KROGSTAD: [*with a searching look at her*] Is that what it all means?—that you want to save your friend at any cost? Tell me frankly. Is that it?

MRS. LINDE: Nils, a woman who has once sold herself for another's sake, doesn't do it a second time.

KROGSTAD: I'll ask for my letter back.

MRS. LINDE: No, no.

KROGSTAD: Yes, of course I will. I'll wait here till Torvald comes; I will tell him he must give me my letter back—that it only concerns my dismissal—that he's not to read it.

MRS. LINDE: No, Nils, you must not recall your letter.

KROGSTAD: But, tell me, wasn't it for that very purpose that you asked me to meet you here?

MRS. LINDE: In my first moment of fright, it was. But twenty-four hours have elapsed since then, and in that time I've witnessed incredible things in this house. Torvald must know all about it. This unhappy secret must be disclosed; they must have a complete understanding between them, which is impossible with all this concealment and falsehood going on.

KROGSTAD: Very well, if you will take the responsibility. But there's one thing I can do in any case, and I shall do it at once.

MRS. LINDE: [*listening*] You must be quick and go! The dance is over; we are not safe a moment longer.

KROGSTAD: I'll wait for you below.

MRS. LINDE: Yes, do. You must see me back to my door.

KROGSTAD: I have never had such an amazing piece of good fortune in my life! [*goes out through the outer door. The door between the room and the hall remains open.*]

MRS. LINDE: [*tidying up the room and laying her hat and cloak ready*] What a difference! What a difference! Someone to work for and live for—a home to bring comfort into. That I will do, indeed. I wish they would be quick and come—[*listens*] Ah, there they are now. I must put on my things. [*Takes up her hat and cloak.* HELMER's *and* NORA's *voices are heard outside; a key is turned, and* HELMER *brings* NORA *almost by force into the hall. She is in an Italian costume with a large black shawl around her; he is in evening dress, and a black cloak which is flying open.*]

NORA: [*hanging back in the doorway, and struggling with him*] No, no, no!—don't take me in. I want to go upstairs again; I don't want to leave so early.

HELMER: But, my dearest Nora—

NORA: Please, Torvald dear—please, *please*—only an hour more.

HELMER: Not a single minute, my sweet Nora. You know that was our agreement. Come along into the room; you are catching cold standing there. [*He brings her gently into the room, in spite of her resistance.*]

MRS. LINDE: Good-evening.

NORA: Christine!

HELMER: You here, so late, Mrs. Linde?

MRS. LINDE: Yes, you must excuse me; I was so anxious to see Nora in her dress.

NORA: Have you been sitting here waiting for me?

MRS. LINDE: Yes, unfortunately I came too late; you had already gone upstairs, and I thought I couldn't go away again without having seen you.

HELMER: [*taking off* NORA's *shawl*] Yes, take a good look at her. I think she's worth looking at. Isn't she charming, Mrs. Linde?

MRS. LINDE: Yes, indeed she is.

HELMER: Doesn't she look remarkably pretty? Everyone thought so at the dance. But she is terribly self-willed, this sweet little person. What are we to do with her? You will hardly believe that I had almost to bring her away by force.

NORA: Torvald, you will repent not having let me stay, even if it were only for half an hour.

HELMER: Listen to her, Mrs. Linde! She had danced her Tarantella, and it had been a tremendous success, as it deserved—although possibly the performance was a trifle too realistic—a little more so, I mean, than was strictly compatible with propriety. But never mind about that! The chief thing is, she had made a success—she had made a tremendous success. Do you think I was going to let her remain there after that, and spoil the effect? No, indeed! I took my charming little Capri maiden—my capricious little Capri maiden, I should say—on my arm; took one quick turn around the room; a curtsy on either side, and, as they say in novels, the beautiful apparition disappeared. An exit ought always to be effective, Mrs. Linde; but that's what I cannot make Nora understand. Pooh! this room is hot. [*throws his cloak on a chair, and opens the door of his room*] Hullo! it's all dark in here. Oh, of course—excuse me— [*He goes in, and lights some candles.*]

NORA: [*in a hurried and breathless whisper*] Well?

MRS. LINDE: [*in a low voice*] I have had a talk with him.

NORA: Yes, and—

MRS. LINDE: Nora, you must tell your husband all about it.

NORA: [*in an expressionless voice*] I knew it.

MRS. LINDE: You have nothing to be afraid of as far as Krogstad is concerned; but you must tell him.

NORA: I won't tell him.

MRS. LINDE: Then the letter will.

NORA: Thank you, Christine. Now I know what I must do. Hush—!

HELMER: [*coming in again*] Well, Mrs. Linde, have you admired her?

MRS. LINDE: Yes, and now I will say good-night.

HELMER: What, already? Is this yours, this knitting?

MRS. LINDE: [*taking it*] Yes, thank you, I had very nearly forgotten it.

HELMER: So you knit?

MRS. LINDE: Of course.

HELMER: Do you know, you ought to embroider.

MRS. LINDE: Really? Why?

HELMER: Yes, it's far more becoming. Let me show you. You hold the embroidery thus in your left hand, and use the needle with the right—like this—with a long, easy sweep. Do you see?

MRS. LINDE: Yes, perhaps

HELMER: But in the case of knitting—that can never be anything but ungraceful; look here—the arms close together, the knitting-needles going up and down—it has a sort of Chinese effect. That was really excellent champagne they gave us.

MRS. LINDE: Well—good-night, Nora, and don't be stubborn any more.

HELMER: That's right, Mrs. Linde.

MRS. LINDE: Good-night, Mr. Helmer.

HELMER: [*accompanying her to the door*] Good-night, good-night. I hope you'll get home all right. I should be very happy to—but you haven't any great distance to go. Good-night, good-night. [*She goes out; he shuts the door after her, and comes in again.*] Ah!—at last we have got rid of her. She is a frightful bore, that woman.

NORA: Aren't you very tired, Torvald?

HELMER: No, not in the least.

NORA: Nor sleepy?

HELMER: Not a bit. On the contrary, I feel extraordinarily lively. And you?—you really look both tired and sleepy.

NORA: Yes, I'm very tired. I want to go to sleep at once.

HELMER: There, you see it was quite right of me not to let you stay there any longer.

NORA: Everything you do is quite right, Torvald.

HELMER: [*kissing her on the forehead*] Now my little skylark is speaking reasonably. Did you notice what good spirits Rank was in this evening?

NORA: Really? Was he? I didn't speak to him at all.

HELMER: And I very little, but I haven't seen him in such good form for a long time. [*looks for a while at her and then goes nearer to her*] It's delightful to be at home by ourselves again, to be all alone with you—you fascinating, charming little darling!

NORA: Don't look at me like that, Torvald.

HELMER: Why shouldn't I look at my dearest treasure?—at all the beauty that's mine, all mine?

NORA: [*going to the other side of the table*] You mustn't say things like that to me to-night.

HELMER: [*following her*] You have still got the Tarantella in your blood, I see. And it makes you more captivating than ever. Listen—the guests are beginning to leave now. [*in a lower voice*] Nora—soon the whole house will be quiet.

NORA: Yes, I hope so.

HELMER: Yes, my own darling Nora. Do you know when I'm out at a party with you like this, why I speak so little to you, keep away from you, and only send a stolen glance in your direction now and then?—do you know why I do that? It's because I make believe that we are secretly in love, and you are my secretly promised bride, and that no one suspects there is anything between us.

NORA: Yes, yes—I know very well you're thinking about me all the time.

HELMER: And when we are leaving, and I am putting the shawl over your beautiful young shoulders—on your lovely neck—then I imagine that you are my bride and that we have just come from the wedding, and I am bringing you for the first time into our home—to be alone with you for the first time—quite alone with my shy little darling! All this evening I have longed for nothing but you. When I watched the seductive figures of the Tarantella, my blood was on fire; I could endure it no longer, and that was why I brought you down so early—

NORA: Go away, Torvald! You must let me go. I won't—

HELMER: What's that? You're teasing, my little Nora! You won't—you won't? Am I not your husband? [*A knock is heard at the outer door.*]

NORA: [*starting*] Did you hear—?

HELMER: [*going into the hall*] Who is it?

RANK: [*outside*] It is I. May I come in for a moment?

HELMER: [*in a fretful whisper*]. Oh, what does he want now? [*aloud*] Wait a minute! [*unlocks the door*] Come, that's kind of you not to pass by our door.

RANK: I thought I heard your voice, and felt as if I should like to look in. [*with a swift glance round*] Ah, yes!—these dear familiar rooms. You are very happy and cozy in here, you two.

HELMER: It seems to me that you looked after yourself pretty well upstairs, too.

RANK: Excellently. Why shouldn't I? Why shouldn't one enjoy everything in this world?—at any rate as much as one can, and as long as one can. The wine was capital—

HELMER: Especially the champagne.

RANK: So you noticed that, too? It's almost incredible how much I managed to put away!

NORA: Torvald drank a great deal of champagne to-night, too.

RANK: Did he?

NORA: Yes, and he is always in such good spirits afterwards.

RANK: Well, why should one not enjoy a merry evening after a well-spent day?

HELMER: Well spent: I'm afraid I can't take credit for that.

RANK: [*clapping him on the back*] But I can, you know!

NORA: Doctor Rank, you must have been occupied with some scientific investigation today.

RANK: Exactly.

HELMER: Just listen!—little Nora talking about scientific investigations!

NORA: And may I congratulate you on the result?

RANK: Indeed you may.

NORA: Was it favourable, then?

RANK: The best possible, for both doctor and patient—certainty.

NORA: [*quickly and searchingly*] Certainty?

RANK: Absolute certainty. So wasn't I entitled to make a merry evening of it after that?

NORA: Yes, you certainly were, Doctor Rank.

HELMER: I think so, too, so long as you don't have to pay for it in the morning.

RANK: Oh well, one can't have anything in this life without paying for it.

NORA: Doctor Rank—are you fond of masked balls?

RANK: Yes, if there's a fine lot of pretty costumes.

NORA: Tell me—what shall we two wear at the next?

HELMER: Little featherbrain!—are you thinking of the next already?

RANK: We two? Yes. I can tell you. You shall go as a good fairy—

HELMER: Yes, but what do you suggest as an appropriate costume for that?

RANK: Let your wife go dressed just as she is in everyday life.

HELMER: That was really very prettily turned. But can't you tell us what you'll be?

RANK: Yes, my dear friend, I have quite made up my mind about that.

HELMER: Well?

RANK: At the next fancy-dress ball I shall be invisible.

HELMER: That's a good joke!

RANK: There is a big black hat—have you never heard of hats that make you invisible? If you put one on, no one can see you.

HELMER: [*suppressing a smile*] Yes, you're quite right.

RANK: But I am clean forgetting what I came for. Helmer, give me a cigar—one of the dark Havanas.

HELMER: With the greatest pleasure. [*offers him his case*]

RANK: [*takes a cigar and cuts off the end*] Thanks.

NORA: [*striking a match*] Let me give you a light.

RANK: Thank you. [*She holds the match for him to light his cigar.*] And now good-bye!

HELMER: Good-bye, good-bye, dear old man!

NORA: Sleep well, Doctor Rank.

RANK: Thank you for that wish.

NORA: Wish me the same.

RANK: You? Well, if you want me to sleep well! And thanks for the light. [*He nods to them both and goes out.*]

HELMER: [*in a subdued voice*] He has drunk more than he ought.

NORA: [*absently*] Maybe. [HELMER *takes a bunch of keys out of his pocket and goes into the hall.*] Torvald! what are you going to do there?

HELMER: Empty the mail box; it's quite full; there will be no room for the newspaper, tomorrow morning.

NORA: Are you going to work to-night?

HELMER: You know quite well I'm not. What is this? Some one has been at the lock.

NORA: At the lock—?

HELMER: Yes, someone has. What can it mean? I should never have thought the maid—. Here is a broken hairpin. Nora, it is one of yours.

NORA: [*quickly*] Then it must have been the children—

HELMER: Then you must get them out of those ways. There, at last I have got it open. [*takes out the contents of the mail box, and calls to the kitchen*] Helen! Helen, put out the light over the front door. [*goes back into the room and shuts the door into the hall. He holds out his hand full of letters.*] Look at that—look what a heap of them there are. [*turning them over*] What on earth is that?

NORA: [*at the window*] The letter—No! Torvald, no!

HELMER: Two cards—of Rank's.

NORA: Of Doctor Rank's?

HELMER: [*looking at them*] Doctor Rank. They were on the top. He must have put them in when he went out.

NORA: Is there anything written on them?

HELMER: There is a black cross over the name. Look there—what an uncomfortable idea! It looks as if he were announcing his own death.

NORA: It's just what he's doing.

HELMER: What? Do you know anything about it? Has he said anything to you?

NORA: Yes. He told me that when the cards came it would be his leave-taking from us. He means to shut himself up and die.

HELMER: My poor old friend. Certainly I knew we should not have him very long with us. But so soon! And so he hides himself away like a wounded animal.

NORA: If it has to happen, it's best it should be without a word—don't you think so, Torvald?

HELMER: [*walking up and down*] He had so grown into our lives. I can't think of him as having gone out of them. He, with his sufferings and his loneliness, was like a cloudy background to our sunlit happiness. Well, perhaps it's best so. For him, anyway. [*standing still*] And perhaps for us, too, Nora. We two are thrown quite upon each other now. [*puts his arms round her*] My darling wife, I don't feel as if I could hold you tight enough. Do you know, Nora, I've often wished that you might be threatened by some great danger, so I might risk my life's blood, and everything, for your sake.

NORA: [*disengages herself, and says firmly and decidedly*] Now you must read your letters, Torvald.

HELMER: No, no; not to-night. I want to be with you, my darling wife.

NORA: With the thought of your friend's death—

HELMER: You are right, it has affected us both. Something ugly has come between us—the thought of the horrors of death. We must try and rid our minds of that. Until then—we'll each go to our own room.

NORA: [*hanging on his neck*] Good-night, Torvald—Good-night!

HELMER: [*kissing her on the forehead*] Good-night, my little singing-bird. Sleep sound, Nora. Now I'll read my letters through. [*He takes his letters and goes into his room, shutting the door after him.*]

NORA: [*gropes distractedly about, seizes* HELMER'S *cloak, throws it round her, while she says in quick, hoarse, spasmodic whispers*] Never to see him again. Never! Never! [*puts her shawl over her head*] Never to see my children again, either—never again. Never! Never!—Ah! the icy, black water—the unfathomable depths—if only it were over! He has got it now—now he is reading it. Good-bye, Torvald and my children! [*She is about to rush out through the hall, when* HELMER *opens his door hurriedly and stands with an open letter in his hand.*]

HELMER: Nora!

NORA: Ah!—

HELMER: What's this? Do you know what's in this letter?

NORA: Yes, I know. Let me go! Let me get out!

HELMER: [*holding her back*] Where are you going?

NORA: [*trying to get free*] You shan't save me, Torvald!

HELMER: [*reeling*] True? Is this true, that I read here? Horrible! No, no—it's impossible that it can be true.

NORA: It's true. I have loved you above everything else in the world.

HELMER: Oh, don't let us have any silly excuses.

NORA: [*taking a step towards him*] Torvald—!

HELMER: Miserable creature—what have you done?

NORA: Let me go. You shall not suffer for my sake. You shall not take it upon yourself.

HELMER: No tragedy airs, please. [*locks the hall door*] Here you shall stay and give me an explanation. Do you understand what you've done? Answer me? Do you understand what you've done?

NORA: [*looks steadily at him and says with a growing look of coldness in her face*] Yes, now I am beginning to understand thoroughly.

HELMER: [*walking about the room*] What a horrible awakening! All these eight years—she who was my joy and pride—a hypocrite, a liar—worse, worse—a criminal! The unutterable ugliness of it all!—For shame! For shame! [NORA *is silent and looks steadily at him. He stops in front of her.*] I ought to have suspected that something of the sort would happen. I ought to have foreseen it. All your father's lack of principle—be silent!—all your father's lack of principle has come out in you. No religion, no morality, no sense of duty—. How I'm punished for having winked at what he did! I did it for your sake, and this is how you repay me.

NORA: Yes, that's just it.

HELMER: Now you have destroyed all my happiness. You've ruined my entire future. It is horrible to think of! I'm in the power of an unscrupulous man; he can do what he likes with me, ask anything he likes of me, give me any orders he pleases—I dare not refuse. And I must sink to such miserable depths because of a silly woman!

NORA: When I'm out of the way, you'll be free.

HELMER: No fine speeches, please. Your father had always plenty of those ready, too. What good would it be to me if you were out of the way, as you say? Not the slightest. He can make the affair known everywhere; and if he does, I may be falsely suspected of having been a party to your criminal action. Very likely people will think I was behind it all—that it was I who prompted you! and I have to thank you for all this—you whom I have cherished during the whole of our married life. Do you understand now what it is you have done to me?

NORA: [*coldly and quietly*] Yes.

HELMER: It's so incredible that I can't take it in. But we must come to some understanding. Take off that shawl. Take it off, I tell you. I must try and appease him some way or another. The matter must be hushed up at any cost. And as for you and me, it must appear as if everything between us were just as before—but naturally only in the eyes of the world. You will still remain in my house, that is a matter of course. But I shall not allow you to bring up the children; I dare not trust them to you. To think that I should be obliged to say so to one whom I have loved dearly, and whom I still—. No, that's all over. From this moment happiness is not the question; all that concerns us is to save the remains, the fragments, the appearance—

[*A ring is heard at the front-door bell.*]

HELMER: [*with a start*] What's that? So late? Can the worst—? Can he—? Hide yourself, Nora. Say you are ill.

[NORA *stands motionless.* HELMER *goes and unlocks the hall door.*]

MAID: [*half-dressed, comes to the door*] A letter for the mistress.

HELMER: Give it to me. [*takes the letter, and shuts the door*] Yes, it's from him. You shall not have it; I will read it myself.

NORA: Yes, read it.

HELMER: [*standing by the lamp*] I scarcely have the courage to do it. It may mean ruin for both of us. No, I must know. [*tears open the letter, runs his eye over a few lines, looks at a paper enclosed, and gives a shout of joy*] Nora! [*She looks at him questioningly.*] Nora!—No, I must read it once again—. Yes, it's true! I'm saved! Nora, I'm saved!

NORA: And I?

HELMER: You, too, of course; we are both saved, both you and I. Look, he sends you your bond back. He says he regrets and repents—that a happy change in his life—never mind what he says! We are saved, Nora! No one can do anything to you. Oh, Nora, Nora!—no, first I must destroy these hateful things. Let me see—. [*takes a look at the bond*] No, no, I won't look at it. The whole thing shall be nothing but a bad dream to me. [*tears up the bond and both letters, throws them all into the stove, and watches them burn*] There—now it doesn't exist any longer. He says that since Christmas Eve you—. These must have been three dreadful days for you, Nora.

NORA: I have fought a hard fight these three days.

HELMER: And suffered agonies, and seen no way out but—. No, we won't call any of the horrors to mind. We'll only shout with joy, and keep saying, "It's all over! It's all over!" Listen to me, Nora. You don't seem to realise that it is all over. What is this?—such a cold, set face! My poor little Nora, I quite understand; you don't feel that I have forgiven you. But it's true, Nora, I swear it; I've forgiven you everything. I know that what you did, you did out of love for me.

NORA: That's true.

HELMER: You have loved me as a wife ought to love her husband. Only you hadn't sufficient knowledge to judge of the means you used. But do you suppose you are any the less dear to me, because you don't understand how to act on your own responsibility? No, no; only lean on me; I will advise you and direct you. I should not be a man if this womanly helplessness did not just give you a double attractiveness in my eyes. You mustn't think any more about the hard things I said in my first moment of consternation, when I thought everything was going to overwhelm me. I've forgiven you, Nora; I swear to you I've forgiven you.

NORA: Thank you for your forgiveness. [*She goes out through to the door to the right.*]

HELMER: No, don't go— [*looks in*] What are you doing in there?

NORA: [*from within*] Taking off my costume.

HELMER: [*standing at the open door*] Yes, do. Try and calm yourself, and make your mind easy again, my frightened little singing-bird. Be at rest, and feel secure; I have broad wings to shelter you under. [*walks up and down by the door*] How warm and cozy our home is, Nora. Here is shelter for you; here I'll protect you like a hunted dove that I have saved from a hawk's claws: _I'll bring peace to your poor beating heart. It will come, little by little, Nora, believe me. To-morrow morning you will look upon it all quite differently; soon everything will be just as it was before. Very soon you won't need me to assure you that I've forgiven you; you will feel the certainty that I've done so. Can you suppose I should ever think of such a thing as repudiating you, or even reproaching you? You have no idea what a true man's heart is like, Nora. There is something so indescribably sweet and satisfying, to a man, in the knowledge that he has forgiven his wife—forgiven her freely, and with all his heart. It seems as if that had made her, as it were, doubly his own; he has given her a new life, so to speak; and she has in a way become both wife and child to him. So you shall be for me after this, my little scared, helpless darling. Have no anxiety about anything, Nora; only be frank and open with me, and I'll serve as will and conscience both to you—. What's this? Not gone to bed? Have you changed your clothes?

NORA: [*in everyday dress*] Yes, Torvald, I have changed my clothes now.

HELMER: But what for?—so late as this.

NORA: I shall not sleep to-night.

HELMER: But, my dear Nora—

NORA: [*looking at her watch*] It's not so very late. Sit down here, Torvald. You and I have much to say to one another. [*She sits down at one side of the table.*]

HELMER: Nora—what's this?—this cold, set face!

NORA: Sit down. It'll take some time; I have a lot to talk over with you.

HELMER: [*sits down at the opposite side of the table*] You alarm me, Nora!—and I don't understand you.

NORA: No, that's just it. You don't understand me, and I've never understood you either— before to-night. No, you mustn't interrupt me. You must simply listen to what I say. Torvald, this is a settling of accounts.

HELMER: What do you mean by that?

NORA: [*after a short silence*] Isn't there any thing that strikes you as strange in our sitting here like this?

HELMER: What is that?

NORA: We've been married now eight years. Doesn't it occur to you that this is the first time we two, you and I, husband and wife, have had a serious conversation?

HELMER: What do you mean by "serious"?

NORA: In all these eight years—longer than that—from the beginning of our acquaintance, we've never exchanged a word on any serious subject.

HELMER: Was it likely that I would be continually and for ever telling you about worries that you couldn't help me with?

NORA: I'm not speaking about business matters. I say that we have never sat down in earnest together to try and get at the bottom of anything.

HELMER: But, dearest Nora, would it have been any good to you?

NORA: That's just it; you've never understood me. I have been greatly wronged, Torvald—first by papa and then by you.

HELMER: What! By us two—by us two, who've loved you better than anyone else in the world?

NORA: [*shaking her head*] You've never loved me. You've only thought it pleasant to be in love with me.

HELMER: Nora, what do I hear you saying?

NORA: It's perfectly true, Torvald. When I was at home with papa, he told me his opinion about everything, and so I had the same opinions; and if I differed from him I concealed the fact, because he wouldn't have liked it. He called me his doll-child, and he played with me just as I used to play with my dolls. And when I came to live with you—

HELMER: What sort of an expression is that to use about our marriage?

NORA: [*undisturbed*] I mean that I was simply transferred from papa's hands into yours. You arranged everything according to your own taste, and so I got the same tastes as you—or else I pretended to. I'm really not quite sure which—I think sometimes the one and sometimes the other. When I look back on it, it seems to me as if I'd been living here like a poor woman—just from hand to mouth. I've existed merely to perform tricks for you, Torvald. But you would have it so. You and papa have committed a great sin against me. It's your fault that I have made nothing of my life.

HELMER: How unreasonable and how ungrateful you are, Nora! Have you not been happy here?

NORA: No, I have never been happy. I thought I was, but it's never really been so.

HELMER: Not—not happy!

NORA: No, only merry. And you've always been so kind to me. But our home has been nothing but a playroom. I've been your doll-wife, just as at home I was papa's doll-child; and here the children have been my dolls. I thought it great fun when you played with me, just as they thought it great fun when I played with them. That's what our marriage has been, Torvald.

HELMER: There is some truth in what you say—exaggerated and strained as your view of it is. But for the future it'll be different. Playtime shall be over, and lesson-time shall begin.

NORA: Whose lessons? Mine, or the children's?

HELMER: Both yours and the children's, my darling Nora.

NORA: Alas, Torvald, you're not the man to educate me into being a proper wife for you.

HELMER: And you can say that?

NORA: And I—how am I fitted to bring up the children?

HELMER: Nora!

NORA: Didn't you say so yourself a little while ago—that you dare not trust me to bring them up?

HELMER: In a moment of anger! Why do you pay any heed to that?

NORA: Indeed, you were perfectly right. I'm not fit for the task. There is another task I must undertake first. I must try and educate myself—you're not the man to help me in that. I must do that for myself. And that's why I'm going to leave you now.

HELMER: [*springing up*] What do you say?

NORA: I must stand quite alone, if I'm to understand myself and everything about me. It's for that reason that I cannot remain with you any longer.

HELMER: Now, Nora!

NORA: I'm going away from here now, at once. I'm sure Christine will take me in for the night—

HELMER: You're out of your mind! I won't allow it! I forbid you!

NORA: It's no use forbidding me anything any longer. I'll take with me what belongs to myself. I'll take nothing from you, either now or later.

HELMER: What sort of madness is this!

NORA: To-morrow I'll go home—I mean, to my old home. It will be easiest for me to find something to do there.

HELMER: You blind, foolish woman!

NORA: I must try and get some sense, Torvald.

HELMER: To desert your home, your husband, and your children! And you don't consider what people will say!

NORA: I can't consider that at all. I only know that it is necessary for me.

HELMER: It's shocking. This is how you would neglect your most sacred duties.

NORA: What do you consider my most sacred duties?

HELMER: Do I need to tell you that? Are they not your duties to your husband and your children?

NORA: I have other duties just as sacred.

HELMER: That you have not. What duties could those be?

NORA: Duties to myself.

HELMER: Before all else, you are a wife and a mother.

NORA: I don't believe that any longer. I believe that before all else I'm a reasonable human being, just as you are—or, at all events, that I must try and become one. I know quite well, Torvald, that most people would think you right, and that views of that kind are to be found in books; but I can no longer content myself with what most people say, or with what's found in books. I must think over things for myself and get to understand them.

HELMER: Can't you understand your place in your own home? Haven't you a reliable guide in such matters as that?—have you no religion?

NORA: I'm afraid, Torvald, I do not exactly know what religion is.

HELMER: What're you saying?

NORA: I know nothing but what the clergyman said, when I went to be confirmed. He told us that religion was this, and that, and the other. When I'm away from all this, and am alone, I'll look into that matter, too. I'll see if what the clergyman said is true, or at all events if it is true for me.

HELMER: This is unheard of in a woman of your age! But if religion cannot touch you, let me try and awaken your conscience. I suppose you have some moral sense? Or— answer me—am I to think you have none?

NORA: I assure you, Torvald, that is not an easy question to answer. I really don't know. The thing puzzles me altogether. I only know that you and I look at it in quite a different light. I'm learning, too, that the law is quite another thing from what I supposed; but I find it impossible to convince myself that the law is right. According to it a woman has no right to spare her old dying father, or to save her husband's life. I can't believe that.

HELMER: You talk like a child. You don't understand the conditions of the world in which you live.

NORA: No, I don't. But now I'm going to try. I'm going to see if I can make out who is right, the world or I.

HELMER: You're ill, Nora; you're delirious; I almost think you're out of your mind.

NORA: I've never felt my mind so clear and certain as to-night.

HELMER: And is it with a clear and certain mind that you forsake your husband and your children?

NORA: Yes, it is.

HELMER: Then there is only one possible explanation.

NORA: What is that?

HELMER: You don't love me any more.

NORA: No, that's just it.

HELMER: Nora!—and you can say that?

NORA: It gives me great pain, Torvald, for you have always been so kind to me, but I can't help it. I don't love you any more.

HELMER: [*regaining his composure*] Is that a clear and certain conviction, too?

NORA: Yes, absolutely clear and certain. That's the reason why I'll not stay here any longer.

HELMER: And can you tell me what I've done to forfeit your love?

NORA: Yes, indeed I can. It was to-night, when the wonderful thing did not happen; then I saw you were not the man I had thought you.

HELMER: Explain yourself better—I don't understand you.

NORA: I've waited so patiently for eight years; for, goodness knows, I knew very well that wonderful things don't happen every day. Then this horrible misfortune came upon me; and then I felt quite certain that the wonderful thing was going to happen at last. When Krogstad's letter was lying out there, never for a moment did I imagine that you would consent to accept this man's conditions. I was so absolutely certain that you would say to him: Publish the thing to the whole world. And when that was done—

HELMER: Yes, what then?—when I had exposed my wife to shame and disgrace?

NORA: When that was done, I was so absolutely certain, you would come forward and take everything upon yourself, and say I'm the guilty one.

HELMER: Nora—!

NORA: You mean that I would never have accepted such a sacrifice on your part? No, of course not. But what would my assurances have been worth against yours? That was the wonderful thing which I hoped for and feared; and it was to prevent that, that I wanted to kill myself.

HELMER: I would gladly work night and day for you, Nora—bear sorrow and want for your sake. But no man would sacrifice his honour for the one he loves.

NORA: Millions of women have done it.

HELMER: Oh, you think and talk like a heedless child.

NORA: Maybe. But you neither think nor talk like the man I could bind myself to. As soon as your fear was over—and it was not fear for what threatened me, but for what might happen to you—when the whole thing was past, as far as you were concerned it was exactly as if nothing at all had happened. Exactly as before, I was your little sky-lark, your doll, which you would in future treat with doubly gentle care, because it was so brittle and fragile. [*getting up*] Torvald—it was then it dawned on me that for eight years I'd been living here with a strange man, and had borne him three children—. Oh, I can't bear to think of it! I could tear myself into little bits!

HELMER: [*sadly*] I see, I see. An abyss has opened between us—there's no denying it. But, Nora, wouldn't it be possible to fill it up?

NORA: As I am now, I'm no wife for you.

HELMER: I have it in me to become a different man.

NORA: Perhaps—if your doll is taken away from you.

HELMER: But to part!—to part from you! No, no. Nora, I can't understand that idea.

NORA: [*going out to the right*] That makes it all the more certain that it must be done. [*She comes back with her cloak and hat and a small bag, which she puts on a chair by the table.*]

HELMER: Nora, Nora, not now! Wait till to-morrow.

NORA: [*putting on her cloak*] I can't spend the night in a strange man's room.

HELMER: But can't we live here like brother and sister?

NORA: [*putting on her hat*] You know very well that wouldn't last long. [*puts the shawl round her*] Good-bye, Torvald. I won't see the little ones. I know they are in better hands than mine. As I am now, I can be of no use to them.

HELMER: But some day, Nora—some day?

NORA: How can I tell? I have no idea what is going to become of me.

HELMER: But you are my wife, whatever becomes of you.

NORA: Listen, Torvald. I have heard that when a wife deserts her husband's house, as I'm doing now, he is legally freed from all obligations towards her. In any case I set you free from all your obligations. You're not to feel yourself bound in the slightest way, any more than I shall. There must be perfect freedom on both sides. See, here is your ring back. Give me mine.

HELMER: That, too?

NORA: That, too.

HELMER: Here it is.

NORA: That's right. Now it's all over. I've put the keys here. The maids know all about everything in the house—better than I do. To-morrow, after I've left her, Christine will come here and pack up my own things that I brought with me from home. I'll have them sent to me.

HELMER: All over! all over!—Nora, shall you never think of me again?

NORA: I know I'll often think of you and the children and this house.

HELMER: May I write to you, Nora?

NORA: No—never. You must not do that.

HELMER: But at least let me send you—

NORA: Nothing—nothing—

HELMER: Let me help you if you're in want.

NORA: No. I can receive nothing from a stranger.

HELMER: Nora—can I never be anything more than a stranger to you?

NORA: [*taking her bag*] Ah, Torvald, the most miraculous thing of all would have to happen.

HELMER: Tell me what that would be!

NORA: Both you and I would have to be so changed that—Oh, Torvald, I don't believe any longer in miracles happening.

HELMER: But I will believe in it. Tell me? So changed that—?

NORA: That our life together would be a real wedlock. Good-bye. [*She goes out through the hall.*]

HELMER: [*sinks down on a chair at the door and buries his face in his hands*] Nora! Nora! [*looks round, and rises*] Empty. She is gone. [*A hope flashes across his mind.*] The most miraculous thing of all—?

[*The sound of a door shutting is heard from below.*]

EUGENE O'NEILL (1888–1953)

"The Hairy Ape" (1921)

E ugene O'Neill was the first American dramatist to win widespread international fame. He experimented with many dramatic forms and styles in his twenty-five full-length plays. In *The Hairy Ape* he adopted many conventions of expressionism, an artistic movement that emerged in Germany just prior to World War I. The expressionists proclaimed the supreme importance of the human spirit, which they believed was being crushed or distorted by materialism and industrialism.

"The Hairy Ape" shows the influence of expressionism on American drama. The unity of the play derives from a central theme: humanity's frustrated search for identity in a hostile environment. In the first scene, Yank is confident that he and his fellow stokers are the only ones who belong because it is they who make the ship go (and by extension the factories and machines of modern industrialized society). But when Yank is told that the pampered, anemic daughter of one of the shipowners (who represents power, money, and influence) has called him "a hairy ape," his confidence is shattered. Seeking to reestablish his identity, he first visits Fifth Avenue, the home territory of the rich and powerful, where he proclaims his superiority by physically attacking the men, only to have his very existence go unacknowledged. Thrown into jail, he decides that the answer lies in destroying the steel and machinery over which he originally thought he had power. In jail he learns that the International Workers of the World (IWW) opposes the owners of factories and ships and, when he is released, he offers to blow up the IWW's enemies. Rejected there, too, Yank visits the apes in the zoo, but when he releases a gorilla it crushes him, and he dies without having achieved a sense of belonging. Yank is symbolic of modern humanity in an industrialized society cut off from a past when human beings had an integral relationship with the natural environment and now little better than cogs in the industrial machine.

"The Hairy Ape" is representative of the outlook and techniques of expressionism. The episodic structure and distorted visual elements are typical of the movement, as is the longing for fulfillment, which suggests the need to change society so that the individual can find a coherent, satisfying relationship with the environment.

Eugene O'Neill

"The Hairy Ape"

Characters

ROBERT SMITH, "YANK"
PADDY
LONG
MILDRED DOUGLAS
HER AUNT
SECOND ENGINEER
A GUARD
A SECRETARY OF AN ORGANIZATION
STOKERS, LADIES, GENTLEMEN, ETC.

Scenes

Scene I: The firemen's forecastle of an ocean liner—an hour after sailing from New York.
Scene II: Section of promenade deck, two days out—morning.
Scene III: The stokehole. A few minutes later.
Scene IV: Same as Scene I. Half an hour later.
Scene V: Fifth Avenue, New York. Three weeks later.
Scene VI: An island near the city. The next night.
Scene VII: In the city. About a month later.
Scene VIII: In the city. Twilight of the next day.

SCENE I

The firemen's forecastle of a transatlantic liner an hour after sailing from New York for the voyage across. Tiers of narrow, steel bunks, three deep, on all sides. An entrance in rear. Benches on the floor before the bunks. The room is crowded with men, shouting, cursing, laughing, singing— a confused, inchoate uproar swelling into a sort of unity, a meaning—the bewildered, furious, baffled defiance of a beast in a cage. Nearly all the men are drunk. Many bottles are passed from hand to hand. All are dressed in dungaree pants, heavy, ugly shoes. Some wear singlets, but the majority are stripped to the waist.

The treatment of this scene, or of any other scene in the play, should by no means be naturalistic. The effect sought after is a cramped space in the bowels of a ship, imprisoned by white steel. The lines of bunks, the uprights supporting them, cross each other like the steel framework of a cage. The ceiling crushes down upon the men's heads. They cannot stand upright. This accentuates the natural stooping posture which shoveling coal and the resultant overdevelopment of back and shoulder muscles have given them. The men themselves should resemble those pictures in which the appear-

296

ance of Neanderthal Man is guessed at. All are hairy-chested, with long arms of tremendous power, and low, receding brows above their small, fierce, resentful eyes. All the civilized white races are represented, but except for the slight differentiation in color of hair, skin, eyes, all these men are alike.

The curtain rises on a tumult of sound. YANK *is seated in the foreground. He seems broader, fiercer, more truculent, more powerful, more sure of himself than the rest. They respect his superior strength—the grudging respect of fear. Then, too, he represents to them a self-expression, the very last word in what they are, their most highly developed individual.*

VOICES: Gif me trink dere, you!
    'Ave a wet!
    Salute!
    Gesundheit!
    Skoal!
    Drunk as a lord, God stiffen you!
    Here's how!
    Luck!
    Pass back that bottle, damn you!
    Pourin' it down his neck!
    Ho, Froggy! Where the devil have you been?
    La Touraine.
    I hit him smash in yaw, py Gott!
    Jenkins—the First—he's a rotten swine
    And the coppers nabbed him—and I run—
    I like peer better. It don't pig head gif you.
    A slut, I'm sayin'! She robbed me aslape—
    To hell with 'em all!
    Your're a bloody liar!
    Say dot again!
        [*Commotion. Two men about to fight are pulled apart.*]
    No scrappin' now!
    Tonight—
    See who's the best man!
    Bloody Dutchman!
    Tonight on the for'ard square.
    I'll bet on Dutchy.
    He packa da wallop, I tella you!
    Shut up, Wop!
    No fightin', maties. We're all chums, ain't we?
        [*A voice starts bawling a song.*]
            Beer, beer, glorious beer!
            Fill yourselves right up to here.
YANK: [*for the first time seeming to take notice of the uproar about him, turns around threateningly—in a tone of contemptuous authority*] Choke off dat noise! Where d'yuh get dat beer stuff? Beer, hell! Beer's for goils—and Dutchmen. Me for somep'n wit a kick to it! Gimme a drink, one of youse guys. [*Several bottles are eagerly offered. He takes a tremendous gulp at one of them; then, keeping the bottle in his hand, glares belligerently at the owner, who hastens to acquiesce in this robbery by*

saying] All righto, Yank. Keep it and have another. [YANK *contemptuously turns his back on the crowd again. For a second there is an embarrassed silence. Then—*]

VOICES: We must be passing the Hook.

> She's beginning to roll to it.
>
> Six days in hell—and then Southampton.
>
> Py Yesus, I vish somepody take my first vatch for me!
>
> Gittin seasick, Square-head?
>
> Drink up and forget it!
>
> What's in your bottle?
>
> Gin.
>
> Dot's nigger trink.
>
> Absinthe? It's doped. You'll go off your chump, Froggy!
>
> Cochon!
>
> Whisky, that's the ticket!
>
> Where's Paddy?
>
> Going asleep.
>
> Sing us that whisky song, Paddy.
>
>> [*They all turn to an old, wizened Irishman who is dozing, very drunk, on the benches forward. His face is extremely monkey-like with all the sad, patient pathos of that animal in his small eyes.*]
>
> Singa da song, Caruso Pat!
>
> He's gettin' old. The drink is too much for him.
>
> He's too drunk.

PADDY: [*blinking about him, starts to his feet resentfully, swaying, holding on to the edge of a bunk*] I'm never too drunk to sing. 'Tis only when I'm dead to the world I'd be wishful sing at all. [*with a sort of sad contempt*] "Whisky Johnny," ye want? A chanty, ye want? Now that's a queer wish from the ugly like of you, God help you. But no matther. [*He starts to sing in a thin, nasal, doleful tone.*]

> *Oh, whisky is the life of man!*
>> *Whisky! O Johnny! [They all join in on this.]*
> *Oh, whisky is the life of man!*
>> *Whisky for my Johnny! [Again chorus.]*
> *Oh, whisky drove my old man mad!*
>> *Whisky! O Johnny!*
> *Oh, whisky drove my old man mad!*
>> *Whisky for my Johnny!*

YANK: [*again turning around scornfully*] Aw hell! Nix on dat old sailing ship stuff! All dat bull's dead, see? And you're dead, too, yuh damned old Harp, on'y yuh don't know it. Take it easy, see? Give us a rest. Nix on de loud noise. [*with a cynical grin*] Can't youse see I'm tryin to t'ink?

ALL: [*repeating the word after him as one with the same cynical amused mockery*] Think! [*The chorused word has a brazen metallic quality as if their throats were phonograph horns. It is followed by a general uproar of hard, barking laughter.*]

VOICES: Don't be cracking your head wit ut, Yank.

> You gat headache, py yingo!
>
> One thing about it—it rhymes with drink!
>
> Ha, ha, ha!
>
> Drink, don't think!
>
> Drink, don't think!

Drink, don't think!

[*A whole chorus of voices has taken up this refrain, stamping on the floor, pounding on the benches with fists.*]

YANK: [*taking a gulp from his bottle—good-naturedly*] Aw right. Can de noise. I got yuh de foist time. [*The uproar subsides. A very drunken sentimental tenor begins to sing.*]

> Far away in Canada,
> Far across the sea,
> There's a lass who fondly waits
> Making a home for me—

YANK: [*fiercely contemptuous*] Shut up, yuh lousy boob! Where d'yuh get dat tripe? Home? Home, hell! I'll make a home for yuh! I'll knock yuh dead. Home! T'hell wit home! Where d'yuh get dat tripe? Dis is home, see? What d'yuh want wit home? [*proudly*] I runned away from mine when I was a kid. On'y too glad to beat it, dat was me. Home was lickings for me, dat's all. But yuh can bet your shoit no one ain't never licked me since! Wanter try it, any of youse? Huh! I guess not. [*in a more placated but still contemptuous tone*] Goils waitin' for yuh, huh? Aw, hell! Dat's all tripe. Dey don't wait for no one. Dey'd double-cross yuh for a nickel. Dey're all tarts, get me? Treat 'em rough, dat's me. To hell wit 'em. Tarts, dat's what, de whole bunch of 'em.

LONG: [*very drunk, jumps on a bench excitedly, gesticulating with a bottle in his hand*] Listen 'ere, Comrades! Yank 'ere is right. 'E says this 'ere stinkin' ship is our 'ome. And 'e says as 'ome is 'ell. And 'e's right! This is 'ell. We lives in 'ell, Comrades—and right enough we'll die in it. [*raging*] And who's ter blame, I arsks yer? We ain't. We wasn't born this rotten way. All men is born free and ekal. That's in the bleedin' Bible, maties. But what d'they care for the Bible—them lazy, bloated swine what travels first cabin? Them's the ones. They dragged us down 'til we're on'y wage slaves in the bowels of a bloody ship, sweatin', burnin' up, eatin' coal dust! Hit's them's ter blame—the damned Capitalist clarss!

[*There had been a gradual murmur of contemptuous resentment rising among the men until now he is interrupted by a storm of catcalls, hisses, boos, hard laughter.*]

VOICES: Turn it off!

Shut up!

Sit down!

Closa da face!

Tamn fool! [*Etc.*]

YANK: [*standing up and glaring at* LONG] Sit down before I knock yuh down! [LONG *makes haste to efface himself.* YANK *goes on contemptuously.*] De Bible, huh? De Cap'tlist class, huh? Aw nix on dat Salvation Army–Socialist bull. Git a soapbox! Hire a hall! Come and be saved, huh? Jerk us to Jesus, huh? Aw g'wan! I've listened to lots of guys like you, see. Yuh're all wrong. Wanter know what I t'ink? Yuh ain't no good for no one. Yuh're de bunk. Yuh ain't got no noive, get me? Yuh're yellow, dat's what. Yellow, dat's you. Say! What's dem slobs in de foist cabin got to do wit us? We're better men dan dey are, ain't we? Sure! One of us guys could clean up de whole mob wit one mitt. Put one of 'em down here for one watch in de stokehole, what'd happen? Dey'd carry him off on a stretcher. Dem boids don't amount to nothin'. Dey're just baggage. Who makes dis old tub run? Ain't it us guys? Well den, we belong, don't we? We belong and dey don't. Dat's all. [*A loud chorus of approval.* YANK *goes on.*] As for dis bein' hell—aw, nuts! Yuh lost your noive, dat's what. Dis is a man's job, get me? It belongs. It runs dis tub. No stiffs need apply. But yuh're a stiff, see? Yuh're yellow, dat's you.

VOICES: [*with a great hard pride in them*]
> Righto!
> A man's job!
> Talk is cheap, Long.
> He never could hold up his end.
> Divil take him!
> Yank's right. We make it go.
> Py Gott, Yank say right ting!
> We don't need no one cryin' over us.
> Makin' speeches.
> Throw him out!
> Yellow!
> Chuck him overboard!
> I'll break his jaw for him!
> [*They crowd around* LONG *threateningly.*]

YANK: [*half good-natured again—contemptuously*] Aw, take it easy. Leave him alone. He ain't woith a punch. Drink up. Here's how, whoever owns dis. [*He takes a long swallow from his bottle. All drink with him. In a flash all is hilarious amiability again, back-slapping, loud talk, etc.*]

PADDY: [*who has been sitting in a blinking, melancholy daze—suddenly cries out in a voice full of old sorrow*] We belong to this, you're saying? We make the ship to go, you're saying? Yerra then, that Almighty God have pity on us! [*His voice runs into the wail of a keen, he rocks back and forth on his bench. The men stare at him, startled and impressed in spite of themselves.*] Oh, to be back in the fine days of my youth, ochone! Oh, there was fine beautiful ships them days—clippers wid tall masts touching the sky—fine strong men in them—men that was sons of the sea as if 'twas the mother that bore them. Oh, the clean skins of them, and the clear eyes, the straight backs and full chests of them! Brave men they was, and bold men surely! We'd be sailing out, bound down round the Horn maybe. We'd be making sail in the dawn, with a fair breeze, singing a chanty song wid no care to it. And astern the land would be sinking low and dying out, but we'd give it no heed but a laugh, and never a look behind. For the day that was, was enough, for we was free men—and I'm thinking 'tis only slaves do be giving heed to the day that's gone or the day to come—until they're old like me. [*with a sort of religious exaltation*] Oh, to be scudding south again wid the power of the Trade Wind driving her on steady through the nights and the days! Full sail on her! Nights and days! Nights when the foam of the wake would be flaming wid fire, when the sky'd be blazing and winking wid stars. Or the full of the moon maybe. Then you'd see her driving through the gray night, her sails stretching aloft all silver and white, not a sound on the deck, the lot of us dreaming dreams, till you'd believe 'twas no real ship at all you was on but a ghost ship like the *Flying Dutchman* they say does be roaming the seas forevermore widout touching a port. And there was the days, too. A warm sun on the clean decks. Sun warming the blood of you, and wind over the miles of shiny green ocean like strong drink to your lungs. Work—aye, hard work—but who'd mind that at all? Sure, you worked under the sky and 'twas work wid skill and daring to it. And wid the day done, in the dog watch, smoking me pipe at ease, the lookout would be raising land maybe, and we'd see the mountains of South Americy wid the red fire of the setting sun painting their white tops and the clouds floating by them! [*His tone of exaltation ceases. He goes on mournfully.*] Yerra, what's the use of talking? 'Tis a dead man's whisper. [*to* YANK *resentfully*] 'Twas them days men belonged to ships, not now. 'Twas them days a ship was part of the sea, and a man was part of a ship, and the sea joined all together and made it one. [*scornfully*] Is it one wid this you'd be, Yank—black smoke from the funnels smudging the sea, smudging the decks—the bloody engines pounding and throbbing and shaking—wid divil a sight of sun or a breath of clean air—choking our lungs wid coal dust—breaking our backs and hearts in the hell of the stokehole—feeding the bloody furnace—feeding our lives along wid the coal, I'm thinking—caged in by steel from a sight of the sky like bloody apes in the zoo! [*with a harsh laugh*] Ho-ho, divil mend you! Is it to belong to that you're wishing? Is it a flesh and blood wheel of the engines you'd be?

YANK: [*who has been listening with a contemptuous sneer, barks out the answer*] Sure ting! Dat's me. What about it?

PADDY: [*as if to himself—with great sorrow*] Me time is past due. That a great wave wid sun in the heart of it may sweep me over the side sometime I'd be dreaming of the days that's gone!

YANK: Aw, yuh crazy Mick! [*He springs to his feet and advances on* PADDY *threateningly—then stops, fighting some queer struggle within himself—lets his hands fall to his sides—contemptuously.*] Aw, take it easy. Yuh're aw right, at dat. Yuh're bugs, dat's all—nutty as a cuckoo. All dat tripe yuh been pullin'—Aw, dat's all right. On'y it's dead, get me? Yuh don't belong no more, see. Yuh don't got de stuff. Yuh're too old. [*disgustedly*] But aw say, come up for air onct in a while, can't yuh? See what's happened since yuh croaked. [*He suddenly bursts forth vehemently, growing more and more excited.*] Say! Sure! Sure I meant it! What de hell—Say, lemme talk! Hey! Hey, you old Harp! Hey, youse guys! Say, listen to me—wait a moment—I gotter talk, see. I belong and he don't. He's dead but I'm livin'. Listen to me! Sure I'm part of de engines! Why de hell not! Dey move, don't dey? Dey're speed, ain't dey? Dey smash trou, don't dey? Twenty-five knots a hour! Dat's goin' some! Dat's new stuff! Dat belongs! But him, he's too old. He gets dizzy. Say, listen. All dat crazy tripe about nights and days; all dat crazy tripe about stars and moons; all dat crazy tripe about suns and winds, fresh air and de rest of it—Aw hell, dat's all a dope dream! Hittin' de pipe of de past, dat's what he's doin'. He's old and don't belong no more. But me, I'm young! I'm in de pink! I move wit it! It, get me! I mean de ting dat's de guts of all dis. It ploughs trou all de tripe he's been sayin'. It blows dat up! It knocks dat dead! It slams dat offen de face of de Oith! It, get me! De engines and de coal and de smoke and all de rest of it! He can't breathe and swallow coal dust, but I kin, see? Dat's fresh air for me! Dat's food for me! I'm new, get me? Hell in de stokehole? Sure! It takes a man to work in hell. Hell, sure, dat's my fav'rite climate. I eat it up! I git fat on it! It's me makes it hot! It's me makes it roar! It's me makes it move! Sure, on'y for me everyting stops. It all goes dead, get me? De noise and smoke and all de engines movin' de woild, dey stop. Dere ain't nothin' no more! Dat's what I'm sayin'. Everyting else dat makes de woild move, somep'n makes it move. It can't move without somep'n else, see? Den yuh get down to me. I'm at de bottom, get me! Dere ain't nothin' foither. I'm de end! I'm de start! I start somep'n and de woild moves! It—dat's me!—de new dat's moiderin' de old! I'm de ting in coal dat makes it boin; I'm steam and oil for de engines; I'm de ting in noise dat makes yuh hear it; I'm smoke and express trains and steamers and factory whistles; I'm de ting in gold dat makes it money! And I'm what makes iron into steel! Steel, dat stands for de whole ting! And I'm steel—steel—steel! I'm de muscles in steel, de punch behind it! [*As he says this he pounds with his fist against the steel bunks. All the men, roused to a pitch of frenzied self-glorification by his speech, do likewise. There is a deafening metallic roar, through which* YANK's *voice can be heard bellowing.*] Slaves, hell. We run de whole woiks. All de rich guys dat tink dey're somep'n, dey ain't nothin'! Dey don't belong. But us guys, we're in de move, we're at de bottom, de whole ting is us! [PADDY *from the start of* YANK's *speech has been taking one gulp after another from his bottle, at first frightenedly, as if he were afraid to listen, then desperately, as if to drown his senses, but finally has achieved complete indifferent, even amused, drunkenness.* YANK *sees his lips moving. He quells the uproar with a shout.*] Hey, youse guys, take it easy! Wait a moment! De nutty Harp is sayin' somep'n.

PADDY: [*is heard now—throws his head back a mocking burst of laughter*] Ho-ho-ho-ho-ho—

YANK: [*drawing back his fist, with a snarl*] Aw! Look out who yuh're givin' the bark!

PADDY: [*begins to sing the "Miller of Dee" with enormous good nature*]

I care for nobody, no, not I,
And nobody cares for me.

YANK: [*good-natured himself in a flash, interrupts* PADDY *with a slap on the bare back like a report*] Dat's de stuff! Now yuh're gettin' wise to somep'n. Care for nobody, dat's de dope! To hell wit 'em all. And nix on nobody else carin'. I kin care for myself, get me! [*Eight bells sound, muffled, vibrating through the steel walls as if some enormous brazen gong were imbedded in the heart of the ship. All the men jump up mechanically, file through the door silently close upon each other's heels in what is very like a prisoners' lockstep.* YANK *slaps* PADDY *on the back.*] Our watch, yuh old Harp! [*mockingly*] Come on down in hell. Eat up de coal dust. Drink in de heat. It's it, see! Act like yuh liked it, yuh better—or croak yuhself.

PADDY: [*with jovial defiance*] To the divil wid it! I'll not report this watch. Let them log me and be damned. I'm no slave the like of you. I'll be sittin' here at me ease, and drinking, and thinking, and dreaming dreams.

YANK: [*contemptuously*] Tinkin' and dreamin', what'll that get yuh? What's tinkin' got to do wit it? We move, don't we? Speed, ain't it? Fog, dat's all you stand for. But we drive trou dat, don't we? We split dat up and smash trou—twenty-five knots a hour! [*turns his back on* PADDY *scornfully*] Aw, yuh make me sick! Yuh don't belong! [*He strides out the door in rear.* PADDY *hums to himself, blinking drowsily.*]

CURTAIN

SCENE II

Two days out. A section of the promenade deck, MILDRED DOUGLAS *and her aunt are discovered reclining in deck chairs. The former is a girl of twenty, slender, delicate, with a pale, pretty face marred by a self-conscious expression of disdainful superiority. She looks fretful, nervous, and discontented, bored by her own anemia. Her aunt is a pompous and proud—and fat—old lady. She is a type even to the point of a double chin and lorgnettes. She is dressed pretentiously, as if afraid her face alone would never indicate her position in life.* MILDRED *is dressed all in white.*

The impression to be conveyed by this scene is one of the beautiful, vivid life of the sea all about—sunshine on the deck in a great flood, the fresh sea wind blowing across it. In the midst of this, these two incongruous, artificial figures, inert and disharmonious, the elder like a gray lump of dough touched up with rouge, the younger looking as if the vitality of her stock had been sapped before she was conceived, so that she is the expression not of its life energy but merely of the artificialities that energy had won for itself in the spending.

MILDRED: [*looking up with affected dreaminess*] How the black smoke swirls back against the sky! Is it not beautiful?

AUNT: [*without looking up*] I dislike smoke of any kind.

MILDRED: My great-grandmother smoked a pipe—a clay pipe.

AUNT: [*ruffling*] Vulgar!

MILDRED: She was too distant a relative to be vulgar. Time mellows pipes.

AUNT: [*pretending boredom but irritated*] Did the sociology you took up at college teach you that—to play the ghoul on every possible occasion, excavating old bones? Why not let your great-grandmother rest in her grave?

MILDRED: [*dreamily*] With her pipe beside her—puffing in Paradise.

AUNT: [*with spite*] Yes, you are a natural-born ghoul. You are even getting to look like one, my dear.

MILDRED: [*in a passionless tone*] I detest you, Aunt. [*looking at her critically*] Do you know what you remind me of? Of a cold pork pudding against a background of linoleum tablecloth in the kitchen of a—but the possibilities are wearisome. [*She closes her eyes*]

AUNT: [*with a bitter laugh*] Merci for your candor. But since I am and must be your chaperon—in appearance, at least—let us patch up some sort of armed truce. For my part you are quite free to indulge any pose of eccentricity that beguiles you—as long as you observe the amenities—

MILDRED: [*drawling*] The inanities?

AUNT: [*going on as if she hadn't heard*] After exhausting the morbid thrills of social service work on New York's East Side—how they must have hated you, by the way, the poor that you made so much poorer in their own eyes!—you are now bent on making your slumming international. Well, I hope Whitechapel will provide the needed nerve tonic. Do not ask me to chaperon you there, however. I told your father I would not. I loathe deformity. We will hire an army of detectives and you may investigate everything—they allow you to see.

MILDRED: [*protesting with a trace of genuine earnestness*] Please do not mock at my attempts to discover how the other half lives. Give me credit for some sort of groping sincerity in that at least. I would like to help them. I would like to be some use in the world. Is it my fault I don't know how? I would like to be sincere, to touch life somewhere. [*with weary bitterness*] But I'm afraid I have neither the vitality nor integrity. All that was burnt out in our stock before I was born. Grandfather's blast furnaces, flaming to the sky, melting steel, making millions—then father keeping those home fires burning, making more millions—and little me at the tail-end of it all. I'm a waste product in the Bessemer process—like the millions. Or rather, I inherit the acquired trait of the by-product, wealth, but none of the energy, none of the strength of the steel that made it. I am sired by gold and damned by it, as they say at the race track—damned in more ways than one. [*She laughs mirthlessly.*]

AUNT: [*unimpressed—superciliously*] You seem to be going in for sincerity today. It isn't becoming to you, really—except as an obvious pose. Be as artificial as you are, I advise. There's a sort of sincerity in that, you know. And, after all, you must confess you like that better.

MILDRED: [*again affected and bored*] Yes, I suppose I do. Pardon me for my outburst. When a leopard complains of its spots, it must sound rather grotesque. [*in a mocking tone*] Purr, little leopard. Purr, scratch, tear, kill, gorge yourself and be happy—only stay in the jungle where your spots are camouflage. In a cage they make you conspicuous.

AUNT: I don't know what you are talking about.

MILDRED: It would be rude to talk about anything to you. Let's just talk. [*She looks at her wristwatch.*] Well, thank goodness, it's about time for them to come for me. That ought to give me a new thrill, Aunt.

AUNT: [*affectedly troubled*] You don't mean to say you're really going? The dirt—the heat must be frightful—

MILDRED: Grandfather started as a puddler. I should have inherited an immunity to heat that would make a salamander shiver. It will be fun to put it to the test.

AUNT: But don't you have to have the captain's—or someone's—permission to visit the stokehole?

MILDRED: [*with a triumphant smile*] I have it—both his and the chief engineer's. Oh, they didn't want to at first, in spite of my social service credentials. They didn't seem a bit anxious that I should investigate how the other half lives and works on a ship. So I had to tell them that my father, the president of Nazareth Steel, chairman of the board of directors of this line, had told me it would be all right.

AUNT: He didn't.

MILDRED: How naïve age makes one! But I said he did, Aunt. I even said he had given me a letter to them—which I had lost. And they were afraid to take the chance that I might be lying. [*excitedly*] So it's ho! for the stokehole. The second engineer is to escort me. [*looking at her watch again*] It's time. And here he comes, I think.

[*The* SECOND ENGINEER *enters. He is a husky, fine-looking man of thirty-five or so. He stops before the two and tips his cap, visibly embarrassed and ill-at-ease.*]

SECOND ENGINEER: Miss Douglas?

MILDRED: Yes. [*throwing off her rugs and getting to her feet*] Are we all ready to start?

SECOND ENGINEER: In just a second, ma'am. I'm waiting for the Fourth. He's coming along.

MILDRED: [*with a scornful smile*] You don't care to shoulder this responsibility alone, is that it?

SECOND ENGINEER: [*forcing a smile*] Two are better than one. [*disturbed by her eyes, glances out to sea—blurts out*] A fine day we're having.

MILDRED: Is it?

SECOND ENGINEER: A nice warm breeze—

MILDRED: It feels cold to me.

SECOND ENGINEER: But it's hot enough in the sun—

MILDRED: Not hot enough for me. I don't like Nature. I was never athletic.

SECOND ENGINEER: [*forcing a smile*] Well, you'll find it hot enough where you're going.

MILDRED: Do you mean hell?

SECOND ENGINEER: [*flabbergasted, decides to laugh*] Ho-ho! No, I mean the stokehole.

MILDRED: My grandfather was a puddler. He played with boiling steel.

SECOND ENGINEER: [*all at sea—uneasily*] Is that so? Hum, you'll excuse me, ma'am, but are you intending to wear that dress?

MILDRED: Why not?

SECOND ENGINEER: You'll likely rub against oil and dirt. It can't be helped.

MILDRED: It doesn't matter. I have lots of white dresses.

SECOND ENGINEER: I have an old coat you might throw over—

MILDRED: I have fifty dresses like this. I will throw this one into the sea when I come back. That ought to wash it clean, don't you think?

SECOND ENGINEER: [*doggedly*] There's ladders to climb down that are none too clean— and dark alleyways—

MILDRED: I will wear this very dress and none other.

SECOND ENGINEER: No offense meant. It's none of my business. I was only warning you—

MILDRED: Warning? That sounds thrilling.

SECOND ENGINEER: [*looking down the deck—with a sigh of relief*] There's the Fourth now. He's waiting for us. If you'll come—

MILDRED: Go on. I'll follow you. [*He goes.* MILDRED *turns a mocking smile on her aunt.*] An oaf—but a handsome, virile oaf.

AUNT: [*scornfully*] Poser!

MILDRED: Take care. He said there were dark alleyways—

AUNT: [*in the same tone*] Poser!

MILDRED: [*biting her lips angrily*] You are right. But would that my millions were not so anemically chaste!

AUNT: Yes, for a fresh pose I have no doubt you would drag the name of Douglas in the gutter!

MILDRED: From which it sprang. Good-by, Aunt. Don't pray too hard that I may fall into the fiery furnace.

AUNT: Poser!

MILDRED: [*viciously*] Old hag! [*She slaps her aunt insultingly across the face and walks off, laughing gaily.*]

AUNT: [*screams after her*] I said "poser"!

CURTAIN

SCENE III

The stokehole. In the rear, the dimly-outlined bulks of the furnaces and boilers. High overhead one hanging electric bulb sheds just enough light through the murky air laden with coal dust to pile up masses of shadows everywhere. A line of men, stripped to the waist, is before the furnace doors. They bend over, looking neither to right nor left, handling their shovels as if they were part of their bodies, with a strange, awkward, swinging rhythm. They use the shovels to throw open the furnace doors. Then from these fiery round holes in the black a flood of terrific light and heat pours full upon the men who are outlined in silhouette in the crouching, inhuman attitudes of chained gorillas. The men shovel with a rhythmic motion, swinging as on a pivot from the coal which lies in heaps on the floor behind to hurl it into the flaming mouths before them. There is a tumult of noise—the brazen clang of the furnace doors as they are flung open or slammed shut, the grating, teeth-gritting grind of steel against steel, of crunching coal. This clash of sounds stuns one's ears with its rending dissonance. But there is order in it, rhythm, a mechanical regulated recurrence, a tempo. And rising above all, making the air hum with the quiver of liberated energy, the roar of leaping flames in the furnaces, the monotonous throbbing beat of the engines.

As the curtain rises, the furnace doors are shut. The men are taking a breathing spell. One or two are arranging the coal behind them, pulling it into more accessible heaps. The others can be dimly made out leaning on their shovels in relaxed attitudes of exhaustion.

PADDY: [*from somewhere in the line—plaintively*] Yerra, will this divil's own watch nivir end? Me back is broke. I'm destroyed entirely.

YANK: [*from the center of the line—with exuberant scorn*] Aw, yuh make me sick! Lie down and croak, why don't yuh? Always beefin', dat's you! Say, dis is a cinch! Dis was made for me! It's my meat, get me! [*A whistle is blown—a thin, shrill note from somewhere overhead in the darkness.* YANK *curses without resentment.*] Dere's de damn engineer crackin' de whip. He tinks we're loafin'.

PADDY: [*vindictively*] God stiffen him!

YANK: [*in an exultant tone of command*] Come on, youse guys! Git into de game! She's gittin' hungry. Pile some grub in her. Trow it into her belly! Come on now, all of youse! Open her up!

    [*At this last all the men, who have followed his movements of getting into position, throw open their furnace doors with a deafening clang. The fiery light floods over their shoulders as they bend round for the coal. Rivulets of sooty sweat have traced maps on their backs. The enlarged muscles form bunches of highlight and shadow.*]

YANK: [*chanting a count as he shovels without seeming effort*] One—two—tree— [*his voice rising exultantly in the joy of battle*] Dat's de stuff! Let her have it! All togedder now! Sling it into her! Let her ride! Shoot de piece now! Call de toin on her! Drive her into it! Feel her move! Watch her smoke! Speed, dat's her middle name! Give her coal, youse guys! Coal, dat's her booze! Drink it up, baby! Let's see yuh sprint! Dig in and gain a lap! Dere she go-o-es.

   [*This last in the chanting formula of the gallery gods at the six-day bike race. He slams his furnace door shut. The others do likewise with as much unison as their wearied bodies will permit. The effect is of one fiery eye after another, being blotted out with a series of accompanying bangs.*]

PADDY: [*groaning*] Me back is broke. I'm bate out—bate—

   [*There is a pause. Then the inexorable whistle sounds again from the dim regions above the electric light. There is a growl of cursing rage from all sides.*]

YANK: [*shaking his fist upward—contemptuously*] Take it easy dere, you! Who d'yuh tink's runnin' dis game, me or you? When I git ready, we move. Not before! When I git ready, get me!

VOICES: [*approvingly*]
   That's the stuff!
   Yank tal him, py golly!
   Yank ain't affeerd.
   Goot poy, Yank!
   Give 'im hell!
   Tell 'im 'e's a bloody swine!
   Bloody slave-driver!

YANK: [*contemptuously*] He ain't got no noive. He's yellow, get me? All de engineers is yellow. Dey got streaks a mile wide. Aw, to hell wit him! Let's move, youse guys. We had a rest. Come on, she needs it! Give her pep! It ain't for him. Him and his whistle, dey don't belong. But we belong, see! We gotter feed de baby! Come on!

   [*He turns and flings his furnace door open. They all follow his lead. At this instant the* SECOND *and* FOURTH ENGINEERS *enter from the darkness on the left with* MILDRED *between them. She starts, turns paler, her pose is crumbling, she shivers with fright in spite of the blazing heat, but forces herself to leave the* ENGINEERS *and take a few steps nearer the men. She is right behind* YANK. *All this happens quickly while the men have their backs turned.*]

YANK: Come on, youse guys! [*He is turning to get coal when the whistle sounds again in a peremptory, irritating note. This drives* YANK *into a sudden fury. While the other men have turned full around and stopped dumbfounded by the spectacle of* MILDRED *standing there in her white dress,* YANK *does not turn far enough to see her. Besides, his head is thrown back, he blinks upward through the murk trying to find the owner of the whistle, he brandishes his shovel murderously over his head in one hand, pounding on his chest, gorilla-like, with the other, shouting:*] Toin off dat whistle! Come down outa dere, yuh yellow, brass-buttoned, Belfast bum, yuh! Come down and I'll knock yer brains out! Yuh lousy, stinkin', yellow mutt of a Catholic-moiderin' bastard! Come down and I'll moider yuh! Pullin' dat whistle on me, huh? I'll show yuh! I'll crash yer skull in! I'll drive yer teet' down yer troat! I'll slam yer nose trou de back of yer head! I'll cut yer guts out for a nickel, yuh lousy boob, yuh dirty crummy, muck-eatin' son of a— [*Suddenly he becomes conscious of all the other men staring at something directly behind his back. He whirls defensively with a snarling, murderous growl, crouching to spring, his lips drawn back over his teeth, his small eyes gleaming ferociously. He sees* MILDRED, *like a white apparition in the full light from the open furnace doors. He glares into her eyes, turned to stone. As for her, during his speech she has listened, paralyzed with horror, terror, her whole personality crushed, beaten in, collapsed, by the terrific impact of this unknown, abysmal brutality, naked and shameless. As she looks at his gorilla face, as his eyes bore into hers, she utters a low, choking cry and shrinks away from him, putting both hands up before her eyes to shut out the sight of his face, to protect her own. This startles* YANK *to a reaction. His mouth falls open, his eyes grow bewildered.*]

MILDRED: [*about to faint—to the* ENGINEERS, *who now have her one by each arm—whimperingly*] Take me away! Oh, the filthy beast!

[*She faints. They carry her quickly back, disappearing in the darkness at the left, rear. An iron door clangs shut. Rage and bewildered fury rush back on* YANK. *He feels himself insulted in some unknown fashion in the very heart of his pride. He roars.*]

YANK: God damn yuh! [*And hurls his shovel after them at the door which has just closed. It hits the steel bulkhead with a clang and falls clattering on the steel floor. From overhead the whistle sounds again in a long, angry, insistent command.*]

CURTAIN

SCENE IV

The firemen's forecastle. YANK's *watch has just come off duty and had dinner. Their faces and bodies shine from a soap-and-water scrubbing but around their eyes, where a hasty dousing does not touch, the coal dust sticks like black makeup, giving them a queer, sinister expression.* YANK *has not washed either face or body. He stands out in contrast to them, a blackened, brooding figure. He is seated forward on a bench in the exact attitude of Rodin's "The Thinker." The others, most of them smoking pipes, are staring at* YANK *half-apprehensively, as if fearing an outburst; half-amusedly as if they saw a joke somewhere that tickled them.*

VOICES: He ain't ate nothin'
    Py golly, a fallar gat to gat grub in him.
    Divil a lie.
    Yank feeda da fire, no feeda da face.
    Ha-ha.
    He ain't even washed hisself.
    He's forgot.
    Hey, Yank you forgot to wash.
YANK: [*sullenly*] Forgot nothin'! To hell wit washin'.
VOICES: It'll stick to you.
    It'll get under your skin.
    Give yer the bleedin' itch, that's wot.
    It makes spots on you—like a leopard.
    Like a piebald nigger, you mean.
    Better wash up, Yank.
    You sleep better.
    Wash up, Yank.
    Wash up! Wash up!
YANK: [*resentfully*] Aw say, youse guys. Lemme alone. Can't youse see I'm tryin' to tink?
ALL: [*repeating the word after him as one with cynical mockery*] Think! [*The word has a brazen, metallic quality as if their throats were phonograph horns. It is followed by a chorus of hard, barking laughter.*]

YANK: [*springing to his feet and glaring at them belligerently*] Yes, tink! Tink, dat's what I said! What about it?

> [*They are silent, puzzled by his sudden resentment at what used to be one of his jokes.* YANK *sits down again in the same attitude of "The Thinker."*]

VOICES: Leave him alone.

He's got a grouch on.

Why wouldn't he?

PADDY: [*with a wink at the others*] Sure I know what's the matther. 'Tis aisy to see. He's fallen in love, I'm telling you.

ALL: [*repeating the word after him as one with cynical mockery*] Love! [*The word has a brazen, metallic quality as if their throats were phonograph horns. It is followed by a chorus of hard, barking laughter.*]

YANK: [*with a contemptuous snort*] Love, hell! Hate, dat's what. I've fallen in hate, get me?

PADDY: [*philosophically*] 'Twould take a wise man to tell one from the other. [*with a bitter, ironical scorn, increasing as he goes on*] But I'm telling you it's love that's in it. Sure what else but love for us poor bastes in the stokehole would be bringing a fine lady, dressed like a white quane, down a mile of ladders and steps to be havin' a look at us? [*A growl of anger goes up from all sides.*]

LONG: [*jumping on a bench—hectically*] Hinsultin' us! Hinsultin' us, the bloody cow! And them bloody engineers! What right 'as they got to be exhibitin' us's if we was bleedin' monkeys in a menagerie? Did we sign for hinsults to our dignity as 'onest workers? Is that in the ship's articles? You kin bloody well bet it ain't! But I knows why they done it. I arsked a deck steward 'o she was and 'e told me. 'Er old man's a bleedin' millionaire, a bloody Capitalist! 'E's got enuf bloody gold to sink this bleedin' ship! 'E makes arf the bloody steel in the world! 'E owns this bloody boat! And you and me, Comrades, we're 'is slaves! And the skipper and mates and engineers, they're 'is slaves! And she's 'is bloody daughter and we're all 'er slaves, too! And she gives 'er orders as 'ow she wants to see the bloody animals below decks and down they takes 'er!

> [*There is a roar of rage from all sides.*]

YANK: [*blinking at him bewilderedly*] Say! Wait a moment! Is all dat straight goods?

LONG: Straight as string! The bleedin' steward as waits on 'em, 'e told me about 'er. And what're we goin' ter do, I arsks yer? 'Ave we got ter swaller 'er hinsults like dogs? It ain't in the ship's articles. I tell yer we got a case. We kin go to law—

YANK: [*with abysmal contempt*] Hell! Law!

ALL: [*repeating the word after him as one with cynical mockery*] Law! [*The word has a brazen, metallic quality as if their throats were phonograph horns. It is followed by a chorus of hard, barking laughter.*]

LONG: [*feeling the ground slipping from under his feet—desperately*] As voters and citizens we kin force the bloody governments—

YANK: [*with abysmal contempt*] Hell! Governments!

ALL: [*repeating the word after him as one with cynical mockery*] Governments! [*The word has a brazen, metallic quality as if their throats were phonograph horns. It is followed by a chorus of hard, barking laughter.*]

LONG: [*hysterically*] We're free and equal in the sight of God—

YANK: [*with abysmal contempt*] Hell! God!

ALL: [*repeating the word after him as one with cynical mockery*] God! [*The word has a brazen, metallic quality as if their throats were phonograph horns. It is followed by a chorus of hard, barking laughter.*]

YANK: [*witheringly*] Aw, join de Salvation Army!

ALL: Sit down! Shut up! Damn fool! Sea-lawyer!

> [LONG *slinks back out of sight.*]

PADDY: [*continuing the trend of his thoughts as if he had never been interrupted—bitterly*] And there she was standing behind us, and the Second pointing at us like a man you'd hear in a circus would be saying: In this cage is a queerer kind of baboon than ever you'd find in darkest Africy. We roast them in their own sweat—and be damned if you won't hear some of thim saying they like it! [*He glances scornfully at* YANK.]

YANK: [*with a bewildered uncertain growl*] Aw!

PADDY: And there was Yank roarin' curses and turning round wid his shovel to brain her—and she looked at him, and him at her—

YANK: [*slowly*] She was all white. I tought she was a ghost. Sure.

PADDY: [*with heavy, biting sarcasm*] 'Twas love at first sight, divil a doubt of it! If you'd seen the endearin' look on her pale mug when she shriveled away with her hands over her eyes to shut out the sight of him! Sure, 'twas as if she'd seen a great hairy ape escaped from the Zoo!

YANK: [*stung—with a growl of rage*] Aw!

PADDY: And the loving way Yank heaved his shovel at the skull of her, only she was out the door! [*a grin breaking over his face*] 'Twas touching, I'm telling you! It put the touch of home, swate home in the stokehole. [*There is a roar of laughter from all.*]

YANK: [*glaring at* PADDY *menacingly*] Aw, choke dat off, see!

PADDY: [*not heeding him—to the others*] And her grabbin' at the Second's arm for protection. [*with a grotesque imitation of a woman's voice*] Kiss me, Engineer dear, for it's dark down here and me old man's in Wall Street making money! Hug me tight, darlin', for I'm afeerd in the dark and me mother's on deck makin' eyes at the skipper! [*Another roar of laughter.*]

YANK: [*threateningly*] Say! What yuh tryin' to do, kid me, yuh old Harp?

PADDY: Divil a bit! Ain't I wishin' myself you'd brained her?

YANK: [*fiercely*] I'll brain her! I'll brain her yet, wait 'n' see! [*coming over to* PADDY—*slowly*] Say, is dat what she called me—a hairy ape?

PADDY: She looked it at you if she didn't say the word itself.

YANK: [*grinning horribly*] Hairy ape, huh? Sure! Dat's de way she looked at me, aw right. Hairy ape! So dat's me, huh? [*bursting into rage—as if she were still in front of him*] Yuh skinny tart! Yuh white-faced bum, yuh! I'll show yuh who's a ape! [*turning to the others, bewilderment seizing him again*] Say, youse guys. I was bawlin' him out for pullin' de whistle on us. You heard me. And den I seen youse lookin' at somep'n and I tought he'd sneaked down to come up in back of me, and I hopped round to knock him dead wit de shovel. And dere she was wit de light on her! Christ, yuh coulda pushed me over with a finger! I was scared, get me? Sure! I tought she was a ghost, see? She was all in white like dey wrap around stiffs. You seen her. Kin yuh blame me? She didn't belong, dat's what. And den when I come to and seen it was a real skoit and seen de way she was lookin' at me—like Paddy said—Christ, I was sore, get me? I don't stand for dat stuff from nobody. And I flung de shovel—on'y she'd beat it. [*furiously*] I wished it'd banged her! I wished it'd knocked her block off!

LONG: And be 'anged for murder or 'lectrocuted? She ain't bleedin' well worth it.

YANK: I don't give a damn what! I'd be square wit her, wouldn't I? Tink I wanter let her put somep'n over on me? Tink I'm goin' to let her git away wit dat stuff? Yuh don't know me! No one ain't never put nothin' over on me and got away wit it, see!—not dat kind of stuff—no guy and no skoit neither! I'll fix her! Maybe she'll come down again—

VOICE: No chance, Yank. You scared her out of a year's growth.

YANK: I scared her? Why de hell should I scare her? Who de hell is she? Ain't she de same as me? Hairy ape, huh? [*with his old confident bravado*] I'll show her I'm better'n her, if she on'y knew it. I belong and she don't, see! I move and she's dead! Twenty-five knots a hour, dat's me! Dat carries her but I make dat. She's on'y baggage. Sure! [*again bewilderedly*] But, Christ, she was funny lookin! Did yuh pipe her hands? White and skinny. Yuh could see de bones through 'em. And her mush, dat was dead white, too. And her eyes, dey was like dey'd seen a ghost. Me, dat was! Sure! Hairy ape! Ghost, huh? Look at dat arm! [*He extends his right arm, swelling out the great muscles.*] I coulda took her wit dat, wit just my little finger even, and broke her in two. [*again bewilderedly*] Say, who is dat skoit, huh? What is she? What's she come from? Who made her? Who give her de noive to look at me like dat? Dis ting's got my goat right. I don't get her. She's new to me. What does a skoit like her mean, huh? She don't belong, get me! I can't see her. [*with growing anger*] But one ting I'm wise to, aw right, aw right! Youse all kin bet your shoits I'll git even wit her. I'll show her if she tinks she—She grinds de organ and I'm on de string, huh? I'll fix her! Let her come down again and I'll fling her in de furnace! She'll move den! She won't shiver at nothin', den! Speed, dat'll be her! She'll belong den! [*He grins horribly.*]

PADDY: She'll never come. She's had her bellyful, I'm telling you. She'll be in bed now, I'm thinking, wid ten doctors and nurses feedin' her salts to clean the fear out of her.

YANK: [*enraged*] Yuh tink I made her sick, too, do yuh? Just lookin' at me, huh? Hairy ape, huh? [*in a frenzy of rage*] I'll fix her! I'll tell her where to git off! She'll git down on her knees and take it back or I'll bust de face offen her! [*shaking one fist upward and beating on his chest with the other*] I'll find yuh! I'm comin', d'yuh hear? I'll fix yuh, God damn yuh! [*He makes a rush for the door.*]

VOICES: Stop him!
  He'll get shot!
  He'll murder her!
  Trip him up!
  Hold him!
  He's gone crazy!
  Gott, he's strong!
  Hold him down!
  Look out for a kick!
  Pin his arms!

  [*They have all piled on him and, after a fierce struggle, by sheer weight of numbers have borne him to the floor just inside the door.*]

PADDY: [*who has remained detached*] Kape him down till he's cooled off. [*scornfully*] Yerra, Yank, you're a great fool. Is it payin' attention at all you are to the like of that skinny sow widout one drop of rale blood in her?

YANK: [*frenziedly, from the bottom of the heap*] She done me doit! She done me doit, didn't she? I'll get square wit her! I'll get her some way! Git offen me, youse guys! Lemme up! I'll show her who's a ape!

CURTAIN

SCENE V

Three weeks later. A corner of Fifth Avenue in the Fifties on a fine Sunday morning. A general atmosphere of clean, well-tidied, wide street; a flood of mellow, tempered sunshine; gentle, genteel breezes. In the rear, the show windows of two shops, a jewelry establishment on the corner, a furrier's next to it. Here the adornments of extreme wealth are tantalizingly displayed. The jeweler's window is gaudy with glittering diamonds, emeralds, rubies, pearls, etc., fashioned in ornate tiaras, crowns, necklaces, collars, etc. From each piece hangs an enormous tag from which a dollar sign and numerals in intermittent electric lights wink out the incredible prices. The same in the furrier's. Rich furs of all varieties hang there bathed in a downpour of artificial light. The general effect is of a background of magnificence cheapened and made grotesque by commercialism, a background in tawdry disharmony with the clear light and sunshine on the street itself.

Up the side street YANK *and* LONG *come swaggering.* LONG *is dressed in shore clothes, wears a black Windsor tie, cloth cap.* YANK *is in his dirty dungarees. A fireman's cap with black peak is cocked defiantly on the side of his head. He has not shaved for days and around his fierce, resentful eyes—as around those of* LONG *to a lesser degree—the black smudge of coal dust still sticks like makeup. They hesitate and stand together at the corner, swaggering, looking about them with a forced, defiant contempt.*

LONG: [*indicating it all with an oratorical gesture*] Well, 'ere we are, Fif' Avenoo. This 'ere's their bleedin private lane, as yer might say. [*bitterly*] We're trespassers 'ere. Proletarians keep orf the grass!

YANK: [*dully*] I don't see no grass, yuh boob. [*staring at the sidewalk*] Clean, ain't it? Yuh could eat a fried egg offen it. The white wings got some job sweepin' dis up. [*looking up and down the avenue—surlily*] Where's all de white-collar stiffs yuh said was here—and de skoits—her kind?

LONG: In church, blast 'em! Arskin' Jesus to give 'em more money.

YANK: Choich, huh? I uster go to choich onct—sure—when I was a kid. Me old man and woman, dey made me. Dey never went demselves, dough. Always got too big a head on Sunday mornin', dat was dem. [*with a grin*] Dey was scrappers for fair, bot' of dem. On Satiday nights when dey bot' got a skinful dey could put up a bout oughter been staged at de Garden. When dey got trough dere wasn't a chair or table wit a leg under it. Or else dey bot' jumped on me for somep'n. Dat was where I loined to take punishment. [*with a grin and a swagger*] I'm a chip offen de old block, get me?

LONG: Did yer old man follow the sea?

YANK: Naw. Worked along shore. I runned away when me old lady croaked wit de tremens. I helped at truckin' and in de market. Den I shipped in de stokehole. Sure. Dat belongs. De rest was nothin'. [*looking around him*] I ain't never seen dis before. De Brooklyn waterfront, dat was where I was dragged up. [*taking a deep breath*] Dis ain't so bad at dat, huh?

LONG: Not bad? Well, we pays for it wiv our bloody sweat, if yer wants to know!

YANK: [*with sudden angry disgust*] Aw, hell! I don't see no one, see—like her. All dis gives me a pain. It don't belong. Say, ain't dere a back room around dis dump? Let's go shoot a ball. All dis is too clean and quiet and dolled-up, get me! It gives me a pain.

LONG: Wait and yer'll bloody well see—

YANK: I don't wait for no one. I keep on de move. Say, what yuh drag me up here for, anyway? Tryin' to kid me, yuh simp, yuh?

LONG: Yer wants to get back at 'er, don't yer? That's what yer been sayin' every bloomin' hour since she hinsulted yer.

YANK: [*vehemently*] Sure ting I do! Didn't I try to get even wit her in Southampton? Didn't I sneak on de dock and wait for her by de gangplank? I was goin' to spit in her pale mug, see! Sure, right in her pop-eyes! Dat woulda made me even, see? But no chanct. Dere was a whole army of plainclothes bulls around. Dey spotted me and gimme de bum's rush. I never seen her. But I'll git square wit her yet, you watch! [*furiously*] De lousy tart! She tinks she kin get away wit moider—but not wit me! I'll fix her! I'll tink of a way!

LONG: [*as disgusted as he dares to be*] Ain't that why I brought yer up 'ere—to show yer? Yer been lookin' at this 'ere 'ole affair wrong. Yer been actin' an' talkin' 's if it was all a bleedin' personal matter between yer and that bloody cow. I wants to convince yer she was on'y a representative of 'er clarss. I wants to awaken yer bloody clarss consciousness. Then yer'll see it's 'er clarss yer've got to fight, not 'er alone. There's a 'ole mob of 'em like 'er, Gawd blind 'em!

YANK: [*spitting on his hands—belligerently*] De more de merrier when I gits started. Bring on de gang!

LONG: Yer'll see 'em in arf a mo', when that church lets out. [*He turns and sees the window display in the two stores for the first time.*] Blimey! Look at that, will yer? [*They both walk back and stand looking in the jeweler's.* LONG *flies into a fury.*] Just look at this 'ere bloomin' mess! Just look at it! Look at the bleedin' prices on 'em —more 'n our 'ole bloody stokehole makes in ten voyages sweatin' in 'ell! And they—'er and 'er bloody clarss—buys 'em for toys to dangle on 'em! One of these 'ere would buy scoff for a starvin' family for a year!

YANK: Aw, cut de sob stuff! T'hell wit de starvin' family. Yuh'll be passin' de hat to me next. [*with naïve admiration*] Say, dem tings is pretty, huh? Bet yuh dey'd hock for a piece of change aw right. [*then turning away, bored*] But, aw hell, what good are dey? Let her have 'em. Dey don't belong no more'n she does. [*with a gesture of sweeping the jeweler's into oblivion*] All dat don't count, get me?

LONG: [*who has moved to the furrier's—indignantly*] And I s'pose this 'ere don't, neither—skins of poor, 'armless animals slaughtered so as 'er and 'ers can keep their bleedin' noses warm!

YANK: [*who has been staring at something inside—with queer excitement*] Take a slant at dat! Give it de once-over! Monkey fur—two t'ousand bucks! [*bewilderedly*] Is dat straight goods—monkey fur? What de hell?

LONG: [*bitterly*] It's straight enuf. [*with grim humor*] They wouldn't bloody well pay that for a 'airy ape's skin—no, nor for the 'ole livin' ape with all 'is 'ead, and body, and soul thrown in!

YANK: [*clenching his fists, his face growing pale with rage as if the skin in the window were a personal insult*] Trowin' it up in my face! Christ! I'll fix her!

LONG: [*excitedly*] Church is out. 'Ere they come, the bleedin' swine. [*after a glance at* YANK's *lowering face—uneasily*] Easy goes, Comrade. Keep yer bloomin' temper. Remember force defeats itself. It ain't our weapon. We must impress our demands through peaceful means—the votes of the onmarching proletarians of the bloody world!

YANK: [*with abysmal contempt*] Votes, hell! Votes is a joke, see. Votes for women! Let dem do it!

LONG: [*still more uneasily*] Calm, now. Treat 'em wiv the proper contempt. Observe the bleedin' parasites but 'old yer 'orses.

YANK: [*angrily*] Git away from me! Yuh're yellow, dat's what. Force, dat's me! De punch, dat's me every time, see!

> [*The crowd from church enter from the right, sauntering slowly and affectedly, their heads held stiffly up, looking neither to right nor left, talking in toneless, simpering voices. The women are rouged, calcimined, dyed, overdressed to the nth degree. The men are in Prince Alberts, high hats, spats, canes, etc. A procession of gaudy marionettes, yet with something of the relentless horror of Frankensteins in their detached, mechanical unawareness.*]

VOICES: Dear Doctor Caiaphas! He is so sincere!

What was the sermon? I dozed off.

About the radicals, my dear—and the false doctrines that are being preached.

We must organize a hundred percent American bazaar.

And let everyone contribute one one-hundredth percent of their income tax.

What an original idea!

We can devote the proceeds to rehabilitating the veil of the temple.
But that has been done so many times.

YANK: [*glaring from one to the other of them—with an insulting snort of scorn*] Huh! Huh! [*Without seeming to see him, they make wide detours to avoid the spot where he stands in the middle of the sidewalk.*]

LONG: [*frightenedly*] Keep yer bloomin' mouth shut, I tells yer.

YANK: [*viciously*] G'wan! Tell it to Sweeney! [*He swaggers away and deliberately lurches into a top-hatted gentleman, then glares at him pugnaciously.*] Say, who d'yuh tink yuh're bumpin'? Tink yuh own de Oith?

GENTLEMAN: [*coldly and affectedly*] I beg your pardon. [*He has not looked at* YANK *and passes on without a glance, leaving him bewildered.*]

LONG: [*rushing up and grabbing* YANK's *arm*] 'Ere! Come away! This wasn't what I meant. Yer'll 'ave the bloody coppers down on us.

YANK: [*savagely—giving him a push that sends him sprawling*] G'wan!

LONG: [*picks himself up—hysterically*] I'll pop orf then. This ain't what I meant. And whatever 'appens, yer can't blame me. [*He slinks off left.*]

YANK: T' hell wit youse! [*He approaches a lady—with a vicious grin and a smirking wink.*] Hello, Kiddo. How's every little ting? Got anyting on for tonight? I know an old boiler down to de docks we kin crawl into. [*The lady stalks by without a look, without a change of pace.* YANK *turns to others—insultingly.*] Holy smokes, what a mug! Go hide yuhself before de horses shy at yuh. Gee, pipe de heinie on dat one! Say, youse, yuh look like de stoin of a ferryboat. Paint and powder! All dolled up to kill! Yuh look like stiffs laid out for de boneyard! Aw, g'wan, de lot of youse! Yuh give me de eyeache. Yuh don't belong, get me! Look at me, why don't youse dare? I belong, dat's me! [*pointing to a skyscraper across the street which is in process of construction—with bravado*] See dat building goin' up dere? See de steel work? Steel, dat's me! Youse guys lives on it and tink yuh're somep'n. But I'm in it, see! I'm de hoistin' engine dat makes it go up! I'm it—de inside and bottom of it! Sure! I'm steel and steam and smoke and de rest of it! It moves—speed—twenty-five stories up—and me at de top and bottom—movin'! Youse simps don't move. Yuh're on'y dolls I winds up to see 'm spin. Yuh're de garbage, get me—de leavins—de ashes we dump over de side! Now, what 'a' yuh gotta say? [*But as they seem neither to see nor hear him, he flies into a fury.*] Bums! Pigs! Tarts! Bitches! [*He turns in a rage on the men, bumping viciously into them but not jarring them the least bit. Rather it is he who recoils after each collision. He keeps growling.*] Git off de Oith! G'wan, yuh bum! Look where yuh're goin', can't yuh? Git outa here! Fight, why don't yuh? Put up yer mitts! Don't be a dog! Fight or I'll knock yuh dead!
[*But, without seeming to see him, they all answer with mechanical affected politeness:*] I beg your pardon. [*Then at a cry from one of the women, they all scurry to the furrier's window.*]

THE WOMAN: [*ecstatically, with a gasp of delight*] Monkey fur! [*The whole crowd of men and women chorus after her in the same tone of affected delight.*] Monkey fur!

YANK: [*with a jerk of his head back on his shoulders, as if he had received a punch full in the face—raging*] I see yuh, all in white! I see yuh, yuh white-faced tart, yuh! Hairy ape, huh? I'll hairy ape yuh!
[*He bends down and grips at the street curbing as if to pluck it out and hurl it. Foiled in this, snarling with passion, he leaps to the lamppost on the corner and tries to pull it up for a club. Just at that moment a bus is heard rumbling up. A fat, high-hatted, spatted gentleman runs out from the side street. He calls out plaintively:*] Bus! Bus! Stop there! [*and runs full tilt into the bending, straining* YANK, *who is bowled off his balance*]

YANK: [*seeing a fight—with a roar of joy as he springs to his feet*] At last! Bus, huh? I'll bust yuh! [*He lets drive a terrific swing, his fist landing full on the fat gentleman's face. But the gentleman stands unmoved as if nothing had happened.*]

GENTLEMAN: I beg your pardon. [*then irritably*] You have made me lose my bus. [*He claps his hands and begins to scream.*] Officer! Officer!

> [*Many police whistles shrill out on the instant and a whole platoon of policemen rush in on* YANK *from all sides. He tries to fight but is clubbed to the pavement and fallen upon. The crowd at the window have not moved or noticed this disturbance. The clanging gong of the patrol wagon approaches with a clamoring din.*]

CURTAIN

SCENE VI

Night of the following day. A row of cells in the prison on Blackwells Island. The cells extend back diagonally from right front to left rear. They do not stop, but disappear in the dark background as if they ran on, numberless, into infinity. One electric bulb from the low ceiling of the narrow corridor sheds its light through the heavy steel bars of the cell at the extreme front and reveals part of the interior. YANK *can be seen within, crouched on the edge of his cot in the attitude of Rodin's "The Thinker." His face is spotted with black and blue bruises. A blood-stained bandage is wrapped around his head.*

YANK: [*suddenly starting as if awakening from a dream, reaches out and shakes the bars— aloud to himself, wonderingly*] Steel. Dis is de zoo, huh? [*A burst of hard, barking laughter comes from the unseen occupants of the cells, runs back down the tier, and abruptly ceases.*]

VOICES: [*mockingly*] The zoo? That's a new name for this coop—a damn good name!
Steel, eh? You said a mouthful. This is the old iron house.
Who is that boob talkin'?
He's the bloke they brung in out of his head. The bulls had beat him up fierce.

YANK: [*dully*] I musta been dreamin'. I tought I was in a cage at de zoo—but de apes don't talk, do dey?

VOICES: [*with mocking laughter*] You're in a cage aw right.
A coop!
A pen!
A sty!
A kennel! [*hard laughter—a pause*]
Say, guy! Who are you? No, never mind lying. What are you?
Yes, tell us your sad story. What's your game?
What did they jug yuh for?

YANK: [*dully*] I was a fireman—stokin' on de liners. [*then with sudden rage, rattling his cell bars*] I'm a hairy ape, get me? And I'll bust youse all in de jaw if yuh don't lay off kiddin' me.

VOICES: Huh! You're a hard-boiled duck, ain't you!
When you spit, it bounces! [*laughter*]
Aw, can it. He's a regular guy. Ain't you?
What did he say he was—a ape?

YANK: [*defiantly*] Sure ting! Ain't dat what youse all are—apes?
> [*A silence. Then a furious rattling of bars from down the corridor.*]

A VOICE: [*thick with rage*] I'll show yuh who's a ape, yuh bum!

VOICES: Ssshh! Nix!

Can de noise!

Piano!

You'll have the guard down on us!

YANK: [*scornfully*] De guard? Yuh mean de keeper, don't yuh?

[*angry exclamations from all the cells*]

VOICE: [*placatingly*] Aw, don't pay no attention to him. He's off his nut from the beatin'-up he got. Say, you guy! We're waitin' to hear what they landed you for—or ain't yuh tellin'?

YANK: Sure, I'll tell youse. Sure! Why de hell not? On'y—youse won't get me. Nobody gets me but me, see? I started to tell de judge and all he says was: "Toity days to tink it over." Tink it over! Christ, dat's all I been doin' for weeks! [*after a pause*] I was tryin' to git even wit someone, see? —someone dat done me doit.

VOICES: [*cynically*] De old stuff, I bet. Your goil, huh?

Give yuh the double-cross, huh?

That's them every time!

Did yuh beat up de odder guy?

YANK: [*disgustedly*] Aw, yuh're all wrong! Sure dere was a skoit in it—but not what youse mean, not dat old tripe. Dis was a new kind of skoit. She was dolled up all in white—in de stokehole. I tought she was a ghost. Sure. [*A pause.*]

VOICES: [*whispering*] Gee, he's still nutty.

Let him rave. It's fun listenin'.

YANK: [*unheeding—groping in his thoughts*] Her hands—dey was skinny and white like dey wasn't real but painted on somep'n. Dere was a million miles from me to her—twenty-five knots a hour. She was like some dead ting de cat brung in. Sure, dat's what. She didn't belong. She belonged in de window of a toy store, or on de top of a garbage can, see! Sure! [*He breaks out angrily.*] But would yuh believe it, she had de noive to do me doit. She lamped me like she was seein' somep'n broke loose from de menagerie. Christ, yuh'd oughter seen her eyes! [*He rattles the bars of his cell furiously.*] But I'll get back at her yet, you watch! And if I can't find her I'll take it out on de gang she runs wit. I'm wise to where dey hangs out now. I'll show her who belongs! I'll show her who's in de move and who ain't. You watch my smoke!

VOICES: [*serious and joking*] Dat's de talkin'!

Take her for all she's got!

What was this dame anyway? Who was she, eh?

YANK: I dunno. First cabin stiff. Her old man's a millionaire, dey says—name of Douglas.

VOICES: Douglas? That's the president of the Steel Trust, I bet.

Sure. I seen his mug in de papers.

He's filthy with dough.

VOICE: Hey, feller, take a tip from me. If you want to get back at that dame, you better join the Wobblies. You'll get some action then.

YANK: Wobblies? What de hell's dat?

VOICE: Ain't you ever heard of the I.W.W.?

YANK: Naw. What is it?

VOICE: A gang of blokes—a tough gang. I been readin' about 'em today in the paper. The guard give me the *Sunday Times*. There's a long spiel about 'em. It's from a speech made in the Senate by a guy named Senator Queen. [*He is in the cell next to* YANK's. *There is a rustling of paper.*] Wait'll I see if I got light enough and I'll read you. Listen. [*He reads.*] "There is a menace existing in the country today which threatens the vitals of our fair Republic—as foul a menace against the very life-blood of the American Eagle as was the foul conspiracy of Cataline against the eagles of ancient Rome!"

VOICE: [*disgustedly*] Aw, hell! Tell him to salt de tail of dat eagle!

VOICE: [*reading*] "I refer to that devil's brew of rascals, jailbirds, murderers and cutthroats who libel all honest working men by calling themselves the Industrial Workers of the World; but in the light of their nefarious plots, I call them the Industrious *Wreckers* of the World!"

YANK: [*with vengeful satisfaction*] Wreckers, dat's de right dope! Dat belongs! Me for dem!

VOICE: Ssshh! [*reading*] "This fiendish organization is a foul ulcer on the fair body of our Democracy—"

VOICE: Democracy, hell! Give him the boid, fellers—the raspberry! [*They do.*]

VOICE: Ssshh! [*reading*] "Like Cato I say to this Senate, the I.W.W. must be destroyed! For they represent an ever-present dagger pointed at the heart of the greatest nation the world has ever known, where all men are born free and equal, with equal opportunities to all, where the Founding Fathers have guaranteed to each one happiness, where Truth, Honor, Liberty, Justice, and the Brotherhood of Man are a religion absorbed with one's mother's milk, taught at our father's knee, sealed, signed, and stamped upon the glorious Constitution of these United States!" [*a perfect storm of hisses, catcalls, boos, and hard laughter*]

VOICES: [*scornfully*] Hurrah for de Fort' of July!

Pass de hat!

Liberty!

Justice!

Honor!

Opportunity!

Brotherhood!

ALL: [*with abysmal scorn*] Aw, hell!

VOICE: Give that Queen Senator guy the bark! All togedder now—one—two—tree—[*a terrific chorus of barking and yapping*]

GUARD: [*from a distance*] Quiet there, youse—or I'll git the hose.

       [*The noise subsides.*]

YANK: [*with growling rage*] I'd like to catch dat senator guy alone for a second. I'd loin him some trute!

VOICE: Ssshh! Here's where he gits down to cases on the Wobblies. [*reads*] "They plot with fire in one hand and dynamite in the other. They stop not before murder to gain their ends, nor at the outraging of defenseless womanhood. They would tear down society, put the lowest scum in the seats of the mighty, turn Almighty God's revealed plan for the world topsy-turvy, and make of our sweet and lovely civilization a shambles, a desolation where man, God's masterpiece, would soon degenerate back to the ape!"

VOICE: [*to* YANK] Hey, you guy. There's your ape stuff again.

YANK: [*with a growl of fury*] I got him. So dey blow up tings, do dey? Dey turn tings round, do dey? Hey, lend me dat paper, will yuh?

VOICE: Sure. Give it to him. On'y keep it to yourself, see. We don't wanter listen to no more of that slop.

VOICE: Here you are. Hide it under your mattress.

YANK: [*reaching out*] Tanks. I can't read much but I kin manage. [*He sits, the paper in the hand at his side, in the attitude of Rodin's "The Thinker." A pause. Several snores from down the corridor. Suddenly* YANK *jumps to his feet with a furious groan as if some appalling thought had crashed on him—bewilderedly.*] Sure—her old man—president of de Steel Trust—makes half de steel in de world—steel—where I tought I belonged—drivin' trou—movin'—in dat—to make *her*—and cage me in for her to spit on! Christ! [*He shakes the bars of his cell door till the whole tier trembles. Irritated, protesting exclamations from those awakened or trying to get to sleep.*] He made dis—dis cage! Steel! *It* don't belong, dat's what! Cages, cells, locks, bolts, bars—dat's what it means!—holdin' me down wit him at de top! But I'll drive trou! Fire, dat melts it! I'll be fire—under de heap—fire dat never goes out—hot as hell—breakin' out in de night—[*While he has been saying this last he has shaken his cell door to a clanging accompaniment. As he comes to the "breakin' out" he seizes one bar with both hands and, putting his two feet up against the others so that his position is parallel to the floor like a monkey's, he gives a great wrench backwards. The bar bends like a licorice stick under his tremendous strength. Just at this moment the* PRISON GUARD *rushes in, dragging a hose behind him.*]

GUARD: [*angrily*] I'll loin youse bums to wake me up! [*sees* YANK] Hello, it's you, huh? Got the D. Ts., hey? Well, I'll cure 'em. I'll drown your snakes for yuh! [*noticing the bar*] Hell, look at dat bar bended! On'y a bug is strong enough for dat!

YANK: [*glaring at him*] Or a hairy ape, yuh big yellow bum! Look out! Here I come! [*He grabs another bar.*]

GUARD: [*scared now—yelling off left*] Toin de hose on, Ben—Full pressure! And call de others—and a straitjacket!

        [*The curtain is falling. As it hides* YANK *from view, there is a splattering smash as the stream of water hits the steel of* YANK's *cell.*]

CURTAIN

SCENE VII

Nearly a month later. An I. W. W. local near the waterfront, showing the interior of a front room on the ground floor, and the street outside. Moonlight on the narrow street, buildings massed in black shadow. The interior of the room, which is general assembly room, office, and reading room, resembles some dingy settlement boys' club. A desk and high stool are in one corner. A table with papers, stacks of pamphlets, chairs about it, is at center. The whole is decidedly cheap, banal, commonplace and unmysterious as a room could well be. The SECRETARY *is perched on the stool making entries in a large ledger. An eye shade casts his face into shadows. Eight or ten men, longshoremen, ironworkers, and the like, are grouped about the table. Two are playing checkers. One is writing a letter. Most of them are smoking pipes. A big signboard is on the wall at the rear, "Industrial Workers of the World—Local No. 57."*

        [YANK *comes down the street outside. He is dressed as in Scene Five. He moves cautiously, mysteriously. He comes to a point opposite the door; tiptoes softly up to it, listens, is impressed by the silence within, knocks carefully, as if he were guessing at the password to some secret rite. Listens. No answer. Knocks again a bit louder. No answer. Knocks impatiently, much louder.*]

SECRETARY: [*turning around on his stool*] What the hell is that—someone knocking? [*shouts*] Come in, why don't you?

        [*All the men in the room look up.* YANK *opens the door slowly, gingerly, as if afraid of an ambush. He looks around for secret doors, mystery, is taken aback by the commonplaceness of the room and the men in it, thinks he may have gotten in the wrong place, then sees the signboard on the wall and is reassured.*]

YANK: [*blurts out*] Hello.

MEN: [*reservedly*] Hello.

YANK: [*more easily*] I tought I'd bumped into de wrong dump.

SECRETARY: [*scrutinizing him carefully*] Maybe you have. Are you a member?

YANK: Naw, not yet. Dat's what I come for—to join.

SECRETARY: That's easy. What's your job—longshore?

YANK: Naw. Fireman—stoker on de liners.

SECRETARY: [*with satisfaction*] Welcome to our city. Glad to know you people are waking up at last. We haven't got many members in your line.

YANK: Naw. Dey're all dead to de woild.

SECRETARY: Well, you can help to wake 'em. What's your name? I'll make out your card.

YANK: [*confused*] Name? Lemme tink.

SECRETARY: [*sharply*] Don't you know your own name?

YANK: Sure; but I been just Yank for so long—Bob, dat's it—Bob Smith.

SECRETARY: [*writing*] Robert Smith. [*fills out the rest of card*] Here you are. Cost you half a dollar.

YANK: Is dat all—four bits? Dat's easy. [*gives the* SECRETARY *the money*]

SECRETARY: [*throwing it in drawer*] Thanks. Well, make yourself at home. No introductions needed. There's literature on the table. Take some of those pamphlets with you to distribute aboard ship. They may bring results. Sow the seed, only go about it right. Don't get caught and fired. We got plenty out of work. What we need is men who can hold their jobs—and work for us at the same time.

YANK: Sure. [*But he still stands, embarrassed and uneasy.*]

SECRETARY: [*looking at him—curiously*] What did you knock for? Think we had a coon in uniform to open doors?

YANK: Naw. I tought it was locked—and dat yuh'd wanter give me the once-over trou a peep-hole or somep'n to see if I was right.

SECRETARY: [*alert and suspicious but with an easy laugh*] Think we were running a crap game? That door is never locked. What put that in your nut?

YANK: [*with a knowing grin, convinced that this is all camouflage, a part of the secrecy*] Dis burg is full of bulls, ain't it?

SECRETARY: [*sharply*] What have the cops got to do with us? We're breaking no laws.

YANK: [*with a knowing wink*] Sure. Youse wouldn't for woilds. Sure. I'm wise to dat.

SECRETARY: You seem to be wise to a lot of stuff none of us knows about.

YANK: [*with another wink*] Aw, dat's aw right, see. [*then made a bit resentful by the suspicious glances from all sides*] Aw, can it! Youse needn't put me trou de toid degree. Can't youse see I belong? Sure! I'm reg'lar. I'll stick, get me? I'll shoot de woiks for youse. Dat's why I wanted to join in.

SECRETARY: [*breezily, feeling him out*] That's the right spirit. Only are you sure you understand what you've joined? It's all plain and above board; still, some guys get a wrong slant on us. [*sharply*] What's your notion of the purpose of the I.W.W.?

YANK: Aw, I know all about it.

SECRETARY: [*sarcastically*] Well, give us some of your valuable information.

YANK: [*cunningly*] I know enough not to speak outa my toin. [*then resentfully again*] Aw, say! I'm reg'lar. I'm wise to de game. I know yuh got to watch your step wit a stranger. For all youse know, I might be a plainclothes dick, or somep'n, dat's what yuh're tinkin', huh? Aw, forget it! I belong, see? Ask any guy down to de docks if I don't.

SECRETARY: Who said you didn't?

YANK: After I'm 'nitiated, I'll show yuh.

SECRETARY: [*astounded*] Initiated? There's no initiation.

YANK: [*disappointed*] Ain't there no password—no grip nor nothin'?

SECRETARY: What'd you think this is—the Elks—or the Black Hand?

YANK: De Elks, hell! De Black Hand, dey're a lot of yellow back-stickin' Ginees. Naw. Dis is a man's gang, ain't it?

SECRETARY: You said it! That's why we stand on our two feet in the open. We got no secrets.

YANK: [*surprised but admiringly*] Yuh mean to say yuh always run wide open—like dis?

SECRETARY: Exactly.

YANK: Den yuh sure got your noive wit youse!

SECRETARY: [*sharply*] Just what was it made you want to join us? Come out with that straight.

YANK: Yuh call me? Well, I got noive, too! Here's my hand. Yuh wanter blow tings up, don't yuh? Well, dat's me! I belong!

SECRETARY: [*with pretended carelessness*] You mean change the unequal conditions of society by legitimate direct action—or with dynamite?

YANK: Dynamite! Blow it offen de Oith—steel—all de cages—all de factories, steamers, buildings, jails—de Steel Trust and all dat makes it go.

SECRETARY: So—that's your idea, eh? And did you have any special job in that line you wanted to propose to us? [*He makes a sign to the men, who get up cautiously one by one and group behind* YANK.]

YANK: [*boldly*] Sure, I'll come out wit it. I'll show youse I'm one of de gang. Dere's dat millionaire guy, Douglas—

SECRETARY: President of the Steel Trust, you mean? Do you want to assassinate him?

YANK: Naw, dat don't get yuh nothin'. I mean blow up de factory, de woiks, where he makes de steel. Dat's what I'm after—to blow up de steel, knock all de steel in de woild up to de moon. Dat'll fix tings! [*eagerly, with a touch of bravado*] I'll do it by me lonesome! I'll show yuh! Tell me where his woiks is, how to get there, all de dope. Gimme de stuff, de old butter—and watch me do de rest! Watch de smoke and see it move! I don't give a damn if dey nab me—long as it's done! I'll soive life for it— and give 'em de laugh! [*half to himself*] And I'll write her a letter and tell her de hairy ape done it. Dat'll square tings.

SECRETARY: [*stepping away from* YANK] Very interesting. [*He gives a signal. The men, huskies all, throw themselves on* YANK *and before he knows it they have his legs and arms pinioned. But he is too flabbergasted to make a struggle, anyway. They feel him over for weapons.*]

MAN: No gat, no knife. Shall we give him what's what and put the boots to him?

SECRETARY: No. He isn't worth the trouble we'd get into. He's too stupid. [*He comes closer and laughs mockingly in* YANK's *face.*] Ho-ho! By God, this is the biggest joke they've put up on us yet. Hey, you Joke! Who sent you—Burns or Pinkerton? No, by God, you're such a bonehead I'll bet you're in the Secret Service! Well, you dirty spy, you rotten agent-provocateur, you can go back and tell whatever skunk is paying you blood-money for betraying your brothers that he's wasting his coin. You couldn't catch a cold. And tell him that all he'll ever get on us, or ever has got, is just his own sneaking plots that he's framed up to put us in jail. We are what our manifesto says we are, neither more nor less—and we'll give him a copy of that any time he calls. And as for you—[*He glares scornfully at* YANK, *who is sunk in an oblivious stupor.*] Oh, hell, what's the use of talking? You're a brainless ape.

YANK: [*aroused by the word to fierce-but-futile struggles*] What's dat, yuh Sheeny bum, yuh!

SECRETARY: Throw him out, boys.

[*In spite of his struggles, this is done with gusto and éclat. Propelled by several parting kicks,* YANK *lands sprawling in the middle of the narrow cobbled street. With a growl he starts to get up and storm the closed door, but stops bewildered by the confusions in his brain, pathetically impotent. He sits there brooding, in as near to the attitude of Rodin's "The Thinker" as he can get in his position.*]

YANK: [*bitterly*] So dem boids don't tink I belong, neider. Aw, to hell wit 'em! Dey're in de wrong pew—de same old bull—soapboxes and Salvation Army—no guts! Cut out an hour offen de job a day and make me happy! Gimme a dollar more a day and make me happy! Tree square a day, and cauliflowers in de front yard—ekal rights—a woman and kids—a lousy vote—and I'm all fixed for Jesus, huh? Aw, hell! What does dat get yuh? Dis ting's in your inside, but it ain't your belly. Feedin' your face—sinkers and coffee—dat don't touch it. It's way down—at de bottom. Yuh can't grab it, and yuh can't stop it. It moves, and everything moves. It stops and de whole woild stops. Dat's me now—I don't tick, see?—I'm a busted Ingersoll, dat's what. Steel was me, and I owned de woild. Now I ain't steel, and de woild owns me. Aw, hell! I can't see—it's all dark, get me? It's all wrong! [*He turns a bitter mocking face up like an ape gibbering at the moon.*] Say, youse up dere, Man in de Moon, yuh look so wise, gimme de answer, huh? Slip me de inside dope, de information right from de stable—where do I get off at, huh?

A POLICEMAN: [*who has come up the street in time to hear this last—with grim humor*] You'll get off at the station, you boob, if you don't get up out of that and keep movin'.

YANK: [*looking up at him—with a hard, bitter laugh*] Sure! Lock me up! Put me in a cage! Dat's de on'y answer yuh know. G'wan, lock me up!

POLICEMAN: What you been doin'?

YANK: Enuf to gimme life for! I was born, see? Sure, dat's de charge. Write it in de blotter. I was born, get me!

POLICEMAN: [*jocosely*] God pity your old woman! [*then matter-of-fact*] But I've no time for kidding. You're soused. I'd run you in but it's too long a walk to the station. Come on now, get up, or I'll fan your ears with this club! Beat it now! [*He hauls* YANK *to his feet.*]

YANK: [*in a vague mocking tone*] Say, where do I go from here?

POLICEMAN: [*giving him a push—with a grin, indifferently*] Go to hell.

CURTAIN

SCENE VIII

Twilight of the next day. The monkey house at the zoo. One spot of clear gray light falls on the front of one cage so that the interior can be seen. The other cages are vague, shrouded in shadow from which chatterings pitched in a conversational tone can be heard. On the one cage a sign from which the word "gorilla" stands out. The gigantic animal himself is seen squatting on his haunches on a bench in much the same attitude as Rodin's "The Thinker." YANK *enters from the left. Immediately a chorus of angry chattering and screeching breaks out. The gorilla turns his eyes but makes no sound or move.*

YANK: [*with a hard, bitter laugh*] Welcome to your city, huh? Hail, hail, de gang's all here! [*At the sound of his voice the chattering dies away into an attentive silence.* YANK *walks up to the gorilla's cage and, leaning over the railing, stares in at its occupant, who stares back at him, silent and motionless. There is a pause of dead stillness. Then* YANK *begins to talk in a friendly, confidential tone, half-mockingly, but with a deep undercurrent of sympathy.*] Say, yuh're some hard-lookin' guy, ain't yuh? I seen lots of tough nuts dat de gang called gorillas, but yuh're de foist real one I ever seen. Some chest yuh got, and shoulders, and dem arms and mitts! I bet yuh got a punch in eider fist dat'd knock 'em silly! [*This with genuine admiration. The gorilla, as if he understood, stands upright, swelling out his chest and pounding on it with his fist.* YANK *grins sympathetically.*] Sure, I get yuh. Yuh challenge de whole woild, huh? Yuh got what I was sayin' even if yuh muffed de woids. [*then bitterness creeping in*] And why wouldn't yuh get me? Ain't we both members of de same club—de Hairy Apes? [*They stare at each other—a pause—then* YANK *goes on slowly and bitterly.*] So yuh're what she seen when she looked at me, de white-faced tart! I was you to her, get me? On'y outa de cage— broke out—free to moider her, see? Sure! Dat's what she tought. She wasn't wise dat I was in a cage, too—worser'n yours—sure—a damn sight—'cause you got some chanct to bust loose—but me— [*He grows confused.*] Aw, hell! It's all wrong, ain't it? [*a pause*] I s'pose yuh wanter know what I'm doin' here, huh? I been warmin' a bench down to de Battery—ever since last night. Sure. I seen de sun come up. Dat was pretty, too—all red and pink and green. I was lookin' at de skyscrapers—steel— and all de ships comin' in, sailin' out, all over de Oith—and dey was steel, too. De sun was warm, dey wasn't no clouds, and dere was a breeze blowin'. Sure, it was great stuff. I got it aw right—what Paddy said about dat bein' de right dope—on'y I couldn't get *in* it, see? I couldn't belong in dat. It was over my head. And I kept tin- kin' and den I beat it up here to see what youse was like. And I waited till dey was all gone to git yuh alone. Say, how d'yuh feel sittin' in dat pen all de time, havin' to stand for 'em comin' and starin' at yuh—de white-faced, skinny tarts and de boobs what marry 'em —makin' fun of yuh, laughin' at yuh, gittin' scared of yuh—damn 'em! [*He pounds on the rail with his fist. The gorilla rattles the bars of his cage and snarls. All the other monkeys set up an angry chattering in the darkness.* YANK *goes on excitedly.*] Sure! Dat's de way it hits me, too. On'y yuh're lucky, see? Yuh don't belong wit 'em and yuh know it. But me, I belong wit 'em —but I don't, see? Dey don't belong wit me, dat's what. Get me? Tinkin' is hard—[*He passes one hand across his forehead with a painful gesture. The gorilla growls impatiently.* YANK *goes on gropingly.*] It's dis way, what I'm drivin' at. Youse can sit and dope dream in de past, green woods, de jun- gle, and de rest of it. Den yuh belong and dey don't. Den yuh kin laugh at 'em, see? Yuh're de champ of de woild. But me—I ain't got no past to tink in, nor nothin' dat's comin', on'y what's now—and dat don't belong. Sure, you're de best off! Yuh can't tink, can yuh? Yuh can't talk, neider. But I kin make a bluff at talkin' and tinkin'— a'most git away wit it—a'most! —and dat's where de joker comes in. [*He laughs.*] I ain't on Oith and I ain't in heaven, get me? I'm in de middle tryin' to separate 'em, takin' all de woise punches from bot' of 'em. Maybe dat's what dey call hell, huh? But you, yuh're at de bottom. You belong! Sure! Yuh're de on'y one in de woild dat does, yuh lucky stiff! [*The gorilla growls proudly.*] And dat's why dey gotter put yuh in a cage, see? [*The gorilla roars angrily.*] Sure! Yuh get me. It beats it when you try to tink it or talk it—it's way down—deep—behind—you 'n' me we feel it. Sure! Bot' members of dis club! [*He laughs—then in a savage tone.*] What de hell! T' hell wit it! A little action, dat's our meat! Dat belongs! Knock 'em down and keep bustin' 'em till dey croak yuh wit a gat—wit steel! Sure! Are yuh game? Dey've looked at youse, ain't dey—in a cage? Wanter git even? Wanter wind up like a sport 'stead of croakin' slow in dere? [*The gorilla roars an emphatic affirmative.* YANK *goes on with a sort of furious exultation.*] Sure! Yuh're reg'lar! You'll stick to de finish! Me 'n' you, huh?— bot' members of this club! We'll put up one last star bout dat'll knock 'em offen deir seats! Dey'll have to make de cages stronger after we're trou! [*The gorilla is straining at his bars, growling, hopping from one foot to the other.* YANK *takes a jimmy from under his coat and forces the lock on the cage door. He throws this open.*] Pardon from de gov- ernor! Step out and shake hands. I'll take yuh for a walk down Fif' Avenoo. We'll knock 'em offen de Oith and croak wit' de band playin'. Come on, Brother. [*The gorilla scrambles gingerly out of his cage. Goes to* YANK *and stands looking at him.* YANK *keeps his mocking tone—holds out his hand.*] Shake—de secret grip of our order. [*Something, the tone of mockery, perhaps, suddenly outrages the animal. With a spring he wraps his huge arms around* YANK *in a murderous hug. There is a cracking snap of crushed ribs—a gasping cry, still mocking, from* YANK.] Hey, I didn't say kiss me! [*The gorilla lets the crushed body slip to the floor, stands over it uncertainly, considering; then picks it up, throws it in the cage, shuts the door, and shuffles off menacingly into the darkness at left. A great uproar of frightened chattering and whimpering comes from the other cages. Then* YANK *moves, groaning, opening his eyes, and there is silence. He mutters painfully.*] Say—dey oughter match him—wit Zybszko. He got me, aw right. I'm trou. Even him didn't tink I belonged. [*then, with sudden passionate despair*] Christ, where do I get off at? Where do I fit in? [*checking himself as suddenly*] Aw, what de hell! No squawkin', see! No quittin', get me! Croak wit your boots on! [*He grabs hold of the bars of the cage and hauls himself painfully to his feet—looks around him bewilderedly—forces a mocking laugh.*] In de cage, huh? [*in the strident tones of a circus broker*] Ladies and gents, step forward and take a slant at de one and only—[*his voice weakening*] —one and original—Hairy Ape from de wilds of—

> [*He slips in a heap on the floor and dies. The monkeys set up a chattering, whimpering wail. And, perhaps, the Hairy Ape at last belongs.*]

CURTAIN

The Good Woman of Setzuan

(1940)

he expressionists' idealistic dream of transforming humanity foundered in disillusionment during the 1920s. Some writers came to believe that society could be improved only by adopting a program of concrete political action, and in the theatre they sought to focus attention on the great difference between human needs and existing conditions. Attempts to use the theatre as a weapon took several forms, but the most significant was Epic Theatre, exemplified in the plays of Bertolt Brecht. Brecht used many of the devices of expressionist drama, such as episodic structure, unity derived from theme or thesis, and nonillusionistic visual elements. But Brecht, unlike the expressionists, did not suggest that external appearance is untruthful or insignificant; rather, he wished to provoke audiences to reflect on the immediate world and its injustices, and he believed that he could do so most effectively if his audience remained conscious that it was in a theatre. Rejecting the theatre of illusion on the basis that it merely lulls the spectator's critical faculties, Brecht devised several techniques (such as projected captions, songs, and presentational acting) to interrupt the empathetic response and intensify the spectator's awareness of social, economic, and political injustices. It was his hope that the spectator would become aware of the need for change outside the theatre.

The Good Woman of Setzuan is a parable about the difficulties of remaining good under existing social and economic conditions. The "good" person, Shen Te, is generous and well-intentioned, but she soon finds herself exploited and betrayed. Her solution is to disguise herself as her cousin Shui Ta—that is, to let the exploitative side of her character direct her actions. As time passes, she finds herself more and more frequently forced into taking on the role of the ruthless capitalist. Brecht uses this device to suggest the progressive deterioration of morality. The play ends in a stalemate, for the gods leave Shen Te with the same simplistic message they delivered in the prologue—"Be good"—and she is no nearer to knowing how to accomplish this under the present economic system. Throughout the play Brecht skillfully and persistently reminds the audience that Shen Te's predicament is a universal human condition—and one that might be solved by taking the right economic and political action.

The Good Woman of Setzuan by Bertolt Brecht, translated by Eric Bentley, in Parables for the Theatre. © 1947, 1956, 1961 by Eric Bentley. Published by and reprinted by permission of University of Minnesota Press.

The Good Woman of Setzuan

REVISED ENGLISH VERSION BY ERIC BENTLEY

Characters

WONG, *a water seller*
THREE GODS
SHEN TE, *a prostitute, later a shopkeeper*
MRS. SHIN, *former owner of Shen Te's shop*
A FAMILY OF EIGHT *(husband, wife, brother, sister-in-law, grandfather, nephew, niece, boy)*
AN UNEMPLOYED MAN
A CARPENTER
MRS. MI TZU, *Shen Te's landlady*
YANG SUN, *an unemployed pilot, later a factory manager*
AN OLD WHORE
A POLICEMAN
AN OLD MAN
AN OLD WOMAN, *his wife*
MR. SHU FU, *a barber*
MRS. YANG, *mother of Yang Sun*
GENTLEMEN, VOICES, CHILDREN *(three), etc.*

PROLOGUE

At the gates of the half-Westernized city of Setzuan. Evening.

[WONG *the water seller introduces himself to the audience.*]

WONG: I sell water here in the city of Setzuan. It isn't easy. When water is scarce, I have long distances to go in search of it, and when it is plentiful, I have no income. But in our part of the world there is nothing unusual about poverty. Many people think only the gods can save the situation. And I hear from a cattle merchant—who travels a lot— that some of the highest gods are on their way at this very moment. Informed sources have it that heaven is quite disturbed at all the complaining. I've been coming out here to the city gates for three days now to bid these gods welcome. I want to be the first to greet them. What about those fellows over there? No, no, they *work*. And that one there has ink on his fingers, he's no god, he must be a clerk from the cement factory. *Those* two are another story. They look as though they'd like to beat you. But gods don't need to beat you, do they?

[THREE GODS *appear.*]

What about those three? Old-fashioned clothes—dust on their feet—they must be gods! [*He throws himself at their feet.*] Do with me what you will, illustrious ones!

FIRST GOD: [*with an ear trumpet*] Ah! [*He is pleased.*] So we are expected?

WONG: [*giving them water*] Oh, yes. And I *knew* you'd come.

FIRST GOD: We need somewhere to stay the night. You know of a place?

WONG: The whole town is at your service, illustrious ones! What sort of a place would you like?

[*The* GODS *eye each other.*]

FIRST GOD: Just try the first house you come to, my son.

WONG: That would be Mr. Fo's place.

FIRST GOD: Mr. Fo.

WONG: One moment! [*He knocks at the first house.*]

VOICE FROM MR. FO'S: No!

[WONG *returns a little nervously.*]

WONG: It's too bad. Mr. Fo isn't in. And his servants don't dare do a thing without his consent. He'll have a fit when he finds out who they turned away, won't he?

FIRST GOD: [*smiling*] He will, won't he?

WONG: One moment! The next house is Mr. Cheng's. Won't he be thrilled!

FIRST GOD: Mr. Cheng.

[WONG *knocks.*]

VOICE FROM MR. CHENG'S: Keep your gods. We have our own troubles!

WONG: [*back with the* GODS] Mr. Cheng is very sorry, but he has a houseful of relations. I think some of them are a bad lot, and naturally, he wouldn't like you to see them.

THIRD GOD: Are we so terrible?

WONG: Well, only with bad people, of course. Everyone knows the province of Kwan is always having floods.

SECOND GOD: Really? How's that?

WONG: Why, because they're so irreligious.

SECOND GOD: Rubbish. It's because they neglected the dam.

FIRST GOD: [*to* SECOND] Sh! [*to* WONG] You're still in hopes, aren't you, my son?

WONG: Certainly. All Setzuan is competing for the honor! What happened up to now is pure coincidence. I'll be back. [*He walks away, but then stands undecided.*]

SECOND GOD: What did I tell you?

THIRD GOD: It *could* be pure coincidence.

SECOND GOD: The same coincidence in Shun, Kwan, and Setzuan? People just aren't religious any more, let's face the fact. Our mission has failed!

FIRST GOD: Oh come, we might run into a good person any minute.

THIRD GOD: How did the resolution read? [*unrolling a scroll and reading from it*] "The world can stay as it is if enough people are found [*at the word "found" he unrolls it a little more*] living lives worthy of human beings." Good people, that is. Well, what about this water seller himself? *He's* good, or I'm very much mistaken.

SECOND GOD: You're very much mistaken. When he gave us a drink, I had the impression there was something odd about the cup. Well, look! [*He shows the cup to the* FIRST GOD.]

FIRST GOD: A false bottom!

SECOND GOD: The man is a swindler.

FIRST GOD: Very well, count *him* out. That's one man among millions. And as a matter of fact, we only need one on *our* side. These atheists are saying, "The world must be changed because no one can *be* good and *stay* good." No one, eh? I say: let us find one—just one—and we have those fellows where we want them!

THIRD GOD: [*to* WONG] Water seller, is it so hard to find a place to stay?

WONG: Nothing could be easier. It's just me. I don't go about it right.

THIRD GOD: Really?

> [*He returns to the others.* A GENTLEMAN *passes by.*]

WONG: Oh dear, they're catching on. [*He accosts the* GENTLEMAN.] Excuse the intrusion, dear sir, but three gods have just turned up. Three of the very highest. They need a place for the night. Seize this rare opportunity—to have real gods as your guests!

GENTLEMAN: [*laughing*] A new way of finding free rooms for a gang of crooks.

> [*Exit* GENTLEMAN.]

WONG: [*shouting at him*] Godless rascal! Have you no religion, gentleman of Setzuan? [*pause*] Patience, illustrious ones! [*pause*] There's only one person left. Shen Te, the prostitute. She *can't* say no. [*calls up to a window*] Shen Te!

> [SHEN TE *opens the shutters and looks out.*]

WONG: Shen Te, it's Wong. They're here, and nobody wants them. Will you take them?

SHEN TE: Oh, no, Wong, I'm expecting a gentleman.

WONG: Can't you forget about him for tonight?

SHEN TE: The rent has to be paid by tomorrow or I'll be out on the street.

WONG: This is no time for calculation, Shen Te.

SHEN TE: Stomachs rumble even on the Emperor's birthday, Wong.

WONG: Setzuan is one big dunghill!

SHEN TE: Oh, very well! I'll hide till my gentleman has come and gone. Then I'll take them. [*She disappears.*]

WONG: They mustn't see her gentleman or they'll know what she is.

FIRST GOD: [*who hasn't heard any of this*] I think it's hopeless.

> [*They approach* WONG.]

WONG: [*jumping, as he finds them behind him*] A room has been found, illustrious ones! [*He wipes sweat off his brow.*]

SECOND GOD: Oh, good.

THIRD GOD: Let's see it.

WONG: [*nervously*] Just a minute. It has to be tidied up a bit.

THIRD GOD: Then we'll sit down here and wait.

WONG: [*still more nervous*] No, no! [*holding himself back*] Too much traffic, you know.

THIRD GOD: [*with a smile*] Of course, if you *want* us to move.

> [*They retire a little. They sit on a doorstep.* WONG *sits on the ground.*]

WONG: [*after a deep breath*] You'll be staying with a single girl—the finest human being in Setzuan!

THIRD GOD: That's nice.

WONG: [*to the audience*] They gave me such a look when I picked up my cup just now.

THIRD GOD: You're worn out, Wong.

WONG: A little, maybe.

FIRST GOD: Do people have a hard time of it?

WONG: The good ones do.

FIRST GOD: What about yourself?

WONG: You mean I'm not good. That's true. And I don't have an easy time, either!

> [*During this dialogue, a* GENTLEMAN *has turned up in front of* SHEN TE's *house, and has whistled several times. Each time* WONG *has given a start.*]

THIRD GOD: [*to* WONG, *softly*] Psst! I think he's gone now.

WONG: [*confused and surprised*] Ye-e-es.

> [*The* GENTLEMAN *has left now, and* SHEN TE *has come down in the street.*]

SHEN TE: [*softly*] Wong!

> [*Getting no answer, she goes off down the street.* WONG *arrives just too late, forgetting his carrying pole.*]

WONG: [*softly*] Shen Te! Shen Te! [*to himself*] So she's gone off to earn the rent. Oh dear, I can't go to the gods *again* with no room to offer them. Having failed in the service of the gods, I shall run to my den in the sewer pipe down by the river and hide from their sight!

> [*He rushes off.* SHEN TE *returns, looking for him, but finding the* GODS. *She stops in confusion.*]

SHEN TE: You are the illustrious ones? My name is Shen Te. It would please me very much if my simple room could be of use to you.

THIRD GOD: Where is the water seller, Miss . . . Shen Te?

SHEN TE: I missed him, somehow.

FIRST GOD: Oh, he probably thought you weren't coming, and was afraid of telling us.

THIRD GOD: [*picking up the carrying pole*] We'll leave this with you. He'll be needing it.

> [*Led by* SHEN TE, *they go into the house. It grows dark, then light. Dawn. Again escorted by* SHEN TE, *who leads them through the half-light with a little lamp, the* GODS *take their leave.*]

FIRST GOD: Thank you, thank you, dear Shen Te, for your elegant hospitality! We shall not forget! And give our thanks to the water seller—he showed us a good human being.

SHEN TE: Oh, *I'm* not good. Let me tell you something: when Wong asked me to put you up, I hesitated.

FIRST GOD: It's all right to hesitate if you then go ahead! And in giving us that room you did much more than you knew. You proved that good people still exist, a point that has been disputed of late—even in heaven. Farewell!

SECOND GOD: Farewell!

THIRD GOD: Farewell!

SHEN TE: Stop, illustrious ones! I'm not sure you're right. I'd like to be good, it's true, but there's the rent to pay. And that's not all: I sell myself for a living. Even so I can't make ends meet, there's too much competition. I'd like to honor my father and mother and speak nothing but the truth and not covet my neighbor's house. I should love to stay with one man. But how? How is it done? Even breaking a few of your command-ments, I can hardly manage.

FIRST GOD: [*clearing his throat*] These thoughts are but, um, the misgivings of an unusu-ally good woman!

THIRD GOD: Good-bye, Shen Te! Give our regards to the water seller!

SECOND GOD: And above all: be good! Farewell!

FIRST GOD: Farewell!

THIRD GOD: Farewell!

> [*They start to wave good-bye.*]

SHEN TE: But everything is so expensive. I don't feel sure I can do it!

SECOND GOD: That's not in our sphere. We never meddle with economics.

THIRD GOD: One moment. [*They stop.*] Isn't it true she might do better if she had more money?

SECOND GOD: Come, come! How could we ever account for it Up Above?

FIRST GOD: Oh, there are ways. [*They put their heads together and confer in dumb show. To* SHEN TE, *with embarrassment:*] As you say you can't pay your rent, well, um, we're not paupers, so of course we *insist* on paying for our room. [*Awkwardly thrusting money into her hand.*] There! [*quickly*] But don't tell anyone! The incident is open to misinterpretation.

SECOND GOD: It certainly is!

FIRST GOD: [*defensively*] But there's no law against it! It was never decreed that a god must-n't pay hotel bills!

> [*The* GODS *leave.*]

SCENE I————*A small tobacco shop. The shop is not as yet completely furnished and hasn't started doing business.*

SHEN TE: [*to the audience*] It's three days now since the gods left. When they wanted to pay for the room, I looked down at my hand, and there was more than a thousand silver dollars! I bought a tobacco shop with the money, and moved in yesterday. I don't own the building, of course, but I can pay the rent, and I hope to do a lot of good here. Beginning with Mrs. Shin, who's just coming across the square with her pot. She had the shop before me, and yesterday she dropped in to ask for rice for her children. [*Enter* MRS. SHIN. *Both women bow.*] How do you do, Mrs. Shin.

MRS. SHIN: How do you do, Miss Shen Te. You like your new home?

SHEN TE: Indeed, yes. Did your children have a good night?

MRS. SHIN: In that hovel? The youngest is coughing already.

SHEN TE: Oh, dear!

MRS. SHIN: You're going to learn a thing or two in these slums.

SHEN TE: Slums? That's not what you said when you sold me the shop!

MRS. SHIN: Now don't start nagging! Robbing me and my innocent children of their home and then calling it a slum! That's the limit! [*She weeps.*]

SHEN TE: [*tactfully*] I'll get your rice.

MRS. SHIN: And a little cash while you're at it.

SHEN TE: I'm afraid I haven't sold anything yet.

MRS. SHIN: [*screeching*] I've got to have it. Strip the clothes from my back and then cut my throat, will you? I know what I'll do: I'll dump my children on your doorstep! [*She snatches the pot out of* SHEN TE'S *hands.*]

SHEN TE: Please don't be angry. You'll spill the rice.

[*Enter an elderly* HUSBAND *and* WIFE *with their shabbily dressed* NEPHEW.]

WIFE: Shen Te, dear! You've come into money, they tell me. And we haven't a roof over our heads! A tobacco shop. We had one, too. But it's gone. Could we spend the night here, do you think?

NEPHEW: [*appraising the shop*] Not bad!

WIFE: He's our nephew. We're inseparable!

MRS. SHIN: And who are these . . . ladies and gentlemen?

SHEN TE: They put me up when I first came in from the country. [*to the audience*] Of course, when my small purse was empty, they put me out on the street, and they may be afraid I'll do the same to them. [*to the newcomers, kindly*] Come in, and welcome, though I've only one little room for you—it's behind the shop.

HUSBAND: That'll do. Don't worry.

WIFE: [*bringing* SHEN TE *some tea*] We'll stay over here, so we won't be in your way. Did you make it a tobacco shop in memory of your first real home? We can certainly give you a hint or two! That's one reason we came.

MRS. SHIN: [*to* SHEN TE] Very nice! As long as you have a few customers, too!

HUSBAND: Sh! A customer!

[*Enter an* UNEMPLOYED MAN, *in rags.*]

UNEMPLOYED MAN: Excuse me. I'm unemployed.

[MRS. SHIN *laughs.*]

SHEN TE: Can I help you?

UNEMPLOYED MAN: Have you any damaged cigarettes? I thought there might be some damage when you're unpacking.

WIFE: What nerve, begging for tobacco! [*rhetorically*] Why don't they ask for bread?

UNEMPLOYED MAN: Bread is expensive. One cigarette butt and I'll be a new man.

SHEN TE: [*giving him cigarettes*] That's very important—to be a new man. You'll be my first customer and bring me luck.

[*The* UNEMPLOYED MAN *quickly lights a cigarette, inhales, and goes off, coughing.*]

WIFE: Was that right, Shen Te, dear?

MRS. SHIN: If this is the opening of a shop, you can hold the closing at the end of the week.

HUSBAND: I bet he had money on him.

SHEN TE: Oh, no, he said he hadn't!

NEPHEW: How d'you know he wasn't lying?

SHEN TE: [*angrily*] How do you know he was?

WIFE: [*wagging her head*] You're too good, Shen Te, dear. If you're going to keep this shop, you'll have to learn to say no.

HUSBAND: Tell them the place isn't yours to dispose of. Belongs to . . . some relative who insists on all accounts being strictly in order. . . .

MRS. SHIN: That's right! What do you think you are—a philanthropist?

SHEN TE: [*laughing*] Very well, suppose I ask you for my rice back, Mrs. Shin?

WIFE: [*combatively, at* MRS. SHIN] So that's *her* rice?

[Enter the CARPENTER, *a small man.*]

MRS. SHIN: [*who, at the sight of him, starts to hurry away*] See you tomorrow, Miss Shen Te!

[*Exit* MRS. SHIN.]

CARPENTER: Mrs. Shin, it's you I want!

WIFE: [*to* SHEN TE] Has she some claim on you?

SHEN TE: She's hungry. That's a claim.

CARPENTER: Are you the new tenant? And filling up the shelves already? Well, they're not yours till they're paid for, ma'am. I'm the carpenter, so I should know.

SHEN TE: I took the shop "furnishings included."

CARPENTER: You're in league with that Mrs. Shin, of course. All right. I demand my hundred silver dollars.

SHEN TE: I'm afraid I haven't got a hundred silver dollars.

CARPENTER: Then you'll find it. Or I'll have you arrested.

WIFE: [*whispering to* SHEN TE] That relative, make it a cousin.

SHEN TE: Can't it wait till next month?

CARPENTER: No!

SHEN TE: Be a little patient, Mr. Carpenter, I can't settle all claims at once.

CARPENTER: Who's patient with me? [*He grabs a shelf from the wall.*] Pay up—or I take the shelves back!

WIFE: Shen Te! Dear! Why don't you let your . . . cousin settle this affair? [*to* CARPENTER] Put your claim in writing. Shen Te's cousin will see you get paid.

CARPENTER: [*derisively*] Cousin, eh?

HUSBAND: Cousin, yes.

CARPENTER: I know these cousins!

NEPHEW: Don't be silly. He's a personal friend of mine.

HUSBAND: What a man! Sharp as a razor!

CARPENTER: All right. I'll put my claim in writing. [*Puts shelf on floor, sits on it, writes out bill.*]

WIFE: [*to* SHEN TE] He'd tear the dress off your back to get his shelves. Never recognize a claim. That's my motto.

SHEN TE: He's done a job, and wants something in return. It's shameful that I can't give it to him. What will the gods say?

HUSBAND: You did your bit when you took *us* in.

[*Enter the* BROTHER, *limping, and the* SISTER-IN-LAW, *pregnant.*]

BROTHER: [*to* HUSBAND *and* WIFE] So this is where you're hiding out! There's family feeling for you! Leaving us on the corner!

WIFE: [*embarrassed, to* SHEN TE] It's my brother and his wife. [*to them*] Now stop grumbling, and sit quietly in that corner. [*to* SHEN TE] It can't be helped. She's in her fifth month.

SHEN TE: Oh yes. Welcome!

WIFE: [*to the couple*] Say "thank you." [*They mutter something.*] The cups are there. [*to* SHEN TE] Lucky you bought this shop when you did!

SHEN TE: [*laughing and bringing tea*] Lucky indeed!

[*Enter* MRS. MI TZU, *the landlady.*]

MRS. MI TZU: Miss Shen Te? I am Mrs. Mi Tzu, your landlady. I hope our relationship will be a happy one. I like to think I give my tenants modern, personalized service. Here is your lease. [*to the others, as* SHEN TE *reads the lease*] There's nothing like the opening of a little shop, is there? A moment of true beauty! [*she is looking around*] Not very much on the shelves, of course. But everything in the gods' good time! Where are your references, Miss Shen Te?

SHEN TE: Do I *have* to have references?

MRS. MI TZU: After all, I haven't a notion who you are!

HUSBAND: Oh, *we'd* be glad to vouch for Miss Shen Te! We'd go through fire for her!

MRS. MI TZU: And who may you be?

HUSBAND: [*stammering*] Ma Fu, tobacco dealer.

MRS. MI TZU: Where is your shop, Mr. . . . Ma Fu?

HUSBAND: Well, um, I haven't got a shop—I've just sold it.

MRS. MI TZU: I see. [*to* SHEN TE] Is there no one else that knows you?

WIFE: [*whispering to* SHEN TE] Your cousin! Your cousin!

MRS. MI TZU: This is a respectable house, Miss Shen Te. I never sign a lease without certain assurances.

SHEN TE: [*slowly, her eyes downcast*] I have . . . a cousin.

MRS. MI TZU: On the square? Let's go over and see him. What does he do?

SHEN TE: [*as before*] He lives . . . in another city.

WIFE: [*prompting*] Didn't you say he was in Shung?

SHEN TE: That's right. Shung.

HUSBAND: [*prompting*] I had his name on the tip of my tongue, Mr. . . .

SHEN TE: [*with an effort*] Mr. . . . Shui . . . Ta.

HUSBAND: That's it! Tall, skinny fellow!

SHEN TE: Shui Ta!

NEPHEW: [*to* CARPENTER] *You* were in touch with him, weren't you? About the shelves?

CARPENTER: [*surlily*] Give him this bill. [*He hands it over.*] I'll back in the morning. [*Exit* CARPENTER.]

NEPHEW: [*calling after him, but with his eyes on* MRS. MI TZU] Don't worry! Mr. Shui Ta pays on the nail!

MRS. MI TZU: [*looking closely at* SHEN TE] I'll be happy to make his acquaintance, Miss Shen Te. [*Exit* MRS. MI TZU.]

[*pause*]

WIFE: By tomorrow morning she'll know more about you than you do yourself.

SISTER-IN-LAW: [*to* NEPHEW] This thing isn't built to last.

[*Enter* GRANDFATHER.]

WIFE: It's Grandfather! [*to* SHEN TE] Such a good old soul!

[*The* BOY *enters.*]

BOY: [*over his shoulder*] Here they are!

WIFE: And the boy, how he's grown! But he always could eat enough for ten.

[*Enter the* NIECE.]

WIFE: [*to* SHEN TE] Our little niece from the country. There are more of us now than in your time. The less we had, the more there were of us; the more there were of us, the less we had. Give me the key. We must protect ourselves from unwanted guests. [*She takes the key and locks the door.*] Just make yourself at home. I'll light the little lamp.

NEPHEW: [*a big joke*] I hope her cousin doesn't drop in tonight! The strict Mr. Shui Ta! [SISTER-IN-LAW *laughs.*]

BROTHER: [*reaching for a cigarette*] One cigarette more or less . . .

HUSBAND: One cigarette more or less.
[*They pile into the cigarettes. The* BROTHER *hands a jug of wine round.*]

NEPHEW: Mr. Shui Ta'll pay for it!

GRANDFATHER: [*gravely, to* SHEN TE] How do you do?
[SHEN TE, *a little taken aback by the belatedness of the greeting, bows. She has the* CARPENTER's *bill in one hand, the landlady's lease in the other.*]

WIFE: How about a bit of song? To keep Shen Te's spirits up?

NEPHEW: Good idea. Grandfather, you start!

SONG OF THE SMOKE

GRANDFATHER:

> *I used to think (before old age beset me)*
> *That brains could fill the pantry of the poor.*
> *But where did all my cerebration get me?*
> *I'm just as hungry as I was before.*
> *So what's the use?*
> *See the smoke float free*
> *Into ever colder coldness!*
> *It's the same with me.*

HUSBAND:

> *The straight and narrow path leads to disaster*
> *And so the crooked path I tried to tread.*
> *That got me to disaster even faster.*
> *(They say we shall be happy when we're dead.)*
> *So what's the use?*
> *See the smoke float free*
> *Into ever colder coldness!*
> *It's the same with me.*

NIECE:

> *You older people, full of expectation,*
> *At any moment now you'll walk the plank!*
> *The future's for the younger generation!*
> *Yes, even if that future is a blank.*
> *So what's the use?*
> *See the smoke float free*
> *Into ever colder coldness!*
> *It's the same with me.*

NEPHEW: [*to the* BROTHER] Where'd you get that wine?

SISTER-IN-LAW: [*answering for the* BROTHER] He pawned the sack of tobacco.

HUSBAND: [*stepping in*] What? That tobacco was all we had to fall back on! You pig!

BROTHER: *You'd* call a man a pig because your wife was frigid! Did you refuse to drink it?
[*They fight. The shelves fall over.*]

SHEN TE: [*imploringly*] Oh don't! Don't break everything! Take it, take it, take it all, but don't destroy a gift from the gods!

WIFE: [*disparagingly*] This shop isn't big enough. I should never have mentioned it to Uncle and the others. When *they* arrive, it's going to be disgustingly overcrowded.

SISTER-IN-LAW: And did you hear our gracious hostess? She cools off quick!

[*Voices outside. Knocking at the door.*]

UNCLE'S VOICE: Open the door!

WIFE: Uncle! Is that you, Uncle?

UNCLE'S VOICE: Certainly, it's me. Auntie says to tell you she'll have the children here in ten minutes.

WIFE: [*to* SHEN TE] I'll have to let him in.

SHEN TE: [*who scarcely hears her*]

The little lifeboat is swiftly sent down
Too many men too greedily
Hold on to it as they drown.

SCENE Ia————WONG's *den in a sewer pipe.*

WONG: [*crouching there*] All quiet! It's four days now since I left the city. The gods passed this way on the second day. I heard their steps on the bridge over there. They must be a long way off by this time, so I'm safe. [*Breathing a sigh of relief, he curls up and goes to sleep. In his dream the pipe becomes transparent, and the* GODS *appear. Raising an arm, as if in self-defense.*] I know, I know, illustrious ones! I found no one to give you a room—not in all Setzuan! There, it's out. Please continue on your way!

FIRST GOD: [*mildly*] But you did find someone. Someone who took us in for the night, watched over us in our sleep, and in the early morning lighted us down to the street with a lamp.

WONG: It was . . . Shen Te that took you in?

THIRD GOD: Who else?

WONG: And I ran away! "She isn't coming," I thought, "she just can't afford it."

GODS: [*singing*]

O you feeble, well-intentioned, and yet feeble chap
Where there's need the fellow thinks there is no goodness!
When there's danger he thinks courage starts to ebb away!
Some people only see the seamy side!
What hasty judgment! What premature desperation!

WONG: I'm *very* ashamed, illustrious ones.

FIRST GOD: Do us a favor, water seller. Go back to Setzuan. Find Shen Te, and give us a report on her. We hear that she's come into a little money. Show interest in her goodness—for no one can be good for long if goodness is not in demand. Meanwhile we shall continue the search, and find other good people. After which, the idle chatter about the impossibility of goodness will stop!

[*The* GODS *vanish.*]

SCENE II

[*a knocking*]

WIFE: Shen Te! Someone at the door. Where is she, anyway?

NEPHEW: She must be getting the breakfast. Mr. Shui Ta will pay for it.

[*The* WIFE *laughs and shuffles to the door. Enter* MR. SHUI TA *and the* CARPENTER.]

WIFE: Who is it?

SHUI TA: I am Miss Shen Te's cousin.

WIFE: What?

SHUI TA: My name is Shui Ta.

WIFE: Her cousin?

NEPHEW: Her cousin?

NIECE: But that was a joke. She hasn't got a cousin.

HUSBAND: So early in the morning?

BROTHER: What's all the noise?

SISTER-IN-LAW: This fellow says he's her cousin.

BROTHER: Tell him to prove it.

NEPHEW: Right. If you're Shen Te's cousin, prove it by getting the breakfast.

SHUI TA: [*whose regime begins as he puts out the lamp to save oil; loudly, to all present, asleep or awake*] Would you all please get dressed! Customers will be coming! I wish to open my shop!

HUSBAND: *Your* shop? Doesn't it belong to our good friend Shen Te?

[SHUI TA *shakes his head.*]

SISTER-IN-LAW: So we've been cheated. Where is the little liar?

SHUI TA: Miss Shen Te has been delayed. She wishes me to tell you there will be nothing she can do—now I am here.

WIFE: [*bowled over*] I thought she was good!

NEPHEW: Do you have to believe him?

HUSBAND: I don't.

NEPHEW: Then do something.

HUSBAND: Certainly! I'll send out a search party at once. You, you, you, and you, go out and look for Shen Te. [as the GRANDFATHER *rises and makes for the door*] Not you, Grandfather, you and I will hold the fort.

SHUI TA: You won't find Miss Shen Te. She has suspended her hospitable activity for an unlimited period. There are too many of you. She asked me to say: this is a tobacco shop, not a gold mine.

HUSBAND: Shen Te never said a thing like that. Boy, food! There's a bakery on the corner. Stuff your shirt full when they're not looking!

SISTER-IN-LAW: Don't overlook the raspberry tarts.

HUSBAND: And don't let the policeman see you.

[*The* BOY *leaves.*]

SHUI TA: Don't you depend on this shop now? Then why give it a bad name by stealing from the bakery?

NEPHEW: Don't listen to him. Let's find Shen Te. She'll give him a piece of her mind.

SISTER-IN-LAW: Don't forget to leave us some breakfast.

[BROTHER, SISTER-IN-LAW, *and* NEPHEW *leave.*]

SHUI TA: [*to the* CARPENTER] You see, Mr. Carpenter, nothing has changed since the poet, eleven hundred years ago, penned these lines:

A governor was asked what was needed
To save the freezing people in the city.
He replied:
"A blanket ten thousand feet long
to cover the city and all its suburbs."

[*He starts to tidy up the shop.*]

CARPENTER: Your cousin owes me money. I've got witnesses. For the shelves.

SHUI TA: Yes, I have your bill. [*He takes it out of his pocket.*] Isn't a hundred silver dollars rather a lot?

CARPENTER: No deductions! I have a wife and children.

SHUI TA: How many children?

CARPENTER: Three.

SHUI TA: I'll make you an offer. Twenty silver dollars.

> [*The* HUSBAND *laughs.*]

CARPENTER: You're crazy. Those shelves are real walnut.

SHUI TA: Very well, take them away.

CARPENTER: What?

SHUI TA: They cost too much. Please take them away.

WIFE: Not bad! [*And she, too, is laughing.*]

CARPENTER: [*a little bewildered*] Call Shen Te, someone! [*to* SHUI TA] She's *good!*

SHUI TA: Certainly. She's ruined.

CARPENTER: [*provoked into taking some of the shelves*] All right, you can keep your tobacco on the floor.

SHUI TA: [*to the* HUSBAND] Help him with the shelves.

HUSBAND: [*grins and carries one shelf over to the door where the* CARPENTER *now is*] Goodbye, shelves!

CARPENTER: [*to the* HUSBAND] You dog! You want my family to starve?

SHUI TA: I repeat my offer. I have no desire to keep my tobacco on the floor. Twenty silver dollars.

CARPENTER: [*with desperate aggressiveness*] One hundred!

> [SHUI TA *shows indifference, looks through the window. The* HUSBAND *picks up several shelves.*]

CARPENTER: [*to* HUSBAND] You needn't smash them against the doorposts, you idiot! [*to* SHUI TA] These shelves were made to measure. They're no use anywhere else!

SHUI TA: Precisely.

> [*The* WIFE *squeals with pleasure.*]

CARPENTER: [*giving up, sullenly*] Take the shelves. Pay what you want to pay.

SHUI TA: [*smoothly*] Twenty silver dollars.

> [*He places two large coins on the table. The* CARPENTER *picks them up.*]

HUSBAND: [*brings the shelves in*] And quite enough, too!

CARPENTER: [*slinking off*] Quite enoug h to get drunk on.

HUSBAND: [*happily*] Well, we got rid of him!

WIFE: [*weeping with fun, gives a rendition of the dialogue just spoken*] "Real walnut," says he. "Very well, take them away," says his lordship. "I have three children," says he. "Twenty silver dollars," says his lordship. "They're no use anywhere else," says he. "Pre-cisely," said his lordship! [*She dissolves into shrieks of merriment.*]

SHUI TA: And now: go!

HUSBAND: What's that?

SHUI TA: You're thieves, parasites. I'm giving you this chance. Go!

HUSBAND: [*summoning all his ancestral dignity*] That sort deserves no answer. Besides, one should never shout on an empty stomach.

WIFE: Where's that boy?

SHUI TA: Exactly. The boy. I want no stolen goods in this shop. [*very loudly*] I strongly advise you to leave! [*But they remain seated, noses in the air. Quietly.*] As you wish. [SHUI TA *goes to the door.* A POLICEMAN *appears.* SHUI TA *bows.*] I am addressing the officer in charge of this precinct?

POLICEMAN: That's right, Mr., um, what was the name, sir?

SHUI TA: Mr. Shui Ta.

POLICEMAN: Yes, of course, sir.

> [*They exchange a smile.*]

SHUI TA: Nice weather we're having.

POLICEMAN: A little on the warm side, sir.

SHUI TA: Oh, a little on the warm side.

HUSBAND: [*whispering to the* WIFE] If he keeps it up till the boy's back, we're done for. [*Tries to signal* SHUI TA.]

SHUI TA: [*ignoring the signal*] Weather, of course, is one thing indoors, another out on the dusty street!

POLICEMAN: Oh, quite another, sir!

WIFE: [*to the* HUSBAND] It's all right as long as he's standing in the doorway—the boy will see him.

SHUI TA: Step inside for a moment! It's quite cool indoors. My cousin and I have just opened the place. And we attach the greatest importance to being on good terms with the, um, authorities.

POLICEMAN: [*entering*] Thank you, Mr. Shui Ta. It *is* cool.

HUSBAND: [*whispering to the* WIFE] And now the boy won't see him.

SHUI TA: [*showing* HUSBAND *and* WIFE *to the* POLICEMAN] Visitors, I think my cousin knows them. They were just leaving.

HUSBAND: [*defeated*] Ye-e-es, we were . . . just leaving.

SHUI TA: I'll tell my cousin you couldn't wait.

[*Noise from the street. Shouts of* "Stop, Thief!"]

POLICEMAN: What's that?

[*The* BOY *is in the doorway with cakes and buns and rolls spilling out of his shirt. The* WIFE *signals desperately to him to leave. He gets the idea.*]

POLICEMAN: No, you don't! [*he grabs the* BOY *by the collar*] Where's all this from?

BOY: [*vaguely pointing*] Down the street.

POLICEMAN: [*grimly*] So that's it. [*prepares to arrest the* BOY]

WIFE: [*stepping in*] And we knew nothing about it. [*to the* BOY] Nasty little thief!

POLICEMAN: [*dryly*] Can you clarify the situation, Mr. Shui Ta?

[SHUI TA *is silent.*]

POLICEMAN: [*who understands silence*] Aha. You're all coming with me—to the station.

SHUI TA: I can hardly say how sorry I am that my establishment . . .

WIFE: Oh, he saw the boy leave not ten minutes ago!

SHUI TA: And to conceal the theft asked a policeman in?

POLICEMAN: Don't listen to her, Mr. Shui Ta. I'll be happy to relieve you of their presence one and all! [*to all three*] Out! [*He drives them before him.*]

GRANDFATHER: [*leaving last, gravely*] Good morning!

POLICEMAN: Good morning!

[SHUI TA, *left alone, continues to tidy up.* MRS. MI TZU *breezes in.*]

MRS. MI TZU: You're her cousin, are you? Then have the goodness to explain what all this means—police dragging people from a respectable house! By what right does your Miss Shen Te turn my property into a house of assignation? Well, as you see, I know all!

SHUI TA: Yes. My cousin has the worst possible reputation: that of being poor.

MRS. MI TZU: No sentimental rubbish, Mr. Shui Ta. Your cousin was a common . . .

SHUI TA: Pauper. Let's use the uglier word.

MRS. MI TZU: I'm speaking of her conduct, not her earnings. But there must have *been* earnings, or how did she buy all this? Several elderly gentlemen took care of it, I suppose. I repeat: this is a respectable house! I have tenants who prefer not to live under the same roof with such a person.

SHUI TA: [*quietly*] How much do you want?

MRS. MI TZU: [*he is ahead of her now*] I beg your pardon.

SHUI TA: To reassure yourself. To reassure your tenants. How much will it cost?

MRS. MI TZU: You're a cool customer.

SHUI TA: [*picking up the lease*] The rent is high. [*He reads on.*] I assume it's payable by the month?

MRS. MI TZU: Not in her case.

SHUI TA: [*looking up*] What?

MRS. MI TZU: Six months' rent payable in advance. Two hundred silver dollars.

SHUI TA: Six . . . ! Sheer usury! And where am I to find it?

MRS. MI TZU: You should have thought of that before.

SHUI TA: Have you no heart, Mrs. Mi Tzu? It's true Shen Te acted foolishly, being kind to all those people, but she'll improve with time. I'll see to it she does. She'll work her fingers to the bone to pay her rent, and all the time be as quiet as a mouse, as humble as a fly.

MRS. MI TZU: Her social background . . .

SHUI TA: Out of the depths! She came out of the depths! And before she'll go back there, she'll work, sacrifice, shrink from nothing. . . . Such a tenant is worth her weight in gold, Mrs. Mi Tzu.

MRS. MI TZU: It's silver dollars we were talking about, Mr. Shui Ta. Two hundred silver dollars or . . .

[*Enter the* POLICEMAN.]

POLICEMAN: Am I intruding, Mr. Shui Ta?

MRS. MI TZU: This tobacco shop is well known to the police, I see.

POLICEMAN: Mr. Shui Ta has done us a service, Mrs. Mi Tzu. I am here to present our official felicitations!

MRS. MI TZU: That means less than nothing to me, sir. Mr. Shui Ta, all I can say is: I hope your cousin will find my terms acceptable. Good day, gentlemen. [*Exit.*]

SHUI TA: Good day, ma'am.

[*pause*]

POLICEMAN: Mrs. Mi Tzu a bit of a stumbling block, sir?

SHUI TA: She wants six months' rent in advance.

POLICEMAN: And you haven't got it, eh? [SHUI TA *is silent.*] But surely you can get it, sir? A man like you?

SHUI TA: What about a woman like Shen Te?

POLICEMAN: You're not staying, sir?

SHUI TA: No, and I won't be back. Do you smoke?

POLICEMAN: [*taking two cigars, and placing them both in his pocket*] Thank you, sir—I see your point. Miss Te—let's mince no words—Miss Shen Te lived by selling herself. "What else could she have done?" you ask. "How else was she to pay the rent?" True. But the fact remains, Mr. Shui Ta, it is not respectable. Why not? A very deep question. But, in the first place, love—love isn't bought and sold like cigars, Mr. Shui Ta. In the second place, it isn't respectable to go waltzing off with someone that's paying his way, so to speak—it must be for love! Thirdly, and lastly, as the proverb has it: not for a handful of rice but for love! [*Pause. He is thinking hard.*] "Well," you may say, "and what good is all this wisdom if the milk's already spilt?" Miss Shen Te is what she is. Is *where* she is. We have to face the fact that if she doesn't get hold of six months' rent pronto, she'll be back on the streets. The question then as I see it— everything in this world is a matter of opinion—the question as I see it is: *how* is she to get hold of this rent? How? Mr. Shui Ta: I don't know. [*pause*] I take that back, sir. It's just come to me. A husband. We must find her a husband!

[*Enter a little* OLD WOMAN.]

OLD WOMAN: A good cheap cigar for my husband; we'll have been married forty years tomorrow and we're having a little celebration.

SHUI TA: Forty years? And you still want to celebrate?

OLD WOMAN: As much as we can afford to. We have the carpet shop across the square. We'll be good neighbors, I hope?

SHUI TA: I hope so, too.

POLICEMAN: [*who keeps making discoveries*] Mr. Shui Ta, you know what we need? We need capital. And how do we acquire capital? We get married.

SHUI TA: [*to* OLD WOMAN] I'm afraid I've been pestering this gentleman with my personal worries.

POLICEMAN: [*lyrically*] We can't pay six months' rent, so what do we do? We marry money.

SHUI TA: That might not be easy.

POLICEMAN: Oh, I don't know. She's a good match. Has a nice, growing business. [*to the* OLD WOMAN] What do you think?

OLD WOMAN: [*undecided*] Well—

POLICEMAN: Should she put an ad in the paper?

OLD WOMAN: [*not eager to commit herself*] Well, if *she* agrees—

POLICEMAN: I'll write it for her. *You* lend us a hand, and *we* write an ad for you!
[*He chuckles away to himself, takes out his notebook, wets the stump of a pencil between his lips, and writes away.*]

SHUI TA: [*slowly*] Not a bad idea.

POLICEMAN: "What . . . *respectable* . . . man . . . with small capital . . . widower . . . not excluded . . . desires . . . marriage . . . into flourishing . . . tobacco shop?" And now let's add: "Am . . . pretty . . . " No! . . . "Prepossessing appearance."

SHUI TA: If you don't think that's an exaggeration?

OLD WOMAN: Oh, not a bit. I've seen her.
[*The* POLICEMAN *tears the page out of his notebook, and hands it over to* SHUI TA.]

SHUI TA: [*with horror in his voice*] How much luck we need to keep our heads above water! How many ideas! How many friends! [*to the* POLICEMAN] Thank you, sir, I think I see my way clear.

SCENE III———*Evening in the municipal park. Noise of a plane overhead.*

[YANG SUN, *a young man in rags, is following the plane with his eyes: one can tell that the machine is describing a curve above the park.* YANG SUN *then takes a rope out of his pocket, looking anxiously about him as he does so. He moves toward a large willow. Enter two prostitutes, one the* OLD WHORE, *the other the* NIECE *whom we have already met.*]

NIECE: Hello. Coming with me?

YANG SUN: [*taken aback*] If you'd like to buy me a dinner.

OLD WHORE: Buy you a dinner! [*to the* NIECE] Oh, we know him—it's the unemployed pilot. Waste no time on him!

NIECE: But he's the only man left in the park. And it's going to rain.

OLD WHORE: Oh, how do you know?
[*As they pass by,* YANG SUN *again looks about him, again takes his rope, and this time throws it round a branch of the willow tree. Again he is interrupted. It is the two prostitutes returning—and in such a hurry they don't notice him.*]

NIECE: It's going to pour!
[*Enter* SHEN TE.]

OLD WHORE: There's that *gorgon* Shen Te! That *drove* your family out into the cold!

NIECE: It wasn't her. It was that cousin of hers. She offered to pay for the cakes. I've nothing against her.

OLD WHORE: I have, though. [*so that* SHEN TE *can hear*] Now where would the little lady be off to? She may be rich now but that won't stop her snatching our young men, will it?

SHEN TE: I'm going to the tearoom by the pond.

NIECE: Is it true what they say? You're marrying a widower—with three children?

SHEN TE: Yes. I'm just going to see him.

YANG SUN: [*his patience at breaking point*] Move on there! This is a park, not a whorehouse!

OLD WHORE: Shut your mouth!

　　　　[*But the two prostitutes leave.*]

YANG SUN: Even in the farthest corner of the park, even when it's raining, you can't get rid of them! [*He spits.*]

SHEN TE: [*overhearing this*] And what right have you to scold them? [*But at this point she sees the rope.*] Oh!

YANG SUN: Well, what are you staring at?

SHEN TE: That rope. What is it for?

YANG SUN: Think! Think! I haven't a penny. Even if I had, I wouldn't spend it on you. I'd buy a drink of water.

　　　　[*The rain starts.*]

SHEN TE: [*still looking at the rope*] What is the rope for? You mustn't!

YANG SUN: What's it to you? Clear out!

SHEN TE: [*irrelevantly*] It's raining.

YANG SUN: Well, don't try to come under this tree.

SHEN TE: Oh, no. [*She stays in the rain.*]

YANG SUN: Now go away. [*pause*] For one thing, I don't like your looks, you're bowlegged.

SHEN TE: [*indignantly*] That's not true!

YANG SUN: Well, don't show 'em to me. Look, it's raining. You better come under this tree.

　　　　[*Slowly, she takes shelter under the tree.*]

SHEN TE: Why did you want to do it?

YANG SUN: You really want to know? [*pause*] To get rid of you! [*pause*] You know what a flyer is?

SHEN TE: Oh yes, I've met a lot of pilots. At the tearoom.

YANG SUN: You call *them* flyers? Think they know what a machine is? Just 'cause they have leather helmets? They gave the airfield director a bribe, that's the way *those* fellows got up in the air! Try one of them out sometime. "Go up to two thousand feet," tell them, "then let it fall, then pick it up again with a flick of the wrist at the last moment." Know what he'll say to that? "It's not in my contract." Then again, there's the landing problem. It's like landing on your own backside. It's no different, planes are human. Those fools don't understand. [*pause*] And I'm the biggest fool for reading the book on flying in the Peking school and skipping the page where it says, "We've got enough flyers and we don't need you." I'm a mail pilot with no mail. You understand that?

SHEN TE: [*shyly*] Yes. I do.

YANG SUN: No, you don't. You'd never understand that.

SHEN TE: When we were little we had a crane with a broken wing. He made friends with us and was very good-natured about our jokes. He would strut along behind us and call out to stop us going too fast for him. But every spring and autumn when the cranes flew over the villages in great swarms, he got quite restless. [*pause*] I understand that. [*She bursts out crying.*]

YANG SUN: Don't!

SHEN TE: [*quieting down*] No.

YANG SUN: It's bad for the complexion.

SHEN TE: [*sniffing*] I've stopped.

> [*She dries her tears on her big sleeve. Leaning against the tree, but not looking at her, he reaches for her face.*]

YANG SUN: You can't even wipe your own face. [*He is wiping it for her with his handkerchief. Pause.*]

SHEN TE: [*still sobbing*] I don't know *anything!*

YANG SUN: You interrupted me! What for?

SHEN TE: It's such a rainy day. You only wanted to do . . . *that* because it's such a rainy day.

> [*To the audience.*]
>
> In our country
> The evenings should never be somber
> High bridges over rivers
> The gray hour between night and morning
> And the long, long winter:
> Such things are dangerous
> For, with all the misery,
> A very little is enough
> And men throw away an unbearable life.
>
> [*pause*]

YANG SUN: Talk about yourself for a change.

SHEN TE: What about me? I have a shop.

YANG SUN: [*incredulous*] You have a shop, have you? Never thought of walking the streets?

SHEN TE: I did walk the streets. Now I have a shop.

YANG SUN: [*ironically*] A gift of the gods, I suppose!

SHEN TE: How did you know?

YANG SUN: [*even more ironically*] One fine evening the gods turned up saying: here's some money!

SHEN TE: [*quickly*] One fine morning.

YANG SUN: [*fed up*] This isn't much of an entertainment.

> [*pause*]

SHEN TE: I can play the zither a little. [*pause*] And I can mimic men. [*pause*] I got the shop, so the first thing I did was to give my zither away. So I can be as stupid as a fish now, I said to myself, and it won't matter.

> I'm rich now, I said
> I walk alone, I sleep alone
> For a whole year, I said
> I'll have nothing to do with a man.

YANG SUN: And now you're marrying one! The one at the tearoom by the pond?

> [SHEN TE *is silent.*]

YANG SUN: What do you know about love?

SHEN TE: Everything.

YANG SUN: Nothing. [*pause*] Or d'you just mean you enjoyed it?

SHEN TE: No.

YANG SUN: [*again without turning to look at her, he strokes her cheek with his hand*] You like that?

SHEN TE: Yes.

YANG SUN: [*breaking off*] You're easily satisfied, I must say. [*pause*] What a town!

SHEN TE: You have no friends?

YANG SUN: [*defensively*] Yes, I have! [*change of tone*] But they don't want to hear I'm still unemployed. "What?" they ask. "Is there still water in the sea?" You have friends?

SHEN TE: [*hesitating*] Just a . . . cousin.

YANG SUN: Watch him carefully.

SHEN TE: He only came once. Then he went away. He won't be back. [YANG SUN *is looking away.*] But to be without hope, they say, is to be without goodness!

    [*pause*]

YANG SUN: Go on talking. A voice is a voice.

SHEN TE: Once, when I was a little girl, I fell, with a load of brushwood. An old man picked me up. He gave me a penny, too. Isn't it funny how people who don't have very much like to give some of it away? They must like to show what they can do, and how could they show it better than by being kind? Being wicked is just like being clumsy. When we sing a song, or build a machine, or plant some rice, we're being kind. You're kind.

YANG SUN: You make it sound easy.

SHEN TE: Oh, no. [*little pause*] Oh! A drop of rain!

YANG SUN: Where'd you feel it?

SHEN TE: Right between the eyes.

YANG SUN: Near the right eye? Or the left?

SHEN TE: Near the left eye.

YANG SUN: Oh, good. [*He is getting sleepy.*] So you're through with men, eh?

SHEN TE: [*with a smile*] But I'm not bowlegged.

YANG SUN: Perhaps not.

SHEN TE: Definitely not.

    [*pause*]

YANG SUN: [*leaning wearily against the willow*] I haven't had a drop to drink all day, I haven't eaten anything for two days. I couldn't love you if I tried.

    [*pause*]

SHEN TE: I like it in the rain.

    [*Enter* WONG *the water seller, singing.*]

THE SONG OF THE WATER SELLER IN THE RAIN

    "Buy my water," I am yelling
    And my fury restraining
    For no water I'm selling
    'Cause it's raining, 'cause it's raining!
      I keep yelling: "Buy my water!"
    But no one's buying
    Athirst and dying
    And drinking and paying!
    Buy water!
    Buy water, you dogs!

    Nice to dream of lovely weather!
    Think of all the consternation
    Were there no precipitation
    Half a dozen years together!
      Can't you hear them shrieking: "Water!"

> *Pretending they adore me?*
> *They all would go down on their knees before me!*
> *Down on your knees!*
> *Go down on your knees, you dogs!*

> *What are lawns and hedges thinking?*
> *What are fields and forests saying?*
> *"At the cloud's breast we are drinking!*
> *And we've no idea who's paying!"*
> > *I keep yelling: "Buy my water!"*
> > *But no one's buying*
> > *Athirst and dying*
> > *And drinking and paying!*
> > *Buy water*
> > *Buy water, you dogs!*

[*The rain has stopped now.* SHEN TE *sees* WONG *and runs toward him.*]

SHEN TE: Wong! You're back! Your carrying pole's at the shop.

WONG: Oh, thank you, Shen Te. And how is life treating *you*?

SHEN TE: I've just met a brave and clever man. And I want to buy him a cup of your water.

WONG: [*bitterly*] Throw back your head and open your mouth and you'll have all the water you need—

SHEN TE: [*tenderly*]

> *I want your water, Wong*
> *That water that has tired you so*
> *The water that you carried all this way*
> *The water that is hard to sell because*
> > *it's been raining.*
> *I need it for the young man over there—he's a flyer!*
> > *A flyer is a bold man:*
> > *Braving the storms*
> > *In company with the clouds*
> > *He crosses the heavens*
> > *And brings to friends in faraway lands*
> > *The friendly mail!*

[*She pays* WONG, *and runs over to* YANG SUN *with the cup. But* YANG SUN *is fast asleep.*]

SHEN TE: [*calling to* WONG, *with a laugh*] He's fallen asleep! Despair and rain and I have worn him out!

SCENE IIIa————WONG's den.

[*The sewer pipe is transparent, and the* GODS *again appear to* WONG *in a dream.*]

WONG: [*radiant*] I've seen her, illustrious ones! And she hasn't changed!

FIRST GOD: That's good to hear.

WONG: She loves someone.

FIRST GOD: Let's hope the experience gives her the strength to stay good!

WONG: It does. She's doing good deeds all the time.

FIRST GOD: Ah? What sort? What sort of good deeds, Wong?

WONG: Well, she has a kind word for everybody.

FIRST GOD: [*eagerly*] And then?

WONG: Hardly anyone leaves her shop without tobacco in his pocket—even if he can't pay for it.

FIRST GOD: Not bad at all. Next?

WONG: She's putting up a family of eight.

FIRST GOD: [*gleefully, to the* SECOND GOD] Eight! [*to* WONG] And that's not all, of course!

WONG: She bought a cup of water from me even though it was raining.

FIRST GOD: Yes, yes, yes, all these smaller good deeds!

WONG: Even they run into money. A little tobacco shop doesn't make so much.

FIRST GOD: [*sententiously*] A prudent gardener works miracles on the smallest plot.

WONG: She hands out rice every morning. That eats up half her earnings.

FIRST GOD: [*a little disappointed*] Well, as a beginning . . .

WONG: They call her the Angel of the Slums—whatever the carpenter may say!

FIRST GOD: What's this? A carpenter speaks ill of her?

WONG: Oh, he only says her shelves weren't paid for in full.

SECOND GOD: [*who has a bad cold and can't pronounce his* n's *and* m's] What's this? Not paying a carpenter? Why was that?

WONG: I suppose she didn't have the money.

SECOND GOD: [*severely*] One pays what one owes, that's in our book of rules! First the letter of the law, then the spirit.

WONG: But it wasn't Shen Te, illustrious ones, it was her cousin. She called *him* in to help.

SECOND GOD: Then her cousin must never darken her threshold again!

WONG: Very well, illustrious ones! But in fairness to Shen Te, let me say that her cousin is a businessman.

FIRST GOD: Perhaps we should inquire what is customary? I find business quite unintelligible. But everybody's doing it. Business! Did the Seven Good Kings do business? Did King the Just sell fish?

SECOND GOD: In any case, such a thing must not occur again!

[*The* GODS *start to leave.*]

THIRD GOD: Forgive us for taking this tone with you, Wong, we haven't been getting enough sleep. The rich recommended us to the poor, and the poor tell us they haven't enough room.

SECOND GOD: Feeble, feeble, the best of them!

FIRST GOD: No great deeds! No heroic daring!

THIRD GOD: On such a *small* scale.

SECOND GOD: Sincere, yes, but what is actually *achieved*?

[*One can no longer hear them.*]

WONG: [*calling after them*] I've thought of something, illustrious ones: Perhaps you shouldn't ask—too—much—all—at—once!

SCENE IV———— *The square in front of* SHEN TE's *tobacco shop. Besides* SHEN TE's *place, two other shops are seen: the carpet shop and a barber's. Morning.*

[*Outside* SHEN TE's *the* GRANDFATHER, *the* SISTER-IN-LAW, *the* UNEMPLOYED MAN, *and* MRS. SHIN *stand waiting.*]

SISTER-IN-LAW: She's been out all night again.

MRS. SHIN: No sooner did we get rid of that crazy cousin of hers than Shen Te herself starts carrying on! Maybe she does give us an ounce of rice now and then, but can you depend on her? Can you depend on her?

[*loud voices from the barber's*]

VOICE OF SHU FU: What are you doing in my shop? Get out—at once!

VOICE OF WONG: But, sir. They all let me sell . . .

> [WONG *comes staggering out of the barber's shop pursued by* MR. SHU FU, *the barber, a fat man carrying a heavy curling iron.*]

SHU FU: Get out, I said! Pestering my customers with your slimy old water! Get out! Take your cup!

> [*He holds out the cup.* WONG *reaches out for it.* MR. SHU FU *strikes his hand with the curling iron, which is hot.* WONG *howls.*]

SHU FU: You had it coming, my man!

> [*Puffing, he returns to his shop. The* UNEMPLOYED MAN *picks up the cup and gives it to* WONG.]

UNEMPLOYED MAN: You can report that to the police.

WONG: My hand! It's smashed up!

UNEMPLOYED MAN: Any bones broken?

WONG: I can't move my fingers.

UNEMPLOYED MAN: Sit down. I'll put some water on it.

> [WONG *sits.*]

MRS. SHIN: The water won't cost you anything.

SISTER-IN-LAW: You might have got a bandage from Miss Shen Te till she took to staying out all night. It's a scandal.

MRS. SHIN: [*despondently*] If you ask me, she's forgotten we ever existed!

> [*Enter* SHEN TE *down the street, with a dish of rice.*]

SHEN TE: [*to the audience*] How wonderful to see Setzuan in the early morning! I always used to stay in bed with my dirty blanket over my head afraid to wake up. This morning I saw the newspapers being delivered by little boys, the streets being washed by strong men, and fresh vegetables coming in from the country on ox carts. It's a long walk from where Yang Sun lives, but I feel lighter at every step. They say you walk on air when you're in love, but it's even better walking on the rough earth, on the hard cement. In the early morning, the old city looks like a great heap of rubbish! Nice, though, with all its little lights. And the sky, so pink, so transparent, before the dust comes and muddies it! What a lot you miss if you never see your city rising from its slumbers like an honest old craftsman pumping his lungs full of air and reaching for his tools as the poet says! [*cheerfully, to her waiting guests*] Good morning, everyone, here's your rice! [*Distributing the rice, she comes upon* WONG.] Good morning, Wong, I'm quite lightheaded today. On my way over, I looked at myself in all the shop windows. I'd love to be beautiful.

> [*She slips into the carpet shop.* MR. SHU FU *has just emerged from his shop.*]

SHU FU: [*to the audience*] It surprises me how beautiful Miss Shen Te is looking today! I never gave her a passing thought before. But now I've been gazing upon her comely form for exactly three minutes! I begin to suspect I am in love with her. She is overpoweringly attractive! [*crossly, to* WONG] Be off with you, rascal!

> [*He returns to his shop.* SHEN TE *comes back out of the carpet shop with the* OLD MAN, *its proprietor, and his wife—whom we have already met—the* OLD WOMAN. SHEN TE *is wearing a shawl. The* OLD MAN *is holding up a looking glass for her.*]

OLD WOMAN: Isn't it lovely? We'll give you a reduction because there's a little hole in it.

SHEN TE: [*looking at another shawl on the* OLD WOMAN'S *arm*] The other one's nice, too.

OLD WOMAN: [*smiling*] Too bad there's no hole in that!

SHEN TE: That's right. My shop doesn't make very much.

OLD WOMAN: And your good deeds eat it all up! Be more careful, my dear . . .

SHEN TE: [*trying on the shawl with the hole*] Just now, I'm lightheaded! Does the color suit me?

OLD WOMAN: You'd better ask a man.

SHEN TE: [*to the* OLD MAN] Does the color suit me?

OLD MAN: You'd better ask your young friend.

SHEN TE: I'd like to have your opinion.

OLD MAN: It suits you very well. But wear it this way: the dull side out.

[SHEN TE *pays up.*]

OLD WOMAN: If you decide you don't like it, you can exchange it. [*She pulls* SHEN TE *to one side.*] Has he got money?

SHEN TE: [*with a laugh*] Yang Sun? Oh, no.

OLD WOMAN: Then how're you going to pay your rent?

SHEN TE: I'd forgotten about that.

OLD WOMAN: And next Monday is the first of the month! Miss Shen Te, I've got something to say to you. After we [*indicating her husband*] got to know you, we had our doubts about that marriage ad. We thought it would be better if you'd let us help you. Out of our savings. We reckon we could lend you two hundred silver dollars. We don't need anything in writing—you could pledge us your tobacco stock.

SHEN TE: You're prepared to lend money to a person like me?

OLD WOMAN: It's folks like you that need it. We'd think twice about lending anything to your cousin.

OLD MAN: [*coming up*] All settled, my dear?

SHEN TE: I wish the gods could have heard what your wife was just saying, Mr. Ma. They're looking for good people who're happy—and helping me makes you happy because you know it was love that got me into difficulties!

[*The* OLD COUPLE *smile knowingly at each other.*]

OLD MAN: And here's the money, Miss Shen Te.

[*He hands her an envelope.* SHEN TE *takes it. She bows. They bow back. They return to their shop.*]

SHEN TE: [*holding up her envelope*] Look, Wong, here's six months' rent! Don't you believe in miracles now? And how do you like my new shawl?

WONG: For the young fellow I saw you with in the park?

[SHEN TE *nods.*]

MRS. SHIN: Never mind all that. It's time you took a look at his hand!

SHEN TE: Have you hurt your hand?

MRS. SHIN: That barber smashed it with his curling iron. Right in front of our eyes.

SHEN TE: [*shocked at herself*] And I never noticed! We must get you to a doctor this minute or who knows what will happen?

UNEMPLOYED MAN: It's not a doctor he should see, it's a judge. He can ask for compensation. The barber's filthy rich.

WONG: You think I have a chance?

MRS. SHIN: [*with relish*] If it's really good and smashed. But is it?

WONG: I think so. It's very swollen. Could I get a pension?

MRS. SHIN: You'd need a witness.

WONG: Well, you all saw it. You could all testify.

[*He looks around. The* UNEMPLOYED MAN, *the* GRANDFATHER, *and the* SISTER-IN-LAW *are all sitting against the wall of the shop eating rice. Their concentration on eating is complete.*]

SHEN TE: [*to* MRS. SHIN] You saw it yourself.

MRS. SHIN: I want nothing to do with the police. It's against my principles.

SHEN TE: [*to* SISTER-IN-LAW] What about you?

SISTER-IN-LAW: Me? I wasn't looking.

SHEN TE: [*to the* GRANDFATHER, *coaxingly*] Grandfather, *you'll* testify, won't you?

SISTER-IN-LAW: And a lot of good that will do. He's simple-minded.

SHEN TE: [*to the* UNEMPLOYED MAN] You seem to be the only witness left.

UNEMPLOYED MAN: My testimony would only hurt him. I've been picked up twice for begging.

SHEN TE: Your brother is assaulted, and you shut your eyes?
He is hit, cries out in pain, and you are silent?
The beast prowls, chooses, and seizes his victim, and you say:
"Because we showed no displeasure, he has spared us."
If no one present will be a witness, I will. I'll say
I saw it.

MRS. SHIN: [*solemnly*] The name for that is perjury.

WONG: I don't know if I can accept that. Though maybe I'll have to. [*looking at his hand*] Is it swollen enough, do you think? The swelling's not going down?

UNEMPLOYED MAN: No, no. The swelling's holding up well.

WONG: Yes. It's *more* swollen if anything. Maybe my wrist is broken after all. I'd better see a judge at once.
[*Holding his hand very carefully, and fixing his eyes on it, he runs off.* MRS. SHIN *goes quickly into the barber's shop.*]

UNEMPLOYED MAN: [*seeing her*] She is getting on the right side of Mr. Shu Fu.

SISTER-IN-LAW: You and I can't change the world, Shen Te.

SHEN TE: Go away! Go away, all of you!
[*The* UNEMPLOYED MAN, *the* SISTER-IN-LAW, *and the* GRANDFATHER *stalk off, eating and sulking.*]
[*To the audience:*]
They've stopped answering
They stay put
They do as they're told
They don't care
Nothing can make them look up
But the smell of food.
[*Enter* MRS. YANG, YANG SUN's *mother, out of breath.*]

MRS. YANG: Miss Shen Te. My son has told me everything. I am Mrs. Yang, Sun's mother. Just think. He's got an offer. Of a job as a pilot. A letter has just come. From the director of the airfield in Peking!

SHEN TE: So he can fly again? Isn't that wonderful!

MRS. YANG: [*less breathlessly all the time*] They won't give him the job for nothing. They want five hundred silver dollars.

SHEN TE: We can't let money stand in his way, Mrs. Yang!

MRS. YANG: If only you could help him out!

SHEN TE: I have the shop. I can try! [*She embraces* MRS. YANG.] I happen to have two hundred with me now. Take it. [*She gives her the old couple's money.*] It was a loan but they said I could repay it with my tobacco stock.

MRS. YANG: And they were calling Sun the Dead Pilot of Setzuan! A friend in need!

SHEN TE: We must find another three hundred.

MRS. YANG: How?

SHEN TE: Let me think. [*slowly*] I know someone who can help. I didn't want to call on his services again, he's hard and cunning. But a flyer must fly. And I'll make this the last time.
[*distant sound of a plane*]

MRS. YANG: If the man you mentioned can do it . . . Oh, look, there's the morning mail
plane, heading for Peking!
SHEN TE: The pilot can see us, let's wave!
[*They wave. The noise of the engine is louder.*]
MRS. YANG: You know that pilot up there?
SHEN TE: Wave, Mrs. Yang! I know the pilot who will be up there. He gave up hope. But
he'll do it now. One man to raise himself above the misery, above us all.
[*To the audience:*]
Yang Sun, my lover:
Braving the storms
In company with the clouds
Crossing the heavens
And bringing to friends in faraway lands
The friendly mail!

SCENE IVa————*In front of the inner curtain.*

[*Enter* SHEN TE, *carrying* SHUI TA's *mask. She sings:*]

THE SONG OF DEFENSELESSNESS

> *In our country*
> *A useful man needs luck*
> *Only if he finds strong backers*
> *Can he prove himself useful.*
> *The good can't defend themselves and*
> *Even the gods are defenseless.*
>
> *Oh, why don't the gods have their own ammunition*
> *And launch against badness their own expedition*
> *Enthroning the good and preventing sedition*
> *And bringing the world to a peaceful condition?*
>
> *Oh, why don't the gods do the buying and selling*
> *Injustice forbidding, starvation dispelling*
> *Give bread to each city and joy to each dwelling?*
> *Oh, why don't the gods do the buying and selling?*
> [*She puts on* SHUI TA's *mask and sings in his voice.*]
> *You can only help one of your luckless brothers*
> *By trampling down a dozen others.*
>
> *Why is it the gods do not feel indignation*
> *And come down in fury to end exploitation*
> *Defeat all defeat and forbid desperation*
> *Refusing to tolerate such toleration?*
>
> *Why is it?*

SCENE V———SHEN TE's *tobacco shop.*

> [*Behind the counter,* MR. SHUI TA, *reading the paper.* MRS. SHIN *is cleaning up.*
> *She talks and he takes no notice.*]

MRS. SHIN: And when certain rumors get about, what happens to a little place like this? It goes to pot. I know. So, if you want my advice, Mr. Shui Ta, find out just what has been going on between Miss Shen Te and that Yang Sun from Yellow Street. And remember: a certain interest in Miss Shen Te has been expressed by the barber next door, a man with twelve houses and only one wife, who, for that matter, is likely to drop off at any time. A certain interest has been expressed. He was even inquiring about her means and, if that doesn't prove a man is getting serious, what would? [*Still getting no response, she leaves with her bucket.*]

YANG SUN'S VOICE: Is that Miss Shen Te's tobacco shop?

MRS. SHIN'S VOICE: Yes, it is, but it's Mr. Shui Ta who's here today.

> [SHUI TA *runs to the mirror with the short, light steps of* SHEN TE, *and is just about to start primping, when he realizes his mistake, and turns away, with a short laugh. Enter* YANG SUN. MRS. SHIN *enters behind him and slips into the back room to eavesdrop.*]

YANG SUN: I am Yang Sun. [SHUI TA *bows*] Is Shen Te in?

SHUI TA: No.

YANG SUN: I guess you know our relationship? [*He is inspecting the stock.*] Quite a place! And I thought she was just talking big. I'll be flying again, all right. [*He takes a cigar, solicits and receives a light from* SHUI TA.] You think we can squeeze the other three hundred out of the tobacco stock?

SHUI TA: May I ask if it is your intention to sell at once?

YANG SUN: It was decent of her to come out with the two hundred, but they aren't much use with the other three hundred still missing.

SHUI TA: Shen Te was overhasty promising so much. She might have to sell the shop itself to raise it. Haste, they say, is the wind that blows the house down.

YANG SUN: Oh, she isn't a girl to keep a man waiting. For one thing or the other, if you take my meaning.

SHUI TA: I take your meaning.

YANG SUN: [*leering*] Uh, huh.

SHUI TA: Would you explain what the five hundred silver dollars are for?

YANG SUN: Want to sound me out? Very well. The director of the Peking airfield is a friend of mine from flying school. I give him five hundred: he gets me the job.

SHUI TA: The price is high.

YANG SUN: Not as these things go. He'll have to fire one of the present pilots—for negligence. Only the man he has in mind isn't negligent. Not easy, you understand. You needn't mention that part of it to Shen Te.

SHUI TA: [*looking intently at* YANG SUN] Mr. Yang Sun, you are asking my cousin to give up her possessions, leave her friends, and place her entire fate in your hands. I presume you intend to marry her?

YANG SUN: I'd be prepared to.

> [*slight pause*]

SHUI TA: Those two hundred silver dollars would pay the rent here for six months. If you were Shen Te wouldn't you be tempted to continue in business?

YANG SUN: What? Can you imagine Yang Sun the flyer behind a counter? [*in an oily voice*] "A strong cigar or a mild one, worthy sir?" Not in this century!

SHUI TA: My cousin wishes to follow the promptings of her heart, and, from her own point of view, she may even have what is called the right to love. Accordingly, she has commissioned me to help you to this post. There is nothing here that I am not empowered to turn immediately into cash. Mrs. Mi Tzu, the landlady, will advise me about the sale.

> [*Enter* MRS. MI TZU.]

MRS. MI TZU: Good morning, Mr. Shui Ta, you wish to see me about the rent? As you know it falls due the day after tomorrow.

SHUI TA: Circumstances have changed, Mrs. Mi Tzu: my cousin is getting married. Her future husband here, Mr. Yang Sun, will be taking her to Peking. I am interested in selling the tobacco stock.

MRS. MI TZU: How much are you asking, Mr. Shui Ta?

YANG SUN: Three hundred sil—

SHUI TA: Five hundred silver dollars.

MRS. MI TZU: How much did she pay for it, Mr. Shui Ta?

SHUI TA: A thousand. And very little has been sold.

MRS. MI TZU: She was robbed. But I'll make you a special offer if you'll promise to be out by the day after tomorrow. Three hundred silver dollars.

YANG SUN: [*shrugging*] Take it, man, take it.

SHUI TA: It is not enough.

YANG SUN: Why not? Why not? Certainly, it's enough.

SHUI TA: Five hundred silver dollars.

YANG SUN: But why? We only need three!

SHUI TA: [*to* MRS. MI TZU] Excuse me. [*takes* YANG SUN *on one side*] The tobacco stock is pledged to the old couple who gave my cousin the two hundred.

YANG SUN: Is it in writing?

SHUI TA: No.

YANG SUN: [*to* MRS. MI TZU] Three hundred will do.

MRS. MI TZU: Of course, I need an assurance that Miss Shen Te is not in debt.

YANG SUN: Mr. Shui Ta?

SHUI TA: She is not in debt.

YANG SUN: When can you let us have the money?

MRS. MI TZU: The day after tomorrow. And remember: I'm doing this because I have a soft spot in my heart for young lovers! [*Exit.*]

YANG SUN: [*calling after her*] Boxes, jars, and sacks—three hundred for the lot and the pain's over! [*to* SHUI TA] Where else can we raise money by the day after tomorrow?

SHUI TA: Nowhere. Haven't you enough for the trip and the first few weeks?

YANG SUN: Oh, certainly.

SHUI TA: How much, exactly.

YANG SUN: Oh, I'll dig it up, even if I have to steal it.

SHUI TA: I see.

YANG SUN: Well, don't fall off the roof. I'll get to Peking somehow.

SHUI TA: Two people can't travel for nothing.

YANG SUN: [*not giving* SHUI TA *a chance to answer*] I'm leaving *her* behind. No millstones round my neck!

SHUI TA: Oh.

YANG SUN: Don't look at me like that!

SHUI TA: How precisely is my cousin to live?

YANG SUN: Oh, you'll think of something.

SHUI TA: A small request, Mr. Yang Sun. Leave the two hundred silver dollars here until you can show me two tickets for Peking.

YANG SUN: You learn to mind your own business, Mr. Shui Ta.

SHUI TA: I'm afraid Miss Shen Te may not wish to sell the shop when she discovers that .

YANG SUN: You don't know women. She'll want to. Even then.

SHUI TA: [*a slight outburst*] She is a human being, sir! And not devoid of common sense!

YANG SUN: Shen Te is a woman: she *is* devoid of common sense. I only have to lay my hand on her shoulder, and church bells ring.

SHUI TA: [*with difficulty*] Mr. Yang Sun!

YANG SUN: Mr. Shui Whatever-it-is!

SHUI TA: My cousin is devoted to you . . . because . . .

YANG SUN: Because I have my hands on her breasts. Give me a cigar. [*He takes one for himself, stuffs a few more in his pocket, then changes his mind and takes the whole box.*] Tell her I'll marry her, then bring me the three hundred. Or let her bring it. One or the other. [*Exit.*]

MRS. SHIN: [*sticking her head out of the back room*] Well, he has your cousin under his thumb, and doesn't care if all Yellow Street knows it!

SHUI TA: [*crying out*] I've lost my shop! And he doesn't love me! [*He runs berserk through the room, repeating these lines incoherently. Then stops suddenly, and addresses* MRS. SHIN.] Mrs. Shin, you grew up in the gutter, like me. Are we lacking in hardness? I doubt it. If you steal a penny from me, I'll take you by the throat till you spit it out! You'd do the same to me. The times are bad, this city is hell, but we're like ants, we keep coming, up and up the walls, however smooth! Till bad luck comes. Being in love, for instance. One weakness is enough, and love is the deadliest.

MRS. SHIN: [*emerging from the back room*] You should have a little talk with Mr. Shu Fu, the barber. He's a real gentleman and just the thing for your cousin. [*She runs off.*]

SHUI TA: A caress becomes a stranglehold

A sigh of love turns to a cry of fear

Why are there vultures circling in the air?

A girl is going to meet her lover.

[SHUI TA *sits down and* MR. SHU FU *enters with* MRS. SHIN.]

SHUI TA: Mr. Shu Fu?

SHU FU: Mr. Shui Ta.

[*They both bow.*]

SHUI TA: I am told that you have expressed a certain interest in my cousin Shen Te. Let me set aside all propriety and confess: she is at this moment in grave danger.

SHU FU: Oh, dear!

SHUI TA: She has lost her shop, Mr. Shu Fu.

SHU FU: The charm of Miss Shen Te, Mr. Shui Ta, derives from the goodness, not of her shop, but of her heart. Men call her the Angel of the Slums.

SHUI TA: Yet her goodness has cost her two hundred silver dollars in a single day: we must put a stop to it.

SHU FU: Permit me to differ, Mr. Shui Ta. Let us, rather, open wide the gates to such goodness! Every morning, with pleasure tinged by affection, I watch her charitable ministrations. For they are hungry, and she giveth them to eat! Four of them, to be precise. Why only four? I ask. Why not four hundred? I hear she has been seeking shelter for the homeless. What about my humble cabins behind the cattle run? They are at her disposal. And so forth. And so on. Mr. Shui Ta, do you think Miss Shen Te could be persuaded to listen to certain ideas of mine? Ideas like these?

SHUI TA: Mr. Shu Fu, she would be honored.

[*Enter* WONG *and the* POLICEMAN. MR. SHU FU *turns abruptly away and studies the shelves.*]

WONG: Is Miss Shen Te here?

SHUI TA: No.

WONG: I am Wong the water seller. You are Mr. Shui Ta?

SHUI TA: I am.

WONG: I am a friend of Shen Te's.

SHUI TA: An intimate friend, I hear.

WONG: [*to the* POLICEMAN] You see? [*to* SHUI TA] It's because of my hand.

POLICEMAN: He hurt his hand, sir, that's a fact.

SHUI TA: [*quickly*] You need a sling, I see. [*He takes a shawl from the back room, and throws it to* WONG.]

WONG: But that's her new shawl!

SHUI TA: She has no more use for it.

WONG: But she bought it to please someone!

SHUI TA: It happens to be no longer necessary.

WONG: [*making the sling*] She is my only witness.

POLICEMAN: Mr. Shui Ta, your cousin is supposed to have seen the barber hit the water seller with a curling iron.

SHUI TA: I'm afraid my cousin was not present at the time.

WONG: But she was, sir! Just ask her! Isn't she in?

SHUI TA: [*gravely*] Mr. Wong, my cousin has her own troubles. You wouldn't wish her to add to them by committing perjury?

WONG: But it was she that told me to go to the judge!

SHUI TA: Was the judge supposed to heal your hand?

[MR. SHU FU *turns quickly around.* SHUI TA *bows to* SHU FU, *and vice versa.*]

WONG: [*taking the sling off, and putting it back*] I see how it is.

POLICEMAN: Well, I'll be on my way. [*to* WONG] And you be careful. If Mr. Shu Fu wasn't a man who tempers justice with mercy, as the saying is, you'd be in jail for libel. Be off with you!

[*Exit* WONG, *followed by* POLICEMAN.]

SHUI TA: Profound apologies, Mr. Shu Fu.

SHU FU: Not at all, Mr. Shui Ta. [*pointing to the shawl*] The episode is over?

SHUI TA: It may take her time to recover. There are some fresh wounds.

SHU FU: We shall be discreet. Delicate. A short vacation could be arranged. . . .

SHUI TA: First, of course, you and she would have to talk things over.

SHU FU: At a small supper in a small, but high-class, restaurant.

SHUI TA: I'll go and find her. [*Exit into back room.*]

MRS. SHIN: [*sticking her head in again*] Time for congratulations, Mr. Shu Fu?

SHU FU: Ah, Mrs. Shin! Please inform Miss Shen Te's guests they may take shelter in the cabins behind the cattle run!

[MRS. SHIN *nods, grinning.*]

SHU FU: [*to the audience*] Well? What do you think of me, ladies and gentlemen? What could a man do more? Could he be less selfish? More farsighted? A small supper in a small but . . . Does that bring rather vulgar and clumsy thoughts into your mind? Ts, ts, ts. Nothing of the sort will occur. She won't even be touched. Not even accidentally while passing the salt. An exchange of ideas only. Only the flowers on the table—white chrysanthemums, by the way [*He writes down a note of this*]—yes, over the white chrysanthemums, two young souls will . . . shall I say "find each other"? We shall *not* exploit the misfortune of others. Understanding? Yes. An offer of assistance?

Certainly. But quietly. Almost inaudibly. Perhaps with a single glance. A glance that could also—also mean more.

MRS. SHIN: [*coming forward*] Everything under control, Mr. Shu Fu?

SHU FU: Oh, Mrs. Shin, what do you know about this worthless rascal Yang Sun?

MRS. SHIN: Why, he's the most worthless rascal. . . .

SHU FU: Is he really? You're sure? [*as she opens her mouth*] From now on, he doesn't exist! Can't be found anywhere!

    [*Enter* YANG SUN.]

YANG SUN: What's been going on here?

MRS. SHIN: Shall I call Mr. Shui Ta, Mr. Shu Fu? He wouldn't want strangers in here!

SHU FU: Mr. Shui Ta is in conference with Miss Shen Te. Not to be disturbed.

YANG SUN: Shen Te here? I didn't see her come in. What kind of conference?

SHU FU: [*not letting him enter the back room*] Patience, dear sir! And if by chance I have an inkling who you are, pray take note that Miss Shen Te and I are about to announce our engagement.

YANG SUN: What?

MRS. SHIN: You didn't expect that, did you?

    [YANG SUN *is trying to push past the barber into the back room when* SHEN TE *comes out.*]

SHU FU: My dear Shen Te, ten thousand apologies! Perhaps you . . .

YANG SUN: What is it, Shen Te? Have you gone crazy?

SHEN TE: [*breathless*] My cousin and Mr. Shu Fu have come to an understanding. They wish me to hear Mr. Shu Fu's plans for helping the poor.

YANG SUN: Your cousin wants to part us.

SHEN TE: Yes.

YANG SUN: And you've agreed to it?

SHEN TE: Yes.

YANG SUN: They told you I was bad. [SHEN TE *is silent.*] And suppose I am. Does that make me need you less? I'm low, Shen Te, I have no money, I don't do the right thing but at least I put up a fight! [*He is near her now, and speaks in an undertone.*] Have you no eyes? Look at him. Have you forgotten already?

SHEN TE: No.

YANG SUN: How it was raining?

SHEN TE: No.

YANG SUN: How you cut me down from the willow tree? Bought me water? Promised me money to fly with?

SHEN TE: [*shakily*] Yang Sun, what do you want?

YANG SUN: I want you to come with me.

SHEN TE: [*in a small voice*] Forgive me, Mr. Shu Fu, I want to go with Mr. Yang Sun.

YANG SUN: We're lovers you know. Give me the key to the shop. [SHEN TE *takes the key from around her neck.* YANG SUN *puts it on the counter. To* MRS. SHIN:] Leave it under the mat when you're through. Let's go, Shen Te.

SHU FU: But this is rape! Mr. Shui Ta!

YANG SUN: [*to* SHEN TE] Tell him not to shout.

SHEN TE: Please don't shout for my cousin, Mr. Shu Fu. He doesn't agree with me, I know, but he's wrong. [*To the audience:*]

I want to go with the man I love
I don't want to count the cost
I don't want to consider if it's wise
I don't want to know if he loves me
I want to go with the man I love.

YANG SUN: That's the spirit.
          [*And the couple leave.*]

SCENE Va————*In front of the inner curtain.*

          [SHEN TE *in her wedding clothes, on the way to her wedding.*]
SHEN TE: Something terrible has happened. As I left the shop with Yang Sun, I found the
    old carpet dealer's wife waiting on the street, trembling all over. She told me her hus-
    band had taken to his bed sick with all the worry and excitement over the two hun-
    dred silver dollars they lent me. She said it would be best if I gave it back now. Of
    course, I had to say I would. She said she couldn't quite trust my cousin Shui Ta or even
    my fiancé Yang Sun. There were tears in her eyes. With my emotions in an uproar, I
    threw myself into Yang Sun's arms, I couldn't resist him. The things he'd said to Shui
    Ta had taught Shen Te nothing. Sinking into his arms, I said to myself:

    To let no one perish, not even oneself
    To fill everyone with happiness, even oneself
    Is so good

    How could I have forgotten those two old people? Yang Sun swept me away like a
    small hurricane. But he's not a bad man, and he loves me. He'd rather work in the
    cement factory than owe his flying to a crime. Though, of course, flying is a great
    passion with Sun. Now, on the way to my wedding, I waver between fear and joy.

SCENE VI————*The "private dining room" on the upper floor of a cheap restaurant in a poor
section of town.*

          [*With* SHEN TE: *the* GRANDFATHER, *the* SISTER-IN-LAW, *the* NIECE, MRS. SHIN, *the*
          UNEMPLOYED MAN. *In a corner, alone, a* PRIEST. A WAITER *pouring wine. Down-
          stage,* YANG SUN *talking to his* MOTHER. *He wears a dinner jacket.*]
YANG SUN: Bad news, Mamma. She came right out and told me she can't sell the shop
    for me. Some idiot is bringing a claim because he lent her the two hundred she
    gave you.
MRS. YANG: What did you say? Of course, you can't marry her now.
YANG SUN: It's no use saying anything to *her.* I've sent for her cousin, Mr. Shui Ta. He said
    there was nothing in writing.
MRS. YANG: Good idea. I'll go and look for him. Keep an eye on things.
          [*Exit* MRS. YANG. SHEN TE *has been pouring wine.*]
SHEN TE: [*to the audience, pitcher in hand*] I wasn't mistaken in him. He's bearing up well.
    Though it must have been an awful blow—giving up flying. I do love him so. [*call-
    ing across the room to him*] Sun, you haven't drunk a toast with the bride!
YANG SUN: What do we drink to?
SHEN TE: Why, to the future!
YANG SUN: When the bridegroom's dinner jacket won't be a hired one!
SHEN TE: But when the bride's dress will still get rained on sometimes!
YANG SUN: To everything we ever wished for!
SHEN TE: May all our dreams come true!
          [*They drink.*]
YANG SUN: [*with loud conviviality*] And now, friends, before the wedding gets under way,
    I have to ask the bride a few questions. I've no idea what kind of wife she'll make, and

it worries me. [*wheeling on* SHEN TE] For example. Can you make five cups of tea with three tea leaves?

SHEN TE: No.

YANG SUN: So I won't be getting very much tea. Can you sleep on a straw mattress the size of that book? [*He points to the large volume the* PRIEST *is reading.*]

SHEN TE: The two of us?

YANG SUN: The one of you.

SHEN TE: In that case, no.

YANG SUN: What a wife! I'm shocked!

> [*While the audience is laughing, his* MOTHER *returns. With a shrug of her shoulders, she tells* YANG SUN *the expected guest hasn't arrived. The* PRIEST *shuts the book with a bang, and makes for the door.*]

MRS. YANG: Where are you off to? It's only a matter of minutes.

PRIEST: [*watch in hand*] Time goes on, Mrs. Yang, and I've another wedding to attend to. Also a funeral.

MRS. YANG: [*irately*] D'you think we planned it this way? I was hoping to manage with one pitcher of wine, and we've run through two already. [*Points to empty pitcher. Loudly*] My dear Shen Te, I don't know where your cousin can be keeping himself!

SHEN TE: My cousin?!

MRS. YANG: Certainly. I'm old-fashioned enough to think such a close relative should attend the wedding.

SHEN TE: Oh, Sun, is it the three hundred silver dollars?

YANG SUN: [*not looking her in the eye*] Are you deaf? Mother says she's old-fashioned. And I say I'm considerate. We'll wait another fifteen minutes.

HUSBAND: Another fifteen minutes.

MRS. YANG: [*addressing the company*] Now you all know, don't you, that my son is getting a job as a mail pilot?

SISTER-IN-LAW: In Peking, too, isn't it?

MRS. YANG: In Peking, too! The two of us are moving to Peking!

SHEN TE: Sun, tell your mother Peking is out of the question now.

YANG SUN: Your cousin'll tell her. If he agrees. I don't agree.

SHEN TE: [*amazed, and dismayed*] Sun!

YANG SUN: I hate this godforsaken Setzuan. What people! Know what they look like when I half close my eyes? Horses! Whinnying, fretting, stamping, screwing their necks up! [*loudly*] And what is it the thunder says? They are su-per-flu-ous! [*He hammers out the syllables.*] They've run their last race! They can go trample themselves to death! [*pause*] I've got to get out of here.

SHEN TE: But I've promised the money to the old couple.

YANG SUN: And since you always do the wrong thing, it's lucky your cousin's coming. Have another drink.

SHEN TE: [*quietly*] My cousin can't be coming.

YANG SUN: How d'you mean?

SHEN TE: My cousin can't be where I am.

YANG SUN: Quite a conundrum!

SHEN TE: [*desperately*] Sun, I'm the one that loves you. Not my cousin. He was thinking of the job in Peking when he promised you the old couple's money—

YANG SUN: Right. And that's why he's bringing the three hundred silver dollars. Here—to my wedding.

SHEN TE: He is not bringing the three hundred silver dollars.

YANG SUN: Huh? What makes you think that?

SHEN TE: [*looking into his eyes*] He says you only bought one ticket to Peking. [*short pause*]

YANG SUN: That was yesterday. [*He pulls two tickets part way out of his inside pocket, making her look under his coat.*] Two tickets. I don't want Mother to know. She'll get left behind. I sold her furniture to buy these tickets, so you see . . .

SHEN TE: But what's to become of the old couple?

YANG SUN: What's to become of me? Have another drink. Or do you believe in moderation? If I drink, I fly again. If you drink, you may learn to understand me.

SHEN TE: You want to fly. But I can't help you.

YANG SUN: "Here's a plane, my darling—but it's only got one wing!" [*The* WAITER *enters.*]

WAITER: Mrs. Yang!

MRS. YANG: Yes?

WAITER: Another pitcher of wine, ma'am?

MRS. YANG: We have enough, thanks. Drinking makes me sweat.

WAITER: Would you mind paying, ma'am?

MRS. YANG: [*to everyone*] Just be patient a few moments longer, everyone, Mr. Shui Ta is on his way over! [*to the* WAITER] Don't be a spoilsport.

WAITER: I can't let you leave till you've paid your bill, ma'am.

MRS. YANG: But they know me here!

WAITER: That's just it.

PRIEST: [*ponderously getting up*] I humbly take my leave. [*And he does.*]

MRS. YANG: [*to the others, desperately*] Stay where you are, everybody! The priest says he'll be back in two minutes!

YANG SUN: It's no good, Mamma. Ladies and gentlemen, Mr. Shui Ta still hasn't arrived and the priest has gone home. We won't detain you any longer. [*They are leaving now.*]

GRANDFATHER: [*in the doorway, having forgotten to put his glass down*] To the bride! [*He drinks, puts down the glass, and follows the others.*] [*pause*]

SHEN TE: Shall I go, too?

YANG SUN: You? Aren't you the bride? Isn't this your wedding? [*He drags her across the room, tearing her wedding dress.*] If we can wait, you can wait. Mother calls me her falcon. She wants to see me in the clouds. But I think it may be St. Nevercome's Day before she'll go to the door and see my plane thunder by. [*Pause. He pretends the guests are still present.*] Why such a lull in the conversation, ladies and gentlemen? Don't you like it here? The ceremony is only slightly postponed—because an important guest is expected at any moment. Also because the bride doesn't know what love is. While we're waiting, the bridegroom will sing a little song. [*He does so:*]

THE SONG OF ST. NEVERCOME'S DAY

> On a certain day, as is generally known,
>   One and all will be shouting: Hooray, hooray!
> For the beggar maid's son has a solid-gold throne
>   And the day is St. Nevercome's Day
> On St. Nevercome's, Nevercome's, Nevercome's Day
>   He'll sit on his solid-gold throne
>
> Oh, hooray, hooray! That day goodness will pay!

That day badness will cost you your head!
And merit and money will smile and be funny
While exchanging salt and bread
On St. Nevercome's, Nevercome's, Nevercome's Day
While exchanging salt and bread

And the grass, oh, the grass will look down at the sky
And the pebbles will roll up the stream
And all men will be good without batting an eye
They will make of our Earth a dream
On St. Nevercome's, Nevercome's, Nevercome's Day
They will make of our Earth a dream

And as for me, that's the day I shall be
A flyer and one of the best
Unemployed man, you will have work to do
Washerwoman, you'll get your rest
On St. Nevercome's, Nevercome's, Nevercome's Day
Washerwoman you'll get your rest

MRS. YANG: It looks like he's not coming.
[*The three of them sit looking at the door.*]

SCENE VIa———WONG's *den.*

[*The sewer pipe is again transparent and again the* GODS *appear to* WONG *in a dream.*]

WONG: I'm so glad you've come, illustrious ones. It's Shen Te. She's in great trouble from following the rule about loving thy neighbor. Perhaps she's too good for this world!

FIRST GOD: Nonsense! You are eaten up by lice and doubts!

WONG: Forgive me, illustrious one, I only meant you might deign to intervene.

FIRST GOD: Out of the question! My colleague here intervened in some squabble or other only yesterday. [*He points to the* THIRD GOD, *who has a black eye.*] The results are before us!

WONG: She had to call on her cousin again. But not even he could help. I'm afraid the shop is done for.

THIRD GOD: [*a little concerned*] Perhaps we should help after all?

FIRST GOD: The gods help those that help themselves.

WONG: What if we *can't* help ourselves, illustrious ones?
[*slight pause*]

SECOND GOD: Try, anyway! Suffering ennobles!

FIRST GOD: Our faith in Shen Te is unshaken!

THIRD GOD: We certainly haven't found any *other* good people. You can see where we spend our nights from the straw on our clothes.

WONG: You might help her find her way by—

FIRST GOD: The good man finds his own way here below!

SECOND GOD: The good woman, too.

FIRST GOD: The heavier the burden, the greater her strength!

THIRD GOD: We're only onlookers, you know.

FIRST GOD: And everything will be all right in the end, O ye of little faith!
[*They are gradually disappearing through these last lines.*]

SCENE VII———*The yard behind* SHEN TE's *shop. A few articles of furniture on a cart.*

[SHEN TE *and* MRS. SHIN *are taking the washing off the line.*]

MRS. SHIN: If you ask me, you should fight tooth and nail to keep the shop.

SHEN TE: How can I? I have to sell the tobacco to pay back the two hundred silver dollars today.

MRS. SHIN: No husband, no tobacco, no house and home! What are you going to live on?

SHEN TE: I can work. I can sort tobacco.

MRS. SHIN: Hey, look. Mr. Shui Ta's trousers! He must have left here stark naked!

SHEN TE: Oh, he may have another pair, Mrs. Shin.

MRS. SHIN: But if he's gone for good as you say, why has he left his pants behind?

SHEN TE: Maybe he's thrown them away.

MRS. SHIN: Can I take them?

SHEN TE: Oh, no.

[*Enter* MR. SHU FU, *running.*]

SHU FU: Not a word! Total silence! I know all. You have sacrificed your own love and happiness so as not to hurt a dear old couple who had put their trust in you! Not in vain does this district—for all its malevolent tongues—call you the Angel of the Slums! That young man couldn't rise to your level, so you left him. And now, when I see you closing up the little shop, that veritable heaven of rest for the multitude, well, I cannot, I cannot let it pass. Morning after morning I have stood watching in the doorway not unmoved—while you graciously handed out rice to the wretched. Is that never to happen again? Is the good woman of Setzuan to disappear? If only you would allow *me* to assist you! Now don't say anything! No assurances, no exclamations of gratitude! [*He has taken out his checkbook.*] Here! A blank check. [*He places it on the cart.*] Just my signature. Fill it out as you wish. Any sum in the world. I herewith retire from the scene, quietly, unobtrusively, making no claims, on tiptoe, full of veneration, absolutely selflessly . . . [*He has gone.*]

MRS. SHIN: Well! You're saved. There's always some idiot of a man. . . . Now hurry! Put down a thousand silver dollars and let me fly to the bank before he comes to his senses.

SHEN TE: I can pay you for the washing without any check.

MRS. SHIN: What? You're not going to cash it just because you might have to marry him? Are you crazy? Men like him want to be led by the nose! Are you still thinking of that flyer? All Yellow Street knows how he treated you!

SHEN TE: When I heard his cunning laugh, I was afraid
But when I saw the holes in his shoes, I loved him dearly.

MRS. SHIN: Defending that good-for-nothing after all that's happened!

SHEN TE: [*staggering as she holds some of the washing*] Oh!

MRS. SHIN: [*taking the washing from her, dryly*] So you feel dizzy when you stretch and bend? There couldn't be a little visitor on the way? If that's it, you can forget Mr. Shu Fu's blank check: it wasn't meant for a christening present!

[*She goes to the back with a basket.* SHEN TE's *eyes follow* MRS. SHIN *for a moment. Then she looks down at her own body, feels her stomach, and a great joy comes into her eyes.*]

SHEN TE: O joy! A new human being is on the way. The world awaits him. In the cities the people say: he's got to be reckoned with, this new human being! [*She imagines a little boy to be present, and introduces him to the audience.*] This is my son, the well-known flyer!
Say: "Welcome"

To the conqueror of unknown mountains and unreachable regions
Who brings us our mail across the impassable deserts!
     [*She leads him up and down by the hand.*]
Take a look at the world, my son. That's a tree. Tree, yes. Say: "Hello, tree!" And bow.
Like this. [*She bows.*] Now you know each other. And, look, here comes the water
seller. He's a friend, give him your hand. A cup of fresh water for my little son, please.
Yes, it *is* a warm day. [*handing the cup*] Oh dear, a policeman, we'll have to make a
circle round *him*. Perhaps we can pick a few cherries over there in the rich Mr. Pung's
garden. But we mustn't be seen. You want cherries? Just like children with fathers. No,
no, you can't go straight at them like that. Don't pull. We must learn to be reasonable. Well, have it your own way. [*She has let him make for the cherries.*] Can you
reach? Where to put them? Your mouth is the best place. [*She tries one herself.*] Mmm,
they're good. But the policeman, we must run! [*They run.*] Yes, back to the street.
Calm now, so no one will notice us. [*Walking the street with her child, she sings.*]
             Once a plum—'twas in Japan—
             Made a conquest of a man
             But the man's turn soon did come
             For he gobbled up the plum
     [*Enter* WONG, *with a* CHILD *by the hand. He coughs.*]
SHEN TE: Wong!
WONG: It's about the carpenter, Shen Te. He's lost his shop, and he's been drinking. His
     children are on the streets. This is one. Can you help?
SHEN TE: [*to the* CHILD] Come here, little man. [*Takes him down to the footlights. To the
     audience:*]
     You there! A man is asking you for shelter!
     A man of tomorrow says: what about today?
     His friend the conqueror, whom you know,
     Is his advocate!
     [*to* WONG] He can live in Mr. Shu Fu's cabins. I may have to go there myself. I'm going
     to have a baby. That's a secret—don't tell Yang Sun—we'd only be in his way. Can
     you find the carpenter for me?
WONG: I knew you'd think of something. [*to the* CHILD] Good-bye, son, I'm going for your
     father.
SHEN TE: What about your hand, Wong? I wanted to help, but my cousin . . .
WONG: Oh, I can get along with one hand, don't worry. [*He shows how he can handle his
     pole with his left hand alone.*]
SHEN TE: But your right hand! Look, take this cart, sell everything that's on it, and go to
     the doctor with the money . . .
WONG: She's still good. But first I'll bring the carpenter. I'll pick up the cart when I get
     back. [*Exit* WONG.]
SHEN TE: [*to the* CHILD] Sit down over here, son, till your father comes. [*The* CHILD *sits cross-
     legged on the ground. Enter the* HUSBAND *and* WIFE, *each dragging a large, full sack.*]
WIFE: [*furtively*] You're alone, Shen Te, dear?
     [SHEN TE *nods. The* WIFE *beckons to the* NEPHEW *offstage. He comes on with
     another sack.*]
WIFE: Your cousin's away? [SHEN TE *nods*] He's not coming back?
SHEN TE: No. I'm giving up the shop.
WIFE: That's why we're here. We want to know if we can leave these things in your new
     home. Will you do us this favor?
SHEN TE: Why, yes, I'd be glad to.

HUSBAND: [*cryptically*] And if anyone asks about them, say they're yours.

SHEN TE: Would anyone ask?

WIFE: [*with a glance at her husband*] Oh, someone might. The police, for instance. They don't seem to like us. Where can we put it?

SHEN TE: Well, I'd rather not get in any more trouble . . .

WIFE: Listen to her. The good woman of Setzuan!

[SHEN TE *is silent.*]

HUSBAND: There's enough tobacco in those sacks to give us a new start in life. We could have our own tobacco factory!

SHEN TE: [*slowly*] You'll have to put them in the back room.

[*The sacks are taken offstage, while the* CHILD *is alone. Shyly glancing about him, he goes to the garbage can, starts playing with the contents, and eating some of the scraps. The others return.*]

WIFE: We're counting on you, Shen Te!

SHEN TE: Yes. [*She sees the* CHILD *and is shocked.*]

HUSBAND: We'll see you in Mr. Shu Fu's cabins.

NEPHEW: The day after tomorrow.

SHEN TE: Yes. Now, go. Go! I'm not feeling well.

[*Exeunt all three, virtually pushed off.*]

He is eating the refuse in the garbage can!

Only look at his little gray mouth!

[*Pause. Music.*]

As this is the world my son will enter

I will study to defend him.

To be good to you, my son,

I shall be a tigress to all others

If I have to.

And I shall have to.

[*She starts to go.*]

One more time, then. I hope really the last.

[*Exit* SHEN TE, *taking* SHUI TA'S *trousers.* MRS. SHIN *enters and watches her with marked interest. Enter the* SISTER-IN-LAW *and the* GRANDFATHER.]

SISTER-IN-LAW: So it's true, the shop has closed down. And the furniture's in the back yard. It's the end of the road!

MRS. SHIN: [*pompously*] The fruit of high living, selfishness, and sensuality! Down the primrose path to Mr. Shu Fu's cabins—with you!

SISTER-IN-LAW: Cabins? Rat holes! He gave them to us because his soap supplies only went moldy there!

[*Enter the* UNEMPLOYED MAN.]

UNEMPLOYED MAN: Shen Te is moving?

SISTER-IN-LAW: Yes. She was sneaking away.

MRS. SHIN: She's ashamed of herself, and no wonder!

UNEMPLOYED MAN: Tell her to call Mr. Shui Ta or she's done for this time!

SISTER-IN-LAW: Tell her to call Mr. Shui Ta or *we're* done for this time.

[*Enter* WONG *and* CARPENTER, *the latter with a* CHILD *on each hand.*]

CARPENTER: So we'll have a roof over our heads for a change!

MRS. SHIN: Roof? Whose roof?

CARPENTER: Mr. Shu Fu's cabins. And we have little Feng to thank for it. [FENG, *we find, is the name of the* CHILD *already there; his* FATHER *now takes him. To the other two:*] Bow to your little brother, you two!

[*The* CARPENTER *and the two new arrivals bow to* FENG. *Enter* SHUI TA.]

UNEMPLOYED MAN: Sst! Mr. Shui Ta!

    [*pause*]

SHUI TA: And what is this crowd here for, may I ask?

WONG: How do you do, Mr. Shui Ta? This is the carpenter. Miss Shen Te promised him space in Mr. Shu Fu's cabins.

SHUI TA: That will not be possible.

CARPENTER: We can't go there after all?

SHUI TA: All the space is needed for other purposes.

SISTER-IN-LAW: You mean we have to get out? But we've got nowhere to go.

SHUI TA: Miss Shen Te finds it possible to provide employment. If the proposition interests you, you may stay in the cabins.

SISTER-IN-LAW: [*with distaste*] You mean work? Work for Miss Shen Te?

SHUI TA: Making tobacco, yes. There are three bales here already. Would you like to get them?

SISTER-IN-LAW: [*trying to bluster*] We have our own tobacco! We were in the tobacco business before you were born!

SHUI TA: [*to the* CARPENTER *and the* UNEMPLOYED MAN] You don't have your own tobacco. What about you?

    [*The* CARPENTER *and the* UNEMPLOYED MAN *get the point, and go for the sacks. Enter* MRS. MI TZU.]

MRS. MI TZU: Mr. Shui Ta? I've brought you your three hundred silver dollars.

SHUI TA: I'll sign your lease instead. I've decided not to sell.

MRS. MI TZU: What? You don't need the money for that flyer?

SHUI TA: No.

MRS. MI TZU: And you can pay six months' rent?

SHUI TA: [*takes the barber's blank check from the cart and fills it out*] Here is a check for ten thousand silver dollars. On Mr. Shu Fu's account. Look! [*He shows her the signature on the check.*] Your six months' rent will be in your hands by seven this evening. And now, if you'll excuse me.

MRS. MI TZU: So it's Mr. Shu Fu now. The flyer has been given his walking papers. These modern girls! In my day they'd have said she was flighty. That poor, deserted Mr. Yang Sun!

    [*Exit* MRS. MI TZU. *The* CARPENTER *and the* UNEMPLOYED MAN *drag the three sacks back on the stage.*]

CARPENTER: [*to* SHUI TA] I don't know why I'm doing this for you.

SHUI TA: Perhaps your children want to eat, Mr. Carpenter.

SISTER-IN-LAW: [*catching sight of the sacks*] Was my brother-in-law here?

MRS. SHIN: Yes, he was.

SISTER-IN-LAW: I thought as much. I know those sacks! That's our tobacco!

SHUI TA: Really? I thought it came from my back room! Shall we consult the police on the point?

SISTER-IN-LAW: [*defeated*] No.

SHUI TA: Perhaps you will show me the way to Mr. Shu Fu's cabins?

    [*Taking* FENG *by the hand,* SHUI TA *goes off, followed by the* CARPENTER *and his two older children, the* SISTER-IN-LAW, *the* GRANDFATHER, *and the* UNEMPLOYED MAN. *Each of the last three drags a sack. Enter* OLD MAN *and* OLD WOMAN.]

MRS. SHIN: A pair of pants—missing from the clothesline one minute—and next minute on the honorable backside of Mr. Shui Ta.

OLD WOMAN: We thought Miss Shen Te was here.

MRS. SHIN: [*preoccupied*] Well, she's not.

OLD MAN: There was something she was going to give us.

WONG: She was going to help me, too. [*looking at his hand*] It'll be too late soon. But she'll be back. This cousin has never stayed long.

MRS. SHIN: [*approaching a conclusion*] No, he hasn't, has he?

SCENE VIIa———*The sewer pipe.*

[WONG *asleep. In his dream, he tells the* GODS *his fears. The* GODS *seem tired from all their travels. They stop for a moment and look over their shoulders at the water seller.*]

WONG: Illustrious ones. I've been having a bad dream. Our beloved Shen Te was in great distress in the rushes down by the river—the spot where the bodies of suicides are washed up. She kept staggering and holding her head down as if she was carrying something and it was dragging her down into the mud. When I called out to her, she said she had to take your book of rules to the other side, and not get it wet, or the ink would all come off. You had talked to her about the virtues, you know, the time she gave you shelter in Setzuan.

THIRD GOD: Well, but what do you suggest, my dear Wong?

WONG: Maybe a little relaxation of the rules, Benevolent One, in view of the bad times.

THIRD GOD: As for instance?

WONG: Well, um, goodwill, for instance, might do instead of love?

THIRD GOD: I'm afraid that would create new problems.

WONG: Or instead of justice, good sportsmanship?

THIRD GOD: That would only mean more work.

WONG: Instead of honor, outward propriety?

THIRD GOD: Still more work! No, no! The rules will have to stand, my dear Wong!

[*Wearily shaking their heads, all three journey on.*]

SCENE VIII———SHUI TA's *tobacco factory in* SHU FU's *cabins.*

[*Huddled together behind bars, several families, mostly women and children. Among these people the* SISTER-IN-LAW, *the* GRANDFATHER, *the* CARPENTER, *and his* THREE CHILDREN. *Enter* MRS. YANG *followed by* YANG SUN.]

MRS. YANG: [*to the audience*] There's something I just *have* to tell you: strength and wisdom are wonderful things. The strong and wise Mr. Shui Ta has transformed my son from a dissipated good-for-nothing into a model citizen. As you may have heard, Mr. Shui Ta opened a small tobacco factory near the cattle runs. It flourished. Three months ago—I shall never forget it—I asked for an appointment, and Mr. Shui Ta agreed to see us—me and my son. I can see him now as he came through the door to meet us. . . .

[*Enter* SHUI TA *from a door.*]

SHUI TA: What can I do for you, Mrs. Yang?

MRS. YANG: This morning the police came to the house. We find you've brought an action for breach of promise of marriage. In the name of Shen Te. You also claim that Sun came by two hundred silver dollars by improper means.

SHUI TA: That is correct.

MRS. YANG: Mr. Shui Ta, the money's all gone. When the Peking job didn't materialize, he ran through it all in three days. I know he's a good-for-nothing. He sold my furniture. He was moving to Peking without me. Miss Shen Te thought highly of him at one time.

SHUI TA: What do *you* say, Mr. Yang Sun?

YANG SUN: The money's gone.

SHUI TA: [*to* MRS. YANG] Mrs. Yang, in consideration of my cousin's incomprehensible weakness for your son, I am prepared to give him another chance. He can have a job—here. The two hundred silver dollars will be taken out of his wages.

YANG SUN: So it's the factory or jail?

SHUI TA: Take your choice.

YANG SUN: May I speak with Shen Te?

SHUI TA: You may not.

> [*pause*]

YANG SUN: [*sullenly*] Show me where to go.

MRS. YANG: Mr. Shui Ta, you are kindness itself: the gods will reward you! [*to* YANG SUN] And honest work will make a man of you, my boy. [YANG SUN *follows* SHUI TA *into the factory.* MRS. YANG *comes down again to the footlights.*] Actually, honest work didn't agree with him—at first. And he got no opportunity to distinguish himself till—in the third week—when the wages were being paid . . .

> [SHUI TA *has a bag of money. Standing next to his foreman—the former* UNEMPLOYED MAN—HE *counts out the wages. It is* YANG SUN'S *turn.*]

UNEMPLOYED MAN: [*reading*] Carpenter, six silver dollars. Yang Sun, six silver dollars.

YANG SUN: [*quietly*] Excuse me, sir. I don't think it can be more than five. May I see? [*He takes the foreman's list.*] It says six working days. But that's a mistake, sir. I took a day off for court business. And I won't take what I haven't earned, however miserable the pay is!

UNEMPLOYED MAN: Yang Sun. Five silver dollars. [*to* SHUI TA] A rare case, Mr. Shui Ta!

SHUI TA: How is it the book says six when it should say five?

UNEMPLOYED MAN: I must've made a mistake, Mr. Shui Ta. [*with a look at* YANG SUN] It won't happen again.

SHUI TA: [*taking* YANG SUN *aside*] You don't hold back, do you? You give your all to the firm. You're even honest. Do the foreman's mistakes always favor the workers?

YANG SUN: He does have . . . friends.

SHUI TA: Thank you. May I offer you any little recompense?

YANG SUN: Give me a trial period of one week, and I'll prove my intelligence is worth more to you than my strength.

MRS. YANG: [*still down at the footlights*] Fighting words, fighting words! That evening, I said to Sun: "If you're a flyer, then fly, my falcon! Rise in the world!" And he got to be foreman. Yes, in Mr. Shui Ta's tobacco factory, he worked real miracles.

> [*We see* YANG SUN *with his legs apart standing behind the workers who are handing along a basket of raw tobacco above their heads.*]

YANG SUN: Faster! Faster! You, there, d'you think you can just stand around, now you're not foreman any more? It'll be your job to lead us in song. Sing!

> [UNEMPLOYED MAN *starts singing. The others join in the refrain.*]

SONG OF THE EIGHTH ELEPHANT

> *Chang had seven elephants—all much the same—*
> *But then there was Little Brother*
> *The seven, they were wild, Little Brother, he was tame*
> *And to guard them Chang chose Little Brother*
> *Run faster!*
> *Mr. Chang has a forest park*
> *Which must be cleared before tonight*
> *And already it's growing dark!*

When the seven elephants cleared that forest park
Mr. Chang rode high on Little Brother
While the seven toiled and moiled till dark
On his big behind sat Little Brother
Dig faster!
Mr. Chang has a forest park
Which must be cleared before tonight
And already it's growing dark!

And the seven elephants worked many an hour
Till none of them could work another
Old Chang, he looked sour, on the seven he did glower
But gave a pound of rice to Little Brother
What was that?
Mr. Chang has a forest park
Which must be cleared before tonight
And already it's growing dark!

And the seven elephants hadn't any tusks
The one that had the tusks was Little Brother
Seven are no match for one, if the one has a gun!
How old Chang did laugh at Little Brother!
Keep on digging!
Mr. Chang has a forest park
Which must be cleared before tonight
And already it's growing dark!

[*Smoking a cigar,* SHUI TA *strolls by* YANG SUN, *laughing, has joined in the refrain of the third stanza and speeded up the tempo of the last stanza by clapping his hands.*]

MRS. YANG: And that's why I say: strength and wisdom are wonderful things. It took the strong and wise Mr. Shui Ta to bring out the best in Yang Sun. A real superior man is like a bell. If you ring it, it rings, and if you don't, it don't, as the saying is.

SCENE IX————SHEN TE's *shop, now an office with club chairs and fine carpets. It is raining.*

[SHUI TA, *now fat, is just dismissing the* OLD MAN *and* OLD WOMAN. MRS. SHIN, *in obviously new clothes, looks on, smirking.*]

SHUI TA: No! I can *not* tell you when we expect her back.

OLD WOMAN: The two hundred silver dollars came today. In an envelope. There was no letter, but it must be from Shen Te. We want to write and thank her. May we have her address?

SHUI TA: I'm afraid I haven't got it.

OLD MAN: [*pulling* OLD WOMAN's *sleeve*] Let's be going.

OLD WOMAN: She's got to come back some time!

[*They move off, uncertainly, worried.* SHUI TA *bows.*]

MRS. SHIN: They lost the carpet shop because they couldn't pay their taxes. The money arrived too late.

SHUI TA: They could have come to me.

MRS. SHIN: People don't like coming to you.

SHUI TA: [*sits suddenly, one hand to his head*] I'm dizzy.

MRS. SHIN: After all, you are in your seventh month. But old Mrs. Shin will be there in your hour of trial! [*She cackles feebly.*]

SHUI TA: [*in a stifled voice*] Can I count on that?

MRS. SHIN: We all have our price, and mine won't be too high for the great Mr. Shui Ta! [*She opens* SHUI TA'*s collar.*]

SHUI TA: It's for the child's sake. All of this.

MRS. SHIN: "All for the child," of course.

SHUI TA: I'm so fat. People must notice.

MRS. SHIN: Oh no, they think it's 'cause you're rich.

SHUI TA: [*more feelingly*] What will happen to the child?

MRS. SHIN: You ask that nine times a day. Why, it'll have the best that money can buy!

SHUI TA: He must never see Shui Ta.

MRS. SHIN: Oh, no. Always Shen Te.

SHUI TA: What about the neighbors? There are rumors, aren't there?

MRS. SHIN: As long as Mr. Shu Fu doesn't find out, there's nothing to worry about. Drink this.

[*Enter* YANG SUN *in a smart business suit, and carrying a businessman's briefcase.* SHUI TA *is more or less in* MRS. SHIN'*s arms.*]

YANG SUN: [*surprised*] I guess I'm in the way.

SHUI TA: [*ignoring this, rises with an effort*] Till tomorrow, Mrs. Shin.

[MRS. SHIN *leaves with a smile, putting her new gloves on.*]

YANG SUN: Gloves now! She couldn't be fleecing you? And since when did you have a private life? [*taking a paper from the briefcase*] You haven't been at your desk lately, and things are getting out of hand. The police want to close us down. They say that at the most they can only permit twice the lawful number of workers.

SHUI TA: [*evasively*] The cabins are quite good enough.

YANG SUN: For the workers maybe, not for the tobacco. They're too damp. We must take over some of Mrs. Mi Tzu's buildings.

SHUI TA: Her price is double what I can pay.

YANG SUN: Not unconditionally. If she has me to stroke her knees she'll come down.

SHUI TA: I'll never agree to that.

YANG SUN: What's wrong? Is it the rain? You get so irritable whenever it rains.

SHUI TA: Never! I will never . . .

YANG SUN: Mrs. Mi Tzu'll be here in five minutes. *You* fix it. And Shu Fu will be with her. . . . What's all that noise?

[*During the above dialogue,* WONG *is heard offstage, calling:* "The good Shen Te, where is she? Which of you has seen Shen Te, good people? Where is Shen Te?" *A knock. Enter* WONG.]

WONG: Mr. Shui Ta, I've come to ask when Miss Shen Te will be back, it's six months now. . . . There are rumors. People say something's happened to her.

SHUI TA: I'm busy. Come back next week.

WONG: [*excited*] In the morning there was always rice on her doorstep—for the needy. It's been there again lately!

SHUI TA: And what do people conclude from this?

WONG: That Shen Te is still in Setzuan! She's been . . . [*He breaks off.*]

SHUI TA: She's been what? Mr. Wong, if you're Shen Te's friend, talk a little less about her, that's my advice to you.

WONG: I don't want your advice! Before she disappeared, Miss Shen Te told me something very important—she's pregnant!

YANG SUN: What? What was that?

SHUI TA: [*quickly*] The man is lying.

WONG: A good woman isn't so easily forgotten, Mr. Shui Ta.

> [*He leaves.* SHUI TA *goes quickly into the back room.*]

YANG SUN: [*to the audience*] Shen Te's pregnant? So that's why. Her cousin sent her away, so I wouldn't get wind of it. I have a son, a Yang appears on the scene, and what happens? Mother and child vanish into thin air! That scoundrel, that unspeakable . . . [*The sound of sobbing is heard from the back room.*] What was that? Someone sobbing? Who was it? Mr. Shui Ta the Tobacco King doesn't weep his heart out. And where does the rice come from that's on the doorstep in the morning? [SHUI TA *returns. He goes to the door and looks out into the rain.*] Where is she?

SHUI TA: Sh! It's nine o'clock. But the rain's so heavy, you can't hear a thing.

YANG SUN: What do you want to hear?

SHUI TA: The mail plane.

YANG SUN: What?!

SHUI TA: I've been told *you* wanted to fly at one time. Is that all forgotten?

YANG SUN: Flying mail is night work. I prefer the daytime. And the firm is very dear to me—after all, it belongs to my ex-fiancé, even if she's not around. And she's not, is she?

SHUI TA: What do you mean by that?

YANG SUN: Oh, well, let's say I haven't altogether—lost interest.

SHUI TA: My cousin might like to know that.

YANG SUN: I might not be indifferent—if I found she was being kept under lock and key.

SHUI TA: By whom?

YANG SUN: By you.

SHUI TA: What could you do about it?

YANG SUN: I could submit for discussion—my position in the firm.

SHUI TA: You are now my manager. In return for a more . . . appropriate position, you might agree to drop the inquiry into your ex-fiancé's whereabouts?

YANG SUN: I might.

SHUI TA: What position *would* be more appropriate?

YANG SUN: The one at the top.

SHUI TA: My own? [*silence*] And if I preferred to throw you out on your neck?

YANG SUN: I'd come back on my feet. With suitable escort.

SHUI TA: The police?

YANG SUN: The police.

SHUI TA: And when the police found no one?

YANG SUN: I might ask them not to overlook the back room. [*ending the pretense*] In short, Mr. Shui Ta, my interest in this young woman has not been officially terminated. I should like to see more of her. [*into* SHUI TA's *face*] Besides, she's pregnant and needs a friend. [*He moves to the door.*] I shall talk about it with the water seller.

> [*Exit.* SHUI TA *is rigid for a moment, then he quickly goes into the back room. He returns with* SHEN TE's *belongings: underwear, etc. He takes a long look at the shawl of the previous scene. He then wraps the things in a bundle, which, upon hearing a noise, he hides under the table. Enter* MRS. MI TZU *and* MR. SHU FU. *They put away their umbrellas and galoshes.*]

MRS. MI TZU: I thought your manager was here, Mr. Shui Ta. He combines charm with business in a way that can only be to the advantage of all of us.

SHU FU: You sent for us, Mr. Shui Ta?

SHUI TA: The factory is in trouble.

SHU FU: It always is.

SHUI TA: The police are threatening to close us down unless I can show that the extension of our facilities is imminent.

SHU FU: Shui Ta, I'm sick and tired of your constantly expanding projects. I place cabins at your cousin's disposal; you make a factory of them. I hand your cousin a check; you present it. Your cousin disappears; you find the cabins too small and start talking of yet more—

SHUI TA: Mr. Shu Fu, I'm authorized to inform you that Miss Shen Te's return is now imminent.

SHU FU: Imminent? It's becoming his favorite word.

MRS. MI TZU: Yes, what does it mean?

SHUI TA: Mrs. Mi Tzu, I can pay you exactly half what you asked for your buildings. Are you ready to inform the police that I am taking them over?

MRS. MI TZU: Certainly, if I can take over your manager.

SHU FU: What?

MRS. MI TZU: He's so efficient.

SHUI TA: I'm afraid I need Mr. Yang Sun.

MRS. MI TZU: So do I.

SHUI TA: He will call on you tomorrow.

SHU FU: So much the better. With Shen Te likely to turn up at any moment, the presence of that young man is hardly in good taste.

SHUI TA: So we have reached a settlement. In what was once the good Shen Te's little shop we are laying the foundation for the great Mr. Shui Ta's twelve magnificent super tobacco markets. You will bear in mind that though they call me the Tobacco King of Setzuan, it is my cousin's interests that have been served . . .

VOICES: [*off*] The police, the police! Going to the tobacco shop! Something must have happened!

[*Enter* YANG SUN, WONG, *and the* POLICEMAN.]

POLICEMAN: Quiet there, quiet, quiet! [*They quiet down.*] I'm sorry, Mr. Shui Ta, but there's a report that you've been depriving Miss Shen Te of her freedom. Not that I believe all I hear, but the whole city's in an uproar.

SHUI TA: That's a lie.

POLICEMAN: Mr. Yang Sun has testified that he heard someone sobbing in the back room.

SHU FU: Mrs. Mi Tzu and myself will testify that no one here has been sobbing.

MRS. MI TZU: We have been quietly smoking our cigars.

POLICEMAN: Mr. Shui Ta, I'm afraid I shall have to take a look at that room. [*He does so. The room is empty.*] No one there, of course, sir.

YANG SUN: But I heard sobbing. What's that? [*He finds the clothes.*]

WONG: Those are Shen Te's things. [*to crowd*] Shen Te's clothes are here!

VOICES: [*off, in sequence*]
—Shen Te's clothes!
—They've been found under the table!
—Body of murdered girl still missing!
—Tobacco King suspected!

POLICEMAN: Mr. Shui Ta, unless you can tell us where the girl is, I'll have to ask you to come along.

SHUI TA: I do not know.

POLICEMAN: I can't say how sorry I am, Mr. Shui Ta. [*He shows him the door.*]

SHUI TA: Everything will be cleared up in no time. There are still judges in Setzuan.

YANG SUN: I heard sobbing!

SCENE IXa————WONG's *den.*

> [*For the last time, the* GODS *appear to the water seller in his dream. They have changed and show signs of a long journey, extreme fatigue, and plenty of mishaps. The* FIRST *no longer has a hat; the* THIRD *has lost a leg; all three are barefoot.*]

WONG: Illustrious ones, at last you're here. Shen Te's been gone for months and today her cousin's been arrested. They think he murdered her to get the shop. But I had a dream and in this dream Shen Te said her cousin was keeping her prisoner. You must find her for us, illustrious ones!

FIRST GOD: We've found very few good people anywhere, and even they didn't keep it up. Shen Te is still the only one that stayed good.

SECOND GOD: If she *has* stayed good.

WONG: Certainly she has. But she's vanished.

FIRST GOD: That's the last straw. All is lost!

SECOND GOD: A little moderation, dear colleague!

FIRST GOD: [*plaintively*] What's the good of moderation now? If she can't be found, we'll have to resign! The world is a terrible place! Nothing but misery, vulgarity, and waste! Even the countryside isn't what it used to be. The trees are getting their heads chopped off by telephone wires, and there's such a noise from all the gunfire, and I can't stand those heavy clouds of smoke, and—

THIRD GOD: The place is absolutely unlivable! Good intentions bring people to the brink of the abyss, and good deeds push them over the edge. I'm afraid our book of rules is destined for the scrap heap—

SECOND GOD: It's people! They're a worthless lot!

THIRD GOD: The world is too cold!

SECOND GOD: It's people! They're too weak!

FIRST GOD: Dignity, dear colleagues, dignity! Never despair! As for this world, didn't we agree that we only have to find one human being who can stand the place? Well, we found her. True, we lost her again. We must find her again, that's all. And at once!

> [*They disappear.*]

SCENE X————*Courtroom.*

> [*Groups:* SHU FU *and* MRS. MI TZU; YANG SUN *and* MRS. YANG; WONG, *the* CARPENTER, *the* GRANDFATHER, *the* NIECE, *the* OLD MAN, *the* OLD WOMAN; MRS. SHIN, *the* POLICEMAN; *the* UNEMPLOYED MAN, *the* SISTER-IN-LAW.]

OLD MAN: So much power isn't good for one man.

UNEMPLOYED MAN: And he's going to open twelve super tobacco markets!

WIFE: One of the judges is a friend of Mr. Shu Fu's.

SISTER-IN-LAW: Another one accepted a present from Mr. Shui Ta only last night. A great fat goose.

OLD WOMAN: [*to* WONG] And Shen Te is nowhere to be found.

WONG: Only the gods will ever know the truth.

POLICEMAN: Order in the court! My lords the judges!

> [*Enter the* THREE GODS *in judges' robes. We overhear their conversation as they pass along the footlights to their bench.*]

THIRD GOD: We'll never get away with it, our certificates were so badly forged.

SECOND GOD: My predecessor's "sudden indigestion" will certainly cause comment.

FIRST GOD: But he had just eaten a whole goose.

UNEMPLOYED MAN: Look at that! New judges.

WONG: New judges. And what good ones!

[*The* THIRD GOD *hears this, and turns to smile at* WONG. *The* GODS *sit. The* FIRST GOD *beats on the bench with his gavel. The* POLICEMAN *brings in* SHUI TA, *who walks with lordly steps. He is whistled at.*]

POLICEMAN: [*to* SHUI TA] Be prepared for a surprise. The judges have been changed.

[SHUI TA *turns quickly round, looks at them, and staggers.*]

NIECE: What's the matter now?

WIFE: The great Tobacco King nearly fainted.

HUSBAND: Yes, as soon as he saw the new judges.

WONG: Does he know who they are?

[SHUI TA *picks himself up, and the proceedings open.*]

FIRST GOD: Defendant Shui Ta, you are accused of doing away with your cousin Shen Te in order to take possession of her business. Do you plead guilty or not guilty?

SHUI TA: Not guilty, my lord.

FIRST GOD: [*thumbing through the documents of the case*] The first witness is the policeman. I shall ask him to tell us something of the respective reputations of Miss Shen Te and Mr. Shui Ta.

POLICEMAN: Miss Shen Te was a young lady who aimed to please, my lord. She liked to live and let live, as the saying goes. Mr. Shui Ta, on the other hand, is a man of principle. Though the generosity of Miss Shen Te forced him at times to abandon half measures, unlike the girl he was always on the side of the law, my lord. One time, he even unmasked a gang of thieves to whom his too-trustful cousin had given shelter. The evidence, in short, my lord, proves that Mr. Shui Ta was *incapable* of the crime of which he stands accused!

FIRST GOD: I see. And are there others who could testify along, shall we say, the same lines?

[SHU FU *rises.*]

POLICEMAN: [*whispering to* GODS] Mr. Shu Fu—a very important person.

FIRST GOD: [*inviting him to speak*] Mr. Shu Fu!

SHU FU: Mr. Shui Ta is a businessman, my lord. Need I say more?

FIRST GOD: Yes.

SHU FU: Very well, I will. He is Vice President of the Council of Commerce and is about to be elected a Justice of the Peace. [*He returns to his seat.*]

[MRS. MI TZU *rises.*]

WONG: Elected! *He* gave him the job!

[*With a gesture the* FIRST GOD *asks who* MRS. MI TZU *is.*]

POLICEMAN: Another very important person. Mrs. Mi Tzu.

MRS. MI TZU: My lord, as Chairman of the Committee on Social Work, I wish to call attention to just a couple of eloquent facts: Mr. Shui Ta not only has erected a model factory with model housing in our city, he is a regular contributor to our home for the disabled. [*She returns to her seat.*]

POLICEMAN: [*whispering*] And she's a great friend of the judge that ate the goose!

FIRST GOD: [*to the* POLICEMAN] Oh, thank you. What's next? [*to the Court, genially*] Oh, yes. We should find out if any of the evidence is less favorable to the defendant.

[WONG, *the* CARPENTER, *the* OLD MAN, *the* OLD WOMAN, *the* UNEMPLOYED MAN, *the* SISTER-IN-LAW, *and the* NIECE *come forward.*]

POLICEMAN: [*whispering*] Just the riffraff, my lord.

FIRST GOD: [*addressing the "riffraff"*] Well, um, riffraff—do you know anything of the defendant, Mr. Shui Ta?

WONG: Too much, my lord.

UNEMPLOYED MAN: What don't we know, my lord.

CARPENTER: He ruined us.

SISTER-IN-LAW: He's a cheat.

NIECE: Liar.

WIFE: Thief.

BOY: Blackmailer.

BROTHER: Murderer.

FIRST GOD: Thank you. We should now let the defendant state his point of view.

SHUI TA: I only came on the scene when Shen Te was in danger of losing what I had understood was a gift from the gods. Because I did the filthy jobs which someone had to do, they hate me. My activities were restricted to the minimum, my lord.

SISTER-IN-LAW: He had us arrested!

SHUI TA: Certainly. You stole from the bakery!

SISTER-IN-LAW: Such concern for the bakery! You didn't want the shop for yourself, I suppose!

SHUI TA: I didn't want the shop overrun with parasites.

SISTER-IN-LAW: We had nowhere else to go.

SHUI TA: There were too many of you.

WONG: What about this old couple. Were *they* parasites?

OLD MAN: We lost our shop because of you!

OLD WOMAN: And we gave your cousin money!

SHUI TA: My cousin's fiancé was a flyer. The money had to go to him.

WONG: Did you care whether he flew or not? Did you care whether she married him or not? You wanted her to marry someone else! [*He points at* SHU FU.]

SHUI TA: The flyer unexpectedly turned out to be a scoundrel.

YANG SUN: [*jumping up*] Which was the reason you made him your manager?

SHUI TA: Later on he improved.

WONG: And when he improved, you sold him to her? [*He points out* MRS. MI TZU.]

SHUI TA: She wouldn't let me have her premises unless she had him to stroke her knees!

MRS. MI TZU: What? The man's a pathological liar. [*to him*] Don't mention my property to me as long as you live! Murderer! [*She rustles off, in high dudgeon.*]

YANG SUN: [*pushing in*] My lord, I wish to speak for the defendant.

SISTER-IN-LAW: Naturally. He's your employer.

UNEMPLOYED MAN: And the worst slave driver in the country.

MRS. YANG: That's a lie! My lord, Mr. Shui Ta is a great man. He . . .

YANG SUN: He's this and he's that, but he is not a murderer, my lord. Just fifteen minutes before his arrest I heard Shen Te's voice in his own back room.

FIRST GOD: Oh? Tell us more!

YANG SUN: I heard sobbing, my lord!

FIRST GOD: But lots of women sob, we've been finding.

YANG SUN: Could I fail to recognize her voice?

SHU FU: No, you made her sob so often yourself, young man!

YANG SUN: Yes. But I also made her happy. Till he [*pointing at* SHUI TA] decided to sell her to you!

SHUI TA: Because you didn't love her.

WONG: Oh, no: it was for the money, my lord!

SHUI TA: And what was the money for, my lord? For the poor! And for Shen Te so she could go on being good!

WONG: For the poor? That he sent to his sweatshops? And why didn't you let Shen Te be good when you signed the big check?

SHUI TA: For the child's sake, my lord.

CARPENTER: What about *my* children? What did he do about them?

> [SHUI TA *is silent.*]

WONG: The shop was to be a fountain of goodness. That was the gods' idea. You came and spoiled it!

SHUI TA: If I hadn't, it would have run dry!

MRS. SHIN: There's a lot in that, my lord.

WONG: What have you done with the good Shen Te, bad man? She was good, my lords, she was, I swear it! [*He raises his hand in an oath.*]

THIRD GOD: What's happened to your hand, water seller?

WONG: [*pointing to* SHUI TA] It's all his fault, my lord, *she* was going to send me to a doctor—[*to* SHUI TA] You were her worst enemy!

SHUI TA: I was her only friend!

WONG: Where is she then? Tell us where your good friend is!

> [*The excitement of this exchange has run through the whole crowd.*]

ALL: Yes, where is she? Where is Shen Te? [*etc.*]

SHUI TA: Shen Te . . . had to go.

WONG: Where? Where to?

SHUI TA: I cannot tell you! I cannot tell you!

ALL: Why? Why did she have to go away? [*etc.*]

WONG: [*into the din with the first words, but talking on beyond the others*] Why not, why not? Why did she have to go away?

SHUI TA: [*shouting*] Because you'd all have torn her to shreds, that's why! My lords, I have a request. Clear the court! When only the judges remain, I will make a confession.

ALL: [*except* WONG, *who is silent, struck by the new turn of events*] So he's guilty? He's confessing! [*etc.*]

FIRST GOD: [*using the gavel*] Clear the court!

POLICEMAN: Clear the court!

WONG: Mr. Shui Ta has met his match this time.

MRS. SHIN: [*with a gesture toward the judges*] You're in for a little surprise.

> [*The court is cleared. Silence.*]

SHUI TA: Illustrious ones!

> [*The* GODS *look at each other, not quite believing their ears.*]

SHUI TA: Yes, I recognize you!

SECOND GOD: [*taking matters in hand, sternly*] What have you done with our good woman of Setzuan?

SHUI TA: I have a terrible confession to make: I am she! [*He takes off his mask, and tears away his clothes.* SHEN TE *stands there.*]

SECOND GOD: Shen Te!

SHEN TE: Shen Te, yes. Shui Ta *and* Shen Te. Both.

> Your injunction
> To be good and yet to live
> Was a thunderbolt:
> It has torn me in two
> I can't tell how it was
> But to be good to others
> And myself at the same time
> I could not do it
> Your world is not an easy one, illustrious ones!
> When we extend our hand to a beggar, he tears it off for us

When we help the lost, we are lost ourselves
And so
Since not to eat is to die
Who can long refuse to be bad?
As I lay prostrate beneath the weight of good intentions
Ruin stared me in the face
It was when I was unjust that I ate good meat
And hobnobbed with the mighty
Why?
Why are bad deeds rewarded?
Good ones punished?
I enjoyed giving
I truly wished to be the Angel of the Slums
But washed by a foster mother in the water of the gutter
I developed a sharp eye
The time came when pity was a thorn in my side
And, later, when kind words turned to ashes in my mouth
And anger took over
I became a wolf
Find me guilty, then, illustrious ones,
But know:
All that I have done I did
To help my neighbor
To love my lover
And to keep my little one from want
For your great, godly deeds, I was too poor, too small.
> [*pause*]

FIRST GOD: [*shocked*] Don't go making yourself miserable, Shen Te! We're overjoyed to have found you!

SHEN TE: I'm telling you I'm the bad man who committed all those crimes!

FIRST GOD: [*using—or failing to use—his ear trumpet*] The good woman who did all those good deeds?

SHEN TE: Yes, but the bad man, too!

FIRST GOD: [*as if something had dawned*] Unfortunate coincidences! Heartless neighbors!

THIRD GOD: [*shouting in his ear*] But how is she to continue?

FIRST GOD: Continue? Well, she's a strong, healthy girl . . .

SECOND GOD: You didn't hear what she said!

FIRST GOD: I heard every word! She is confused, that's all! [*He begins to bluster.*] And what about this book of rules—we can't renounce our rules, can we? [*more quietly*] Should the world be changed? How? By whom? The world should not be changed! [*At a sign from him, the lights turn pink, and music plays.*[1]]
And now the hour of parting is at hand.
Dost thou behold, Shen Te, yon fleecy cloud?
It is our chariot. At a sign from me
'Twill come and take us back from whence we came
Above the azure vault and silver stars. . . .

---

[1]The rest of this scene has been adapted by many American theatres that do not have "fly-space" to lower things from ropes.

SHEN TE: No! Don't go, illustrious ones!

FIRST GOD: Our cloud has landed now in yonder field
From which it will transport us back to heaven.
Farewell, Shen Te, let not thy courage fail thee. . . .
[*Exeunt* GODS.]

SHEN TE: What about the old couple? They've lost their shop! What about the water seller and his hand? And I've got to defend myself against the barber, because I don't love him! And against Sun, because I do love him! How? How?
[SHEN TE's *eyes follow the* GODS *as they are imagined to step into a cloud which rises and moves forward over the orchestra and up beyond the balcony.*]

FIRST GOD: [*from on high*] We have faith in you, Shen Te!

SHEN TE: There'll be a child. And he'll have to be fed. I can't stay here. Where shall I go?

FIRST GOD: Continue to be good, good woman of Setzuan!

SHEN TE: I need my bad cousin!

FIRST GOD: But not very often!

SHEN TE: Once a week at least!

FIRST GOD: Once a month will be quite enough!

SHEN TE: [*shrieking*] No, no! Help!
[*But the cloud continues to recede as the* GODS *sing.*]

VALEDICTORY HYMN

> *What a rapture, oh, it is to know*
> *A good thing when you see it*
> *And having seen a good thing, oh,*
> *What rapture 'tis to flee it*
>
> *Be good, sweet maid of Setzuan*
> *Let Shui Ta be clever*
> *Departing, we forget the man*
> *Remember your endeavor*
>
> *Because through all the length of days*
> *Her goodness faileth never*
> *Sing hallelujah! Make Shen Te's*
> *Good name live on forever!*

SHEN TE: Help!

EPILOGUE

You're thinking, aren't you, that this is no right
Conclusion to the play you've seen tonight?[2]
After a tale, exotic, fabulous,
A nasty ending was slipped up on us.
We feel deflated, too. We, too, are nettled
To see the curtain down and nothing settled.
How could a better ending be arranged?

---

[2]*At afternoon performances:*
We quite agree, our play this afternoon
Collapsed upon us like a pricked balloon

Could one change people? Can the world be changed?
Would new gods do the trick? Will atheism?
Moral rearmament? Materialism?
It is for you to find a way, my friends,
To help good men arrive at happy ends.
You write the happy ending to the play!
There must, there must, there's got to be a way![3]

[3]When I first received the German manuscript of *Good Woman* from Brecht in 1945 it had no Epilogue. He wrote it a little later, influenced by misunderstandings of the ending in the press on the occasion of the Viennese première of the play. I believe that the Epilogue has sometimes been spoken by the actress playing Shen Te, but the actor playing Wong might be a shrewder choice, since the audience has already accepted him as a kind of chorus. On the other hand, it is not Wong who should deliver the Epilogue: whichever actor delivers it should drop the character he has been playing—E. B.

Cat on a Hot Tin Roof (1955)

For several years following World War II, the most successful American plays were written in a style that can be called modified realism. Tennessee Williams helped to popularize this style with *The Glass Menagerie* (1944), in which scenes and characters are called up out of the narrator-character's memory. The emphasis in this play, as in Williams' *A Streetcar Named Desire* (1949) and Arthur Miller's *Death of a Salesman* (1949), is on the psychological truth of character and situation played out in minimal and symbolic settings.

Cat on a Hot Tin Roof is in this tradition. The action, which is continuous, takes place in a bed-sitting room in a large plantation house in Mississippi. Within this restricted time and space, the characters are engulfed in mendacity—deception both of themselves and others. Two of the characters, Big Daddy and Brick, are forced to face truths that threaten the very core of their being: that Big Daddy is actually dying of cancer though he has been told he is free of it; and that Brick's friend Skipper loved him and died when Brick rejected him.

Brick's wife Maggie and his brother Gooper (along with Gooper's wife Mae) are primarily concerned with gaining control over Big Daddy's estate. Maggie, whose description of her position gives the play its title, seeks desperately to convince Brick to impregnate her because she believes a child will help overcome the doubts about Brick's reliability raised by his alcoholism. Ironically, it is a new deception, Maggie's false announcement that she is pregnant, that forces her to find the means to make Brick sleep with her (taking away his alcohol until he does so). Despite the play's denunciation of deception, the ending seems to condone Maggie's mendacity.

With its powerful psychological portraits, compelling conflicts, and its insights into a world dominated by self-interest, *Cat on a Hot Tin Roof* is an excellent example of postwar realism.

Tennessee Williams

Cat on a Hot Tin Roof

Charcters

MARGARET
BRICK
MAE, *sometimes called Sister Woman*
BIG MAMA
DIXIE, *a little girl*
BIG DADDY
REVEREND TOOKER
GOOPER, *sometimes called Brother Man*
DOCTOR BAUGH, *pronounced "Baw"*
LACEY, *a Negro servant*
SOOKEY, *another*
Another little girl and two small boys

The set is the bed-sitting room of a plantation house in the Mississippi Delta. It is along an upstairs gallery that probably runs around the entire house; it has two pairs of very wide doors opening onto the gallery, showing white balustrades against a fair summer sky that fades into dusk and night during the course of the play. . . . The bathroom door, showing only pale-blue tile and silver towel racks, is in one side wall; the hall door in the opposite wall. Two articles of furniture need mention: a big double bed . . . ; and against the wall space between the two huge double doors upstage . . . a huge console combination of radio-phonograph (hi-fi with three speakers), TV set, and liquor cabinet, bearing and containing many glasses and bottles. . . . The walls below the ceiling should dissolve mysteriously into air; the set should be roofed by the sky. . . .
   An evening in summer. The action is continuous, with two intermissions.

ACT ONE

At the rise of the curtain someone is taking a shower in the bathroom, the door of which is half open. A pretty young woman, with anxious lines in her face, enters the bedroom and crosses to the bathroom door.

MARGARET: [*shouting above roar of water*] One of those no-neck monsters hit me with a
   hot buttered biscuit so I have t' change!
   [MARGARET*'s voice is both rapid and drawling. In her long speeches she has the vocal tricks of a priest delivering a liturgical chant, the lines are almost sung, always continuing a little beyond her breath so she has to gasp for another. Sometimes she intersperses the lines with a little wordless singing, such as* "DA-DA-DAAAA!"]
   [*Water turns off and* BRICK *calls out to her, but is still unseen. A tone of politely feigned interest, masking indifference, or worse, is characteristic of his speech with* MARGARET.]
BRICK: Wha'd you say, Maggie? Water was on s' loud I couldn't hearya. . . .

MARGARET: Well, I!—just remarked that!—one of th' no-neck monsters messed up m' lovely lace dress so I got t'—cha-a-ange. . . .

[*She opens and kicks shut drawers of the dresser.*]

BRICK: Why d'ya call Gooper's kiddies "no-neck monsters"?

MARGARET: Because they've got no necks! Isn't that a good enough reason?

BRICK: Don't they have any necks?

MARGARET: None visible. Their fat little heads are set on their fat little bodies without a bit of connection.

BRICK: That's too bad.

MARGARET: Yes, it's too bad because you can't wring their necks if they've got no necks to wring! Isn't that right, honey?

[*She steps out of her dress, stands in a slip of ivory satin and lace.*]

Yep, they're no-neck monsters, all no-neck people are monsters. . . .

[*Children shriek downstairs.*]

Hear them? Hear them screaming? I don't know where their voice boxes are located since they don't have necks. I tell you I got so nervous at that table tonight I thought I would throw back my head and utter a scream you could hear across the Arkansas border an' parts of Louisiana an' Tennessee. I said to your charming sister-in-law, Mae, honey, couldn't you feed those precious little things at a separate table with an oilcloth cover? They make such a mess an' the lace cloth looks so pretty! She made enormous eyes at me and said, "Ohhh, nooooo! On Big Daddy's birthday? Why, he would never forgive me!" Well, I want you to know, Big Daddy hadn't been at the table two minutes with those five no-neck monsters slobbering and drooling over their food before he threw down his fork an' shouted, "Fo' God's sake, Gooper, why don't you put them pigs at a trough in th' kitchen?"—Well, I swear, I simply could have di-ieed!

Think of it, Brick, they've got five of them and number six is coming They've brought the whole bunch down here like animals to display at a county fair. Why they have those children doin' tricks all the time! "Junior, show Big Daddy how you do this, show Big Daddy how you do that, say your little piece fo' Big Daddy, Sister. Show your dimples, Sugar. Brother, show Big Daddy how you stand on your head!"—It goes on all the time along, with constant little remarks and innuendos about the fact that you and I have not produced any children, are totally childless, and therefore totally useless!—Of course it's comical but it's also disgusting since it's so obvious what they're up to!

BRICK: [*without interest*] What are they up to, Maggie?

MARGARET: Why, you know what they're up to!

BRICK: [*appearing*] No, I don't know what they're up to.

[*He stands there in the bathroom doorway drying his hair with a towel and hanging onto the towel rack because one ankle is broken, plastered and bound. He is still slim and firm as a boy. His liquor hasn't started tearing him down outside. He has the additional charm of that cool air of detachment that people have who have given up the struggle. But now and then, when disturbed, something flashes behind it, like lightning in a fair sky, which shows that at some deeper level he is far from peaceful. Perhaps in a stronger light he would show some signs of deliquescence, but the fading, still warm, light from the gallery treats him gently.*]

MARGARET: I'll tell you what they're up to, boy of mine!—They're up to cutting you out of your father's estate, and—

[*She freezes momentarily before her next remark. Her voice drops as if it were somehow a personally embarrassing admission.*]

—Now we know that Big Daddy's dyin' of—*cancer.* . . .

[*There are voices on the lawn below: long-drawn calls across distance.* MARGARET *raises her lovely bare arms and powders her armpits with a light sigh.*]

[*She adjusts the angle of a magnifying mirror to straighten an eyelash, then rises fretfully saying:*]

There's so much light in the room it—

BRICK: [*softly but sharply*] Do we?

MARGARET: Do we what?

BRICK: Know Big Daddy's dyin' of cancer?

MARGARET: Got the report today.

BRICK: Oh . . .

MARGARET: [*letting down bamboo blinds which cast long, gold-fretted shadows over the room*] Yep, got th' report just now . . . It didn't surprise me, Baby. . . .

[*Her voice has range and music; sometimes it drops low as a boy's and you have a sudden image of her playing boy's games as a child.*]

I recognized the symptoms soon's we got here last spring and I'm willin' to bet you that Brother Man and his wife were pretty sure of it, too. That more than likely explains why their usual summer migration to the coolness of the Great Smokies was passed up this summer in favor of—hustlin' down here ev'ry whipstitch with their whole screamin' tribe! And why so many allusions have been made to Rainbow Hill lately. You know what Rainbow Hill is? Place that's famous for treatin' alcoholics an' dope fiends in the movies!

BRICK: I'm not in the movies.

MARGARET: No, and you don't take dope. Otherwise you're a perfect candidate for Rainbow Hill, Baby, and that's where they aim to ship you—over my dead body! Yep, over my dead body they'll ship you there, but nothing would please them better. Then Brother Man could get a-hold of the purse strings and dole out remittances to us, maybe get power of attorney and sign checks for us and cut off our credit wherever, whenever he wanted! Son-of-a-bitch!—How'd you like that, Baby?—Well, you've been doin' just about ev'rything in your power to bring it about, you've just been doin' ev'rything you can think of to aid and abet them in this scheme of theirs! Quittin' work, devoting yourself to the occupation of drinkin'!—Breakin' your ankle last night on the high school athletic field: doin' what? Jumpin' hurdles? At two or three in the morning? Just fantastic! Got in the paper. *Clarksdale Register* carried a nice little item about it, human interest story about a well-known former athlete stagin' a one-man track meet on the Glorious Hill High School athletic field last night, but was slightly out of condition and didn't clear the first hurdle! Brother Man Gooper claims he exercised his influence t' keep it from goin' out over AP or UP or every goddam *"P."*

But, Brick? You still have one big advantage!

[*During the above swift flood of words,* BRICK *has reclined with contrapuntal leisure on the snowy surface of the bed and has rolled over carefully on his side or belly.*]

BRICK: [*wryly*] Did you say something, Maggie?

MARGARET: Big Daddy dotes on you, honey. And he can't stand Brother Man and Brother Man's wife, that monster of fertility, Mae; she's downright odious to him! Know how I know? By little expressions that flicker over his face when that woman is holding fo'th on one of her choice topics such as—how she refused twilight sleep!—when the twins were delivered! Because she feels motherhood's an experience that a woman ought to experience fully!—in order to fully appreciate the wonder and beauty of it! HAH!

[*This loud "HAH!" is accompanied by a violent action such as slamming a drawer shut.*]

—and how she made Brother Man come in an' stand beside her in the delivery room so he would not miss out on the "wonder and beauty" of it, either!—producin' those no-neck monsters . . . .

[*A speech of this kind would be antipathetic from almost anybody but* MARGARET; *she makes it oddly funny, because her eyes constantly twinkle and her voice shakes with laughter which is basically indulgent.*]

—Big Daddy shares my attitude toward those two! As for me, well—I give him a laugh now and then and he tolerates me. In fact!—I sometimes suspect that Big Daddy harbors a little unconscious "lech" fo' me. . . .

BRICK: What makes you think that Big Daddy has a lech for you, Maggie?

MARGARET: Way he always drops his eyes down my body when I'm talkin' to him, drops his eyes to my boobs an' licks his old chops! Ha ha!

BRICK: That kind of talk is disgusting.

MARGARET: Did anyone ever tell you that you're an ass-aching Puritan, Brick? I think it's mighty fine that that ole fellow, on the doorstep of death, still takes in my shape with what I think is deserved appreciation!

And you wanta know something else? Big Daddy didn't know how many little Maes and Goopers had been produced! "How many kids have you got?" he asked at the table, just like Brother Man and his wife were new acquaintances to him! Big Mama said he was jokin', but that old boy wasn't jokin', Lord, no!

And when they infawmed him that they had five already and were turning out number six!—the news seemed to come as a sort of unpleasant surprise. . . .

[*Children yell below.*]

Scream, monsters!

[*Turns to* BRICK *with a sudden, gay, charming smile which fades as she notices that he is not looking at her but into fading gold space with a troubled expression.*]

[*It is constant rejection that makes her humor "bitchy."*]

Yes, you should of been at that supper table, Baby.

[*Whenever she calls him "Baby" the word is a soft caress.*]

Y'know, Big Daddy, bless his ole sweet soul, he's the dearest ole thing in the world, but he does hunch over his food as if he preferred not to notice anything else. Well, Mae an' Gooper were side by side at the table, direckly across from Big Daddy, watchin' his face like hawks while they jawed an' jabbered about the cuteness an' brilliance of th' no-neck monsters!

[*She giggles with a hand fluttering at her throat and her breast and her long throat arched.*]

[*She comes downstage and re-creates the scene with voice and gesture.*]

And the no-neck monsters were ranged around the table, some in high chairs and some on th' *Books of Knowledge*, all in fancy little paper caps in honor of Big Daddy's birthday, and all through dinner, well, I want you to know that Brother Man an' his partner never once, for one moment, stopped exchanging pokes an' pinches an' kicks an' signs an' signals!—Why, they were like a couple of cardsharps fleecing a sucker.— Even Big Mama, bless her ole sweet soul, she isn't th' quickest an' brightest thing in the world, she finally noticed, at last, an' said to Gooper, "Gooper, what are you an' Mae makin' all these signs at each other about?"—I swear t' goodness, I nearly choked on my chicken!

[MARGARET, *back at the dressing table, still doesn't see* BRICK. *He is watching her with a look that is not quite definable—Amused? shocked? contemptuous?—part of those and part of something else.*]

Y'know—your brother Gooper still cherishes the illusion he took a giant step up on the social ladder when he married Miss Mae Flynn of the Memphis Flynns.

[MARGARET *moves about the room as she talks, stops before the mirror, moves on.*] But I have a piece of Spanish news for Gooper. The Flynns never had a thing in this world but money and they lost that, they were nothing at all but fairly successful climbers. Of course, Mae Flynn came out in Memphis eight years before I made my debut in Nashville, but I had friends at Ward-Belmont who came from Memphis and they used to come to see me and I used to go to see them for Christmas and spring vacations, and so I know who rates an' who doesn't rate in Memphis society. Why, y'know ole Papa Flynn, he barely escaped doing time in the federal pen for shady manipulations on th' stock market when his chain stores crashed, and as for Mae having been a cotton carnival queen, as they remind us so often, lest we forget, well, that's one honor that I don't envy her for!—Sit on a brass throne on a tacky float an' ride down Main Street, smilin', bowin', and blowin' kisses to all the trash on the street—

[*She picks out a pair of jeweled sandals and rushes to the dressing table.*]

Why, year before last, when Susan McPheeters was singled out fo' that honor, y'know what happened to her? Y'know what happened to poor little Susie McPheeters?

BRICK: [*absently*] No. What happened to little Susie McPheeters?

MARGARET: Somebody spit tobacco juice in her face.

BRICK: [*dreamily*] Somebody spit tobacco juice in her face?

MARGARET: That's right, some old drunk leaned out of a window in the Hotel Gayoso and yelled, "Hey, Queen, hey, hey, there, Queenie!" Poor Susie looked up and flashed him a radiant smile and he shot out a squirt of tobacco juice right in poor Susie's face.

BRICK: Well, what d'you know about that.

MARGARET: [*gaily*] What do I know about it? I was there, I saw it!

BRICK: [*absently*] Must have been kind of funny.

MARGARET: Susie didn't think so. Had hysterics. Screamed like a banshee. They had to stop th' parade an' remove her from her throne an' go on with—

[*She catches sight of him in the mirror, gasps slightly, wheels about to face him. Count ten.*]

—Why are you looking at me like that?

BRICK: [*whistling softly, now*] Like what, Maggie?

MARGARET: [*intensely, fearfully*] The way y' were looking at me just now, befo' I caught your eye in the mirror and you started t' whistle! I don't know how t' describe it but it froze my blood!—I've caught you lookin' at me like that so often lately. What are you thinkin' of when you look at me like that?

BRICK: I wasn't conscious of lookin' at you, Maggie.

MARGARET: Well, I was conscious of it! What were you thinkin'?

BRICK: I don't remember thinking of anything, Maggie.

MARGARET: Don't you think I know that—? Don't you—?—Think I know that—?

BRICK: [*coolly*] Know *what*, Maggie?

MARGARET: [*struggling for expression*] That I've gone through this—*hideous!*—transformation, become—hard! Frantic!

[*Then she adds, almost tenderly:*]

—cruel!!

That's what you've been observing in me lately. How could y' help but observe it? That's all right. I'm not—thin-skinned any more, can't afford t' be thin-skinned any more.

[*She is now recovering her power.*]

—But Brick? Brick?

BRICK: Did you say something?

MARGARET: I was *goin' t'* say something: that I get—lonely. Very!

BRICK: Ev'rybody gets that. . . .

MARGARET: Living with someone you love can be lonelier—than living entirely *alone!*—
if the one that y' love doesn't love you. . . .

> [*There is a pause.* BRICK *hobbles downstage and asks, without looking at her:*]

BRICK: Would you like to live alone, Maggie?

> [*Another pause: then—after she has caught a quick, hurt breath:*]

MARGARET: No!—God!—I wouldn't!

> [*Another gasping breath. She forcibly controls what must have been an impulse to cry out. We see her deliberately, very forcibly, going all the way back to the world in which you can talk about ordinary matters.*]

Did you have a nice shower?

BRICK: Uh-huh.

MARGARET: Was the water cool?

BRICK: No.

MARGARET: But it made y' feel fresh, huh?

BRICK: Fresher. . . .

MARGARET: I know something would make y' feel *much* fresher!

BRICK: What?

MARGARET: An alcohol rub. Or cologne, a rub with cologne!

BRICK: That's good after a workout but I haven't been workin' out, Maggie.

MARGARET: You've kept in good shape, though.

BRICK: [*indifferently*] You think so, Maggie?

MARGARET: I always thought drinkin' men lost their looks, but I was plainly mistaken.

BRICK: [*wryly*] Why; thanks, Maggie.

MARGARET: You're the only drinkin' man I know that it never seems t' put fat on.

BRICK: I'm gettin' softer, Maggie.

MARGARET: Well, sooner or later it's bound to soften you up. It was just beginning to
soften up Skipper when—

> [*She stops short.*]

I'm sorry. I never could keep my fingers off a sore—I wish you would lose your looks.
If you did it would make the martyrdom of Saint Maggie a little more bearable. But
no such goddam luck. I actually believe you've gotten better looking since you've
gone on the bottle. Yeah, a person who didn't know you would think you'd never had
a tense nerve in your body or a strained muscle.

> [*There are sounds of croquet on the lawn below: the click of mallets, light voices, near and distant.*]

Of course, you always had that detached quality as if you were playing a game without much concern over whether you won or lost, and now that you've lost the game,
not lost but just quit playing, you have that rare sort of charm that usually only happens in very old or hopelessly sick people, the charm of the defeated.—You look so
cool, so cool, so enviably cool.

> [*Music is heard.*]

They're playing croquet. The moon has appeared and it's white, just beginning to turn
a little bit yellow. . . .

You were a wonderful lover. . . .

Such a wonderful person to go to bed with, and I think mostly because you
were really indifferent to it. Isn't that right? Never had any anxiety about it, did it naturally, easily, slowly, with absolute confidence and perfect calm, more like opening a
door for a lady or seating her at a table than giving expression to any longing for her.
Your indifference made you wonderful at lovemaking—*strange?*—but true. . . .

You know, if I thought you would never, never, never make love to me again—
I would go downstairs to the kitchen and pick out the longest and sharpest knife I
could find and stick it straight into my heart, I swear that I would!

But one thing I don't have is the charm of the defeated, my hat is still in the ring, and I am determined to win!

[*There is the sound of croquet mallets hitting croquet balls.*]

—What is the victory of a cat on a hot tin roof?—I wish I knew. . . . Just staying on it, I guess, as long as she can. . . .

[*more croquet sounds*]

Later tonight I'm going to tell you I love you an' maybe by that time you'll be drunk enough to believe me. Yes, they're playing croquet. . . .

Big Daddy is dying of cancer. . . .

What were you thinking of when I caught you looking at me like that? Were you thinking of Skipper?

[BRICK *takes up his crutch, rises.*]

Oh, excuse me, forgive me, but laws of silence don't work! No, laws of silence don't work. . . .

[BRICK *crosses to the bar, takes a quick drink, and rubs his head with a towel.*]

Laws of silence don't work. . . .

When something is festering in your memory or your imagination, laws of silence don't work, it's just like shutting a door and locking it on a house on fire in hope of forgetting that the house is burning. But not facing a fire doesn't put it out. Silence about a thing just magnifies it. It grows and festers in silence, becomes malignant. . . .

Get dressed, Brick.

[*He drops his crutch.*]

BRICK: I've dropped my crutch.

[*He has stopped rubbing his hair dry but still stands hanging onto the towel rack in a white towel-cloth robe.*]

MARGARET: Lean on me.

BRICK: No, just give me my crutch.

MARGARET: Lean on my shoulder.

BRICK: *I don't want to lean on your shoulder, I want my crutch!*

[*This is spoken like sudden lightning.*]

Are you going to give me my crutch or do I have to get down on my knees on the floor and—

MARGARET: *Here, here, take it, take it!*

[*She has thrust the crutch at him.*]

BRICK: [*hobbling out*] Thanks. . . .

MARGARET: We mustn't scream at each other, the walls in this house have ears. . . .

[*He hobbles directly to liquor cabinet to get a new drink.*]

—but that's the first time I've heard you raise your voice in a long time, Brick. A crack in the wall?—Of composure?

—I think that's a good sign. . . .

A sign of nerves in a player on the defensive!

[BRICK *turns and smiles at her coolly over his fresh drink.*]

BRICK: It just hasn't happened yet, Maggie.

MARGARET: What?

BRICK: The click I get in my head when I've had enough of this stuff to make me peaceful. . . . Will you do me a favor?

MARGARET: Maybe I will. What favor?

BRICK: Just, just keep your voice down!

MARGARET: [*in a hoarse whisper*] I'll do you that favor, I'll speak in a whisper, if not shut up completely, if *you* will do *me* a favor and make that drink your last one till after the party.

BRICK: What party?

MARGARET: Big Daddy's birthday party.

BRICK: Is this Big Daddy's birthday?

MARGARET: You know this is Big Daddy's birthday!

BRICK: No, I don't, I forgot it.

MARGARET: Well, I remembered it for you. . . .

> [*They are both speaking as breathlessly as a pair of kids after a fight, drawing deep exhausted breaths and looking at each other with faraway eyes, shaking and panting together as if they had broken apart from a violent struggle.*]

BRICK: Good for you, Maggie.

MARGARET: You just have to scribble a few lines on this card.

BRICK: You scribble something, Maggie.

MARGARET: It's got to be your handwriting; it's your present, I've given him my present; it's got to be your handwriting!

> [*The tension between them is building again, the voices becoming shrill once more.*]

BRICK: I didn't get him a present.

MARGARET: I got one for you.

BRICK: All right. You write the card, then.

MARGARET: And have him know you didn't remember his birthday?

BRICK: I didn't remember his birthday.

MARGARET: You don't have to prove you didn't!

BRICK: I don't want to fool him about it.

MARGARET: Just write "Love, Brick!" for God's—

BRICK: No.

MARGARET: You've *got* to!

BRICK: I don't have to do anything I don't want to do. You keep forgetting the conditions on which I agreed to stay on living with you.

MARGARET: [*out before she knows it*] I'm not living with you. We occupy the same cage.

BRICK: You've got to remember the conditions agreed on.

MARGARET: They're impossible conditions!

BRICK: Then why don't you—?

MARGARET: HUSH! Who is out there? Is somebody at the door?

> [*There are footsteps in hall.*]

MAE: [*outside*] May I enter a moment?

MARGARET: Oh, you! Sure. Come in, Mae.

> [MAE *enters bearing aloft the bow of a young lady's archery set.*]

MAE: Brick, is this thing yours?

MARGARET: Why, Sister Woman—that's my Diana Trophy. Won it at the intercollegiate archery contest on the Ole Miss campus.

MAE: It's a mighty dangerous thing to leave exposed round a house full of nawmal rid-blooded children attracted t' weapons.

MARGARET: "Nawmal rid-blooded children attracted t' weapons" ought t' be taught to keep their hands off things that don't belong to them.

MAE: Maggie, honey, if you had children of your own you'd know how funny that is. Will you please lock this up and put the key out of reach?

MARGARET: Sister Woman, nobody is plotting the destruction of your kiddies.—Brick and I still have our special archers' license. We're goin' deer-huntin' on Moon Lake as soon as the season starts. I love to run with dogs through chilly woods, run, run leap over obstructions—

> [*She goes into the closet carrying the bow.*]

MAE: How's the injured ankle, Brick?

BRICK: Doesn't hurt. Just itches.

MAE: Oh my! Brick—Brick, you should've been downstairs after supper! Kiddies put on a show. Polly played the piano, Buster an' Sonny drums, an' then they turned out the lights an' Dixie an' Trixie puhfawmed a toe dance in fairy costume with *spahkluhs!* Big Daddy just beamed! He just beamed!

MARGARET: [*from the closet with a sharp laugh*] Oh, I bet. It breaks my heart that we missed it! [*She reenters.*]

But Mae? Why did y'give dawgs' names to all your kiddies?

MAE: *Dogs'* names?

[MARGARET *has made this observation as she goes to raise the bamboo blinds, since the sunset glare has diminished. In crossing she winks at* BRICK.]

MARGARET: [*sweetly*] Dixie, Trixie, Buster, Sonny, Polly!—Sounds like four dogs and a parrot . . . animal act in a circus!

MAE: Maggie?

[MARGARET *turns with a smile.*]

Why are you so catty?

MARGARET: 'Cause I'm a cat! But why can't you take a joke, Sister Woman?

MAE: Nothin' pleases me more than a joke that's funny. You know the real names of our kiddies. Buster's real name is Robert. Sonny's real name is Saunders. Trixie's real name is Marlene and Dixie's—

[*Someone downstairs calls for her.* "HEY, MAE!"—*She rushes to door, saying:*]

Intermission is over!

MARGARET: [*as* MAE *closes door*] I wonder what Dixie's real name is?

BRICK: Maggie, being catty doesn't help things any. . . .

MARGARET: I know! *WHY!*—Am I so catty?—'Cause I'm consumed with envy an' eaten up with longing?—Brick, I've laid out your beautiful Shantung silk suit from Rome and one of your monogrammed silk shirts. I'll put your cuff links in it, those lovely star sapphires I get you to wear so rarely. . . .

BRICK: I can't get trousers on over this plaster cast.

MARGARET: Yes, you can, I'll help you.

BRICK: I'm not going to get dressed, Maggie.

MARGARET: Will you just put on a pair of white silk pajamas?

BRICK: Yes, I'll do that, Maggie.

MARGARET: *Thank* you, thank you *so much!*

BRICK: Don't mention it.

MARGARET: *Oh, Brick!* How long does it have t' go on? This punishment? Haven't I done time enough, haven't I served my term, can't I apply for a—pardon?

BRICK: Maggie, you're spoiling my liquor. Lately your voice always sounds like you'd been running upstairs to warn somebody that the house was on fire!

MARGARET: Well, no wonder, no wonder. Y'know what I feel like, Brick?

[*Children's and grown-ups' voices are blended, below, in a loud-but-uncertain rendition of* "My Wild Irish Rose."]

I feel all the time like a cat on a hot tin roof!

BRICK: Then jump off the roof, jump off it, cats can jump off roofs and land on their four feet uninjured!

MARGARET: Oh, yes!

BRICK: Do it!—Fo' God's sake, do it. . . .

MARGARET: Do what?

BRICK: Take a lover!

MARGARET: I can't see a man but you! Even with my eyes closed, I just see you!

Why don't you get ugly, Brick, why don't you please get fat or ugly or something so I could stand it?

[*She rushes to hall door, opens it, listens.*]

The concert is still going on! Bravo, no-necks, bravo!

[*She slams and locks door fiercely.*]

BRICK: What did you lock the door for?

MARGARET: To give us a little privacy for a while.

BRICK: You know better, Maggie.

MARGARET: No, I don't know better. . . .

[*She rushes to gallery doors, draws the rose-silk drapes across them.*]

BRICK: Don't make a fool of yourself.

MARGARET: I don't mind makin' a fool of myself over you!

BRICK: I mind, Maggie. I feel embarrassed for you.

MARGARET: Feel embarrassed! But don't continue my torture. I can't live on and on under these circumstances.

BRICK: You agreed to—

MARGARET: I know but—

BRICK: Accept that condition!

MARGARET: *I CAN'T! CAN'T! CAN'T!*

[*She seizes his shoulder.*]

BRICK: Let go!

[*He breaks away from her and seizes the small boudoir chair and raises it like a lion-tamer facing a big circus cat.*]

[*Count five. She stares at him with her fist pressed to her mouth, then bursts into shrill, almost hysterical laughter. He remains grave for a moment, then grins and puts the chair down.*]

[BIG MAMA *calls through closed door.*]

BIG MAMA: Son? Son? Son?

BRICK: What is it, Big Mama?

BIG MAMA: [*outside*] Oh, son! We got the most wonderful news about Big Daddy. I just had t' run up an' tell you right this—

[*She rattles the knob.*]

—What's this door doin', locked, faw? You all think there's robbers in the house?

MARGARET: Big Mama, Brick is dressin', he's not dressed yet.

BIG MAMA: That's all right, it won't be the first time I've seen Brick not dressed. Come on, open this door!

[MARGARET, *with a grimace, goes to unlock and open the hall door, as* BRICK *hobbles rapidly to the bathroom and kicks the door shut.* BIG MAMA *has disappeared from the hall.*]

MARGARET: Big Mama?

[BIG MAMA *appears through the opposite gallery doors behind* MARGARET, *huffing and puffing like an old bulldog. She is a short, stout woman; her sixty years and 170 pounds have left her somewhat breathless most of the time; she's always tensed like a boxer, or rather, a Japanese wrestler. Her "family" was maybe a little superior to* BIG DADDY'*s, but not much. She wears a black or silver lace dress and at least half a million in flashy gems. She is very sincere.*]

BIG MAMA: [*loudly, startling* MARGARET] Here—I come through Gooper's and Mae's gall'ry door. Where's Brick? *Brick*—Hurry on out of there, son, I just have a second and want to give you the news about Big Daddy.—I hate locked doors in a house. . . .

MARGARET: [*with affected lightness*] I've noticed you do, Big Mama, but people have got to have *some* moments of privacy, don't they?

BIG MAMA: No, ma'am, not in *my* house. [*without pause*] Whacha took off you' dress faw? I thought that little lace dress was so sweet on yuh, honey.

MARGARET: I thought it looked sweet on me, too, but one of m' cute little table partners used it for a napkin so—!

BIG MAMA: [*picking up stockings on floor*] What?

MARGARET: You know, Big Mama, Mae and Gooper's so touchy about those children—thanks, Big Mama . . .

> [BIG MAMA *has thrust the picked-up stockings in* MARGARET'*s hand with a grunt.*]

—that you just don't dare to suggest there's any room for improvement in their—

BIG MAMA: Brick, hurry out!—Shoot, Maggie, you just don't like children.

MARGARET: I do SO like children! Adore them!—well brought up!

BIG MAMA: [*gentle—loving*] Well, why don't you have some and bring them up well, then, instead of all the time pickin' on Gooper's an' Mae's?

GOOPER: [*shouting up the stairs*] Hey, hey, Big Mama, Betsy an' Hugh got to go, waitin' t' tell yuh g'by!

BIG MAMA: Tell 'em to hold their hawses, I'll be right down in a jiffy!

> [*She turns to the bathroom door and calls out.*]

Son? Can you hear me in there?

> [*There is a muffled answer.*]

We just got the full report from the laboratory at the Ochsner Clinic, completely negative, son, ev'rything negative, right on down the line! Nothin' a-tall's wrong with him but some little functional thing called a spastic colon. Can you hear me, son?

MARGARET: He can hear you, Big Mama.

BIG MAMA: Then why don't he say something? God Almighty, a piece of news like that should make him shout. It made me shout, I can tell you. I shouted and sobbed and fell right down on my knees!—Look!

> [*She pulls up her skirt.*]

See the bruises where I hit my kneecaps? Took both doctors to haul me back on my feet!

> [*She laughs—she always laughs like hell at herself.*]

Big Daddy was furious with me! But ain't that wonderful news?

> [*Facing bathroom again, she continues:*]

After all the anxiety we been through to git a report like that on Big Daddy's birthday? Big Daddy tried to hide how much of a load that news took off his mind, but didn't fool *me*. He was mighty close to crying about it *himself!*

> [*Goodbyes are shouted downstairs, and she rushes to door.*]

Hold those people down there, don't let them go!—Now, git dressed, we're all comin' up to this room fo' Big Daddy's birthday party because of your ankle.—How's his ankle, Maggie?

MARGARET: Well, he broke it, Big Mama.

BIG MAMA: I know he broke it.

> [*A phone is ringing in hall. A Negro voice answers: "Mistuh Polly's res'dence."*]

I mean does it hurt him much still.

MARGARET: I'm afraid I can't give you that information, Big Mama. You'll have to ask Brick if it hurts much still or not.

SOOKEY: [*in the hall*] It's Memphis, Mizz Polly, it's Miss Sally in Memphis.

BIG MAMA: Awright, Sookey.

> [BIG MAMA *rushes into the hall and is heard shouting on the phone:*]

Hello, Miss Sally. How are you, Miss Sally?—Yes, well, I was just gonna call you about it. *Shoot!*—

> [*She raises her voice to a bellow.*]

Miss Sally? Don't ever call me from the Gayoso Lobby, too much talk goes on in that hotel lobby, no wonder you can't hear me! Now listen, Miss Sally. They's nothin' serious wrong with Big Daddy. We got the report just now, they's nothin' wrong but a thing called a—spastic! *SPASTIC!*—colon. . . .

[*She appears at the hall door and calls to* MARGARET.]

—Maggie, come out here and talk to that fool on the phone. I'm shouted breathless!

MARGARET: [*goes out and is heard sweetly at phone*] Miss Sally? This is Brick's wife, Maggie. So nice to hear your voice. Can you hear mine? Well, good!—Big Mama just wanted you to know that they've got the report from the Ochsner Clinic and what Big Daddy has is a spastic colon. Yes. Spastic colon, Miss Sally. That's right, spastic colon. *G'bye, Miss Sally, hope I'll see you real soon!*

[*Hangs up a little before* MISS SALLY *was probably ready to terminate the talk. She returns through the hall door.*]

She heard me perfectly. I've discovered with deaf people the thing to do is not shout at them but just enunciate clearly. My rich old Aunt Cornelia was deaf as the dead but I could make her hear me just by sayin' each word slowly, distinctly, close to her ear. I read her the *Commercial Appeal* ev'ry night, read her the classified ads in it, even, she never missed a word of it. But was she a mean ole thing! Know what I got when she died? Her unexpired subscriptions to five magazines and the Book-of-the-Month Club and a LIBRARY full of ev'ry dull book ever written! All else went to her hellcat of a sister . . . meaner than she was, even!

[BIG MAMA *has been straightening things up in the room during this speech.*]

BIG MAMA: [*closing closet door on discarded clothes*] Miss Sally sure is a case! Big Daddy says she's always got her hand out fo' something. He's not mistaken. That poor ole thing always has her hand out fo' somethin'. I don't think Big Daddy gives her as much as he should.

[*Somebody shouts for her downstairs and she shouts:*]

I'm comin'!

[*She starts out. At the hall door, turns and jerks a forefinger, first toward the bathroom door, then toward the liquor cabinet, meaning: "Has Brick been drinking?"* MARGARET *pretends not to understand, cocks her head and raises her brows as if the pantomimic performance was completely mystifying to her.*]

[BIG MAMA *rushes back to* MARGARET:]

Shoot! Stop playin' so dumb!—I mean has he been drinkin' that stuff much yet?

MARGARET: [*with a little laugh*] Oh! I think he had a highball after supper.

BIG MAMA: Don't laugh about it!—Some single men stop drinkin' when they git married and others start! Brick never touched liquor before he—!

MARGARET: [*crying out*] *THAT'S NOT FAIR!*

BIG MAMA: Fair or not fair I want to ask you a question, one question: D'you make Brick happy in bed?

MARGARET: Why don't you ask if he makes *me* happy in bed?

BIG MAMA: Because I know that—

MARGARET: *It works both ways!*

BIG MAMA: Something's not right! You're childless and my son drinks!

[*Someone has called her downstairs and she has rushed to the door on the line above. She turns at the door and points at the bed.*]

When a marriage goes on the rocks, the rocks are *there*, right *there!*

MARGARET: *That's*—

[BIG MAMA *has swept out of the room and slammed the door.*]

—not *fair* . . .

[MARGARET *is alone, completely alone, and she feels it. She draws in, hunches her shoulders, raises her arms with fists clenched, shuts her eyes tight as a child about to be stabbed with a vaccination needle. When she opens her eyes again, what she sees is the long oval mirror and she rushes straight to it, stares into it with a grimace and says: "Who are you?"—Then she crouches a little and answers herself in a different voice which is high, thin, mocking: "I am Maggie the Cat!"—Straightens quickly as bathroom door opens a little and* BRICK *calls out to her.*]

BRICK: Has Big Mama gone?

MARGARET: She's gone.

[*He opens the bathroom door and hobbles out, with his liquor glass now empty, straight to the liquor cabinet. He is whistling softly.* MARGARET's *head pivots on her long, slender throat to watch him.*]

[*She raises a hand uncertainly to the base of her throat, as if it was difficult for her to swallow, before she speaks:*]

You know, our sex life didn't just peter out in the usual way, it was cut off short, long before the natural time for it to, and it's going to revive again, just as sudden as that. I'm confident of it. That's what I'm keeping myself attractive for. For the time when you'll see me again like other men see me. Yes, like other men see me. They still see me, Brick, and they like what they see. Uh-huh. Some of them would give their—

Look, Brick!

[*She stands before the long oval mirror, touches her breast and then her hips with her two hands.*]

How high my body stays on me!—Nothing has fallen on me—not a fraction. . . .

[*Her voice is soft and trembling: a pleading child's. At this moment as he turns to glance at her—a look which is like a player passing a ball to another player, third down and goal to go—she has to capture the audience in a grip so tight that she can hold it till the first intermission without any lapse of attention.*]

Other men still want me. My face looks strained, sometimes, but I've kept my figure as well as you've kept yours, and men admire it. I still turn heads on the street. Why, last week in Memphis everywhere that I went men's eyes burned holes in my clothes, at the country club and in restaurants and department stores, there wasn't a man I met or walked by that didn't just eat me up with his eyes and turn around when I passed him and look back at me. Why, at Alice's party for her New York cousins, the best-lookin' man in the crowd—followed me upstairs and tried to force his way in the powder room with me, followed me to the door and tried to force his way in!

BRICK: Why didn't you let him, Maggie?

MARGARET: Because I'm not that common, for one thing. Not that I wasn't almost tempted to. You like to know who it was? It was Sonny Boy Maxwell, that's who!

BRICK: Oh, yeah, Sonny Boy Maxwell, he was a good end-runner but had a little injury to his back and had to quit.

MARGARET: He has no injury now and has no wife and still has a lech for me!

BRICK: I see no reason to lock him out of a powder room in that case.

MARGARET: And have someone catch me at it? I'm not that stupid. Oh, I might sometime cheat on you with someone, since you're so insultingly eager to have me do it!—But if I do, you can be damned sure it will be in a place and time where no one but me and the man could possibly know. Because I'm not going to give you any excuse to divorce me for being unfaithful or anything else. . . .

BRICK: Maggie, I wouldn't divorce you for being unfaithful or anything else. Don't you know that? Hell. I'd be relieved to know that you'd found yourself a lover.

MARGARET: Well, I'm taking no chances. No, I'd rather stay on this hot tin roof.

BRICK: A hot tin roof's 'n uncomfo'table place t' stay on. . . .
> [*He starts to whistle softly.*]

MARGARET: [*through his whistle*] Yeah, but I can stay on it just as long as I have to.

BRICK: You could leave me, Maggie.
> [*He resumes whistle. She wheels about to glare at him.*]

MARGARET: Don't want to and will not! Besides if I did, you don't have a cent to pay for it but what you get from Big Daddy and he's dying of cancer!
> [*For the first time a realization of* BIG DADDY's *doom seems to penetrate to* BRICK's *consciousness, visibly, and he looks at* MARGARET.]

BRICK: Big Mama just said he *wasn't*, that the report was okay.

MARGARET: That's what she thinks because she got the same story that they gave Big Daddy. And was just as taken in by it as he was, poor ole things. . . .

But tonight they're going to tell her the truth about it. When Big Daddy goes to bed, they're going to tell her that he is dying of cancer.
> [*She slams the dresser drawer.*]

—It's malignant and it's terminal.

BRICK: Does Big Daddy know it?

MARGARET: Hell, do they *ever* know it? Nobody says, "You're dying." You have to fool them. They have to fool *themselves*.

BRICK: Why?

MARGARET: *Why?* Because human beings dream of life everlasting, that's the reason! But most of them want it on earth and not in heaven.
> [*He gives a short, hard laugh at her touch of humor.*]

Well. . . . [*She touches up her mascara.*] That's how it is, anyhow. . . . [*She looks about.*] Where did I put down my cigarette? Don't want to burn up the home place, at least not with Mae and Gooper and their five monsters in it!
> [*She has found it and sucks at it greedily. Blows out smoke and continues:*]

So this is Big Daddy's last birthday. And Mae and Gooper, they know it, oh, *they* know it, all right. They got the first information from the Ochsner Clinic. That's why they rushed down here with their no-neck monsters. Because. Do you know something? Big Daddy's made no will? Big Daddy's never made out any will in his life, and so this campaign's afoot to impress him, forcibly as possible, with the fact that you drink and I've borne no children!
> [*He continues to stare at her a moment, then mutters something sharp but not audible and hobbles rather rapidly out onto the long gallery in the fading, much faded, gold light.*]

MARGARET: [*continuing her liturgical chant*] Y'know, I'm *fond* of Big Daddy, I am genuinely fond of that old man, I really *am*, you know. . . .

BRICK: [*faintly, vaguely*] Yes, I know you are. . . .

MARGARET: I've always sort of admired him in spite of his coarseness, his four-letter words, and so forth. Because Big Daddy *is* what he *is*, and he makes no bones about it. He hasn't turned gentleman farmer, he's still a Mississippi redneck, as much of a redneck as he must have been when he was just overseer here on the old Jack Straw and Peter Ochello place. But he got hold of it an' built it into th' biggest an' finest plantation in the Delta.—I've always *liked* Big Daddy. . . .
> [*She crosses to the proscenium.*]

Well, this is Big Daddy's last birthday. I'm sorry about it. But I'm facing the facts. It takes money to take care of a drinker and that's the office that I've been elected to lately.

BRICK: You don't have to take care of me.

MARGARET: Yes, I do. Two people in the same boat have got to take care of each other. At least you want money to buy more Echo Spring when this supply is exhausted, or will you be satisfied with a ten-cent beer?

Mae an' Gooper are plannin' to freeze us out of Big Daddy's estate because you drink and I'm childless. But we can defeat that plan. We're going to defeat that plan!

Brick, y'know, I've been so goddam disgustingly poor all my life!—That's the *truth*, Brick!

BRICK: I'm not sayin' it isn't.

MARGARET: Always had to suck up to people I couldn't stand because they had money and I was poor as Job's turkey. You don't know what that's like. Well, I'll tell you, it's like you would feel a thousand miles away from Echo Spring!—And had to get back to it on that broken ankle . . . without a crutch!

That's how it feels to be as poor as Job's turkey and have to suck up to relatives that you hated because they had money and all you had was a bunch of hand-me-down clothes and a few old moldly three-percent government bonds. My daddy loved his liquor, he fell in love with his liquor the way you've fallen in love with Echo Spring!—And my poor Mama, having to maintain some semblance of social position, to keep appearances up, on an income of one hundred and fifty dollars a month on those old government bonds!

When I came out, the year that I made my debut, I had just two evening dresses! One Mother made me from a pattern in *Vogue*, the other a hand-me-down from a snotty rich cousin I hated!

—The dress that I married you in was my grandmother's weddin' gown. . . . So that's why I'm like a cat on a hot tin roof!

[BRICK *is still on the gallery. Someone below calls up to him in a warm Negro voice,* "Hiya, Mistuh Brick, how yuh feelin'?" BRICK *raises his liquor glass as if that answered the question.*]

MARGARET: You can be young without money, but you can't be old without it. You've got to be old *with* money because to be old without it is just too awful, you've got to be one or the other, either *young* or *with money*, you can't be old and *without* it.—That's the *truth*, Brick. . . .

[BRICK *whistles softly, vaguely.*]

Well, now I'm dressed, I'm all dressed, there's nothing else for me to do.

[*forlornly, almost fearfully*]

I'm dressed, all dressed, nothing else for me to do. . . .

[*She moves about restlessly, aimlessly, and speaks, as if to herself.*]

I know when I made my mistake.—What am I—? Oh!—my bracelets. . . .

[*She starts working a collection of bracelets over her hands onto her wrists, about six on each, as she talks.*]

I've thought a whole lot about it and now I know when I made my mistake. Yes, I made my mistake when I told you the truth about that thing with Skipper. Never should have confessed it, a fatal error, tellin' you about that thing with Skipper.

BRICK: Maggie, shut up about Skipper. I mean it, Maggie; you got to shut up about Skipper.

MARGARET: You ought to understand that Skipper and I—

BRICK: You don't think I'm serious, Maggie? You're fooled by the fact that I am saying this quiet? Look, Maggie. What you're doing is a dangerous thing to do. You're— you're—you're—

MARGARET: This time I'm going to finish what I have to say to you. Skipper and I made love, if love you could call it, because it made both of us feel a little bit closer to you. You see, you son of a bitch, you asked too much of people, of me, of him, of all the unlucky poor damned sons of bitches that happen to love you, and there was a whole pack of them, yes, there was a pack of them besides me and Skipper, you asked too goddam much of people that loved you, you—superior creature!—you godlike being!—And so we made love to each other to dream it was you, both of us! Yes, yes, yes! Truth, truth! What's so awful about it? I like it, I think the truth is—yeah! I shouldn't have told you. . . .

BRICK: [*holding his head unnaturally still and uptilted a bit*] It was Skipper that told me about it. Not you, Maggie.

MARGARET: I told you!

BRICK: After he told me!

MARGARET: What does it matter who?

[BRICK *turns suddenly out upon the gallery and calls:*]

BRICK: Little girl! Hey, little girl!

LITTLE GIRL: [*at a distance*] What, Uncle Brick?

BRICK: Tell the folks to come up!—Bring everybody upstairs!

MARGARET: I can't stop myself! I'd go on telling you this in front of them all, if I had to!

BRICK: Little girl! Go on, go on, will you? Do what I told you, call them!

MARGARET: Because it's got to be told and you, you!—you never let me!

[*She sobs, then controls herself, and continues almost calmly.*]

It was one of those beautiful, ideal things they tell about in the Greek legends, it couldn't be anything else, you being you, and that's what made it so sad, that's what made it so awful, because it was love that never could be carried through to anything satisfying or even talked about plainly. Brick, I tell you, you got to believe me, Brick, I *do* understand all about it! I—I think it was—*noble!* Can't you tell I'm sincere when I say I respect it? My only point, the only point that I'm making, is life has got to be allowed to continue even after the *dream* of life is—all—over. . . .

[BRICK *is without his crutch. Leaning on furniture, he crosses to pick it up as she continues as if possessed by a will outside herself.*]

Why, I remember when we double-dated at college, Gladys Fitzgerald and I and you and Skipper, it was more like a date between you and Skipper. Gladys and I were just sort of tagging along as if it was necessary to chaperone you!—to make a good public impression—

BRICK: [*turns to face her, half lifting his crutch*] Maggie, you want me to hit you with this crutch? Don't you know I could kill you with this crutch?

MARGARET: Good Lord, man, d' you think I'd care if you did?

BRICK: One man has one great good true thing in his life. One great good thing which is true!—I had friendship with Skipper.—You are naming it dirty!

MARGARET: I'm not naming it dirty! I am naming it clean.

BRICK: Not love with you, Maggie, but friendship with Skipper was that one great true thing, and you are naming it dirty!

MARGARET: Then you haven't been listenin', not understood what I'm saying! I'm naming it so damn clean that it killed poor Skipper!—You two had something that had to be kept on ice, yes, incorruptible, yes!—and death was the only icebox where you could keep it. . . .

BRICK: I married you, Maggie. Why would I marry you, Maggie, if I was—?

MARGARET: Brick, don't brain me yet, let me finish!—I know, believe me I know, that it was only Skipper that harbored even any *unconscious* desire for anything not perfectly pure between you two!—Now let me skip a little. You married me early that summer we graduated out of Ole Miss, and we were happy, weren't we, we were blissful, yes, hit heaven together ev'ry time that we loved! But that fall you an' Skipper turned down wonderful offers of jobs in order to keep on bein' football heroes—pro football heroes. You organized the Dixie Stars that fall, so you could keep on bein' teammates forever! But somethin' was not right with it!—*Me included!*—between you. Skipper began hittin' the bottle . . . you got a spinal injury—couldn't play the Thanksgivin' game in Chicago, watched it on TV from a traction bed in Toledo. I joined Skipper. The Dixie Stars lost because poor Skipper was drunk. We drank together that night all night in the bar of the Blackstone and when cold day was comin' up over the lake an' we were comin' out drunk to take a dizzy look at it, I said, "SKIPPER! STOP LOVIN' MY HUSBAND OR TELL HIM HE'S GOT TO LET YOU ADMIT IT TO HIM!"—one way or another!

HE SLAPPED ME HARD ON THE MOUTH!—then turned and ran without stopping once, I am sure, all the way back into his room at the Blackstone. . . .

—When I came to his room that night, with a little scratch like a shy little mouse at his door, he made that pitiful, ineffectual little attempt to prove that what I had said wasn't true. . . .

[BRICK *strikes at her with crutch, a blow that shatters the gemlike lamp on the table.*]

—In this way, I destroyed him, by telling him truth that he and his world which he was born and raised in, yours and his world, had told him could not be told?

—From then on Skipper was nothing at all but a receptacle for liquor and drugs. . . .

Who shot Cock Robin? I with my—

[*She throws back her head with tight shut eyes.*]

—*merciful arrow!*

[BRICK *strikes at her; misses.*]

Missed me!—Sorry—I'm not tryin' to whitewash my behavior, Christ, no! Brick, I'm not good. I don't know why people have to pretend to be good, nobody's good. The rich or the well-to-do can afford to respect moral patterns, conventional moral patterns, but I could never afford to, yeah, but—I'm honest! Give me credit for just that, will you *please?*—Born poor, raised poor, expect to die poor unless I manage to get us something out of what Big Daddy leaves when he dies of cancer! But Brick?!—*Skipper is dead! I'm alive! Maggie the Cat is—*

[BRICK *hops awkwardly forward and strikes at her again with his crutch.*]

—*alive! I am alive, alive! I am . . .*

[*He hurls the crutch at her, across the bed she took refuge behind, and pitches forward on the floor as she completes her speech.*]

—*alive!*

[*A little girl,* DIXIE, *bursts into the room, wearing an Indian war bonnet and firing a cap pistol at* MARGARET *and shouting:* "Bang, bang, bang!"]

[*Laughter downstairs floats through the open hall door.* MARGARET *had crouched gasping to bed at child's entrance. She now rises and says with cool fury:*]

Little girl, your mother or someone should teach you—[*gasping*]—to knock at a door before you come into a room. Otherwise people might think that you—lack—good breeding. . . .

DIXIE: Yanh, yanh, yanh, what is Uncle Brick doin' on th' floor?

BRICK: I tried to kill your Aunt Maggie, but I failed—and I fell. Little girl, give me my crutch so I can get up off th' floor.

MARGARET: Yes, give your uncle his crutch, he's a cripple, honey, he broke his ankle last night jumping hurdles on the high school athletic field!

DIXIE: What were you jumping hurdles for, Uncle Brick?

BRICK: Because I used to jump them, and people like to do what they used to do, even after they've stopped being able to do it. . . .

MARGARET: That's right, that's your answer, now go away, little girl.

[DIXIE *fires cap pistol at* MARGARET *three times.*]

Stop, you stop that, monster! You little no-neck monster!

[*She seizes the cap pistol and hurls it through gallery doors.*]

DIXIE: [*with a precocious instinct for the cruelest thing*] You're *jealous!*—You're just jealous because you can't have babies!

[*She sticks out her tongue at* MARGARET *as she sashays past her with her stomach stuck out, to the gallery.* MARGARET *slams the gallery doors and leans panting against them. There is a pause.* BRICK *has replaced his spilt drink and sits, faraway, on the great four-poster bed.*]

MARGARET: You see?—they gloat over us being childless, even in front of their five little no-neck monsters!

[*Pause. Voices approach on the stairs.*]

Brick?—I've been to a doctor in Memphis, a—a gynecologist. . . .

I've been completely examined, and there is no reason why we can't have a child whenever we want one. And this is my time by the calendar to conceive. Are you listening to me? Are you? Are you LISTENING TO ME!

BRICK: Yes. I hear you, Maggie.

[*His attention returns to her inflamed face.*]

—But how in hell on Earth do you imagine—that you're going to have a child by a man that can't stand you?

MARGARET: That's a problem that I will have to work out.

[*She wheels about to face the hall door.*]

Here they come!

[*The lights dim.*]

CURTAIN

ACT TWO

There is no lapse of time. MARGARET *and* BRICK *are in the same positions they held at the end of Act I.*

MARGARET: [*at door*]: *Here they come!*

[BIG DADDY *appears first, a tall man with a fierce, anxious look, moving carefully not to betray his weakness even, or especially, to himself.*]

BIG DADDY: Well, Brick.

BRICK: Hello, Big Daddy.—Congratulations!

BIG DADDY: —Crap. . . .

[*Some of the people are approaching through the hall, others along the gallery: voices from both directions.* GOOPER *and* REVEREND TOOKER *become visible outside gallery doors, and their voices come in clearly.*]

[*They pause outside as* GOOPER *lights a cigar.*]

REVEREND TOOKER: [*vivaciously*] Oh, but St. Paul's in Grenada has three memorial windows, and the latest one is a Tiffany stained-glass window that cost twenty-five hundred dollars, a picture of Christ the Good Shepherd with a Lamb in His arms.

GOOPER: Who give that window, Preach?

REVEREND TOOKER: Clyde Fletcher's widow. Also presented St. Paul's with a baptismal font.

GOOPER: Y'know what somebody ought t' give your church is a *coolin'* system, Preach.

REVEREND TOOKER: Yes, siree, Bob! And y'know what Gus Hamma's family gave in his memory to the church at Two Rivers? A complete new stone parish-house with a basketball court in the basement and a—

BIG DADDY: [*uttering a loud barking laugh, which is far from truly mirthful*] Hey, Preach! What's all this talk about memorials, Preach? Y' think somebody's about t' kick off around here? 'S that it?

> [*Startled by this interjection,* REVEREND TOOKER *decides to laugh at the question almost as loud as he can.*]
>
> [*How he would answer the question we'll never know, as he's spared that embarrassment by the voice of* GOOPER's *wife,* MAE, *rising high and clear as she appears with "*DOC*"* BAUGH, *the family doctor, through the hall door.*]

MAE: [*almost religiously*]—Let's see now, they've had their *tyyy*-phoid shots, and their tetanus shots, their diphtheria shots and their hepatitis shots and their polio shots, they got *those* shots every month from May through September and—Gooper? Hey! Gooper!—What all have the kiddies been shot faw?

MARGARET: [*overlapping a bit*] Turn on the hi-fi, Brick! Let's have some music t' start off th' party with!

> [*The talk becomes so general that the room sounds like a great aviary of chattering birds. Only* BRICK *remains unengaged, leaning upon the liquor cabinet with his faraway smile, an ice cube in a paper napkin with which he now and then rubs his forehead. He doesn't respond to* MARGARET's *command. She bounds forward and stoops over the instrument panel of the console.*]

GOOPER: We gave 'em that thing for a third anniversary present, got three speakers in it.

> [*The room is suddenly blasted by the climax of a Wagnerian opera or a Beethoven symphony.*]

BIG DADDY: *Turn that dam thing off!*

> [*Almost instant silence, almost instantly broken by the shouting charge of* BIG MAMA, *entering through hall door like a charging rhino.*]

BIG MAMA: *Wha's my Brick, wha's mah precious baby!!*

BIG DADDY: *Sorry! Turn it back on!*

> [*Everyone laughs very loud.* BIG DADDY *is famous for his jokes at* BIG MAMA's *expense, and nobody laughs louder at these jokes than* BIG MAMA *herself, though sometimes they're pretty cruel and* BIG MAMA *has to pick up or fuss with something to cover the hurt that the loud laugh doesn't quite cover.*]
>
> [*On this occasion, a happy occasion because the dread in her heart has also been lifted by the false report on* BIG DADDY's *condition, she giggles, grotesquely, coyly, in* BIG DADDY's *direction and bears down upon* BRICK, *all very quick and alive.*]

BIG MAMA: Here he is, here's my precious baby! What's that you've got in your hand? You put that liquor down, son, your hand was made fo' holdin' somethin' better than that!

GOOPER: Look at Brick put it down!

> [BRICK *has obeyed* BIG MAMA *by draining the glass and handing it to her. Again everyone laughs, some high, some low.*]

BIG MAMA: Oh, you bad boy, you're my bad little boy. Give Big Mama a kiss, you bad boy, you!—Look at him shy away, will you? Brick never liked bein' kissed or made a fuss over, I guess because he's always had too much of it!

> Son, you turn that thing off!
>
> [BRICK *has switched on the TV set.*]

I can't stand TV, radio was bad enough but TV has gone it one better, I mean—[*plops wheezing in chair*]—one worse, ha ha! Now what'm I sittin' down here faw? I want t' sit next to my sweetheart on the sofa, hold hands with him and love him up a little!

> [BIG MAMA *has on a black-and-white–figured chiffon. The large irregular patterns, like the markings of some massive animal, the luster of her great diamonds and many pearls, the brilliants set in the silver frames of her glasses, her riotous voice, booming laugh, have dominated the room since she entered.* BIG DADDY *has been regarding her with a steady grimace of chronic annoyance.*]

BIG MAMA: [*still louder*] Preacher, Preacher, hey, Preach! Give me you' hand an' help me up from this chair!

REVEREND TOOKER: None of your tricks, Big Mama!

BIG MAMA: What tricks? You give me you' hand so I can get up an'—

> [REVEREND TOOKER *extends her his hand. She grabs it and pulls him into her lap with a shrill laugh that spans an octave in two notes.*]

Ever seen a preacher in a fat lady's lap? Hey, hey, folks! Ever seen a preacher in a fat lady's lap?

> [BIG MAMA *is notorious throughout the Delta for this sort of inelegant horseplay.* MARGARET *looks on with indulgent humor, sipping Dubonnet "on the rocks" and watching* BRICK, *but* MAE *and* GOOPER *exchange signs of humorless anxiety over these antics, the sort of behavior which* MAE *thinks may account for their failure to quite get in with the smartest young married set in Memphis, despite all. One of the negroes,* LACY *or* SOOKEY, *peeks in, cackling. They are waiting for a sign to bring in the cake and champagne. But* BIG DADDY'S *not amused. He doesn't understand why, in spite of the infinite mental relief he's received from the doctor's report, he still has these same old fox teeth in his guts. "This spastic thing sure is something," he says to himself, but aloud he roars at* BIG MAMA:]

BIG DADDY: *BIG MAMA, WILL YOU QUIT HORSIN'?*—You're too old an' too fat fo' that sort of crazy kid stuff an' besides a woman with your blood pressure—she had two hundred last spring!—is riskin' a stroke when you mess around like that. . . .

BIG MAMA: Here comes Big Daddy's birthday!

> [*Negroes in white jackets enter with an enormous birthday cake ablaze with candles and carrying buckets of champagne with satin ribbons about the bottle necks.*]
> [MAE *and* GOOPER *strike up song, and everybody, including the Negroes and* CHILDREN, *joins in. Only* BRICK *remains aloof.*]

EVERYONE: *Happy birthday to you.*
              Happy birthday to you.
              Happy birthday, Big Daddy

> [*Some sing:* "Dear, Big Daddy!"]

              Happy birthday to you.

> [*Some sing:* "How old are you?"]
> [MAE *has come down center and is organizing her children like a chorus. She gives them a barely audible:* "One, two, three!" *and they are off in the new tune.*]

CHILDREN: *Skinamarinka—dinka—dink*
              Skinamarinka—do
              We love you.
              Skinamarinka—dinka—dink
              Skinamarinka—do.

> [*All together, they turn to* BIG DADDY.]

              Big Daddy, you!

> [*They turn back front, like a musical comedy chorus.*]

              We love you in the morning;
              We love you in the night.
              We love you when we're with you,
              And we love you out of sight.
              Skinamarinka—dinka—dink
              Skinamarinka—do.

> [MAE *turns to* BIG MAMA.]

              Big Mama, too!

> [BIG MAMA *bursts into tears. The Negroes leave.*]

BIG DADDY: Now Ida, what the hell is the matter with you?

MAE: She's just so happy.

BIG MAMA: I'm just so happy, Big Daddy, I have to cry or something.

> [*Sudden and loud in the hush:*]
> Brick, do you know the wonderful news that Doc Baugh got from the clinic about Big Daddy? Big Daddy's one hundred percent!

MARGARET: Isn't that wonderful?

BIG MAMA: He's just one hundred percent. Passed the examination with flying colors. Now that we know there's nothing wrong with Big Daddy but a spastic colon, I can tell you something. I was worried sick, half out of my mind, for fear that Big Daddy might have a thing like—

> [MARGARET *cuts through this speech, jumping up and exclaiming shrilly:*]

MARGARET: Brick, honey, aren't you going to give Big Daddy his birthday present?

> [*Passing by him, she snatches his liquor glass from him.*]
> [*She picks up a fancily wrapped package.*]
> *Here it is, Big Daddy, this is from Brick!*

BIG MAMA: This is the biggest birthday Big Daddy's ever had, a hundred presents and bushels of telegrams from—

MAE: [*at same time*] What is it, Brick?

GOOPER: I bet 500 to 50 that Brick don't know what it is.

BIG MAMA: The fun of presents is not knowing what they are till you open the package. Open your present, Big Daddy.

BIG DADDY: Open it you'self. I want to ask Brick somethin! Come here, Brick.

MARGARET: Big Daddy's callin' you, Brick.

> [*She is opening the package.*]

BRICK: Tell Big Daddy I'm crippled.

BIG DADDY: I see you're crippled. I want to know how you got crippled.

MARGARET: [*making diversionary tactics*] Oh, look, oh, look, why, it's a cashmere robe!

> [*She holds the robe up for all to see.*]

MAE: You sound surprised, Maggie.

MARGARET: I never saw one before.

MAE: That's funny.—*Hah!*

MARGARET: [*turning on her fiercely, with a brilliant smile*] Why is it funny? All my family ever had was family—and luxuries such as cashmere robes still surprise me!

BIG DADDY: [*ominously*] Quiet!

MAE: [*heedless in her fury*] I don't see how you could be so surprised when you bought it yourself at Loewenstein's in Memphis last Saturday. You know how I know?

BIG DADDY: I said, "Quiet!"

MAE: —I know because the salesgirl that sold it to you waited on me and said, "Oh, Mrs. Pollitt, your sister-in-law just bought a cashmere robe for your husband's father!"

MARGARET: Sister Woman! Your talents are wasted as a housewife and mother, you really ought to be with the FBI or—

BIG DADDY: QUIET!

> [REVEREND TOOKER'*s reflexes are slower than the others'. He finishes a sentence after the bellow.*]

REVEREND TOOKER: [*to* DOC BAUGH]—the Stork and the Reaper are running neck and neck!

> [*He starts to laugh gaily when he notices the silence and* BIG DADDY'*s glare. His laugh dies falsely.*]

BIG DADDY: Preacher, I hope I'm not butting in on more talk about memorial stained-glass windows, am I, Preacher?

> [REVEREND TOOKER *laughs feebly, then coughs dryly in the embarrassed silence.*]
> Preacher?

BIG MAMA: Now, Big Daddy, don't you pick on Preacher!

BIG DADDY: [*raising his voice*] You ever hear that expression "all hawk and no spit"? You bring that expression to mind with that little dry cough of yours, all hawk an' no spit. . . .

> [*The pause is broken only by a short startled laugh from* MARGARET, *the only one there who is conscious of and amused by the grotesque.*]

MAE: [*raising her arms and jangling her bracelets*] I wonder if the mosquitoes are active tonight?

BIG DADDY: What's that, Little Mama? Did you make some remark?

MAE: Yes, I said I wondered if the mosquitoes would eat us alive if we went out on the gallery for a while.

BIG DADDY: Well, if they do, I'll have your bones pulverized for fertilizer!

BIG MAMA: [*quickly*] Last week we had an airplane spraying the place and I think it done some good, at least I haven't had a—

BIG DADDY: [*cutting her speech*] Brick, they tell me, if what they tell me is true, that you done some jumping last night on the high school athletic field?

BIG MAMA: Brick, Big Daddy is talking to you, son.

BRICK: [*smiling vaguely over his drink*] What was that, Big Daddy?

BIG DADDY: They said you done some jumping on the high school track field last night.

BRICK: That's what they told me, too.

BIG DADDY: Was it jumping or humping that you were doing out there? What were you doing out there at three A.M., layin' a woman on that cinder track?

BIG MAMA: Big Daddy, you are off the sick-list, now, and I'm not going to excuse you for talkin' so—

BIG DADDY: Quiet!

BIG MAMA: —*nasty* in front of Preacher and—

BIG DADDY: QUIET!—I ast you, Brick, if you was cuttin' you'self a piece o' poon-tang last night on that cinder track? I thought maybe you were chasin poon-tang on that track an' tripped over something in the heat of the chase—'sthat it?

> [GOOPER *laughs, loud and false, others nervously following suit.* BIG MAMA *stamps her foot, and purses her lips, crossing to* MAE *and whispering something to her as* BRICK *meets his father's hard, intent, grinning stare with a slow, vague smile that he offers all situations from behind the screen of his liquor.*]

BRICK: No, sir, I don't think so. . . .

MAE: [*at the same time, sweetly*] Reverend Tooker, let's you and I take a stroll on the widow's walk.

> [*She and the preacher go out on the gallery as* BIG DADDY *says:*]

BIG DADDY: Then what the hell were you doing out there at three o'clock in the morning?

BRICK: Jumping the hurdles, Big Daddy, runnin' and jumpin' the hurdles, but those high hurdles have gotten too high for me, now.

BIG DADDY: 'Cause you was drunk?

BRICK: [*his vague smile fading a little*] Sober I wouldn't have tried to jump the *low* ones. . . .

BIG MAMA: [*quickly*] Big Daddy, blow out the candles on your birthday cake!

MARGARET: [*at the same time*] I want to propose a toast to Big Daddy Pollitt on his sixty-fifth birthday, the biggest cotton planter in—

BIG DADDY: [*bellowing with fury and disgust*] *I told you to stop it, now stop it, quit this!*

BIG MAMA: [*coming in front of* BIG DADDY *with the cake*] Big Daddy, I will not allow you to talk that way, not even on your birthday, I—

BIG DADDY: I'll talk like I want to on my birthday, Ida, or any other goddam day of the year and anybody here that don't like it knows what they can do!

BIG MAMA: You don't mean that!

BIG DADDY: What makes you think I don't mean it?

> [*Meanwhile various discreet signals have been exchanged and* GOOPER *has also gone out on the gallery.*]

BIG MAMA: I just know you don't mean it.

BIG DADDY: You don't know a goddam thing and you never did!

BIG MAMA: Big Daddy, you don't mean that.

BIG DADDY: Oh, yes, I do, oh, yes, I do, I mean it! I put up with a whole lot of crap around here because I thought I was dying. And you thought I was dying and you started taking over, well, you can stop taking over now, Ida, because I'm not gonna die, you can just stop now this business of taking over because you're not taking over because I'm not dying, I went through the laboratory and the goddam exploratory operation and there's nothing wrong with me but a spastic colon. And I'm not dying of cancer which you thought I was dying of. Ain't that so? Didn't you think that I was dying of cancer, Ida?

> [*Almost everybody is out on the gallery but the two old people glaring at each other across the blazing cake.*]
>
> [BIG MAMA's *chest heaves and she presses a fat fist to her mouth.*]
>
> [BIG DADDY *continues, hoarsely:*]

Ain't that so, Ida? Didn't you have an idea I was dying of cancer and now you could take control of this place and everything on it? I got that impression, I seemed to get that impression. Your loud voice everywhere, your fat old body butting in here and there!

BIG MAMA: Hush! The preacher!

BIG DADDY: Rut the goddam preacher!

> [BIG MAMA *gasps loudly and sits down on the sofa, which is almost too small for her.*]

Did you hear what I said? I said rut the goddam preacher!

> [*Somebody closes the gallery doors from outside just as there is a burst of fireworks and excited cries from the children.*]

BIG MAMA: I never seen you act like this before and I can't think what's got in you!

BIG DADDY: I went through all that laboratory and operation and all just so I would know if you or me was boss here! Well, now it turns out that I am and you ain't—and that's my birthday present—and my cake and champagne!—because for three years now you been gradually taking over. Bossing. Talking. Sashaying your fat old body around the place I made! I made this place! I was overseer on it! I was the overseer on the old Straw and Ochello plantation. I quit school at ten! I quit school at ten years old and went to work like a nigger in the fields. And I rose to be overseer of the Straw and Ochello plantation. And old Straw died and I was Ochello's partner and the place got bigger and bigger and bigger and bigger and bigger! I did all that myself with no goddam help from you, and now you think you're just about to take over. Well, I am just about to tell you that you are not just about to take over, you are not just about to take over a goddam thing. Is that clear to you, Ida? Is that very plain to you, now? Is that understood completely? I been through the laboratory from A to Z. I've had the goddam exploratory operation, and nothing is wrong with me but a spastic colon—made spastic, I guess, by *disgust!* By all the goddam lies and liars that I have had to put up with, and all the goddam hypocrisy that I lived with all these forty years that we been livin' together!

> Hey! Ida!! Blow out the candles on the birthday cake! Purse up your lips and draw a deep breath and blow out the goddam candles on the cake!

BIG MAMA: Oh, Big Daddy, oh, oh, oh, Big Daddy!

BIG DADDY: What's the matter with you?

BIG MAMA: *In all these years you never believed that I loved you??*

BIG DADDY: Huh?

BIG MAMA: *And I did, I did so much, I did love you!*—I even loved your hate and your hardness, Big Daddy!

[*She sobs and rushes awkwardly out onto the gallery.*]

BIG DADDY: [*to himself*] Wouldn't it be funny if that was true. . . .

[*A pause is followed by a burst of light in the sky from the fireworks.*]

BRICK! HEY, BRICK

[*He stands over his blazing birthday cake.*]

[*After some moments,* BRICK *hobbles in on his crutch, holding his glass.*]

[MARGARET *follows him with a bright, anxious smile.*]

I didn't call you, Maggie. I called Brick.

MARGARET: I'm just delivering him to you.

[*She kisses* BRICK *on the mouth, which he immediately wipes with the back of his hand. She flies girlishly back out.* BRICK *and his father are alone.*]

BIG DADDY: Why did you do that?

BRICK: Do what, Big Daddy?

BIG DADDY: Wipe her kiss off your mouth like she'd spit on you.

BRICK: I don't know. I wasn't conscious of it.

BIG DADDY: That woman of yours has a better shape on her than Gooper's but somehow or other they got the same look about them.

BRICK: What sort of look is that, Big Daddy?

BIG DADDY: I don't know how to describe it but it's the same look.

BRICK: They don't look peaceful, do they?

BIG DADDY: No, they sure in hell don't.

BRICK: They look nervous as cats?

BIG DADDY: That's right, they look nervous as cats.

BRICK: Nervous as a couple of cats on a hot tin roof?

BIG DADDY: That's right, boy, they look like a couple of cats on a hot tin roof. It's funny that you and Gooper being so different would pick out the same type of woman.

BRICK: Both of us married into society, Big Daddy.

BIG DADDY: Crap . . . I wonder what gives them both that look?

BRICK: Well. They're sittin' in the middle of a big piece of land, Big Daddy, twenty-eight thousand acres is a pretty big piece of land and so they're squaring off on it, each determined to knock off a bigger piece of it than the other whenever you let it go.

BIG DADDY: I got a surprise for those women. I'm not gonna let it go for a long time yet if that's what they're waiting for.

BRICK: That's right, Big Daddy. You just sit tight and let them scratch each other's eyes out. . . .

BIG DADDY: You bet your life I'm going to sit tight on it and let those sons of bitches scratch their eyes out, ha ha ha. . . .

But Gooper's wife's a good breeder, you got to admit she's fertile. Hell, at supper tonight she had them all at the table and they had to put a couple of extra leafs in the table to make room for them, she's got five head of them, now, and another one's comin'.

BRICK: Yep, number six is comin'. . . .

BIG DADDY: Brick, you know, I swear to God, I don't know the way it happens?

BRICK: The way what happens, Big Daddy?

BIG DADDY: You git you a piece of land, by hook or crook, an' things start growin' on it, things accumulate on it, and the first thing you know it's completely out of hand, completely out of hand!

BRICK: Well, they say nature hates a vacuum, Big Daddy.

BIG DADDY: That's what they say, but sometimes I think that a vacuum is a hell of a lot better than some of the stuff that nature replaces it with.

Is someone out there by that door?

BRICK: Yep.

BIG DADDY: Who?

[*He has lowered his voice.*]

BRICK: Someone int'rested in what we say to each other.

BIG DADDY: Gooper?—*GOOPER!*

[*After a discreet pause,* MAE *appears in the gallery door.*]

MAE: Did you call Gooper, Big Daddy?

BIG DADDY: Aw, it was you.

MAE: Do you want Gooper, Big Daddy?

BIG DADDY: No, and I don't want you. I want some privacy here, while I'm having a confidential talk with my son Brick. Now it's too hot in here to close them doors, but if I have to close those rutten doors in order to have a private talk with my son Brick, just let me know and I'll close 'em. Because I hate eavesdroppers, I don't like any kind of sneakin' an' spyin'.

MAE: Why, Big Daddy—

BIG DADDY: You stood on the wrong side of the moon, it threw your shadow!

MAE: I was just—

BIG DADDY: You was just nothing but *spyin'* an' you *know* it!

MAE: [*begins to sniff and sob*] Oh, Big Daddy, you're so unkind for some reason to those that really love you!

BIG DADDY: Shut up, shut up, shut up! I'm going to move you and Gooper out of that room next to this! It's none of your goddam business what goes on in here at night between Brick an' Maggie. You listen at night like a couple of rutten peekhole spies and go and give a report on what you hear to Big Mama an' she comes to me and says they say such and such and so and so about what they heard goin' on between Brick an' Maggie, and Jesus, it makes me sick. I'm goin' to move you an' Gooper out of that room, I can't stand sneakin' an' spyin', it makes me sick. . . .

[MAE *throws back her head and rolls her eyes heavenward and extends her arms as if invoking God's pity for this unjust martyrdom; then she presses a handkerchief to her nose and flies from the room with a loud swish of skirts.*]

BRICK: [*now at the liquor cabinet*] They listen, do they?

BIG DADDY: Yeah. They listen and give reports to Big Mama on what goes on in here between you and Maggie. They say that—

[*He stops as if embarrassed.*]

—You won't sleep with her, that you sleep on the sofa. Is that true or not true? If you don't like Maggie, get rid of Maggie!—What are you doin' there now?

BRICK: Fresh'nin' up my drink.

BIG DADDY: Son, you know you got a real liquor problem?

BRICK: Yes, sir, yes, I know.

BIG DADDY: Is that why you quit sports announcing, because of this liquor problem?

BRICK: Yes, sir, yes, sir, I guess so.

[*He smiles vaguely and amiably at his father across his replenished drink.*]

BIG DADDY: Son, don't guess about it, it's too important.

BRICK: [*vaguely*] Yes, sir.

BIG DADDY: And listen to me, don't look at the damn chandelier. . . .

[*Pause.* BIG DADDY'*s voice is husky.*]

—Somethin' else we picked up at th' big fire sale in Europe.

[*another pause*]

Life is important. There's nothing else to hold onto. A man that drinks is throwing his life away. Don't do it, hold onto your life. There's nothing else to hold onto. . . .

Sit down over here so we don't have to raise our voices, the walls have ears in this place.

BRICK: [*hobbling over to sit on the sofa beside him*] All right, Big Daddy.

BIG DADDY: Quit!—how'd that come about? Some disappointment?

BRICK: I don't know. Do you?

BIG DADDY: I'm askin' you, goddam it! How in hell would I know if you don't?

BRICK: I just got out there and found that I had a mouth full of cotton. I was always two or three beats behind what was goin' on on the field and so I—

BIG DADDY: Quit!

BRICK: [*amiably*] Yes, quit.

BIG DADDY: Son?

BRICK: Huh?

BIG DADDY: [*inhales loudly and deeply from his cigar; then bends suddenly a little forward, exhaling loudly and raising a hand to his forehead*]

—Whew!—ha ha!—I took in too much smoke, it made me a little light-headed. . . .

[*The mantel clock chimes.*]

Why is it so damn hard for people to talk?

BRICK: Yeah. . . .

[*The clock goes on sweetly chiming till it has completed the stroke of ten.*]

—Nice peaceful-soundin' clock, I like to hear it all night. . . .

[*He slides low and comfortable on the sofa;* BIG DADDY *sits up straight and rigid with some unspoken anxiety. All his gestures are tense and jerky as he talks. He wheezes and pants and sniffs through his nervous speech, glancing quickly, shyly, from time to time, at his son.*]

BIG DADDY: We got that clock the summer we wint to Europe, me an' Big Mama on that damn Cook's Tour, never had such an awful time in my life, I'm tellin' you, son, those gooks over there, they gouge your eyeballs out in their grand hotels. And Big Mama bought more stuff than you could haul in a couple of boxcars, that's no crap. Everywhere she wint on this whirlwind tour, she bought, bought, bought. Why, half that stuff she bought is still crated up in the cellar, under water last spring!

[*He laughs.*]

That Europe is nothin' on earth but a great big auction, that's all it is, that bunch of worn-out places, it's just a big fire sale, the whole rutten thing, an' Big Mama wint wild in it, why, you couldn't hold that woman with a mule's harness! Bought, bought, bought!—lucky I'm a rich man, yes, siree, Bob, an' half that stuff is mildewin' in th' basement. It's lucky I'm a rich man, it sure is lucky, well, I'm a rich man, Brick, yep, I'm a mighty rich man.

[*His eyes light up for a moment.*]

Y'know how much I'm worth? Guess, Brick! Guess how much I'm worth!

[BRICK *smiles vaguely over his drink.*]

Close on ten million in cash an' blue-chip stocks, outside, mind you, of twenty-eight thousand acres of the richest land this side of the valley Nile!

[*A puff and crackle and the night sky blooms with an eerie greenish glow. Children shriek on the gallery.*]

But a man can't buy his life with it, he can't buy back his life with it when his life has been spent, that's one thing not offered in the Europe fire sale or in the American markets or any markets on earth, a man can't buy his life with it, he can't buy back his life when his life is finished. . . .

That's a sobering thought, a very sobering thought, and that's a thought that I was turning over in my head, over and over and over—until today. . . .

I'm wiser and sadder, Brick, for this experience which I just gone through. They's one thing else that I remember in Europe.

BRICK: What is that, Big Daddy?

BIG DADDY: The hills around Barcelona in the country of Spain and the children running over those bare hills in their bare skins beggin' like starvin' dogs with howls and screeches, and how fat the priests are on the streets of Barcelona, so many of them and so fat and so pleasant, ha ha!—Y'know I could feed that country? I got money enough to feed that goddam country, but the human animal is a selfish beast and I don't reckon the money I passed out there to those howling children in the hills around Barcelona would more than upholster one of the chairs in this room, I mean pay to put a new cover on this chair!

Hell, I threw them money like you'd scatter feed corn for chickens, I threw money at them just to get rid of them long enough to climb back into th' car and— drive away. . . .

And then in Morocco, them Arabs, why, prostitution begins at four or five, that's no exaggeration, why, I remember one day in Marrakech, that old walled Arab city, I set on a broken-down wall to have a cigar, it was fearful hot there and this Arab woman stood in the road and looked at me till I was embarrassed, she stood stock still in the dusty hot road and looked at me till I was embarrassed. But listen to this. She had a naked child with her, a little naked girl with her, barely able to toddle, and after a while she set this child on the ground and give her a push and whispered something to her.

This child come toward me, barely able t' walk, come toddling up to me and— Jesus, it makes you sick t' remember a thing like this!

It stuck out its hand and tried to unbutton my trousers!

That child was not yet five! Can you believe me? Or do you think that I am making this up? I wint back to the hotel and said to Big Mama, "Git packed! We're clearing out of this country." . . .

BRICK: Big Daddy, you're on a talkin' jag tonight.

BIG DADDY: [*ignoring this remark*] Yes, sir, that's how it is, the human animal is a beast that dies but the fact that he's dying don't give him pity for others, no, sir, it— —Did you say something?

BRICK: Yes.

BIG DADDY: What?

BRICK: Hand me over that crutch so I can get up.

BIG DADDY: Where you goin'?

BRICK: I'm takin' a little short trip to Echo Spring.

BIG DADDY: To where?

BRICK: Liquor cabinet. . . .

BIG DADDY: Yes, sir, boy—

[*He hands* BRICK *the crutch.*]

—the human animal is a beast that dies and if he's got money he buys and buys and buys and I think the reason he buys everything he can buy is that in the back of his mind he has the crazy hope that one of his purchases will be life everlasting!—Which it never can be. . . . The human animal is a beast that—

BRICK: [*at the liquor cabinet*] Big Daddy, you sure are shootin' th' breeze here tonight.

[*There is a pause and voices are heard outside.*]

BIG DADDY: I been quiet here lately, spoke not a word, just sat and stared into space. I had something heavy weighing on my mind but tonight that load was took off me. That's why I'm talking.—The sky looks diff'rent to me. . . .

BRICK: You know what I like to hear most?

BIG DADDY: What?

BRICK: Solid quiet. Perfect unbroken quiet.

BIG DADDY: Why?

BRICK: Because it's more peaceful.

BIG DADDY: Man, you'll hear a lot of that in the grave.

[*He chuckles agreeably.*]

BRICK: Are you through talkin' to me?

BIG DADDY: Why are you so anxious to shut me up?

BRICK: Well, sir, ever so often you say to me, "Brick, I want to have a talk with you," but when we talk, it never materializes. Nothing is said. You sit in a chair and gas about this and that and I look like I listen. I try to look like I listen, but I don't listen, not much. Communication is—awful hard between people an'—somehow between you and me, it just don't—

BIG DADDY: Have you ever been scared? I mean have you ever felt downright terror of something?

[*He gets up.*]

Just one moment. I'm going to close these doors. . . .

[*He closes doors on gallery as if he were going to tell an important secret.*]

BRICK: What?

BIG DADDY: Brick?

BRICK: Huh?

BIG DADDY: Son, I thought I had it!

BRICK: Had what? Had what, Big Daddy?

BIG DADDY: Cancer!

BRICK: Oh . . .

BIG DADDY: I thought the old man made out of bones had laid his cold and heavy hand on my shoulder!

BRICK: Well, Big Daddy, you kept a tight mouth about it.

BIG DADDY: A pig squeals. A man keeps a tight mouth about it, in spite of a man not having a pig's advantage.

BRICK: What advantage is that?

BIG DADDY: Ignorance—of mortality—is a comfort. A man don't have that comfort, he's the only living thing that conceives of death, that knows what it is. The others go without knowing, which is the way that anything living should go, go without knowing, without any knowledge of it, and yet a pig squeals, but a man sometimes, he can keep a tight mouth about it. Sometimes he—

[*There is a deep, smoldering ferocity in the old man.*]

—can keep a tight mouth about it. I wonder if—

BRICK: What, Big Daddy?

BIG DADDY: A whiskey highball would injure this spastic condition?

BRICK: No, sir, it might do it good.

BIG DADDY: [*grins suddenly, wolfishly*] Jesus, I can't tell you! The sky is open! Christ it's open again! It's open, boy, it's open!

[BRICK *looks down at his drink.*]

BRICK: You feel better, Big Daddy?

BIG DADDY: Better? Hell! I can breathe!—All of my life I been like a doubled-up fist. . . .

[*He pours a drink.*]

—Poundin', smashin', drivin'!—now I'm going to loosen these doubled-up hands and touch things easy with them. . . .

[*He spreads his hands as if caressing the air.*]

You know what I'm contemplating?

BRICK: [*vaguely*] No, sir. What are you contemplating?

BIG DADDY: Ha ha!—*Pleasure!*—pleasure with *women!*

> [BRICK'*s smile fades a little but lingers.*]

Brick, this stuff burns me!—

—Yes, boy. I'll tell you something that you might not guess. I still have desire for women and this is my sixty-fifth birthday.

BRICK: I think that's mighty remarkable, Big Daddy.

BIG DADDY: Remarkable?

BRICK: *Admirable,* Big Daddy.

BIG DADDY: You're damn right it is, remarkable and admirable both. I realize now that I never had me enough. I let many chances slip by because of scruples about it, scruples, convention—crap. . . . All that stuff is bull, bull, bull!—It took the shadow of death to make me see it. Now that shadow's lifted, I'm going to cut loose and have, what is it they call it, have me a—ball!

BRICK: A ball, huh?

BIG DADDY: That's right, a ball, a ball! Hell!—I slept with Big Mama till, let's see, five years ago, till I was sixty and she was fifty-eight, and never even liked her, never did!

> [*The phone has been ringing down the hall.* BIG MAMA *enters, exclaiming.*]

BIG MAMA: Don't you men hear that phone ring? I heard it way out on the gall'ry.

BIG DADDY: There's five rooms off this front gall'ry that you could go through. Why do you go through this one?

> [BIG MAMA *makes a playful face as she bustles out the hall door.*]

Hunh!—Why, when Big Mama goes out of a room, I can't remember what that woman looks like, but when Big Mama comes back into the room, boy, then I see what she looks like, and I wish I didn't!

> [*Bends over laughing at this joke till it hurts his guts and he straightens with a grimace. The laugh subsides to a chuckle as he puts the liquor glass a little distrustfully down on the table.*]

> [BRICK *has risen and hobbled to the gallery doors.*]

Hey! Where you goin'?

BRICK: Out for a breather.

BIG DADDY: Not yet you ain't. Stay here till this talk is finished, young fellow.

BRICK: I thought it was finished, Big Daddy.

BIG DADDY: It ain't even begun.

BRICK: My mistake. Excuse me. I just wanted to feel that river breeze.

BIG DADDY: Turn on the ceiling fan and set back down in that chair.

> [BIG MAMA'*s voice rises, carrying down the hall.*]

BIG MAMA: Miss Sally, you're a case! You're a caution, Miss Sally. Why didn't you give me a chance to explain it to you?

BIG DADDY: Jesus, she's talking to my old maid sister again.

BIG MAMA: Well, goodbye, now, Miss Sally. You come down real soon, Big Daddy's dying to see you! Yaisss, goodbye, Miss Sally. . . .

> [*She hangs up and bellows with mirth.* BIG DADDY *groans and covers his ears as she approaches.*]

> [*Bursting in:*]

Big Daddy, that was Miss Sally callin' from Memphis again! You know what she done, Big Daddy? She called her doctor in Memphis to git him to tell her what that spastic thing is! Ha-*HAAAA!*—And called back to tell me how relieved she was that—Hey! Let me in!

> [BIG DADDY *has been holding the door half closed against her.*]

BIG DADDY: Naw I ain't. I told you not to come and go through this room. You just back
out and go through those five other rooms.

BIG MAMA: Big Daddy? Big Daddy? Oh, Big Daddy!—You didn't mean those things you
said to me, did you?

[*He shuts door firmly against her but she still calls.*]

Sweetheart? Sweetheart? Big Daddy? You didn't mean those awful things you said to
me?—I know you didn't. I know you didn't mean those things in your heart. . . .

[*The childlike voice fades with a sob and her heavy footsteps retreat down the hall.*
BRICK *has risen once more on his crutches and starts for the gallery again.*]

BIG DADDY: All I ask of that woman is that she leave me alone. But she can't admit to herself that she makes me sick. That comes of having slept with her too many years.
Should of quit much sooner but that old woman she never got enough of it—and I
was good in bed. . . . I never should of wasted so much of it on her. . . . They say you
got just so many and each one is numbered. Well, I got a few left in me, a few, and
I'm going to pick me a good one to spend 'em on! I'm going to pick me a choice one,
I don't care how much she costs, I'll smother her in—minks! Ha ha! I'll strip her
naked and smother her in minks and choke her with diamonds! Ha ha! I'll strip her
naked and choke her with diamonds and smother her with minks and hump her
from hell to breakfast. *Ha aha ha ha ha!*

MAE: [*gaily at door*] Who's that laughin' in there?

GOOPER: Is Big Daddy laughin' in there?

BIG DADDY: Crap!—them two—*drips*. . . .

[*He goes over and touches* BRICK's *shoulder.*]

Yes, son. Brick, boy.—I'm—*happy!* I'm happy, son, I'm happy!

[*He chokes a little and bites his under lip, pressing his head quickly, shyly against his
son's head and then, coughing with embarrassment, goes uncertainly back to the
table where he set down the glass. He drinks and makes a grimace as it burns his guts.*
BRICK *sighs and rises with effort.*]

What makes you so restless? Have you got ants in your britches?

BRICK: Yes, sir. . . .

BIG DADDY: Why?

BRICK: —Something—hasn't happened. . . .

BIG DADDY: Yeah? What is that!

BRICK: [*sadly*]—the click. . . .

BIG DADDY: Did you say "click"?

BRICK: Yes, click.

BIG DADDY: What click?

BRICK: A click that I get in my head that makes me peaceful.

BIG DADDY: I sure in hell don't know what you're talking about, but it disturbs me.

BRICK: It's just a mechanical thing.

BIG DADDY: What is a mechanical thing?

BRICK: This click that I get in my head that makes me peaceful. I got to drink till I get it.
It's just a mechanical thing, something like a—like a—like a—

BIG DADDY: Like a—

BRICK: Switch clicking off in my head, turning the hot light off and the cool night on and—

[*He looks up, smiling sadly.*]

—all of a sudden there's—peace!

BIG DADDY: [*whistles long and soft with astonishment; he goes back to* BRICK *and clasps his
son's two shoulders*] Jesus! I didn't know it had gotten that bad with you. Why, boy,
you're—*alcoholic!*

BRICK: That's the truth, Big Daddy. I'm alcoholic.

BIG DADDY: This shows how I—let things go!

BRICK: I have to hear that little click in my head that makes me peaceful. Usually I hear it sooner than this, sometimes as early as—noon, but—

—Today it's—dilatory. . . .

—I just haven't got the right level of alcohol in my bloodstream yet!

[*This last statement is made with energy as he freshens his drink.*]

BIG DADDY: Uh—huh. Expecting death made me blind. I didn't have no idea that a son of mine was turning into a drunkard under my nose.

BRICK: [*gently*] Well, now you do, Big Daddy, the news has penetrated.

BIG DADDY: Uh-huh, yes, now I do, the news has—penetrated. . . .

BRICK: And so if you'll excuse me—

BIG DADDY: No, I won't excuse you.

BRICK: —I'd better sit by myself till I hear that click in my head, it's just a mechanical thing but it don't happen except when I'm alone or talking to no one. . . .

BIG DADDY: You got a long, long time to sit still, boy, and talk to no one, but now you're talkin' to me. At least I'm talking to you. And you set there and listen until I tell you the conversation is over!

BRICK: But this talk is like all the others we've ever had together in our lives! It's nowhere, nowhere!—it's—it's *painful*, Big Daddy. . . .

BIG DADDY: All right, then let it be painful, but don't you move from that chair!—I'm going to remove that crutch. . . .

[*He seizes the crutch and tosses it across room.*]

BRICK: I can hop on one foot, and if I fall, I can crawl!

BIG DADDY: If you ain't careful you're gonna crawl off this plantation and then, by Jesus, you'll have to hustle your drinks along Skid Row!

BRICK: That'll come, Big Daddy.

BIG DADDY: Naw, it won't. You're my son and I'm going to straighten you out; now that *I'm* straightened out, I'm going to straighten out you!

BRICK: Yeah?

BIG DADDY: Today the report come in from Ochsner Clinic. Y'know what they told me?

[*His face glows with triumph.*]

The only thing that they could detect with all the instruments of science in that great hospital is a little spastic condition of the colon! And nerves torn to pieces by all that worry about it.

[*A little girl bursts into room with a sparkler clutched in each fist, hops and shrieks like a monkey gone mad and rushes back out again as* BIG DADDY *strikes at her.*]

[*Silence. The two men stare at each other. A woman laughs gaily outside.*]

I want you to know I breathed a sigh of relief almost as powerful as the Vicksburg tornado!

BRICK: You weren't ready to go?

BIG DADDY: GO WHERE?—crap. . . .

—When you are gone from here, boy, you are long gone and no where! The human machine is not no different from the animal machine or the fish machine or the bird machine or the reptile machine or the insect machine! It's just a whole goddam lot more complicated and consequently more trouble to keep together. Yep. I thought I had it. The earth shook under my foot, the sky come down like the black lid of a kettle and I couldn't breathe!—Today!!—that lid was lifted, I drew my first free breath in—how many years?—*God!—three*. . . .

[*There is laughter outside, running footsteps, the soft, plushy sound and light of exploding rockets.*]

[BRICK *stares at him soberly for a long moment; then makes a sort of startled sound in his nostrils and springs up on one foot and hops across the room to grab his crutch, swinging on the furniture for support. He gets the crutch and flees as if in horror for the gallery. His father seizes him by the sleeve of his white silk pajamas.*]

Stay here, you son of a bitch!—till I say go!

BRICK: I can't.

BIG DADDY: You sure in hell will, goddamn it.

BRICK: No, I can't. We talk, you talk, in—circles! We get no where, no where! It's always the same, you say you want to talk to me and don't have a ruttin' thing to say to me!

BIG DADDY: Nothin' to say when I'm tellin' you I'm going to live when I thought I was dying?!

BRICK: Oh—*that!*—Is that what you have to say to me?

BIG DADDY: Why, you son of a bitch! Ain't that, ain't that—*important?!*

BRICK: Well, you said that, that's said, and now I—

BIG DADDY: Now you set back down.

BRICK: You're all balled up, you—

BIG DADDY: I ain't balled up!

BRICK: You are, you're all balled up!

BIG DADDY: Don't tell me what I am, you drunken whelp! I'm going to tear this coat sleeve off if you don't set down!

BRICK: Big Daddy—

BIG DADDY: Do what I tell you! I'm the boss here, now! I want you to know I'm back in the driver's seat now!

[BIG MAMA *rushes in, clutching her great heaving bosom.*]

What in hell do you want in here, Big Mama?

BIG MAMA: Oh, Big Daddy! Why are you shouting like that? I just cain't *stainnnnnnnd—it.* . . .

BIG DADDY: [*raising the back of his hand above his head*] GIT!—outa here.

[*She rushes back out, sobbing.*]

BRICK: [*softly, sadly*] Christ. . . .

BIG DADDY: [*fiercely*] Yeah! Christ!—is right. . . .

[BRICK *breaks loose and hobbles toward the gallery.*]

[BIG DADDY *jerks his crutch from under* BRICK *so he steps with the injured ankle. He utters a hissing cry of anguish, clutches a chair and pulls it over on top of him on the floor.*]

Son of a—tub of—hog fat. . . .

BRICK: Big Daddy! Give me my crutch.

[BIG DADDY *throws the crutch out of reach.*]

Give me that crutch, Big Daddy.

BIG DADDY: Why do you drink?

BRICK: Don't know, give me my crutch!

BIG DADDY: You better think why you drink or give up drinking!

BRICK: Will you please give me my crutch so I can get up off this floor?

BIG DADDY: First you answer my question. Why do you drink? Why are you throwing your life away, boy, like somethin' disgusting you picked up on the street?

BRICK: [*getting onto his knees*] Big Daddy, I'm in pain, I stepped on that foot.

BIG DADDY: Good! I'm glad you're not too numb with the liquor in you to feel some pain!

BRICK: You—spilled my—drink. . . .

BIG DADDY: I'll make a bargain with you. You tell me why you drink and I'll hand you one. I'll pour you the liquor myself and hand it to you.

BRICK: Why do I drink?

BIG DADDY: Yea! Why?

BRICK: Give me a drink and I'll tell you.

BIG DADDY: Tell me first!

BRICK: I'll tell you in one word.

BIG DADDY: What word?

BRICK: DISGUST!

> [*The clock chimes softly, sweetly.* BIG DADDY *gives it a short, outraged glance.*]
> Now how about that drink?

BIG DADDY: What are you disgusted with? You got to tell me that, first. Otherwise being disgusted don't make no sense!

BRICK: Give me my crutch.

BIG DADDY: You heard me, you got to tell me what I asked you first.

BRICK: I told you, I said to kill my disgust!

BIG DADDY: DISGUST WITH WHAT!

BRICK: You strike a hard bargain.

BIG DADDY: What are you disgusted with?—an' I'll pass you the liquor.

BRICK: I can hop on one foot, and if I fall, I can crawl.

BIG DADDY: You want liquor that bad?

BRICK: [*dragging himself up, clinging to bedstead*] Yeah, I want it that bad.

BIG DADDY: If I give you a drink, will you tell me what it is you're disgusted with, Brick?

BRICK: Yes, sir, I will try to.

> [*The old man pours him a drink and solemnly passes it to him.*]
> [*There is silence as* BRICK *drinks.*]
> Have you ever heard the word "mendacity"?

BIG DADDY: Sure. Mendacity is one of them five-dollar words that cheap politicians throw back and forth at each other.

BRICK: You know what it means?

BIG DADDY: Don't it mean lying and liars?

BRICK: Yes, sir, lying and liars.

BIG DADDY: Has someone been lying to you?

CHILDREN: [*chanting in chorus offstage*]
> We want Big Dad-dee!
> We want Big Dad-dee!
> [GOOPER *appears in the gallery door.*]

GOOPER: Big Daddy, the kiddies are shouting for you out there.

BIG DADDY: [*fiercely*] Keep out, Gooper!

GOOPER: 'Scuse *me!*

> [BIG DADDY *slams the doors after* GOOPER.]

BIG DADDY: Who's been lying to you, has Margaret been lying to you, has your wife been lying to you about something, Brick?

BRICK: Not her. That wouldn't matter.

BIG DADDY: Then who's been lying to you, and what about?

BRICK: No one single person and no one lie. . . .

BIG DADDY: Then what, what then, for Christ's sake?

BRICK: The whole, the whole—thing. . . .

BIG DADDY: Why are you rubbing your head? You got a headache?

BRICK: No, I'm tryin' to—

BIG DADDY: —Concentrate, but you can't because your brain's all soaked with liquor, is that the trouble? Wet brain!

> [*He snatches the glass from* BRICK's *hand.*]

What do you know about this mendacity thing? Hell! I could write a book on it! Don't you know that? I could write a book on it and still not cover the subject? Well, I could, I could write a goddam book on it and still not cover the subject anywhere near enough!!—Think of all the lies I got to put up with!—Pretenses! Ain't that mendacity? Having to pretend stuff you don't think or feel or have any idea of? Having for instance to act like I care for Big Mama!—I haven't been able to stand the sight, sound, or smell of that woman for forty years now!—even when I *laid* her!—regular as a piston. . . .

    Pretend to love that son of a bitch of a Gooper and his wife Mae and those five same screechers out there like parrots in a jungle? Jesus! Can't stand to look at 'em!

    Church!—it bores the bejesus out of me but I go!—I go an' sit there and listen to the fool preacher!

    Clubs!—Elks! Masons! Rotary!—*crap!*

    [*A spasm of pain makes him clutch his belly. He sinks into a chair and his voice is softer and hoarser.*]

You I *do* like for some reason, did always have some kind of real feeling for—affection—respect yes, always. . . .

    You and being a success as a planter is all I ever had any devotion to in my whole life!and that's the truth. . . .

    I don't know why, but it is!

    I've lived with mendacity!—Why can't *you* live with it? Hell, you *got* to live with it, there's nothing *else* to *live* with except mendacity, is there?

BRICK: Yes, sir. Yes, sir, there is something else that you can live with!

BIG DADDY: What?

BRICK: [*lifting his glass*] This!—Liquor. . . .

BIG DADDY: That's not living, that's dodging away from life.

BRICK: I want to dodge away from it.

BIG DADDY: Then why don't you kill yourself, man?

BRICK: I like to drink. . . .

BIG DADDY: Oh, God, I can't talk to you. . . .

BRICK: I'm sorry, Big Daddy.

BIG DADDY: Not as sorry as I am. I'll tell you something. A little while back when I thought my number was up—

    [*This speech should have torrential pace and fury.*]

—before I found out it was just this—spastic—colon. I thought about you. Should I or should I not, if the jig was up, give you this place when I go—since I hate Gooper an' Mae an' know that they hate me, and since all five same monkeys are little Maes an' Goopers.—And I thought, No!—Then I thought, Yes!—I couldn't make up my mind. I hate Gooper and his five same monkeys and that bitch Mae! Why should I turn over twenty-eight thousand acres of the richest land this side of the valley Nile to not my kind?—But why in hell, on the other hand, Brick—should I subsidize a goddam fool on the bottle?—Liked or not liked, well, maybe even—*loved!*—Why should I do that?—Subsidize worthless behavior? Rot? Corruption?

BRICK: [*smiling*] I understand.

BIG DADDY: Well, if you do, you're smarter than I am, goddam it, because I don't understand. And this I will tell you frankly. I didn't make up my mind at all on that question and still to this day I ain't made out no will!—Well, now I don't have to. The pressure is gone. I can just wait and see if you pull yourself together or if you don't.

BRICK: That's right, Big Daddy.

BIG DADDY: You sound like you thought I was kidding.

BRICK: [*rising*] No, sir, I know you're not kidding.

BIG DADDY: But you don't care—?

BRICK: [*hobbling toward the gallery door*] No, sir, I don't care. . . .
Now how about taking a look at your birthday fireworks and getting some of that cool breeze off the river?
[*He stands in the gallery doorway as the night sky turns pink and green and gold with successive flashes of light.*]

BIG DADDY: WAIT!—Brick. . . .
[*His voice drops. Suddenly there is something shy, almost tender, in his restraining gesture.*]
Don't let's—leave it like this, like them other talks we've had, we've always—talked around things, we've—just talked around things for some rutten reason, I don't know what, it's always like something was left not spoken, something avoided because neither of us was honest enough with the—other. . . .

BRICK: I never lied to you, Big Daddy.

BIG DADDY: Did I ever to *you?*

BRICK: No, sir. . . .

BIG DADDY: Then there is at least two people that never lied to each other.

BRICK: But we've never *talked* to each other.

BIG DADDY: We can *now.*

BRICK: Big Daddy, there don't seem to be anything much to say.

BIG DADDY: You say that you drink to kill your disgust with lying.

BRICK: You said to give you a reason.

BIG DADDY: Is liquor the only thing that'll kill this disgust?

BRICK: Now. Yes.

BIG DADDY: But not once, huh?

BRICK: Not when I was still young an' believing. A drinking man's someone who wants to forget he isn't still young an' believing.

BIG DADDY: Believing what?

BRICK: Believing. . . .

BIG DADDY: Believing *what?*

BRICK: [*stubbornly evasive*] Believing. . . .

BIG DADDY: I don't know what the hell you mean by "believing" and I don't think you know what you mean by "believing" but if you still got sports in your blood, go back to sports announcing and—

BRICK: Sit in a glass box watching games I can't play? Describing what I can't do while players do it? Sweating out their disgust and confusion in contests I'm not fit for? Drinkin' a Coke, half bourbon, so I can stand it? That's no goddam good any more, no help—time just outran me, Big Daddy—got there first. . . .

BIG DADDY: I think you're passing the buck.

BRICK: You know many drinkin' men?

BIG DADDY: [*with a slight, charming smile*] I have known a fair number of that species.

BRICK: Could any of them tell you why he drank?

BIG DADDY: Yep, you're passin' the buck to things like time and disgust with "mendacity" and—crap!—if you got to use that kind of language about a thing, it's ninety-proof bull, and I'm not buying any.

BRICK: I had to give you a reason to get a drink!

BIG DADDY: You started drinkin' when your friend Skipper died.
[*Silence for five beats. Then* BRICK *makes a startled movement, reaching for his crutch.*]

BRICK: What are you suggesting?

BIG DADDY: I'm suggesting nothing.

[*The shuffle and clop of* BRICK's *rapid hobble away from his father's steady, grave attention.*]

—But Gooper an' Mae suggested that there was something not right exactly in your—

BRICK: [*stopping short downstage as if backed to a wall*] "Not right"?

BIG DADDY: Not, well, exactly normal in your friendship with—

BRICK: They suggested that, too? I thought that was Maggie's suggestion.

[BRICK's *detachment is at last broken through. His heart is accelerated; his forehead sweat-beaded; his breath becomes more rapid and his voice hoarse. The thing they're discussing, timidly and painfully on the side of* BIG DADDY, *fiercely, violently on* BRICK's *side, is the inadmissible thing that Skipper died to disavow between them. The fact that if it existed it had to be disavowed to "keep face" in the world they lived in, may be at the heart of the "mendacity" that* BRICK *drinks to kill his disgust with. It may be the root of his collapse. Or maybe it is only a single manifestation of it, not even the most important. The bird that I hope to catch in the net of this play is not the solution of one man's psychological problem. I'm trying to catch the true quality of experience in a group of people, that cloudy, flickering, evanescent—fiercely charged!—interplay of live human beings in the thundercloud of a common crisis. Some mystery should be left in the revelation of character in a play, just as a great deal of mystery is always left in the revelation of character in life, even in one's own character to himself. This does not absolve the playwright of his duty to observe and probe as clearly and deeply as he* legitimately *can: but it should steer him away from "pat" conclusions, facile definitions which make a play just a play, not a snare for the truth of human experience.*]

[*The following scene should be played with great concentration, with most of the power leashed but palpable in what is left unspoken.*]

Who else's suggestion is it, is it yours? How many others thought that Skipper and I were—

BIG DADDY: [*gently*] Now, hold on, hold on a minute, son.—I knocked around in my time.

BRICK: What's that got to do with—

BIG DADDY: I said "Hold on!"—I bummed, I bummed this country till I was—

BRICK: Whose suggestion, who else's suggestion is it?

BIG DADDY: Slept in hobo jungles and railroad Y's and flophouses in all cities before I—

BRICK: Oh, *you* think so, too, you call me your son and a queer. Oh! Maybe that's why you put Maggie and me in this room that was Jack Straw's and Peter Ochello's, in which that pair of old sisters slept in a double bed where both of 'em died!

BIG DADDY: *Now just don't go throwing rocks at*—

[*Suddenly* REVEREND TOOKER *appears in the gallery doors, his head slightly, playfully, fatuously cocked, with a practiced clergyman's smile, sincere as a bird call blown on a hunter's whistle, the living embodiment of the pious, conventional lie.*]

[BIG DADDY *gasps a little at this perfectly timed, but incongruous, apparition.*]

—What're you lookin' for, Preacher?

REVEREND TOOKER: The gentleman's lavatory, ha ha!—heh, heh . . .

BIG DADDY: [*with strained courtesy*]—Go back out and walk down to the other end of the gallery, Reverend Tooker, and use the bathroom connected with my bedroom, and if you can't find it, ask them where it is!

REVEREND TOOKER: Ah, thanks.

[*He goes out with a deprecatory chuckle.*]

BIG DADDY: It's hard to talk in this place. . . .

BRICK: Son of a—!

BIG DADDY: [*leaving a lot unspoken*]—I seen all things and understood a lot of them, till 1910. Christ, the year that—I had worn my shoes through, hocked my—I hopped off a yellow dog freight car half a mile down the road, slept in a wagon of cotton out-side the gin—Jack Straw an' Peter Ochello took me in. Hired me to manage this place which grew into this one. When Jack Straw died—why, old Peter Ochello quit eatin' like a dog does when its master's dead, and died, too!

BRICK: Christ!

BIG DADDY: I'm just saying I understand such—

BRICK: [*violently*] Skipper is dead. I have not quit eating!

BIG DADDY: No, but you started drinking.

> [BRICK *wheels on his crutch and hurls his glass across the room shouting.*]

BRICK: YOU THINK SO, TOO?

BIG DADDY: *Shhh!*

> [*Footsteps run on the gallery. There are women's calls.*]
>
> [BIG DADDY *goes toward the door.*]

Go way!—Just broke a glass. . . .

> [BRICK *is transformed, as if a quiet mountain blew suddenly up in volcanic flame.*]

BRICK: You think so, too? You think so, too? You think me an' Skipper did, did, did!—*sodomy!*—together?

BIG DADDY: Hold—!

BRICK: That what you—

BIG DADDY: —*ON*—a minute!

BRICK: You think we did dirty things between us, Skipper an'—

BIG DADDY: Why are you shouting like that? Why are you—

BRICK: —Me, is that what you think of Skipper, is that—

BIG DADDY: —so excited? I don't think nothing. I don't know nothing. I'm simply telling you what—

BRICK: You think that Skipper and me were a pair of dirty old men?

BIG DADDY: Now that's—

BRICK: Straw? Ochello? A couple of—

BIG DADDY: Now just—

BRICK: —ducking sissies? Queers? Is that what you—

BIG DADDY: Shhh.

BRICK: —think?

> [*He loses his balance and pitches to his knees without noticing the pain. He grabs the bed and drags himself up.*]

BIG DADDY: Jesus!—Whew. . . . Grab my hand!

BRICK: Naw, I don't want your hand. . . .

BIG DADDY: Well, I want yours. Git up!

> [*He draws him up, keeps an arm about him with concern and affection.*]

You broken out in a sweat! You're panting like you'd run a race with—

BRICK: [*freeing himself from his father's hold*] Big Daddy, you shock me, Big Daddy, you, you—shock me! Talkin' so—

> [*He turns away from his father.*]

—casually!—about a—thing like that. . . .

—Don't you know how people *feel* about things like that? How, how *disgusted* they are by things like that? Why, at Ole Miss when it was discovered a pledge to our fraternity, Skipper's and mine, did a, attempted to do a, unnatural thing with—

We not only dropped him like a hot rock!—We told him to git off the campus, and he did, he got!—All the way to—

> [*He halts, breathless.*]

BIG DADDY: —Where?

BRICK: —North Africa, last I heard!

BIG DADDY: Well, I have come back from further away than that, I have just now returned from the other side of the moon, death's country, son, and I'm not easy to shock by anything here.

[*He comes downstage and faces out.*]

Always, anyhow, lived with too much space around me to be infected by ideas of other people. One thing you can grow on a big place more important than cotton! —is *tolerance!*—I grown it.

[*He returns toward* BRICK.]

BRICK: Why can't exceptional friendship, *real, real, deep, deep friendship!* between two men be respected as something clean and decent without being thought of as—

BIG DADDY: It can, it is, for God's sake.

BRICK: —*Fairies.* . . .

[*In his utterance of this word, we gauge the wide and profound reach of the conventional mores he got from the world that crowned him with early laurel.*]

BIG DADDY: I told Mae an' Gooper—

BRICK: Frig Mae and Gooper, frig all dirty lies and liars!—Skipper and me had a clean, true thing between us!—had a clean friendship, practically all our lives, till Maggie got the idea you're talking about. Normal? No!—It was too rare to be normal, any true thing between two people is too rare to be normal. Oh, once in a while he put his hand on my shoulder or I'd put mine on his, oh, maybe even, when we were touring the country in pro football an' shared hotel rooms we'd reach across the space between the two beds and shake hands to say goodnight, yeah, one or two times we—

BIG DADDY: Brick, nobody thinks that that's not normal!

BRICK: Well, they're mistaken, it was! It was a pure an' true thing an' that's not normal.

[*They both stare straight at each other for a long moment. The tension breaks and both turn away as if tired.*]

BIG DADDY: Yeah, it's—hard t'—talk. . . .

BRICK: All right, then, let's—let it go. . . .

BIG DADDY: Why did Skipper crack up? Why have you?

[BRICK *looks back at his father again. He has already decided, without knowing that he has made this decision, that he is going to tell his father that he is dying of cancer. Only this could even the score between them: one inadmissible thing in return for another.*]

BRICK: [*ominously*] All right. You're asking for it, Big Daddy. We're finally going to have that real true talk you wanted. It's too late to stop it, now, we got to carry it through and cover every subject.

[*He hobbles back to the liquor cabinet.*]

Uh-huh.

[*He opens the ice bucket and picks up the silver tongs with slow admiration of their frosty brightness.*]

Maggie declares that Skipper and I went into pro football after we left Ole Miss because we were scared to grow up. . . .

[*He moves downstage with the shuffle and clop of a cripple on a crutch. As* MARGARET *did when her speech became "recitative," he looks out into the house, commanding its attention by his direct, concentrated gaze—a broken, "tragically elegant" figure telling simply as much as he knows of "the Truth":*]

—Wanted to—keep on tossing—those long, long!—high, high!—passes that—couldn't be intercepted except by time, the aerial attack that made us famous! And so we did, we did, we kept it up for one season, that aerial attack, we held it high!—Yeah, but—

   —that summer, Maggie, she laid the law down to me, said, Now or never, and so I married Maggie. . . .

BIG DADDY: How was Maggie in bed?

BRICK: [*wryly*] Great! the greatest!

   [BIG DADDY *nods as if he thought so.*]

She went on the road that fall with the Dixie Stars. Oh, she made a great show of being the world's best sport. She wore a—wore a—tall bearskin cap! A "shako," they call it, a dyed moleskin coat, a moleskin coat dyed red!—Cut up crazy! Rented hotel ballrooms for victory celebrations, wouldn't cancel them when it—turned out—defeat. . . .

   MAGGIE THE CAT! Ha ha!

   [BIG DADDY *nods.*]

—But Skipper, he had some fever which came back on him which doctors couldn't explain and I got that injury—turned out to be just a shadow on the X-ray plate—and a touch of bursitis. . . .

   I lay in a hospital bed, watched our games on TV, saw Maggie on the bench next to Skipper when he was hauled out of a game for stumbles, fumbles!—Burned me up the way she hung on his arm!—Y'know, I think that Maggie had always felt sort of left out because she and me never got any closer together than two people just get in bed, which is not much closer than two cats on a—fence humping. . . .

   So! She took this time to work on poor dumb Skipper. He was a less-than-average student at Ole Miss, you know that, don't you?!—Poured in his mind the dirty, false idea that what we were, him and me, was a frustrated case of that ole pair of sisters that lived in this room, Jack Straw and Peter Ochello!—He, poor Skipper, went to bed with Maggie to prove it wasn't true, and when it didn't work out, he thought it was true!—Skipper broke in two like a rotten stick—nobody ever turned so fast to a lush—or died of it so quick. . . .

   —Now are you satisfied?

   [BIG DADDY *has listened to this story, dividing the grain from the chaff. Now he looks at his son.*]

BIG DADDY: Are *you* satisfied?

BRICK: With what?

BIG DADDY: That half-ass story!

BRICK: What's half-ass about it?

BIG DADDY: Something's left out of that story. What did you leave out?

   [*The phone has started ringing in the hall. As if it reminded him of something,* BRICK *glances suddenly toward the sound and says:*]

BRICK: Yes!—I left out a long-distance call which I had from Skipper, in which he made a drunken confession to me and on which I hung up!—last time we spoke to each other in our lives. . . .

   [*Muted ring stops as someone answers phone in a soft, indistinct voice in hall.*]

BIG DADDY: You hung up?

BRICK: Hung up. Jesus! Well—

BIG DADDY: Anyhow now!—we have tracked down the lie with which you're disgusted and which you are drinking to kill your disgust with, Brick. You been passing the buck. This disgust with mendacity is disgust with yourself.

   You!—dug the grave of your friend and kicked him in it!—before you'd face truth with him!

BRICK: *His* truth, not *mine!*

BIG DADDY: His truth, okay! But you wouldn't face it with him!

BRICK: Who *can* face truth? Can *you?*

BIG DADDY: Now don't start passin' the rotten buck again, boy!

BRICK: *How about these birthday congratulations, these many, many happy returns of the day, when ev'rybody but you knows there won't be any!*

> [*Whoever has answered the hall phone lets out a high, shrill laugh; the voice becomes audible saying:* "No, no, you got it all wrong! Upside down! Are you crazy?"]
> [BRICK *suddenly catches his breath as he realizes that he has made a shocking disclosure. He hobbles a few paces, then freezes, and without looking at his father's shocked face, says:*]

Let's let's—go out, now, and—

> [BIG DADDY *moves suddenly forward and grabs hold of the boy's crutch like it was a weapon for which they were fighting for possession.*]

BIG DADDY: Oh, no, no! No one's going out! What did you start to say?

BRICK: I don't remember.

BIG DADDY: "Many happy returns when they know there won't be any"?

BRICK: Aw, hell, Big Daddy, forget it. Come on out on the gallery and look at the fireworks they're shooting off for your birthday. . . .

BIG DADDY: First you finish that remark you were makin' before you cut off. "Many happy returns when they know there won't be any"?—Ain't that what you just said?

BRICK: Look, now. I can get around without that crutch if I have to but it would be a lot easier on the furniture an' glassware if I didn' have to go swinging along like Tarzan of th'—

BIG DADDY: FINISH! WHAT YOU WAS SAYIN'!

> [*An eerie green glow shows in sky behind him.*]

BRICK: [*sucking the ice in his glass, speech becoming thick*] Leave th' place to Gooper and Mae an' their five little same little monkeys. All I want is—

BIG DADDY: "LEAVE TH' PLACE," did you say?

BRICK: [*vaguely*] All twenty-eight thousand acres of the richest land this side of the valley Nile.

BIG DADDY: Who said I was "leaving the place" to Gooper or anybody? This is my sixty-fifth birthday! I got fifteen years or twenty years left in me! I'll outlive *you!* I'll bury you an' have to pay for your coffin!

BRICK: Sure. Many happy returns. Now let's go watch the fireworks, come on, let's—

BIG DADDY: Lying, have they been lying? About the report from th'—clinic? did they, did they—find something?—*Cancer.* Maybe?

BRICK: Mendacity is a system that we live in. Liquor is one way out an' death's the other. . . .

> [*He takes the crutch from* BIG DADDY*'s loose grip and swings out on the gallery leaving the doors open.*]
> [*A song, "Pick a Bale of Cotton," is heard.*]

MAE: [*appearing in door*] Oh, Big Daddy, the field hands are singin' fo' you!

BIG DADDY: [*shouting hoarsely*] BRICK! BRICK!

MAE: He's outside drinkin', Big Daddy.

BIG DADDY: *BRICK!*

> [MAE *retreats, awed by the passion of his voice. Children call* "Brick" *in tones mocking* BIG DADDY. *His face crumbles like broken yellow plaster about to fall into dust.*]
> [*There is a glow in the sky.* BRICK *swings back through the doors, slowly, gravely, quite soberly.*]

BRICK: I'm sorry, Big Daddy. My head don't work any more and it's hard for me to understand how anybody could care if he lived or died or was dying or cared about anything but whether or not there was liquor left in the bottle and so I said what I said without thinking. In some ways I'm no better than the others, in some ways worse because I'm less alive. Maybe it's being alive that makes them lie, and being almost not alive makes me sort of accidentally truthful—I don't know but—anyway—we've been friends. . . .

—And being friends is telling each other the truth. . . .

[*There is a pause.*]

You told *me!* I told *you!*

[*A child rushes into the room and grabs a fistful of firecrackers and runs out again.*]

CHILD: [*screaming*] Bang, bang, bang, bang, bang, bang, bang, bang, bang!

BIG DADDY: [*slowly and passionately*]

CHRIST—DAMN—ALL—LYING SONS OF—LYING BITCHES!

[*He straightens at last and crosses to the inside door. At the door he turns and looks back as if he had some desperate question he couldn't put into words. Then he nods reflectively and says in a hoarse voice:*]

Yes, all liars, all liars, all lying dying liars!

[*This is said slowly, slowly, with a fierce revulsion. He goes on out.*]

—Lying! Dying! Liars!

[*His voice dies out. There is a sound of a child being slapped. It rushes, hideously bawling, through room and out the hall door.*]

[BRICK *remains motionless as the lights dim out and the curtain falls.*]

CURTAIN

ACT THREE

There is no lapse of time. MAE *enters with* REVEREND TOOKER.

MAE: Where is Big Daddy! Big Daddy?

BIG MAMA: [*entering*] Too much smell of burnt fireworks makes me feel a little bit sick at my stomach.—Where is Big Daddy?

MAE: That's what I want to know, where has Big Daddy gone?

BIG MAMA: He must have turned in, I reckon he went to baid. . . .

[GOOPER *enters.*]

GOOPER: Where is Big Daddy?

MAE: We don't know where he is!

BIG MAMA: I reckon he's gone to baid.

GOOPER: Well, then, now we can talk.

BIG MAMA: What *is* this talk, *what* talk?

[MARGARET *appears on gallery, talking to* DR. BAUGH.]

MARGARET: [*musically*] My family freed their slaves ten years before abolition, my great-great-grandfather gave his slaves their freedom five years before the War between the States started!

MAE: Oh, for God's sake! Maggie's climbed back up in her family tree!

MARGARET: [*sweetly*] What, Mae?—Oh, where's Big Daddy?!

[*The pace must be very quick. Great Southern animation.*]

BIG MAMA: [*addressing them all*] I think Big Daddy was just worn out. He loves his family, he loves to have them around him, but it's a strain on his nerves. He wasn't himself tonight, Big Daddy wasn't himself, I could tell he was all worked up.

REVEREND TOOKER: I think he's remarkable.

BIG MAMA: Yaisss! Just remarkable. Did you all notice the food he ate at that table? Did you all notice the supper he put away? Why, he ate like a hawss!

GOOPER: I hope he doesn't regret it.

BIG MAMA: Why, that man—ate a huge piece of cawn-bread with molasses on it! Helped himself twice to hoppin' john.

MARGARET: Big Daddy loves hoppin' john.—We had a real country dinner.

BIG MAMA: [*overlapping* MARGARET] Yais, he simply adores it! An' candied yams? That man put away enough food at that table to stuff a nigger *field* hand!

GOOPER: [*with grim relish*] I hope he don't have to pay for it later on. . . .

BIG MAMA: [*fiercely*] What's *that*, Gooper?

MAE: Gooper says he hopes Big Daddy doesn't suffer tonight.

BIG MAMA: Oh, shoot, Gooper says, Gooper says! Why should Big Daddy suffer for satisfying a normal appetite? There's nothin' wrong with that man but nerves, he's sound as a dollar! And now he knows he is an' that's why he ate such a supper. He had a big load off his mind, knowin' he wasn't doomed t'—what he thought he was doomed to. . . .

MARGARET: [*sadly and sweetly*] Bless his old sweet soul. . . .

BIG MAMA: [*vaguely*] Yais, bless his heart, where's Brick?

MAE: Outside.

GOOPER: —Drinkin' . . .

BIG MAMA: I know he's drinkin'. You all don't have to keep tellin' *me* Brick is drinkin'. Cain't I see he's drinkin' without you continually tellin' me that boy's drinkin'?

MARGARET: Good for you, Big Mama!

[*She applauds.*]

BIG MAMA: Other people *drink* and *have* drunk an' will *drink*, as long as they make that stuff an' put it in bottles.

MARGARET: That's the truth. I never trusted a man that didn't drink.

MAE: Gooper never drinks. Don't you trust Gooper?

MARGARET: Why, Gooper, don't you drink? If I'd known you didn't drink, I wouldn't of made that remark—

BIG MAMA: *Brick?*

MARGARET: —at least not in your presence.

[*She laughs sweetly.*]

BIG MAMA: *Brick!*

MARGARET: He's still on the gall'ry. I'll go bring him in so we can talk.

BIG MAMA: [*worriedly*] I don't know what this mysterious family conference is about.

[*Awkward silence.* BIG MAMA *looks from face to face, then belches slightly and mutters,* "Excuse me. . . ." *She opens an ornamental fan suspended about her throat, a black lace fan to go with her black lace gown, and fans her wilting corsage, sniffing nervously and looking from face to face in the uncomfortable silence as* MARGARET *calls* "Brick?" *and* BRICK *sings to the moon on the gallery.*]

I don't know what's wrong here, you all have such long faces! Open that door on the hall and let some air circulate through here, will you please, Gooper?

MAE: I think we'd better leave that door closed, Big Mama, till after the talk.

BIG MAMA: Reveren' Tooker, will *you* please open that door?!

REVEREND TOOKER: I sure will, Big Mama.

MAE: I just didn't think we ought t' take any chance of Big Daddy hearin' a word of this discussion.

BIG MAMA: I *swan!* Nothing's going to be said in Big Daddy's house that he cain't hear if he wants to!

GOOPER: Well, Big Mama, it's—

[MAE *gives him a quick, hard poke to shut him up. He glares at her fiercely as she circles before him like a burlesque ballerina, raising her skinny bare arms over her head, jangling her bracelets, exclaiming:*]

MAE: *A breeze! A breeze!*

REVEREND TOOKER: I think this house is the coolest house in the Delta.—Did you all know that Halsey Banks' widow put air-conditioning units in the church and rectory at Friar's Point in memory of Halsey?

> [*General conversation has resumed; everybody is chatting so that the stage sounds like a big bird cage.*]

GOOPER: Too bad nobody cools your church off for you. I bet you sweat in that pulpit these hot Sundays, Reverend Tooker.

REVEREND TOOKER: Yes, my vestments are drenched.

MAE: [*at the same time to* DR. BAUGH] You think those vitamin B$_{12}$ injections are what they're cracked up t' be, Doc Baugh?

DOCTOR BAUGH: Well, if you want to be stuck with something I guess they're as good to be stuck with as anything else.

BIG MAMA: [*at gallery door*] *Maggie, Maggie, aren't you comin' with Brick?*

MAE: [*suddenly and loudly, creating a silence*] *I have a strange feeling, I have a peculiar feeling!*

BIG MAMA: [*turning from gallery*] What feeling?

MAE: That Brick said somethin' he shouldn't of said t' Big Daddy.

BIG MAMA: Now what on earth could Brick of said t' Big Daddy that he shouldn't say?

GOOPER: Big Mama, there's somethin'—

MAE: NOW, WAIT!

> [*She rushes up to* BIG MAMA *and gives her a quick hug and kiss.* BIG MAMA *pushes her impatiently off as the* REVEREND TOOKER'*s voice rises serenely in a little pocket of silence.*]

REVEREND TOOKER: Yes, last Sunday the gold in my chasuble faded into th' purple. . . .

GOOPER: Reveren', you must of been preachin' hell's fire last Sunday!

> [*He guffaws at this witticism but the* REVEREND *is not sincerely amused. At the same time* BIG MAMA *has crossed over to* DR. BAUGH *and is saying to him:*]

BIG MAMA: [*her breathless voice rising high-pitched above the others*]
In my day they had what they call the Keeley cure for heavy drinkers. But now I understand they just take some kind of tablets, they call them "Annie Bust" tablets. But *Brick* don't need to take *nothin'*.

> [BRICK *appears in gallery doors with* MARGARET *behind him.*]

BIG MAMA: [*unaware of his presence behind her*] That boy is just broken up over Skipper's death. You know how poor Skipper died. They gave him a big, big dose of that sodium amytal stuff at his home and then they called the ambulance and give him another big, big dose of it at the hospital and that and all of the alcohol in his system fo' months an' months an' months just proved too much for his heart. . . . I'm scared of needles! I'm more scared of a needle than the knife. . . . I think more people have been needled out of this world than—

> [*She stops short and wheels about.*]

OH!—here's Brick! My precious baby—

> [*She turns upon* BRICK *with short, fat arms extended, at the same time uttering a loud, short sob, which is both comic and touching.*]
> [BRICK *smiles and bows slightly, making a burlesque gesture of gallantry for* MAGGIE *to pass before him into the room. Then he hobbles on his crutch directly to the liquor cabinet and there is absolute silence, with everybody looking at* BRICK *as everybody has always looked at* BRICK *when he spoke or moved or appeared. One by one he drops ice cubes in his glass, then suddenly, but not quickly, looks back over his shoulder with a wry, charming smile, and says:*]

BRICK: I'm sorry! Anyone else?

BIG MAMA: [*sadly*] No, son. I *wish* you wouldn't!

BRICK: I wish I didn't have to, Big Mama, but I'm still waiting for that click in my head which makes it all smooth out!

BIG MAMA: Aw, Brick, you—BREAK MY HEART!

MARGARET: [*at the same time*] Brick, go sit with Big Mama!

BIG MAMA: I just cain't *staiiiiiiii-nnnnnd*—it. . . .
> [*She sobs.*]

MAE: Now that we're all assembled—

GOOPER: We kin talk. . . .

BIG MAMA: Breaks my heart. . . .

MARGARET: Sit with Big Mama, Brick, and hold her hand.
> [BIG MAMA *sniffs very loudly three times, almost like three drum beats in the pocket of silence.*]

BRICK: You do that, Maggie. I'm a restless cripple. I got to stay on my crutch.
> [BRICK *hobbles to the gallery door; leans there as if waiting.* MAE *sits beside* BIG MAMA, *while* GOOPER *moves in front and sits on the end of the couch, facing her.* REVEREND TOOKER *moves nervously into the space between them; on the other side,* DR. BAUGH *stands looking at nothing in particular and lights a cigar.* MARGARET *turns away.*]

BIG MAMA: Why're you all *surroundin'* me—like this? Why're you all starin' at me like this an' makin' signs at each other?
> [REVEREND TOOKER *steps back startled.*]

MAE: Calm yourself, Big Mama.

BIG MAMA: Calm you'self, *you'self*, Sister Woman. How could I calm myself with everyone starin' at me as if big drops of blood had broken out on m' face? What's this all about, annh! What?
> [GOOPER *coughs and takes a center position.*]

GOOPER: Now, Doc Baugh.

MAE: Doc Baugh?

BRICK: [*suddenly*] SHHH!
> [*Then he grins and chuckles and shakes his head regretfully.*]
—Naw!—that wasn't th' click.

GOOPER: Brick, shut up or stay out there on the gallery with your liquor! We got to talk about a serious matter. Big Mama wants to know the complete truth about the report we got today from the Ochsner Clinic.

MAE: [*eagerly*] —on Big Daddy's condition!

GOOPER: Yais, on Big Daddy's condition, we got to face it.

DOCTOR BAUGH: Well. . . .

BIG MAMA: [*terrified, rising*] Is there? Something? Something that I? Don't—Know?
> [*In these few words, this startled, very soft, question,* BIG MAMA *reviews the history of her forty-five years with* BIG DADDY, *her great, almost embarrassingly true-hearted and simple-minded devotion to* BIG DADDY, *who must have had something* BRICK *has, who made himself loved so much by the "simple expedient" of not loving enough to disturb his charming detachment, also once coupled, like* BRICK'*s, with virile beauty.*]
> [BIG MAMA *has a dignity at this moment: she almost stops being fat.*]

DOCTOR BAUGH: [*after a pause, uncomfortably*] Yes?—Well—

BIG MAMA: I!!!—want to—*knowwwwwww*. . . .
> [*Immediately she thrusts her fist to her mouth as if to deny that statement.*]
> [*Then, for some curious reason, she snatches the withered corsage from her breast and hurls it on the floor and steps on it with her short, fat feet.*]
—Somebody must be lyin'!—I want to know!

MAE: Sit down, Big Mama, sit down on this sofa.

MARGARET: [*quickly*] Brick, go sit with Big Mama.

BIG MAMA: *What is it, what is it?*

DOCTOR BAUGH: I never have seen a more thorough examination than Big Daddy Pollitt was given in all my experience with the Ochsner Clinic.

GOOPER: It's one of the best in the country.

MAE: It's *THE* best in the country—bar *none!*

> [*For some reason she gives* GOOPER *a violent poke as she goes past him. He slaps at her hand without removing his eyes from his mother's face.*]

DOCTOR BAUGH: Of course, they were ninety-nine and nine-tenths percent sure before they even started.

BIG MAMA: Sure of what, sure of what, sure of—*what?*—*what!*

> [*She catches her breath in a startled sob.* MAE *kisses her quickly. She thrusts* MAE *fiercely away from her, staring at the doctor.*]

MAE: Mommy, be a brave girl!

BRICK: [*in the doorway, softly*]
> "By the light, by the light,
> Of the sil-ve-ry mo-ooo-n . . . "

GOOPER: Shut up!—Brick.

BRICK: —Sorry. . . .

> [*He wanders out on the gallery.*]

DOCTOR BAUGH: But now, you see, Big Mama, they cut a piece off this growth, a specimen of the tissue and—

BIG MAMA: Growth? You told Big Daddy—

DOCTOR BAUGH: Now wait.

BIG MAMA: [*fiercely*] You told me and Big Daddy there wasn't a thing wrong with him but—

MAE: Big Mama, they always—

GOOPER: Let Doc Baugh talk, will yuh?

BIG MAMA: —little spastic condition of—

> [*Her breath gives out in a sob.*]

DOCTOR BAUGH: Yes, that's what we told Big Daddy. But we had this bit of tissue run through the laboratory and I'm sorry to say the test was positive on it. It's—well—malignant. . . .

> [*Pause.*]

BIG MAMA: —Cancer?! Cancer?!

> [DR. BAUGH *nods gravely.*]
> [BIG MAMA *gives a long gasping cry.*]

MAE AND GOOPER: Now, now, now, Big Mama, you had to know. . . .

BIG MAMA: *WHY DIDN'T THEY CUT IT OUT OF HIM? HANH? HANH?*

DOCTOR BAUGH: Involved too much, Big Mama, too many organs affected.

MAE: Big Mama, the liver's affected and so's the kidneys, both! It's gone way past what they call a—

GOOPER: A Surgical risk.

MAE: —Uh-huh. . . .

> [BIG MAMA *draws a breath like a dying gasp.*]

REVEREND TOOKER: Tch, tch, tch, tch, tch!

DOCTOR BAUGH: Yes, it's gone past the knife.

MAE: *That's why he's turned yellow, Mommy!*

BIG MAMA: *Git away from me, git away from me, Mae!*
> [*She rises abruptly.*]
>> *I want Brick! Where's Brick? Where is my only son?*

MAE: Mama! Did she say "*only* son"?

GOOPER: What does that make *me*?

MAE: A sober responsible man with five precious children!—*Six!*

BIG MAMA: I want Brick to tell me! Brick! Brick!

MARGARET: [*rising from her reflections in a corner*] Brick was so upset he went back out.

BIG MAMA: *Brick!*

MARGARET: Mama, let *me* tell you!

BIG MAMA: No, no, leave me alone, you're not my blood!

GOOPER: *Mama, I'm your son!* Listen to *me!*

MAE: Gooper's your son, Mama, he's your first-born!

BIG MAMA: Gooper never liked Daddy.

MAE: [*as if terribly shocked*] *That's not TRUE!*
> [*There is a pause. The minister coughs and rises.*]

REVEREND TOOKER: [*to* MAE] I think I'd better slip away at this point.

MAE: [*sweetly and sadly*] Yes, Doctor Tooker, you go.

REVEREND TOOKER: [*discreetly*] Goodnight, goodnight, everybody, and God bless you all . . . on this place. . . .
> [*He slips out.*]

DOCTOR BAUGH: That man is a good man but lacking in tact. Talking about people giving memorial windows—if he mentioned one memorial window, he must have spoke of a dozen, and saying how awful it was when somebody died intestate, the legal wrangles, and so forth.
> [MAE *coughs, and points at* BIG MAMA.]

DOCTOR BAUGH: Well, Big Mama. . . .
> [*He sighs.*]

BIG MAMA: It's all a mistake, I know it's just a bad dream.

DOCTOR BAUGH: We're gonna keep Big Daddy as comfortable as we can.

BIG MAMA: Yes, it's just a bad dream, that's all it is, it's just an awful dream.

GOOPER: In my opinion Big Daddy is having some pain but won't admit that he has it.

BIG MAMA: Just a dream, a bad dream.

DOCTOR BAUGH: That's what lots of them do, they think if they don't admit they're having the pain they can sort of escape the fact of it.

GOOPER: [*with relish*] Yes, they get sly about it, they get real sly about it.

MAE: Gooper and I think—

GOOPER: Shut up, Mae!—Big Daddy ought to be started on morphine.

BIG MAMA: Nobody's going to give Big Daddy morphine.

DOCTOR BAUGH: Now, Big Mama, when that pain strikes it's going to strike mighty hard and Big Daddy's going to need the needle to bear it.

BIG MAMA: I tell you, nobody's going to give him morphine.

MAE: Big Mama, you don't want to see Big Daddy suffer, you know you—
> [GOOPER *standing beside her gives her a savage poke.*]

DOCTOR BAUGH: [*placing a package on the table*] I'm leaving this stuff here, so if there's a sudden attack you all won't have to send out for it.

MAE: I know how to give a hypo.

GOOPER: Mae took a course in nursing during the war.

MARGARET: Somehow I don't think Big Daddy would want Mae to give him a hypo.

MAE: You think he'd want *you* to do it?

> [DR. BAUGH *rises.*]

GOOPER: Doctor Baugh is goin'.

DOCTOR BAUGH: Yes, I got to be goin'. Well, keep your chin up, Big Mama.

GOOPER: [*with jocularity*] She's gonna keep *both* chins up, aren't you, Big Mama?

> [BIG MAMA *sobs.*]

Now stop that, Big Mama.

MAE: Sit down with me, Big Mama.

GOOPER: [*at door with* DR. BAUGH] Well, Doc, we sure do appreciate all you done. I'm telling you, we're surely obligated to you for—

> [DR. BAUGH *has gone out without a glance at him.*]

GOOPER: I guess that doctor has got a lot on his mind but it wouldn't hurt him to act a little more human. . . .

> [BIG MAMA *sobs.*]

Now be a brave girl, Mommy.

BIG MAMA: It's not true, I know that it's just not true!

GOOPER: Mama, those tests are infallible!

BIG MAMA: Why are you so determined to see your father daid?

MAE: Big Mama!

MARGARET: [*gently*] I know what Big Mama means.

MAE: [*fiercely*] Oh, do you?

MARGARET: [*quietly and very sadly*] Yes, I think I do.

MAE: For a newcomer in the family you sure do show a lot of understanding.

MARGARET: Understanding is needed on this place.

MAE: I guess you must have needed a lot of it in your family, Maggie, with your father's liquor problem and now you've got Brick with his!

MARGARET: Brick does not have a liquor problem at all. Brick is devoted to Big Daddy. This thing is a terrible strain on him.

BIG MAMA: Brick is Big Daddy's boy, but he drinks too much and it worries me and Big Daddy, and, Margaret, you've got to cooperate with us, you've got to cooperate with Big Daddy and me in getting Brick straightened out. Because it will break Big Daddy's heart if Brick don't pull himself together and take hold of things.

MAE: Take hold of *what* things, Big Mama?

BIG MAMA: The place.

> [*There is a quick violent look between* MAE *and* GOOPER.]

GOOPER: Big Mama, you've had a shock.

MAE: Yais, we've all had a shock, but . . .

GOOPER: Let's be realistic—

MAE: —Big Daddy would never, would never, be foolish enough to—

GOOPER: —put this place in irresponsible hands!

BIG MAMA: Big Daddy ain't going to leave the place in anybody's hands; Big Daddy is *not* going to die. I want you to get that in your heads, all of you!

MAE: Mommy, Mommy, Big Mama, we're just as hopeful an' optimistic as you are about Big Daddy's prospects, we have faith in *prayer*—but nevertheless there are certain matters that have to be discussed an' dealt with, because otherwise—

GOOPER: Eventualities have to be considered and now's the time. . . . Mae, will you please get my briefcase out of our room?

MAE: Yes, honey.

> [*She rises and goes out through the hall door.*]

GOOPER: [*standing over* BIG MAMA] Now, Big Mom. What you said just now was not at all true and you know it. I've always loved Big Daddy in my own quiet way. I never made a show of it, and I know that Big Daddy has always been fond of me in a quiet way, too, and he never made a show of it, neither.

[MAE *returns with* GOOPER'*s briefcase.*]

MAE: Here's your briefcase, Gooper, honey.

GOOPER: [*handing the briefcase back to her*] Thank you. . . . Of ca'use, my relationship with Big Daddy is different from Brick's.

MAE: You're eight years older'n Brick an' always had t'carry a bigger load of th' responsibilities than Brick ever had t' carry. He never carried a thing in his life but a football or a highball.

GOOPER: Mae, will y' let me talk, please?

MAE: Yes, honey.

GOOPER: Now, a twenty-eight thousand-acre plantation's a mighty big thing t' run.

MAE: Almost singlehanded.

[MARGARET *has gone out onto the gallery, and can be heard calling softly* BRICK.]

BIG MAMA: You never had to run this place! What are you talking about? As if Big Daddy was dead and in his grave, you had to run it? Why, you just helped him out with a few business details and had your law practice at the same time in Memphis!

MAE: Oh, Mommy, Mommy, Big Mommy! Let's be fair! Why, Gooper has given himself body and soul to keeping this place up for the past five years since Big Daddy's health started failing. Gooper won't say it, Gooper never thought of it as a duty, he just did it. And what did Brick do? Brick kept living in his past glory at college! Still a football player at twenty-seven!

MARGARET: [*returning alone*] Who are you talking about, now? Brick? A football player? He isn't a football player and you know it. Brick is a sports announcer on TV and one of the best-known ones in the country!

MAE: I'm talking about what he was.

MARGARET: Well, I wish you would just stop talking about my husband.

GOOPER: I've got a right to discuss my brother with other members of MY OWN family which don't include *you.* Why don't you go out there and drink with Brick?

MARGARET: I've never seen such malice toward a brother.

GOOPER: How about his for me? Why, he can't stand to be in the same room with me!

MARGARET: This is a deliberate campaign of vilification for the most disgusting and sordid reason on earth, and I know what it is! It's *avarice, avarice, greed, greed!*

BIG MAMA: *Oh, I'll scream! I will scream in a moment unless this stops!*

[GOOPER *has stalked up to* MARGARET *with clenched fists at his sides as if he would strike her.* MAE *distorts her face again into a hideous grimace behind* MARGARET'*s back.*]

MARGARET: We only remain on the place because of Big Mom and Big Daddy. If it is true what they say about Big Daddy we are going to leave here just as soon as it's over. Not a moment later.

BIG MAMA: [*sobs*] Margaret. Child. Come here. Sit next to Big Mama.

MARGARET: Precious Mommy. I'm sorry, I'm so sorry, I—!

[*She bends her long graceful neck to press her forehead to* BIG MAMA'*s bulging shoulder under its black chiffon.*]

GOOPER: How beautiful, how touching, this display of devotion!

MAE: Do you know why she's childless? She's childless because that big beautiful athlete husband of hers won't go to bed with her!

GOOPER: You jest won't let me do this in a nice way, will yah? Aw right—Mae and I have five kids with another one coming! I don't give a goddam if Big Daddy likes me or don't like me or did or never did or will or will never! I'm just appealing to a sense of common decency and fair play. I'll tell you the truth. I've resented Big Daddy's partiality to Brick ever since Brick was born, and the way I've been treated like I was just barely good enough to spit on and sometimes not even good enough for that. Big Daddy is dying of cancer, and it's spread all through him and it's attacked all his vital organs including the kidneys and right now he is sinking into uremia, and you all know what uremia is, it's poisoning of the whole system due to the failure of the body to eliminate its poisons.

MARGARET: [*to herself, downstage, hissingly*] *Poisons, poisons! Venomous thoughts and words! In hearts and minds!—That's poisons!*

GOOPER: [*overlapping her*] I am asking for a square deal, and I expect to get one. But if I don't get one, if there's any peculiar shenanigans going on around here behind my back, or before me, well, I'm not a corporation lawyer for nothing, I know how to protect my own interests.—*OH! A late arrival!*

> [BRICK *enters from the gallery with a tranquil, blurred smile, carrying an empty glass with him.*]

MAE: Behold the conquering hero comes!

GOOPER: The fabulous Brick Pollitt! Remember him?—Who could forget him!

MAE: He looks like he's been injured in a game!

GOOPER: Yep, I'm afraid you'll have to warm the bench at the Sugar Bowl this year, Brick!

> [MAE *laughs shrilly.*]

Or was it the Rose Bowl that he made that famous run in?

MAE: The punch bowl, honey. It was in the punch bowl, the cut-glass punch bowl!

GOOPER: Oh, that's right, I'm getting the bowls mixed up!

MARGARET: Why don't you stop venting your malice and envy on a sick boy?

BIG MAMA: *Now you two hush, I mean it, hush, all of you, hush!*

GOOPER: All right, Big Mama. A family crisis brings out the best and the worst in every member of it.

MAE: *That's* the truth.

MARGARET: *Amen!*

BIG MAMA: *I said, "hush!"* I won't tolerate any more catty talk in my house.

> [MAE *gives* GOOPER *a sign indicating briefcase.*]
> [BRICK's *smile has grown both brighter and vaguer. As he prepares a drink, he sings softly.*]

BRICK: *Show me the way to go home,*
                         I'm tired and I wanta go to bed,
                         I had a little drink about an hour ago—

GOOPER: [*at the same time*] Big Mama, you know it's necessary for me t' go back to Memphis in th' mornin' t' represent the Parker estate in a lawsuit.

> [MAE *sits on the bed and arranges papers she has taken from the briefcase.*]

BRICK: [*continuing the song*]
                         Wherever I may roam,
                         On land or sea or foam.

BIG MAMA: Is it, Gooper?

MAE: Yaiss.

GOOPER: That's why I'm forced to—to bring up a problem that—

MAE: Somethin' that's too important t' be put off!

GOOPER: If Brick was sober, he ought to be in on this.

MARGARET: Brick is present; we're here.

GOOPER: Well, good. I will now give you this outline my partner, Tom Bullitt, an' me have drawn up—a sort of dummy—trusteeship.

MARGARET: Oh, that's it! You'll be in charge an' dole out remittances, will you?

GOOPER: This we did as soon as we got the report on Big Daddy from th' Ochsner Laboratories. We did this thing, I mean we drew up this dummy outline with the advice and assistance of the Chairman of the Boa'd of Directors of th' Southern Plantahs Bank and Trust Company in Memphis, C. C. Bellowes, a man who handles estates for all th' prominent fam'lies in West Tennessee and th' Delta.

BIG MAMA: Gooper?

GOOPER: [*crouching in front of* BIG MAMA] Now this is not—not final, or anything like it. This is just a preliminary outline. But it does provide a basis—a design—a—possible, feasible—*plan!*

MARGARET: Yes, I'll bet.

MAE: It's a plan to protect the biggest estate in the Delta from irresponsibility an'—

BIG MAMA: Now you listen to me, all of you, you listen here! They's not goin' to be any more catty talk in my house! And Gooper, you put that away before I grab it out of your hand and tear it right up! I don't know what the hell's in it, and I don't want to know what the hell's in it. I'm talkin' in Big Daddy's language now; I'm his *wife*, not his *widow*, I'm still his *wife!* And I'm talkin' to you in his language an'—

GOOPER: Big Mama, what I have here is—

MAE: Gooper explained that it's just a plan. . . .

BIG MAMA: I don't care what you got there. Just put it back where it came from, an' don't let me see it again, not even the outside of the envelope of it! Is that understood? Basis! Plan! Preliminary! Design! I say—what is it Big Daddy always says when he's disgusted?

BRICK: [*from the bar*] Big Daddy says "crap" when he's disgusted.

BIG MAMA: [*rising*] That's right—*CRAP!* I say *CRAP*, too, like Big Daddy!

MAE: Coarse language doesn't seem called for in this—

GOOPER: Somethin' in me is *deeply outraged* by hearin' you talk like this.

BIG MAMA: *Nobody's goin' to take nothin'!*—till Big Daddy lets go of it, and maybe, just possibly, not—not even then! No, not even then!

BRICK: *You can always hear me singin' this song,*
            Show me the way to go home.

BIG MAMA: Tonight Brick looks like he used to look when he was a little boy, just like he did when he played wild games and used to come home all sweaty and pink-cheeked and sleepy, with his—red curls shining. . . .

> [*She comes over to him and runs her fat shaky hand through his hair. He draws aside as he does from all physical contact and continues the song in a whisper, opening the ice bucket and dropping in the ice cubes one by one as if he were mixing some important chemical formula.*]

BIG MAMA: [*continuing*] Time goes by so fast. Nothin' can outrun it. Death commences too early—almost before you're half acquainted with life—you meet with the other. . . . Oh, you know we just got to love each other an' stay together, all of us, just as close as we can, especially now that such a *black* thing has come and moved into this place without invitation.

> [*Awkwardly embracing* BRICK, *she presses her head to his shoulder.*]
> [GOOPER *has been returning papers to* MAE, *who has restored them to briefcase with an air of severely tried patience.*]

GOOPER: Big Mama? Big Mama?

> [*He stands behind her, tense with sibling envy.*]

BIG MAMA: [*oblivious of* GOOPER] Brick, you hear me, don't you?

MARGARET: Brick hears you, Big Mama, he understands what you're saying.

BIG MAMA: Oh, Brick, son of Big Daddy! Big Daddy does so love you! Y'know what would be his fondest dream come true? If before he passed on, if Big Daddy has to pass on, you gave him a child of yours, a grandson as much like his son as his son is like Big Daddy!

MAE: [*zipping briefcase shut: an incongruous sound*] *Such a pity that Maggie an' Brick can't oblige!*

MARGARET: [*suddenly and quietly but forcefully*] Everybody listen.
　　　[*She crosses to the center of the room, holding her hands rigidly together.*]

MAE: Listen to what, Maggie?

MARGARET: I have an announcement to make.

GOOPER: A sports announcement, Maggie?

MARGARET: Brick and I are going to—*have a child!*
　　　[BIG MAMA *catches her breath in a loud gasp.*]
　　　[*Pause.* BIG MAMA *rises.*]

BIG MAMA: Maggie! Brick! This is too good to believe!

MAE: That's right, too good to believe.

BIG MAMA: Oh, my, my! This is Big Daddy's dream, his dream come true! I'm going to tell him right now before he—

MARGARET: We'll tell him in the morning. Don't disturb him now.

BIG MAMA: I want to tell him before he goes to sleep, I'm going to tell him his dream's come true this minute! And Brick! A child will make you pull yourself together and quit this drinking!
　　　[*She seizes the glass from his hand.*]
　　　The responsibilities of a father will—
　　　[*Her face contorts and she makes an excited gesture; bursting into sobs, she rushes out, crying.*]
　　　I'm going to tell Big Daddy right this minute!
　　　[*Her voice fades out down the hall.*]
　　　[BRICK *shrugs slightly and drops an ice cube into another glass.* MARGARET *crosses quickly to his side, saying something under her breath, and she pours the liquor for him, staring up almost fiercely into his face.*]

BRICK: [*coolly*] Thank you, Maggie, that's a nice big shot.
　　　[MAE *has joined* GOOPER *and she gives him a fierce poke, making a low hissing sound and a grimace of fury.*]

GOOPER: [*pushing her aside*] Brick, could you possibly spare me one small shot of that liquor?

BRICK: Why, help yourself, Gooper boy.

GOOPER: I will.

MAE: [*shrilly*] Of course we know that this is—

GOOPER: *Be still, Mae!*

MAE: I won't be still! I know she's made this up!

GOOPER: Goddam it, I said to shut up!

MARGARET: Gracious! I didn't know that my little announcement was going to provoke such a storm!

MAE: *That* woman isn't *pregnant!*

GOOPER: Who said she was?

MAE: *She* did.

GOOPER: The doctor didn't. Doc Baugh didn't.

MARGARET: I haven't gone to Doc Baugh.

GOOPER: Then who'd you go to, Maggie?

MARGARET: One of the best gynecologists in the South.

GOOPER: Uh huh, uh huh!—I see. . . .

[*He takes out pencil and notebook.*]

   —May we have his name, please?

MARGARET: No, you may not, Mister Prosecuting Attorney!

MAE: He doesn't have any name, he doesn't exist!

MARGARET: Oh, he exists all right, and so does my child, Brick's baby!

MAE: You can't conceive a child by a man that won't sleep with you unless you think you're—

   [BRICK *has turned on the phonograph. A scat song cuts* MAE'*s speech.*]

GOOPER: *Turn that off!*

MAE: We know it's a lie because we hear you in here; he won't sleep with you, we hear you! So don't imagine you're going to put a trick over on us, to fool a dying man with a—

   [*A long drawn cry of agony and rage fills the house.* MARGARET *turns phonograph down to a whisper.*]

   [*The cry is repeated.*]

MAE: [*awed*] Did you hear that, Gooper, did you hear that?

GOOPER: Sounds like the pain has struck.

MAE: Go see, Gooper!

GOOPER: Come along and leave these lovebirds together in their nest!

   [*He goes out first.* MAE *follows but turns at the door, contorting her face and hissing at* MARGARET.]

MAE: Liar!

   [*She slams the door.*]

   [MARGARET *exhales with relief and moves a little unsteadily to catch hold of* BRICK'*s arm.*]

MARGARET: Thank you for—keeping still. . . .

BRICK: Okay, Maggie.

MARGARET: It was gallant of you to save my face!

BRICK: —It hasn't happened yet.

MARGARET: What?

BRICK: The click. . . .

MARGARET: —the click in your head that makes you peaceful, honey?

BRICK: Uh-huh. It hasn't happened. . . . I've got to make it happen before I can sleep. . . .

MARGARET: —I—know what you—mean. . . .

BRICK: Give me that pillow in the big chair, Maggie.

MARGARET: I'll put it on the bed for you.

BRICK: No, put it on the sofa, where I sleep.

MARGARET: Not tonight, Brick.

BRICK: I want it on the sofa. That's where I sleep.

   [*He has hobbled to the liquor cabinet. He now pours down three shots in quick succession and stands waiting, silent. All at once he turns with a smile and says:*]

   There!

MARGARET: What?

BRICK: The *click.* . . .

   [*His gratitude seems almost infinite as he hobbles out on the gallery with a drink. We hear his crutch as he swings out of sight. Then, at some distance, he begins singing to himself a peaceful song.*]

   [MARGARET *holds the big pillow forlornly as if it were her only companion, for a few moments, then throws it on the bed. She rushes to the liquor cabinet, gathers all the bottles in her arms, turns about undecidedly, then runs out of the room with them, leaving the door ajar on the dim yellow hall.* BRICK *is heard hobbling back along the gallery, singing his peaceful song. He comes back in, sees the pillow on the bed, laughs lightly, sadly, picks it up. He has it under his arm as* MARGARET *returns to the room.* MARGARET *softly shuts the door and leans against it, smiling softly at* BRICK.]

MARGARET: Brick, I used to think that you were stronger than me and I didn't want to be overpowered by you. But now, since you've taken to liquor—you know what?—I guess it's bad, but now I'm stronger than you and I can love you more truly!

Don't move that pillow. I'll move it right back if you do!

—Brick?

[*She turns out all the lamps but a single rose-silk-shaded one by the bed.*]

I really have been to a doctor and I know what to do and—Brick?—this is my time by the calendar to conceive!

BRICK: Yes, I understand, Maggie. But how are you going to conceive a child by a man in love with his liquor?

MARGARET: By locking his liquor up and making him satisfy my desire before I unlock it!

BRICK: Is that what you've done, Maggie?

MARGARET: Look and see. That cabinet's mighty empty compared to before!

BRICK: Well, I'll be a son of a—

[*He reaches for his crutch but she beats him to it and rushes out on the gallery, hurls the crutch over the rail and comes back in, panting.*]

[*There are running footsteps.* BIG MAMA *bursts into the room, her face all awry, gasping, stammering.*]

BIG MAMA: Oh, my God, oh, my God, oh, my God, where is it?

MARGARET: Is this what you want, Big Mama?

[MARGARET *hands her the package left by the doctor.*]

BIG MAMA: I can't bear it, oh, God! Oh, Brick! Brick, baby!

[*She rushes at him. He averts his face from her sobbing kisses.* MARGARET *watches with a tight smile.*]

My son, Big Daddy's boy! Little Father!

[*The groaning cry is heard again. She runs out, sobbing.*]

MARGARET: And so tonight we're going to make the lie true, and when that's done, I'll bring the liquor back here and we'll get drunk together, here, tonight, in this place that death has come into. . . .

—What do you say?

BRICK: I don't say anything. I guess there's nothing to say.

MARGARET: Oh, you weak people, you weak, beautiful people!—who give up.—What you want is someone to—

[*She turns out the rose-silk lamp.*]

—take hold of you.—Gently, gently, with love! And—

[*The curtain begins to fall slowly.*]

I *do* love you, Brick, I *do!*

BRICK: [*smiling with charming sadness*] Wouldn't it be funny if that was true?

CURTAIN—THE END

Happy Days (1961)

everal postwar dramatists (among them Samuel Beckett, Eugene Ionesco, and Jean Genet) were dubbed "absurdists" by Martin Esslin because their work conveyed "the sense that the certitudes and unshakable basic assumptions of former ages have been swept away, that they have been . . . discredited as cheap and somewhat childish illusions." Or, as Ionesco put it, "cut off from his religious, metaphysical, and transcendental roots, man is lost; all his actions become senseless, absurd and useless." Most absurdist plays, rather than telling a story, explore this human condition, in which characters seek to insulate themselves against the void by indulging in meaningless activities or abortive attempts at communication.

Beckett's *Happy Days* embodies most of the traits of absurdism. It has virtually abandoned action. The first act shows a woman, Winnie, trapped up to her waist in a mound of earth. She does not struggle against her physical entrapment but fills her days with a routine built around objects she keeps in a shopping bag; she speaks often to her husband, who for the most part remains unseen behind the mound and who responds only rarely. In the second act, Winnie is buried up to her neck and able to move only her eyes and mouth; at first she is not even sure that her husband is still alive, but eventually he crawls up the mound into her view. Despite her situation, Winnie remains determinedly cheerful; she speaks often of her blessings and the small things that will make this "another happy day." She never questions why she is in this situation, nor does she wonder at her isolation. She apparently accepts her lot as no more to be questioned than existence itself.

As in others of his plays, in *Happy Days* Beckett uses visual imagery to sum up his vision of the human condition. He shows human beings trapped in a symbolic landscape, cut off from all but the most minimal contact, passing time as best they can while waiting doggedly or hoping desperately for something that will give meaning to the moment or to life itself. Occasionally they reveal flashes of anxiety, but they quickly divert themselves with games, memories, and speculations. The plays explore a state of being rather than show a developing action.

Samuel Beckett

Happy Days

Characters

WINNIE, *a woman about fifty*
WILLIE, *a man about sixty*

ACT I

Expanse of scorched grass rising centre to low mound. Gentle slopes down to front and either side of stage. Back an abrupter fall to stage level. Maximum of simplicity and symmetry.
   Blazing light.
   Very pompier trompe-l'oeil backcloth to represent unbroken plain and sky receding to meet in far distance.
   Embedded up to above her waist in exact centre of mound, WINNIE. *About fifty, well preserved, blond for preference, plump, arms and shoulders bare, low bodice, big bosom, pearl necklet. She is discovered sleeping, her arms on the ground before her, her head, on her arms. Beside her on ground to her left a capacious black bag, shopping variety and to her right a collapsible collapsed parasol, beak of handle emerging from sheath.*
   To her right and rear, lying asleep on ground, hidden by mound, WILLIE.
   Long pause. A bell rings piercingly, say ten seconds, stops. She does not move. Pause. Bell more piercingly, say five seconds. She wakes. Bell stops. She raises her head, gazes front. Long pause. She straightens up, lays her hands flat on ground, throws back her head and gazes at zenith. Long pause.

WINNIE: [*gazing at zenith*] Another heavenly day. [*Pause. Head back level, eyes front, pause.
   She clasps hands to breast, closes eyes. Lips move in unaudible prayer, say ten seconds. Lips
   still. Hands remain clasped. Low.*] For Jesus Christ sake Amen. [*Eyes open, hands
   unclasp, return to mound. Pause. She clasps hands to breast again, closes eyes, lips move
   again in inaudible addendum, say five seconds. Low.*] World without end Amen. [*Eyes
   open, hands unclasp, return to mound. Pause.*] Begin, Winnie. [*pause*] Begin your day,
   Winnie. [*Pause. She turns to bag, rummages in it without moving it from its place, brings
   out toothbrush, rummages again, brings out flat tube of toothpaste, turns back front,
   unscrews cap of tube, lays cap on ground, squeezes with difficulty small blob of paste on
   brush, holds tube in one hand and brushes teeth with other. She turns modestly aside and
   back to her right to spit out behind mound. In this position her eyes rest on* WILLIE. *She
   spits out. She cranes a little further back and down. Loud.*] Hoo-oo! [*Pause. Louder.*]
   Hoo-oo! [*Pause. Tender smile as she turns back front, lays down brush.*] Poor Willie—
   [*examines tube, smile off*]—running out—[*looks for cap*] —ah well—[*finds cap*]—
   can't be helped—[*screws on cap*]—just one of those old things—[*lays down
   tube*]—another of those old things—[*turns towards bag*]—just can't be cured—[*rummages in bag*]—cannot be cured—[*brings out small mirror, turns back front*]—ah
   yes—[*inspects teeth in mirror*]—poor dear Willie—[*testing upper front teeth with*

thumb, indistinctly]—good Lord!—[*pulling back upper lip to inspect gums, do.*]—good God!—[*pulling back corner of mouth, mouth open, do.*]—ah well—[*other corner, do.*]—no worse—[*abandons inspection, normal speech*]—no better, no worse—[*lays down mirror*]—no change—[*wipes fingers on grass*]—no pain—[*looks for toothbrush*]—hardly any—[*takes up toothbrush*]—great thing that—[*examines handle of brush*]—nothing like it—[*examines handle, reads*]—pure . . . what?—[*pause*]—what?—[*lays down brush*]—ah yes—[*turns toward bag*]—poor Willie—[*rummages in bag*]—no zest—[*rummages*]—for anything—[*brings out spectacles in case*]—no interest—[*turns back front*]—in life—[*takes spectacles from case*]—poor dear Willie—[*lays down case*]—sleep for ever—[*opens spectacles*]—marvelous gift—[*puts on spectacles*]—nothing to touch it—[*looks for toothbrush*]—in my opinion—[*takes up toothbrush*]—always said so[*examines handle of brush*]wish I had it[*examines handle, reads*]genuine . . . pure . . . what?—[*lays down brush*]—blind next—[*takes off spectacles*]—ah well—[*lays down spectacles*]—seen enough—[*feels in bodice for handkerchief*]—I suppose—[*takes out folded handkerchief*]—by now—[*shakes out handkerchief*]—what are those wonderful lines—[*wipes one eye*]—woe woe is me—[*wipes the other*]—to see what I see—[*looks for spectacles*]—ah yes—[*takes up spectacles*]—wouldn't miss it—[*starts polishing spectacles, breathing on lenses*]—or would I?— [*polishes*]—holy light—[*polishes*]—bob up out of dark—[*polishes*]—blaze of hellish light. [*stops polishing, raises face to sky, pause, head back level, resumes polishing, stops polishing, cranes back to her right and down*] Hoo-oo! [*Pause. Tender smile as she turns back front and resumes polishing. Smile off.*] Marvelous gift—[*stops polishing, lays down spectacles*]—wish I had it—[*folds handkerchief*]—ah well—[*puts handkerchief back in bodice*]—can't complain—[*looks for spectacles*]—no no—[*takes up spectacles*]—mustn't complain—[*holds up spectacles, looks through lens*]—so much to be thankful for—[*looks through other lens*]—no pain—[*puts on spectacles*]—hardly any—[*looks for toothbrush*]—wonderful thing that—[*takes up toothbrush*]—nothing like it— [*examines handle of brush*]—slight headache sometimes—[*examines handle, reads*]—guaranteed . . . genuine . . . pure . . . what?—[*looks closer*]—genuine pure . . .—[*takes handkerchief from bodice*]—ah yes—[*shakes out handkerchief*]—occasional mild migraine—[*starts wiping handle of brush*]—it comes—[*wipes*]—then goes—[*wiping mechanically*]—ah yes—[*wiping*]—many mercies—[*wiping*]—great mercies—[*stops wiping, fixed lost gaze, brokenly*]—prayers perhaps not for naught—[*Pause. Do.*]—first thing—[*Pause. Do.*]—last thing—[*head down, resumes wiping, stops wiping, head up, calmed, wipes eyes, folds handkerchief, puts it back in bodice, examines handle of brush, reads*]fully guaranteed . . . genuine pure . . . —[*looks closer*]—genuine pure . . . —[*takes off spectacles, lays them and brush down, gazes before her*] Old things. [*pause*] Old eyes. [*long pause*] On, Winnie. [*She casts about her, sees parasol, considers it at length, takes it up, and develops from sheath a handle of surprising length. Holding butt of parasol in right hand she cranes back and down to her right to hand over* WILLIE.] Hoo-oo! [*pause*] Willie! [*pause*] Wonderful gift. [*She strikes down at him with beak of parasol.*] Wish I had it. [*She strikes again. The parasol slips from her grasp and falls behind mound. It is immediately restored to her by* WILLIE*'s invisible hand.*] Thank you, dear. [*She transfers parasol to left hand, turns back front and examines right palm.*] Damp. [*returns parasol to right hand, examines left palm*] Ah well, no worse. [*head up, cheerfully*] No better, no worse, no change. [*Pause. Do.*] No pain. [*cranes back to look down at* WILLIE, *holding parasol by butt as before*] Don't go off on me again now, dear, will you please, I may need you. [*pause*] No hurry, no hurry, just don't curl up on me again. [*turns back front, lays down parasol, examines palms together, wipes them on grass*] Perhaps a shade off colour just the same. [*turns to bag, rummages in it, brings out revolver, holds it up, kisses it rapidly, puts it back, rummages, brings out almost-empty bottle of red medicine, turns back front, looks for spectacles, puts them on, reads label*] Loss of spirits . . . lack of keenness . . . want of appetite . . . infants . . . children . . . adults . . . six level . . . tablespoonfuls daily—[*head up, smile*]—the old style!—[*smile off, head down, reads*]—daily . . . before and after . . . meals . . . instantaneous . . . [*looks closer*] improvement. [*Takes off spectacles, lays them down, holds up bottle at arm's length to see level, unscrews cap, swigs it off head well back, tosses cap and bottle away in* WILLIE*'s direction. Sound of breaking glass.*] Ah that's better! [*turns to bag, rummages in it, brings out lipstick, turns back front, examines lipstick*] Running out. [*looks for spectacles*] Ah well. [*puts on spectacles, looks for mirror*] Musn't complain. [*takes up mirror, starts doing lips*] What is that wonderful line? [*lips*] Oh fleeting joys—[*lips*]—oh something lasting woe. [*Lips. She is interrupted by disturbance from* WILLIE. *He is sitting up. She lowers lipstick and mirror and cranes back and down to look at him. Pause. Top back of* WILLIE*'s bald head, trickling blood, rises to view above slope, comes to rest.* WINNIE *pushes up her spectacles. Pause. His hand appears with handkerchief, spreads it on skull, disappears. Pause. The hand appears with boater, club ribbon, settles it on head, rakish angle, disappears. Pause.* WINNIE *cranes a little further back and down.*] Slip on your drawers, dear, before you get singed. [*pause*] No? [*pause*] Oh I see, you still have some of that stuff left. [*pause*] Work it well in, dear. [*pause*] Now the other. [*Pause. She turns back front, gazes before her. Happy expression.*] Oh this is going to be another happy day! [*Pause. Happy expression off. She pulls down spectacles and resumes lips.* WILLIE *opens newspaper, hands invisible. Tops of yellow sheets appear on either side of his head.* WINNIE *finishes lips, inspects them in mirror held a little further away.*] Ensign crimson. [WILLIE *turns page.* WINNIE *lays down lipstick and mirror, turns towards bag.*] Pale flag.

> [WILLIE *turns page.* WINNIE *rummages in bag, brings out small ornate brimless hat with crumpled feather, turns back front, straightens hat, smooths feather, raises it towards head, arrests gesture as* WILLIE *reads.*]

WILLIE: His Grace and Most Reverend Father in God Dr. Carolus Hunter dead in tub.

WINNIE: [*gazing front, hat in hand, tone of fervent reminiscence*] Charlie Hunter! [*pause*] I close my eyes— [*She takes off spectacles and does so, hat in one hand, spectacles in other.* WILLIE *turns page.*] —and am sitting on his knees again, in the back garden at Borough Green, under the horse-beech. [*Pause. She opens eyes, puts on spectacles, fiddles with hat.*] Oh the happy memories!

> [*Pause. She raises hat towards head, arrests gesture as* WILLIE *reads.*]

WILLIE: Opening for smart youth.

> [*Pause. She raises hat towards head, arrests gesture, takes off spectacles, gazes front, hat in one hand, spectacles in other.*]

WINNIE: My first ball! [*long pause*] My second ball! [*Long pause. Closes eyes.*] My first kiss! [*Pause.* WILLIE *turns page.* WINNIE *opens eyes.*] A Mr. Johnson, or Johnston, or perhaps I should say Johnstone. Very bushy moustache, very tawny. [*reverently*] Almost ginger! [*pause*] Within a toolshed, though whose I cannot conceive. We had no toolshed and he most certainly had no toolshed. [*closes eyes*] I see the piles of pots. [*pause*] The tangles of bast. [*pause*] The shadows deepening among the rafters.

> [*Pause. She opens eyes, puts on spectacles, raises hat towards head, arrests gesture as* WILLIE *reads.*]

WILLIE: Wanted bright boy.

> [*Pause.* WINNIE *puts on hat hurriedly, looks for mirror.* WILLIE *turns page.* WINNIE *takes up mirror, inspects hat, lays down mirror, turns towards bag. Paper disappears.* WINNIE *rummages in bag, brings out magnifying glass, turns back front,*]

looks for toothbrush. Paper reappears, folded, and begins to fan WILLIE'*s face, hand invisible.* WINNIE *takes up toothbrush and examines handle through glass.*]

WINNIE: Fully guaranteed . . . [WILLIE *stops fanning.*] . . . genuine pure . . . [*Pause.* WILLIE *resumes fanning.* WINNIE *looks closer, reads.*] Fully guaranteed . . . [WILLIE *stops fanning.*] . . . genuine pure . . . [*Pause.* WILLIE *resumes fanning.* WINNIE *lays down glass and brush, takes handkerchief from bodice, takes off and polishes spectacles, puts on spectacles, looks for glass, takes up and polishes glass, lays down glass, looks for brush, takes up brush and wipes handle, lays down brush, puts handkerchief back in bodice, looks for glass, takes up glass, looks for brush, takes up brush and examines handle through glass.*] Fully guaranteed . . . [WILLIE *stops fanning.*] . . . genuine pure . . . [*Pause.* WILLIE *resumes fanning.*] . . . hog's [WILLIE *stops fanning. Pause.*] . . . setae. [*Pause.* WINNIE *lays down glass and brush. Paper disappears.* WINNIE *takes off spectacles, lays them down, gazes front.*] Hog's setae. [*pause*] That is what I find so wonderful, that not a day goes by—[*smile*]—to speak in the old style—[*smile off*]—hardly a day, without some addition to one's knowledge however trifling, the addition I mean, provided one takes the pains. [WILLIE'*s hand reappears with a postcard which he examines close to eyes.*] And if for some strange reason no further pains are possible, why then just close the eyes—[*She does so.*]—and wait for the day to come—[*opens eyes*]—the happy day to come when flesh melts at so many degrees and the night of the moon has so many hundred hours. [*pause*] That is what I find so comforting when I lose heart and envy the brute beast. [*turning towards* WILLIE] I hope you are taking in—[*She sees postcard, bends lower.*] What is that you have there, Willie, may I see? [*She reaches down with hand and* WILLIE *hands her card. The hairy forearm appears above slope, raised in gesture of giving, the hand open to take back, and remains in this position till card is returned.* WINNIE *turns back front and examines card.*] Heavens, what are they up to! [*She looks for spectacles, puts them on and examines card.*] No but this is just genuine pure filth! [*examines card*] Make any nice-minded person want to vomit! [*Impatience of* WILLIE'*s fingers. She looks for glass, takes it up and examines card through glass. Long pause.*] What does the creature in the background think he's doing? [*looks closer*] Oh no really! [*Impatience of fingers. Last long look. She lays down glass, takes edge of card between right forefinger and thumb, averts head, takes nose between left forefinger and thumb.*] Pah! [*drops card*] Take it away! [WILLIE'*s arm disappears. His hand reappears immediately, holding card.* WINNIE *takes off spectacles, lays them down, gazes before her. During what follows* WILLIE *continues to relish card, varying angles and distance from his eyes.*] Hog's setae. [*puzzled expression*] What exactly is a hog? [*Pause. Do.*] A sow, of course, I know, but a hog . . . [*puzzled expression off*] Oh well what does it matter, that is what I always say, it will come back, that is what I find so wonderful, all comes back. [*pause*] All? [*pause*] No, not all. [*smile*] No no. [*smile off*] Not quite. [*pause*] A part. [*pause*] Floats up, one fine day, out of the blue. [*pause*] That is what I find so wonderful. [*Pause. She turns towards bag. Hand and card disappear. She makes to rummage in bag, arrests gesture.*] No. [*She turns back front. Smile.*] No no. [*smile off*] Gently Winnie. [*She gazes front.* WILLIE'*s hand reappears, takes off hat, disappears with hat.*] What then? [*Hand reappears, takes handkerchief from skull, disappears with handkerchief. Sharply, as to one not paying attention.*] Winnie! [WILLIE *bows head out of sight.*] What is the alternative? [*pause*] What is the al—[WILLIE *blows nose loud and long, head and hands invisible. She turns to look at him. Pause. Head reappears. Pause. Hand reappears with handkerchief, spreads it on skull, disappears. Pause. Hand reappears with boater, settles it on head, rakish angle, disappears. Pause.*] Would I had let you sleep on. [*She turns back front. Intermittent plucking at grass, head up and down, to animate following.*] Ah yes, if only I could bear to be alone, I mean prattle away with not a soul to hear. [*pause*] Not that I flatter myself you hear much, no Willie, God forbid. [*pause*] Days perhaps when you hear nothing. [*pause*] But days, too, when you answer. [*pause*] So that I may say at all times, even when you do not answer and perhaps hear nothing, something of this is being heard, I am not merely talking to myself, that is in the wilderness, a thing I could never bear to do—for any length of time. [*pause*] That is what enables me to go on, go on talking, that is. [*pause*] Whereas if you were to die—[*smile*]—to speak in the old style—[*smile off*]—or go away and leave me, then what would I do, what could I do, all day long, I mean between the bell for waking and the bell for sleep? [*pause*] Simply gaze before me with compressed lips. [*Long pause while she does so. No more plucking.*] Not another word as long as I drew breath, nothing to break the silence of this place. [*pause*] Save possibly, now and then, every now and then, a sigh into my looking glass. [*pause*] Or a brief . . . gale of laughter, should I happen to see the old joke again. [*Pause. Smile appears, broadens and seems about to culminate in laugh when suddenly replaced by expression of anxiety.*] My hair! [*pause*] Did I brush and comb my hair? [*pause*] I may have done. [*pause*] Normally I do. [*pause*] There is so little one can do. [*pause*] One does it all. [*pause*] All one can. [*pause*] 'Tis only human. [*pause*] Human nature. [*She begins to inspect mound, looks up.*] Human weakness. [*She resumes inspection of mound, looks up.*] Natural weakness. [*She resumes inspection of mound.*] I see no comb. [*inspects*] Nor any hairbrush. [*Looks up. Puzzled expression. She turns to bag, rummages in it.*] The comb is here. [*Back front. Puzzled expression.*] Perhaps I put them back after use. [*Pause. Do.*] But normally I do not put things back, after use, no, I leave them lying about and put them back all together, at the end of the day. [*smile*] To speak in the old style. [*pause*] The sweet old style. [*smile off*] And yet . . . I seem . . . to remember . . . [*suddenly careless*] Oh well, what does it matter, that is what I always say, I shall simply brush and comb them later on, purely and simply, I have the whole—[*Pause. Puzzled.*] Them? [*pause*] Or it? [*pause*] Brush and comb it? [*pause*] Sounds improper somehow. [*Pause. Turning a little towards* WILLIE.] What would you say, Willie? [*Pause. Turning a little further.*] What would you say, Willie, speaking of your hair, them or it? [*pause*] The hair on your head, I mean. [*Pause. Turning a little further.*] The hair on your head, Willie, what would you say speaking of the hair on your head, them or it?

[*long pause*]

WILLIE: It.

WINNIE: [*turning back front, joyfully*] Oh you are going to talk to me today, this is going to be a happy day! [*Pause. Joy off.*] Another happy day. [*pause*] Ah well, where was I, my hair, yes, later on, I shall be thankful for it later on. [*pause*] I have my—[*raises hand to hat*]—yes, on, my hat on—[*lowers hands*]—I cannot take it off now. [*pause*] To think there are times one cannot take off one's hat, not if one's life were at stake. Times one cannot put it on, times one cannot take it off. [*pause*] How often I have said, Put on your hat now, Winnie, there is nothing else for it, take off your hat now, Winnie, like a good girl, it will do you good, and did not. [*pause*] Could not. [*Pause. She raises hand, frees a strand of hair from under hat, draws it towards eye, squints at it, lets it go, hand down.*] Golden you called it, that day, when the last guest was gone— [*hand up in gesture of raising a glass*]—to your golden . . . may it never . . . [*voice breaks*] . . . may it never . . . [*Hand down. Head down. Pause. Low.*] That day. [*Pause. Do.*] What day? [*Pause. Head up. Normal voice.*] What now? [*pause*] Words fail, there are times when even they fail. [*turning a little towards* WILLIE] Is that not so, Willie? [*Pause. Turning a little further.*] Is not that so, Willie, that even words fail, at times? [*Pause. Back front.*] What is one to do then, until they come again? Brush and comb the hair, if it has not been done, or if there is some doubt, trim the nails if they are in need of trimming, these things tide one over. [*pause*] That is what I mean. [*pause*] That is all I mean. [*pause*] That is what I find so wonderful, that not a day goes by— [*smile*]—to speak in the old style—[*smile off*]—without some blessing—[WILLIE *collapses behind slope, his head disappears.* WINNIE *turns towards event.*]—in disguise. [*She cranes back and down.*] Go back into your hole now, Willie, you've exposed yourself enough. [*pause*] Do as I say, Willie, don't lie sprawling there in this hellish sun, go back into your hole. [*pause*] Go on now, Willie. [WILLIE, *invisible, starts crawling left towards hole.*] That's the man. [*She follows his progress with her eyes.*] Not head first, stupid, how are you going to turn? [*pause*] That's it . . . right round . . . now . . . back in. [*pause*] Oh I know it is not easy, dear, crawling backwards, but it is rewarding in the end. [*pause*] You have left your Vaseline behind. [*She watches as he crawls back for Vaseline.*] The lid! [*She watches as he crawls back towards hole. Irritated.*] Not head first, I tell you! [*pause*] More to the right. [*pause*] The right, I said. [*Pause. Irritated.*] Keep your tail down, can't you! [*pause*] Now. [*pause*] There! [*All these directions loud. Now in her normal voice, still turned towards him.*] Can you hear me? [*pause*] I beseech you, Willie, just yes or no, can you hear me, just yes or nothing.

     [*pause*]

WILLIE: Yes.

WINNIE: [*turning front, same voice*] And now?

WILLIE: [*irritated*] Yes.

WINNIE: [*less loud*] And now?

WILLIE: [*more irritated*] Yes.

WINNIE: [*still less loud*] And now? [*A little louder.*] And now?

WILLIE: [*violently*] Yes!

WINNIE: [*same voice*] Fear no more the heat o' the sun. [*pause*] Did you hear that?

WILLIE: [*irritated*] Yes.

WINNIE: [*same voice*] What? [*pause*] What?

WILLIE: [*more irritated*] Fear no more.

     [*pause*]

WINNIE: [*same voice*] No more what? [*pause*] Fear no more what?

WILLIE: [*violently*] Fear no more!

WINNIE: [*normal voice, gabbled*] Bless you Willie I do appreciate your goodness I know what an effort it costs you, now you may relax I shall not trouble you again unless I am obliged to, by that I mean unless I come to the end of my own resources which is most unlikely, just to know that in theory you can hear me even though in fact you don't is all I need, just to feel you there within earshot and conceivably on the qui vive is all I ask, not to say anything I would not wish you to hear or liable to cause you pain, not to be just babbling away on trust as it is were not knowing and something gnawing at me. [*pause for breath*] Doubt. [*places index and second finger on heart area, moves them about, brings them to rest*] Here. [*moves them slightly*] Abouts. [*hand away*] Oh no doubt the time will come when before I can utter a word I must make sure you heard the one that went before and then no doubt another come another time when I must learn to talk to myself a thing I could never bear to do such wilderness. [*pause*] Or gaze before me with compressed lips. [*She does so.*] All day long. [*gaze and lips again*] No. [*smile*] No no. [*smile off*] There is, of course, the bag. [*turns towards it*] There will always be the bag. [*back front*] Yes, I suppose so. [*pause*] Even when you are gone, Willie. [*She turns a little towards him.*] You are going, Willie, aren't you? [*Pause. Louder.*] You will be going soon, Willie, won't you? [*Pause. Louder.*] Willie! [*Pause. She cranes back and down to look at him.*] So you have taken off your straw, that is wise. [*pause*] You do look snug, I must say, with your chin on your hands and the

old blue eyes like saucers in the shadows. [*pause*] Can you see me from there I wonder, I still wonder. [*pause*] No? [*back front*] Oh I know it does not follow when two are gathered together—[*faltering*]—in this way—[*normal*] —that because one sees the other the other sees the one, life has taught me that . . . too. [*pause*] Yes, life I suppose, there is no other word. [*She turns a little towards him.*] Could you see me, Willie, do you think, from where you are, if you were to raise your eyes in my direction? [*turns a little further*] Lift up your eyes to me, Willie, and tell me can you see me, do that for me, I'll lean back as far as I can. [*Does so. Pause.*] No? [*pause*] Well never mind. [*turns back painfully front*] The earth is very tight today, can it be I have put on flesh, I trust not. [*Pause. Absently, eyes lowered.*] The great heat possibly. [*starts to pat and stroke ground*] All things expanding, some more than others. [*Pause. Patting and stroking.*] Some less. [*Pause. Do.*] Oh I can well imagine what is passing through your mind, it is not enough to have to listen to the woman, now I must look at her as well. [*Pause. Do.*] Well it is very understandable. [*Pause. Do.*] One does not appear to be asking a great deal, indeed at times it would seem hardly possible—[*voice breaks, falls to a murmur*]—to ask less—of a fellow creature—to put it mildly—whereas actually—when you think about it—look into your heart—see the other—what he needs—peace—to be left in peace—then perhaps the moon—all this time—asking for the moon. [*Pause. Stroking hand suddenly still. Lively.*] Oh I say, what have we here? [*Bending head to ground, incredulous.*] Looks like life of some kind! [*Looks for spectacles, puts them on, bends closer. Pause.*] An emmet! [*Recoils. Shrill.*] Willie, an emmet, a live emmet! [*Seizes magnifying glass, bends to ground again, inspects through glass.*] Where's it gone? [*inspects*] Ah! [*follows its progress through grass*] Has like a little white ball in its arms. [*Follows progress. Hand still. Pause.*] It's gone in. [*Continues a moment to gaze at spot through glass, then slowly straightens up, lays down glass, takes off spectacles and gazes before her, spectacles in hand. Finally.*] Like a little white ball.
[*Long pause. Gesture to lay down spectacles.*]

WILLIE: Eggs.

WINNIE: [*arresting gesture*] What?
[*pause*]

WILLIE: Eggs. [*Pause. Gesture to lay down glass.*] Formication.

WINNIE: [*arresting gesture*] What!
[*pause*]

WILLIE: Formication.
[*Pause. She lays down spectacles, gazes before her. Finally.*]

WINNIE: [*murmur*] God. [*Pause.* WILLIE *laughs quietly. After a moment she joins in. They laugh quietly together.* WILLIE *stops. She laughs on a moment alone.* WILLIE *joins in. They laugh together. She stops.* WILLIE *laughs on a moment alone. He stops. Pause. Normal voice.*] Ah well what a joy in any case to hear you laugh again, Willie, I was convinced I never would, you never would. [*pause*] I suppose some people might think us a trifle irreverent, but I doubt it. [*pause*] How can one better magnify the Almighty than by sniggering with him at his little jokes, particularly the poorer ones? [*pause*] I think you would back me up there, Willie. [*pause*] Or were we perhaps diverted by two quite different things? [*pause*] Oh well, what does it matter, that is what I always say, so long as one . . . you know . . . what is that wonderful line . . . laughing wild . . . something something laughing wild amid severest woe. [*pause*] And now? [*long pause*] Was I lovable once, Willie? [*pause*] Was I ever lovable? [*pause*] Do not misunderstand my question, I am not asking you if you loved me, we know all about that, I am asking you if you found me lovable—at one stage. [*pause*] No? [*pause*] You can't? [*pause*] Well I admit it is a teaser. And you have done more than your bit already, for

the time being, just lie back now and relax, I shall not trouble you again unless I am compelled to, just to know you are there within hearing and conceivably on the semi-alert is . . . er . . . paradise enow. [*pause*] The day is now well advanced. [*smile*] To speak in the old style. [*smile off*] And yet it is perhaps a little soon for my song. [*pause*] To sing too soon is a great mistake, I find. [*turning towards bag*] There is, of course, the bag. [*looking at bag*] The bag. [*back front*] Could I enumerate its contents? [*pause*] No. [*pause*] Could I, if some kind person were to come along and ask, What all have you got in that big black bag, Winnie? give an exhaustive answer? [*pause*] No. [*pause*] The depths in particular, who knows what treasures. [*pause*] What comforts. [*turns to look at bag*] Yes, there is the bag. [*back front*] But something tells me, Do not overdo the bag, Winnie, make use of it, of course, let it help you . . . along, when stuck, by all means, but cast your mind forward, something tells me, cast your mind forward, Winnie, to the time when words must fail—[*She closes eyes, pause, opens eyes.*]—and do not overdo the bag. [*Pause. She turns to look at bag.*] Perhaps just one quick dip. [*She turns back front, closes eyes, throws out left arm, plunges hand in bag and brings out revolver. Disgusted.*] You again! [*She opens eyes, brings revolver front and contemplates it. She weighs it in her palm.*] You'd think the weight of this thing would bring it down among the . . . last rounds. But no. It doesn't. Ever uppermost, like Browning. [*pause*] Brownie . . . [*turning a little toward* WILLIE] Remember Brownie, Willie? [*pause*] Remember how you used to keep on at me to take it away from you? Take it away, Winnie, take it away, before I put myself out of my misery. [*Back front. Derisive.*] *Your* misery! [*to revolver*] Oh I suppose it's a comfort to know you're there, but I'm tired of you. [*pause*] I'll leave you out, that's what I'll do. [*She lays revolver on ground to her right.*] There, that's your home from this day out. [*smile*] The old style! [*smile off*] And now? [*long pause*] Is gravity what it was, Willie, I fancy not. [*pause*] Yes, the feeling more and more that if I were not held—[*gesture*]—in this way, I would simply float up into the blue. [*pause*] And that perhaps some day the earth will yield and let me go, the pull is so great, yes, crack all round me and let me out. [*pause*] Don't you ever have that feeling, Willie, of being sucked up? [*pause*] Don't you have to cling on sometimes, Willie? [*Pause. She turns a little towards him.*] Willie.
   [*pause*]

WILLIE: Sucked up?

WINNIE: Yes, love, up into the blue, like gossamer. [*pause*] No? [*pause*] You don't [*pause*] Ah well, natural laws, natural laws, I suppose it's like everything else, it all depends on the creature you happen to be. All I can say for my part is that for me they are not what they were when I was young and . . . foolish and . . . [*faltering, head down*] . . . beautiful . . . possibly . . . lovely . . . in a way . . . to look at. [*Pause. Head up.*] Forgive me, Willie, sorrow keeps breaking in. [*Normal voice.*] Ah well what a joy in any case to know you are there, as usual, and perhaps awake, and perhaps taking all this in, some of all this, what a happy day for me . . . it will have been. [*pause*] So far. [*pause*] What a blessing nothing grows, imagine if all this stuff were to start growing. [*pause*] Imagine. [*pause*] Ah yes, great mercies. [*long pause*] I can say no more. [*pause*] For the moment. [*Pause. Turns to look at bag. Back front. Smile.*] No no. [*Smile off. Looks at parasol.*] I suppose I might—[*takes up parasol*]—yes, I suppose I might . . . hoist this thing now. [*Begins to unfurl it. Following punctuated by mechanical difficulties overcome.*] One keeps putting off—putting up—for fear of putting up—too soon—and the day goes by—quite by—without one's having put up—at all. [*Parasol now fully open. Turned to her right she twirls it idly this way and that.*] Ah yes, so little to say, so little to do, and the fear so great, certain days, of finding oneself . . . left, with hours still to run, before the bell for sleep, and nothing more to say, nothing more to do, that the days go by, certain days go by, quite by, the bell goes, and little or nothing said, little or nothing done. [*raising parasol*] That is the danger. [*turning front*] To be guarded against. [*She gazes front, holding up parasol with right hand. Maximum pause.*] I used to perspire freely. [*pause*] Now hardly at all. [*pause*] The heat is much greater. [*pause*] The perspiration much less. [*pause*] That is what I find so wonderful. [*pause*] The way man adapts himself. [*pause*] To changing conditions. [*She transfers parasol to left hand. Long pause.*] Holding up wearies the arm. [*pause*] Not if one is going along. [*pause*] Only if one is at rest. [*pause*] That is a curious observation. [*pause*] I hope you heard that, Willie, I should be grieved to think you had not heard that. [*She takes parasol in both hands. Long pause.*] I am weary, holding it up, and I cannot put it down. [*pause*] I am worse off with it up than with it down, and I cannot put it down. [*pause*] Reason says, Put it down, Winnie, it is not helping you, put the thing down and get on with something else. [*pause*] I cannot. [*pause*] I cannot move. [*pause*] No, something must happen, in the world, take place, some change, I cannot, if I am to move again. [*pause*] Willie. [*mildly*] Help. [*pause*] No? [*pause*] Bid me put this thing down, Willie, I would obey you instantly, as I have always done, honoured, and obeyed. [*pause*] Please, Willie. [*mildly*] For pity's sake. [*pause*] No? [*pause*] You can't? [*pause*] Well I don't blame you, no, it would ill become me, who cannot move, to blame my Willie because he cannot speak. [*pause*] Fortunately I am in tongue again. [*pause*] That is what I find so wonderful, my two lamps, when one goes out the other burns brighter. [*pause*] Oh yes, great mercies. [*Maximum pause. The parasol goes on fire. Smoke, flames if feasible. She sniffs, looks up, throws parasol to her right behind mound, cranes back to watch it burning. Pause.*] Ah earth you old extinguisher. [*back front*] I presume this has occurred before, though I cannot recall it. [*pause*] Can you, Willie? [*turns a little towards him*] Can you recall this having occurred before? [*Pause. Cranes to look at him.*] Do you know what has occurred, Willie? [*pause*] Have you gone off on me again? [*pause*] I do not ask if you are alive to all that is going on, I merely ask if you have not gone off on me again. [*pause*] Your eyes appear to be closed, but that has no particular significance, we know. [*pause*] Raise a finger, dear, will you please, if you are not quite senseless. [*pause*] Do that for me, Willie, please, just the little finger, if you are still conscious. [*Pause. Joyful.*] Oh all five, you are a darling today, now I may continue with an easy mind. [*back front*] Yes, what ever occurred that did not occur before and yet . . . I wonder, yes, I confess I wonder. [*pause*] With the sun blazing so much fiercer down, and hourly fiercer, is it not natural things should go on fire never known to do so, in this way I mean, spontaneous like. [*pause*] Shall I myself not melt perhaps in the end, or burn, oh I do not mean necessarily burst into flames, no, just little by little be charred to a black cinder, all this—[*ample gesture of arms*]—visible flesh. [*pause*] On the other hand, did I ever know a temperate time? [*pause*] No. [*pause*] I speak of temperate times and torrid times, they are empty words. [*pause*] I speak of when I was not yet caught—in this way—and had my legs and had the use of my legs, and could seek out a shady place, like you, when I was tired of the sun, or a sunny place when I was tired of the shade, like you, and they are all empty words. [*pause*] It is no hotter today than yesterday, it will be no hotter tomorrow than today, how could it, and so on back into the far past, forward into the far future. [*pause*] And should one day the earth cover my breasts, then I shall never have seen my breasts, no one ever seen my breasts. [*pause*] I hope you caught something of that, Willie, I should be sorry to think you had caught nothing of all that, it is not every day I rise to such heights. [*pause*] Yes, something seems to have occurred, something has seemed to occur, and nothing has occurred, nothing at all, you are quite right, Willie. [*pause*] The sunshade will be there again tomorrow, beside me on this mound, to help me through the day. [*Pause. She takes up mirror.*] I take up this little glass, I shiver it on a stone—[*does so*]—I throw it away—[*does so far behind her*]—it will be in the bag again tomorrow, without a scratch, to help me through the day. [*pause*] No, one can do nothing. [*pause*] That is what I find so wonderful, the way things . . . [*voice breaks, head down*] . . . things . . . so wonderful. [*Long pause, head down. Finally turns, still bowed, to bag, brings out unidentifiable odds and ends, stuffs them back, fumbles deeper, brings out finally musical box, winds it up, turns it on, listens for a moment holding it in both hands, huddled over it, turns back front, straightens up and listens to tune, holding box to breast with both hands. It plays the waltz duet "I Love You So" from* The Merry Widow. *Gradually happy expression. She sways to the rhythm. Music stops. Pause. Brief burst of hoarse song without words—musical box tune—from* WILLIE. *Increase of happy expression. She lays down box.*] Oh this will have been a happy day! [*She claps hands.*] Again, Willie, again! [*claps*] Encore, Willie, please! [*Pause. Happy expression off.*] No? You won't do that for me? [*pause*] Well it is very understandable, very understandable. One cannot sing just to please someone, however much one loves them, no, song must come from the heart, that is what I always say, pour out from the inmost, like a thrush. [*pause*] How often I have said, in evil hours, Sing now, Winnie, sing your song, there is nothing else for it, and did not. [*pause*] Could not. [*pause*] No, like the thrush, or the bird of dawning, with no thought of benefit, to oneself or anyone else. [*pause*] And now? [*Long pause. Low.*] Strange feeling. [*Pause. Do.*] Strange feeling that someone is looking at me. I am clear, then dim, then gone, then dim again, then clear again, and so on, back and forth, in and out of someone's eye. [*Pause. Do.*] Strange? [*Pause. Do.*] No, here all is strange. [*Pause. Normal voice.*] Something says, Stop talking now, Winnie, for a minute, don't squander all your words for the day, stop talking and do something for a change, will you? [*She raises hands and holds them open before her eyes. Apostrophic.*] Do something! [*She closes hands.*] What claws! [*She turns to bag, rummages in it, brings out finally a nail file, turns back front and begins to file nails. Files for a time in silence, then the following punctuated by filing.*] There floats up—into my thoughts—a Mr. Shower—a Mr. and perhaps a Mrs. Shower—no—they are holding hands—his fiancée then more likely—or just some—loved one. [*looks closer at nails*] Very brittle today. [*resumes filing*] Shower—Shower—does the name mean anything—to you, Willie—evoke any reality, I mean—for you, Willie—don't answer if you don't—feel up to it—you have done more—than your bit—already—Shower—Shower. [*inspects filed nails*] Bit more like it. [*raises head, gazes front*] Keep yourself nice, Winnie, that's what I always say, come what may, keep yourself nice. [*Pause. Resumes filing.*] Yes—Shower—Shower—[*stops filing, raises head, gazes front, pause*]—or Cooker, perhaps I should say Cooker, [*turning a little towards* WILLIE] Cooker, Willie, does Cooker strike a chord? [*Pause. Turns a little further. Louder.*] Cooker, Willie, does Cooker ring a bell, the name Cooker? [*Pause. She cranes back to look at him. Pause.*] Oh really! [*pause*] Have you no handkerchief, darling? [*pause*] Have you no delicacy? [*pause*] Oh, Willie, you're not eating it! Spit it out, dear, spit it out! [*Pause. Back front.*] Ah well, I suppose it's only natural. [*break in voice*] Human. [*Pause. Do.*] What is one to do? [*Head down. Do.*] All day long. [*Pause. Do.*] Day after day. [*Pause. Head up. Smile. Calm.*] The old style! [*Smile off. Resumes nails.*] No, done him. [*passes on to next*] Should have put on my glasses. [*pause*] Too late now. [*finishes left hand, inspects it.*] Bit more human. [*Starts right hand. Following punctuated as before.*] Well anyway—this man Shower—or Cooker—no matter—and the woman—hand in hand—in the other hands bags—kind of big brown grips—standing there gaping at me—and at last this man Shower—or Cooker—

ends in "er" anyway—stake my life on that—What's she doing? he says—What's the idea? he says—stuck up to her diddies in the bleeding ground—coarse fellow—What does it mean? he says—What's it meant to mean—and so on—lot more stuff like that—usual drivel—Do you hear me? he says—I do, she says, God help me—What do you mean, he says, God help you? [*stops filing, raises head, gazes front*] And you, she says, what's the idea of you, she says, what are you meant to mean? It is because you're still on your two flat feet, with your old ditty full of tinned muck and changes of underwear, dragging me up and down this fornicating wilderness, coarse creature, fit mate—[*with sudden violence*]—let go of my hand and drop for God's sake, she says, drop! [*Pause. Resumes filing.*] Why doesn't he dig her out? he says—referring to you, my dear—What good is she to him like that?—What good is he to her like that?—and so on—usual tosh—Good! she says, have a heart for God's sake—Dig her out, he says, dig her out, no sense in her like that—Dig her out with what? she says— I'd dig her out with my bare hands, he says—must have been man and—wife. [*files in silence*] Next thing they're away—hand in hand—and the bags—dim—then gone—last human kind—to stray this way. [*finishes right hand, inspects it, lays down file, gazes front*] Strange thing, time like this, drift up into the mind. [*pause*] Strange? [*pause*]. No, here all is strange. [*pause*] Thankful for it in any case. [*voice breaks*] Most thankful. [*Head down. Pause. Head up. Calm.*] Bow and raise the head, bow and raise, always that. [*pause*] And now? [*Long pause. Starts putting things back in bag, toothbrush last. This operation, interrupted by pauses as indicated, punctuates following.*] It is per- haps a little soon—to make ready—for the night—[*stops tidying, head up, smile*]— the old style!—[*smile off, resumes tidying*]—and yet I do—make ready for the night—feeling it at hand—the bell for sleep—saying to myself—Winnie—it will not be long now, Winnie—until the bell for sleep. [*stops tidying, head up*] Sometimes I am wrong. [*smile*] But not often. [*smile off*] Sometimes all is over, for the day, all done, all said, all ready for the night, and the day not over, far from over, the night not ready, far, far from ready. [*smile*] But not often. [*smile off*] Yes, the bell for sleep, when I feel it at hand, and so make ready for the night—[*gesture*]—in this way, some- times I am wrong—[*smile*]—but not often. [*Smile off. Resumes tidying.*] I used to think—I say I used to think—that all these things—put back into the bag—if too soon—put back too soon—could be taken out again—if necessary—if needed—and so on—indefinitely—back into the bag—back out of the bag—until the bell—went. [*Stops tidying, head up, smile.*] But no. [*smile broader*] No no. [*Smile off. Resumes tidy- ing.*] I suppose this—might seem strange—this—what shall I say—this what I have said—yes—[*She takes up revolver.*]—strange—[*She turns to put revolver in bag.*]— were it not—[*about to put revolver in bag she arrests gesture and turns back front*]—were it not—[*She lays down revolver to her right, stops tidying, head up.*]—that all seems strange. [*pause*] Most strange. [*pause*] Never any change. [*pause*] And more and more strange. [*Pause. She bends to mound again, takes up last object, i.e. toothbrush, and turns to put it in bag when her attention is drawn to disturbance from* WILLIE. *She cranes back and to her right to see. Pause.*] Weary of your hole, dear? [*pause*] Well I can under- stand that. [*pause*] Don't forget your straw. [*pause*] Not the crawler you were, poor darling. [*pause*] No, not the crawler I gave my heart to. [*pause*] The hands and knees, love, try the hands and knees. [*pause*] The knees! The knees! [*pause*] What a curse, mobility! [*She follows with eyes his progress towards her behind mound, i.e. towards place he occupied at beginning of act.*] Another foot, Willie, and you're home. [*pause as he observes last foot*] Ah! [*turns back front laboriously, rubs neck*] Crick in my neck admir- ing you. [*rubs neck*] But it's worth it, well worth it. [*turns slightly towards him*] Do you know what I dream sometimes? [*pause*] What I dream sometimes, Willie. [*pause*]

That you'll come round and live this side where I could see you. [*Pause. Back front.*] I'd be a different woman. [*pause*] Unrecognizable. [*turning slightly toward him*] Or just now and then, come round this side just every now and then and let me feast on you. [*back front*] But you can't, I know. [*head down*] I know. [*Pause. Head up.*] Well anyway—[*looks at toothbrush in her hand*]—can't be long now—[*looks at brush*]—until the bell. [*Top back of* WILLIE'*s head appears above slope.* WINNIE *looks closer at brush.*] Fully guaranteed . . . [*head up*] . . . what's this it was? [WILLIE'*s hand appears with handkerchief, spreads it on skull, disappears.*] Genuine pure . . . fully guaranteed . . . [WILLIE'*s hand appears with boater, settles it on head, rakish angle, disappears.*] . . . genuine pure . . . ah! hog's setae. [*pause*] What is a hog exactly? [*Pause. Turns slightly towards* WILLIE.] What exactly is a hog, Willie, do you know, I can't remember. [*Pause. Turning a little further, pleading.*] What is a hog, Willie, please!

    [*pause*]

WILLIE: Castrated male swine. [*Happy expression appears on* WINNIE'*s face.*] Reared for slaughter.

    [*Happy expression increases.* WILLIE *opens newspaper, hands invisible. Tops of yellow sheets appear on either side of his head.* WINNIE *gazes before her with happy expression.*]

WINNIE: Oh this is a happy day! This will have been another happy day! [*pause*] After all. [*pause*] So far.

    [*Pause. Happy expression off.* WILLIE *turns page. Pause. He turns another page. Pause.*]

WILLIE: Opening for smart youth.

    [*Pause.* WINNIE *takes off hat, turns to put it in bag, arrests gesture, turns back front. Smile.*]

WINNIE: No. [*smile broader*] No no. [*Smile off. Puts on hat again, gazes front, pause.*] And now? [*pause*] Sing. [*pause*] Sing your song, Winnie. [*pause*] No? [*pause*] Then pray. [*pause*] Pray your prayer, Winnie.

    [*Pause.* WILLIE *turns page.*]

WILLIE: Wanted bright boy.

    [*Pause.* WINNIE *gazes before her.* WILLIE *turns page. Pause. Newspaper disappears. Long pause.*]

WINNIE: Pray your old prayer, Winnie.

    [*Long pause.*]

CURTAIN

ACT II

Scene as before.
    WINNIE *embedded up to neck, hat on head, eyes closed. Her head, which she can no longer turn, nor bow, nor raise, faces front motionless throughout act. Movements of eyes as indicated. Bag and parasol as before. Revolver conspicuous to her right on mound.*
Long pause.
Bell rings loudly. She opens eyes at once. Bell stops. She gazes front. Long pause.

WINNIE: Hail, holy light. [*Long pause. She closes her eyes. Bell rings loudly. She opens eyes at once. Bell stops. She gazes front. Long smile. Smile off. Long pause.*] Someone is looking at me still. [*pause*] Caring for me still. [*pause*] That is what I find so wonderful. [*pause*] Eyes on my eyes. [*pause*] What is that unforgettable line? [*Pause. Eyes right.*] Willie. [*Pause. Louder.*] Willie. [*Pause. Eyes front.*] May one still speak of time? [*pause*] Say it is a long time now, Willie, since I saw you. [*pause*] Since I heard you. [*pause*]

May one? [*pause*] One does. [*smile*] The old style! [*smile off*] There is so little one
can speak of. [*pause*] One speaks of it all. [*pause*] All one can. [*pause*] I used to think
. . . [*pause*] . . . I say I used to think that I would learn to talk alone. [*pause*] By that
I mean to myself, the wilderness. [*smile*] But no. [*smile broader*] No no. [*smile off*]
Ergo you are there. [*pause*] Oh no doubt you are dead like the others, no doubt you
have died, or gone away and left me, like the others, it doesn't matter, you are there.
[*Pause. Eyes left.*] The bag, too, is there, the same as ever, I can see it. [*Pause. Eyes
right. Louder.*] The bag is there, Willie, as good as ever, the one you gave me that day
. . . to go to market. [*Pause. Eyes front.*] That day. [*pause*] What day? [*pause*] I used
to pray. [*pause*] I say I used to pray. [*pause*] Yes, I must confess I did. [*smile*] Not now.
[*smile broader*] No no. [*Smile off. Pause.*] Then . . . now . . . what difficulties here,
for the mind. [*pause*] To have been always what I am—and so changed from what I
was. [*pause*] I am the one, I say the one, then the other. [*pause*] Now the one, then
the other. [*pause*] Now the one, then the other. [*pause*] There is so little one can say,
one says it all. [*pause*] All one can. [*pause*] And no truth in it anywhere. [*pause*] My arms.
[*pause*] My breasts. [*pause*] What arms? [*pause*] What breasts? [*pause*] Willie. [*pause*]
What Willie? [*sudden vehement affirmation*] My Willie! [*eyes right, calling*] Willie! [*Pause.
Louder.*] Willie! [*Pause. Eyes front.*] Ah well, not to know, not to know for sure, great
mercy, all I ask. [*pause*] Ah yes . . . then . . . now . . . beechen green . . . . this . . . Charlie . . . kisses . . . this . . . all that . . . deep trouble for the mind. [*pause*] But it does
not trouble mine. [*smile*] Not now. [*smile broader*] No no. [*Smile off. Long pause. She
closes eyes. Bell rings loudly. She opens eyes. Pause.*] Eyes float up that seem to close in
peace . . . to see . . . in peace. [*pause*] Not mine. [*smile*] Not now. [*smile broader*] No
no. [*Smile off. Long pause.*] Willie. [*pause*] Do you think the earth has lost its atmosphere, Willie? [*pause*] Do you, Willie? [*pause*] You have no opinion? [*pause*] Well that
is like you, you never had any opinion about anything. [*pause*] It's understandable.
[*pause*] Most. [*pause*] The earth-ball. [*pause*] I sometimes wonder. [*pause*] Perhaps not
quite all. [*pause*] There always remains something. [*pause*] Of everything. [*pause*]
Some remains. [*pause*] If the mind were to go. [*pause*] It won't, of course. [*pause*] Not
quite. [*pause*] Not mine. [*smile*] Now now. [*smile broader*] No no. [*Smile off. Long
pause.*] It might be the eternal cold. [*pause*] Everlasting perishing cold. [*pause*] Just
chance, I take it, happy chance. [*pause*] Oh yes, great mercies, great mercies. [*pause*]
And now? [*Long pause*] The face. [*pause*] The nose. [*She squints down.*] I can see
it. . . . [*squinting down*] . . . the tip . . . the nostrils . . . breath of life . . . that curve
you so admired . . . [*pouts*] . . . a hint of lip . . . [*pouts again*] . . . if I pout them out
. . . [*sticks out tongue*] . . . the tongue, of course . . . you so admired . . . if I stick it
out . . . [*sticks it out again*]. . . the tip . . . [*eyes up*] . . . suspicion of brow . . . eye-
brow . . . imagination possibly . . . [*eyes left*] . . . cheek . . . no . . . [*eyes right*] . . . no
. . . [*distends cheeks*] . . . even if I puff them out . . . [*eyes left, distends cheeks again*]
. . . no . . . no damask. [*eyes front*] That is all. [*pause*] The bag, of course . . . [*eyes
left*] . . . little blurred perhaps . . . but the bag. [*Eyes front. Offhand.*] The Earth, of
course, and sky. [*eyes right*] The sunshade you gave me . . . that day . . . [*pause*] . . .
that day . . . the lake . . . the reeds. [*Eyes front. Pause.*] What day? [*pause*] What
reeds? [*Long pause. Eyes close. Bell rings loudly. Eyes open. Pause. Eyes right.*] Brownie,
of course. [*pause*] You remember Brownie, Willie, I can see him. [*pause*] Brownie is
there, Willie, beside me. [*Pause. Eyes front.*] That is all. [*pause*] What would I do
without them? [*pause*] What would I do without them, when words fail? [*pause*]
Gaze before me, with compressed lips. [*long pause while she does so*] I cannot. [*pause*]
Ah yes, great mercies, great mercies. [*Long pause. Low.*] Sometimes I hear sounds.

[*Listening expression. Normal voice.*] But not often. [*pause*] They are a boon, sounds are a boon, they help me . . . through the day. [*smile*] The old style! [*smile off*] Yes, those are happy days, when there are sounds. [*pause*] When I hear sounds. [*pause*] I used to think . . . [*pause*] . . . I say I used to think they were in my head. [*smile*] But no. [*smile broader*] No no. [*smile off*] That was just logic. [*pause*] Reason. [*pause*] I have not lost my reason. [*pause*] Not yet. [*pause*] Not all. [*pause*] Some remains. [*pause*] Sounds. [*pause*] Like little . . . sunderings, little falls . . . apart. [*Pause. Low.*] It's things, Willie. [*Pause. Normal voice.*] In the bag, outside the bag. [*pause*] Ah yes, things have their life, that is what I always say, things have a life. [*pause*] Take my looking glass, it doesn't need me. [*pause*] The bell. [*pause*] It hurts like a knife. [*pause*] A gouge. [*pause*] One cannot ignore it. [*pause*] How often . . . [*pause*] . . . I say how often I have said, Ignore it, Winnie, ignore the bell, pay no heed, just sleep and wake, sleep and wake, as you please, open and close the eyes, as you please, or in the way you find most helpful. [*pause*] Open and close the eyes, Winnie, open and close, always that. [*pause*] But no. [*smile*] Not now. [*smile broader*] No no. [*Smile off. Pause.*] What now? [*pause*] What now, Willie? [*long pause*] There is my story, of course, when all else fails. [*pause*] A life. [*smile*] A long life. [*smile off*] Beginning in the womb, where life used to begin, Mildred has memories, she will have memories, of the womb, before she dies, the mother's womb. [*pause*] She is now four or five already and has recently been given a big waxen dolly. [*pause*] Fully clothed, complete outfit. [*pause*] Shoes, socks, undies, complete set, frilly frock, gloves. [*pause*] White mesh. [*pause*] A little white straw hat with a chin elastic. [*pause*] Pearly necklet. [*pause*] A little picture book with legends in real print to go under her arm when she takes her walk. [*pause*] China blue eyes that open and shut. [*Pause. Narrative.*] The sun was not well up when Milly rose, descended the steep . . . [*pause*] . . . slipped on her nightgown, descended all along the steep wooden stairs, backwards on all fours, though she had been forbidden to do so, entered the . . . [*pause*] . . . tiptoed down the silent passage, entered the nursery and began to undress Dolly. [*pause*] Crept under the table and began to undress Dolly. [*pause*] Scolding her . . . the while. [*pause*] Suddenly a mouse—[*long pause*] Gently, Winnie. [*Long pause. Calling.*] Willie! [*Pause. Louder.*] Willie! [*Pause. Mild reproach.*] I sometimes find your attitude a little strange, Willie, all this time, it is not like you to be wantonly cruel. [*pause*] Strange? [*pause*] No. [*smile*] Not here. [*smile broader*] Not now. [*smile off*] And yet . . . [*suddenly anxious*] I do hope nothing is amiss. [*eyes right, loud*] Is all well, dear? [*Pause. Eyes front. To herself.*] God grant he did not go in head foremost [*Eyes right, loud.*] You're not stuck, Willie? [*Pause. Do.*] You're not jammed, Willie? [*eyes front, distressed*] Perhaps he is crying out for help all this time and I do not hear him! [*pause*] I do, of course, hear cries. [*pause*] But they are in my head surely. [*pause*] Is it possible that . . . [*Pause. With finality.*] No no, my head was always full of cries. [*pause*] Faint confused cries. [*pause*] They come. [*pause*] Then go. [*pause*] As on a wind. [*pause*] That is what I find so wonderful. [*pause*] They cease. [*pause*] Ah yes, great mercies, great mercies. [*pause*] The day is now well advanced. [*Smile. Smile off.*] And yet it is perhaps a little soon for my song. [*pause*] To sing too soon is fatal, I always find. [*pause*] On the other hand it is possible to leave it too late. [*pause*] The bell goes for sleep and one has not sung. [*pause*] The whole day has flown—[*smile, smile off*]—flown by, quite by, and no song of any class, kind, or description. [*pause*] There is a problem here. [*pause*] One cannot sing . . . just like that, no. [*pause*] It bubbles up, for some unknown reason, the time is ill chosen, one chokes it back. [*pause*] One says, Now is the time, it is now or never, and one cannot. [*pause*] Simply cannot sing. [*pause*] Not a note. [*pause*] Another thing, Willie, while we are on this subject. [*pause*] The sadness after song. [*pause*] Have you run across that, Willie? [*pause*] In the course of your experience. [*pause*] No? [*pause*] Sadness after intimate sexual intercourse one is familiar with, of course. [*pause*] You would concur with Aristotle there, Willie, I fancy. [*pause*] Yes, that one knows and is prepared to face. [*pause*] But after song . . . [*pause*] It does not last, of course. [*pause*] That is what I find so wonderful. [*pause*] It wears away. [*pause*] What are those exquisite lines? [*pause*] Go forget me why should something o'er that some-thing shadow fling . . . go forget me . . .why should sorrow . . . brightly smile . . . go forget me . . . never hear me . . . sweetly smile . . . brightly sing . . . [*Pause. With a sigh.*] One loses one's classics. [*pause*] Oh not all. [*pause*] A part. [*pause*] A part remains. [*pause*] That is what I find so wonderful, a part remains, of one's classics, to help one through the day. [*pause*] Oh yes, many mercies, many mercies. [*pause*] And now? [*pause*] And now, Willie? [*long pause*] I call to the eye of the mind . . . Mr. Shower—or Cooker. [*She closes her eyes. Bell rings loudly. She opens her eyes. Pause.*] Hand in hand, in the other hands bags. [*pause*] Getting on . . . in life. [*pause*] No longer young, not yet old. [*pause*] Standing there gaping at me. [*pause*] Can't have been a bad bosom, he says, in its day. [*pause*] Seen worse shoulders, he says, in my time. [*pause*] Does she feel her legs? he says. [*pause*] Is there any life in her legs? he says. [*pause*] Has she anything on underneath? he says. [*pause*] Ask her, he says, I'm shy. [*pause*] Ask her what? she says. [*pause*] Is there any life in her legs. [*pause*] Has she anything on underneath. [*pause*] Ask her yourself, she says. [*Pause. With sudden violence.*] Let go of me for Christ sake and drop! [*Pause. Do.*] Drop dead! [*smile*] But no. [*smile broader*] No no. [*smile off*] I watch them recede. [*pause*] Hand in hand—and the bags. [*pause*] Dim. [*pause*] Then gone. [*pause*] Last human kind—to stray this way. [*pause*] Up to date. [*pause*] And now? [*Pause. Low.*] Help. [*Pause. Do.*] Help, Willie. [*Pause. Do.*] No? [*Long pause. Narrative.*] Suddenly a mouse . . . [*pause*] Suddenly a mouse ran up her little thigh and Mildred, dropping Dolly in her fright, began to scream—[WINNIE *gives a sudden piercing scream.*]—and screamed and screamed—[WINNIE *screams twice.*]—screamed and screamed and screamed and screamed till all came running, in their night attire, papa, mamma, Bibby and . . . old Annie, to see what was the matter . . . [*pause*] . . . what on earth could possibly be the matter. [*pause*] Too late. [*pause*] Too late. [*Long pause. Just audible.*] Willie. [*Pause. Normal voice.*] Ah well, not long now, Winnie, can't be long now, until the bell for sleep. [*pause*] Then you may close your eyes, then you must close your eyes—and keep them closed. [*pause*] Why say that again? [*pause*] I used to think . . . [*pause*] . . . I say I used to think there was no difference between one fraction of a second and the next. [*pause*] I used to say . . . [*pause*] . . . I say I used to say, Winnie, you are changeless, there is never any difference between one fraction of a second and the next. [*pause*] Why bring that up again? [*pause*] There is so little one can bring up, one brings up all. [*pause*] All one can. [*pause*] My neck is hurting me! [*pause*] Ah that's better. [*with mild irritation*] Everything within reason. [*long pause*] I can do no more. [*pause*] Say no more. [*pause*] But I must say more. [*pause*] Problem here. [*pause*] No, something must move, in the world, I can't any more. [*pause*] A zephyr. [*pause*] A breath. [*pause*] What are those immortal lines? [*pause*] It might be the eternal dark. [*pause*] Black night without end. [*pause*] Just chance, I take it, happy chance. [*pause*] Oh yes, abounding mercies. [*long pause*] And now? [*pause*] And now, Willie? [*long pause*] That day. [*pause*] The pink fizz. [*pause*] The flute glasses. [*pause*]

The last guest gone. [*pause*] The last bumper with the bodies nearly touching. [*pause*] The look. [*long pause*] I hear cries. [*pause*] Sing. [*pause*] Sing your old song, Winnie. [*Long pause. Suddenly alert expression. Eyes switch right.* WILLIE*'s head appears to her right round corner of mound. He is on all fours, dressed to kill—top hat, morning coat, striped trousers, etc., white gloves in hand. Very long bushy white Battle of Britain moustache. He halts, gazes front, smoothes moustache. He emerges completely from behind mound, turns to his left, halts, looks up at* WIN-NIE*. He advances on all fours towards centre, halts, turns head front, gazes front, strokes moustache, straightens tie, adjusts hat, advances a little further, halts, takes off hat and looks up at* WINNIE*. He is now not far from centre and within her field of vision. Unable to sustain effort of looking up he sinks head to ground.*]

WINNIE: [*mondaine*] Well this is an unexpected pleasure! [*pause*] Reminds me of the day you came whining for my hand. [*pause*] I worship you, Winnie, be mine. [*He looks up.*] Life a mockery without Win. [*She goes off into a giggle.*] What a getup, you do look a sight! [*giggles*] Where are the flowers? [*pause*] That smile today. [WILLIE *sinks head.*] What's that on your neck, an anthrax? [*pause*] Want to watch that, Willie, before it gets a hold on you. [*pause*] Where were you all this time? [*pause*] What were you doing all this time? [*pause*] Changing? [*pause*] Did you not hear me screaming for you? [*pause*] Did you get stuck in your hole? [*Pause. He looks up.*] That's right, Willie, look at me. [*pause*] Feast your old eyes, Willie. [*pause*] Does anything remain? [*pause*] Any remains? [*pause*] No? [*pause*] I haven't been able to look after it, you know. [*He sinks his head.*] You are still recognizable, in a way. [*pause*] Are you thinking of coming to live this side now . . . for a bit maybe? [*pause*] No? [*pause*] Just a brief call? [*pause*] Have you gone deaf, Willie? [*pause*] Dumb? [*pause*] Oh I know you were never one to talk, I worship you Winnie be mine and then nothing from that day forth only tidbits from *Reynold's News*. [*Eyes front. Pause.*] Ah well, what matter, that's what I always say, it will have been a happy day, after all, another happy day. [*pause*] Not long now, Winnie. [*pause*] I hear cries. [*pause*] Do you ever hear cries, Willie? [*pause*] No? [*Eyes back on* WILLIE.] [*pause*] Look at me again, Willie. [*pause*] Once more, Willie. [*He looks up. Happily.*] Ah! [*Pause. Shocked.*] What ails you, Willie, I never saw such an expression! [*pause*] Put on your hat, dear, it's the sun, don't stand on ceremony, I won't mind. [*He drops hat and gloves and starts to crawl up mound towards her. Gleeful.*] Oh I say, this is terrific! [*He halts, clinging to mound with one hand, reaching up with the other.*] Come on, dear, put a bit of jizz into it, I'll cheer you on. [*pause*] Is it me you're after, Willie . . . or is it something else? [*pause*] Do you want to touch my face . . . again? [*pause*] Is it a kiss you're after, Willie . . . or is it something else? [*pause*] There was a time when I could have given you a hand. [*pause*] And then a time before that when I did give you a hand. [*pause*] You were always in dire need of a hand, Willie. [*He slithers back to foot of mound and lies with face to ground.*] Brrum! [*Pause. He rises to hands and knees, raises his face towards her.*] Have another go, Willie, I'll cheer you on. [*pause*] Don't look at me like that! [*Pause. Vehement.*] Don't look at me like that! [*Pause. Low.*] Have you gone off your head, Willie? [*Pause. Do.*] Out of your poor old wits, Willie?

[*pause*]

WILLIE: [*just audible*] Win.

[*Pause.* WINNIE*'s eyes front. Happy expression appears, grows.*]

WINNIE: Win! [*pause*] Oh this is a happy day, this will have been another happy day! [*pause*] After all. [*pause*] So far.

[*Pause. She hums tentatively beginning of song, then sings softly, musical box tune.*]

Though I say not
What I may not
Let you hear,
Yet the swaying
Dance is saying,
Love me dear!
Every touch of fingers
Tells me what I know,
Says for you,
It's true, it's true,
You love me so!

[*Pause. Happy expression off. She closes her eyes. Bell rings loudly. She opens her eyes. She smiles, gazing front. She turns her eyes, smiling, to* WILLIE, *still on his hands and knees looking up at her. Smile off. They look at each other. Long pause.*]

CURTAIN

Ma Rainey's Black Bottom (1984)

MA RAINEY'S BLACK BOTTOM was the first in a cycle of plays that August Wilson set out to write, one play for each decade, about the black experience in twentieth-century America. Set in Chicago in 1927, the action of *Ma Rainey's Black Bottom* is confined to a recording studio where white managers have arranged to record Ma Rainey, queen of the blues, and her band. As the play develops, it becomes clear that the white managers have little respect for the black musicians or their music. Rather, they are interested primarily in exploiting the blacks and seek to dictate both what is to be recorded and how it is to be done. All of the musicians in the band, except for the newcomer Levee, are used to doing what they are told in order to avoid stirring up trouble. But Ma Rainey recognizes that she also has an important weapon, for although the white managers may not respect her, they cannot proceed without her cooperation. Through small demands (for a soft drink, that her nephew introduce her song—even though he has a persistent stutter, threats to walk out), she gradually establishes her power and is able to maintain the integrity of her music, even though what she eventually does is quite contrary to what the white managers had planned.

All might have concluded peaceably were it not for Levee, who has little respect for Ma Rainey's music and has reached a tentative agreement with the white managers to follow his advice on today's recording, as well as to record some of Levee's own music, which he considers a great improvement over the blues popular at the time. When it becomes clear to the managers that Levee is both out of favor with Ma Rainey and a potential troublemaker, they back out of their promise to him. His disappointment and frustration lead Levee to provoke a fight with one of the band members, whom he stabs to death.

The relationship between whites and blacks in the play is symbolic of that in the larger society outside the recording studio. Virtually powerless, blacks like Ma Rainey have learned to defend their integrity in subtle and roundabout ways. But as the relationship between Levee and the other musicians indicates, not all have that ability, and the price they pay is high.

Wilson went on to write several other plays, two of which (*Fences* and *The Piano Lesson*) won Pulitzer Prizes. He is now considered one of America's major playwrights and a leader in seeking better opportunities for blacks in the theatre.

Ma Rainey's Black Bottom

Characters

STURDYVANT, *studio owner*
IRVIN, *Ma Rainey's manager*
CUTLER, *guitar and trombone player*
TOLEDO, *piano player*
SLOW DRAG, *bass player*
LEVEE, *trumpet player*
MA RAINEY, *blues singer*
POLICEMAN
DUSSIE MAE, *Ma Rainey's companion*
SYLVESTER, *Ma Rainey's nephew*

> *They tore the railroad down*
> *so the Sunshine Special can't run*
> *I'm going away baby*
> *build me a railroad of my own*
> —Blind Lemon Jefferson

THE SETTING

There are two playing areas: what is called the "band room," and the recording studio. The band room is at stage left and is in the basement of the building. It is entered through a door up left. There are benches and chairs scattered about, a piano, a row of lockers, and miscellaneous paraphernalia stacked in a corner and long since forgotten. A mirror hangs on a wall with various posters.

The studio is upstairs at stage right, and resembles a recording studio of the late 1920s. The entrance is from a hall on the right wall. A small control booth is at the rear and its access is gained by means of a spiral staircase. Against one wall there is a line of chairs, and a horn through which the control room communicates with the performers. A door in the rear wall allows access to the band room.

THE PLAY

It is early March in Chicago, 1927. There is a bit of a chill in the air. Winter has broken but the wind coming off the lake does not carry the promise of spring. The people of the city are bundled and brisk in their defense against such misfortunes as the weather, and the business of the city proceeds largely undisturbed.

Chicago in 1927 is a rough city, a bruising city, a city of millionaires and derelicts, gangsters and roughhouse dandies, whores and Irish grandmothers who move through its streets fingering long black rosaries. Somewhere a man is wrestling with the taste of a woman in his cheek. Somewhere a dog is barking. Somewhere the moon has fallen through a window and broken into thirty pieces of silver.

It is one o'clock in the afternoon. Secretaries are returning from their lunch, the noon Mass at St. Anthony's is over, and the priest is mumbling over his vestments while the altar boys practice their Latin. The procession of cattle cars through the stockyards continues unabated. The busboys in Mac's Place are cleaning away the last of the corned beef and cabbage, and on the city's Southside, sleepy-eyed negroes move lazily toward their small cold-water flats and rented rooms to await the onslaught of night, which will find them crowded in the bars and juke joints both dazed and dazzling in their rapport with life. It is with these negroes that our concern lies most heavily: their values, their attitudes, and particularly their music.

It is hard to define this music. Suffice it to say that it is music that breathes and touches. That connects. That is in itself a way of being, separate and distinct from any other. This music is called blues. Whether this music came from Alabama or Mississippi or other parts of the South doesn't matter anymore. The men and women who make this music have learned it from the narrow crooked streets of East St. Louis, or the streets of the city's Southside, and the Alabama or Mississippi roots have been strangled by the northern manners and customs of free men of definite and sincere worth, men for whom this music often lies at the forefront of their conscience and concerns. Thus they are laid open to be consumed by it; its warmth and redress, its braggadocio and roughly poignant comments, its vision and prayer, which would instruct and allow them to reconnect, to reassemble and gird up for the next battle in which they would be both victim and the ten thousand slain.

ACT 1

The lights come up in the studio. IRVIN *enters, carrying a microphone. He is a tall, fleshy man who prides himself on his knowledge of blacks and his ability to deal with them. He hooks up the microphone, blows into it, taps it, etc. He crosses over to the piano, opens it, and fingers a few keys.* STURDYVANT *is visible in the control booth. Preoccupied with money, he is insensitive to black performers and prefers to deal with them at arm's length. He puts on a pair of earphones.*

STURDYVANT: [*Over speaker*] Irv . . . let's crack that mike, huh? Let's do a check on it.

IRVIN: [*Crosses to mike, speaks into it*] Testing . . . one . . . two . . . three . . .
> [*There is a loud feedback.* STURDYVANT *fiddles with the dials.*]
> Testing . . . one . . . two . . . three . . . testing. How's that Mel?
> [STURDYVANT *doesn't respond.*]
> Testing . . . one . . . two . . .

STURDYVANT: [*Taking off the earphones*] Okay . . . that checks. We got a good reading.
> [*Pause.*] You got that list, Irv?

IRVIN: Yeah . . . yeah, I got it. Don't worry about nothing.

STURDYVANT: Listen, Irv . . . you keep her in line, okay? I'm holding you responsible for her . . . If she starts any of her . . .

IRVIN: Mel, what's with the goddamn horn? You wanna talk to me . . . okay! I can't talk to you over the goddamn horn . . . Christ!

STURDYVANT: I'm not putting up with any shenanigans. You hear, Irv?
> [IRVIN *crosses over to the piano and mindlessly runs his fingers over the keys.*]

I'm just not gonna stand for it. I want you to keep her in line. Irv?

[STURDYVANT *enters from the control booth.*]

Listen, Irv . . . you're her manager . . . she's your responsibility . . .

IRVIN: Okay, okay, Mel . . . let me handle it.

STURDYVANT: She's your responsibility. I'm not putting up with any Royal Highness . . . Queen of the Blues bullshit!

IRVIN: Mother of the Blues, Mel. Mother of the Blues.

STURDYVANT: I don't care what she calls herself. I'm not putting up with it. I just want to get her in here . . . record those songs on that list . . . and get her out. Just like clockwork, huh?

IRVIN: Like clockwork, Mel. You just stay out of the way and let me handle it.

STURDYVANT: Yeah . . . yeah . . . You handled it last time. Remember? She marches in here like she owns the damn place . . . doesn't like the songs we picked out . . . says her throat is sore . . . doesn't want to do more than one take . . .

IRVIN: Okay . . . okay . . . I was here! I know all about it.

STURDYVANT: Complains about the building being cold . . . and then . . . trips over the mike wire and threatens to sue me. That's taking care of it?

IRVIN: I've got it all worked out this time. I talked with her last night. Her throat is fine . . . We went over the songs together . . . I got everything straight, Mel.

STURDYVANT: Irv, that horn player . . . the one who gave me those songs . . . is he gonna be here today? Good. I want to hear more of that sound. Times are changing. This is a tricky business now. We've got to jazz it up . . . put in something different. You know, something wild . . . with a lot of rhythm. [*Pause.*] You know what we put out last time, Irv? We put out garbage last time. It was garbage. I don't even know why I bother with this anymore.

IRVIN: You did all right last time, Mel. Not as good as you did before, but you did all right.

STURDYVANT: You know how many records we sold in New York? You wanna see the sheet? And you know what's in New York, Irv? Harlem. Harlem's in New York, Irv.

IRVIN: Okay, so they didn't sell in New York. But look at Memphis . . . Birmingham . . . Atlanta. Christ, you made a bundle.

STURDYVANT: It's not the money, Irv. You know I couldn't sleep last night? This business is bad for my nerves. My wife is after me to slow down and take a vacation. Two more years and I'm gonna get out . . . get into something respectable. Textiles. That's a respectable business. You know what you could do with a shipload of textiles from Ireland?

[*A buzzer is heard offstage.*]

IRVIN: Why don't you go upstairs and let me handle it, Mel?

STURDYVANT: Remember . . . you're responsible for her.

> [STURDYVANT *exits to the control booth.* IRVIN *crosses to get the door.* CUTLER, SLOW DRAG, *and* TOLEDO *enter.* CUTLER *is in his mid-fifties, as are most of the others. He plays guitar and trombone and is the leader of the group, possibly because he is the most sensible. His playing is solid and almost totally unembellished. His understanding of his music is limited to the chord he is playing at the time he is playing it. He has all the qualities of a loner except the introspection.* SLOW DRAG, *the bass player, is perhaps the one most bored by life. He resembles* CUTLER, *but lacks* CUTLER's *energy. He is deceptively intelligent, though, as his name implies, he appears to be slow. He is a rather large man with a wicked smile. Innate African rhythms underlie everything he plays, and he plays with an ease that is at times startling.* TOLEDO *is the piano player. In control of his instrument, he understands and recognizes that its limitations are an extension of himself. He is the only one in the group*

who can read. He is self-taught but misunderstands and misapplies his knowledge, though he is quick to penetrate to the core of a situation and his insights are thought-provoking. All of the men are dressed in a style of clothing befitting the members of a successful band of the era.]

IRVIN: How you boys doing, Cutler? Come on in. [*Pause.*] Where's Ma? Is she with you?

CUTLER: I don't know, Mr. Irvin. She told us to be here at one o'clock. That's all I know.

IRVIN: Where's . . . huh . . . the horn player? Is he coming with Ma?

CUTLER: Levee's supposed to be here same as we is. I reckon he'll be here in a minute. I can't rightly say.

IRVIN: Well, come on . . . I'll show you to the band room, let you get set up and rehearsed. You boys hungry? I'll call over to the deli and get some sandwiches. Get you fed and ready to make some music. Cutler . . . here's the list of songs we're gonna record.

STURDYVANT: [*Over speaker*] Irvin, what's happening? Where's Ma?

IRVIN: Everything under control, Mel. I got it under control.

STURDYVANT: Where's Ma? How come she isn't with the band?

IRVIN: She'll be here in a minute, Mel. Let me get these fellows down to the band room, huh?

> [*They exit the studio. The lights go down in the studio and up in the band room.* IRVIN *opens the door and allows them to pass as they enter.*]

You boys go ahead and rehearse. I'll let you know when Ma comes.

> [IRVIN *exits.* CUTLER *hands* TOLEDO *the list of songs.*]

CUTLER: What we got here, Toledo?

TOLEDO: [*Reading*] We got . . . "Prove It on Me" . . . "Hear Me Talking To You" . . . "Ma Rainey's Black Bottom" . . . and "Moonshine Blues."

CUTLER: Where Mr. Irvin go? Them ain't the songs Ma told me.

SLOW DRAG: I wouldn't worry about it if I were you, Cutler. They'll get it straightened out. Ma will get it straightened out.

CUTLER: I just don't want no trouble about these songs, that's all. Ma ain't told me them songs. She told me something else.

SLOW DRAG: What she tell you?

CUTLER: This "Moonshine Blues" wasn't in it. That's one of Bessie's songs.

TOLEDO: Slow Drag's right . . . I wouldn't worry about it. Let them straighten it up.

CUTLER: Levee know what time he supposed to be here?

SLOW DRAG: Levee gone out to spend your four dollars. He left the hotel this morning talking about he was gonna go buy some shoes. Say it's the first time he ever beat you shooting craps.

CUTLER: Do he know what time he supposed to be here? That's what I wanna know. I ain't thinking about no four dollars.

SLOW DRAG: Levee sure was thinking about it. That four dollars liked to burn a hole in his pocket.

CUTLER: Well, he's supposed to be here at one o'clock. That's what time Ma said. That nigger get out in the streets with that four dollars and ain't no telling when he's liable to show. You ought to have seen him at the club last night, Toledo. Trying to talk to some gal Ma had with her.

TOLEDO: You ain't got to tell me. I know how Levee do.

> [*Buzzer is heard offstage.*]

SLOW DRAG: Levee tried to talk to that gal and got his feelings hurt. She didn't want no part of him. She told Levee he'd have to turn his money green before he could talk with her.

CUTLER: She out for what she can get. Anybody could see that.

SLOW DRAG: That's why Levee run out to buy some shoes. He's looking to make an impression on that gal.

CUTLER: What the hell she gonna do with his shoes? She can't do nothing with the nigger's shoes.

[SLOW DRAG *takes out a pint bottle and drinks.*]

TOLEDO: Let me hit that, Slow Drag.

SLOW DRAG: [*Handing him the bottle*] This some of that good Chicago bourbon!

[*The door opens and* LEVEE *enters, carrying a shoe box. In his early thirties,* LEVEE *is younger than the other men. His flamboyance is sometimes subtle and sneaks up on you. His temper is rakish and bright. He lacks fuel for himself and is somewhat of a buffoon. But it is an intelligent buffoonery, clearly calculated to shift control of the situation to where he can grasp it. He plays trumpet. His voice is strident and totally dependent on his manipulation of breath. He plays wrong notes frequently. He often gets his skill and talent confused with each other.*]

CUTLER: Levee . . . where Mr. Irvin go?

LEVEE: Hell, I don't know. I ain't none of his keeper.

SLOW DRAG: What you got there, Levee?

LEVEE: Look here, Cutler . . . I got me some shoes!

CUTLER: Nigger, I ain't studying you.

[LEVEE *takes the shoes out of the box and starts to put them on.*]

TOLEDO: How much you pay for something like that, Levee?

LEVEE: Eleven dollars. Four dollars of it belong to Cutler.

SLOW DRAG: Levee say if it wasn't for Cutler . . . he wouldn't have no new shoes.

CUTLER: I ain't thinking about Levee or his shoes. Come on . . . let's get ready to rehearse.

SLOW DRAG: I'm with you on that score, Cutler. I wanna get out of here. I don't want to be around here all night. When it comes time to go up there and record them songs . . . I just wanna go up there and do it. Last time it took us all day and half the night.

TOLEDO: Ain't but four songs on the list. Last time we recorded six songs.

SLOW DRAG: It felt like it was sixteen!

LEVEE: [*Finishes with his shoes*] Yeah! Now I'm ready! I can play some good music now!

[*He goes to put up his old shoes and looks around the room.*]

Damn! They done changed things around. Don't never leave well enough alone.

TOLEDO: Everything changing all the time. Even the air you breathing change. You got, monoxide, hydrogen . . . changing all the time. Skin changing . . . different molecules and everything.

LEVEE: Nigger, what is you talking about? I'm talking about the room. I ain't talking about no skin and air. I'm talking about something I can see! Last time the band room was upstairs. This time it's downstairs. Next time it be over there. I'm talking about what I can see. I ain't talking about no molecules or nothing.

TOLEDO: Hell, I know what you talking about. I just said everything changin'. I know what you talking about, but you don't know what I'm talking about.

LEVEE: That door! Nigger, you see that door? That's what I'm talking about. That door wasn't there before.

CUTLER: Levee, you wouldn't know your right from your left. This is where they used to keep the recording horns and things . . . and damn if that door wasn't there. How in hell else you gonna get in here? Now, if you talking about they done switched rooms, you right. But don't go telling me that damn door wasn't there!

SLOW DRAG: Damn the door and let's get set up. I wanna get out of here.

LEVEE: Toledo started all that about the door. I'm just saying that things change.

TOLEDO: What the hell you think I was saying? Things change. The air and everything. Now you gonna say you was saying it. You gonna fit two propositions on the same track . . . run them into each other, and because they crash, you gonna say it's the same train.

LEVEE: Now this nigger talking about trains! We done went from the air to the skin to the door . . . and now trains. Toledo, I'd just like to be inside your head for five minutes. Just to see how you think. You done got more shit piled up and mixed up in there than the devil got sinners. You been reading too many goddamn books.

TOLEDO: What you care about how much I read? I'm gonna ignore you 'cause you ignorant.

[LEVEE *takes off his coat and hangs it in the locker.*]

SLOW DRAG: Come on, let's rehearse the music.

LEVEE: You ain't gotta rehearse that . . . ain't nothing but old jug-band music. They need one of them jug bands for this.

SLOW DRAG: Don't make me no difference. Long as we get paid.

LEVEE: That ain't what I'm talking about, nigger. I'm talking about art!

SLOW DRAG: What's drawing got to do with it?

LEVEE: Where you get this nigger from, Cutler? He sound like one of them Alabama niggers.

CUTLER: Slow Drag's all right. It's you talking all that weird shit about art. Just play the piece, nigger. You wanna be one of them . . . what you call . . . virtuoso or something, you in the wrong place. You ain't no Buddy Bolden or King Oliver . . . you just an old trumpet player come a dime a dozen. Talking about art.

LEVEE: What is you? I don't see your name in lights.

CUTLER: I just play the piece. Whatever they want. I don't go talking about art and criticizing other people's music.

LEVEE: I ain't like you, Cutler. I got talent! Me and this horn . . . we's tight. If my daddy knowed I was gonna turn out like this, he would've named me Gabriel. I'm gonna get me a band and make me some records. I done give Mr. Sturdyvant some of my songs I wrote and he say he's gonna let me record them when I get my band together. [*Takes some papers out of his pocket.*] I just gotta finish the last part of this song. And Mr. Sturdyvant want me to write another part to this song.

SLOW DRAG: How you learn to write music, Levee?

LEVEE: I just picked it up . . . like you pick up anything. Miss Eula used to play the piano . . . she learned me a lot. I knows how to play *real* music . . . not this old jug-band shit. I got style!

TOLEDO: Everybody got style. Style ain't nothing but keeping the same idea from beginning to end. Everybody got it.

LEVEE: But everybody can't play like I do. Everybody can't have their own band.

CUTLER: Well, until you get your own band where you can play what you want, you just play the piece and stop complaining. I told you when you came on here, this ain't none of them hot bands. This is an accompaniment band. You play Ma's music when you here.

LEVEE: I got sense enough to know that. Hell, I can look at you all and see what kind of band it is. I can look at Toledo and see what kind of band it is.

TOLEDO: Toledo ain't said nothing to you now. Don't let Toledo get started. You can't even spell music, much less play it.

LEVEE: What you talking about? I can spell music. I got a dollar say I can spell it! Put your dollar up. Where your dollar?

[TOLEDO *waves him away.*]

Now come on. Put your dollar up. Talking about I can't spell music.

[LEVEE *peels a dollar off his roll and slams it down on the bench beside* TOLEDO.]

TOLEDO: All right, I'm gonna show you. Cutler. Slow Drag. You hear this? The nigger betting me a dollar he can spell music. I don't want no shit now!

[TOLEDO *lays a dollar down besides* LEVEE's.]

All right. Go ahead. Spell it.

LEVEE: It's a bet then. Talking about I can't spell music.

TOLEDO: Go ahead, then. Spell it. Music. Spell it.

LEVEE: I can spell it, nigger! M-U-S-I-K. There!

> [*He reaches for the money.*]

TOLEDO: Naw! Naw! Leave the money alone! You ain't spelled it.

LEVEE: What you mean I ain't spelled it? I said M-U-S-I-K!

TOLEDO: That ain't how you spell it! That ain't how you spell it! It's M-U-S-I-C! C, nigger. Not K! C! M-U-S-I-C!

LEVEE: What you mean, C? Who say it's C?

TOLEDO: Cutler. Slow Drag. Tell this fool.

> [*They look at each other and then away.*]

> Well, I'll be a monkey's uncle!

> [TOLEDO *picks up the money and hands* LEVEE *his dollar back.*]

> Here's your dollar back, Levee. I done won it, you understand. I done won the dollar. But if don't nobody know but me, how am I gonna prove it to you?

LEVEE: You just mad 'cause I spelled it.

TOLEDO: Spelled what! M-U-S-I-K don't spell nothing. I just wish there was some way I could show you the right and wrong of it. How you gonna know something if the other fellow don't know if you're right or not? Now I can't even be sure that I'm spelling it right.

LEVEE: That's what I'm talking about. You don't know it. Talking about C. You ought to give me that dollar I won from you.

TOLEDO: All right. All right. I'm gonna show you how ridiculous you sound. You know the Lord's Prayer?

LEVEE: Why? You wanna bet a dollar on that?

TOLEDO: Just answer the question. Do you know the Lord's Prayer or don't you?

LEVEE: Yeah, I know it. What of it?

TOLEDO: Cutler?

CUTLER: What you Cutlering me for? I ain't got nothing to do with it.

TOLEDO: I just want to show the man how ridiculous he is.

CUTLER: Both of you all sound like damn fools. Arguing about something silly. Yeah, I know the Lord's Prayer. My daddy was a deacon in the church. Come asking me if I know the Lord's Prayer. Yeah, I know it.

TOLEDO: Slow Drag?

SLOW DRAG: Yeah.

TOLEDO: All right. Now I'm gonna tell you a story to show just how ridiculous he sound. There was these two fellows, see. So, the one of them go up to this church and commence to taking up the church learning. The other fellow see him out on the road and he say, "I done heard you taking up the church learning," say, "Is you learning anything up there?" The other one say, "Yeah, I done take up the church learning and I's learning all kinds of things about the Bible and what it say and all. Why you be asking?" The other one say, "Well, do you know the Lord's Prayer?" And he say "Why, sure I know the Lord's Prayer, I'm taking up learning at the church ain't I? I know the Lord's Prayer backwards and forewards." And the other fellow says, "I bet you five dollars you don't know the Lord's Prayer, 'cause I don't think you knows it. I think you be going up to the church 'cause the Widow Jenkins be going up there and you just wanna be sitting in the same room with her when she cross them big, fine, pretty legs she got." And the other one say, "Well, I'm gonna prove you wrong and I'm gonna bet you that five dollars." So he say, "Well, go on and say it then." So he commenced to saying the Lord's Prayer. He say, "Now I lay me down to sleep, I pray the Lord my soul to keep." The other one say, "Here's your five dollars. I didn't think you knew it."

[*They all laugh.*]

Now that's just how ridiculous Levee sound. Only 'cause I knowed how to spell music, I still got my dollar.

LEVEE: That don't prove nothing. What's that supposed to prove?

[TOLEDO *takes a newspaper out of his back pocket and begins to read.*]

TOLEDO: I'm through with it.

SLOW DRAG: Is you all gonna rehearse this music or ain't you?

[CUTLER *takes out some papers and starts to roll a reefer.*]

LEVEE: How many times you done played them songs? What you gotta rehearse for?

SLOW DRAG: This a recording session. I wanna get it right the first time and get on out of here.

CUTLER: Slow Drag's right. Let's go on and rehearse and get it over with.

LEVEE: You all go and rehearse, then. I got to finish this song for Mr. Sturdyvant.

CUTLER: Come on, Levee . . . I don't want no shit now. You rehearse like everybody else. You in the band like everybody else. Mr. Sturdyvant just gonna have to wait. You got to do that on your own time. This is the band's time.

LEVEE: Well, what is you doing? You sitting there rolling a reefer talking about let's rehearse. Toledo reading a newspaper. Hell, I'm ready if you wanna rehearse. I just say there ain't no point in it. Ma ain't here. What's the point in it?

CUTLER: Nigger, why you gotta complain all the time?

TOLEDO: Levee would complain if a gal ain't laid across his bed just right.

CUTLER: That's what I know. That's what I try to tell him just play the music and forget about it. It ain't no big thing.

TOLEDO: Levee ain't got an eye for that. He wants to tie on to some abstract component and sit down on the elemental.

LEVEE: This is get-on-Levee time, huh? Levee ain't said nothing except this some old jug-band music.

TOLEDO: Under the right circumstances you'd play anything. If you know music, then you play it. Straight on or off to the side. Ain't nothing abstract about it.

LEVEE: Toledo, you sound like you got a mouth full of marbles. You the only cracker-talking nigger I know.

TOLEDO: You ought to have learned yourself to read . . . then you'd understand the basic understanding of everything.

SLOW DRAG: Both of you all gonna drive me crazy with that philosophy bullshit. Cutler, give me a reefer.

CUTLER: Ain't you got some reefer? Where's your reefer? Why you all the time asking me?

SLOW DRAG: Cutler, how long I done known you? How long we been together? Twenty-two years. We been doing this together for twenty-two years. All up and down the back roads, the side roads, the front roads . . . We done played the juke joints, the whorehouses, the barn dances, and city sit-downs . . . I done lied for you and lied with you . . . We done laughed together, fought together, slept in the same bed together, done sucked on the same titty . . . and now you don't wanna give me no reefer.

CUTLER: You see this nigger trying to talk me out of my reefer, Toledo? Running all that about how long he done knowed me and how we done on the same titty. Nigger, you *still* ain't getting none of my reefer!

TOLEDO: That's African.

SLOW DRAG: What? What you talking about? What's African?

LEVEE: I know he ain't talking about me. You don't see me running around in no jungle with no bone between my nose.

TOLEDO: Levee, you worse than ignorant. You ignorant without a premise. [*Pauses.*] Now, what I was saying is what Slow Drag was doing is African. That's what you call an African conceptualization. That's when you name the gods or call on the ancestors to achieve whatever your desires are.

SLOW DRAG: Nigger, I ain't no African! I ain't doing no African nothing!

TOLEDO: Naming all those things you and Cutler done together is like trying to solicit some reefer based on a bond of kinship. That's African. An ancestral retention. Only you forgot the name of the gods.

SLOW DRAG: I ain't forgot nothing, I was telling the nigger how cheap he is. Don't come talking that African nonsense to me.

TOLEDO: You just like Levee. No eye for taking an abstract and fixing it to a specific. There's so much that goes on around you and you can't even see it.

CUTLER: Wait a minute . . . wait a minute. Toledo, now when this nigger . . . when an African do all them things you say and name all the gods and whatnot . . . then what happens?

TOLEDO: Depends on if the gods is sympathetic with his cause for which he is calling them with the right names. Then his success comes with the right proportion of his naming. That's the way that go.

CUTLER: [*Taking out a reefer*] Here, Slow Drag. Here's a reefer. You done talked yourself up on that one.

SLOW DRAG: Thank you. You ought to have done that in the first place and saved me all the aggravation.

CUTLER: What I wants to know is . . . what's the same titty we done sucked on. That's what I want to know.

SLOW DRAG: Oh, I just threw that in there to make it sound good.
    [*They all laugh.*]

CUTLER: Nigger, you ain't right.

SLOW DRAG: I knows it.

CUTLER: Well, come on . . . let's get it rehearsed. Time's wasting.
    [*The musicians pick up their instruments.*]
    Let's do it. "Ma Rainey's Black Bottom." One . . . two . . . you know what to do.
    [*They begin to play.* LEVEE *is playing something different. He stops.*]

LEVEE: Naw! Naw! We ain't doing it that way.
    [TOLEDO *stops playing, then* SLOW DRAG.]
    We doing my version. It say so right there on that piece of paper you got. Ask Toledo. That's what Mr. Irvin told me . . . say it's on the list he gave you.

CUTLER: Let me worry about what's on the list and what ain't on the list. How you gonna tell me what's on the list?

LEVEE: 'Cause I know what Mr. Irvin told me! Ask Toledo!

CUTLER: Let me worry about what's on the list. You just play the song I say.

LEVEE: What kind of sense it make to rehearse the wrong version of the song? That's what I wanna know. Why you wanna rehearse that version.

SLOW DRAG: You supposed to rehearse what you gonna play. That's the way they taught me. Now, *whatever* version we gonna play . . . let's go on and rehearse it.

LEVEE: That's what I'm trying to tell the man.

CUTLER: You trying to tell me what we is and ain't gonna play. And that ain't none of your business. Your business is to play what I say.

LEVEE: Oh, I see now. You done got jealous cause Mr. Irvin using my version. You done got jealous cause I proved I know something about music.

CUTLER: What the hell . . . nigger, you talk like a fool! What the hell I got to be jealous of you about? The day I get jealous of you I may as well lay down and die.

TOLEDO: Levee started all that 'cause he too lazy to rehearse. [*To* LEVEE.] You ought to just go on and play the song . . . What difference does it make?

LEVEE: Where's the paper? Look at the paper! Get the paper and look at it! See what it say. Gonna tell me I'm too lazy to rehearse.

CUTLER: We ain't talking about the paper. We talking about you understanding where you fit in when you around here. You just play what I say.

LEVEE: Look . . . I don't care what you play! All right? It don't matter to me. Mr. Irvin gonna straighten it up! I don't care what you play.

CUTLER: Thank you. [*Pauses.*] Let's play this "Hear Me Talking to You" till we find out what's happening with the "Black Bottom." Slow Drag, you sing Ma's part. [*Pauses.*] "Hear Me Talking to You." Let's do it. One . . . Two . . . You know what to do.

> [*They play.*]

SLOW DRAG: [*Singing*]

> *Rambling man makes no change in me*
> *I'm gonna ramble back to my used-to-be*
> *Ah, you hear me talking to you*
> *I don't bite my tongue*
> *You wants to be my man*
> *You got to fetch it with you when you come.*
>
> *Eve and Adam in the garden taking a chance*
> *Adam didn't take time to get his pants*
> *Ah, you hear me talking to you*
> *I don't bite my tongue*
> *You wants to be my man*
> *You got to fetch it with you when you come.*
>
> *Our old cat swallowed a ball of yarn*
> *When the kittens were born they had sweaters on*
> *Ah, you hear me talking to you*
> *I don't bite my tongue*
> *You wants to be my man*
> *You got to fetch it with you when you come.*

> [IRVIN *enters. The musicians stop playing.*]

IRVIN: Any of you boys know what's keeping Ma?

CUTLER: Can't say, Mr. Irvin. She'll be along directly, I reckon. I talked to her this morning, she say she'll be here in time to rehearse.

IRVIN: Well, you boys go ahead.

> [*He starts to exit.*]

CUTLER: Mr. Irvin, about these songs . . . Levee say . . .

IRVIN: Whatever's on the list, Cutler. You got that list I gave you?

CUTLER: Yessir, I got it right here.

IRVIN: Whatever's on there. Whatever that says.

CUTLER: I'm asking about this "Black Bottom" piece . . . Levee say . . .

IRVIN: Oh, it's on the list. "Ma Rainey's Black Bottom" on the list.

CUTLER: I know it's on the list. I wanna know what version. We got two versions of that song.

IRVIN: Oh, Levee's arrangement. We're using Levee's arrangement.

CUTLER: Ok. I got that straight. Now, this "Moonshine Blues" . . .

IRVIN: We'll work it out with Ma, Cutler. Just rehearse whatever's on the list and use Levee's arrangement on that "Black Bottom" piece.

> [*He exits.*]

LEVEE: See, I told you! It don't mean nothing when I say it. You got to wait for Mr. Irvin to say it. Well, I told you the way it is.

CUTLER: Levee, the sooner you understand it ain't what you say, or what Mr. Irvin say . . . it's what Ma say that counts.

SLOW DRAG: Don't nobody say when it come to Ma. She's gonna do what she wants to do. Ma says what happens with her.

LEVEE: Hell, the man's the one putting out the record! He's gonna put out what he wanna put out!

SLOW DRAG: He's gonna put out what Ma want him to put out.

LEVEE: You heard what the man told you . . . "Ma Rainey's Black Bottom," Levee's arrangement. There you go! That's what he told you.

SLOW DRAG: What you gonna do, Cutler?

CUTLER: Ma ain't told me what version. Let's go on and play it Levee's way.

TOLEDO: See, now . . . I'll tell you something. As long as the colored man look to white folks to put the crown on what he say . . . as long as he looks to white folks for approval . . . then he ain't never gonna find out who he is and what he's about. He's just gonna be about what white folks want him to be about. That's one sure thing.

LEVEE: I'm just trying to show Cutler where he's wrong.

CUTLER: Cutler don't need you to show him nothing.

SLOW DRAG: [*Irritated*] Come on, let's get this shit rehearsed! You all can bicker afterward!

CUTLER: Levee's confused about who the boss is. He don't know Ma's the boss.

LEVEE: Ma's the boss on the road! We at a recording session. Mr. Sturdyvant and Mr. Irvin say what's gonna be here! We's in Chicago, we ain't in Memphis! I don't know why you all wanna pick me about it, shit! I'm with Slow Drag . . . Let's go on and get it rehearsed.

CUTLER: All right. All right. I know how to solve this. "Ma Rainey's Black Bottom." Levee's version. Let's do it. Come on.

TOLEDO: How that first part go again, Levee?

LEVEE: It go like this. [*He plays.*] That's to get the people's attention to the song. That's when you and Slow Drag come in with the rhythm part. Me and Cutler play on the breaks. [*Becoming animated.*] Now we gonna dance it . . . but we ain't gonna countrify it. This ain't no barn dance. We gonna play it like . . .

CUTLER: The man ask you how the first part go. He don't wanna hear all that. Just tell him how the piece go.

TOLEDO: I got it. I got it. Let's go. I know how to do it.

CUTLER: "Ma Rainey's Black Bottom." One . . . two . . . You know what to do.

> [*They begin to play.* LEVEE *stops.*]

LEVEE: You all got to keep up now. You playing in the wrong time. Ma come in over the top. She got to find her own way in.

CUTLER: Nigger, will you let us play this song? When you get your own band . . . then you tell them that nonsense. We know how to play the piece. I was playing music before you was born. Gonna tell me how to play . . . All right. Let's try it again.

SLOW DRAG: Cutler, wait till I fix this. This string started to unravel. [*Playfully.*] And you know I want to play Levee's music right.

LEVEE: If you was any kind of musician, you'd take care of your instrument. Keep it in tip-top order. If you was any kind of musician, I'd let you be in my band.

SLOW DRAG: Shhheeeeet!

> [*He crosses to get his string and steps on* LEVEE's *shoes.*]

LEVEE: Damn, Slow Drag! Watch them big-ass shoes you got.

SLOW DRAG: Boy, ain't nobody done nothing to you.

LEVEE: You done stepped on my shoes.

SLOW DRAG: Move them the hell out the way, then. You was in my way . . . I wasn't in your way.

> [CUTLER *lights up another reefer.* SLOW DRAG *rummages around in his belongings for a string.* LEVEE *takes out a rag and begins to shine his shoes.*]

You can shine these when you get done, Levee.

CUTLER: If I had them shoes Levee got, I could buy me a whole suit of clothes.

LEVEE: What kind of difference it make what kind of shoes I got? Ain't nothing wrong with having nice shoes. I ain't said nothing about your shoes. Why you wanna talk about me and my Florsheims?

CUTLER: Any man who takes a whole week's pay and puts it on some shoes—you understand what I mean, what you walk around on the ground with—is a fool! And I don't mind telling you.

LEVEE: [*Irritated*] What difference it make to you, Cutler?

SLOW DRAG: The man ain't said nothing about your shoes. Ain't nothing wrong with having nice shoes. Look at Toledo.

TOLEDO: What about Toledo?

SLOW DRAG: I said ain't nothing wrong with having nice shoes.

LEVEE: Nigger got them clodhoppers! Old brogans! He ain't nothing but a sharecropper.

TOLEDO: You can make all the fun you want. It don't mean nothing. I'm satisfied with them and that's what counts.

LEVEE: Nigger, why don't you get some decent shoes? Got nerve to put on a suit and tie with them farming boots.

CUTLER: What you just tell me? It don't make no difference about the man's shoes. That's what you told me.

LEVEE: Aw, hell, I don't care what the nigger wear. I'll be honest with you. I don't care if he went barefoot. [SLOW DRAG *has put his string on the bass and is tuning it.*] Play something for me, Slow Drag. [*Slow Drag plays.*] A man got to have some shoes to dance like this! You can't dance like this with them clodhoppers Toledo got.

> [LEVEE *sings.*]

> *Hello Central give me Doctor Jazz*
> *He's got just what I need I'll say he has*
> *When the world goes wrong and I have got the blues*
> *He's the man who makes me get on my dancing shoes.*

TOLEDO: That's the trouble with colored folks . . . always wanna have a good time. Good times done got more niggers killed than God got ways to count. What the hell having a good time mean? That's what I wanna know.

LEVEE: Hell, nigger . . . it don't need explaining. Ain't you never had no good time before?

TOLEDO: The more niggers get killed having a good time, the more good times niggers wanna have.

> [SLOW DRAG *stops playing.*]

There's more to life than having a good time. If there ain't, then this is piss-poor life we're having . . . if that's all there is to be got out of it.

SLOW DRAG: Toledo, just 'cause you like to read them books and study and whatnot . . . that's your good time. People get other things they likes to do to have a good time. Ain't no need you picking them about it.

CUTLER: Niggers been having a good time before you was born, and they gonna keep having a good time after you gone.

TOLEDO: Yeah, but what else they gonna do? Ain't nobody talking about making the lot of the colored man better for him here in America.

LEVEE: Now you gonna be Booker T. Washington.

TOLEDO: Everybody worried about having a good time. Ain't nobody thinking about what kind of world they gonna leave their youngens. "Just give me the good time, that's all I want." It just makes me sick.

SLOW DRAG: Well, the colored man's gonna be all right. He got through slavery, and he'll get through whatever else the white man put on him. I ain't worried about that. Good times is what makes life worth living. Now, you take the white man . . . The white man don't know how to have a good time. That's why he's troubled all the time. He don't know how to have a good time. He don't know how to laugh at life.

LEVEE: That's what the problem is with Toledo . . . reading all them books and things. He done got to the point where he forgot how to laugh and have a good time. Just like the white man.

TOLEDO: I know how to have a good time as well as the next man. I said, there's got to be more to life than having a good time. I said the colored man ought to be doing more than just trying to have a good time all the time.

LEVEE: Well, what is you doing, nigger? Talking all them highfalutin ideas about making a better world for the colored man. What is you doing to make it better? You playing the music and looking for your next piece of pussy same as we is. What is you doing? That's what I wanna know. Tell him, Cutler.

CUTLER: You all leave Cutler out of this. Cutler ain't got nothing to do with it.

TOLEDO: Levee, you just about the most ignorant nigger I know. Sometimes I wonder why I ever bother to try and talk with you.

LEVEE: Well, what is you doing? Talking that shit to me about I'm ignorant! What is you doing? You just a whole lot of mouth. A great big windbag. Thinking you smarter than everybody else. What is you doing, huh?

TOLEDO: It ain't just me, fool! It's everybody! What you think . . . I'm gonna solve the colored man's problems by myself? I said, we. You understand that? We. That's every living colored man in the world got to do his share. Got to do his part. I ain't talking about what I'm gonna do . . . or what you or Cutler or Slow Drag or anybody else. I'm talking about all of us together. What all of us is gonna do. That's what I'm talking about, nigger!

LEVEE: Well, why didn't you say that, then?

CUTLER: Toledo, I don't know why you waste your time on this fool.

TOLEDO: That's what I'm trying to figure out.

LEVEE: Now there go Cutler with his shit. Calling me a fool. You wasn't even in the conversation. Now you gonna take sides and call me a fool.

CUTLER: Hell, I was listening to the man. I got sense enough to know what he was saying. I could tell it straight back to you.

LEVEE: Well, you go on with it. But I'll tell you this . . . I ain't gonna be too many more of your fools. I'll tell you that. Now you put that in your pipe and smoke it.

CUTLER: Boy, ain't nobody studying you. Telling me what to put in my pipe. Who's you to tell me what to do?

LEVEE: All right, I ain't nobody. Don't pay me no mind. I ain't nobody.

TOLEDO: Levee, you ain't nothing but the devil.

LEVEE: There you go! That's who I am. I'm the devil. I ain't nothing but the devil.

CUTLER: I can see that. That's something you know about. You know all about the devil.

LEVEE: I ain't saying what I know. I know plenty. What you know about the devil? Telling me what I know. What you know?

SLOW DRAG: I know a man sold his soul to the devil.

LEVEE: There you go! That's the only thing I ask about the devil . . . to see him coming so I can sell him this one I got. 'Cause if there's a god up there, he done went to sleep.

SLOW DRAG: Sold his soul to the devil himself. Name of Eliza Cotter. Lived in Tuscaloosa County, Alabama. The devil came by and he done upped and sold him his soul.

CUTLER: How you know the man done sold his soul to the devil, nigger? You talking that old-woman foolishness.

SLOW DRAG: Everybody know. It wasn't no secret. He went around working for the devil and everybody knowed it. Carried him a bag . . . one of them carpetbags. Folks say he carried the devil's papers and whatnot where he put your fingerprint on the paper with blood.

LEVEE: Where he at now? That's what I want to know. He can put my whole handprint if he want to!

CUTLER: That's the damnedest thing I ever heard! Folks kill me with that talk.

TOLEDO: Oh, that's real enough, all right. Some folks go arm in arm with the devil, shoulder to shoulder, and talk to him all the time. That's real, ain't nothing wrong in believing that.

SLOW DRAG: That's what I'm saying. Eliza Cotter is one of them. All right. The man living up in an old shack on Ben Foster's place, shoeing mules and horses, making them charms and things in secret. He done hooked up with the devil, showed up one day all fancied out with just the finest clothes you ever seen on a colored man . . . dressed just like one of them crackers . . . and carrying this bag with them papers and things. All right. Had a pocketful of money, just living the life of a rich man. Ain't done no more work or nothing. Just had him a string of women he run around with and throw his money away on. Bought him a big fine house . . . Well, it wasn't all that big, but it did have one of them white picket fences around it. Used to hire a man once a week just to paint that fence. Messed around there and one of the fellows of them gals he was messing with got fixed on him wrong and Eliza killed him. And he laughed about it. Sheriff come and arrest him, and then let him go. And he went around in that town laughing about killing this fellow. Trial come up, and the judge cut him loose. He must have been in converse with the devil too . . . 'cause he cut him loose and give him a bottle of whiskey! Folks ask what done happened to make him change, and he'd tell them straight out he done sold his soul to the devil and ask them if they wanted to sell theirs 'cause he could arrange it for them. Preacher see him coming, used to cross on the other side of the road. He'd just stand there and laugh at the preacher and call him a fool to his face.

CUTLER: Well, whatever happened to this fellow? What come of him? A man who, as you say, done sold his soul to the devil is bound to come to a bad end.

TOLEDO: I don't know about that. The devil's strong. The devil ain't no pushover.

SLOW DRAG: Oh, the devil had him under his wing, all right. Took good care of him. He ain't wanted for nothing.

CUTLER: What happened to him? That's what I want to know.

SLOW DRAG: Last I heard, he headed north with that bag of his, handing out hundred-dollar bills on the spot to whoever wanted to sign on with the devil. That's what I hear tell of him.

CUTLER: That's a bunch of fool talk. I don't know how you fix your mouth to tell that story. I don't believe that.

SLOW DRAG: I ain't asking you to believe it. I'm just telling you the facts of it.

LEVEE: I sure wish I knew where he went. He wouldn't have to convince me long. Hell, I'd even help him sign people up.

CUTLER: Nigger, God's gonna strike you down with that blasphemy you talking.

LEVEE: Oh, shit! God don't mean nothing to me. Let him strike me! Here I am, standing right here. What you talking about he's gonna strike me? Here I am! Let him strike me! I ain't scared of him. Talking that stuff to me.

CUTLER: All right. You gonna be sorry. You gonna fix yourself to have bad luck. Ain't nothing gonna work for you.

[*Buzzer sounds offstage.*]

LEVEE: Bad luck? What I care about some bad luck? You talking simple. I ain't knowed nothing but bad luck all my life. Couldn't get no worse. What the hell I care about some bad luck? Hell, I eat it everyday for breakfast! You dumber than I thought you was . . . talking about bad luck.

CUTLER: All right, nigger, you'll see! Can't tell a fool nothing. You'll see!

IRVIN: [IRVIN *enters the studio, checks his watch, and calls down the stairs.*] Cutler . . . you boys' sandwiches are up here . . . Cutler?

CUTLER: Yessir, Mr. Irvin . . . be right there.

TOLEDO: I'll walk up there and get them.

[TOLEDO *exits. The lights go down in the band room and up in the studio.* IRVIN *paces back and forth in an agitated manner.* STURDYVANT *enters.*]

STURDYVANT: Irv, what's happening? Is she here yet? Was that her?

IRVIN: It's the sandwiches, Mel. I told you . . . I'll let you know when she comes, huh?

STURDYVANT: What's keeping her? Do you know what time it is? Have you looked at the clock? You told me she'd be here. You told me you'd take care of it.

IRVIN: Mel, for Chrissakes! What do you want from me? What do you want me to do?

STURDYVANT: Look what time it is, Irv. You told me she'd be here.

IRVIN: She'll be here, okay? I don't know what's keeping her. You know they're always late, Mel.

STURDYVANT: You should have went by the hotel and made sure she was on time. You should have taken care of this. That's what you told me, huh? "I'll take care of it."

IRVIN: Okay! Okay! I didn't go by the hotel! What do you want me to do? She'll be here, okay? The band's here . . . she'll be here.

STURDYVANT: Okay, Irv. I'll take your word. But if she doesn't come . . . if she doesn't come . . .

[STURDYANT *exits to the control booth as* TOLEDO *enters.*]

TOLEDO: Mr. Irvin . . . I come up to get the sandwiches.

IRVIN: Say . . . uh . . . look . . . one o'clock, right? She said one o'clock.

TOLEDO: That's what time she told us. Say be here at one o'clock.

IRVIN: Do you know what's keeping her? Do you know why she ain't here?

TOLEDO: I can't say, Mr Irvin. Told us one o'clock.

[*The buzzer sounds.* IRVIN *goes to the door. There is a flurry of commotion as* MA RAINEY *enters, followed closely by the* POLICEMAN, DUSSIE MAE, *and* SYLVESTER. MA RAINEY *is a short, heavy woman. She is dressed in a full-length fur coat with matching hat, an emerald-green dress, and several strands of pearls of varying lengths. Her hair is secured by a headband that matches her dress. Her manner is simple and direct, and she carries herself in a royal fashion.* DUSSIE MAE *is a young, dark-skinned woman whose greatest asset is the sensual energy which seems to flow from her. She is dressed in a fur jacket and a tight-fitting canary-yellow dress.* SYLVESTER *is an Arkansas country boy, the size of a fullback. He wears a new suit and coat, in which he is obviously uncomfortable. Most of the time, he stutters when he speaks.*]

MA RAINEY: Irvin . . . you better tell this man who I am! You better get him straight!

IRVIN: Ma, do you know what time it is? Do you have any idea? We've been waiting . . .

DUSSIE MAE: [*To* SYLVESTER] If you was watching where you was going . . .

SYLVESTER: I was watching . . . What you mean?

IRVIN: [*Notices* POLICEMAN] What's going on here? Officer, what's the matter?

MA RAINEY: Tell the man who he's messing with!

POLICEMAN : Do you know this lady?

MA RAINEY: Just tell the man who I am! That's all you gotta do.

POLICEMAN : Lady, will you let me talk, huh?

MA RAINEY: Tell the man who I am!

IRVIN: Wait a minute . . . wait a minute! Let me handle it. Ma, will you let me handle it?

MA RAINEY: Tell him who he's messing with!

IRVIN: Okay! Okay! Give me a chance! Officer, this is one of our recording artists . . . Ma Rainey.

MA RAINEY: Madame Rainey! Get it straight! Madame Rainey! Talking about taking me to jail!

IRVIN: Look, Ma . . . give me a chance, okay? Here . . . sit down. I'll take care of it. Officer, what's the problem?

DUSSIE MAE: [*To* SYLVESTER] It's all your fault.

SYLVESTER: I ain't done nothing . . . Ask Ma.

POLICEMAN: Well . . . when I walked up on the incident . . .

DUSSIE MAE: Sylvester wrecked Ma's car.

SYLVESTER: I d-d-did not! The m-m-man ran into me!

POLICEMAN: [*To* IRVIN] Look, buddy . . . if you want it in a nutshell, we got her charged with assault and battery.

MA RAINEY: Assault and what for what!

DUSSIE MAE: See . . . we was trying to get a cab . . . and so Ma . . .

MA RAINEY: Wait a minute! I'll tell you if you wanna know what happened. [*She points to* SYLVESTER] Now, that's Sylvester. That's my nephew. He was driving my car . . .

POLICEMAN: Lady, we don't know whose car he was driving.

MA RAINEY: That's my car!

DUSSIE MAE & SYLVESTER: That's Ma's car!

MA RAINEY: What you mean you don't know whose car it is? I bought and paid for that car.

POLICEMAN: That's what you say, lady . . . We still gotta check. [*To* IRVIN.] They hit a car on Market Street. The guy said the kid ran a stoplight.

SYLVESTER: What you mean? The man c-c-come around the corner and hit m-m-me!

POLICEMAN: While I was calling a paddy wagon to haul them to the station, they try to hop into a parked cab. The cabbie said he was waiting on a fare . . .

MA RAINEY: The man was just sitting there. Wasn't waiting for nobody. I don't know why he wanna tell that lie.

POLICEMAN: Look, lady . . . will you let me tell the story?

MA RAINEY: Go ahead and tell it then. But tell it right!

POLICEMAN: Like I say . . . she tries to get in this cab. The cabbies waiting on a fare. She starts creating a disturbance. The cabbie gets out to try to explain the situation to her . . . and she knocks him down.

DUSSIE MAE: She ain't hit him! He just fell!

SYLVESTER: He just s-s-s-slipped!

POLICEMAN: He claims she knocked him down. We got her charged with assault and battery.

MA RAINEY: If that don't beat all to hell. I ain't touched the man! The man was trying to reach around me to keep his car door closed. I opened the door and it hit him and he fell down. I ain't touched the man!

IRVIN: Okay. Okay . . . I got it straight now, Ma. You didn't touch him. All right? Officer, can I see you for a minute?

DUSSIE MAE: Ma was just trying to open the door.

SYLVESTER: He j-j-just got in t-t-the way!

MA RAINEY: Said he wasn't gonna haul no colored folks . . . if you want to know the truth of it.

IRVIN: Okay, Ma . . . I got it straight now . . . Officer?

> [IRVIN *pulls the* POLICEMAN *off to the side.*]

MA RAINEY: [*Noticing* TOLEDO] Toledo, Cutler and everybody here?

TOLEDO: Yeah, they down in the band room. What happened to your car?

STURDYVANT: [*Entering*] Irv, what's the problem? What's going on? Officer . . .

IRVIN: Mel, let me take care of it. I can handle it.

STURDYVANT: What's happening? What the hell's going on?

IRVIN: Let me handle it, Mel, huh?

> [STURDYVANT *crosses over to* MA RAINEY.]

STURDYVANT: What's going on, Ma. What'd you do?

MA RAINEY: Sturdyvant, get on away from me! That's the last thing I need . . . to go through some of your shit!

IRVIN: Mel, I'll take care of it. I'll explain it all to you. Let me handle it, huh?

> [STURDYVANT *reluctantly returns to the control booth.*]

POLICEMAN: Look, buddy, like I say . . . we got her charged with assault and battery . . . and the kid with threatening the cabbie.

SYLVESTER: I ain't done n-n-nothing!

MA RAINEY: You leave the boy out of it. He ain't done nothing. What's he supposed to have done?

POLICEMAN: He threatened the cabbie, lady! You just can't go around threatening people!

SYLVESTER: I ain't done nothing to him! He's the one talking about he g-g-gonna get a b-b-baseball bat on me! I just told him what I'd do with it. But I ain't done nothing 'cause he didn't get the b-b-bat!

IRVIN: [*Pulling the* POLICEMAN *aside.*] Officer . . . look here . . .

POLICEMAN: We was on our way down to the precinct . . . but I figured I'd do you a favor and bring her by here. I mean, if she's as important as she says she is . . .

IRVIN: [*Slides a bill from his pocket*] Look, Officer . . . I'm Madame Rainey's manager . . . It's good to meet you. [*He shakes the* POLICEMAN's *hand and passes him the bill.*] As soon as we're finished with the recording session, I'll personally stop by the precinct house and straighten up this misunderstanding.

POLICEMAN: Well . . . I guess that's all right. As long as someone is responsible for them.

> [*He pockets the bill and winks at* IRVIN.]

No need to come down . . . I'll take care of it myself. Of course, we wouldn't want nothing like this to happen again.

IRVIN: Don't worry, Officer . . . I'll take care of everything. Thanks for your help.

> [IRVIN *escorts the* POLICEMAN *to the door and returns. He crosses over to* MA RAINEY.]

Here, Ma . . . let me take your coat. [*To* SYLVESTER.] I don't believe I know you.

MA RAINEY: That's my nephew, Sylvester.

IRVIN: I'm very pleased to meet you. Here . . . you can give me your coat.

MA RAINEY: That there is Dussie Mae.

IRVIN: Hello . . .

> [DUSSIE MAE *hands* IRVIN *her coat.*]

Listen, Ma, just sit there and relax. The boys are in the band room rehearsing. You just sit and relax a minute.

MA RAINEY: I ain't for no sitting. I ain't never heard of such. Talking about taking me to jail. Irvin, call down there and see about my car.

IRVIN: Okay, Ma . . . I'll take care of it. You just relax.

> [IRVIN *exits with the coats.*]

MA RAINEY: Why you all keep it so cold in here? Sturdyvant try and pinch every penny he can. You all wanna make some records, you better put some heat on in here or give me back my coat.

IRVIN: [*Entering*] We got the heat turned up, Ma. It's warming up. It'll be warm in a minute.

DUSSIE MAE: [*Whispering to* MA RAINEY] Where's the bathroom?

MA RAINEY: It's in the back. Down the hall next to Sturdyvant's office. Come on, I'll show you where it is. Irvin, call down there and see about my car. I want my car fixed today.

IRVIN: I'll take care of everything, Ma.

> [*He notices* TOLEDO.]

Say . . . uh . . . uh . . .

TOLEDO: Toledo.

IRVIN: Yeah . . . Toledo. I got the sandwiches, you can take down to the rest of the boys. We'll be ready to go in a minute. Give you boys a chance to eat and then we'll be ready to go.

> [IRVIN *and* TOLEDO *exit. The lights go down in the studio and come up in the band room.*]

LEVEE: Slow Drag, you ever been to New Orleans?

SLOW DRAG: What's in New Orleans that I want?

LEVEE: How you call yourself a musician and ain't never been to New Orleans.

SLOW DRAG: You ever been to Fat Back, Arkansas? [*Pauses.*] All right, then. Ain't never been nothing in New Orleans that I couldn't get in Fat Back.

LEVEE: That's why you backwards. You just an old country boy talking about Fat Back, Arkansas, and New Orleans in the same breath.

CUTLER: I been to New Orleans. What about it?

LEVEE: You ever been to Lula White's?

CUTLER: Lula White's? I ain't never heard of it.

LEVEE: Man, they got some gals in there just won't wait! I seen a man get killed in there once. Got drunk and grabbed one of the gals wrong . . . I don't know what the matter of it was. But he grabbed her and she stuck a knife in him all the way up to the hilt. He ain't even fell. He just stood there and choked on his own blood. I was just asking Slow Drag 'cause I was gonna take him to Lula White's when we get down to New Orleans and show him a good time. Introduce him to one of them gals I know down there.

CUTLER: Slow Drag don't need you to find him no pussy. He can take care of his own self. Fact is . . . you better watch your gal when Slow Drag's around. They don't call him Slow Drag for nothing. [*He laughs.*] Tell him how you got your name Slow Drag.

SLOW DRAG: I ain't thinking about Levee.

CUTLER: Slow Drag break a woman's back when he dance. They had this contest one time in this little town called Bolingbroke about a hundred miles outside of Macon. We was playing for this dance and they was giving twenty dollars to the best slow draggers. Slow Drag looked over the competition, got down off the bandstand, grabbed hold of one of them gals, and stuck to her like a fly to jelly. Like wood to glue. Man had that gal whooping and hollering so . . . everybody stopped to watch. This fellow come in . . . this gal's fellow . . . and pulled a knife a foot long on Slow Drag. 'Member that, Slow Drag?

SLOW DRAG: Boy that mama was hot! The front of her dress was wet as a dishrag!

LEVEE: So what happened? What the man do?

CUTLER: Slow Drag ain't missed a stroke. The gal, she just look at her man with that sweet dizzy look in her eye. She ain't about to stop! Folks was clearing out, ducking and hiding under tables, figuring there's gonna be a fight. Slow Drag just looked over the gal's shoulder at the man and said, "Mister, if you'd quit hollering and wait a minute . . . you'll see I'm doing you a favor. I'm helping this gal win ten dollars so she can buy you a gold watch." The man just stood there and looked at him, all the while stroking that knife. Told Slow Drag, say, "All right, then, nigger. You just better make damn sure you win." That's when folks started calling him Slow Drag. The women got to hanging around him so bad after that, them fellows in that town ran us out of there.

[TOLEDO *enters, carrying a small cardboard box with the sandwiches.*]

LEVEE: Yeah . . . well, them gals in Lula White's will put a harness on his ass.

TOLEDO: Ma's up there. Some kind of commotion with the police.

CUTLER: Police? What the police up there for?

TOLEDO: I couldn't get it straight. Something about her car. They gone now . . . she's all right. Mr. Irvin sent some sandwiches.

[LEVEE *springs across the room.*]

LEVEE: Yeah, all right. What we got here?

[*He takes two sandwiches out of the box.*]

TOLEDO: What you doing grabbing two? There ain't but five in there . . . How you figure you get two?

LEVEE: 'Cause I grabbed them first. There's enough for everybody . . . What you talking about? It ain't like I'm taking food out of nobody's mouth.

CUTLER: That's all right. He can have mine too. I don't want none.

[LEVEE *starts toward the box to get another sandwich.*]

TOLEDO: Nigger, you better get out of here. Slow Drag, you want this?

SLOW DRAG: Naw, you can have it.

TOLEDO: With Levee around, you don't have to worry about no leftovers. I can see that.

LEVEE: What's the matter with you? Ain't you eating two sandwiches? Then why you wanna talk about me? Talking about there won't be no leftovers with Levee around. Look at your own self before you look at me.

TOLEDO: That's what you is. That's what we all is. A leftover from history. You see now, I'll show you.

LEVEE: Aw, shit . . . I done got the nigger started now.

TOLEDO: Now, I'm gonna show how this goes . . . where you just a leftover from history. Everybody come from different places in Africa, right? Come from different tribes and things. Soonawhile they began to make one big stew. You had the carrots, the peas, and potatoes and whatnot over here. And over there you had the meat, the nuts, the okra, corn . . . and then you mix it up and let it cook right through to get the flavors flowing together . . . then you got one thing. You got a stew.

Now you take and eat the stew. You take and make your history with that stew. All right, Now it's over. Your history's over and you done ate the stew. But you look around and you see some carrots over here, some potatoes over there. That stew's still there. You done made your history and it's still there. You can't eat it all. So what you got? You got some leftovers. That's what it is. You got leftovers and you can't do nothing with it. You already making you another history . . . cooking you another meal, and you don't need them leftovers no more. What to do?

See, we's the leftovers. The colored man is the leftovers. Now, what's the colored man gonna do with himself? That's what we waiting to find out. But first we gotta know we the leftovers. Now, who knows that? You find me a nigger that knows that and I'll turn any whichaway you want me to. I'll bend over for you. You ain't gonna find that. And that's what the problem is. The problem ain't with the white man. The white man knows you just a leftover. 'Cause he the one who done the eating and he know what he done ate. But we don't know that we been took and made history out of. Done went and filled the white man's belly and now he's full and tired and wants you to get out the way and let him be by himself. Now, I know what I'm talking about. And if you wanna find out, you just ask Mr. Irvin what he had for supper yesterday. And if he's an honest white man . . . which is asking for a whole heap of a lot . . . he'll tell you he done ate your black ass and if you please I'm full up with you . . . so go on and get off the plate and let me eat something else.

SLOW DRAG: What that mean? What's eating got to do with how the white man treat you? He don't treat you no different according to what he ate.

TOLEDO: I ain't said it had nothing to do with how he treat you.

CUTLER: The man's trying to tell you something, fool!

SLOW DRAG: What he trying to tell me? Ain't you here. Why you say he was trying to tell *me* something? Wasn't he trying to tell you too?

LEVEE: He was trying all right. He was trying a whole heap. I'll say that for him. But trying ain't worth a damn. I got lost right there trying to figure out who puts nuts in their stew.

SLOW DRAG: I knowed that before. My grandpappy used to put nuts in his stew. He and my grandmama both. That ain't nothing new.

TOLEDO: They put nuts in their stew all over Africa. But the stew they eat, and the stew your grandpappy made, and all the stew that you and me eat, and the stew Mr. Irvin eats . . . ain't in no way the same stew. That's the way that go. I'm through with it. That's the last you know me to ever try and explain something to you.

CUTLER: [*After a pause.*] Well, time's getting along . . . Come on, let's finish rehearsing.

LEVEE: [*Stretching out on a bench*] I don't feel like rehearsing. I ain't nothing but a left over. You go and rehearse with Toledo . . . He's gonna teach you how to make a stew.

SLOW DRAG: Cutler, what you gonna do? I don't want to be around here all day.

LEVEE: I know my part. You all go on and rehearse your part. You all need some rehearsal.

CUTLER: Come on, Levee, get up off your ass and rehearse the songs.

LEVEE: I already know them songs . . . What I wanna rehearse them for?

SLOW DRAG: You in the band, ain't you? You supposed to rehearse when the band rehearse.

TOLEDO: Levee think he the king of the barnyard. He thinks he's the only rooster know how to crow.

LEVEE: All right! All right! Come on, I'm gonna show you I know them songs. Come on, let's rehearse. I bet you the first one mess be Toledo. Come on . . . I wanna see if he know how to crow.

CUTLER: "Ma Rainey's Black Bottom," Levee's version. Let's do it.

> [*They begin to rehearse. The lights go down in the band room and up in the studio.* MA RAINEY *sits and takes off her shoe, rubs her feet.* DUSSIE MAE *wanders about looking at the studio.* SYLVESTER *is over by the piano.*]

MA RAINEY: [*Singing to herself*]

> *Oh, Lord, these dogs of mine*
> *They sure do worry me all the time*
> *The reason why I don't know*
> *Lord, I beg to be excused*
> *I can't wear me no sharp-toed shoes.*
> *I went for a walk*
> *I stopped to talk*
> *Oh, how my corns did bark.*

DUSSIE MAE: It feels kinda spooky in here. I ain't never been in no recording studio before. Where's the band at?

MA RAINEY: They off somewhere rehearsing. I don't know where Irvin went to. All this hurry up and he goes off back there with Sturdyvant. I know he better come on 'cause Ma ain't gonna be waiting. Come here . . . let me see that dress.

> [DUSSIE MAE *crosses over.* MA RAINEY *tugs at the dress around the waist, appraising the fit.*]

That dress looks nice. I'm gonna take you tomorrow and get you some more things before I take you down to Memphis. They got clothes up here you can't get in

Memphis. I want you to look nice for me. If you gonna travel with the show you got to look nice.

DUSSIE MAE: I need me some more shoes. These hurt my feet.

MA RAINEY: You get you some shoes that fit your feet. Don't you be messing around with no shoes that pinch your feet. Ma know something about bad feet. Hand me my slippers out my bag over yonder.

[DUSSIE MAE *brings the slippers.*]

DUSSIE MAE: I just want to get a pair of them yellow ones. About a half-size bigger.

MA RAINEY: We'll get you whatever you need. Sylvester, too . . . I'm gonna get him some more clothes. Sylvester, tuck your clothes in. Straighten them up and look nice. Look like a gentleman.

DUSSIE MAE: Look at Sylvester with that hat on.

MA RAINEY: Sylvester, take your hat off inside. Act like your mama taught you something. I know she taught you better than that.

[SYLVESTER *bangs on the piano.*]

Come on over here and leave that piano alone.

SYLVESTER: I ain't d-d-doing nothing to the p-p-piano. I'm just l-l-looking at it.

MA RAINEY: Well. Come on over here and sit down. As soon as Mr. Irvin comes back, I'll have him take you down and introduce you to the band.

[SYLVESTER *comes over.*]

He's gonna take you down there and introduce you in a minute . . . have Cutler show you how your part go. And when you get your money, you gonna send some of it home to your mama. Let her know you doing all right. Make her feel good to know you doing all right in the world.

[DUSSIE MAE *wanders about the studio and opens the door leading to the band room. The strains of* LEVEE's *version of "Ma Rainey's Black Bottom" can be heard.* IRVIN *enters.*]

IRVIN: Ma, I called down to the garage and checked on your car. It's just a scratch. They'll have it ready for you this afternoon. They're gonna send it over with one of their fellows.

MA RAINEY: They better have my car fixed right too. I ain't going for that. Brand-new car . . . they better fix it like new.

IRVIN: It was just a scratch on the fender, Ma . . . They'll take care of it . . . don't worry . . . they'll have it like new.

MA RAINEY: Irvin, what is that I hear? What is that the band's rehearsing? I know they ain't rehearsing Levee's "Black Bottom." I know I ain't hearing that?

IRVIN: Ma, listen . . . that's what I wanted to talk to you about. Levee's version of that song . . . it's got a nice arrangement . . . a nice horn intro . . . It really picks it up . . .

MA RAINEY: I ain't studying Levee nothing. I know what he done to that song and I don't like to sing it that way. I'm doing it the old way. That's why I brought my nephew to do the voice intro.

IRVIN: Ma, that's what the people want now. They want something they can dance to. Times are changing. Levee's arrangement gives the people what they want. It gets them excited . . . makes them forget about their troubles.

MA RAINEY: I don't care what you say, Irvin. Levee ain't messing up my song. If he got what the people want, let him take it somewhere else. I'm singing Ma Rainey's song. I ain't singing Levee's song. Now that's all there is to it. Carry my nephew on down there and introduce him to the band. I promised my sister I'd look out for him and he's gonna do the voice intro on the song my way.

IRVIN: Ma, we just figured that . . .

MA RAINEY: Who's this "we"? What you mean "we"? I ain't studying Levee nothing. Come talking this "we" stuff. Who's "we"?

IRVIN: Me and Sturdyvant. We decided that it would . . .

MA RAINEY: You decided, huh? I'm just a bump on the log. I'm gonna go which ever way the river drift. Is that it? You and Sturdyvant decided.

IRVIN: Ma, it was just that we thought it would be better.

MA RAINEY: I ain't got good sense. I don't know nothing about music. I don't know what's a good song and what ain't. You know more about my fans than I do.

IRVIN: It's not that, Ma. It would just be easier to do. It's more what the people want.

MA RAINEY: I'm gonna tell you something, Irvin . . . and you go on up there and tell Sturdyvant. What you all say don't count with me. You understand? Ma listens to her heart. Ma listens to the voice inside her. That's what counts with Ma. Now, you carry my nephew on down there . . . tell Cutler he's gonna do the voice intro on that "Black Bottom" song and that Levee ain't messing up my song with none of his music shit. Now, if that don't set right with you and Sturdyvant . . . then I can carry my black bottom on back down South to my tour, 'cause I don't like it up here no ways.

IRVIN: Okay, Ma . . . I don't care. I just thought . . .

MA RAINEY: Damn what you thought! What you look like telling me how to sing my song? This Levee and Sturdyvant nonsense . . . I ain't going for it! Sylvester, go on down there and introduce yourself. I'm through playing with Irvin.

SYLVESTER: Which way you go? Where they at?

MA RAINEY: Here . . . I'll carry you down there myself.

DUSSIE MAE: Can I go? I wanna see the band.

MA RAINEY: You stay your behind up here. Ain't no cause in you being down there. Come on, Sylvester.

IRVIN: Okay, Ma. Have it your way. We'll be ready to go in fifteen minutes.

MA RAINEY: We'll be ready to go when Madame says we're ready. That's the way it goes around here.

[MA RAINEY *and* SYLVESTER *exit. The lights go down in the studio and up in the band room.* MA RAINEY *enters with* SYLVESTER.]

Cutler, this here is my nephew Sylvester. He's gonna do that voice intro on the "Black Bottom" song using the old version.

LEVEE: What you talking about? Mr. Irvin says he's using my version. What you talking about?

MA RAINEY: Levee, I ain't studying you or Mr. Irvin. Cutler, get him straightened out on how to do his part. I ain't thinking about Levee. These folks done messed with the wrong person this day. Sylvester, Cutler gonna teach you your part. You go ahead and get it straight. Don't worry about what nobody else say.

[MA RAINEY *exits.*]

CUTLER: Well, come on in, boy. I'm Cutler. You got Slow Drag . . . Levee . . . and that's Toledo over there. Sylvester, huh?

SYLVESTER: Sylvester Brown.

LEVEE: I done wrote a version of that song what picks it up and sets it down in the people's lap! Now she come talking this! You don't need that old circus bullshit! I know what I'm talking about. You gonna mess up the song Cutler and you know it.

CUTLER: I ain't gonna mess up nothing. Ma say . . .

LEVEE: I don't care what Ma say! I'm talking about what the intro gonna do to the song. The peoples in the North ain't gonna buy all that tent-show nonsense. They wanna hear some music!

CUTLER: Nigger, I done told you time and again . . . you just in the band. You plays the piece . . . whatever they want! Ma says what to play! Not you! You ain't here to be doing no creating. Your job is to play whatever Ma says!

LEVEE: I might not play nothing! I might quit!

CUTLER: Nigger, don't nobody care if you quit. Whose heart you gonna break?

TOLEDO: Levee ain't gonna quit. He got to make some money to keep him in shoe polish.

LEVEE: I done told you all . . . you all don't know me. You don't know what I'll do.

CUTLER: I don't think nobody too much give a damn! Sylvester, here's the way your part go. The band plays the intro . . . I'll tell you where to come in. The band plays the intro and then you say, "All right, boys, you done seen the rest . . . Now I'm gonna show you the best. Ma Rainey's gonna show you her black bottom." You got that? [SYLVESTER *nods.*] Let me hear you say it one time.

SYLVESTER: "All right, boys, you done s-s-seen the rest n-n-now I'm gonna show you the best. M-m-m-m-m-m-ma Rainey's gonna s-s-show you her black b-b-bottom."

LEVEE: What kind of . . . All right, Cutler! Let me see you fix that! You straighten that out! You hear that shit, Slow Drag? How in the hell the boy gonna do the part and he can't even talk!

SYLVESTER: W-w-w-who's you to tell me what to do, nigger! This ain't your band! Ma tell me to d-d-d-do it and I'm gonna do it. You can go to hell, n-n-n-nigger!

LEVEE: B-b-b-boy, ain't nobody studying you. You go on and fix that one, Cutler. You fix that one and I'll . . . I'll shine your shoes for you. You go on and fix that one!

TOLEDO: You say you Ma's nephew, huh?

SYLVESTER: Yeah. So w-w-what that mean?

TOLEDO: Oh, I ain't mean nothing . . . I was just asking.

SLOW DRAG: Well, come on and let's rehearse so the boy can get it right.

LEVEE: I ain't rehearsing nothing! You just wait till I get my band. I'm gonna record that song and show you how it supposed to go!

CUTLER: We can do it without Levee. Let him sit on over there. Sylvester, you remember your part?

SYLVESTER: I remember it pretty g-g-g-good.

CUTLER: Well, come on, let's do it, then.

    [*The band begins to play.* LEVEE *sits and pouts.* STURDYVANT *enters the band room.*]

STURDYVANT: Good . . . you boys are rehearsing, I see.

LEVEE: [*Jumping up.*] Yessir! We rehearsing. We know them songs real good.

STURDYVANT: Good! Say, Levee, did you finish that song?

LEVEE: Yessir, Mr. Sturdyvant. I got it right here. I wrote that other part just like you say. It go like:

> *You can shake it, you can break it*
> *You can dance at any hall*
> *You can slide across the floor*
> *You'll never have to stall*
> *My jelly, my roll*
> *Sweet Mama, don't you let it fall.*

Then I put that part in there for the people to dance, like you say, for them to forget about their troubles.

STURDYVANT: Good! Good! I'll just take this. I wanna see you about your songs as soon as I get the chance.

LEVEE: Yessir! As soon as you get the chance, Mr. Sturdyvant.

    [STURDYVANT *exits.*]

CUTLER: You hear, Levee? You hear this nigger? "Yessuh, we's rehearsing, boss."

SLOW DRAG: I heard him. Seen him too. Shuffling them feet.

TOLEDO: Aw, Levee can't help it none. He's like all of us. Spooked up with the white man.

LEVEE: I'm spooked up with him, all right. You let one of them crackers fix on me wrong. I'll show you how spooked up I am with him.

TOLEDO: That's the trouble of it. You wouldn't know if he was fixed on you wrong or not. You so spooked up by him you ain't had the time to study him.

LEVEE: I studies the white man. I got him studied good. The first time one fixes on me wrong, I'm gonna let him know just how much I studied. Come telling me I'm spooked up with the white man. You let one of them mess with me, I'll show you how spooked up I am.

CUTLER: You talking out your hat. The man come in here, call you a boy, tell you to get up off your ass and rehearse, and you ain't had nothing to say to him, except "Yessir!"

LEVEE: I can say "yessir" to whoever I please. What you got to do with it? I know how to handle white folks. I been handling them for thirty-two years, and now you gonna tell me how to do it. Just 'cause I say "yessir" don't mean I'm spooked up with him. I know what I'm doing. Let me handle him my way.

CUTLER: Well, go on and handle it, then.

LEVEE: Toledo, you always messing with somebody! Always agitating somebody with that old philosophy bullshit you be talking. You stay out of my way about what I do and say. I'm my own person. Just let me alone.

TOLEDO: You right, Levee. I apologize. It ain't none of my business that you spooked up by the white man.

LEVEE: All right! See! That's the shit I'm talking about. You all back up and leave Levee alone.

SLOW DRAG: Aw, Levee, we was all just having fun. Toledo ain't said nothing about you he ain't said about me. You just taking it all wrong.

TOLEDO: I ain't meant nothing by it Levee. [*Pauses.*] Cutler, you ready to rehearse?

LEVEE: Levee got to be Levee! And he don't need nobody messing with him about the white man—cause you don't know nothing about me. You don't know Levee. You don't know nothing about what kind of blood I got! What kind of heart I got beating here! [*He pounds his chest.*] I was eight years old when I watched a gang of white mens come into my daddy's house and have to do with my mama any way they wanted. [*Pauses.*] We was living in Jefferson County, about eighty miles outside of Natchez. My daddy's name was Memphis . . . Memphis Lee Green . . . had him near fifty acres of good farming land. I'm talking about good land! Grow anything you want! He done gone off of shares and bought this land from Mr. Hallie's widow woman after he done passed on. Folks called him an uppity nigger 'cause he done saved and borrowed to where he could buy this land and be independent. [*Pauses.*] It was coming on planting time and my daddy went into Natchez to get him some seed and fertilizer. Called me, say, "Levee you the man of the house now. Take care of your mama while I'm gone." I wasn't but a little boy, eight years old. [*Pauses.*] My mama was frying up some chicken when them mens come in that house. Must have been eight or nine of them. She standing there frying that chicken and them mens come and took hold of her just like you take hold of a mule and make him do what you want. [*Pauses.*] There was my mama with a gang of white mens. She tried to fight them off, but I could see where it wasn't gonna do her any good, I didn't know what they were doing to her . . . but I figured whatever it was they may as well do to me too. My daddy had a knife that he kept around there for hunting and working and whatnot. I knew where he kept it and I went and got it.

I'm gonna show you how spooked up I was by the white man. I tried my damn-dest to cut one of them's throat! I hit him on the shoulder with it. He reached back and grabbed hold of that knife and whacked me across the chest with it.

[LEVEE *raises his shirt to show a long ugly scar.*]

That's what made them stop. They was scared I was gonna bleed to death. My mama wrapped a sheet around me and carried me two miles down to the Furlow place and they drove me up to Doc Albans. He was waiting on a calf to be born, and say he ain't had time to see me. They carried me up to Miss Etta, the midwife, and she fixed me up.

My daddy came back and acted like he done accepted the facts of what happened. But he got the names of them mens from mama. He found out who they was and then we announced we was moving out of that county. Said good-bye to everybody . . . all the neighbors. My daddy went and smiled in the face of one of them crackers who had been with my mama. Smiled in his face and sold him our land. We moved over with relations in Caldwell. He got us settled in and then he took off one day. I ain't never seen him since. He sneaked back, hiding up in the woods, laying to get them eight or nine men. [*Pauses.*] He got four of them before they got him. They tracked him down in the woods. Caught up with him and hung him and set him afire. [*Pauses.*] My daddy wasn't spooked up by the white man. No sir! And that taught me how to handle them. I seen my daddy go up and grin in this cracker's face . . . smile in his face and sell him his land. All the while he's planning how he's gonna get him and what he's gonna do to him. That taught me how to handle them. So you all just back up and leave Levee alone about the white man. I can smile and say yessir to whoever I please. I got time coming to me. You all just leave Levee alone about the white man.

[*There is a long pause.* SLOW DRAG *begins playing on the bass and sings.*]

SLOW DRAG: [*Singing*]

> *If I had my way*
> *If I had my way*
> *If I had my way*
> *I would tear this old building down.*

ACT 2

[*The lights come up in the studio. The musicians are setting up their instruments.* MA RAINEY *walks about shoeless, singing softly to herself.* LEVEE *stands near* DUSSIE MAE, *who hikes up her dress and crosses her leg.* CUTLER *speaks to* IRVIN *off to the side.*]

CUTLER: Mr. Irvin, I don't know what you gonna do. I ain't got nothing to do with it, but the boy can't do the part. He stutters. He can't get it right. He stutters right through it every time.

IRVIN: Christ! Okay. We'll . . . Shit! We'll just do it like we planned. We'll do Levee's version. I'll handle it, Cutler. Come on, let's go. I'll think of something.

[*He exits to the control booth.*]

MA RAINEY: [*Calling* CUTLER *over*] Levee's got his eyes in the wrong place. You better school him, Cutler.

CUTLER: Come on, Levee . . . let's get ready to play! Get your mind on your work!

IRVIN: [*Over speaker*] Okay, boys, we're gonna do "Moonshine Blues" first. "Moonshine Blues," Ma.

MA RAINEY: I ain't doing no "Moonshine" nothing. I'm doing the "Black Bottom" first. Come on, Sylvester. [*To* IRVIN.] Where's Sylvester's mike? You need a mike for Sylvester. Irvin . . . get him a mike.

IRVIN: Uh . . . Ma, the boys say he can't do it. We'll have to do Levee's version.

MA RAINEY: What you mean he can't do it? Who say he can't do it? What boys say he can't do it?

IRVIN: The band, Ma . . . the boys in the band.

MA RAINEY: What band? The band work for me! I say what goes! Cutler, what's he talking about? Levee, this some of your shit?

IRVIN: He stutters, Ma. They say he stutters.

MA RAINEY: I don't care if he do. I promised the boy he could do the part . . . and he's gonna do it! That's all there is to it. He don't stutter all the time. Get a microphone down here for him.

IRVIN: Ma, we don't have time. We can't . . .

MA RAINEY: If you wanna make a record, you gonna find time. I ain't playing with you, Irvin. I can walk out of here and go back to my tour. I got plenty fans. I don't need to go through all of this. Just go and get the boy a microphone.

[IRVIN *and* STURDYVANT *consult in the booth,* IRVIN *exits.*]

STURDYVANT: All right, Ma . . . we'll get him a microphone. But if he messes up . . . He's only getting one chance . . . The cost . . .

MA RAINEY: Damn the cost. You always talking about the cost. I make more money for this outfit than anybody else you got put together. If he messes up he'll just do it till he gets it right. Levee, I know you had something to do with this. You better watch yourself.

LEVEE: It was Cutler!

SYLVESTER: It was you! You the only one m-m-mad about it.

LEVEE: The boy stutter. He can't do the part. Everybody see that. I don't know why you want the boy to do the part no ways.

MA RAINEY: Well, can or can't . . . he's gonna do it! You ain't got nothing to do with it!

LEVEE: I don't care what you do! He can sing the whole goddamned song for all I care!

MA RAINEY: Well, all right. Thank you.

[IRVIN *enters with a microphone and hooks it up. He exits to the control booth.*]

MA RAINEY: Come on, Sylvester. You just stand here and hold your hands like I told you. Just remember the words and say them . . . That's all there is to it. Don't worry about messing up. If you mess up, we'll do it again. Now, let me hear you say it. Play for him, Cutler.

CUTLER: One . . . two . . . you know what to do.

[*The band begins to play and* SYLVESTER *curls his fingers and clasps his hands together in front of his chest, pulling in opposite directions as he says his lines.*]

SYLVESTER: "All right, boys, you d-d-done s-s-seen the best . . .

[LEVEE *stops playing.*]

Now I'm g-g-gonna show you the rest . . . Ma R-r-rainey's gonna show you her b-b-b-black b-b-b-bottom."

[*The rest of the band stops playing.*]

MA RAINEY: That's all right. That's real good. You take your time, you'll get it right.

STURDYVANT: [*Over speaker*] Listen, Ma . . . now, when you come in, don't wait so long to come in. Don't take so long on the intro, huh?

MA RAINEY: Sturdyvant, don't you go trying to tell me how to sing. You just take care of that up there and let me take care of this down here. Where's my Coke?

IRVIN: Okay, Ma. We're all set up to go up here. "Ma Rainey's Black Bottom," boys.

MA RAINEY: Where's my Coke? I need a Coke. You ain't got no Coke down here? Where's my Coke?

IRVIN: What's the matter, Ma? What's . . .

MA RAINEY: Where's my Coke? I need a Coca-Cola.

IRVIN: Uh . . . Ma, look, I forgot the Coke, huh? Let's do it without it, huh? Just this one song. What say, boys?

MA RAINEY: Damn what the band say! You know I don't sing nothing without my Coca-Cola!

STURDYVANT: We don't have any, Ma. There's no Coca-Cola here. We're all set up and we'll just go ahead and . . .

MA RAINEY: You supposed to have Coca-Cola. Irvin knew that. I ain't singing nothing without my Coca-Cola!

> [*She walks away from the mike, singing to herself.* STURDYVANT *enters from the control booth.*]

STURDYVANT: Now, just a minute here, Ma. You come in an hour late . . . we're way behind schedule as it is . . . the band is set up and ready to go . . . I'm burning my lights . . . I've turned up the heat . . . We're ready to make a record and what? You decide you want a Coca-Cola?

MA RAINEY: Sturdyvant, get out of my face.

> [IRVIN *enters.*]

Irvin . . . I told you keep him away from me.

IRVIN: Mel, I'll handle it.

STURDYVANT: I'm tired of her nonsense, Irv. I'm not gonna put up with this!

IRVIN: Let me handle it, Mel. I know how to handle her. [IRVIN *to* MA RAINEY.] Look, Ma . . . I'll call down to the deli and get you a Coke. But let's get started, huh? Sylvester's standing there ready to go . . . the band's set up . . . let's do this one song, huh?

MA RAINEY: If you too cheap to buy me a Coke, I'll buy my own. Slow Drag! Sylvester, go with Slow Drag and get me a Coca-Cola.

> [SLOW DRAG *comes over.*]

Slow Drag, walk down to that store on the corner and get me three bottles of Coca-Cola. Get out of my face, Irvin. You all just wait until I get my Coke. It ain't gonna kill you.

IRVIN: Okay, Ma. Get your Coke, for Chrissakes! Get your Coke!

> [IRVIN *and* STURDYVANT *exit into the hallway followed by* SLOW DRAG *and* SYLVESTER. TOLEDO, CUTLER, *and* LEVEE *head for the band room.*]

MA RAINEY: Cutler, come here a minute. I want to talk to you.

> [CUTLER *crosses over somewhat reluctantly.*]

What's all this about "the boys in the band say"? I tells you what to do. I says what the matter is with the band. I say who can and can't do what.

CUTLER: We just say 'cause the boy stutter . . .

MA RAINEY: I know he stutters. Don't you think I know he stutters. This is what's gonna help him.

CUTLER: Well, how can he do the part if he stutters? You want him to stutter through it? We just thought it be easier to go on and let Levee do it like we planned.

MA RAINEY: I don't care if he stutters or not! He's doing the part and I don't wanna hear any more of this shit about what the band says. And I want you to find somebody to replace Levee when we get to Memphis. Levee ain't nothing but trouble.

CUTLER: Levee's all right. He plays good music when he puts his mind to it. He knows how to write music too.

MA RAINEY: I don't care what he know. He ain't nothing but bad news. Find somebody else. I know it was his idea about who to say who can do what.

> [DUSSIE MAE *wanders over to where they are sitting.*]

Dussie Mae, go sit your behind down somewhere and quit flaunting yourself around.

DUSSIE MAE: I ain't doing nothing.

MA RAINEY: Well, just go on somewhere and stay out of the way.

CUTLER: I been meaning to ask you, Ma . . . about these songs. This "Moonshine Blues" . . . that's one of them songs Bessie Smith sang, I believes.

MA RAINEY: Bessie what? Ain't nobody thinking about Bessie. I taught Bessie. She ain't doing nothing but imitating me. What I care about Bessie? I don't care if she sell a million records. She got her people and I got mine. I don't care what nobody else do. Ma was the *first* and don't you forget it!

CUTLER: Ain't nobody said nothing about that. I just said that's the same song she sang.

MA RAINEY: I been doing this a long time. Ever since I was a little girl. I don't care what nobody else do. That's what gets me so mad with Irvin. White folks try to be put out with you all the time. Too cheap to buy me a Coca-Cola. I lets them know it, though. Ma don't stand for no shit. Wanna take my voice and trap it in them fancy boxes with all them buttons and dials . . . and then too cheap to buy me a Coca-Cola. And it don't cost but a nickle a bottle.

CUTLER: I knows what you mean about that.

MA RAINEY: They don't care nothing about me. All they want is my voice. Well, I done learned that, and they gonna treat me like I want to be treated no matter how much it hurt them. They back there now calling me all kinds of names . . . calling me everything but a child of god. But they can't do nothing else. They ain't got what they wanted yet. As soon as they get my voice down on them recording machines, then it's just like if I'd be some whore and they roll over and put their pants on. Ain't got no use for me then. I know what I'm talking about. You watch. Irvin right there with the rest of them. He don't care nothing about me either. He's been my manager for six years, always talking about sticking together, and the only time he had me in his house was to sing for some of his friends.

CUTLER: I know how they do.

MA RAINEY: If you colored and can make them some money, then you all right with them. Otherwise, you just a dog in the alley. I done made this company more money from my records than all other recording artists they got put together. And they wanna balk about how much this session is costing them.

CUTLER: I don't see where it's costing them all what they say.

MA RAINEY: It ain't! I don't pay that kind of talk no mind.

[*The lights go down on the studio and come up on the band room.* TOLEDO *sits reading a newspaper.* LEVEE *sings and hums his song.*]

LEVEE: [*Singing*]

You can shake it, you can break it
You can dance at any hall
You can slide across the floor
You'll never have to stall
My jelly, my roll,
Sweet Mama, don't you let it fall.

Wait till Sturdyvant hear me play that! I'm talking about some real music, Toledo! I'm talking about *real* music!

[*The door opens and* DUSSIE MAE *enters.*]

Hey, mama! Come on in.

DUSSIE MAE: Oh, hi! I just wanted to see what it looks like down here.

LEVEE: Well, come on in . . . I don't bite.

DUSSIE MAE: I didn't know you could really write music. I thought you was just jiving me at the club last night.

LEVEE: Naw, baby . . . I knows how to write music. I done give Mr. Sturdyvant some of my songs and he says he's gonna let me record them. Ask Toledo. I'm gonna have my own band! Toledo, ain't I give Mr. Sturdyvant some of my songs I wrote?

TOLEDO: Don't get Toledo mixed up in nothing.

[*He exits.*]

DUSSIE MAE: You gonna get your own band sure enough?

LEVEE: That's right! Levee Green and his Footstompers.

DUSSIE MAE: That's real nice.

LEVEE: That's what I was trying to tell you last night. A man what's gonna get his own band need to have a woman like you.

DUSSIE MAE: A woman like me wants somebody to bring it and put it in my hand. I don't need nobody wanna get something for nothing and leave me standing in my door.

LEVEE: That ain't Levee's style sugar. I got more style than that. I knows how to treat a woman. Buy her presents and things . . . treat her like she wants to be treated.

DUSSIE MAE: That's what they all say . . . till it come time to be buying the presents.

LEVEE: When we get down to Memphis, I'm gonna show you what I'm talking about. I'm gonna take you out and show you a good time. Show you Levee knows how to treat a woman.

DUSSIE MAE: When you getting your own band?

LEVEE: [*Moves closer to slip his arm around her*] Soon as Mr. Sturdyvant say. I done got my fellows already picked out. Getting me some good fellows know how to play real sweet music.

DUSSIE MAE: [*Moves away*] Go on now, I don't go for all that pawing and stuff. When you get your own band, maybe we can see about this stuff you talking.

LEVEE: [*Moving toward her*] I just wanna show you I know what the women like. They don't call me Sweet Lemonade for nothing.

    [LEVEE *takes her in his arms and attempts to kiss her.*]

DUSSIE MAE: Stop it now. Somebody's gonna come in here.

LEVEE: Naw they ain't. Look here, sugar . . . what I wanna know is . . . can I introduce my red rooster to your brown hen?

DUSSIE MAE: You get your band, then we'll see if that rooster know how to crow.

    [*He grinds up against her and feels her buttocks.*]

LEVEE: Now I know why my grandpappy sat on the back porch with his straight razor when grandma hung out the wash.

DUSSIE MAE: Nigger, you crazy!

LEVEE: I bet you sound like the midnight train from Alabama when it crosses the Mason-Dixon line.

DUSSIE MAE: How's you get so crazy?

LEVEE: It's women like you . . . drives me that way.

    [*He moves to kiss her as the lights go down in the band room and up in the studio.* MA RAINEY *sits with* CUTLER *and* TOLEDO.]

MA RAINEY: It sure done got quiet in here. I never could stand no silence. I always got to have some music going on in my head somewhere. It keeps things balanced. Music will do that. It fills things up. The more music you got in the world, the fuller it is.

CUTLER: I can agree with that. I got to have my music too.

MA RAINEY: White folks don't understand about the blues. They hear it come out, but they don't know how it got there. They don't understand that's life's way of talking. You don't sing to feel better. You sing 'cause that's a way of understanding life.

CUTLER: That's right. You get that understanding and you done got a grip on life to where you can hold your head up and go on to see what else life got to offer.

MA RAINEY: The blues help you get out of bed in the morning. You get up knowing you ain't alone. There's something else in the world. Something's been added by that song. This be an empty world without the blues. I take that emptiness and try to fill it up with something.

TOLEDO: You fill it up with something people can't be without, Ma. That's why they call you the Mother of the Blues. You fill up that emptiness in a way ain't nobody ever thought of doing before. And now they can't be without it.

MA RAINEY: I ain't started the blues way of singing. The blues always been here.

CUTLER: In the church sometimes you find that way of singing. They got blues in the church.

MA RAINEY: They say I started it . . . but I didn't. I just helped it out. Filled up that empty space a little bit. That's all. But if they wanna call me the Mother of the Blues, that's all right with me. It don't hurt none.

[SLOW DRAG *and* SYLVESTER *enter with the Cokes.*]

It sure took you long enough. That store ain't but on the corner.

SLOW DRAG: That one was closed. We had to find another one.

MA RAINEY: Sylvester, go and find Mr. Irvin and tell him we ready to go.

[SYLVESTER *exits. The lights in the band room come up while the lights in the studio stay on.* LEVEE *and* DUSSIE MAE *are kissing.* SLOW DRAG *enters. They break their embrace.* DUSSIE MAE *straightens up her clothes.*]

SLOW DRAG: Cold out. I just wanted to warm up with a little sip.

[*He goes to his locker, takes out his bottle and drinks.*]

Ma got her Coke, Levee. We about ready to start.

[SLOW DRAG *exits.* LEVEE *attempts to kiss* DUSSIE MAE *again.*]

DUSSIE MAE: No . . . Come on! I got to go. You gonna get me in trouble.

[*She pulls away and exits up the stairs.* LEVEE *watches after her.*]

LEVEE: Good God! Happy birthday to the lady with the cakes!

[*The lights go down in the band room and come up in the studio.* MA RAINEY *drinks her Coke.* LEVEE *enters from the band room. The musicians take their places.* SYLVESTER *stands by his mike.* IRVIN *and* STURDYVANT *look on from the control booth.*]

IRVIN: We're all set up here, Ma. We're all set to go. You ready down there?

MA RAINEY: Sylvester you just remember your part and say it. That's all there is to it. [*To* IRVIN.] Yeah, we ready.

IRVIN: Okay, boys. "Ma Rainey's Black Bottom." Take one.

CUTLER: One . . . two . . . You know what to do.

[*The band plays.*]

SYLVESTER: All right boys, you d-d-d-done s-s-seen the rest . . .

IRVIN: Hold it!

[*The band stops.* STURDYVANT *changes the recording disk and nods to* IRVIN.]

Okay. Take two.

CUTLER: One . . . two . . . You know what to do.

[*The band plays.*]

SYLVESTER: All right, boys, you done seen the rest . . . now I'm gonna show you the best. Ma Rainey's g-g-g-gonna s-s-show you her b-b-black bottom.

IRVIN: Hold it! Hold it!

[*The band stops.* STURDYVANT *changes the recording disk.*]

Okay. Take three. Ma, let's do it without the intro, huh? No voice intro . . . you just come in singing.

MA RAINEY: Irvin, I done told you . . . the boy's gonna do the part. He don't stutter all the time. Just give him a chance. Sylvester, hold your hands like I told you and just relax. Just relax and concentrate.

IRVIN: All right. Take three.

CUTLER: One . . . two . . . You know what to do.

[*The band plays.*]

SYLVESTER: All right, boys, you done seen the rest . . . now, I'm gonna show you the best. Ma Rainey's gonna show you her black bottom.

MA RAINEY: [*Singing*]

> *Way down south in Alabamy*
> *I got a friend they call dancing Sammy*
> *Who's crazy about all the latest dances*
> *Black Bottom stomping, two babies prancing*

The other night at a swell affair
As soon as the boys found out that I was there
They said, come on, Ma, let's go to the cabaret.
When I got there, you ought to hear them say,

I want to see the dance you call the black bottom
I want to learn that dance
I want to see the dance you call your big black bottom
It'll put you in a trance.

All the boys in the neighborhood
They say your black bottom is really good
Come on and show me your black bottom
I want to learn that dance

I want to see the dance you call the black bottom
I want to learn that dance
Come on and show the dance you call your big black bottom
It puts you in a trance.

Early last morning about the break of day
Grandpa told my grandma, I heard him say,
Get up and show your old man your black bottom
I want to learn that dance.

[*Instrumental break.*]

I done showed you all my black bottom
You ought to learn that dance.

IRVIN: Okay, that's good Ma. That sounded great! Good job, boys!

MA RAINEY: [*To* SYLVESTER] See! I told you. I knew you could do it. You just have to put your mind to it. Didn't he do good, Cutler? Sound real good. I told him he could do it.

CUTLER: He sure did. He did better than I thought he was gonna do.

IRVIN: [*Entering to remove* SYLVESTER's *mike*] Okay, boys . . . Ma . . . let's do "Moonshine Blues" next, huh? "Moonshine Blues," boys

STURDYVANT: [*Over speaker*] Irv! Something's wrong down there. We don't have it right.

IRVIN: What? What's the matter Mel . . .

STURDYVANT: We don't have it right. Something happened. We don't have the goddamn song recorded!

IRVIN: What's the matter? Mel, what happened? You sure you don't have nothing?

STURDYVANT: Check that mike, huh, Irv. It's the kid's mike. Something's wrong with the mike. We've got everything all screwed up here.

IRVIN: Christ almighty! Ma, we got to do it again. We don't have it. We didn't record the song.

MA RAINEY: What you mean you didn't record it? What was you and Sturdyvant doing up there?

IRVIN: [*Following the mike wire.*] Here . . . Levee must have kicked the plug out.

LEVEE: I ain't done nothing. I ain't kicked nothing!

SLOW DRAG: If Levee had his mind on what he's doing . . .

MA RAINEY: Levee, if it ain't one thing, it's another. You better straighten yourself up!

LEVEE: Hell . . . it ain't my fault. I ain't done nothing!

STURDYVANT: What's the matter with that mike, Irv? What's the problem?

IRVIN: It's the cord, Mel. The cord's all chewed up. We need another cord.

MA RAINEY: This is the most disorganized . . . Irvin, I'm going home! Come on. Come on, Dussie.

> [MA RAINEY *walks past* STURDYVANT *as he enters from the control booth. She exits off-stage to get her coat.*]

STURDYVANT: [*To* IRVIN] Where's she going?

IRVIN: She said she's going home.

STURDYVANT: Irvin, you get her! If she walks out of here . . .

> [MA RAINEY *enters carrying her and* DUSSIE MAE's *coat.*]

MA RAINEY: Come on, Sylvester.

IRVIN: [*Helping her with her coat.*] Ma . . . Ma . . . listen. Fifteen minutes! All I ask is fifteen minutes!

MA RAINEY: Come on, Sylvester, get your coat.

STURDYVANT: Ma, if you walk out of this studio . . .

IRVIN: Fifteen minutes, Ma!

STURDYVANT: You'll be through . . . washed up! If you walk out on me . . .

IRVIN: Mel, for Chrissakes, shut up and let me handle it!

> [*He goes after* MA RAINEY, *who has started for the door.*]

Ma, listen. These records are gonna be hits! They're gonna sell like crazy! Hell, even Sylvester will be a star. Fifteen minutes. That's all I'm asking! Fifteen minutes.

MA RAINEY: [*Crossing to a chair and sits with her coat on.*] Fifteen minutes! You hear me, Irvin? Fifteen minutes . . . and then I'm gonna take my black bottom on back down to Georgia. Fifteen minutes. Then Madame Rainey is leaving!

IRVIN: [*Kisses her*] All right, Ma . . . fifteen minutes. I promise. [*To the band.*] You boys go ahead and take a break. Fifteen minutes and we'll be ready to go.

CUTLER: Slow Drag, you got any of that bourbon left?

SLOW DRAG: Yeah, there's some down there.

CUTLER: I could use a little nip.

> [CUTLER *and* SLOW DRAG *exit to the band room, followed by* LEVEE, *and* TOLEDO. *The lights go down in the studio and up in the band room.*]

SLOW DRAG: Don't make no difference if she leave or not. I was kinda hoping she would leave.

CUTLER: I'm like Mr. Irvin . . . After all this time we done put in here, it's best to go ahead and get something out of it.

TOLEDO: Ma gonna do what she wanna do, that's for sure. If I was Mr. Irvin, I'd best go on and get them cords and things hooked up right. And I wouldn't take no longer than fifteen minutes doing it.

CUTLER: If Levee had his mind on his work, we wouldn't be in this fix. We'd be up there finishing up. Now we got to go back and see if that boy get that part right. Ain't no telling if he ever get that right again in his life.

LEVEE: Hey, Levee ain't done nothing!

SLOW DRAG: Levee up there got one eye on the gal and the other on his trumpet.

CUTLER: Nigger, don't you know that's Ma's gal?

LEVEE: I don't care whose gal it is. I ain't done nothing to her. I just talk to her like I talk to anybody else.

CUTLER: Well, that being Ma's gal, and that being that boy's gal, is one and two different things. The boy is liable to kill you . . . but you' ass gonna be out there scraping the concrete looking for a job if you messing with Ma's gal.

LEVEE: How am I messing with her? I ain't done nothing to the gal. I just asked her her name. Now, if you telling me I can't do that, then Ma will just have to go to hell.

CUTLER: All I can do is warn you.

SLOW DRAG: Let him hang himself, Cutler. Let him string his neck out.

LEVEE: I ain't done nothing to the gal! You all talk like I done went and done something to her. Leave me go with my business.

CUTLER: I'm through with it. Try and talk to a fool . . .

TOLEDO: Some mens got it worse than others . . . this foolishness I'm talking about. Some mens is excited to be fools. That excitement is something else. I know about it. I done experienced it. It makes you feel good to be a fool. But it don't last long. It's over in a minute. Then you got to tend with the consequences. You got to tend with what comes after. That's when you wish you had learned something about it.

LEVEE: That's the best sense you made all day. Talking about being a fool. That's the only sensible thing you said today. Admitting you was a fool.

TOLEDO: I admits it, all right. Ain't nothing wrong with it. I done been a little bit of everything.

LEVEE: Now you're talking. You's as big a fool as they make.

TOLEDO: Gonna be a bit more things before I'm finished with it. Gonna be foolish again. But I ain't never been the same fool twice. I might be a different kind of fool, but I ain't gonna be the same fool twice. That's where we parts ways.

SLOW DRAG: Toledo, you done been a fool about a woman?

TOLEDO: Sure. Sure I have. Same as everybody.

SLOW DRAG: Hell, I ain't never seen you mess with no woman. I thought them books was your woman.

TOLEDO: Sure I messed with them. Done messed with a whole heap of them. And gonna mess with some more. But I ain't gonna be no fool about them. What you think? I done come in the world full-grown, with my head in a book? I done been young. Married. Got kids. I done been around and I done loved women to where you shake in your shoes just at the sight of them. Feel it all up and down your spine.

SLOW DRAG: I didn't know you was married.

TOLEDO: Sure. Legally. I been married legally. Got the papers and all. I done been through life. Made my marks. Followed some signs on the road. Ignored some others. I done been all through it. I touched and been touched by it. But I ain't never been the same fool twice. That's what I can say.

LEVEE: But you been a fool. That's what counts. Talking about I'm a fool for asking the gal her name and here you is one yourself.

TOLEDO: Now, I married a woman. A good woman. To this day I can't say she wasn't a good woman. I can't say nothing bad about her. I married that woman with all the good graces and intentions of being hooked up and bound to her for the rest of my life. I was looking for her to put me in my grave. But, you see . . . it ain't all the time what you' intentions and wishes are. She went out and joined the church. All right. There ain't nothing wrong with that. A good Christian woman going to church and wanna do right by her god. There ain't nothing wrong with that. But she got up there, got to seeing them good Christian mens and wonder why I ain't like that. Soon she figure she got a heathen on her hands. She figured she couldn't live like that. The church was more important than I was. So she left. Packed up one day and moved out. To this day I ain't never said another word to her. Come home one day and my house was empty! And I sat down and figured out that I was a fool not to see that she needed something that I wasn't giving her. Else she wouldn't have been up there at the church in the first place. I ain't blaming her. I just said it wasn't gonna happen to me again. So, yeah, Toledo been a fool about a woman. That's part of making life.

CUTLER: Well, yeah, I been a fool too. Everybody done been a fool once or twice. But, you see, Toledo, what you call a fool and what I call a fool is two different things. I can't see where you was being a fool for that. You ain't done nothing foolish. You can't help what happened, and I wouldn't call you a fool for it. A fool is responsible for what happens to him. A fool cause it to happen. Like Levee . . . if he keeps messing with Ma's gal and his feet be out there scraping the ground. That's a fool.

LEVEE: Ain't nothing gonna happen to Levee. Levee ain't gonna let nothing happen to him. Now, I'm gonna say it again. I asked the gal her name. That's all I done. And if that's being a fool, then you looking at the biggest fool in the world . . . 'cause I sure as hell asked her.

SLOW DRAG: You just better not let Ma see you ask her. That's what the man's trying to tell you.

LEVEE: I don't need nobody to tell me nothing.

CUTLER: Well, Toledo, all I gots to say is that from the looks of it . . . from your story . . . I don't think life did you fair.

TOLEDO: Oh, life is fair. It's just in the taking what it gives you.

LEVEE: Life ain't shit. You can put it in a paper bag and carry it around with you. It ain't got no balls. Now, death . . . death got some style! Death will kick your ass and make you wish you never been born! That's how bad death is! But you can rule over life. Life ain't nothing.

TOLEDO: Cutler, how's your brother doing?

CUTLER: Who, Nevada? Oh, he's doing all right. Staying in St. Louis. Got a bunch of kids, last I heard.

TOLEDO: Me and him was all right with each other. Done a lot of farming together down in Plattsville.

CUTLER: Yeah, I know you all was tight. He in St. Louis now. Running an elevator, last I hear about it.

SLOW DRAG: That's better than stepping in muleshit.

TOLEDO: Oh, I don't know now. I liked farming. Get out there in the sun . . . smell that dirt. Be out there by yourself . . . nice and peaceful. Yeah, farming was all right by me. Sometimes I think I'd like to get me a little old place . . . but I done got too old to be following behind one of them balky mules now.

LEVEE: Nigger talking about life is fair. And ain't got a pot to piss in.

TOLEDO: See, now, I'm gonna tell you something. A nigger gonna be dissatisfied no matter what. Give a nigger some bread and butter . . . and he'll cry 'cause he ain't got no jelly. Give him some jelly, and he'll cry 'cause he ain't got no knife to put it on with. If there's one thing I done learned in this life, it's that you can't satisfy a nigger no matter what you do. A nigger's gonna make his own dissatisfaction.

LEVEE: Niggers got a right to be dissatisfied. Is you gonna be satisfied with a bone somebody done throwed you when you see them eating the whole hog?

TOLEDO: You lucky they let you be an entertainer. They ain't got to accept your way of entertaining. You lucky and you don't even know it. You's entertaining and the rest of the people is hauling wood. That's the only kind of job for the colored man.

SLOW DRAG: Ain't nothing wrong with hauling wood. I done hauled plenty wood. My daddy used to haul wood. Ain't nothing wrong with that. That's honest work.

LEVEE: That ain't what I'm talking about. I ain't talking about hauling no wood. I'm talking about being satisfied with a bone somebody done throwed you. That's what's the matter with you all. You satisfied sitting in one place. You got to move on down the road from where you sitting . . . and all the time you got to keep an eye out for that devil who's looking to buy up souls. And hope you get lucky and find him!

CUTLER: I done told you about that blasphemy. Talking about selling your soul to the devil.

TOLEDO: We done the same thing, Cutler. There ain't no difference. We done sold Africa for the price of tomatoes. We done sold ourselves to the white man in order to be like him. Look at the way you dressed . . . That ain't African. That's the white man. We trying to be just like him. We done sold who we are in order to become someone else. We's imitation white men.

CUTLER: What else we gonna be, living over here?

LEVEE: I'm Levee. Just me. I ain't no imitation nothing!

SLOW DRAG: You change who you are by how you dress. That's what I got to say.

TOLEDO: It ain't all how you dress. It's how you act, how you see the world. It's how you follow life.

LEVEE: It don't matter what you talking about. I ain't no imitation white man. And I don't want to be no white man. As soon as I get my band together and make them records like Mr. Sturdyvant done told me I can make, I'm gonna be like Ma and tell the white man just what he can do. Ma tell Mr. Irvin she gonna leave . . . and Mr. Irvin get down on his knees and beg her to stay! That's the way I'm gonna be! Make the white man respect me!

CUTLER: The white man don't care nothing about Ma. The colored folks made Ma a star. White folks don't care nothing about who she is . . . what kind of music she make.

SLOW DRAG: That's the truth about that. You let her go down to one of them white-folks hotels and see how big she is.

CUTLER: Hell, she ain't got to do that. She can't even get a cab up here in the North. I'm gonna tell you something. Reverend Gates . . . you know Reverend Gates? . . . Slow Drag know who I'm talking about. Reverend Gates . . . now I'm gonna show you how this go where the white man don't care a thing about who you is. Reverend Gates was coming from Tallahassee to Atlanta, going to see his sister, who was sick at that time with the consumption. The train come up through Thomasville, then past Moultrie, and stopped in this little town called Sigsbee . . .

LEVEE: You can stop telling that right there! That train don't stop in Sigsbee. I know what train you talking about. That train got four stops before it reach Macon to go on to Atlanta. One in Thomasville, one in Moultrie, one in Cordele . . . and it stop in Centerville.

CUTLER: Nigger, I know what I'm talking about. You gonna tell me where the train stop?

LEVEE: Hell, yeah, if you talking about it stop in Sigsbee. I'm gonna tell you the truth.

CUTLER: I'm talking about *this* train! I don't know what train you been riding. I'm talking about *this* train!

LEVEE: Ain't but one train. Ain't but one train come out of Tallahassee heading north to Atlanta, and it don't stop at Sigsbee. Tell him, Toledo . . . that train don't stop at Sigsbee. The only train that stops at Sigsbee is the Yazoo Delta, and you have to transfer at Moultrie to get it!

CUTLER: Well, hell, maybe that what he done! I don't know. I'm just telling you the man got off the train at Sigsbee . . .

LEVEE: All right . . . you telling it. Tell it your way. Just make up anything.

SLOW DRAG: Levee, leave the man alone and let him finish.

CUTLER: I ain't paying Levee no never mind.

LEVEE: Go on and tell it your way.

CUTLER: Anyway . . . Reverend Gates got off his train in Sigsbee. The train done stopped there and he figured he'd get off and check the schedule to be sure he arrive in time for somebody to pick him up. All right. While he's there checking the schedule, it come upon him that he had to go to the bathroom. Now, they ain't had no colored rest rooms at the station. The only colored rest room is an outhouse they got sitting way back two hundred yards or so from the station. All right. He in the outhouse and train go off and leave him there. He don't know nothing about this town. Ain't never been there before—in fact, ain't never even heard of it before.

LEVEE: I heard of it! I know just where it's at . . . and he ain't got off no train coming out of Tallahassee in Sigsbee!

CUTLER: The man standing there, trying to figure out what he's gonna do . . . where this train done left him in this strange town. It started getting dark. He see where the sun's getting low in the sky and he's trying to figure out what he's gonna do, when he noticed a couple of white fellows standing across the street from this station. Just standing there, watching him. And then two or three more come up and joined the other one. He look around, ain't seen no colored folks nowhere. He didn't know what was getting in these here fellows' minds, so he commence to walking. He ain't knowed where he was going. He just walking down the railroad tracks when he hear them call him. "Hey, nigger!" See, just like that. "Hey, nigger!" He kept on walking. They called him some more and he just keep walking. Just going down the tracks. And then he heard a gunshot where somebody done fired a gun in the air. He stopped then, you know.

TOLEDO: You don't even have to tell me no more. I know the facts of it. I done heard the same story a hundred times. It happened to me too. Same thing.

CUTLER: Naw, I'm gonna show how the white folks don't care nothing about who or what you is. They crowded around him. These gang of mens made a circle around him. Now, he's standing there, you understand . . . got his cross around his neck like them preachers wear. Had his little Bible with him what he carry all the time. So they crowd on around him and one of them ask who he is. He told them he was Reverend Gates and that he was going to see his sister who was sick and the train left without him. And they said, "Yeah, nigger . . . but can you dance?" He looked at them and commenced to dancing. One of them reached up and tore his cross off his neck. Said he was committing a heresy by dancing with a cross and Bible. Took his Bible and tore it up and had him dancing till they got tired of watching him.

SLOW DRAG: White folks ain't never had no respect for the colored minister.

CUTLER: That's the only way he got out of there alive . . . was to dance. Ain't even had no respect for a man of God! Wanna make him into a clown. Reverend Gates sat right in my house and told me that story from his own mouth. So . . . the white folks don't care nothing about Ma Rainey. She's just another nigger who they can use to make some money.

LEVEE: What I wants to know is . . . if he's a man of God, then where the hell was God when all of this was going on? Why wasn't God looking out for him. Why didn't God strike down them crackers with some this lightning you talk about to me?

CUTLER: Levee, you gonna burn in hell.

LEVEE: What I care about burning in hell? You talk like a fool . . . burning in hell. Why didn't God strike some of them crackers down? Tell me that! That's the question! Don't come telling me this burning-in-hell shit! He a man of God . . . why didn't God strike some of them crackers down? I'll tell you why! I'll tell you the truth! It's sitting out there as plain as day! 'Cause he a white man's God. That's why! God ain't never listened to no nigger's prayers. God take a nigger's prayers and throw them in the garbage. God don't pay niggers no mind. In fact . . . God hate niggers! Hate them with all the fury in his heart. Jesus don't love you, nigger! Jesus hate your black ass! Come talking that shit to me. Talking about burning in hell! God can kiss my ass.

[CUTLER *can stand no more. He jumps up and punches* LEVEE *in the mouth. The force of the blow knocks* LEVEE *down and* CUTLER *jumps on him.*]

CUTLER: You worthless . . . That's my God! That's my God! That's my God! You wanna blaspheme my God!

[TOLEDO *and* SLOW DRAG *grab* CUTLER *and try to pull him off* LEVEE.]

SLOW DRAG: Come on, Cutler . . . let it go! It don't mean nothing!

[CUTLER *has* LEVEE *down on the floor and pounds on him with a fury.*]

CUTLER: Wanna blaspheme my God! You worthless . . . talking about my God!

[TOLEDO *and* SLOW DRAG *succeed in pulling* CUTLER *off* LEVEE, *who is bleeding at the nose and mouth.*]

LEVEE: Naw, let him go! Let him go!

[*He pulls out a knife.*]

That's your God, huh? That's your God, huh? Is that right? Your God, huh? All right. I'm gonna give your God a chance. I'm gonna give him a chance to save your black ass.

[LEVEE *circles* CUTLER *with the knife.* CUTLER *picks up a chair to protect himself.*]

TOLEDO: Come on, Levee . . . put the knife up!

LEVEE: Stay out of this, Toledo!

TOLEDO: That ain't no way to solve nothing.

[LEVEE *alternately swipes at* CUTLER *during the following.*]

LEVEE: I'm calling Cutler's God! I'm talking to Cutler's God! You hear me? Cutler's God! I'm calling Cutler's God. Come on and save this nigger! Strike me down before I cut his throat!

SLOW DRAG: Watch him, Cutler! Put that knife up, Levee!

LEVEE: [*To* CUTLER] I'm calling your God! I'm gonna give him a chance to save you! I'm calling your God! We gonna find out whose God he is!

CUTLER: You gonna burn in hell, nigger!

LEVEE: Cutler's God! Come on and save this nigger! Come on and save him like you did my mama! Save him like you did my mama! I heard her when she called you! I heard her when she said, "Lord, have mercy! Jesus, help me! Please, God, have mercy on me, Lord Jesus, help me!" And did you turn your back? Did you turn your back, motherfucker? Did you turn your back?

[LEVEE *becomes so caught up in his dialogue with God that he forgets about* CUTLER *and begins to stab upward in the air, trying to reach God.*]

Come on! Come on and turn your back on me! Turn your back on me! Come on! Where is you? Come on and turn your back on me! Turn your back on me, motherfucker! I'll cut your heart out! Come on, turn your back on me! Come on! What's the matter? Where is you? Come on and turn your back on me! Come on, what you scared of? Turn your back on me! Come on! Coward, motherfucker?

[LEVEE *folds his knife and stands triumphantly.*]

Your God ain't shit, Cutler.

[*The lights fade to black.*]

MA RAINEY: [*Singing*]

> *Ah, you hear me talking to you*
> *I don't bite my tongue*
> *You wants to be my man*
> *You got to fetch it with you when you come.*

[*Lights come up in the studio. The last bars of the last song of the session are dying out.*]

IRVIN: [*Over speaker*] Good! Wonderful! We have that, boys. Good session. That's great, Ma. We've got ourselves some winners.

TOLEDO: Well, I'm glad that's over.

MA RAINEY: Slow Drag, where you learn to play the bass at? You had it singing! I heard you! Had that bass jumping all over the place.

SLOW DRAG: I was following Toledo. Nigger got them long fingers striding all over the piano. I was trying to keep up with him.

TOLEDO: That's what you supposed to do, ain't it? Play the music. Ain't nothing abstract about it.

MA RAINEY: Cutler, you hear Slow Drag on that bass? He make it do what he want it to do! Spank it just like you spank a baby.

CUTLER: Don't be telling him that. Nigger's head get so big his hat won't fit him.

SLOW DRAG: If Cutler tune that guitar up, we would really have something!

CUTLER: You wouldn't know what a tuned-up guitar sounded like if you heard one.

TOLEDO: Cutler was talking. I heard him moaning. He was all up in it.

MA RAINEY: Levee . . . what is that you doing? Why you playing all them notes? You play ten notes for every one you supposed to play. It don't call for that.

LEVEE: You supposed to improvise on the theme. That's what I was doing.

MA RAINEY: You supposed to play the song the way I sing it. The way everybody else play it. You ain't supposed to go off by yourself and play what you want.

LEVEE: I was playing the song. I was playing it the way I felt it.

MA RAINEY: I couldn't keep up with what was going on. I'm trying to sing the song and you up there messing up my ear. That's what you was doing. Call yourself playing music.

LEVEE: Hey . . . I know what I'm doing. I know what I'm doing, all right. I know how to play music. You all back up and leave me alone about my music.

CUTLER: I done told you . . . it ain't about *your* music. It's about *Ma's* music.

MA RAINEY: That's all right, Cutler. I done told you what to do.

LEVEE: I don't care what you do. You supposed to improvise on the theme. Not play note for note the same thing over and over again.

MA RAINEY: You just better watch yourself. You hear me?

LEVEE: What I care what you or Cutler do? Come telling me to watch myself. What's that supposed to mean?

MA RAINEY: All right . . . you gonna find out what it means.

LEVEE: Go ahead and fire me. I don't care. I'm gonna get my own band anyway.

MA RAINEY: You keep messing with me.

LEVEE: Ain't nobody studying you. You ain't gonna do nothing to me. Ain't nobody gonna do nothing to Levee.

MA RAINEY: All right, nigger . . . you fired!

LEVEE: You think I care about being fired? I don't care nothing about that. You doing me a favor.

MA RAINEY: Cutler, Levee's out! He don't play in my band no more.

LEVEE: I'm fired . . . Good! Best thing that ever happened to me. I don't need this shit!

[LEVEE *exits to the band room.* IRVIN *enters from the control booth.*]

MA RAINEY: Cutler, I'll see you back at the hotel.

IRVIN: Okay, boys . . . you can pack up. I'll get your money for you.

CUTLER: That's cash money, Mr. Irvin. I don't want no check.

IRVIN: I'll see what I can do. I can't promise you nothing.

CUTLER: As long as it ain't no check. I ain't got no use for a check.

IRVIN: I'll see what I can do, Cutler.

[CUTLER, TOLEDO, *and* SLOW DRAG *exit to the band room.*]

Oh, Ma, listen . . . I talked to Sturdyvant, and he said . . . Now, I tried to talk him out of it . . . He said the best he can do is to take your twenty-five dollars of your money and give it to Sylvester.

MA RAINEY: Take what and do what? If I wanted the boy to have twenty-five dollars of my money, I'd give it to him. He supposed to get his own money. He supposed to get paid like everybody else.

IRVIN: Ma, I talked to him . . . He said . . .

MA RAINEY: Go talk to him again! Tell him if he don't pay that boy, he'll never make another record of mine again. Tell him that. You supposed to be my manager. All this talk about sticking together. Start sticking! Go on up there and get that boy his money!

IRVIN: Okay, Ma . . . I'll talk to him again. I'll see what I can do.

MA RAINEY: Ain't no see about it! You bring that boy's money back here!

[IRVIN *exits. The lights stay on in the studio and come up in the band room. The men have their instruments packed and sit waiting for* IRVIN *to come and pay them.* SLOW DRAG *has a pack of cards.*]

SLOW DRAG: Come on, Levee, let me show you a card trick.

LEVEE: I don't need want to see no card trick. What you wanna show me for? Why you wanna bother me with that?

SLOW DRAG: I was just trying to be nice.

LEVEE: I don't need you to be nice to me. What I need you to be nice to me for? I ain't gonna be nice to you. I ain't even gonna let you be in my band no more.

SLOW DRAG: Toledo, let me show you a card trick.

CUTLER: I just hope Mr. Irvin don't bring no check down here. What the hell I'm gonna do with a check?

SLOW DRAG: All right now . . . pick a card. Any card . . . go on . . . take any of them. I'm gonna show you something.

TOLEDO: I agrees with you, Cutler. I don't want no check either.

CUTLER: It don't make no sense to give a nigger a check.

SLOW DRAG: Okay, now. Remember your card. Remember which one you got. Now . . . put it back in the deck. Anywhere you want. I'm gonna show you something.

[TOLEDO *puts the card in the deck.*]

You remember your card? All right. Now I'm gonna shuffle the deck. Now . . . I'm gonna show you what card you picked. Don't say nothing now. I'm gonna tell you what card you picked.

CUTLER: Slow Drag, that trick is as old as my mama.

SLOW DRAG: Naw, naw . . . wait a minute! I'm gonna show him his card . . . There it go! The six of diamonds. Ain't that your card? Ain't that it?

TOLEDO: Yeah, that's it . . . the six of diamonds.

SLOW DRAG: Told you! Told you I'd show him what it was!

[*The lights fade in the band room and come up full on the studio.* STURDYVANT *enters with* IRVIN.]

STURDYVANT: Ma, is there something wrong? Is there a problem?

MA RAINEY: Sturdyvant, I want you to pay that boy his money.

STURDYVANT: Sure, Ma. I got it right here. Two hundred for you and twenty-five for the kid, right?

[STURDYVANT *hands the money to* IRVIN, *who hands it to* MA RAINEY *and* SYLVESTER.]

Irvin misunderstood me. It was all a mistake. Irv made a mistake.

MA RAINEY: A mistake, huh?

IRVIN: Sure, Ma. I made a mistake. He's paid, right? I straightened it out.

MA RAINEY: The only mistake was when you found out I hadn't signed the release forms. That was the mistake. Come on, Sylvester.

[*She starts to exit.*]

STURDYVANT: Hey, Ma . . . come on, sign the forms, huh?

IRVIN: Ma . . . come on now.

MA RAINEY: Get your coat, Sylvester. Irvin, where's my car?

IRVIN: It's right out front, Ma. Here . . . I got the keys right here. Come on, sign the forms, huh?

MA RAINEY: Irvin, give me my car keys!

IRVIN: Sure, Ma . . . just sign the forms, huh?

> [*He gives her the keys, expecting a trade-off.*]

MA RAINEY: Send them to my address and I'll get around to them.

IRVIN: Come on, Ma . . . I took care of everything, right? I straightened everything out.

MA RAINEY: Give me the pen, Irvin.

> [*She signs the forms.*]
>
> You tell Sturdyvant . . . one more mistake like that and I can make my records some-place else.
>
> [*She turns to exit.*]
>
> Sylvester, straighten up your clothes. Come on, Dussie Mae.
>
> [*She exits, followed by* DUSSIE MAE *and* SYLVESTER. *The lights go down in the studio and come up on the band room.*]

CUTLER: I know what's keeping him so long. He up there writing out checks. You watch. I ain't gonna stand for it. He ain't gonna bring me no check down here. If he do, he's gonna take it right back upstairs and get some cash.

TOLEDO: Don't get yourself all worked up about it. Wait and see. Think positive.

CUTLER: I am thinking positive. He positively gonna give me some cash. Man give me a check last time . . . you remember . . . we went all over Chicago trying to get it cashed. See a nigger with a check, the first thing they think is he done stole it someplace.

LEVEE: I ain't had no trouble cashing mine.

CUTLER: I don't visit no whorehouses.

LEVEE: You don't know about my business. So don't start nothing. I'm tired of you as it is. I ain't but two seconds off your ass no way.

TOLEDO: Don't you all start nothing now.

CUTLER: What the hell I care what you tired of. I wasn't even talking to you. I was talking to this man right here.

> [IRVIN *and* STURDYVANT *enter.*]

IRVIN: Okay boys. Mr. Sturdyvant has your pay.

CUTLER: As long as it's cash money, Mr. Sturdyvant. 'Cause I have too much trouble trying to cash a check.

STURDYVANT: Oh, yes . . . I'm aware of that. Mr. Irvin told me you boys prefer cash, and that's what I have for you.

> [*He starts handing out money.*]
>
> That was a good session you boys put in . . . That's twenty-five for you. Yessir, you boys really know your business and we are going to . . . Twenty-five for you . . . We are going to get you back in here real soon . . . twenty-five . . . and have another session so you can make some more money . . . and twenty-five for you. Okay, thank you, boys. You can get your things together and Mr. Irvin will make sure you find your way out.

IRVIN: I'll be out front when you get your things together, Cutler.

> [IRVIN *exits,* STURDYVANT *starts to follow.*]

LEVEE: Mr. Sturdyvant, sir. About them songs I give you? . . .

STURDYVANT: Oh, yes, . . . uh . . . Levee. About them songs you gave me. I've thought about it and I just don't think the people will buy them. They're not the type of songs we're looking for.

LEVEE: Mr. Sturdyvant, sir . . . I done got my band picked out and they's real good fellows. They knows how to play real good. I know if the peoples hear the music, they'll buy it.

STURDYVANT: Well, Levee, I'll be fair with you . . . but they're just not the right songs.

LEVEE: Mr. Sturdyvant, you got to understand about that music. That music is what the people is looking for. They's tired of jug-band music. They wants something that excites them. Something with some fire to it.

STURDYVANT: Okay, Levee. I'll tell you what I'll do. I'll give you five dollars a piece for them. Now that's the best I can do.

LEVEE: I don't want no five dollars, Mr. Sturdyvant. I wants to record them songs, like you say.

STURDYVANT: Well, Levee, like I say . . . they just aren't the kind of songs we're looking for.

LEVEE: Mr. Sturdyvant, you asked me to write them songs. Now, why didn't you tell me that before when I first gave them to you? You told me you was gonna let me record them. What's the difference between then and now?

STURDYVANT: Well, look . . . I'll pay you for your trouble . . .

LEVEE: What's the difference, Mr. Sturdyvant? That's what I wanna know.

STURDYVANT: I had my fellows play your songs, and when I heard them, they just didn't sound like the kind of songs I'm looking for right now.

LEVEE: You got to hear *me* play them, Mr. Sturdyvant! You ain't heard *me* play them. That's what's gonna make them sound right.

STURDYVANT: Well, Levee, I don't doubt that really. It's just that . . . well, I don't think they'd sell like Ma's records. But I'll take them off your hands for you.

LEVEE: The people's tired of jug-band music, Mr. Sturdyvant. They wants something that's gonna excite them! They wants something with some fire! I don't know what fellows you had playing them songs . . . but if I could play them! I'd set them down in the people's lap! Now you told me I could record them songs!

STURDYVANT: Well, there's nothing I can do about that. Like I say, it's five dollars a piece. That's what I'll give you. I'm doing you a favor. Now, if you write any more, I'll help you out and take them off your hands. The price is five dollars a piece. Just like now.

[*He attempts to hand* LEVEE *the money, finally shoves it in* LEVEE's *coat pocket and is gone in a flash.* LEVEE *follows him to the door and it slams in his face. He takes the money from his pocket, balls it up and throws it on the floor. The other musicians silently gather up their belongings.* TOLEDO *walks past* LEVEE *and steps on his shoe.*]

LEVEE: Hey! Watch it . . . Shit Toledo! You stepped on my shoe!

TOLEDO: Excuse me there, Levee.

LEVEE: Look at that! Look at that! Nigger, you stepped on my shoe. What you do that for?

TOLEDO: I said I'm sorry.

LEVEE: Nigger gonna step on my goddamn shoe! You done fucked up my shoe! Look at that! Look at what you done to my shoe, nigger! I ain't stepped on your shoe! What you wanna step on my shoe for?

CUTLER: The man said he's sorry.

LEVEE: Sorry! How the hell he gonna be sorry after he gone ruint my shoe! Come talking about sorry!

[*Turns his attention back to* TOLEDO.]

Nigger, you stepped on my shoe! You know that!

[LEVEE *snatches his shoe off his foot and holds it up for* TOLEDO *to see.*]

See what you done?

TOLEDO: What you want me to do about it? It's done now. I said excuse me.

LEVEE: Wanna go and fuck up my shoe like that. I ain't done nothing to your shoe. Look at this!

[TOLEDO *turns and continues to gather up his things.* LEVEE *spins him around by his shoulder.*]

LEVEE: Naw . . . naw . . . look what you done!

[*He shoves the shoe in* TOLEDO'*s face.*]

Look at that! That's my shoe! Look at that! You did it! You did it! You fucked up my shoe! You stepped on my shoe with them raggedy-ass clodhoppers!

TOLEDO: Nigger, ain't nobody studying you and your shoe! I said excuse me. If you can't accept that, then the hell with it. What you want me to do?

[LEVEE *is in near rage, breathing hard. He is trying to get a grip on himself, as even he senses, or perhaps only he senses, he is about to lose control. He looks around, uncertain of what to do.* TOLEDO *has gone back to packing, as have* CUTLER *and* SLOW DRAG. *They purposefully avoid looking at* LEVEE *in hopes he'll calm down if he doesn't have an audience. All the weight in the world suddenly falls on* LEVEE *and he rushes at* TOLEDO *with his knife in his hand.*]

LEVEE: Nigger, you stepped on my shoe!

[*He plunges the knife into* TOLEDO'*s back up to the hilt.* TOLEDO *lets out a sound of surprise and agony.* CUTLER *and* SLOW DRAG *freeze.* TOLEDO *falls backward with* LEVEE, *his hand still on the knife, holding him up.* LEVEE *is suddenly faced with the realization of what he has done. He shoves* TOLEDO *forward and takes a step back.* TOLEDO *slumps to the floor.*]

He . . . he stepped on my shoe. He did. Honest, Cutler, he stepped on my shoe. What he do that for? Toledo, what you do that for? Cutler, help me. He stepped on my shoe, Cutler.

[*He turns his attention to* TOLEDO.]

Toledo! Toledo, get up.

[*He crosses to* TOLEDO *and tries to pick him up.*]

It's okay, Toledo. Come on . . . I'll help you. Come on, stand up now. Levee'll help you.

[TOLEDO *is limp and heavy and awkward. He slumps back to the floor.* LEVEE *gets mad at him.*]

Don't look at me like that! Toledo! Nigger, don't look at me like that! I'm warning you nigger! Close your eyes! Don't you look at me like that! [*He turns to* CUTLER] Tell him to close his eyes. Cutler. Tell him don't look at me like that.

CUTLER: Slow Drag, get Mr. Irvin down here.

[*The sound of a trumpet is heard,* LEVEE'*s trumpet, a muted trumpet struggling for the highest of possibilities and blowing pain and warning.*]

BLACK OUT.

Roosters (1987)

ike African American drama, Latino drama has become increasingly well known since the mid-1960s, when Luis Valdez achieved wide recognition with plays designed to help migrant farm workers gain better working conditions. Although the number of Latino playwrights thereafter grew significantly, few prior to the 1980s were female. Among recent Latina playwrights, Milcha Sanchez-Scott has been one of the most successful.

Sanchez-Scott's *Roosters*, first produced jointly by INTAR Hispanic Arts Center and the New York Shakespeare Festival in 1987, uses cockfighting as its central metaphor. Set in the desert Southwest, the major action focuses on a struggle between the father of a family, Gallo ("rooster," "macho"), whose life is given meaning by cockfighting (winning at which in his eyes justifies any behavior, including cheating, con games, and even murder) and his son Hector, who wishes to escape the kind of life his father has led. Their struggle is focused on their rival claims to Zapata, a fighting cock. Eventually Gallo (apparently willing to kill his own son in order to gain possession of the rooster), using a stiletto, forces Hector to fight him.

Caught in this struggle between males are the three women of the family: Juana, Gallo's worn-down wife who supports the family, always deferring to her adored husband; Chata, Gallo's promiscuous sister; and Angela, Gallo's adolescent daughter who wears angel wings and clings to childhood and religion as buffers against hurt. Angela's faith is shattered when her father, after cajoling her into revealing the whereabouts of Zapata, abandons her after he recovers the rooster. During a superhuman effort to regain her faith, she levitates. The atmosphere of the play moves easily between realism and fantasy in the manner of Latino "magic realism." Overall, *Roosters* is a powerful play that has much to say about machismo, women, love, and psychological need in a male-dominated Latino culture.

MILCHA SANCHEZ-SCOTT

Roosters

Characters

GALLO
ZAPATA
HECTOR
ANGELA
JUANA
CHATA
ADAN
SHADOW #1
SHADOW #2
SAN JUAN

TIME:————*The Present*
PLACE:————*The Southwest*

ACT ONE

SCENE I

Stage and house are dark. Slowly a narrow pinspot of light comes up. We hear footsteps. Enter GALLO, *a very, very handsome man in his forties. He is wearing a cheap dark suit, with a white open-neck shirt. He carries a suitcase. He puts the suitcase down. He faces the audience.*

GALLO: Lord Eagle, Lord Hawk, sainted ones, spirits and winds, Santa María Aurora of the Dawn . . . I want no resentment, I want no rancor. . . . I had an old red Cuban hen. She was squirrel-tailed and sort of slab-sided and you wouldn't have given her a second look. But she was a queen. She could be thrown with any cock and you would get a hard-kicking stag every time.

I had a vision, of a hard-kicking flyer, the ultimate bird. The Filipinos were the ones with the pedigree Bolinas, the high flyers, but they had no real kick. To see those birds fighting in the air like dark avenging angels . . . well like my father use to say, "Son nobles . . . finos. . . . " I figured to mate that old red Cuban. This particular Filipino had the best. A dark burgundy flyer named MacArthur. He wouldn't sell. I began borrowing MacArthur at night, bringing him back before dawn, no one the wiser, but one morning the Filipino's son caught me. He pulled out his blade. I pulled out mine. I was faster. I went up on manslaughter. . . . They never caught on . . . thought I was in the henhouse trying to steal their stags. . . . It took time—refining, inbreeding, cross-breeding, brother to sister, mother to son, adding power, rapid attack . . . but I think we got him.

[GALLO *stands still for a beat, checks his watch, takes off his jacket and faces center stage. A slow, howling drumbeat begins. As it gradually goes higher in pitch and*

490

excitement mounts, we see narrow beams of light, the first light of dawn, filtering through chicken wire. The light reveals a heap of chicken feathers which turns out to be an actor/dancer who represents the rooster ZAPATA. ZAPATA *stretches his wings, then his neck, to greet the light. He stands and struts proudly, puffs his chest and crows his salutation to the sun.* GALLO *stalks* ZAPATA, *as drums follow their movements.*]

Ya, ya, mi lindo . . . yeah, baby . . . you're a beauty, a real beauty. Now let's see whatcha got. [*He pulls out a switchblade stiletto. It gleams in the light as he tosses it from hand to hand.*] Come on baby boy. Show Daddy whatcha got.

[GALLO *lunges at* ZAPATA. *The rooster parries with his beak and wings. This becomes a slow, rhythmic fight-dance, which continues until* GALLO *grabs* ZAPATA *by his comb, bending his head backwards until he is forced to sit.* GALLO *stands behind* ZAPATA, *straddling him, one hand still holding the comb, the other holding the knife against the rooster's neck.*]

Oh yeah, you like to fight? Huh? You gonna kill for me baby boy? Huh?

[GALLO *sticks the tip of the knife into* ZAPATA. *The rooster squawks in pain.*]

Sssh! Baby boy, you gotta learn. Daddy's gotta teach you.

[GALLO *sticks it to* ZAPATA *again. This time the rooster snaps back in anger.*]

That's right beauty. . . . Now you got it. . . . Come on, come.

[GALLO *waves his knife and hand close to* ZAPATA's *face. The rooster's head and eyes follow.*]

Oh yeah . . . that's it baby, take it! Take it!

[*Suddenly* ZAPATA *attacks, drawing blood.* GALLO's *body contracts in orgasmic pleasure/pain.*]

Ay precioso! . . . Mi lindo. . . . You like that, eh? Taste good, huh? [*He waves the gleaming knife in a slow hypnotic movement which calms the rooster.*] Take my blood, honey. . . . I'm in you now. . . . Morales blood, the blood of kings . . . and you're my rooster . . . a Morales rooster. [*He slowly backs away from the rooster. He picks up his suitcase, still pointing the knife at* ZAPATA.] Kill. You're my son. Make me proud.

[GALLO *exits.* ZAPATA *puffs his chest and struts upstage. Lights go up a little on upstage left area as the rooster goes into the chicken-wire henhouse. He preens and scratches. Enter* HECTOR, *a young man of about twenty. He is very handsome. He wears gray sweatpants and no shirt. On his forehead is a sweatband. His hair and body are dripping wet. He has been running. Now he is panting as he leans on the henhouse looking at* ZAPATA.]

HECTOR: I saw what you did to those chicks. Don't look at me like you have a mind, or a soul, or feelings. You kill your young . . . and we are so proud of your horrible animal vigor. . . . But you are my inheritance . . . Abuelo's gift to me . . . to get me out. Oh, Abuelo, Grandfather . . . you should have left me your courage, your sweet pacific strength.

[*A ray of light hits downstage right. In a semi-shadow, we see a miniature cemetery, with small white headstones and white crosses. We see the profile of a young angel/girl with wings and a pale dress.* ANGELA *is kneeling next to a bare desert tree with low scratchy branches. She has a Buster Brown haircut and a low tough voice. She is fifteen, but looks twelve.*]

ANGELA: [*loudly*]

Angel of God
My Guardian Dear
To whom God's love
Commits me here
Ever this day be

At my side
To light and guard
To rule and guide
Amen.
[*Her paper wings get caught in a tree branch.*] Aw, shit! [*She exits.*]

SCENE II

As the light changes we hear the clapping of women making tortillas. Lights come up full. Center stage is a faded wood-frame house, with a porch that is bare except for a table and a few chairs. The house sits in the middle of a desert agricultural valley somewhere in the Southwest. Everything is sparse. There is a feeling of blue skies and space. One might see off on the horizon tall Nopales or Century cactus. JUANA, *a thin, worn-out–looking woman of thirty-five, comes out of the house. She is wearing a faded housedress. She goes to mid-yard, faces front and stares out.*

JUANA: It's dry. Bone dry. There's a fire in the mountains . . . up near Jacinto Pass. [*The clapping stops for a beat, then continues. She starts to go back into the house, then stops. She sniffs the air, sniffs again, and again.*] Tres Rosas . . . I smell Tres Rosas. [*She hugs her body and rocks.*] Tres Rosas. . . . Ay, St. Anthony let him come home. . . . Let him be back.
    [*The clapping stops.* CHATA *enters from the house. She is a fleshy woman of forty, who gives new meaning to the word "blowsy." She has the lumpy face of a hard boozer. She walks with a slight limp. She wears a black kimono, on the back of which is embroidered in red a dragon and the words "Korea, U.S.S. Perkins, 7th Fleet." A cigarette hangs from her lips. She carries a bowl containing balls of tortilla dough.*]
    I smell Tres Rosas. . . . The brilliantine for his hair. . . . He musta been here. Why did he go?
CHATA: Men are shit.
JUANA: Where could he be?
CHATA: First day out of jail! My brother never comes home first day. You should know that. Gotta sniff around . . . gotta get use to things. See his friends.
JUANA: Sí, that's right. . . . He just gotta get used to things. I'll feel better when I see him. . . . I gotta keep busy.
CHATA: You been busy all morning.
JUANA: I want him to feel good, be proud of us. . . . You hear anything when you come in yesterday?
CHATA: Who's gonna know anything at the Trailways bus station?
JUANA: You ain't heard anything?
CHATA: Juanita, he knows what he's doing. If there was gonna be any trouble he'd know. Ay, mujer, he's just an old warrior coming home.
JUANA: Ain't that old.
CHATA: For a fighting man, he's getting up there.
    [JUANA *slaps tortillas.* CHATA *watches her.*]
    Who taught you to make tortillas?
JUANA: I don't remember. I never make 'em. Kids don't ask.
CHATA: Look at this. You call this a tortilla? Have some pride. Show him you're a woman.
JUANA: Chata, you've been here one day, and you already—
CHATA: Ah, you people don't know what it is to eat fresh handmade tortillas. My grandmother Hortensia, the one they used to call "La India Condensada" . . . she would start making them at five o'clock in the morning. So the men would have something to

eat when they went into the fields. Hijo! She was tough. . . . Use to break her own horses . . . and her own men. Every day at five o'clock she would wake me up. "Buenos pinchi días," she would say. I was twelve or thirteen years old, still in braids. . . . "Press your hands into the dough," "Con fuerza," "Put your stamp on it." One day I woke up, tú sabes, con la sangre. "Ah! So you're a woman now. Got your own cycle like the moon. Soon you'll want a man, well this is what you do. When you see the one you want, you roll the tortilla on the inside of your thigh and then you give it to him nice and warm. Be sure you give it to him and nobody else." Well, I been rolling tortillas on my thighs, on my nalgas, and God only knows where else, but I've been giving my tortillas to the wrong men . . . and that's been the problem with my life. First there was Emilio. I gave him my first tortilla. Ay Mamacita, he use to say, these are delicious. Aye, he was handsome, a real lady-killer! After he did me the favor he didn't even have the cojones to stick around . . . took my TV set, too. They're all shit . . . the Samoan bartender, what was his name . . .

JUANA: Nicky, Big Nicky.

CHATA: The guy from Pep Boys—

JUANA: Chata, you really think he'll be back?

CHATA: His son's first time in the pit? With "the" rooster? A real Morales rooster? Honey, he'll be back. Stop worrying.

JUANA: Let's put these on the griddle. Angela, Hector . . . breakfast.

SCENE III

ANGELA *slides out from under the house, wearing her wings. She carries a white box which contains her cardboard tombstones, paper and crayons, a writing tablet, and a pen. She, too, sniffs the air. She runs to the little cemetery and looks up, as* HECTOR *appears at the window behind her.*

ANGELA: Tres Rosas. . . . Did you hear? Sweet Jesus, Abuelo, Queen of Heaven, all the Saints, all the Angels. It is true. It is certain. He is coming, coming to stay forever and ever. Amen.

HECTOR: Don't count on it!

ANGELA: [*to Heaven*] Protect me from those of little faith and substance.

HECTOR: I'm warning you. You're just going to be disappointed.

ANGELA: [*to Heaven*] Guard me against the enemies of my soul.

HECTOR: Your butt's getting bigger and bigger!

ANGELA: And keep me from falling in with low companions.

HECTOR: Listen, little hummingbird woman, you gotta be tough, and grown-up today.
[ANGELA *digs up her collection can and two dolls. Both dolls are dressed in nuns' habits. One, the St. Lucy doll, has round sunglasses. She turns a box over to make a little tea table on which she places a doll's teapot and cups.*]

ANGELA: As an act of faith and to celebrate her father's homecoming, Miss Angela Ester Morales will have a tea party.

HECTOR: No more tea parties.

ANGELA: Dancing in attendance will be that charming martyr St. Lucy.

HECTOR: He will not be impressed.

ANGELA: Due to the loss of her eyes and the sensitivity of her alabaster skin, St. Lucy will sit in the shade. [*She sits St. Lucy in the shade and picks up the other doll.*]

HECTOR: Who's that?

ANGELA: St. Teresa of Avignon, you will sit over here. [*She seats St. Teresa doll.*]

HECTOR: Just don't let him con you, Angela.

ANGELA: [*pouring pretend tea*] One lump or two, St. Lucy? St. Teresa has hyperglycemia, and only takes cream in her tea. Isn't that right, St. Teresa?

HECTOR: He's not like Abuelo.

[ANGELA *animates the dolls like puppets and uses two different voices as St. Lucy and St. Teresa.*]

ANGELA: [*as St. Teresa*] Shouldn't we wait for St. Luke?

HECTOR: Stop hiding. You can't be a little girl forever.

ANGELA: [*as St. Lucy*] St. Luke! St. Luke! Indeed! How that man got into Heaven I'll never know. That story about putting peas in his boots and offering the discomfort up to God is pure bunk. I happen to know he boiled the peas first.

HECTOR: I don't want you hurt. It's time to grow up.

ANGELA: [*as St. Teresa*] St. Lucy! I can only think that it is the loss of your eyes that makes you so disagreeable. Kindly remember that we have all suffered to be saints.

HECTOR: Are you listening to me, Angie?

ANGELA: [*as St. Lucy*] Easy for you to say! They took my eyes because I wouldn't put out! They put them on a plate. A dirty, chipped one, thank you very much indeed! To this day no true effort has been made to find them.

HECTOR: Excuse me! . . . Excuse me, St. Teresa, St. Lucy, I just thought I should tell you . . . a little secret. . . . Your hostess, Miss Angela Ester Morales, lies in her little, white, chaste, narrow bed, underneath the crucifix, and masturbates.

ANGELA: Heretic! Liar!

HECTOR: Poor Jesus, up there on the cross, right over her bed, his head tilted down. He sees everything.

ANGELA: Lies! Horrible lies!

HECTOR: Poor saint of the month, watching from the night table.

ANGELA: I hate you! I hate you! Horrible, horrible Hector.

JUANA: [*from offstage*] Breakfast!

[HECTOR *leaves the window.* ANGELA *sits on the ground writing on a tombstone.*]

ANGELA: [*lettering a tombstone*] Here lies Horrible Hector Morales. Died at age twenty, in great agony, for tormenting his little sister.

JUANA: [*offstage*] You kids . . . breakfast!

HECTOR: [*pops up at window*] Just be yourself. A normal sex-crazed fifteen-year-old girl with a big gigantic enormous butt. [*He exits.*]

ANGELA: [*to Heaven*]
Send me to Alaska
Let me be frozen
Send me a contraction
A shrinking antidote
Make me little again
Please make my legs
Like tiny pink Vienna sausages
Give me back my little butt.

[JUANA *and* CHATA *bring breakfast out on the porch and set it on the table.*]

JUANA: Angie! Hector! We ain't got all day.

[ANGELA *goes to the breakfast table with the St. Lucy doll and the collection can.*]

And take your wings off before you sit at the table. Ain't you kids got any manners?

[ANGELA *removes her wings, sits down, bows her head in prayer.* CHATA *stares at St. Lucy. St. Lucy stares at* CHATA. JUANA *shoos flies and stares at the distant fire.*]

I hope he's on this side of the fire.

CHATA: That doll's staring at me.

ANGELA: She loves you.

> [*Lights fade on the women, come up on the henhouse,* ADAN, *a young man of twenty, is talking to* ZAPATA—*now a real rooster, not the actor/dancer—and preparing his feed.*]

ADAN: Hola Zapata . . . ya mi lindo . . . mi bonito En Inglés. Tengo que hablar en English . . . pinchi English . . . verdad Zapata? En Español más romántico pero Hector say I must learned di English. [ZAPATA *starts squawking.*] Qué te pasa? Orita vas a comer. [HECTOR *enters.*]

HECTOR: English, Adan . . . English.

ADAN: No English . . . pinchi English.

HECTOR: Good morning, Adan.

ADAN: A que la fregada! . . . Okay this morning in the fields, I talk English pero this after-noon for fight I talk puro Español.

HECTOR: Good morning, Adan.

ADAN: Sí, sí, good morning, muy fine. . . . Hector el Filipino he say . . . [*He moves away from* ZAPATA, *so bird will not hear him.*] He say to tell you que Zapata no win. Porque Filipino bird fight more y your bird first fight y your first fight y you got no ex . . . ex . . .

HECTOR: Experience.

ADAN: Sí eso, he say you sell bird to him y no fight. . . . He say is not true Morales bird porque Gallo not here. El Filipino say if you fight bird . . . bird dead. If bird still alive after Filipino bird beat him. . . . Bird still dead porque nobody pay money for bird that lose.

HECTOR: But if he wins, everybody wants him.

ADAN: I say, ay di poor, poor Hector. His abuelo leave him bird. He can no sell. El Filipino say, "Good!" Inside, in my heart I am laughing so hard porque he not know Gallo gonna be here. We win, we make much money.

HECTOR: It's my bird, I have to do it myself.

ADAN: You tonto! You stupido! You mulo! Like donkey. . . . He help you, he the king . . . he you papa. For him all birds fight.

HECTOR: No!

ADAN: Why? Why for you do this? You no even like bird. Zapata he knows this, he feel this thing in his heart. You just want money to go from the fields, to go to the other side of the mountains . . . to go looking . . . to go looking for what? On the other side is only more stupid people like us.

HECTOR: How could you think I just wanted money? I want him to see me.

ADAN: Sorry. . . . I am sorry my friend. . . . I know. . . . I stay with you y we win vas a ver! Okay Zapata! We win y esta noche estamos tomando Coors, Ripple, Lucky Lager, unas Buds, Johnnie Walkers, oh sí, y las beautiful señoritas. [*He gives* ZAPATA *his food.*] Eat Zapata! Be strong.

HECTOR: I almost forgot, look what I have for you . . . fresh, warm homemade tortillas.

ADAN: Oh, how nice.

HECTOR: Yes, how nice. Aunt Chata made them.

ADAN: Oh, much nice.

HECTOR: Today she woke up at five o'clock, spit a green booger the size of a small frog into a wad of Kleenex. She wrapped her soiled black "7th Fleet" kimono around her loose, flaccid, tortured, stretch-marked body and put her fattoed, corned yellow hooves into a pair of pink satin slippers. She slap-padded over to the sink, where she opened her two hippo lips and looked into the mirror. She looked sad. I looked at those lips

. . . those lips that had wrapped themselves warmly and lovingly around the cocks of a million campesinos, around thousands upon thousands of Mexicanos, Salvadoreños, Guatemaltecos. For the tide of brown men that flooded the fields of this country, she was there with her open hippo whore's lips, saying, "Bienvenidos," "Welcome," "Hola," "Howdy." Those are legendary lips, Adan.

ADAN: Yes . . . muy yes.

HECTOR: What a woman, what a comfort. Up and down the state in her beat-up station wagon. A '56 Chevy with wood panels on the sides, in the back a sad, abused mattress. She followed the brown army of pickers through tomatoes, green beans, zucchinis, summer squash, oranges, and finally Castroville, the artichoke capital of the world, where her career was stopped by the fists of a sun-crazed compañero. The ingratitude broke her heart.

ADAN: Oh my gooseness!

HECTOR: She was a river to her people, she should be rewarded, honored. No justice in the world.

ADAN: Pinchi world. [*He and* HECTOR *look to mountains.*] You look mountains. In my country I look mountains to come here. I am here and everybody still look mountains.

HECTOR: I want to fly right over them.

ADAN: No, my friend, we are here, we belong . . . la tierra.

JUANA: [*from offstage*] Hector, I ain't calling you again.

> [*Lights up on the porch.* JUANA *and* CHATA *are sitting at the table.* ANGELA *is sitting on the steps. She has her wings back on. St. Lucy and the collection can are by her side. She is writing on her tablet.*]

JUANA: Oh Gallo, what's keeping you?

CHATA: Men are shit! That's all. And it's Saturday. When do they get drunk? When do they lose their money? When do they shoot each other? Saturdays, that's when the shit hits the fan.

> [*Enter* HECTOR *and* ADAN *with* ZAPATA *in a traveling carrier.*]

JUANA: It's because I'm so plain.

HECTOR: We're better off without him.

CHATA: Buenos días Adan. Un cafecito?

ADAN: Ah. Good morning, Mrs. Chata, no gracias, ah good morning, Mrs. Morales y Miss Angelita.

> [ANGELA *sticks out her collection can.* ADAN *automatically drops coins in.*]

JUANA: Angela!

ADAN: No, is good, is for the poor. Miss Angela, she good lady . . . eh, girl. [*He pats* ANGELA *on the head.*]

JUANA: Why don't you leave the bird, so your father can see him when he gets home.

HECTOR: He's my bird. He can see it later.

JUANA: I can't believe you would do this to your own father. Birds are his life . . . and he's so proud of you.

HECTOR: This is news. How would he know, he hasn't seen me in years.

JUANA: It isn't his fault.

HECTOR: It never is.

JUANA: Your father is with us all the time, he got his eye on us, he knows everything we're doing.

ANGELA: Everything!?

JUANA: I brag about you kids in my letters. . . . His friends they tell him what a smart boy you are . . . that you're good-looking like him. . . . He's proud. . . . "A real Morales," that's what he says.

HECTOR: And did he call me a winner? A champ? A prince? And did you tell him I was in the fields?

ANGELA: What did he say about me, Mama?

HECTOR: Nothing, you're a girl and a retard. What possible use could he have for you? Grow up!

CHATA: No, you grow up.

> [ANGELA *buries herself in* CHATA'*s lap.*]

JUANA: Hector, please, Hector, for me.

HECTOR: No, Mother. Not even for you.

JUANA: You give him a chance.

HECTOR: What chance did he give us? Fighting his birds, in and out of trouble. He was never here for us, never a card, a little present for Angela. He forgot us.

JUANA: You don't understand him. He's different.

HECTOR: Just make it clear to him. Abuelo left the bird to me, not to him, to me.

JUANA: Me, me, me. You gonna choke on this me, me. Okay, okay, I'm not going to put my nose in the bird business. I just ask you for me, for Angie, be nice to him.

HECTOR: As long as we all understand the "bird business," I'll be nice to him even if it kills me, Mother.

JUANA: Now you're feeling sorry for yourself. Just eat. You can feel sorry for yourself later.

HECTOR: Why didn't I think of that. I'll eat now and feel sorry for myself later.

JUANA: Now, you kids gotta be nice and clean, you papa don't like dirty people.

CHATA: Me, too, I hate dirty people.

JUANA: Angie, you take a bath.

HECTOR: Oh, Angela, how . . . how long has it been since you and water came together? [ANGELA *hits him.*] Oww!

JUANA: You put on a nice clean dress, and I don't wanna see you wearing no dirty wings.

HECTOR: Right, Angie, put on the clean ones.

JUANA: You say "please" and "excuse me" . . . and you watch your table manners. . . . I don't want to see any pigs at my table.

HECTOR: [*making pig noises*] What a delicious breakfast! Cold eggs, sunny-side up. How cheery! How uplifting! Hmm, hmmm! [*He turns so* ANGELA *can see him. He picks up eggs with his hands and stuffs them in his mouth.*] Look, Angela, refried beans in a delicate pool of congealed fat. [*Still making pig noises, he picks up gobs of beans, stuffs them into his mouth.*]

CHATA: A que la fregada! Hector, stop playing with your food. You're making us sick.

JUANA: [*looking at watch*] 7: 20, you got ten minutes before work.

> [HECTOR *drums his fingers on the table.*]

HECTOR: Nine minutes. . . . I will now put on the same old smelly, shit-encrusted boots, I will walk to the fields. The scent of cow dung and rotting vegetation will fill the air. I will wait with the same group of beaten-down, pathetic men . . . taking their last piss against a tree, dropping hard warm turds in the bushes. All adding to this fertile whore of a valley. At 7: 30 that yellow mechanical grasshopper, the Deerfield tractor, will belch and move. At this exact moment, our foreman, John Knipe, will open his pig-sucking mouth, exposing his yellow, pointy, plaque-infested teeth. He yells, "Start picking, boys." The daily war begins . . . the intimidation of violent growth . . . the expanding melons and squashes, the hardiness of potatoes, the waxy purple succulence of eggplant, the potency of ripening tomatoes. All so smug, so rich, so ready to burst with sheer generosity and exuberance. They mock me. . . . I hear them. . . . "Hey Hector," they say, "show us whatcha got," and "Yo Hector we got bacteria out here more productive than you." . . . I look to the ground. Slugs, snails, worms slithering in the earth with such ferocious hunger they devour their own tails, flies oozing out larvae, aphids, bees, gnats, caterpillars their prolification only slightly dampened by our sprays. We still find eggsacks hiding, ready to burst forth. Their teeming life, their lust, is shameful . . . a mockery of me and my slender spirit. . . . Well it's time . . . . Bye Ma. [*He exits.*]

JUANA: [*yelling*] Hector! You gotta do something about your attitude. [*to herself.*] Try to see the bright side.

> [JUANA *and* CHATA *exit into the house, leaving* ANGELA *on the porch steps.* ADAN *runs up to her.*]

ADAN: Pssst! Miss Angelita! . . . di . . . di cartas?

ANGELA: Oh, the letters . . . that will be one dollar.

ADAN: One dollar! Adan very poor man. . . .

> [ANGELA *sticks the collection can out and shakes it.* ADAN *reaches into his pockets and drops coins into the can.*]

Oh, sí, you are very good.

> [ANGELA *puts on glasses and pulls out a letter.*]

ANGELA: [*reading letter*] Adored Señora Acosta: The impulses of my heart are such that they encourage even the most cautious man to commit indiscretion. My soul is carried to the extreme with the love that only you could inspire. Please know that I feel a true passion for your incomparable beauty and goodness. I tremulously send this declaration and anxiously await the result. Your devoted slave, Adan.

ADAN: [*sighing*] Ay, que beautiful.

ANGELA: P.S. With due respect Señora, if your husband should be home, do not turn on the porch light.

ADAN: Ah, thank you . . . thank you very much.

> [ADAN *hurriedly exits.* ANGELA *gathers her St. Lucy doll and her collection can, and exits quickly.* CHATA *enters from the house wearing "colorful" street clothes. She looks around, then swiftly exits.* HECTOR *enters, picks up* ZAPATA, *hurries off.*]
> [*The stage darkens, as if smoke from the distant fire has covered the sun. Drum rolls are heard. In the distance we hear a rooster crow and sounds of excited chickens as the henhouse comes to life.* GALLO *appears.*]

GALLO: Easy hens, shshsh! My beauties. [*He puts his suitcase down, cups his hands to his mouth, and yells to the house.*] Juana! Juana! Juana! [JUANA *opens the door.*] How many times, in the fever of homesickness, have I written out that name on prison walls, on bits of paper, on the skin of my arms. . . . Let me look at you . . . my enduring rock, my anchor made from the hard parts of the earth—minerals, rocks, bits of glass, ground shells, the brittle bones of dead animals.

JUANA: I never seen you so pale, so thin. . . .

GALLO: I'm home to rest, to fatten up, to breathe, to mend, to you.

JUANA: How long? How long will you stay?

GALLO: Here. Here is where I'll put my chair. . . . I will sit here basking in the sun, like a fat old iguana catching flies, and watching my grandchildren replant the little cemetery with the bones of tiny sparrows. Here. Here I will build the walks for my champions. Morales roosters. The brave and gallant red Cubans, the hard and high-kicking Irish Warhorses, the spirited high-flying Bolinas.

JUANA: Don't say nothing you don't mean. . . . You really gonna stay?

GALLO: [*gently*] Here. Here is where I'll plant a garden of herbs. Blessed laurel to cure fright, wild marjoram for the agony of lovesickness, cempasuchie flowers for the grief of loneliness.

[GALLO *gently kisses* JUANA, *picks her up and carries her into the house. The door slams shut.* ANGELA *enters, her wings drooping behind her. She trips over* GALLO's *suitcase. She examines it. She smells it.*]

ANGELA: Tres Rosas!

[ANGELA *looks at the house. She sits on the suitcase, crosses her arms over her chest as if she were ready to wait an eternity. The shadows of two strangers fall on her.*]

ANGELA: What do you want?

SHADOW #1: Where's Gallo?

ANGELA: Nobody's home to you, rancor.

SHADOW #2: Just go in, tell him we got something for him.

ANGELA: Nobody's home to you, resentment.

SHADOW #1: Who are you supposed to be?

ANGELA: [*holding St. Lucy doll*]
I am the angel of this yard
I am the angel of this door
I am the angel of light
I am the angel who shouts
I am the angel who thunders

SHADOW #1: She is pure crazy.

SHADOW #2: Don't play with it, it's serious.

ANGELA: You are the shadow of resentment
You are the shadow of rancor
I am the angel of acid saliva
I will spit on you.

SHADOW #1: There's time.

SHADOW #2: Yeah, later.

[ANGELA *spits. The shadows leave.* ANGELA *crosses her hands over her chest and looks to Heaven.*]

ANGELA: Holy Father. . . . Listen, you don't want him, you want me. Please take me, claim me, launch me and I will be your shooting-star woman. I will be your comet woman. I will be your morning-star woman.

SCENE IV

Lights become brighter. ANGELA *exits under the house. The door opens.* GALLO *comes out in T-shirt and pants and goes to his suitcase.* JUANA *comes to the door in slip and tight robe.*

GALLO: I never sent him to the fields.

JUANA: I know.

GALLO: I never said for you to put him there.

JUANA: No, you never said. . . .

GALLO: Then why is my son in the fields? [*They look at each other. He looks away.*] Don't look at me. I see it in your eyes. You blame me. Just like the old man.

JUANA: Abuelo never said a word against you.

GALLO: I never let him down with the birds, nobody could match me. They were the best.

JUANA: He knew that. . . .

GALLO: So, he left the bird to Hector.

JUANA: He wanted him out of the fields. We didn't know when you would be out or maybe something would happen to you.

GALLO: He let the boy into the fields, that was his sin. He allowed a Morales into the fields.

JUANA: He was old, tired, heartbroken.

GALLO: Heartbroken, he wasn't a woman to be heartbroken.

JUANA: His only son was in jail.

GALLO: Yes, we know that, the whole valley knows that. You . . . what did you do? Didn't you lay out your hard, succulent, bitch's teat at the breakfast table? So he would have the strength to stand behind a hoe, with his back bent and his eyes on the mud for ten hours a day.

JUANA: Hard work never killed anybody.

GALLO: Ay, mujer! Can't you think what you've done, you bowed his head down.

JUANA: What was I suppose to do? There ain't no other work here. I can't see anything wrong with it for a little while.

GALLO: The difference between them and us, is we never put a foot into the fields. We stayed independent—we worked for nobody. They have to respect us, to respect our roosters.

[HECTOR *and* ADAN *enter. They are both very dirty.* HECTOR *has* ZAPATA, *in his carrier.* ADAN *has a carrier containing a second rooster.* GALLO *and* HECTOR *stare at each other.*]

Well . . . you are taller. This offshoot . . . this little bud has grown.

HECTOR: Yeah, well . . . that must be why you seem . . . smaller.

GALLO: Un abrazo!

HECTOR: I'm dirty, I'm sweaty.

GALLO: I see that.

HECTOR: I'm afraid I smell of the fields.

GALLO: Yes.

HECTOR: Of cheap abundant peon labor . . . the scent would gag you.

GALLO: It's going to kill you.

HECTOR: Mama says hard work never killed anyone . . . isn't that right, Mother?

JUANA: It's only for a little while. Your papa thinks that—

GALLO: I'll tell him what I think. Now what about those tamales you promised me?

JUANA: Ah sí, con permiso . . . I got some work in the kitchen.

ADAN: Oh sí, Mrs. Juana, los tamales . . . que rico.

JUANA: [*smiling at* ADAN] I hope they're the kind you like. [*She exits into house.*]

GALLO: Hijo, you always take the bird with you into the fields?

HECTOR: No, not always.

GALLO: This bird has to look like he's got secrets . . . no one but us should be familiar with him.

HECTOR: This is Adan.

ADAN: Es un honor, Mr. El Gallo.

[ANGELA *sticks her head out from under the house.* ADAN *and* GALLO *shake hands and greet each other.*]

GALLO: [*referring to* ZAPATA] Let him out. . . . He needs a bigger carrier. . . . He's a flyer.

ADAN: Como Filipino birds?

GALLO: Yes, but this baby boy, he's got a surprise. He's got a kick.

ADAN: Like Cuban bird?

GALLO: He'll fight in the air, he'll fight on the ground. You can put spurs or razors on that kick and he'll cut any bird to ribbons. You can put money on that.

ADAN: Hijo! Señor . . . how you know? He never fight. Maybe he only kick in cage.

GALLO: I know because I'm his papa. . . . [*pointing to the other carrier*] That your bird?

ADAN: Sí, pero no good . . . no fight. San Juan, he run away.

GALLO: I'll make him fight. Just let him out.

ADAN: Mr. El Gallo, you give this pendejo bird too much honor. Gracias Señor, pero this poor bird, he no can fight.

GALLO: Is it the bird, or you who will not fight?

HECTOR: The bird is too young. He doesn't want him to fight.

GALLO: I've never seen a bird that won't fight, but there are men who are cowards.

HECTOR: He is not a coward.

ADAN: This is true, pero I am not El Gallo. In my country all men who love di rooster know Mr. El Gallo. They tell of di famoso día de los muertos fight in Jacinto Park.

GALLO: Ah, you heard about that fight. You remember that fight, Hector?

HECTOR: No.

GALLO: First time you saw a real cockfight. . . . Abuelo took you. . . . How could you forget your first cockfight? [to ADAN] Go on, take your bird out. I'll make him fight.

[GALLO *takes a drink from a bottle, then blows on* SAN JUAN. *As he does this, lights go down almost to black. Pinspot comes up center stage, as other lights come up to a dark red. During this process, we hear* GALLO's *voice—*"Ready," *then a few beats later* "Pit!" *On this cue two dancer/roosters jump into the pinspot. This rooster dance is savage. The dancers wear razors on their feet. The* ZAPATA *dancer jumps very high. The poor* SAN JUAN *dancer stays close to the ground. Throughout the dance, we hear drums and foot-stomping. At every hit, there is a big drum pound. During the fight,* HECTOR *appears on the porch.*]

HECTOR: [*to himself*] It was in Jacinto Park. . . . The crowd was a monster, made up of individual human beings stuck together by sweat and spittle. Their gaping mouths let out screams, curses, and foul gases, masticating, smacking eager for the kill. You stood up. The monster roared. Quasimoto, your bird, in one hand. You lifted him high, "Pit!" went the call. "Pit!" roared the monster. And you threw him into the ring . . . soaring with the blades on his heels flashing I heard the mighty rage of his wings and my heart soared with him. He was a whirlwind flashing and slashing like a dark avenging angel then like some distant rainbow star exploding he was hit. The monster crowd inhaled, sucking back their hopes. . . . In that vacuum he was pulled down. My heart went down the same dark shaft, my brains slammed against the earth's hard crust . . . my eyes clouded . . . my arteries gushed . . . my lungs collapsed. "Get up," said Abuelo, "up here with me, and you will see a miracle." You, Father, picked up Quasimoto, a lifeless pile of bloody feathers, holding his head oh so gently, you closed your eyes, and like a great wave receding, you drew a breath that came from deep within your ocean floor. I heard the stones rumble, the mountains shift, the topsoil move, and as your breath slammed on the beaches, Quasimoto sputtered back to life. Oh Papi, breathe on me.

[ANGELA *appears and stands behind her brother. Her wings are spread very far out. Drums and stomping crescendo as* ZAPATA *brutally kills* SAN JUAN. *Blackout.*]

ACT TWO

SCENE I

Early afternoon. The table is set up in the middle of the yard in a festive way, with tablecloth, flowers, a bowl of peaches, and bottles of whiskey and wine. GALLO *is in the henhouse with* ADAN. HECTOR *is in the bathroom,* JUANA *and* CHATA *are in the kitchen.* ANGELA *is by the little cemetery writing on a tombstone.*

ANGELA: Here lies Angela Ester Morales died of acute neglect. Although she is mourned by many, she goes to a far, far, better place, where they have better food.

[ANGELA *slides under the house as* JUANA *comes out wearing a fresh housedress and carrying a steaming pot.*]

JUANA: [*yelling*] Hector! Angela! You kids wash up, it's time to eat.

[JUANA *hurries back into the house, almost knocking* CHATA *down as she comes out with a tray of tortillas. She is heavily made up, wearing tight clothes, dangling earrings, high-heeled shoes. A cigarette dangles from her mouth.*]

CHATA: Why are you eating out here?

JUANA: He wants it. Says he don't wanta hide in the house.

CHATA: Begging for trouble.

JUANA: What can I do, he's the man. [*She goes into the house.*]

CHATA: Ah, they're all shit! Just want trouble. Soup's on!

> [CHATA *pours herself a quick shot of whiskey, shoots it down and makes a face.* JUANA *comes out with another pot.*]

JUANA: You better tell 'em that the food's ready. [CHATA *goes to henhouse.*] Hector!

HECTOR: [*coming out on porch*] What?

JUANA: It's time to eat. . . . You look real nice, honey. Makes me proud to have your papa see you all dressed up.

HECTOR: Okay. Okay. Don't make a big deal about it. I just don't want him to think—

JUANA: I just feel so happy—

HECTOR: I just don't want him to think—

JUANA: Hijito! You love your papa . . . don't you?

HECTOR: Mother!

JUANA: I know you a little mad at him . . . pero when he comes home it's like the sun when it—

HECTOR: Shshshsh!

> [CHATA, GALLO, *and* ADAN *come out of the henhouse.*]

GALLO: We have to sharpen and polish those spurs. I want them to flash.

JUANA: [*to* GALLO] The food's ready. . . . We fixed what you like . . . mole, rice, frijolitos . . . tamales.

GALLO: Tamales estilo Jalisco!

CHATA: [*looking* HECTOR *over*] Ay Papi que rico estás! [HECTOR *quickly sits down.*] Honey! You gonna have to beat all them women off with a stick, when they see you and that rooster tonight.

ADAN: No worry, Hector, I be there . . . down you mujeres, women leave de Mr. Hector and me alone. . . . Ay Mama! [*He has a giggling fit.*]

GALLO: [*kissing* JUANA] It's wonderful to be in love . . . to be touched by the noble fever.

CHATA: Ah, you're better off with a touch of typhoid.

JUANA: I . . . gracias al Señor que . . . my whole family is here. [*She looks around. She yells.*] Angela! Angie!

HECTOR: Mom!

JUANA: Where is she? Where is your sister?

HECTOR: Talking to the saints! I don't know.

> [JUANA *gets up, goes to the spot where* ANGELA *slides under the house, gets down on her hands and knees and yells.*]

JUANA: Angela! Angela! You leave them saints alone. You hear me!

> [*As everybody looks at* JUANA, ANGELA *comes from behind the house and tiptoes toward the henhouse.* HECTOR *is the only one to see her. Using hand signals, she pleads to him to be quiet.* JUANA *peers under the house.*]

Angie! Honey . . . your mama worked for days to fix this food and now it's getting cold. [*to* GALLO] You should see how sweet she looks when she's all dressed up. [*to under the house*] You ain't got no manners . . . ain't even said hello to your father. [*to* GALLO] She prays a lot . . . and she's got real pretty eyes.

CHATA: [*to* GALLO] She's sorta . . . the bashful type . . . you know.

JUANA: [*to* GALLO] And she ain't spoiled.

CHATA: [*taking a drink*] Nah, all them kids smell like that.

JUANA: [*to under the house*] Angie!

GALLO: Juana, leave her alone.

JUANA: Okay. Angie, I'm gonna ignore you, 'cause you spoiled my day, this day that I been looking forward to for years and years and now you making me look like a bad mama, what's your papa gonna think of us.

GALLO: Juana, she'll come out when she's ready.

[JUANA *goes back to the table.*]

CHATA: Maybe was them roosters fighting got her scared.

ADAN: Poor San Juan.

GALLO: Adan, drink up and I'll see you get one of our famous Champion Morales birds.

HECTOR: What famous Champion Morales birds?

GALLO: The ones I paid for dearly, the ones I came home to raise . . . isn't that right, mi amor?

JUANA: Yes . . . you see, honey, your papa's gonna stay home . . . raise birds. . . . I think Abuelo would want that.

GALLO: And after they see our bird tonight . . . See, first I want them to think it's just you and the bird up there. After the bets are down, I'll take over and they're gonna know we got roosters. A toast . . .

[*As* GALLO *stands up, everybody raises a glass, except* HECTOR. ANGELA *tiptoes from the henhouse carrying* ZAPATA. *She goes behind and under the house. Only* HECTOR *sees her.*]

To the finest fighting cocks ever to be seen. [*He slides bottle to* HECTOR.]

HECTOR: [*sliding bottle back.*] No.

[*pause*]

GALLO: Too good to drink with your old man.

HECTOR: I only drink with people I trust.

CHATA: Me . . . I drink with anybody. Maybe that's my problem.

GALLO: I am your father.

HECTOR: Yes. You are my father.

CHATA: I like it better when I drink alone. Ya meet a better class of people that way.

HECTOR: But it's my bird. Abuelo left it to me.

GALLO: Abuelo was my father, and you are my son. I see no problem. Now let's eat.

HECTOR: Mother!

JUANA: Let's eat, honey, and we can talk about it later.

ADAN: Ay the mole muy delicious . . . the mole muy rico . . . the mole muy beautiful y Mrs. Juana. Today, you look beautiful, like the mole.

GALLO: Hm, sabroso, exquisito.

JUANA: I bet you been in plenty of fancy places got better food than this.

GALLO: This is home cooking, I know that your hands made it. . . . These . . . these are the hands of a beautiful woman. . . .

HECTOR: Ha! Bullshit.

GALLO: We say your mother is beautiful and you call it bullshit! I find that very disrespectful.

JUANA: Hijo, you're right. . . . It's just the way people talk, I know I ain't beautiful.

GALLO: I say you are beautiful.

ADAN: Sí, muy beautiful.

GALLO: Ya ves! . . . If your son doesn't have the eyes, the soul, the imagination to see it . . . it's his loss.

HECTOR: That's right. I just can't seem to stretch my imagination that far.

GALLO: This is an insult to your mother.

HECTOR: It's the truth. That is a plain, tired, worn-out woman.

GALLO: Shut up.

HECTOR: The hands of a beautiful woman! Those aren't hands, they're claws because she has to scratch for her living.

JUANA: Please, Hector, let him say what he wants. . . . I know I ain't beautiful. It don't go to my head.

HECTOR: But it goes to your heart which is worse. Did he ever really take care of you? Did he ever go out and work to put food on the table, to buy you a dress? All he has is words, and he throws a few cheap words to you and you come to life. Don't you have any pride?

GALLO: Your mother has great courage to trust and believe in me.

HECTOR: Stupidity!

GALLO: You know nothing!

HECTOR: You don't seem to realize that it is my rooster. And that after the fight, depending on the outcome, I will sell him or eat him. I have made a deal with the Filipinos.

JUANA: Ay, Hector! You've spoiled everything. All this food . . . I worked so hard . . . for this day.

GALLO: You're not selling anything to anybody. This is nothing to joke about.

HECTOR: I don't want to spend my life training chickens to be better killers. And I don't want to spend my whole life in this valley. Mother, Aunt Chata, excuse me.

CHATA: Ah? . . . O sí hijo pase . . . sometimes Hector can be a real gentleman.
[HECTOR *starts to leave.*]

GALLO: Son! . . . You have no courage, no juice. . . . You are a disgrace to me.

JUANA: Ay, Gallo, don't say that to him.

HECTOR: Do you think I care what you think . . . Father.

JUANA: Hijo no . . . for me, just once for me. I don't wanna be alone no more.

HECTOR: What about me? You have me, you'll always have me, I'll work, I've always worked, I can take care of you. I won't leave you.

JUANA: It ain't the same, honey.

HECTOR: Yeah. . . . He comes first for you, he will always come first.

GALLO: If you sell that bird, it will be over your dead body.

HECTOR: You can't stop me.
[*Exit* HECTOR. CHATA *takes a plate of food and bowl of peaches to the under-the-house area and tries to tempt* ANGELA *out.*]

GALLO: He doesn't seem to realize . . . coward . . . too bad.
[GALLO *goes to the henhouse.* JUANA *starts to follow him.*]

JUANA: Talk to him. . . . He's a good boy. . . . If you just talk . . . [*Seeing* ADAN *still eating.*] Is it good? You really like it?

ADAN: Hm! Sabroso!

CHATA: Come on, Angie. . . . It's real good.
[GALLO *returns running.*]

GALLO: He's gone. . . . The bird is gone. . . .

ADAN: Yo no see nada, nada.

JUANA: He'll bring it back, he's a good boy. He's just a little upset . . . you know.

GALLO: Nobody fools with my roosters. Not even this over-petted, over-pampered viper you spawned. Go and pray to your Dark Virgin. You know what I'm capable of.
[*Exit* GALLO. ADAN *stops eating and tries to comfort* JUANA *as she puts her head down on the table and cries.*]

ADAN: No cry, no cry, Mrs. Juana. Di women cry y Adan, he not know what to do. [JUANA *cries louder.*] Ay, Mrs. Juana, for sure di flowers will die . . . di trees will be torn from di ground, freshness will leave di morning, softness will leave di night . . . [JUANA's *cries increase.*] Ay Dios! [*From his pocket, he brings out the letter* ANGELA

wrote for him. He crosses himself.] Mrs. di Juana . . . [*reading with great difficulty*]
Di . . . impulses . . . of my . . . heart . . . are such . . . [*throwing letter aside*] A que
la fregada! Mrs. Juana, Adan have mucho amor for you. My heart break to see you
cry. I will not a breathe. When you no cry then I will breathe.

> [ADAN *takes a big breath and holds it. Slowly* JUANA *stops crying and lifts her head.*
> ADAN, *suffering some discomfort, continues to hold his breath.*]

JUANA: I been dreaming. Nothing's gonna change. I gotta face facts.

> [ADAN *lets his breath out in a great whoosh.* ANGELA *pops out from under the house
> and takes a peach from* CHATA's *hand. She stares at the peach with great intensity.*]

CHATA: Angie, ain't it nice to have the family all together again?

ANGELA: There is no pit in this peach. It is hollow. Instead of the pit, there is a whole little world, a little blue-green crystal-clear ocean, with little schools of tiny darting silver fish. On a tiny rock sits a mermaid with little teenie-weenie kinky yellow hair. A
tiny sun is being pulled across a little china-blue sky by teenie-weenie white horses
with itty-bitty wings. There is an island with tiny palm trees and tiny thatched hut.
Next to the hut stand a tiny man and woman. She is wearing flowers and leaves. He
is wearing one single leaf. On their heads are little bitty halos. In their arms is a little bitsy baby. He isn't wearing anything.

CHATA: Let me see. . . . [*Looking at peach.*] I can't see dick!

BLACKOUT

SCENE II

Later in the afternoon. CHATA *sits on the porch steps, her legs spread out, fanning herself.* JUANA
sits on a straight-back chair, her hands folded on her lap. She rocks herself gently. She watches
ANGELA, *who is sitting on the ground drawing circles in the dirt and humming softly. The circles get deeper and deeper.*

CHATA: It's hot. . . . I am waiting for a cool breeze. . . .

ANGELA: Uh ha uh ha uh ha uh haa.

CHATA: Aire fresco . . . come on, cool breeze, come right over here.

ANGELA: Uh ha uh ha uh haa.

CHATA: Women! We're always waiting.

> [ANGELA *hums for a beat, then there is silence for a beat.*]

JUANA: It's because I'm so plain.

CHATA: Ah, you just work too much.

JUANA: Plainness runs in my family. My mother was plain, my grandmother was plain, my
great-grandmother—

CHATA: It was the hard times . . . the hard work that did it.

JUANA: My Aunt Chona was the plainest.

CHATA: I don't remember her.

JUANA: The one with the crossed eyes and the little mustache.

CHATA: Ay, Juanita, that woman had a beautiful soul, sewing those little tiny outfits for the
statues of the saints. That woman was a saint.

JUANA: She's the one told on you that time you was drinking beer with them sailors at the
cockfight.

CHATA: Disgusting old bitch!

> [ANGELA *hums for a beat as she continues drawing circles.*]

JUANA: I get up at six, I brush my teeth, no creams, no lotions, what they gonna do for me?
I work, that's all. I take care of people and I work. People look at me, they know that's

all I do. I ain't got no secrets. No hidden gardens. I keep busy, that's what I do. Don't stop, that's what I say to myself. Don't stop, 'cause you're not pretty enough, exciting enough, smart enough to just stand there.

ANGELA: Mama, I don't wanna be plain.

CHATA: Honey, you're too colorful to be plain.

ANGELA: Yeah, that's what I thought.

CHATA: Your mama forgets . . . those years when her heart was filled with wild dreams when she use to weave white star jasmine vines in her hair and drive all the men crazy.

JUANA: It ain't true. . . . She was the one always getting me in trouble.

CHATA: I wasn't the one they called Juanita la Morenita Sabrosita.

JUANA: Oh, Chata. We was young girls together . . . in the summer, at Jacinto Park . . . cock-fights, fistfights, the music. At night we would jump out of our bedroom windows in our party dresses. With our good shoes in one hand, our hearts in the other, we ran barefoot through the wet grass, above us all the stars twinkling go, go, go.

CHATA: Nothing could stop us. . . . We had a short time being girls.

JUANA: Now, all I am is an old hag.

CHATA: It ain't true.

JUANA: Sí, it's true enough. I carry burdens, I hang sheets, I scrub, I gather, I pick up, "Here sit down," "I'll wash it," "Here's fifty cents," "Have my chair," "Take my coat," "Here's a piece of my own live flesh"!

CHATA: Es la menopause, that's what it is. You getting it early. I knew this woman once, use to pull out her hair.

JUANA: I don't care, I don't want any stories, I don't care what happens to Fulano Mangano. . . . I just wanna stand still, I wanna be interesting, exciting enough to stand still.

CHATA: Ay, mujer!

JUANA: And I want to look like I got secrets.

CHATA: Juana!

JUANA: Don't call me Juana. Juana is a mule's name.

CHATA: Ah, you're crazy! That new gray hen, the kids named her Juana. See, they think of you.

JUANA: A gray hen! An old gray hen, that's all I am. An old gray hen in a family of roosters. No more! I want feathers, I wanna strut, too. I wanna crow.

ANGELA: Mama!

JUANA: Don't! Don't call me "Mama." I am not Mama. . . . I am . . . I am that movie star, that famous dancer and heartbreaker "Morenita Sabrosita" . . . and now if my fans will excuse me I'm gonna take a bath in champagne, eat cherry bonbons and paint my toenails. [*She goes into the house.*]

CHATA: [*to* JUANA] We got champagne?

> [CHATA *goes into the house as* ANGELA *goes to the little cemetery and puts up a new tombstone.*]

ANGELA: [*printing on tombstone*] Here lies Juana Morales. Beloved Wife of El Gallo, Blessed Mother to Angela and Horrible Hector. Died of acute identity crisis sustained during la menopause.

SCENE III

Lights go down, as ANGELA *sits on her box/table at the little cemetery. The long shadows of men fall on* ANGELA *and the cemetery.*

SHADOW #1: There's that spooky kid. You go, brother.

SHADOW #2: Ah, it's just a weird kid. Hey! You! Kid!

[ANGELA *does not acknowledge them.*]

SHADOW #1: Call her "Angel."

SHADOW #2: Hey, Angel.

[ANGELA *looks up.*]

SHADOW #1: See what I mean.

SHADOW #2: Listen kid, tell your old man, we got business to discuss.

SHADOW #1: Yeah, and you make sure he gets the message.

ANGELA: My old man, my Holy Father, my all-powerful Father, sees no problems. If there are problems, I am the angel of this yard. I am the comet. I am the whirlwind. I am the shooting stars. Feel my vibrance.

SHADOW #1: I feel it, right behind my ears, like . . . like . . .

ANGELA: Locust wings.

SHADOW #1: Let's get outta here.

SHADOW #2: Tell Gallo some pals dropped by to settle an old score.

SHADOW #1: Come on!

SHADOW #2: [*voice trailing off*] Hey! That kid don't scare me, see.

SHADOW #1: [*voice trailing off*] I'm telling ya, my ears hurt.

[*Exit shadows. Lights go back up.* ANGELA *folds her hands in prayer.*]

ANGELA: Holy Father, please help me, I feel the illumination, the fever of grace slipping away. I need to know that you are with me, that you take an interest in my concerns. Send me a little demonstration, a sign. Any sign . . . I don't care. Stigmata, visions, voices, send an angel, burn a bush. . . . I am attracted to levitation . . . but you choose . . . . I'll just lay here and wait.

[ANGELA *lies on the ground waiting. After a few beats* HECTOR *enters. He slowly walks up to* ANGELA *and looks down on her for a beat.*]

HECTOR: What are you doing?

ANGELA: [*sitting up*] Ohhh . . . you're no sign.

HECTOR: What is going on?

ANGELA: Weird, shady men came here looking for Gallo. Two of them. They were not polite.

HECTOR: I see. . . . So your reaction is to lay stretched out on the dirt instead of going into the house.

ANGELA: Hector, please, I am scared. . . . I wanted a sign.

[HECTOR *sits down next to* ANGELA.]

HECTOR: Hey, you're the shooting-star woman, you can't be scared.

ANGELA: I am scared. Really scared. If I grow up will I still be scared? Are grown-ups scared?

HECTOR: Always scared, trembling . . . cowering . . . this . . . this second, now . . . this planet that we are sitting on is wobbling precariously on its lightning path around the sun and every second the sun is exploding . . . stars are shooting at us from deep distant space, comets zoom around us, meteor rocks are being hurled through distances we measure in light. . . . This very earth which we call our home, our mother, has catastrophic moods, she keeps moving mountains, receding oceans, shifting poles, bucking and reeling like an overburdened beast trying to shake us off. . . . Life is violent.

ANGELA: You're scared about the fight . . . huh?

HECTOR: No. Whatever happens, Papi will still only care about the rooster. That's his son, that's who gets it all.

ANGELA: Maybe if we gave him the rooster he'd stay here and be happy.

HECTOR: He has to stay for us, not the rooster. . . . Angela . . . you . . . you were great taking the rooster.

ANGELA: He kept killing the little chicks. How could he do that, Hector? He's their papa.

HECTOR: Training. Look, Angela, you're the angel of this yard. You keep a close guard on that rooster. Don't let anyone near him . . . promise me.

ANGELA: Yes.

HECTOR: That's a real promise now. No crossed fingers behind your back.

ANGELA: I promise already. [*She spreads her hands out in front of her, then kisses the tip of her thumb.*] May God strike me dumb, make me a plain whiny person and take away my gift of faith. Forever and ever, throughout my mortal years on earth, and throughout the everlasting fires of hell. Amen. Satisfied?

HECTOR: Yes.

ANGELA: Gee, maybe I should have given myself a little leeway, a little room for error. [CHATA *enters from the house with a bottle and glass.*]

HECTOR: Too late now. Can't take it back.

CHATA: Oh, oh, look who's here. Angie, your mama needs some cheering up, a nice hug, an angel's kiss, maybe a little song.

ANGELA: Litany to the Virgin. That's her favorite. [*She exits.*]

CHATA: Men are shit. Pure shit.

HECTOR: And you're still drinking.

CHATA: Stay outta my drinking. You hurt your mama, Hector.

HECTOR: Too bad.

CHATA: Ay Dios, what a man he is now.

HECTOR: Yeah, well, what about you? Didn't you break Abuelo's heart when you became a whore?

CHATA: They called me the encyclopedia of love. You want to turn a few pages? Your Aunt Chata could show you a few things.

HECTOR: You're disgusting.

CHATA: Is that what fascinates you, honey? Is that why I always find you peeping at me, mirrors at the keyhole, your eyeballs in the cracks, spying when I'm sleeping, smelling my kimono.

HECTOR: You're drunk.

CHATA: I ain't drunk, honey.

HECTOR: You drink too much. It's not . . . good for you . . . It makes you ugly.

CHATA: Ain't none of your business. Don't tell me what to do, Hector.

HECTOR: I have to, it's for your own good.

CHATA: You got nothing to say about it, you ain't my man, and you ain't your mama's man. The sooner you learn that the better. . . . Take your bird, leave it, eat or sell it, but get out of here. [HECTOR *stands alone in the yard, as she goes to the door. She turns. They look at each other.*] What are you hanging around here for? Go on! Get out! It ain't your home anymore. [*She takes a broom and shoos* HECTOR *from the yard.*] Shoo! Shoo! You don't belong here, it ain't your place anymore.

HECTOR: Stop it, stop it, stop it.

[HECTOR *goes to the outside boundary of the yard, where he falls to his knees and buries his face in his hands, as* CHATA *comes slowly up behind him.*]

CHATA: I feel like I'm tearing my own flesh from my bones. . . . He's back. Honey, we got too many roosters in this yard.

HECTOR: Did you sleep with my father? Did he yearn for you as you slept in your little white, chaste, narrow bed? Did he steal you when you were dreaming?

CHATA: [*embracing him*] Shshsh . . .

HECTOR: I'm not like him.

CHATA: You're just like him, so handsome you make my teeth ache.

HECTOR: Whore, mother, sister, saint-woman, moon-woman, give me the shelter of your darkness, fold me like a fan and take me into your stillness, submerge me beneath the water, beneath the sea, beneath the mysteries, baptize me, bear me up, give me life, breathe on me.

> [CHATA *enfolds him as the lights fade. We hear* ANGELA *reciting the litany.*]

ANGELA: [*offstage*] She is the Gate of Heaven, the Mystical Rose, the Flower of Consolation, the Fire of Transcendence, and the Queen of Love.

SCENE IV

Lights come up to indicate that time has passed. ANGELA *is alone in the yard. She sniffs the air.*

ANGELA: Tres Rosas!

> [ANGELA *slides under the house as* GALLO *enters. He sees a brief flash of* ANGELA *from the corner of his eye. He walks slowly into the yard. He stops by the little cemetery and reads the tombstones. Feeling the urge for a drink, he goes to the table and has a shot. He sits.*]

GALLO: Acute neglect? . . . uh-huh . . . I thought I felt a little spirit, slight, delicate . . . yes, I feel it. A little tenderness . . . a little greenness . . . [*examining the ground*] What's this? Tracks . . . little tiny paws . . . there . . . [*following tracks*] and there . . .

> [GALLO *pretends to be following tracks to the porch. Then with one great leap he jumps in the opposite direction, surprising the hell out of* ANGELA, *and pulls her from under the house by her heels.*]

Ah, ha!

ANGELA: Shit! Hey! You're ripping my wings! You shithead! Put me down! Don't touch me!

> [GALLO *puts* ANGELA *down, throws his hands up to indicate he won't touch her. They stand and stare at each other.* ANGELA *goes to the little cemetery, never taking her eyes off* GALLO. *They continue to stare for a beat, then* ANGELA *looks up to Heaven, slapping her hands together in prayer.*]

There is a person here trying to con me, but I don't con that easy.

GALLO: [*slapping his hands in prayer*] There is a person here who swallows saints but defecates devils.

ANGELA: [*to Heaven*] He comes here smelling of rosas using sweet oily words. . . . It's phony, it's obnoxious, it's obscene. . . . I wanna throw up.

GALLO: I came here to see my baby, my little angel, my little woman of the shooting stars, my light delicate splendorous daughter. But she is as light, as delicate, as splendid as an angel's fart.

ANGELA: Angels do not fart. They do not have a digestive system. That's why they can all scrunch together on the head of a pin.

GALLO: Oh . . . I only come with my love—

ANGELA: You only came with words. . . . Well, where were these words on my birthday, Christmas, my saint's day? Where's my Easter outfit, my trip to Disneyland, the orthodontist. . . . You owe me.

GALLO: Sweet Jesus. . . . What a monster! I owe you . . . but Angela! Angela! Angela! How many times have I written that name on prison walls. On bits of paper, on the skin of my arms.

ANGELA: [*to Heaven*] He's hopeless! You write everybody's name on your arms.

GALLO: Women like to know that they're on your flesh.

ANGELA: I am not a woman. I'm your baby daughter. You said so yourself.

GALLO: I'm afraid . . . fathers to daughters . . . that's so delicate. I don't know . . . what to do . . . help me, Angela. How do I know what to do?

ANGELA: Instinct! Ain't ya got no instinct? Don't you feel anything?

GALLO: [*moving closer to* ANGELA] When you were a little baby, you were a miracle of tiny fingers and toes and dimples and you had a soft spot on the top of your head.

ANGELA: I still have it, see.

GALLO: I wanted to take you into my arms and crush you against my chest so that I could keep you forever and nobody, and nothing, could ever, ever hurt you because you would be safe . . . my little offshoot, my little bud, my little flower growing inside my chest.

ANGELA: Papi . . .

GALLO: Sí, sí, hijita. Your papi's here.

ANGELA: And Papi, these men come all the—

GALLO: [*holding* ANGELA] Shshsh . . . it's nothing, nothing and you thought I forgot about you. . . . Well, it just hurt too much, do you understand?

ANGELA: You had to pull down some hard time and the only way to survive was to cut off all feelings and become an animal just like the rest of them.

GALLO: Well, something like that. Honey, you know what I wish—

ANGELA: Papa, did the lights really go down when they put the people in the electric chair?

GALLO: Angela, what a . . . Honey, you know what I wish—

ANGELA: Did they force you to make license plates? Hector and I would look real close at the ones that started with a G. We thought you made them. "What craftsmanship!" Hector used to say.

GALLO: Don't you have any normal interests?

ANGELA: Like what?

GALLO: Like swimming. . . . You know what I wish? That we could take a trip and see the ocean together.

ANGELA: I've never seen the ocean. When?

GALLO: Just you and me. Laying on our bellies, feeding the seagulls, riding the waves.

ANGELA: I can't swim.

GALLO: I will teach you, that's what fathers are for—

ANGELA: [*to Heaven*] Angels and saints, did you hear? My father's going to teach me to swim!

GALLO: Now Angela, I didn't promise.

ANGELA: But you said—

GALLO: I want to but I have to hurry and fix things. I have to find Hector, talk to him and find that rooster fast before Hector sells him. Honey, you pray to St. Anthony, your prayers are powerful . . . unless . . . St. Anthony, he listen to you?

ANGELA: [*crossing her fingers*] Hey, we're like that.

GALLO: Ask St. Anthony, Angela . . . then we can go to the ocean.

ANGELA: Truly, Papi? Just you and me? And will you stay with us forever and ever?

GALLO: Wild horses couldn't drag me away.

ANGELA: Close your eyes. Tony! Tony! Look around, Zapata's lost and can't be found. [*She goes under the house, gets* ZAPATA, *and gives him to* GALLO.] I found him, Papi, he was—

GALLO: Ya lindo, ya. [*to bird*] Papa's got you now. Angela, you keep quiet now, honey, this is our secret.

ANGELA: What about Hector?

GALLO: I'm going to talk to Hector now. You go inside and get all dressed up. So I can be proud of my girl. I'll pick you up after the fight. [*He exits.*]

ANGELA: Your girl! [*singing*] *We are going to the ocean, we are going to the sea, we are going to the ocean to see what we can see* . . .

    [ANGELA *goes into the house. We hear cha-cha music.*]

CHATA: [*offstage*] One, two . . . not like that . . . I'm getting tired. . . . What time's "Zorro" on?

JUANA: [*offstage*] No, no. . . . Just one more. [*singing*] Cha, cha, cha, que rico . . . cha, cha, cha. . . . Ay, I could do it all night.

> [*Enter* GALLO *running, breathing hard. He has* ZAPATA's *carrier. He goes to the door and yells.*]

GALLO: Juana! Juana!

> [JUANA *and* CHATA *come to the door.*]

I need money . . . and my stuff. I gotta leave. . . . Something's come up. . . . Do you hear me? I need money now.

JUANA: I hear ya. . . . You ain't even been here a day and already you're gone. . . . Nothing's going to change with you . . . nothing. I was having fun, dancing, remembering old times, do you know how long—

GALLO: I don't have time for this, just give me the money.

JUANA: I ain't got any!

CHATA: I got some. [*She goes in the house.*]

GALLO: The Filipino, somebody told him about the bird. Oh, ya, ya my little hen, don't you ruffle those pretty feathers, I'll be back.

JUANA: No, you always gonna be running.

GALLO: If it was just me, I'd stay. You know that, Juana? You know I'd stay, but I got the bird to think of, gotta hide him, breed him good, soon as I get some good stags I'll come home. . . . This is just a little setback.

> [CHATA *returns with suitcase and money.*]

JUANA: You know how long it's been since I went dancing?

CHATA: Here, you're gonna need this. [*Gives him the suitcase.*] And this is all the cash I got.

> [ANGELA *enters as* GALLO *counts the money. She is dressed in a red strapless dress made tight by large visible safety pins, high heels, and a great deal of heavy makeup and jewelry. The effect is that of a young girl dressed like a tart for a costume party. She carries a suitcase, purse, and her collection can.*]

GALLO: Is this all you got?

ANGELA: [*shaking the can*] Don't worry, Papa, I got my donation-can money.

> [*They all stare at her for a beat.*]

JUANA AND CHATA: Angela?!!

JUANA: Angie, you got on your mama's old party dress.

CHATA: Yeah, and all my jewelry. . . . Where you going?

ANGELA: Papa, didn't you hear me? I have money. [*She shakes the can.*]

GALLO: Oh honey, don't you look pretty. . . . Now you got a little bit too much lipstick on, let your mama wipe some off.

ANGELA: Are we leaving now?

JUANA: Gallo!

GALLO: Shshsh Juana . . . Angela, I gotta talk to your mama for a few minutes. You go in the house and I'll come and get you.

ANGELA: Are you sure?

GALLO: Don't you trust me, Angie?

CHATA: Come on, Angie, I'll show you how to draw eyebrows. First you draw a straight line across your forehead and then spit on your finger and rub out the middle. Let's go in and try it.

ANGELA: Really, Aunt Chata, I'm not a child, you don't have to patronize me.

CHATA: Okay, I'll give you the low-down on blow-jobs.

> [ANGELA *and* CHATA *go into the house.*]

Now, don't tell your mama . . .

GALLO: Juana, keep her in the house until I leave.

JUANA: You promised to take her with you?

GALLO: I had to get the bird. I said I would take her to the ocean.

JUANA: Ay bruto! How could you do it?

GALLO: How was I to know this would happen . . . and Juanita, it hurts me to say this but that kid is crazy. . . .

JUANA: No, no, Señor, she is not crazy and I ain't gonna let you call her crazy. She got the spirit they broke in me. I ain't gonna let it happen to her.

GALLO: Shshsh! Don't get so excited. It isn't important.

JUANA: It's important. . . . It's her spirit, her soul and you ain't gonna stomp on it . . . you hear me.

[ADAN *enters running.*]

ADAN: Mr. El Gallo . . . bad men! Mucho bad, y mucho ugly. Looking for you y Zapata. All over they look for you . . . Big Nicky's, Castro Fields, Don Pancho's. . . . You leave, Mr. El Gallo. You go far away. I take you. I go for my truck.

GALLO: You are a good friend, Adan, and my new partner.

ADAN: Oh, thank you, Mr. El Gallo. I am proud. But is better I come back here to Mrs. Juana y Hector.

JUANA: Thank you, Adan.

GALLO: We better hurry.

ADAN: Sí, sí, I come back with truck. [*He exits.*]

[JUANA *goes into the house.* HECTOR *enters as* GALLO *starts to pack his suitcase.*]

HECTOR: [*seeing* ZAPATA] You must have really sold her a bill of goods to get Zapata.

GALLO: Look, there's trouble. . . . The Filipino send you?

HECTOR: No, how could you think I would work for him, but I came to get Zapata.

GALLO: You're the one told him about the bird.

HECTOR: Yes. I made a deal with the Filipino. He'll leave you alone if I give him the rooster.

GALLO: That's a lie and you fell for it.

HECTOR: No, he is an honorable man, we were here unprotected for seven years and he never bothered us. It's his bird, Papi.

GALLO: No, I paid seven years of my life for this baby.

HECTOR: And he lost his son. It's the right thing to do.

[*A truck horn is heard.* ANGELA *comes out of the house with her suitcase,* JUANA *and* CHATA *follow after her.*]

ANGELA: Papa? Are we leaving now, Papa?

JUANA: Angie! No!

HECTOR: So that's it. . . . Angela, get back in the house.

ANGELA: I'm going with him, Hector.

HECTOR: Get back in the house, nobody's going anywhere.

ANGELA: No! I don't have to listen to you anymore. You're not my father.

JUANA: Angie . . . he's not going to the ocean. . . . He can't take you.

[*We hear the sound of* ADAN'S *truck. The horn is heard as* GALLO *starts backing away, picking up* ZAPATA'S *carrier.*]

ANGELA: Papi, wait for me! Papa, you promised.

GALLO: You're all grown up now, you don't need your old man.

CHATA: Hector!

[GALLO *turns, tries to run out.* ANGELA *grabs him, knocking* ZAPATA'S *carrier out of his hand.* HECTOR *picks up the carrier.*]

ANGELA: No, Papa, we need you and Mama needs you, we've been waiting, and waiting, you can't leave, you promised me.

JUANA: They'll kill you, Gallo.

GALLO: [*throwing* ANGELA *off*] Stop sucking off me. I got nothing for you.

ANGELA: [*beating her fists on the ground.*] No, no, Papa! You promised me! . . . Oh, Hector
. . . . No, no, I promised Hector.
> [*Drums begin as punctuation of the pounding of* ANGELA'*s fists on the ground. Lights
> change. A special on* ANGELA *and another on* GALLO *and* HECTOR *come up, as shad-
> ows appear.* ANGELA *sees them.*]
Ah . . . Holy Father, Abuelo.

GALLO: [*to* HECTOR] Give me that bird.

ANGELA: Saints, Angels, Mama.

JUANA: [*trying to pick up* ANGELA] Come on, Angie, get up.

GALLO: [*to* HECTOR] What do you want?

HECTOR: You, alive, Papi.

CHATA: Careful, Hector.

ANGELA: I've lost my faith. I am splintered.

GALLO: [*imitating* HECTOR] You Papi. . . . Give me life. . . . Make me a man. [*He whips out
his stiletto.*] This is how you become a man. [*The drums get louder. We hear howling.*]
Come on, baby boy, show Daddy whatcha got.

JUANA: Are you crazy! That's your son!

ANGELA: I am cast down! Exiled!
> [GALLO *stalks* HECTOR *as drums follow their movements.*]

JUANA: Oh Gallo, you're killing your own children.

CHATA: Move, Hector, don't think, move!

GALLO: Oh yeah, mi lindo, you like to fight . . . eh?

JUANA: No, stop them! Please, please stop this.

ANGELA: Fallen from the light, condemned to the mud, to the shadows.

GALLO: You gotta learn, baby boy.

CHATA: Look at him, Hector. He's getting old, his hand is shaking. . . . Take the knife! Stay
down, old warrior. Stay down.

ANGELA: Alone and diminished. This loneliness is unendurable.

JUANA: Hector!

HECTOR: Do I have it? Is this what you want me to be . . .

ANGELA: [*looking to Heaven*]
My brains are slammed against the earth's hard crust.
My eyes are clouded.
My arteries gush
My lungs collapsed.

HECTOR: [*letting go of* GALLO] No! I am your son.
> [*Drums and cries stop.*]

ANGELA: Holy Father, Abuelo, Hector, breathe on me.
> [*Celestial sound as a white narrow shaft of light falls on* ANGELA. *She levitates, her
> wings spreading. Only* CHATA *and* JUANA *see this.*]

HECTOR: [*taking a deep breath*] Oh sweet air! [*He gets the rooster and sees* ANGELA.] Angela!

ADAN: [*rushing in*] I am here, I have truck. . . . [*Seeing* ANGELA, *he crosses himself.*] Ay Dios.
[*He kneels.*]

JUANA: [*at* GALLO'*s side*] Gallo, look!

GALLO: Did you see the hands on that kid, just like steel, never seen finer hands . . . [*seeing* ANGELA] Sweet Jesus, my beautiful monster. [*He crosses himself.*]

CHATA: No, it ain't true.

HECTOR: [*standing before* ANGELA *holding the rooster*] Oh sweet hummingbird woman,
shooting star, my comet, you are launched.

ANGELA: Abuelo, Queen of Heaven, All the Saints, All the Angels. It is true, I am back. I
am restored. I am . . . Hector, take me with you.

HECTOR: Everywhere. . . . Over the mountains, up to the stars.

ANGELA: To the very edge.

ADAN: Hector! Angelita! You take Adan. [*He goes to* ANGELA.]

CHATA: [*looking at* ANGELA] Shit happens. . . . Been happening all my life, that's all I know.

JUANA: [*holding* GALLO *like the Pietà*] We seen it, Gallo, with our own eyes.

ANGELA: [to HECTOR and ADAN] And I want my doorstep heaped with floral offerings . . . and . . .

> [HECTOR, ADAN, *and* ANGELA *freeze.* CHATA *removes the flower from her hair and holds it in her hand, trying to decide what to do. She freezes.*]

GALLO: Ay, Juanita, I had a vision of a hard-kicking flyer . . . [*He yawns.*] the ultimate bird, noble, fino. [*He falls asleep.*]

> [JUANA *looks at* GALLO, *smiles, then looks out half-smiling.*]

END OF PLAY

PAULA VOGEL (1951–)

How I Learned to Drive (1997)

OW I LEARNED TO DRIVE uses the metaphor of learning to drive a car to draw a parallel with learning to make one's way through the difficulties of growing up, and especially ways of steering around the hazards created by a pedophile who uses driving lessons as a prime opportunity to seduce his pupil, who is also his wife's niece. The situation is made especially complex by the fact that the would-be seducer, Uncle Peck, is basically a sympathetic character who seems truly to love his niece, Li'l Bit, and who has far more concern for her than do the other members of her family who constantly tease her and make her miserable with comments about her physical appearance, especially about the size of her breasts. It seems clear that Uncle Peck himself has been a victim of pedophilia and that he sees in Li'l Bit some hope for emotional fulfillment.

How I Learned to Drive is basically a memory play. It moves easily back and forth through many years of time as Li'l Bit recalls scenes of family life but mostly her relationship with Uncle Peck, mostly while learning to drive. There are only two clearly developed characters: Li'l Bit and Uncle Peck. The numerous other roles are taken by what the script labels the Greek Chorus—one male and two female actors who play all the numerous characters that come and go in the script. They change identities quickly and are present for brief moments, filling in the context of family, students, waiters, and others needed to make the script function effectively.

Li'l Bit and Uncle Peck share a deep emotional relationship that is always more painful than fulfilling, one that can never be forgotten. As Li'l Bit says of her first understanding of what was happening between them: "That day was the last day I lived in my body. I retreated above the neck, and I've lived inside the 'fire' in my head ever since. . . . The nearest sensation I feel—of flight in the body—I guess I feel when I'm driving." And at the end of the play as she prepares to drive, she recalls and obeys all the rules that Uncle Peck had taught her. At this point she seems near to accepting what has happened in the past and to be as near reconciliation as it is possible.

How I Learned to Drive won the Pulitzer Prize for Drama in 1998.

How I Learned to Drive by Paula Vogel. From *The Mammary Plays* by Paula Vogel. © 1998 by Paula Vogel. Published by Theatre Communications Group.

How I Learned to Drive

Characters

LI'L BIT—*A woman who ages forty-something to eleven years old. (See Notes on the New York Production)*

PECK—*Attractive man in his forties. Despite a few problems, he should be played by an actor one might cast in the role of Atticus in* To Kill A Mockingbird.

THE GREEK CHORUS—*If possible, these three members should be able to sing three-part harmony.*

MALE GREEK CHORUS—*Plays Grandfather, Waiter, High School Boys. Thirties-Forties. (See Notes on the New York Production)*

FEMALE GREEK CHORUS—*Plays Mother, Aunt Mary, High School Girls. Thirty-Fifty (See Notes on the New York Production)*

TEENAGE GREEK CHORUS—*Plays Grandmother, High School Girls and the voice of eleven-year-old Li'l Bit. Note on the casting of this actor: I would strongly recommend casting a young woman who is of "legal age," that is, twenty-one to twenty-five years old who can look as close to eleven as possible. The contrast with the other cast members will help. If the actor is too young, the audience may feel uncomfortable. (See notes on the New York Production)*

PRODUCTION NOTES

I urge directors to use the Greek Chorus in staging as environment and, well, part of the family—with the exception of the Teenage Greek Chorus member who, after the last time she appears onstage, should perhaps disappear.

As For Music: Please have fun. I wrote sections of the play listening to music like Roy Orbison's "Dream Baby" and The Mamas and the Papa's "Dedicated to the One I Love." The vaudeville sections go well to the Tijuana Brass or any music that sounds like a Laugh-In soundtrack. Other sixties music is rife with pedophilish (?) reference: the "You're Sixteen" genre hits; The Beach Boys' "Little Surfer Girl"; Gary Puckett and the Union Gap's "This Girl Is a Woman Now"; "Come Back When You Grow Up," etc.

And whenever possible, please feel free to punctuate the action with traffic signs: "No Passing," "Slow Children," "Dangerous Curves," "One Way," and the visual signs for children, deer crossings, hills, school buses, etc. (See Notes on the New York Production.)

This script uses the notion of slides and projections, which were not used in the New York production of the play.

On Titles: Throughout the script there are boldfaced titles. In production these should be spoken in a neutral voice (the type of voice that driver education films employ). In the New York production these titles were assigned to various members of the Greek Chorus and were done live.

NOTES ON THE NEW YORK PRODUCTION

The role of Li'l Bit was originally written as a character who is forty-something. When we cast Mary-Louise Parker in the role of Li'l Bit, we cast the Greek Chorus members with younger actors as the Female Greek and the Male Greek, and cast the Teenage Greek with an older (that is, mid-twenties) actor as well. There is a great deal of flexibility in age. Directors should change the age in the last monologue for Li'l Bit ("And before you know it, I'll be thirty-five . . . ") to reflect the actor's age who is playing Li'l Bit.

As the house lights dim, a VOICE *announces:*

Safety first—You and Driver Education.

[*Then the sound of a key turning the ignition of a car.* LI'L BIT *steps into a spotlight on the stage; "well-endowed," she is a softer-looking woman in the present time than she was at seventeen.*]

LI'L BIT: Sometimes to tell a secret, you first have to teach a lesson. We're going to start our lesson tonight on an early, warm summer evening.

In a parking lot overlooking the Beltsville Agricultural Farms in suburban Maryland.

Less than a mile away, the crumbling concrete of U.S. One wends its way past one-room revival churches, the porno drive-in, and boarded up motels with For Sale signs tumbling down.

Like I said, it's a warm summer evening.

Here on the land the Department of Agriculture owns, the smell of sleeping farm animal is thick in the air. The smells of clover and hay mix in with the smells of the leather dashboard. You can still imagine how Maryland used to be, before the malls took over. This countryside was once dotted with farmhouses—from their porches you could have witnessed the Civil War raging in the front fields.

Oh yes. There's a moon over Maryland tonight, that spills into the car where I sit beside a man old enough to be—did I mention how still the night is? Damp soil and tranquil air. It's the kind of night that makes a middle-aged man with a mortgage feel like a country boy again.

It's 1969. And I am very old, very cynical of the world, and I know it all. In short, I am seventeen years old, parking off a dark lane with a married man on an early summer night.

[*Lights up on two chairs facing front—or a Buick Riviera, if you will. Waiting patiently, with a smile on his face,* PECK *sits sniffing the night air.* LI'L BIT *climbs in beside him, seventeen years old and tense. Throughout the following, the two sit facing directly front. They do not touch. Their bodies remain passive. Only their facial expressions emote.*]

PECK: Ummm. I love the smell of your hair.

LI'L BIT: Uh-huh.

PECK: Oh, Lord. Ummmm. [*Beat*] A man could die happy like this.

LI'L BIT: Well, *don't*.

PECK: What shampoo is this?

LI'L BIT: Herbal Essence.

PECK: Herbal Essence. I'm gonna buy me some. Herbal Essence. And when I'm all alone in the house, I'm going to get into the bathtub, and uncap the bottle and—

LI'L BIT: —Be good.

PECK: What?

LI'L BIT: Stop being . . . bad.

PECK: What did you think I was going to say? What do you think I'm going to do with the shampoo?

LI'L BIT: I don't want to know. I don't want to hear it.

PECK: I'm going to wash my hair. That's all.

LI'L BIT: Oh.

PECK: What did you think I was going to do?

LI'L BIT: Nothing . . . I don't know. Something . . . nasty.

PECK: With shampoo? Lord, gal—your mind!

LI'L BIT: And whose fault is it?

PECK: Not mine. I've got the mind of a boy scout.

LI'L BIT: Right. A horny boy scout.

PECK: Boy scouts are always horny. What do you think the first Merit Badge is for?

LI'L BIT: There. You're going to be nasty again.

PECK: Oh, no. I'm good. Very good.

LI'L BIT: It's getting late.

PECK: Don't change the subject. I was talking about how good I am. [*Beat*] Are you ever gonna let me show you how good I am?

LI'L BIT: Don't go over the line now.

PECK: I won't. I'm not gonna do anything you don't want me to do.

LI'L BIT: That's right.

PECK: And I've been good all week.

LI'L BIT: You have?

PECK: Yes. All week. Not a single drink.

LI'L BIT: Good boy.

PECK: Do I get a reward? For not drinking?

LI'L BIT: A small one. It's getting late.

PECK: Just let me undo you. I'll do you back up.

LI'L BIT: All right. But be quick about it. [PECK *pantomimes undoing* LI'L BIT'*s brassiere with one hand*] You know, that's amazing. The way you can undo the hooks through my blouse with one hand.

PECK: Years of practice.

LI'L BIT: You would make an incredible brain surgeon with that dexterity.

PECK: I'll bet Clyde—what's the name of the boy taking you to the prom?

LI'L BIT: Claude Souders.

PECK: Claude Souders. I'll bet it takes him two hands, lights on, and you helping him on to get to first base.

LI'L BIT: Maybe.

> [*Beat.*]

PECK: Can I . . . kiss them? Please?

LI'L BIT: I don't know.

PECK: Don't make a grown man beg.

LI'L BIT: Just one kiss.

PECK: I'm going to lift your blouse.

LI'L BIT: It's a little cold.

> [PECK *laughs gently*]

PECK: That's not why you're shivering. [*They sit, perfectly still, for a long moment of silence.* PECK *makes gentle, concentric circles with his thumbs in the air in front of him*] How does that feel?

> [LI'L BIT *closes her eyes, carefully keeps her voice calm:*]

LI'L BIT: It's . . . okay.

> [*Sacred music, organ music or a boy's choir swells beneath the following.*]

PECK: I tell you, you can keep all the cathedrals of Europe. Just give me a second with these—these celestial orbs—

[PECK *bows his head as if praying. But he is kissing her nipple.* LI'L BIT, *eyes still closed, rears back her head on the leather Buick car seat.*]

LI'L BIT: Uncle Peck—we've got to go. I've got graduation rehearsal at school tomorrow morning. And you should get on home to Aunt Mary—

PECK: —All right, Li'l Bit.

LI'L BIT: —*Don't* call me that no more. [*Calmer*] Any more. I'm a big girl now, Uncle Peck. As you know.

[LI'L BIT *pantomimes refastening her bra behind her back.*]

PECK: That you are. Going on eighteen. Kittens will turn into cats.

[*Sighs*] I live all week long for these few minutes with you—you know that?

LI'L BIT: I'll drive.

[A VOICE *cuts in with:*]

Idling in the Neutral Gear.

[*Sound of a car revving cuts off the sacred music;* LI'L BIT, *now an adult, rises out of the car and comes to us.*]

LI'L BIT: In most families, relatives get names like "Junior," or "Brother," or "Bubba." In my family, if we call someone "Big Papa," it's not because he's tall. In my family, folks tend to get nicknamed for their genitalia. Uncle Peck, for example. My mama's adage was "the titless wonder," and my cousin Bobby got branded for life as "B.B."

[*In unison with Greek Chorus:*]

LI'L BIT: For blue balls.	GREEK CHORUS: For blue balls.

FEMALE GREEK CHORUS: [*As Mother*] And of course, we were so excited to have a baby girl that when the nurse brought you in and said, "It's a girl! It's a baby girl!" I just had to see for myself. So we whipped your diapers down and parted your chubby little legs—and right between your legs there was—

[PECK *has come over during the above and chimes along:*]

PECK: Just a little bit.	GREEK CHORUS: Just a little bit.

FEMALE GREEK CHORUS: [*As Mother*] And when you were born, you were so tiny that you fit in Uncle Peck's outstretched hand.

[PECK *stretches his hand out.*]

PECK: Now that's a fact. I held you, one day old, right in this hand.

[*A traffic signal is projected of a bicycle in a circle with a diagonal red slash.*]

LI'L BIT: Even with my family background, I was sixteen or so before I realized that pedophilia did not mean people who loved to bicycle . . .

[A VOICE *intrudes:*]

Driving in First Gear.

LI'L BIT: 1969. A typical family dinner.

FEMALE GREEK CHORUS: [*As Mother*] Look, Grandma. Li'l Bit's getting to be as big in the bust as you are.

LI'L BIT: Mother! Could we please change the subject?

TEENAGE GREEK CHORUS: [*As Grandmother*] Well, I hope you are buying her some decent bras. I never had a decent bra, growing up in the Depression, and now my shoulders are just crippled—crippled from the weight hanging on my shoulders—the dents

from my bra straps are big enough to put your finger in.—Here, let me show you—
[*As Grandmother starts to open her blouse:*]

LI'L BIT: Grandma! Please don't undress at the dinner table.

PECK: I thought the entertainment came *after* the dinner.

LI'L BIT: [*To the audience*] This is how it always starts. My grandfather, Big Papa, will chime in next with—

MALE GREEK CHORUS: [*As Grandfather*] Yup. If Li'l Bit gets any bigger, we're gonna haveta buy her a wheelbarrow to carry in front of her—

LI'L BIT: —Damn it—

PECK: —How about those Redskins on Sunday, Big Papa?

LI'L BIT: [*To the audience*] The only sports Big Papa followed was chasing Grandma around the house—

MALE GREEK CHORUS: [*As Grandfather*] —Or we could write to Kate Smith. Ask her for somma her used brassieres she don't want anymore—she could maybe give to Li'l Bit here—

LI'L BIT: —I can't stand it. I can't.

PECK: Now, honey, that's just their way—

FEMALE GREEK CHORUS: [*As Mother*] I tell you, Grandma, Li'l Bit's at that age. She's so sensitive, you can't say boo—

LI'L BIT: I'd like some privacy, that's all. Okay? Some goddamn privacy—

PECK: —Well, at least she didn't use the savior's name—

LI'L BIT: [*To the audience*] And Big Papa wouldn't let a dead dog lie. No sirree.

MALE GREEK CHORUS: [*As Grandfather*] Well, she'd better stop being so sensitive. 'Cause five minutes before Li'l Bit turns the corner, her tits turn first—

LI'L BIT: [*Starting to rise from the table*] —That's it. That's it.

PECK: Li'l Bit, you can't let him get to you. Then he wins.

LI'L BIT: I hate him. *Hate* him.

PECK: That's fine. But hate him and eat a good dinner at the same time.
[LI'L BIT *calms down and sits with perfect dignity*]

LI'L BIT: The gumbo is really good, Grandma.

MALE GREEK CHORUS: [*As Grandfather*] A'course, Li'l Bit's got a big surprise coming for her when she goes to that fancy college this fall—

PECK: Big Papa—let it go.

MALE GREEK CHORUS: [*As Grandfather*] What does she need a college degree for? She's got all the credentials she'll need on her chest—

LI'L BIT: —Maybe I want to learn things. Read. Rise above my cracker background—

PECK: —Whoa, now, Li'l Bit—

MALE GREEK CHORUS: [*As Grandfather*] What kind of things do you want to read?

LI'L BIT: There's a whole semester course, for example, on Shakespeare—
[*Greek Chorus, as Grandfather, laughs until he weeps*]

MALE GREEK CHORUS: [*As Grandfather*] Shakespeare. That's a good one. Shakespeare is really going to help you in life.

PECK: I think it's wonderful. And on scholarship!

MALE GREEK CHORUS: [*As Grandfather*] How is Shakespeare going to help her lie on her back in the dark?
[LI'L BIT *is on her feet.*]

LI'L BIT: You're getting old, Big Papa. You are going to die—very very soon. Maybe even *tonight.* And when you get to heaven, God's going to be a beautiful black woman in a long white robe. She's gonna look at your chart and say: Uh-oh. Fornication. Dog-ugly mean with blood relatives. Oh. Uh-oh. Voted for George Wallace. Well, one last chance: If you can name the play, all will be forgiven. And then she'll quote: "The quality of mercy is not strained." Your answer? Oh, too bad—*Merchant of Venice:* Act IV, Scene iii. And then she'll send your ass to fry in hell with all the other crackers. Excuse me, please.

[*To the audience*] And as I left the house, I would always hear Big Papa say:

MALE GREEK CHORUS: [*As Grandfather*] Lucy, your daughter's got a mouth on her. Well, no sense in wasting good gumbo. Pass me her plate, Mama.

LI'L BIT: And Aunt Mary would come up to Uncle Peck:

FEMALE GREEK CHORUS: [*As Aunt Mary*] Peck, go after her, will you? You're the only one she'll listen to when she gets like this.

PECK: She just needs to cool off.

FEMALE GREEK CHORUS: [*As Aunt Mary*] Please, honey—Grandma's been on her feet cooking all day.

PECK: All right.

LI'L BIT: And as he left the room, Aunt Mary would say:

FEMALE GREEK CHORUS: [*As Aunt Mary*] Peck's so good with them when they get to be this age.

[LI'L BIT *has stormed to another part of the stage, her back turned, weeping with a teenage fury.* PECK, *cautiously, as if stalking a deer, comes to her. She turns away even more. He waits a bit.*]

PECK: I don't suppose you're talking to family. [*No response*] Does it help that I'm in-law?

LI'L BIT: Don't you dare make fun of this.

PECK: I'm not. There's nothing funny about this. [*Beat*] Although I'll bet when Big Papa is about to meet his maker, he'll remember *The Merchant of Venice.*

LI'L BIT: I've got to get away from here.

PECK: You're going away. Soon. Here, take this.

[PECK *hands her his folded handkerchief.* LI'L BIT *uses it, noisily. Hands it back. Without her seeing, he reverently puts it back.*]

LI'L BIT: I hate this family

PECK: Your grandfather's ignorant. And you're right—he's going to die soon. But he's fam-ily. Family is . . . family.

LI'L BIT: Grown-ups are always saying that. Family.

PECK: Well, when you get a little older, you'll see what we're saying.

LI'L BIT: Uh-huh. So family is another acquired taste, like French kissing?

PECK: Come again?

LI'L BIT: You know, at first it really grosses you out, but in time you grow to like it?

PECK: Girl, you are . . . a handful.

LI'L BIT: Uncle Peck—you have the keys to your car?

PECK: Where do you want to go?

LI'L BIT: Just up the road.

PECK: I'll come with you.

LI'L BIT: No—please? I just need to . . . to drive for a little bit. Alone.

[PECK *tosses her the keys.*]

PECK: When can I see you alone again?

LI'L BIT: Tonight.

[LI'L BIT *crosses to center stage while the lights dim around her.* A VOICE *directs:*]

Shifting Forward from First to Second Gear

LI'L BIT: There were a lot of rumors about why I got kicked out of that fancy school in 1970. Some say I got caught with a man in my room. Some say as a kid on scholarship I fooled around with a rich man's daughter.

[LI'L BIT *smiles innocently at the audience*] I'm not talking.

But the real truth was I had a constant companion in my dorm room—who was less than discrete. Canadian V.O. A fifth a day.

1970. A Nixon recession. I slept on the floors of friends who were out of work themselves. Took factory work when I could find it. A string of dead-end day jobs that didn't last very long.

What I did, most nights, was cruise the Beltway and the back roads of Maryland, where there was still country, past the battlefields and farm houses. Racing in a 1965 Mustang—and as long as I had gasoline for my car and whiskey for me, the nights would pass. Fully tanked, I would speed past the churches and the trees on the bend, thinking just one notch of the steering wheel would be all it would take, and yet some . . . reflex took over. My hands on the wheel in the nine and three o'clock position—I never so much as got a ticket. He taught me well.

[A VOICE *announces:*]

You and the Reverse Gear.

LI'L BIT: Back up. 1968. On the Eastern Shore. A celebration dinner.

[LI'L BIT *joins* PECK *at a table in a restaurant.*]

PECK: Feeling better, missy?

LI'L BIT: The bathroom's really amazing here, Uncle Peck! They have these little soaps—instead of borax or something—and they're in the shape of shells.

PECK: I'll have to take a trip to the gentlemen's room just to see.

LI'L BIT: How did you know about this place?

PECK: This inn is famous on the Eastern Shore—it's been open since the seventeenth century. And I know how you like history . . .

[LI'L BIT *is shy and pleased.*]

LI'L BIT: It's great.

PECK: And you've just done your first, legal, long-distance drive. You must be hungry.

LI'L BIT: I'm starved.

PECK: I would suggest a dozen oysters to start, and the crab imperial . . . [LI'L BIT *is genuinely agog*] You might be interested to know the town history. When the British sailed up this very river in the dead of night—see outside where I'm pointing?—They were going to bombard the heck out of this town. But the town fathers were ready for them. They crept up all the trees with lanterns so that the British would think they saw the town lights and they aimed their cannons too high. And that's why the inn is still here for business today.

LI'L BIT: That's a great story.

PECK: [*Casually*] Would you like to start with a cocktail?

LI'L BIT: You're not . . . you're not going to start drinking, are you, Uncle Peck?

PECK: Not me. I told you, as long as you're with me, I'll never drink. I asked you if *you'd* like a cocktail before dinner. It's nice to have a little something with the oysters.

LI'L BIT: But . . . I'm not . . . legal. We could get arrested. Uncle Peck, they'll never believe I'm twenty-one!

PECK: So? Today we celebrate your driver's license—on the first try. This establishment reminds me a lot of places back home.

LI'L BIT: What does that mean?

PECK: In South Carolina, like here on the Eastern Shore, they're . . . [*Searches for the right euphemism*] . . . "European." Not so puritanical. And very understanding if gentlemen wish to escort very attractive young ladies who might want a before-dinner cocktail. If you want one, I'll order one.

LI'L BIT: Well—sure. Just . . . one.

[*The Female Greek Chorus appears in a spot.*]

FEMALE GREEK CHORUS: [*As Mother*] A Mother's Guide to Social Drinking:

A lady never gets sloppy—she may, however, get tipsy and a little gay.

Never drink on an empty stomach. Avail yourself of the bread basket and generous portions of butter. *Slather* the butter on your bread.

Sip your drink, slowly, let the beverage linger in your mouth—interspersed with interesting, fascinating conversation. Sip, never . . . slurp or gulp. Your glass should always be three-quarters full when his glass is empty.

Stay away from *ladies'* drinks: drinks like pink ladies, slow gin fizzes, daiquiris, gold cadillacs, Long Island iced teas, margaritas, pina colada, mai tais, planters punch, white Russians, black Russians, red Russians, melon balls, blue balls, hummingbirds, hemorrhages and hurricanes. In short, avoid anything with sugar, or anything with an umbrella. Get your vitamin C from *fruit.* Don't order anything with Voodoo or Vixen in the title or sexual positions in the name like Dead Man Screw or the Missionary. [*She sort of titters*]

Believe me, they are lethal . . . I think you were conceived after one of those.

Drink, instead, like a man: straight up or on the rocks, with plenty of water in between.

Oh, yes. And never mix your drinks. Stay with one all night long, like the man you came in with: bourbon, gin, or tequila till dawn, damn the torpedoes, full speed ahead!

[*As the* FEMALE GREEK CHORUS *retreats, the* MALE GREEK CHORUS *approaches the table as a Waiter.*]

MALE GREEK CHORUS: [*As Waiter*] I hope you all are having a pleasant evening. Is there something I can bring you, sir, before you order?

[LI'L BIT *waits in anxious fear. Carefully, Uncle* PECK *says with command:*]

PECK: I'll have a plain iced tea. The lady would like a drink, I believe.

[*The* MALE GREEK CHORUS *does a double take; there is a moment when Uncle* PECK *and he are in silent communication.*]

MALE GREEK CHORUS: [*As Waiter*] Very good. What would the . . . lady like?

LI'L BIT: [*A bit flushed*] Is there . . . is there any sugar in a martini?

PECK: None that I know of.

LI'L BIT: That's what I'd like then—a dry martini. And could we maybe have some bread?

PECK: A drink fit for a woman of the world.—Please bring the lady a dry martini, be generous with the olives, straight up.

[*The* MALE GREEK CHORUS *anticipates a large tip.*]

MALE GREEK CHORUS: [*As Waiter*] Right away. Very good, sir.

[*The* MALE GREEK CHORUS *returns with an empty martini glass which he puts in front of* LI'L BIT.]

PECK: Your glass is empty. Another martini, madam?

LI'L BIT: Yes, thank you.

[PECK *signals the* MALE GREEK CHORUS, *who nods*] So why did you leave South Carolina, Uncle Peck?

PECK: I was stationed in D.C. after the war, and decided to stay. Go North, Young Man, someone might have said.

LI'L BIT: What did you do in the service anyway?

PECK: [*Suddenly taciturn*] I . . . I did just this and that. Nothing heroic or spectacular.

LI'L BIT: But did you see fighting? Or go to Europe?

PECK: I served in the Pacific Theater. It's really nothing interesting to talk about.

LI'L BIT: It is to me. [*The Waiter has brought another empty glass*] Oh, goody. I love the color of the swizzle sticks. What were we talking about?

PECK: Swizzle sticks.

LI'L BIT: Do you ever think of going back?

PECK: To the Marines?

LI'L BIT: No—to South Carolina.

PECK: Well, we do go back. To visit.

LI'L BIT: No, I mean to live.

PECK: Not very likely. I think it's better if my mother doesn't have a daily reminder of her disappointment.

LI'L BIT: Are these floorboards slanted?

PECK: Yes, the floor is very slanted. I think this is the original floor.

LI'L BIT: Oh, good.

> [*The* FEMALE GREEK CHORUS *as Mother enters swaying a little, a little past tipsy.*]

FEMALE GREEK CHORUS: [*As Mother*] Don't leave your drink unattended when you visit the ladies' room. There is such a thing as white slavery; the modus operandi is to spike an unsuspecting young girl's drink with a "mickey" when she's left the room to powder her nose.

> But if you feel you have had more than your sufficiency in liquor, do go to the ladies' room—often. Pop your head out of doors for a refreshing breath of the night air. If you must, wet your face and head with tap water. Don't be afraid to dunk your head if necessary. A wet woman is still less conspicuous than a drunk woman.

> [*The* FEMALE GREEK CHORUS *stumbles a little; conspiratorially*] When in the course of human events it becomes necessary, go to a corner stall and insert the index and middle finger down the throat almost to the epiglottis. Divulge your stomach contents by such persuasion, and then wait a few moments before rejoining your beau waiting for you at your table.

> Oh, no. Don't be shy or embarrassed. In the very best of establishments, there's always one or two debutantes crouched in the corner stalls, their beaded purses tossed willy-nilly, sounding like cats in heat, heaving up the contents of their stomachs.

> [*The* FEMALE GREEK CHORUS *begins to wander off*] I wonder what it is they do in the men's rooms . . .

LI'L BIT: So why is your mother disappointed in you, Uncle Peck?

PECK: Every mother in Horry County has Great Expectations.

LI'L BIT: —Could I have another mar-ti-ni, please?

PECK: I think this is your last one.

> [PECK *signals the Waiter. The Waiter looks at* LI'L BIT *and shakes his head no.* PECK *raises his eyebrow, raises his finger to indicate one more, and then rubs his fingers together. It looks like a secret code. The Waiter sighs, shakes his head sadly, and brings over another empty martini glass. He glares at* PECK.]

LI'L BIT: The name of the county where you grew up is "Horry?" [LI'L BIT, *plastered, begins to laugh. Then she stops.*] I think your mother should be proud of you.

> [PECK *signals for the check.*]

PECK: Well, missy, she wanted me to do—to *be* everything my father was not. She wanted me to amount to something.

LI'L BIT: But you have! You've amounted a lot. . . .

PECK: I'm just a very ordinary man.

> [*The Waiter has brought the check and waits.* PECK *draws out a large bill and hands it to the Waiter.* LI'L BIT *is in the soppy stage.*]

LI'L BIT: I'll bet your mother loves you, Uncle Peck.

> [PECK *freezes a bit. To* MALE GREEK CHORUS *as Waiter:*]

PECK: Thank you. The service was exceptional. Please keep the change.

MALE GREEK CHORUS: [*As Waiter, in a tone that could freeze*] Thank you, sir. Will you be needing any help?

PECK: I think we can manage, thank you.

> [*Just then, the* FEMALE GREEK CHORUS *as Mother lurches on stage; the* MALE GREEK CHORUS *as Waiter escorts her off as she delivers:*]

FEMALE GREEK CHORUS: [*As Mother*] Thanks to judicious planning and several trips to the ladies' loo, your mother once out-drank an entire regiment of British officers on a good-will visit to Washington! Every last man of them! Milquetoasts! How'd they ever kick Hitler's cahones, huh? No match for an American lady—I could drink every man in here under the table.

> [*She delivers one last crucial hint before she is gently "bounced"*] As a last resort, when going out for an evening on the town, be sure to wear a skin-tight girdle—so tight that only a surgical knife or acetylene torch can get it off you—so that if you do pass out in the arms of your escort, he'll end up with rubber burns on his fingers before he can steal your virtue—

> [A VOICE *punctures the interlude with:*]

Vehicle Failure.

Even with careful maintenance and preventive operation of your automobile, it is all too common for us to experience an unexpected breakdown. If you are driving at any speed when a breakdown occurs, you must slow down and guide the automobile to the side of the road.

> [PECK *is slowly propping up* LI'L BIT *as they work their way to his car in the parking lot of the inn.*]

PECK: How are you doing, missy?

LI'L BIT: It's so far to the car, Uncle Peck. Like the lanterns in the trees the British fired on . . .

> [LI'L BIT *stumbles.* PECK *swoops her up in his arms.*]

PECK: Okay. I think we're going to take a more direct route.

> [LI'L BIT *closes her eyes*] Dizzy? [*She nods her head*] Don't look at the ground. Almost there—do you feel sick to your stomach? [LI'L BIT *nods. They reach the "car."* PECK *gently deposits her on the front seat*] Just settle here a little while until things stop spinning. [LI'L BIT *opens her eyes*]

LI'L BIT: What are we doing?

PECK: We're just going to sit here until your tummy settles down.

LI'L BIT: It's such nice upholst'ry—

PECK: Think you can go for a ride, now?

LI'L BIT: Where are you taking me?

PECK: Home.

LI'L BIT: You're not taking me—upstairs? There's no room at the inn?

> [LI'L BIT *giggles*]

PECK: Do you want to go upstairs? [LI'L BIT *doesn't answer*] Or home?

LI'L BIT: —This isn't right, Uncle Peck.

PECK: What isn't right?

LI'L BIT: What we're doing. It's wrong. It's very wrong.

PECK: What are we doing? [LI'L BIT *doesn't answer*] We're just going out to dinner.

LI'L BIT: You know. It's not nice to Aunt Mary.

PECK: You let me be the judge of what's nice and not nice to my wife.

> [*Beat.*]

LI'L BIT: Now, you're mad.

PECK: I'm not mad. It's just that I thought you . . . understood me, Li'l Bit. I think you're
the only one who does.

LI'L BIT: Someone will get hurt.

PECK: Have I forced you to do anything?

> [*There is a long pause as* LI'L BIT *tries to get sober enough to think this through.*]

LI'L BIT: . . . I guess not.

PECK: We're just enjoying each other's company. I've told you, nothing is going to happen
between us until you want it to. Do you know that?

LI'L BIT: Yes.

PECK: Nothing is going to happen until you want it to. [*A second more, with* PECK *staring
ahead at the river while seated at the wheel of his car. Then, softly:*] Do you want something to happen?

> [PECK *reaches over and strokes her face, very gently.* LI'L BIT *softens, reaches for him,
and buries her head in his neck. Then she kisses him. Then she moves away, dizzy
again.*]

LI'L BIT: . . . I don't know.

> [PECK *smiles; this has been good news for him—it hasn't been a "no."*]

PECK: Then I'll wait. I'm a very patient man. I've been waiting for a long time. I don't
mind waiting.

LI'L BIT: Someone is going to get hurt.

PECK: No one is going to get hurt. [LI'L BIT *closes her eyes*] Are you feeling sick?

LI'L BIT: Sleepy.

> [*Carefully,* PECK *props* LI'L BIT *up on the seat.*]

PECK: Stay here a second.

LI'L BIT: Where're you going?

PECK: I'm getting something from the back seat.

LI'L BIT: [*Scared; too loud*] What? What are you going to do?

> [PECK *reappears in the front seat with a lap rug.*]

PECK: Shhhh. [PECK *covers* LI'L BIT. *She calms down*] There. Think you can sleep?

> [LI'L BIT *nods. She slides over to rest on his shoulder. With a look of happiness,* PECK
turns the ignition key. Beat. PECK *leaves* LI'L BIT *sleeping in the car and strolls down
to the audience. Wagner's* Flying Dutchman *comes up faintly.*]
>
> [A VOICE *interjects:*]

Idling in the Neutral Gear.

TEENAGE GREEK CHORUS: Uncle Peck Teaches Cousin Bobby How to Fish.

PECK: I get back once or twice a year—supposedly to visit Mama and the family, but the
real truth is to fish. I miss this the most of all. There's a smell in the Low Country—
where the swamp and fresh inlet join the saltwater—a scent of sand and cypress, that
I haven't found anywhere yet.

> I don't say this very often up North because it will just play into the stereotype
everyone has, but I will tell you: I didn't wear shoes in the summertime until I was

sixteen. It's unnatural down here to pen up your feet in leather. Go ahead—take 'em off. Let yourself breathe—it really will make you feel better.

We're going to aim for some pompano today—and I have to tell you, they're a very shy, mercurial fish. Takes patience, and psychology. You have to believe it doesn't matter if you catch one or not.

Sky's pretty spectacular—there's some beer in the cooler next to the crab salad I packed, so help yourself if you get hungry. Are you hungry? Thirsty? Holler if you are.

Okay. You don't want to lean over the bridge like that—pompano feed in shallow water, and you don't want to get too close—they're frisky and shy little things—wait, check your line. Yep, something's been munching while we were talking.

Okay, look: We take the sand flea and you take the hook like this—right through his little sand flea rump. Sand fleas should always keep their backs to the wall. Okay. Cast it in, like I showed you. That's great! I can taste that pompano now, sautéed with some pecans and butter, a little bourbon—now—let it lie on the bottom—now, reel, jerk, reel, jerk—

Look—look at your line. There's something calling, all right. Okay, tip the rod up—not too sharp—hook it—all right, now easy, reel and then rest—let it play. And reel—play it out, that's right—really good! I can't believe it! It's a pompano.—Good work! Way to go! You are an official fisherman now. Pompano are hard to catch. We are going to have a delicious little—

What? Well, I don't know how much pain a fish feels—you can't think of that. Oh, no, don't cry, come on now, it's just a fish—the other guys are going to see you.—No, no you're just real sensitive, and I think that's wonderful at your age—look, do you want me to cut it free? You do?

Okay, hand me those pliers—look—I'm cutting the hook—okay? And we're just going to drop it in—no I'm not mad. It's just for fun, okay? There—it's going to swim back to its lady friend and tell her what a terrible day it had and she's going to stroke him with her fins until he feels better, and then they'll do something alone together that will make them both feel good and sleepy . . .

[PECK *bends down, very earnest*] I don't want you to feel ashamed about crying. I'm not going to tell anyone, okay? I can keep secrets. You know, men cry all the time. They just don't tell anybody, and they don't let anybody catch them. There's nothing you could do that would make me feel ashamed of you. Do you know that? Okay. [PECK *straightens up, smiles*]

Do you want to pack up and call it a day? I tell you what—I think I can still remember—there's a really neat tree house where I used to stay for days. I think it's still here—it was the last time I looked. But it's a secret place—you can't tell anybody we've gone there—least of all your mom or your sisters.—This is something special just between you and me. Sound good? We'll climb up there and have a beer and some crab salad—okay, B.B.? Bobby? Robert . . .

[LI'L BIT *sits at a kitchen table with the two* FEMALE GREEK CHORUS *members.*]

LI'L BIT: [*To the audience*] Three women, three generations, sit at the kitchen table.

On Men, Sex, and Women: Part I:

FEMALE GREEK CHORUS: [*As Mother*] Men only want one thing.

LI'L BIT: [*Wide-Eyed*] But what? What is it they want?

FEMALE GREEK CHORUS: [*As Mother*] And once they have it, they lose all interest. So Don't Give It to Them.

TEENAGE GREEK CHORUS: [*As Grandmother*] I never had the luxury of the rhythm method. Your grandfather is just a big bull. A big bull. Every morning, every evening.

FEMALE GREEK CHORUS: [*As Mother, whispers to* LI'L BIT] And he used to come home for lunch every day.

LI'L BIT: My god, Grandma!

TEENAGE GREEK CHORUS: [*As Grandmother*] Your grandfather only cares that I do two things: have the table set and the bed turned down.

FEMALE GREEK CHORUS: [*As Mother*] And in all that time, Mother, you never have experienced—?

LI'L BIT: [*To the audience*]—Now my grandmother believed in all the sacraments of the church, to the day she died. She believed in Santa Claus and the Easter Bunny until she was fifteen. But she didn't believe in—

TEENAGE GREEK CHORUS: [*As Grandmother*]—Orgasm! That's just something you and Mary have made up! I don't believe you.

FEMALE GREEK CHORUS: [*As Mother*] Mother, it happens to women all the time—

TEENAGE GREEK CHORUS: [*As Grandmother*]—Oh, now you're going to tell me about the G force!

LI'L BIT: No, Grandma, I think that's astronauts—

FEMALE GREEK CHORUS: [*As Mother*] Well, Mama, after all, you were a child bride when Big Papa came and got you—you were a married woman and you still believed in Santa Claus.

TEENAGE GREEK CHORUS: [*As Grandmother*] It was legal, what Daddy and I did! I was fourteen and in those days, fourteen was a grown-up woman—

[*Big Papa shuffles in the kitchen for a cookie.*]

MALE GREEK CHORUS: [*As Grandfather*]—Oh, now we're off on Grandma and the Rape of the Sa-bean Women!

TEENAGE GREEK CHORUS: [*As Grandmother*] Well, you were the one in such a big hurry—

MALE GREEK CHORUS: [*As Grandfather to* LI'L BIT]—I picked your grandmother out of that herd of sisters just like a lion chooses the gazelle—the plump, slow, flaky gazelle dawdling at the edge of the herd—your sisters were too smart and too fast and too scrawny—

LI'L BIT: [*To the audience*]—The family story is that when Big Papa came for Grandma, my Aunt Lily was waiting for him with a broom—and she beat him over the head all the way down the stairs as he was carrying out Grandma's hope chest—

MALE GREEK CHORUS: [*As Grandfather*]—And they were *mean.* 'Specially Lily.

FEMALE GREEK CHORUS: [*As Mother*] Well, you were robbing the baby of the family!

TEENAGE GREEK CHORUS: [*As Grandmother*] I still keep a broom handy in the kitchen! And I know how to use it! So get your hand out of the cookie jar and don't you spoil your appetite for dinner—out of the kitchen!

[MALE GREEK CHORUS *as Grandfather leaves chuckling with a cookie.*]

FEMALE GREEK CHORUS: [*As Mother*] Just one thing a married woman needs to know how to use—the rolling pin or the broom. I prefer a heavy cast-iron fry pan—they're great on a man's head, no matter how thick the skull is.

TEENAGE GREEK CHORUS: [*As Grandmother*] Yes, sir, your father is ruled by only two bosses! Mr. Gut and Mr. Peter! And sometimes, first thing in the morning, Mr. Sphincter Muscle!

FEMALE GREEK CHORUS: [*As Mother*] It's true. Men are like children. Just like little boys.

TEENAGE GREEK CHORUS: [*As Grandmother*] Men are bulls! Big bulls!

[*The* GREEK CHORUS *is getting aroused.*]

FEMALE GREEK CHORUS: [*As Mother*] They'd still be crouched on their haunches over a fire in a cave if we hadn't cleaned them up!

TEENAGE GREEK CHORUS: [*As Grandmother, flushed*] Coming in smelling of sweat—

FEMALE GREEK CHORUS: [*As Mother*]—Looking at those naughty pictures like boys in a dime store with a dollar in their pockets!

TEENAGE GREEK CHORUS: [*As Grandmother; raucous*] No matter to them what they smell like! They've got to have it, right then, on the spot, right there! Nasty!—

FEMALE GREEK CHORUS: [*As Mother*]—Vulgar!—

TEENAGE GREEK CHORUS: [*As Grandmother*] Primitive!—

FEMALE GREEK CHORUS: [*As Mother*]—Hot!—

LI'L BIT: And just about then, Big Papa would shuffle in with—

MALE GREEK CHORUS: [*As Grandfather*]—What are you all cackling about in here?

TEENAGE GREEK CHORUS: [*As Grandmother*] Stay out of the kitchen! This is just for girls!

[*As Grandfather leaves:*]

MALE GREEK CHORUS: [*As Grandfather*] Lucy, you'd better not be filling Mama's head with sex! Every time you and Mary come over and start in about sex, when I ask a simple question like, "What time is dinner going to be ready?," Mama snaps my head off!

TEENAGE GREEK CHORUS: [*As Grandmother*] Dinner will be ready when I'm good and ready! Stay out of this kitchen!

[LI'L BIT *steps out.*]

[A VOICE *directs:*]

When Making a Left Turn, You Must Downshift While Going Forward.

LI'L BIT: 1979. A long bus trip to Upstate New York. I settled in to read, when a young man sat beside me.

MALE GREEK CHORUS: [*As Young Man; voice cracking*] "What are your reading?"

LI'L BIT: He asked. His voice broke into that miserable equivalent of vocal acne, not quite falsetto and not tenor, either. I glanced a side view. He was appealing in an odd way, huge ears at a defiant angle springing forward at ninety degrees. He must have been shaving, because his face, with a peach sheen, was speckled with nicks and styptic. "I have a class tomorrow," I told him.

MALE GREEK CHORUS: [*As Young Man*] "You're taking a class?"

LI'L BIT: "I'm teaching a class." He concentrated on lowering his voice.

MALE GREEK CHORUS: [*As Young Man*] "I'm a senior. Walt Whitman High."

LI'L BIT: The light was fading outside, so perhaps he was—with a very high voice.

I felt his "interest" quicken. Five steps ahead of the hopes in his head, I slowed down, waited, pretended surprise, acted at listening, all the while knowing we would get off the bus, he would just then seem to think to ask me to dinner, he would chivalrously insist on walking me home, he would continue to converse in the street until I would casually invite him up to my room—and—I was only into the second moment of conversation and I could see the whole evening before me.

And dramaturgically speaking, after the faltering and slightly comical "first act," there was the very briefest of intermissions, and an extremely capable and forceful *sustained* second act. And after the second act climax and a gentle denouement—before the post-play discussion—I lay on my back in the dark and I thought about you, Uncle Peck. Oh. Oh—this is the allure. Being older. Being the first. Being the translator, the teacher, the epicure, the already jaded. This is how the giver gets taken.

[LI'L BIT *changes her tone*] On Men, Sex, and Women: Part II:

[LI'L BIT *steps back into the scene as a fifteen year old, gawky and quiet, as the gazelle at the edge of the herd.*]

TEENAGE GREEK CHORUS: [*As Grandmother; to* LI'L BIT] You're being mighty quiet, missy. Cat Got Your Tongue?

LI'L BIT: I'm just listening. Just thinking.

TEENAGE GREEK CHORUS: [*As Grandmother*] Oh, yes, Little Miss Radar Ears? Soaking it all in? Little Miss Sponge? Penny for your thoughts?

[LI'L BIT *hesitates to ask but she really wants to know.*]

LI'L BIT: Does it—when you do it—you know, theoretically when I do it and I haven't done it before—I mean—does it hurt?

FEMALE GREEK CHORUS: [*As Mother*] Does what hurt, honey?

LI'L BIT: When a . . . when a girl does it for the first time—with a man—does it hurt?

TEENAGE GREEK CHORUS: [*As Grandmother; horrified*] *That's* what you're thinking about?

FEMALE GREEK CHORUS: [*As Mother; calm*] Well, just a little bit. Like a pinch. And there's a little blood.

TEENAGE GREEK CHORUS: [*As Grandmother*] Don't tell her that! She's too young to be thinking those things!

FEMALE GREEK CHORUS: [*As Mother*] Well, if she doesn't find out from me, where is she going to find out? In the street?

TEENAGE GREEK CHORUS: [*As Grandmother*] Tell her it hurts! It's agony! You think you're going to die! Especially if you do it before marriage!

FEMALE GREEK CHORUS: [*As Mother*] Mama! I'm going to tell her the truth! Unlike you, you left me and Mary completely in the dark with fairy tales and told us to go to the priest! What does an eighty-year-old priest know about love-making with girls!

LI'L BIT: [*Getting upset*] It's not fair!

FEMALE GREEK CHORUS: [*As Mother*] Now, see, she's getting upset—you're scaring her.

TEENAGE GREEK CHORUS: [*As Grandmother*] Good! Let her be good and scared! It hurts! You bleed like a stuck pig! And you lay there and say, "Why, O Lord, have you forsaken me?!"

LI'L BIT: It's not fair! Why does everything have to hurt for girls? Why is there always blood?

FEMALE GREEK CHORUS: [*As Mother*] It's not a lot of blood—and it feels wonderful after the pain subsides . . .

TEENAGE GREEK CHORUS: [*As Grandmother*] You're encouraging her to just go out and find out with the first drugstore joe who buys her a milk shake!

FEMALE GREEK CHORUS: [*As Mother*] Don't be scared. It won't hurt you—if the man you go to bed with really loves you. It's important that he loves you.

TEENAGE GREEK CHORUS: [*As Grandmother*]—Why don't you just go out and rent a motel room for her, Lucy?

FEMALE GREEK CHORUS: [*As Mother*] I believe in telling my daughter the truth! We have a very close relationship! I want her to be able to ask me anything—I'm not scaring her with stories about Eve's sin and snakes crawling on their bellies for eternity and women's bearing children in mortal pain—

TEENAGE GREEK CHORUS: [*As Grandmother*]—If she stops and thinks before she takes her knickers off, maybe someone in this family will finish high school!

[LI'L BIT *knows what is about to happen and starts to retreat from the scene at this point.*]

FEMALE GREEK CHORUS: [*As Mother*] Mother! If you and Daddy had helped me—I wouldn't have had to marry that—that no-good-son-of-a—

TEENAGE GREEK CHORUS: [*As Grandmother*]—He was good enough for you on a full moon! I hold you responsible!

FEMALE GREEK CHORUS: [*As Mother*]—You could have helped me! You could have told me something about the facts of life!

TEENAGE GREEK CHORUS: [*As Grandmother*]—I told you what my mother told me! A girl with her skirt up can outrun a man with his pants down!

[*The* MALE GREEK CHORUS *enters the fray;* LI'L BIT *edges further downstage.*]

FEMALE GREEK CHORUS: [*As Mother*] And when I turned to you for a little help, all I got afterwards was—

MALE GREEK CHORUS: [*As Grandfather*] You Made Your Bed; Now Lie On It!

[*The* GREEK CHORUS *freezes, mouths open, argumentatively.*]

LI'L BIT: [*To the audience*] Oh, please! I still can't bear to listen to it, after all these years—

[*The* MALE GREEK CHORUS *"unfreezes," but out of his open mouth, as if to his surprise, comes a base refrain from a Motown song.*]

MALE GREEK CHORUS: "Do-Bee-Do-Wah!"

[*The* FEMALE GREEK CHORUS *member is also surprised; but she, too, unfreezes.*]

FEMALE GREEK CHORUS: "Shoo-doo-be-doo-be-doo; shoo-doo-be-doo-be-doo."

[*The* MALE *and* FEMALE GREEK CHORUS *members continue with their harmony, until the* TEENAGE *member of the* CHORUS *starts in with Motown lyrics such as "Dedicated to the One I Love," or "In the Still of the Night," or "Hold Me"— any Sam Cooke will do. The three modulate down into three part harmony, softly, until they are submerged by the actual recording playing over the radio in the car in which Uncle* PECK *sits in the driver's seat, waiting.* LI'L BIT *sits in the passenger seat.*]

LI'L BIT: Ahh. That's better.

[*Uncle* PECK *reaches over and turns the volume down; to* LI'L BIT:]

PECK: How can you hear yourself think?

[LI'L BIT *does not answer.*]

[*A* VOICE *insinuates itself in the pause:*]

Before You Drive.

Always check under your car for obstructions—broken bottles, fallen tree branches, and the bodies of small children. Each year hundreds of children are crushed beneath the wheels of unwary drivers in their own driveways. Children depend on *you* to watch them.

[*Pause. The* VOICE *continues:*]

You and the Reverse Gear.

[*In the following section, it would be nice to have slides of erotic photographs of women and cars: women posed over the hood; women draped along the sideboards; women with water hoses spraying the car; and the actress playing* LI'L BIT *with a Bel Air or any 1950s car one can find for the finale.*]

LI'L BIT: 1967. In a parking lot of the Beltsville Agricultural Farms. The Initiation into a Boy's First Love.

PECK: [*With a soft look on his face*] Of course, my favorite car will always be the '56 Bel Air Sports Coupe. Chevy sold more '55s, but the '56!—a V-8 with Corvette option, 225 horsepower, went from zero to sixty miles per hour in 8.9 seconds.

LI'L BIT: [*To the audience*] Long after a mother's tits, but before a woman's breasts:

PECK: Super-Turbo-Fire! What a Power Pack—mechanical lifters, twin four-barrel carbs, lightweight valves, dual exhausts—

LI'L BIT: [*To the audience*] After the milk but before the beer:

PECK: A specific intake manifold, higher-lift camshaft, and the tightest squeeze Chevy had ever made—

LI'L BIT: [*To the audience*] Long after he's squeezed down the birth canal but before he's pushed his way back in: The boy falls in love with the thing that bears his weight with speed.

PECK: I want you to know your automobile inside and out.—Are you there? Li'l Bit?
　　　[*Slides end here.*]

LI'L BIT: —What?

PECK: You're drifting. I need you to concentrate.

LI'L BIT: Sorry.

PECK: Okay. Get into the driver's seat. [LI'L BIT *does*] Okay. Now. Show me what you're going to do before you start the car.
　　　[LI'L BIT *sits, with her hands in her lap. She starts to giggle.*]

LI'L BIT: I don't know, Uncle Peck.

PECK: Now, come on. What's the first thing you're going to adjust?

LI'L BIT: My bra strap?—

PECK: —Li'l Bit. What's the most important thing to have control of on the inside of the car?

LI'L BIT: That's easy. The radio. I tune the radio from Mama's old fart tunes to—
　　　[LI'L BIT *turns the radio up so we can hear a 1960s tune. With surprising firmness,* PECK *commands:*]

PECK: —Radio off. Right now. [LI'L BIT *turns the radio off*] When you are driving your car, with your license, you can fiddle with the stations all you want. But when you are driving with a learner's permit in my car, I want all your attention to be on the road.

LI'L BIT: Yes, sir.

PECK: Okay. Now the seat—forward and up. [LI'L BIT *pushes it forward*] Do you want a cushion?

LI'L BIT: No—I'm good.

PECK: You should be able to reach all the switches and controls. Your feet should be able to push the accelerator, brake and clutch all the way down. Can you do that?

LI'L BIT: Yes.

PECK: Okay, the side mirrors. You want to be able to see just a bit of the right side of the car in the right mirror—can you?

LI'L BIT: Turn it out more.

PECK: Okay. How's that?

LI'L BIT: A little more . . . Okay, that's good.

PECK: Now the left—again, you want to be able to see behind you—but the left lane— adjust it until you feel comfortable. [LI'L BIT *does so*] Next. I want you to check the rearview mirror. Angle it so you have a clear vision of the back. [LI'L BIT *does so*] Okay. Lock your door. Make sure all the doors are locked.

LI'L BIT: [*Making a joke of it*] But then I'm locked in with you.

PECK: Don't fool.

LI'L BIT: All right. We're locked in.

PECK: We'll deal with the air vents and defroster later. I'm teaching you on a manual—once you learn manual, you can drive anything. I want you to be able to drive any car, any machine. Manual gives you *control*. In ice, if your brakes fail, if you need more power—okay? It's a little harder at first, but then it becomes like breathing. Now. Put your hands on the wheel. I never want to see you driving with one hand. Always two hands. [LI'L BIT *hesitates*] What? What is it now?

LI'L BIT: If I put my hands on the wheel—how do I defend myself?

PECK: [*Softly*] Now listen. Listen up close. We're not going to fool around with this. This is a serious business. I will never touch you when you are driving a car. Understand?

LI'L BIT: Okay.

PECK: Hands on the nine o'clock and three o'clock position gives you maximum control and turn.

> [PECK *goes silent for a while.* LI'L BIT *waits for more instruction*]

Okay. Just relax and listen to me, Li'l Bit, okay? I want you to lift your hands for a second and look at them. [LI'L BIT *feels a bit silly, but does it*]

Those are your two hands. When you are driving, your life is in your own two hands. Understand? [LI'L BIT *nods*]

I don't have any sons. You're the nearest to a son I'll ever have—and I want to give you something. Something that really matters to me.

There's something about driving—when you're in control of the car, just you and the machine and the road—that nobody can take from you. A power. I feel more myself in my car than anywhere else. And that's what I want to give to you.

There's a lot of assholes out there. Crazy men, arrogant idiots, drunks, angry kids, geezers who are blind—and you have to be ready for them. I want to teach you to drive like a man.

LI'L BIT: What does that mean?

PECK: Men are taught to drive with confidence—with aggression. The road belongs to them. They drive defensively—always looking out for the other guy. Women tend to be polite—to hesitate. And that can be fatal.

You're going to learn to think what the other guy is going to do before he does it. If there's an accident, and ten cars pile up, and people get killed, you're the one who's gonna steer through it, put your foot on the gas if you have to, and be the only one to walk away. I don't know how long you or I are going to live, but we're for damned sure not going to die in a car.

So if you're going to drive with me, I want you to take this very seriously.

LI'L BIT: I will, Uncle Peck. I want you to teach me to drive.

PECK: Good. You're going to pass your test on the first try. Perfect score. Before the next four weeks are over, you're going to know this baby inside and out. Treat her with respect.

LI'L BIT: Why is it a "she?"

PECK: Good question. It doesn't have to be a "she"—but when you close your eyes and think of someone who responds to your touch—someone who performs just for you and gives you what you ask for—I guess I always see a "she." You can call her what you like.

LI'L BIT: [*To the audience*] I closed my eyes—and decided not to change the gender.

> [A VOICE:]

Defensive driving involves defending yourself from hazardous and sudden changes in your automotive environment. By thinking ahead, the defensive driver can adjust to weather, road conditions and road kill. Good defensive driving involves mental and physical preparation. Are you prepared?

> [*Another* VOICE *chimes in:*]

You and the Reverse Gear.

LI'L BIT: 1966. The Anthropology of the Female Body in Ninth Grade—Or A Walk Down Mammary Lane.

> [*Throughout the following, there is occasional rhythmic beeping, like a transmitter signaling.* LI'L BIT *is aware of it, but can't figure out where it is coming from. No one else seems to hear it.*]

MALE GREEK CHORUS: In the hallway of Francis Scott Key Middle School.
[*A bell rings; the* GREEK CHORUS *is changing classes and meets in the hall, conspiratorially.*]
TEENAGE GREEK CHORUS: She's coming!
[LI'L BIT *enters the scene; the* MALE GREEK CHORUS *member has a sudden, violent sneezing and lethal allergy attack.*]
FEMALE GREEK CHORUS: Jerome? Jerome? Are you all right?
MALE GREEK CHORUS: I—don't—know. I can't breathe—get Li'l Bit—
TEENAGE GREEK CHORUS: —He needs oxygen!—
FEMALE GREEK CHORUS: —Can you help us here?
LI'L BIT: What's wrong? Do you want me to get the school nurse—
[*The* MALE GREEK CHORUS *member wheezes, grabs his throat and sniffs at* LI'L BIT'*s chest, which is beeping away.*]
MALE GREEK CHORUS: No—it's okay—I only get this way when I'm around an allergy trigger—
LI'L BIT: Golly. What are you allergic to?
MALE GREEK CHORUS: [*With a sudden grab of her breast*] Foam rubber.
[*The* GREEK CHORUS *members break up with hilarity; Jerome leaps away from* LI'L BIT'*s kicking rage with agility; as he retreats:*]
LI'L BIT: Jerome! Creep! Cretin! Cro-Magnon!
TEENAGE GREEK CHORUS: Rage is not attractive in a girl.
FEMALE GREEK CHORUS: Really. Get a Sense of Humor.
[A VOICE *echoes:*]

Good defensive driving involves mental and physical preparation. Were You Prepared?

FEMALE GREEK CHORUS: Gym Class: In the showers.
[*The sudden sound of water; the* FEMALE GREEK CHORUS *members and* LI'L BIT, *while fully clothed, drape towels across their fronts, miming nudity. They stand, hesitate, at an imaginary shower's edge.*]
LI'L BIT: Water looks hot.
FEMALE GREEK CHORUS: Yesss . . . .
[FEMALE GREEK CHORUS *members are not going to make the first move. One dips a tentative toe under the water, clutching the towel around her.*]
LI'L BIT: Well, I guess we'd better shower and get out of here.
FEMALE GREEK CHORUS: Yep. You go ahead. I'm still cooling off.
LI'L BIT: Okay.—Sally? Are you gonna shower?
TEENAGE GREEK CHORUS: After you—
[LI'L BIT *takes a deep breath for courage, drops the towel and plunges in: The two* FEMALE GREEK CHORUS *members look at* LI'L BIT *in the all together, laugh, gasp and high-five each other.*]
TEENAGE GREEK CHORUS: Oh my god! Can you believe—
FEMALE GREEK CHORUS: Told you! It's not foam rubber! I win! Jerome owes me fifty cents!
[A VOICE *editorializes:*]

Were You Prepared?

[LI'L BIT *tries to cover up; she is exposed, as suddenly 1960s Motown fills the room and we segue into:*]
FEMALE GREEK CHORUS: The Sock Hop.
[LI'L BIT *stands up against the wall with her female classmates.* TEENAGE GREEK CHORUS *is mesmerized by the music and just sways alone, lip-synching the lyrics.*]

LI'L BIT: I don't know. Maybe it's just me—but—do you ever feel like you're just a walking Mary Jane joke?

FEMALE GREEK CHORUS: I don't know what you mean.

LI'L BIT: You haven't heard the Mary Jane jokes? [FEMALE GREEK CHORUS *member shakes her head no*] Okay. "Little Mary Jane is walking through the woods, when all of a sudden this man who was hiding behind a tree *jumps* out, *rips* open Mary Jane's blouse, and *plunges* his hands on her breasts. And Little Mary Jane just laughed and laughed because she knew her money was in her shoes."

[LI'L BIT *laughs; the* FEMALE GREEK CHORUS *does not.*]

FEMALE GREEK CHORUS: You're weird.

[*In another space, in a strange light, Uncle* PECK *stands and stares at* LI'L BIT'*s body. He is setting up a tripod, but he just stands, appreciative, watching her.*]

LI'L BIT: Well, don't you ever feel . . . self-conscious? Like you're being looked at all the time?

FEMALE GREEK CHORUS: That's not a problem for me.—Oh—look—Greg's coming over to ask you to dance.

[TEENAGE GREEK CHORUS *becomes attentive, flustered.* MALE GREEK CHORUS *member, as Greg, bends slightly as a very short young man, whose head is at* LI'L BIT'*s chest level. Ardent, sincere and socially inept, Greg will become a successful gynecologist.*]

TEENAGE GREEK CHORUS: [*Softly*] Hi, Greg.

[*Greg does not hear. He is intent on only one thing.*]

MALE GREEK CHORUS: [*As Greg, to* LI'L BIT] Good Evening. Would you care to dance?

LI'L BIT: [*Gently*] Thank you very much, Greg—but I'm going to sit this one out.

MALE GREEK CHORUS: [*As Greg*] Oh. Okay. I'll try my luck later.

[*He disappears.*]

TEENAGE GREEK CHORUS: Oohhh.

[LI'L BIT *relaxes. Then she tenses, aware of* PECK'*s gaze.*]

FEMALE GREEK CHORUS: Take pity on him. Someone should.

LI'L BIT: But he's so short.

TEENAGE GREEK CHORUS: He can't help it.

LI'L BIT: But his head comes up to [LI'L BIT *gestures*] here. And I think he asks me on the fast dances so he can watch me—you know—jiggle.

FEMALE GREEK CHORUS: I wish I had your problems.

[*The tune changes; Greg is across the room in a flash.*]

MALE GREEK CHORUS: [*As Greg*] Evening again. May I ask you for the honor of a spin on the floor?

LI'L BIT: I'm . . . very complimented, Greg. But I . . . I just don't do fast dances.

MALE GREEK CHORUS: [*As Greg*] Oh. No problem. That's okay.

[*He disappears.* TEENAGE GREEK CHORUS *watches him go.*]

TEENAGE GREEK CHORUS: That is just so—sad.

[LI'L BIT *becomes aware of* PECK *waiting.*]

FEMALE GREEK CHORUS: You know, you should take it as a compliment that the guys want to watch you jiggle. They're guys. That's what they're supposed to do.

LI'L BIT: I guess you're right. But sometimes I feel like these alien life forces, these two mounds of flesh have grafted themselves onto my chest, and they're using me until they can "propagate" and take over the world and they'll just keep growing, with a mind of their own until I collapse under their weight and they suck all the nourishment out of my body and I finally just waste away while they get bigger and bigger and— [LI'L BIT'*s classmates are just staring at her in disbelief*]

FEMALE GREEK CHORUS: —You are the strangest girl I have ever met.

[LI'L BIT'*s trying to joke but feels on the verge of tears.*]

LI'L BIT: Or maybe someone's implanted radio transmitters in my chest at a frequency I can't hear, that girls can't detect, but they're sending out these signals to men who get mesmerized, like sirens, calling them to dash themselves on these "rocks"—

[*Just then, the music segues into a slow dance, perhaps a Beach Boys tune like* Little Surfer, *but over the music there's a rhythmic, hypnotic beeping transmitted, which both Greg and* PECK *hear.* LI'L BIT *hears it too, and in horror she stares at her chest. She, too, is almost hypnotized. In a trance, Greg responds to the signals and is called to her side—actually, her front. Like a zombie, he stands in front of her, his eyes planted on her two orbs.*]

MALE GREEK CHORUS: [*As Greg*] This one's a slow dance. I hope your dance card isn't . . . filled?

[LI'L BIT *is aware of* PECK; *but the signals are calling her to him. The signals are no longer transmitters, but an electromagnetic force, pulling* LI'L BIT *to his side, where he again waits for her to join him. She must get away from the dance floor.*]

LI'L BIT: Greg—you really are a nice boy. But I don't like to dance.

MALE GREEK CHORUS: [*As Greg*] That's okay. We don't have to move or anything. I could just hold you and we could just *sway* a little—

LI'L BIT: —No! I'm sorry—but I think I have to leave; I hear someone calling me—

[LI'L BIT *starts across the dance floor, leaving Greg behind. The beeping stops. The lights change, although the music does not. As* LI'L BIT *talks to the audience, she continues to change and prepare for the coming session. She should be wearing a tight tank top or a sheer blouse and very tight pants. To the audience:*]

In every man's home some small room, some zone in his house, is set aside. It might be the attic, or the study, or a den. And there's an invisible sign as if from the old treehouse: Girls Keep Out.

Here, away from female eyes, lace doilies and crochet, he keeps his manly toys: the Vargas pinups, the tackle. A scent of tobacco and WD-40. [*She inhales deeply*] A dash of his Bay Rum. Ahhh . . . [LI'L BIT *savors it for just a moment more*]

Here he keeps his secrets: a violin or saxophone, drum set or darkroom, and the stacks of *Playboy*. [*In a whisper*] Here, in my aunt's home, it was the basement. Uncle Peck's turf.

[A VOICE *commands:*]

You and the Reverse Gear.

LI'L BIT: 1965. The Photo Shoot.

[LI'L BIT *steps into the scene as a nervous but curious thirteen year old. Music, from the previous scene, continues to play, changing into something like Roy Orbison later—something seductive with a beat.* PECK *fiddles, all business, with his camera. As in the driving lesson, he is all competency and concentration.* LI'L BIT *stands awkwardly. He looks through the Leica camera on the tripod, adjusts the back lighting, etc.*]

PECK: Are you cold? The lights should heat up some in a few minutes—

LI'L BIT: —Aunt Mary is?

PECK: At the National Theatre matinee. With your mother. We have time.

LI'L BIT: But—what if—

PECK: —And so what if they return? I told them you and I were going to be working with my camera. They won't come down. [LI'L BIT *is quiet, apprehensive*]—Look, are you sure you want to do this?

LI'L BIT: I said I'd do it. But—

PECK: —I know. You've drawn the line.

LI'L BIT: [*Reassured*] That's right. No frontal nudity.

PECK: Good heavens, girl, where did you pick that up?

LI'L BIT: [*Defensive*] I *read.*

> [PECK *tries not to laugh.*]

PECK: And I read *Playboy* for the interviews. Okay. Let's try some different music.

> [PECK *goes to an expensive reel-to-reel and forwards. Something like "Sweet Dreams" begins to play.*]

LI'L BIT: I didn't know you listened to this.

PECK: I'm not dead, you know. I try to keep up. Do you like this song? [LI'L BIT *nods with pleasure*] Good. Now listen—at professional photo shoots, they always play music for the models. Okay? I want you to just enjoy the music. Listen to it with your body, and just—respond.

LI'L BIT: Respond to the music with my . . . body?

PECK: Right. Almost like dancing. Here—let's get you on the stool, first. [PECK *comes over and helps her up*]

LI'L BIT: But nothing showing—

> [PECK *firmly, with his large capable hands, brushes back her hair, angles her face.* LI'L BIT *turns to him like a plant to the sun.*]

PECK: Nothing showing. Just a peek.

> [*He holds her by the shoulder, looking at her critically. Then he unbuttons her blouse to the midpoint, and runs his hands over the flesh of her exposed sternum, arranging the fabric, just touching her. Deliberately, calmly. Asexually,* LI'L BIT *quiets, sits perfectly still, and closes her eyes*]

> Okay?

LI'L BIT: Yes.

> [PECK *goes back to his camera*]

PECK: I'm going to keep talking to you. Listen without responding to what I'm saying; you want to *listen* to the music. Sway, move just your torso or your head—I've got to check the light meter.

LI'L BIT: But—you'll be watching.

PECK: No—I'm not here—just my voice. Pretend you're in your room all alone on a Friday night with your mirror—and the music feels good—just move for me, Li'l Bit—

> [LI'L BIT *closes her eyes. At first self-conscious; then she gets more into the music and begins to sway. We hear the camera start to whir. Throughout the shoot, there can be a slide montage of actual shots of the actor playing* LI'L BIT—*interspersed with other models à la* Playboy, *Calvin Klein and Victoriana/Lewis Carroll's Alice Liddell*]

> That's it. That looks great. Okay. Just keep doing that. Lift your head up a bit more, good, good, just keep moving, that a girl—you're a very beautiful young woman. Do you know that? [LI'L BIT *looks up, blushes.* PECK *shoots the camera. The audience should see this shot on the screen*]

LI'L BIT: No. I don't know that.

PECK: Listen to the music. [LI'L BIT *closes her eyes again*] Well you are. For a thirteen year old, you have a body a twenty-year-old woman would die for.

LI'L BIT: The boys in school don't think so.

PECK: The boys in school are little Neanderthals in short pants. You're ten years ahead of them in maturity; it's gonna take a while for them to catch up.

> [PECK *clicks another shot; we see a faint smile on* LI'L BIT *on the screen*]

> Girls turn into women long before boys turn into men.

LI'L BIT: Why is that?

PECK: I don't know, Li'l Bit. But it's a blessing for men.

> [LI'L BIT *turns silent*] Keep moving. Try arching your back on the stool, hands behind you, and throw your head back. [*The slide shows a* Playboy *model in this pose*] Oohh, great. That one was great. Turn your head away, same position. [*Whir*] Beautiful.

> [LI'L BIT *looks at him a bit defiantly*]

LI'L BIT: I think Aunt Mary is beautiful.

> [PECK *stands still*]

PECK: My wife is a very beautiful woman. Her beauty doesn't cancel yours out. [*More casually; he returns to the camera*] All the women in your family are beautiful. In fact, I think all women are. You're not listening to the music. [PECK *shoots some more film in silence*] All right, turn your head to the left. Good. Now take the back of your right hand and put it on your right cheek—your elbow angled up—now slowly, slowly, stroke your cheek, draw back your hair with the back of your hand. [*Another classic* Playboy *or Vargas*] Good. One hand above and behind your head; stretch your body; smile. [*Another pose*]

> Li'l Bit. I want you to think of something that makes you laugh—

LI'L BIT: I can't think of anything.

PECK: Okay. Think of Big Papa chasing Grandma around the living room. [LI'L BIT *lifts her head and laughs. Click. We should see this shot*] Good. Both hands behind your head. Great! Hold that! [*From behind his camera*] You're doing great work. If we keep this up, in five years we'll have a really professional portfolio.

> [LI'L BIT *stops.*]

LI'L BIT: What do you mean in five years?

PECK: You can't submit work to *Playboy* until you're eighteen—

> [PECK *continues to shoot; he knows he's made a mistake.*]

LI'L BIT: —Wait a minute. You're joking, aren't you, Uncle Peck?

PECK: Heck, no. You can't get into *Playboy* unless you're the very best. And you are the very best.

LI'L BIT: I would never do that!

> [PECK *stops shooting. He turns off the music.*]

PECK: Why? There's nothing wrong with *Playboy*—it's a very classy maga—

LI'L BIT: [*More upset*] But I thought you said I should go to college!

PECK: Wait—Li'l Bit—it's nothing like that. Very respectable women model for *Playboy*—actresses with major careers—women in college—there's an Ivy League issue every—

LI'L BIT: —I'm never doing anything like that! You'd show other people these—other *men*—these—what I'm doing.—Why would you do that?! Any *boy* around here could just pick up, just go into The Stop & Go and *buy*— Why would you ever want to—to share—

PECK: —Whoa, whoa. Just stop a second and listen to me. Li'l Bit. Listen. There's nothing wrong in what we're doing. I'm very proud of you. I think you have a wonderful body and an even more wonderful mind. And of course I want other people to *appreciate* it. It's not anything shameful.

LI'L BIT: [*Hurt*] But this is something—that I'm only doing for you. This is something—that you said was just between us.

PECK: It is. And if that's how you feel, five years from now, it will remain that way. Okay? I know you're not going to do anything you don't feel like doing.

> [*He walks back to the camera*]

> Do you want to stop now? I've got just a few more shots on this roll—

LI'L BIT: I don't want anyone seeing this.

PECK: I swear to you. No one will. I'll treasure this—that you're doing this only for me.

> [LI'L BIT, *still shaken, sits on the stool. She closes her eyes*]

> Li'l Bit? Open your eyes and look at me. [LI'L BIT *shakes her head no*] Come on. Just open your eyes, honey.

LI'L BIT: If I look at you—if I look at the camera: You're gonna know what I'm thinking. You'll see right through me—

PECK: —No, I won't. I want you to look at me. All right, then. I just want you to listen. Li'l Bit. [*She waits*] I love you. [LI'L BIT *opens her eyes; she is startled.* PECK *captures the shot. On the screen we see right through her.* PECK *says softly*] Do you know that? [LI'L BIT *nods her head yes*] I have loved you every day since the day you were born.

LI'L BIT: Yes.

> [LI'L BIT *and* PECK *just look at each other. Beat. Beneath the shot of herself on screen,* LI'L BIT, *still looking at her uncle, begins to unbutton her blouse.*]
>
> [*A neutral* VOICE *cuts off the above scene with:*]

Implied Consent.

As an individual operating a motor vehicle in the state of Maryland, you must abide by "Implied Consent." If you do not consent to take the blood alcohol content test, there may be severe penalties: a suspension of license, a fine, community service and a possible *jail* sentence.

> [*The* VOICE *shifts tone:*]

Idling in the Neutral Gear.

MALE GREEK CHORUS: [*Announcing*] Aunt Mary on behalf of her husband.

> [FEMALE GREEK CHORUS *checks her appearance, and with dignity comes to the front of the stage and sits down to talk to the audience.*]

FEMALE GREEK CHORUS: [*As Aunt Mary*] My husband was such a good man—is. Is such a good man. Every night, he does the dishes. The second he comes home, he's taking out the garbage, or doing yard work, lifting heavy things I can't. Everyone in the neighborhood borrows Peck—it's true—women with husbands of their own, men who just don't have Peck's abilities—there's always a knock on our door for a jump start on cold mornings, when anyone needs a ride, or help shoveling the sidewalk— I look out, and there Peck is, without a coat, pitching in. I know I'm lucky. The man works from dawn to dusk. And the overtime he does every year—my poor sister. She sits every Christmas when I come to dinner with a new stole, or diamonds, or with tickets to Bermuda.

I know he has troubles. And we don't talk about them. I wonder, sometimes, what happened to him during the war. The men who fought World War II didn't have "rap sessions" to talk about their feelings. Men in his generation were expected to be quiet about it and get on with their lives. And sometimes I can feel him just fighting the trouble—whatever has burrowed deeper than the scar tissue—and we don't talk about it. I know he's having a bad spell because he comes looking for me in the house, and just hangs around me until it passes. And I keep my banter light—I discuss a new recipe, or sales, or gossip—because I think domesticity can be a balm for men when they're lost. We sit in the house and listen to the peace of the clocks ticking in his well-ordered living room, until it passes.

[*Sharply*] I'm not a fool. I know what's going on. I wish you could feel how hard Peck fights against it—he's swimming against the tide, and what he needs is to see me on the shore, believing in him, knowing he won't go under, he won't give up—

And I want to say this about my niece. She's a sly one, that one is. She knows exactly what she's doing; she's twisted Peck around her little finger and thinks it's all a big secret. Yet another one who's borrowing my husband until it doesn't suit her anymore.

Well. I'm counting the days until she goes away to school. And she manipulates someone else. And then he'll come back again, and sit in the kitchen while I bake, or beside me on the sofa when I sew in the evenings. I'm a very patient woman. But I'd like my husband back.

I am counting the days.

[A VOICE *repeats:*]

You and the Reverse Gear.

MALE GREEK CHORUS: Li'l Bit's Thirteenth Christmas. Uncle Peck Does the Dishes. Christmas 1964.

[PECK *stands in a dress shirt and tie, nice pants, with an apron. He is washing dishes. He's in a mood we haven't seen. Quiet, brooding.* LI'L BIT *watches him a moment before seeking him out.*]

LI'L BIT: Uncle Peck? [*He does not answer. He continues to work on the pots*] I didn't know where you'd gone to. [*He nods. She takes this as a sign to come in*] Don't you want to sit with us for a while?

PECK: No. I'd rather do the dishes.

[*Pause.* LI'L BIT *watches him.*]

LI'L BIT: You're the only man I know who does the dishes. [PECK *says nothing*] I think it's really nice.

PECK: My wife has been on her feet all day. So's your grandmother and your mother.

LI'L BIT: I know. [*Beat*] Do you want some help?

PECK: No. [*He softens a bit towards her*] You can help just by talking to me.

LI'L BIT: Big Papa never does the dishes. I think it's nice.

PECK: I think men should be nice to women. Women are always working for us. There's nothing particularly manly in wolfing down food and then sitting around in a stupor while the women clean up.

LI'L BIT: That looks like a really neat camera that Aunt Mary got you.

PECK: It is. It's a very nice one.

[*Pause, as* PECK *works on the dishes and some demon that* LI'L BIT *intuits.*]

LI'L BIT: Did Big Papa hurt your feelings?

PECK: [*Tired*] What? Oh, no—it doesn't hurt me. Family is family. I'd rather have him picking on me than—I don't pay him any mind, Li'l Bit.

LI'L BIT: Are you angry with us?

PECK: No, Li'l Bit. I'm not angry.

[*Another pause.*]

LI'L BIT: We missed you at Thanksgiving. . . . I did. I missed you.

PECK: Well, there were . . . "things" going on. I didn't want to spoil anyone's Thanksgiving.

LI'L BIT: Uncle Peck? [*Very carefully*] Please don't drink anymore tonight.

PECK: I'm not . . . overdoing it.

LI'L BIT: I know. [*Beat*] Why do you drink so much?

[PECK *stops and thinks, carefully*]

PECK: Well, Li'l Bit—let me explain it this way. There are some people who have a . . . a "fire" in the belly. I think they go to work on Wall Street or they run for office. And then there are people who have a "fire" in their heads—and they become writers or scientists or historians. [*He smiles a little at her*] You. You've got a "fire" in the head. And then there are people like me.

LI'L BIT: Where do you have . . . a fire?

PECK: I have a fire in my heart. And sometimes the drinking helps.

LI'L BIT: There's got to be other things that can help.

PECK: I suppose there are.

LI'L BIT: Does it help—to talk to me?

PECK: Yes. It does. [*Quiet*] I don't get to see you very much.

LI'L BIT: I know. [LI'L BIT *thinks*] You could talk to me more.

PECK: Oh?

LI'L BIT: I could make a deal with you, Uncle Peck.

PECK: I'm listening.

LI'L BIT: We could meet and talk—once a week. You could just store up whatever's bothering you during the week—and then we could talk.

PECK: Would you like that?

LI'L BIT: As long as you don't drink. I'd meet you somewhere for lunch or for a walk—on the weekends—as long as you stop drinking. And we could talk about whatever you want.

PECK: You would do that for me?

LI'L BIT: I don't think I'd want Mom to know. Or Aunt Mary. I wouldn't want them to think—

PECK: —No. It would just be us talking.

LI'L BIT: I'll tell Mom I'm going to a girlfriend's. To study. Mom doesn't get home until six, so you can call me after school and tell me where to meet you.

PECK: You get home at four?

LI'L BIT: We can meet once a week. But only in public. You've got to let me—draw the line. And once it's drawn, you mustn't cross it.

PECK: Understood.

LI'L BIT: Would that help?

[PECK *is very moved.*]

PECK: Yes. Very much.

LI'L BIT: I'm going to join the others in the living room now. [LI'L BIT *turns to go*]

PECK: Merry Christmas, Li'l Bit.

[LI'L BIT *bestows a very warm smile on him.*]

LI'L BIT: Merry Christmas, Uncle Peck.

[A VOICE *dictates:*]

Shifting Forward from Second to Third Gear.

[*The* MALE *and* FEMALE GREEK CHORUS *members come forward.*]

MALE GREEK CHORUS: 1969. Days and Gifts: A Countdown:

FEMALE GREEK CHORUS: A note. "September 3, 1969. Li'l Bit: You've only been away two days and it feels like months. Hope your dorm room is cozy. I'm sending you this tape cassette—it's a new model—so you'll have some music in your room. Also that music you're reading about for class—*Carmina Burana*. Hope you enjoy. Only ninety days to go!—Peck."

MALE GREEK CHORUS: September 22. A bouquet of roses. A note: "Miss you like crazy. Sixty-nine days . . . "

TEENAGE GREEK CHORUS: September 25. A box of chocolates. A card: "Don't worry about the weight gain. You still look great. Got a post office box—write to me there. Sixty-six days.—Love, your candy man."

MALE GREEK CHORUS: October 16. A note: "Am trying to get through the Jane Austen you're reading—*Emma*—here's a book in return: *Liaisons Dangereuses*. Hope you're saving time for me." Scrawled in the margin the number: "47."

FEMALE GREEK CHORUS: November 16. "Sixteen days to go!—Hope you like the perfume.—Having a hard time reaching you on the dorm phone. You must be in the library a lot. Won't you think about me getting you your own phone so we can talk?"

TEENAGE GREEK CHORUS: November 18. "Li'l Bit—got a package returned to the P.O. Box. Have you changed dorms? Call me at work or write to the P.O. Am still on the wagon. Waiting to see you. Only two weeks more!"

MALE GREEK CHORUS: November 23. A letter. "Li'l Bit. So disappointed you couldn't come home for the turkey. Sending you some money for a nice dinner out—nine days and counting!"

GREEK CHORUS: [*In unison*] November 25th. A letter:

LI'L BIT: "Dear Uncle Peck: I am sending this to you at work. Don't come up next weekend for my birthday. I will not be here—"

> [A VOICE *directs:*]

Shifting Forward from Third to Fourth Gear.

MALE GREEK CHORUS: December 10, 1969. A hotel room. Philadelphia. There is no moon tonight.

> [PECK *sits on the side of the bed while* LI'L BIT *paces. He can't believe she's in his room, but there's a desperate edge to his happiness.* LI'L BIT *is furious, edgy. There is a bottle of champagne in an ice bucket in a very nice hotel room.*]

PECK: Why don't you sit?

LI'L BIT: I don't want to.—What's the champagne for?

PECK: I thought we might toast your birthday—

LI'L BIT: —I am so pissed off at you, Uncle Peck.

PECK: Why?

LI'L BIT: I mean, are you crazy?

PECK: What did I do?

LI'L BIT: You scared the holy crap out of me—sending me that stuff in the mail—

PECK: —They were gifts! I just wanted to give you some little perks your first semester—

LI'L BIT: —Well, what the hell were those numbers all about! Forty-four days to go—only two more weeks.—And then just numbers—69—68—67—like some serial killer!

PECK: Li'l Bit! Whoa! This is me you're talking to—I was just trying to pick up your spirits, trying to celebrate your birthday.

LI'L BIT: My *eighteenth* birthday. I'm not a child, Uncle Peck. You were counting down to my eighteenth birthday.

PECK: So?

LI'L BIT: So? So statutory rape is not in effect when a young woman turns eighteen. And you and I both know it.

> [PECK *is walking on ice.*]

PECK: I think you misunderstand.

LI'L BIT: I think I understand all too well. I know what you want to do five steps ahead of you doing it. Defensive Driving 101.

PECK: Then why did you suggest we meet here instead of the restaurant?

LI'L BIT: I don't want to have this conversation in public.

PECK: Fine. Fine. We have a lot to talk about.

LI'L BIT: Yeah. We do.

> [LI'L BIT *doesn't want to do what she has to do*] Could I . . . have some of that champagne?

PECK: Of course, madam! [PECK *makes a big show of it*] Let me do the honors. I wasn't sure which you might prefer—Taittingers or Veuve Clicquot—so I thought we'd start out with an old standard—Perrier Jouet. [*The bottle is popped*]

> Quick—Li'l Bit—your glass! [*Uncle* PECK *fills* LI'L BIT*'s glass. He puts the bottle back in the ice and goes for a can of ginger ale*] Let me get some of this ginger ale—my bubbly—and toast you.

> [*He turns and sees that* LI'L BIT *has not waited for him.*]

LI'L BIT: Oh—sorry, Uncle Peck. Let me have another. [PECK *fills her glass and reaches for his ginger ale; she stops him*] Uncle Peck—maybe you should join me in the champagne.

PECK: You want me to—drink?

LI'L BIT: It's not polite to let a lady drink alone.

PECK: Well, missy, if you insist . . . [PECK *hesitates*]—Just one. It's been a while. [PECK *fills another flute for himself*] There. I'd like to propose a toast to you and your birthday! [PECK *sips it tentatively*] I'm not used to this anymore.

LI'L BIT: You don't have anywhere to go tonight, do you?

[PECK *hopes this is a good sign.*]

PECK: I'm all yours.—God, it's good to see you! I've gotten so used to . . . to . . . talking to you in my head. I'm used to seeing you every week—there's so much—I don't quite know where to begin. How's school, Li'l Bit?

LI'L BIT: I—it's hard. Uncle Peck. Harder than I thought it would be. I'm in the middle of exams and papers and—I don't know.

PECK: You'll pull through. You always do.

LI'L BIT: Maybe. I . . . might be flunking out.

PECK: You always think the worse, Li'l Bit, but when the going gets tough—[LI'L BIT *shrugs and pours herself another glass*]—Hey, honey, go easy on that stuff, okay?

LI'L BIT: Is it very expensive?

PECK: Only the best for you. But the cost doesn't matter—champagne should be "sipped." [LI'L BIT *is quiet*] Look—if you're in trouble in school—you can always come back home for a while.

LI'L BIT: *No*—[LI'L BIT *tries not to be so harsh*]—Thanks, Uncle Peck, but I'll figure some way out of this.

PECK: You're supposed to get in scrapes, your first year away from home.

LI'L BIT: Right. How's Aunt Mary?

PECK: She's fine. [*Pause*] Well—how about the new car?

LI'L BIT: It's real nice. What is it, again?

PECK: It's a Cadillac El Dorado.

LI'L BIT: Oh. Well, I'm real happy for you, Uncle Peck.

PECK: I got it for you.

LI'L BIT: What?

PECK: I always wanted to get a Cadillac—but I thought, Peck, wait until Li'l Bit's old enough—and thought maybe you'd like to drive it, too.

LI'L BIT: [*Confused*] Why would I want to drive your car?

PECK: Just because it's the best—I want you to have the best.

[*They are running out of "gas"; small talk.*]

LI'L BIT: Listen, Uncle Peck, I don't know   PECK: I have been thinking of how to say
    how to begin this, but—   this in my head, over and over—

PECK: Sorry.

LI'L BIT: You first.

PECK: Well, your going away—has just made me realize how much I miss you. Talking to you and being alone with you. I've really come to depend on you, Li'l Bit. And it's been so hard to get in touch with you lately—the distance and—and you're never in when I call—I guess you've been living in the library—

LI'L BIT: —No—the problem is, I haven't been in the library—

PECK: —Well, it doesn't matter—I hope you've been missing me as much.

LI'L BIT: Uncle Peck—I've been thinking a lot about this—and I came here tonight to tell you that—I'm not doing very well. I'm getting very confused—I can't concentrate on my work—and now that I'm away—I've been going over and over it in my mind—and I don't want us to "see" each other anymore. Other than with the rest of the family.

PECK: [*Quiet*] Are you seeing other men?

LI'L BIT: [*Getting agitated*] I—no, that's not the reason—I—well, yes I am seeing other—listen, it's not really anybody's business!

PECK: Are you in love with anyone else?

LI'L BIT: That's not what this is about.

PECK: Li'l Bit—you're scared. Your mother and your grandparents have filled your head with all kinds of nonsense about men—I hear them working on you all the time—and you're scared. It won't hurt you—if the man you go to bed with really loves you. [LI'L BIT *is scared. She starts to tremble*] And I have loved you since the day I held you in my hand. And I think everyone's just gotten you frightened to death about something that is just like breathing—

LI'L BIT: Oh, my god—[*She takes a breath*] I can't see you anymore, Uncle Peck.

> [PECK *downs the rest of his champagne.*]

PECK: Li'l Bit. Listen. Open your eyes and look at me. Come on. Just open your eyes, honey. [LI'L BIT, *eyes squeezed shut, refuses*] All right then. I just want you to listen. Li'l Bit—I'm going to ask you just this once. Of your own free will. Just lie down on the bed with me—our clothes on—just lie down with me, a man and a woman . . . and let's . . . hold one another. Nothing else. Before you say anything else. I want the chance to . . . hold you. Because sometimes the body knows things that the mind isn't listening to . . . and after I've held you, then I want you to tell me what you feel.

LI'L BIT: You'll just . . . hold me?

PECK: Yes. And then you can tell me what you're feeling.

> [LI'L BIT—*half wanting to run, half wanting to get it over with, half wanting to be held by him:*]

LI'L BIT: Yes. All right. Just hold. Nothing else.

> [PECK *lies down on the bed and holds his arms out to her.* LI'L BIT *lies beside him, putting her head on his chest. He looks as if he's trying to soak her into his pores by osmosis. He strokes her hair, and she lies very still. The* MALE GREEK CHORUS *member and the* FEMALE GREEK CHORUS *member as Aunt Mary come into the room.*]

MALE GREEK CHORUS: Recipe for a Southern boy:

FEMALE GREEK CHORUS: [*As Aunt Mary*] A drawl of molasses in the way he speaks.

MALE GREEK CHORUS: A gumbo of red and brown mixed in the cream of his skin.

> [*While* PECK *lies, his eyes closed,* LI'L BIT *rises in the bed and responds to her aunt.*]

LI'L BIT: Warm brown eyes—

FEMALE GREEK CHORUS: [*As Aunt Mary*] Bedroom eyes—

MALE GREEK CHORUS: A dash of Southern Baptist Fire and Brimstone—

LI'L BIT: A curl of Elvis on his forehead—

FEMALE GREEK CHORUS: [*As Aunt Mary*] A splash of Bay Rum—

MALE GREEK CHORUS: A closely shaven beard that he razors just for you—

FEMALE GREEK CHORUS: [*As Aunt Mary*] Large hands—rough hands—

LI'L BIT: Warm hands—

MALE GREEK CHORUS: The steel of the military in his walk —

LI'L BIT: The slouch of the fishing skiff in his walk—

MALE GREEK CHORUS: Neatly pressed khakis—

FEMALE GREEK CHORUS: [*As Aunt Mary*] And under the wide leather of the belt —

LI'L BIT: Sweat of cypress and sand—

MALE GREEK CHORUS: Neatly pressed khakis—

LI'L BIT: His heart beating Dixie—

FEMALE GREEK CHORUS: [*As Aunt Mary*] The whisper of the zipper—you could reach out with your hand and—

LI'L BIT: His mouth—

FEMALE GREEK CHORUS: [*As Aunt Mary*] You could just reach out and—
LI'L BIT: Hold him in your hand—
FEMALE GREEK CHORUS: [*As Aunt Mary*] And his mouth—
>   [LI'L BIT *rises above her uncle and looks at his mouth; she starts to lower herself to kiss him—and wrenches herself free. She gets up from the bed.*]
LI'L BIT: —I've got to get back.
PECK: Wait—Li'l Bit. Did you . . . feel nothing?
LI'L BIT: [*Lying*] No. Nothing.
PECK: Do you—do you think of me?
>   [*The* GREEK CHORUS *whispers:*]
FEMALE GREEK CHORUS: Khakis—
MALE GREEK CHORUS: Bay Rum—
FEMALE GREEK CHORUS: The whisper of the—
LI'L BIT: —No.
>   [PECK, *in a rush, trembling, gets something out of his pocket.*]
PECK: I'm forty-five. That's not old for a man. And I haven't been able to do anything else but think of you. I can't concentrate on my work—Li'l Bit. You've got to—I want you to think about what I am about to ask you.
LI'L BIT: I'm listening.
>   [PECK *opens a small ring box.*]
PECK: I want you to be my wife.
LI'L BIT: This isn't happening
PECK: I'll tell Mary I want a divorce. We're not blood-related. It would be legal—
LI'L BIT: —What have you been thinking! You are married to my aunt, Uncle Peck. She's my family. You have—you have gone way over the line. Family is family.
>   [*Quickly,* LI'L BIT *flies through the room, gets her coat*]
I'm leaving. Now. I am not seeing you. Again.
>   [PECK *lies down on the bed for a moment, trying to absorb the terrible news. For a moment, he almost curls into a fetal position*]
I'm not coming home for Christmas. You should go home to Aunt Mary. Go home now, Uncle Peck.
>   [PECK *gets control, and sits, rigid*]
Uncle Peck?—I'm sorry but I have to go.
>   [*Pause*]
Are you all right.
>   [*With a discipline that comes from being told that boys don't cry,* PECK *stands upright.*]
PECK: I'm fine. I just think—I need a real drink.
>   [*The* MALE GREEK CHORUS *has become a bartender. At a small counter, he is lining up shots for* PECK. *As* LI'L BIT *narrates, we see* PECK *sitting, carefully and calmly downing shot glasses.*]
LI'L BIT: [*To the audience*] I never saw him again. I stayed away from Christmas and Thanksgiving for years after.

It took my uncle seven years to drink himself to death. First he lost his job, then his wife, and finally his driver's license. He retreated to his house, and had his bottles delivered.
>   [PECK *stands, and puts his hands in front of him—almost like Superman flying*]
One night he tried to go downstairs to the basement—and he flew down the steep basement stairs. My aunt came by weekly to put food on the porch, and she noticed the mail and the papers stacked up, uncollected.

They found him at the bottom of the stairs. Just steps away from his dark room.

Now that I'm old enough, there are some questions I would have liked to have asked him. Who did it to you, Uncle Peck? How old were you? Were you eleven?

[PECK *moves to the driver's seat of the car and waits*]

Sometimes I think of my uncle as a kind of Flying Dutchman. In the opera, the Dutchman is doomed to wander the sea; but every seven years he can come ashore, and if he finds a maiden who will love him of her own free will—he will be released.

And I see Uncle Peck in my mind, in his Chevy '56, a spirit driving up and down the back roads of Carolina—looking for a young girl who, of her own free will, will love him. Release him.

[A VOICE *states:*]

You and the Reverse Gear.

LI'L BIT: The summer of 1962. On Men, Sex, and Women: Part III

[LI'L BIT *steps, as an eleven year old, into:*]

FEMALE GREEK CHORUS: [*As Mother*] It is out of the question. End of Discussion.

LI'L BIT: But why?

FEMALE GREEK CHORUS: [*As Mother*] Li'l Bit—we are not discussing this. I said no.

LI'L BIT: But I could spend an extra week at the beach! You're not telling me why!

FEMALE GREEK CHORUS: [*As Mother*] Your uncle pays entirely too much attention to you.

LI'L BIT: He listens to me when I talk. And—and he talks to me. He teaches me about things. Mama—he knows an awful lot.

FEMALE GREEK CHORUS: [*As Mother*] He's a small town hick who's learned how to mix drinks from Hugh Hefner.

LI'L BIT: Who's Hugh Hefner?

[*Beat.*]

FEMALE GREEK CHORUS: [*As Mother*] I am not letting an eleven-year-old girl spend seven hours alone in the car with a man. . . . I don't like the way your uncle looks at you.

LI'L BIT: For god's sake, mother! Just because you've gone through a bad time with my father—you think every man is evil!

FEMALE GREEK CHORUS: [*As Mother*] Oh no, Li'l Bit—not all men . . . We . . . we just haven't been very lucky with the men in our family.

LI'L BIT: Just because you lost your husband—I still deserve a chance at having a father! Someone! A man who will look out for me! Don't I get a chance?

FEMALE GREEK CHORUS: [*As Mother*] I will feel terrible if something happens.

LI'L BIT: Mother! It's in your head! Nothing will happen! I can take care of myself. And I can certainly handle Uncle Peck.

FEMALE GREEK CHORUS: [*As Mother*] All right. But I'm warning you—if anything happens, I hold you responsible.

[LI'L BIT *moves out of this scene and toward the car.*]

LI'L BIT: 1962. On the Back Roads of Carolina: The First Driving Lesson.

[*The* TEENAGE GREEK CHORUS *member stands apart on stage. She will speak all of* LI'L BIT*'s lines.* LI'L BIT *sits beside* PECK *in the front seat. She looks at him closely, remembering.*]

PECK: Li'l Bit? Are you getting tired?

TEENAGE GREEK CHORUS: A little.

PECK: It's a long drive. But we're making really good time. We can take the back road from here and see . . . a little scenery. Say—I've got an idea— [PECK *checks his rearview mirror*]

TEENAGE GREEK CHORUS: Are we stopping, Uncle Peck?

PECK: There's no traffic here. Do you want to drive?

TEENAGE GREEK CHORUS: I can't drive.

PECK: It's easy. I'll show you how. I started driving when I was your age. Don't you want to?—

TEENAGE GREEK CHORUS: —But it's against the law at my age!

PECK: And that's why you can't tell anyone I'm letting you do this—

TEENAGE GREEK CHORUS: —But—I can't reach the pedals.

PECK: You can sit in my lap and steer. I'll push the pedals for you. Did your father ever let you drive his car?

TEENAGE GREEK CHORUS: No way.

PECK: Want to try?

TEENAGE GREEK CHORUS: Okay.

[LI'L BIT *moves into* PECK'*s lap. She leans against him, closing her eyes*]

PECK: You're just a little thing, aren't you? Okay—now think of the wheel as a big clock— I want you to put your right hand on the clock where three o'clock would be; and your left hand on the nine—

[LI'L BIT *puts one hand to* PECK'*s face, to stroke him. Then, she takes the wheel.*]

TEENAGE GREEK CHORUS: Am I doing it right?

PECK: That's right. Now, whatever you do, don't let go of the wheel. You tell me whether to go faster or slower—

TEENAGE GREEK CHORUS: Not so fast, Uncle Peck!

PECK: Li'l Bit—I need you to watch the road—

[PECK *puts his hands on* LI'L BIT'*s breasts. She relaxes against him, silent, accepting his touch.*]

TEENAGE GREEK CHORUS: Uncle Peck—what are you doing?

PECK: Keep driving. [*He slips his hands under her blouse*]

TEENAGE GREEK CHORUS: Uncle Peck—please don't do this—

PECK: —Just a moment longer . . . [PECK *tenses against* LI'L BIT]

TEENAGE GREEK CHORUS: [*Trying not to cry*] This isn't happening.

[PECK *tenses more, sharply. He buries his face in* LI'L BIT'*s neck, and moans softly. The* TEENAGE GREEK CHORUS *exits, and* LI'L BIT *steps out of the car.* PECK, *too, disappears.*]

[A VOICE *reflects:*]

Driving in Today's World.

LI'L BIT: That day was the last day I lived in my body. I retreated above the neck, and I've lived inside the "fire" in my head ever since.

And now that seems like a long, long time ago. When we were both very young. And before you know it, I'll be thirty-five. That's getting up there for a woman. And I find myself believing in things that a younger self vowed never to believe in. Things like family and forgiveness.

I know I'm lucky. Although I still have never known what it feels like to jog or dance. Any thing that . . . "jiggles." I do like to watch people on the dance floor, or out on the running paths, just jiggling away. And I say—good for them. [LI'L BIT *moves to the car with pleasure*]

The nearest sensation I feel—of flight in the body—I guess I feel when I'm driving. On a day like today. It's five A.M. The radio says it's going to be clear and crisp. I've got five miles of highway ahead of me—and some back roads too. I filled the tank last night, and had the oil checked. Checked the tires, too. You've got to treat her . . . with respect.

First thing I do is: Check under the car. To see if any two year olds or household cats have crawled beneath, and strategically placed their skulls behind my back tires. [LI'L BIT *crouches*]

Nope. Then I get in the car. [LI'L BIT *does so*]

I lock the doors. And turn the key. Then I adjust the most important control on the dashboard—the radio—[LI'L BIT *turns the radio on: We hear all of the* GREEK CHORUS *overlapping, and static:*]

FEMALE GREEK CHORUS: [*Overlapping*] —"You were so tiny you fit in his hand—"

MALE GREEK CHORUS: [*Overlapping*]—"How is Shakespeare gonna help her lie on her back in the—"

TEENAGE GREEK CHORUS: [*Overlapping*]—"Am I doing it right?"

[LI'L BIT *fine-tunes the radio station. A song like "Dedicated to the One I Love" or Orbison's "Sweet Dreams" comes on, and cuts off the* GREEK CHORUS.]

LI'L BIT: Ahh . . . [*Beat*] I adjust my seat. Fasten my seat belt. Then I check the right side mirror—check the left side. [*She does*] Finally, I adjust the rearview mirror. [*As* LI'L BIT *adjusts the rear view mirror, a faint light strikes the spirit of Uncle* PECK *who is sitting in the back seat of the car. She sees him in the mirror. She smiles at him, and he nods at her. They are happy to be going for a long drive together.* LI'L BIT *slips the car into first gear; to the audience:*] And then—I floor it. [*Sound of a car taking off. Blackout*]

END OF PLAY

The Shrine in the Fields

(15th Century)

HE SHRINE IN THE FIELDS represents one of the five basic types of Noh plays. A "woman play," it is based on episodes from a famous Japanese novel, *The Tale of Genji*, in which Lord Genji is the lover of Lady Rokujo (the protagonist of *The Shrine in the Fields*) but after a time neglects her. At a festival, attendants on Lord Genji's wife publicly humiliate Lady Rokujo by pushing her carriage out of the procession and disabling it. Lady Rokujo then leaves the capital and goes to Nonomiya, where her daughter is being prepared to become priestess of Ise (the Sun Goddess). While at Nonomiya, Lady Rokujo is visited by Lord Genji, who begs her to return to him. Although she refuses, her love and humiliation keep drawing her back to Nonomiya even after her death.

The major influence on Noh is Zen Buddhism, which teaches that ultimate peace comes from overcoming individual desire in order to achieve union with all being. The protagonists of Noh are ghosts, demons, or obsessed humans whose souls cannot find rest because in life they became too devoted to love, honor, or other goals that pull them back into the physical world.

In Noh, each play occurs in a specific season of the year, and the mood throughout must be in keeping with that season. In this play, the season is autumn. The introductory scene drastically compresses time and place: the itinerant priest (the *waki*) travels almost instantaneously from the capital to Nonomiya. The ghost of Lady Rokujo (in the guise of a village girl) appears and, as the priest questions her, it becomes apparent that she is protecting some secret. Later she returns as herself, the Miyasudokoro (Lady Rokujo) of long ago. As she tells her story, the emotion builds until, as in all Noh plays, it finds expression in a dance. In the final scene, the pull between this and the next world are fully symbolized by passing back and forth through the gate of the shrine. At the end, the freeing of the soul is indicated by rushing out of the "burning house," an image for the world, which, in Buddhist teaching, enlightened persons are counseled to flee as willingly as they would a burning building. Thus, at the end, we are asked to believe that Miyasudokoro has broken her attachment to the world. Overall, *The Shrine in the Fields* does not seek to tell a story or to develop a character so much as to capture a particular mood, to distill a powerful emotion, and to express an attitude about the physical world and human existence.

The Shrine in the Fields (Nonomiya), from *Twenty Plays for the Nō Theatre*, edited by Donald Keene and translated by Paul Varley, © 1970. Reprinted by permission of Columbia University Press.

The Shrine in the fields (15th Century)

TRANSLATED BY H. PAUL VARLEY

Persons

A TRAVELING PRIEST
A VILLAGE GIRL
MIYASUDOKORO

PLACE————*Sagano in Yamashiro Province*
TIME————*Late autumn, the seventh day of the ninth month*
>   [*The stage assistant places a* torii *at the front of the stage. To either upright of the* torii *are attached short sections of fence made of brushwood twigs. The* PRIEST *enters. He carries a rosary in his hand. He stands at the naming-place.*]

PRIEST
I am an itinerant priest. Recently I have been staying in the Capital, where I have visited all the famous sites and relics of the past. Autumn is nearing its close and Sagano will be lovely now. I think I shall go there for a visit. [*He turns towards the* torii, *indicating that he has already arrived in Sagano.*] When I asked people about this wood they told me it is the ancient site of the Shrine in the Fields. I would like to visit the place, though I am no more than a passing stranger.
>   [*He advances to stage center, still facing the* torii.]

I enter the wood and I see
A rustic log *torii*
And a fence of brushwood twigs.
Surely nothing has changed from the past!
But why should time have spared this place?
Be that as it may, how lucky I am
To have come at this lovely time of year
And be able to worship at such a place.
>   [*He kneels and presses his palms together.*]

The Great Shrine at Ise
Makes no distinction
Between gods and Buddhas:
The teachings of the Buddhist Law
Have guided me straight along the path,
And I have arrived at the Shrine.
My heart is pure in the evening light,
Pure in the clear evening light!
>   [*The* GIRL *enters. She wears the* fukai *mask and carries a branch of sakaki. She stands at the* shite-*position and faces the musicians.*]

GIRL
Shrine in the Fields
Where I have lived with flowers;
Shrine in the Fields
Where I have lived with flowers—
What will be left when autumn has passed?
                    [*She faces front.*]
Now lonely autumn ends,
But still my sleeves
Wilt in a dew of tears;
The dusk racks my body,
And my heart of itself
Takes on the fading colors
Of the thousand flowers;
It withers, as all things, with neglect.
Each year on this day,
Unknown to anyone else,
I return to the old remains.
In the wood at the Shrine in the Fields
Autumn has drawn to a close
And the harsh winds blow;
Colors so brilliant
They pierced the senses
Have faded and vanished;
What remains now to recall
The memories of the past
What use was it to come here?
                    [*She takes a few steps to her right, then faces front*]
Ahh—how I loathe the attachment
That makes me go back and forth,
Again and again on my journey
To this meaningless, fugitive world.
                    [*The* PRIEST *rises and faces her.*]
PRIEST
As I was resting in the shade of the trees, thinking about the past and refreshing my
mind, a charming young lady has suddenly appeared. Please tell me who you are.
GIRL
It would be appropriate if I had asked who you are. This is Nonomiya, the Shrine in the
Fields, where in ancient days the virgin designated as the Priestess of Ise was temporarily
lodged. The custom has fallen into disuse, but today, the seventh day of the ninth
month, is still a time for recalling the past. Each year, unknown to anyone else, I come to
sweep the shrine and to perform a service. I do not know where you have come from, but
your presence here is an intrusion. Please leave at once.
                    [*She takes two steps towards the* PRIEST.]
PRIEST
No, no. There can be no objection to my being here. I am only a wandering priest who
has renounced the uncertain world. But tell me, why should you return here, to these old
ruins, on this particular day each year in search of the past?
GIRL
This is the day when Genji the Shining One visited this place, the seventh day of the
ninth month. He brought with him a twig of *sakaki* and pushed it through the sacred

fence. Miyasudokoro at once composed this poem:
"This sacred enclosure
Has no cypress to mark the spot;[1]
By some error you have picked
A twig of *sakaki* wood."
It happened on this day!

PRIEST
That was truly a worthy poem.[2]
—And the *sakaki* branch
You hold in your hand
Is the same color it was in the past.

GIRL
The same color as in the past?
How clever to put it that way!
Only the *sakaki* stays green forever,
And in its unvarying shade

PRIEST
On the pathways through the wood,
The autumn deepens

GIRL
And leaves turn crimson only to scatter.

PRIEST
In the weed-grown fields
                    [*She goes to the* torii *and places the* sakaki *branch there. The* PRIEST *kneels.*]

CHORUS
The stalks and leaf tips wither;
Nonomiya, the Shrine in the Fields,
Stands amidst the desolation
Of withered stalks and leaves
The seventh day of the ninth month
Has returned again today
To this place of memories.
                    [*She moves to center stage.*]
How fragile it seemed at the time,
This little fence of brushwood twigs.
                    [*She gazes at the fence.*]
And the house that looked so temporary
Has now become the guardian's hut.
                    [*She turns towards the gazing-pillar.*]
A dim glow shines from inside:
I wonder if the longing within me
Reveals itself outwardly?
How lonely a place is this shrine,
How lonely a place is this palace!

PRIEST
Please tell me more of the story of Miyasudokoro.
                    [*The* GIRL *kneels at center stage.*]

---

[1] Evergreen is associated with enduring love and devotion.

[2] The poem quoted is from *The Tale of Genji*, where it seems to mean that the visitor has come without invitation, pretending to have been invited.

CHORUS
The lady known as Miyasudokoro
Became the wife of the former Crown Prince,
The brother of Kiritsubo's Emperor,[3]
A man at the height of his glory;
They were like the color and perfume
Of the same flower, indissolubly bound.
GIRL
They knew, of course, the truth
That those who must meet part—
CHORUS
Why should it have surprised them?
But it came so soon—like a nightmare—
His death that left her alone.
GIRL
She could not remain in that state,
Helpless and given to tears;
CHORUS
Soon Genji the Shining One
Imposed his love and began
Their clandestine meetings.
GIRL
How did their love affair end?
CHORUS
And why, after they separated,
Did his love never turn to hate?
With customary tenderness
He made his way through the fields
To distant Nonomiya.
The autumn flowers had all withered,
The voices of insects were sparse.
Oh, the loneliness of that journey!
Even the wind echoing in the pines
Reminded him there is no end
To the sadness of autumn.
So the Prince visited her,
And with the deepest affection
Spoke his love in many ways;
How noble and sensitive a man!
GIRL
Later, by the Katsura River,
She performs cleansing rite,
CHORUS
Setting the white-wrapped branches[4]
Adrift on the river waves;
Herself like a drifting weed,

---

[3] Kiritsubo was Genji's mother.
[4] Streamers of paper or mulberry bark were inscribed with prayers and attached to *sakaki* branches, then tossed into the stream.

No roots or destination,
She moved at the water's will.
"Through the waves of the eighty rapids
Of Suzuki River to Ise,
Who will worry if the waves wet me or no?"
She wrote this poem to describe her journey.
Never before had a mother
Escorted her daughter, the Virgin,
All the way to the Také Palace.[5]
Mother and daughter on the way
Felt only the bitterness of regret.
   [*for* PRIEST]
Now that I have heard your tale,
I am sure that you are no ordinary woman.
Please tell me your name.
GIRL
Revealing my name
Would serve no purpose;
In my helplessness
I am ashamed of myself.
Sooner or later
My name will be known,
It can't be helped;
But now say a prayer for one nameless,
And not of this world.
CHORUS
[*for* PRIEST]. Not of this world?
What strange words to hear!
Then, have you died and departed
GIRL
This world, long ago,
A name my only monument:
CHORUS
Miyasudokoro
GIRL
Is myself.
CHORUS
Autumn winds rise at dusk;
   [*She stands.*]
Through the forest branches
The evening moonlight shines
   [*She goes to the* shite-*position.*]
Dimly illuminating,
Under the trees,
   [*She looks at the* torii.]
The rustic logs of the *torii*.
She passes between the two pillars
And vanishes without a trace;

---

[5] The Virgin resided at Ise in the Také Palace.

She has vanished without a trace.

[*She slowly exits. A Villager then enters and performs the* kyōgen *interlude, a lengthy recapitulation of* MIYASUDOKORO'*s story. The* PRIEST *asks the Villager to tell what he knows, and then the two men agree that the* PRIEST *has just seen the ghost of* MIYASUDOKORO. *The* PRIEST *decides to stay and read the sutras and prayers for her. The Villager withdraws.*]

PRIEST

Alone I lie on the forest moss,
A sleeve of my robe spread beneath me—
Under forest trees, a mossy robe:
My mat is grass of the same color.[6]
Unfolding my memories
I shall offer prayers all night long;
I shall pray for her repose.

[*The* GIRL, *now revealed as* MIYASUDOKORO, *enters and stands at the* shite-*position.*]

MIYASUDOKORO

In this carriage,
Lovely as the autumn followers
At Nonomiya,
I too have returned to the past,
To long ago.

PRIEST

How strange!
In the faint moonlight
The soft sounds
Of an approaching carriage,
A courtly carriage
With reed blinds hanging—
A sight of unimagined beauty!
It must be you, Miyasudokoro!
But what is the carriage you ride in?

MIYASUDOKORO

You ask me about my carriage?
I remember now
That scene of long ago—
The Kamo Festival,
The jostling carriages,
No one could tell
Who their owners were,
But thick as dewdrops

PRIEST

The splendid ranks crowded the place.

MIYASUDOKORO

Pleasure carriages of every description,
And one among them of special magnificence,
The Princess Aoi's.

---

6 A priest's robe was frequently called *kokegoromo,* literally meaning "moss robe." Here it also refers to moss and autumn grass that is faded like the priest's robe.

PRIEST
"Make way for Her Highness's carriage!"
The servants cried, clearing the crowd,
And in the confusion
MIYASUDOKORO
I answered, "My carriage is small,
I have nowhere else to put it."
I stood my ground,
PRIEST
But around the carriage
MIYASUDOKORO
Men suddenly swarmed.
            [*Her gestures suggest the actions described.*]
CHORUS
Grasping the shafts,
They pushed my carriage back
Into the ranks of servants.
My carriage had come for no purpose,
My pleasure gone,
And I knew my helplessness.
I realized now
That all that happened
Was surely retribution
For the sins of former lives.
Even now I am in agony:
Like the wheels of my carriage
I return again and again—
How long must I still keep returning?
I beg you, dispel this delusion!
I beg you, dispel this suffering!
            [*She presses her palms together in supplication.*]
MIYASUDOKORO
Remembering the vanished days
I dance, waving at the moon
My flowerlike sleeves,
CHORUS
As if begging it to restore the past.
            [*She goes to the* shite-*position and begins to dance. As her dance ends, the text*
            resumes.]
MIYASUDOKORO
Even the moon
At the Shrine in the Fields
Must remember the past;
CHORUS
Its light forlornly trickles
Through the leaves to the forest dew.
Through the leaves to the forest dew.
MIYASUDOKORO
This place, once my refuge,
This garden, still lingers

CHORUS
Unchanged from long ago,
MIYASUDOKORO
A beauty nowhere else,
CHORUS
Though transient, insubstantial
MIYASUDOKORO
As this little wooden fence
CHORUS
From which he used to brush the dew.
          [*She brushes the fence with her fan.*]
I, whom he visited,
And he, my lover too,
The whole world turned to dreams,
To aging ruins;
Whom shall I pine for now?
The voices of the pine-crickets
Trill *rin, rin,*
The wind howls:
          [*She advances to stage front. She gazes at the* torii.]
How I remember
Nights at the Shrine in the Fields!
          [*Weeping, she withdraws to the area before the musicians and starts to dance. The
          text resumes when her dance has ended.*]
CHORUS
At this shrine we have always worshiped
The divine wind that blows from Ise,
          [*She goes before the* torii.]
The Inner and Outer Shrines.
As I pass to and fro through this *torii*
I seem to wander on the path of delusion:
I waver between life and death.
          [*She passes back and forth through the* torii.]
The gods will surely reject me!
Again she climbs in her carriage and rides out
The gate of the Burning House,
The gate of the Burning House.[7]

7 The Burning House is an image for this world, which an enlightened person should flee as eagerly as from
a burning house.

The Strong Breed (1964)

I n *The Strong Breed*, the dramatic action focuses on a ritual that in one form or another is found in various societies—the selection and expulsion of a scapegoat. This theme exists in *Oedipus the King*, as well as many other plays. In Soyinka's play, the protagonist Eman's mistake lies in thinking the ritual is observed everywhere as it was in his own community where someone willingly allowed the troubles and cares of the village to be loaded into a symbolic vessel that a "carrier" then took away down the river thereby cleansing the community in preparation for the new year. In Eman's village, the carrier was honored for his strength, courage, and wisdom, but in the village to which Eman has recently come, the carrier himself becomes the object of loathing and is driven from the village permanently. Thus, only outsiders are chosen as carriers; they are then drugged and hypnotized, and subjected to beatings, curses, and other forms of abuse. As one of only two outsiders present in the village, Eman becomes an obvious candidate to serve as the carrier.

In the first part of the play, little is revealed about Eman's past or why he is here. But as the villagers begin to close in on him, Eman relives his past and his attempt to escape its unpleasantness. In a flashback, his father reminds him that he comes from a family of carriers (the strong breed) and that he cannot escape his fate. Eventually, the villagers track down Eman and kill him, but the act fills most of them with shame and makes them question following their leaders blindly.

The Strong Breed develops a number of themes common in Soyinka's plays: the conflict between the traditional and the modern; the ongoing need to save society from its tendency to follow custom and mistaken belief unquestioningly; the special individual, who through dedication and vision awakens the people and leads them toward better ways, even though he may become a victim of the society he seeks to benefit.

In this and his other plays, Soyinka draws his material from native sources but reinterprets it, often showing the conflict between traditional customs and modern consciousness. He has sought a balance between appreciation for the culture of the past and the need to alter conditions to achieve a just society. Soyinka's accomplishments were acknowledged when he became the first African dramatist to win the Nobel Prize for Literature.

WOLE SOYINKA

The Strong Breed

Characters

EMAN, *a stranger*
SUNMA, *Jaguna's daughter*
IFADA, *an idiot*
GIRL
JAGUNA
ORAGE
THE VILLAGERS, *attendants stalwarts*

from Eman's past—
OLD MAN, *his father*
OMAE, *his betrothed*
TUTOR
PRIEST
THE VILLAGERS, *attendants*

The scenes are described briefly, but very often a darkened stage with lit areas will not only suffice but is necessary. Except for the one indicated place, there can be no break in the action. A distracting scene-change would be ruinous.

A mud house, with space in front of it. EMAN, *in light buba and trousers stands at the window, looking out. Inside,* SUNMA *is clearing the table of what looks like a modest clinic, putting the things away in the cupboard. Another rough table in the room is piled with exercise books, two or three worn text-books, etc.* SUNMA *appears agitated. Outside, just below the window crouches* IFADA. *He looks up with a shy smile from time to time, waiting for* EMAN *to notice him.*

SUNMA: [*hesitant.*] You will have to make up your mind soon Eman. The lorry leaves very shortly.

[*As* EMAN *does not answer,* SUNMA *continues her work, more nervously. Two villagers, obvious travellers, pass hurriedly in front of the house, the man has a small raffia sack, the woman a cloth-covered basket, the man enters first, turns and urges the woman who is just emerging to hurry.*]

SUNMA: [*seeing them, her tone is more intense.*] Eman, are we going or aren't we? You will leave it till too late.

EMAN: [*quietly.*] There is still time—if you want to go.

SUNMA: If I want to go . . . and you?

[EMAN *makes no reply.*]

SUNMA: [*bitterly.*] You don't really want to leave here. You never want to go away—even for a minute.

[IFADA *continues his antics.* EMAN *eventually pats him on the head and the boy grins happily. Leaps up suddenly and returns with a basket of oranges which he offers to* EMAN.]

EMAN: My gift for today's festival enh?

[IFADA *nods, grinning.*]

EMAN: They look ripe—that's a change.

SUNMA: [*she has gone inside the room. Looks round the door.*] Did you call me?

EMAN: No. [*she goes back.*] And what will you do tonight Ifada? Will you take part in the dancing? Or perhaps you will mount your own masquerade?

[IFADA *shakes his head, regretfully.*]

EMAN: You won't? So you haven't any? But you would like to own one.

[IFADA *nods eagerly.*]

EMAN: Then why don't you make your own?

[IFADA *stares, puzzled by this idea.*]

EMAN: Sunma will let you have some cloth you know. And bits of wool . . .

SUNMA: [*coming out.*] Who are you talking to Eman?

EMAN: Ifada. I am trying to persuade him to join the young maskers.

SUNMA: [*losing control.*] What does he want here? Why is he hanging around us?

EMAN: [*amazed.*] What . . . ? I said Ifada, Ifada.

SUNMA: Just tell him to go away. Let him go and play somewhere else!

EMAN: What is this? Hasn't he always played here?

SUNMA: I don't want him here. [*Rushes to the window.*] Get away idiot. Don't bring your foolish face here any more, do you hear? Go on, go away from here . . .

EMAN: [*restraining her*] Control yourself Sunma. What on earth has got into you?

[IFADA, *hurt and bewildered, backs slowly away.*]

SUNMA: He comes crawling around here like some horrible insect. I never want to lay my eyes on him again.

EMAN: I don't understand. It *is* Ifada you know. Ifada! The unfortunate one who runs errands for you and doesn't hurt a soul.

SUNMA: I cannot bear the sight of him.

EMAN: You can't do what? It can't be two days since he last fetched water for you.

SUNMA: What else can he do except that? He is useless. Just because we have been kind to him . . . Others would have put him in an asylum.

EMAN: You are not making sense. He is not a madman, he is just a little more unlucky than other children. [*Looks keenly at her.*] But what is the matter?

SUNMA: It's nothing. I only wish we had sent him off to one of those places for creatures like him.

EMAN: He is quite happy here. He doesn't bother anyone and he makes himself useful.

SUNMA: Useful! Is that one of any use to anybody? Boys of his age are already earning a living but all he can do is hang around and drool at the mouth.

EMAN: But he does work. You know he does a lot for you.

SUNMA: Does he? And what about the farm you started for him! Does he ever work on it? Or have you forgotten that it was really for Ifada you cleared that brush. Now you have to go and work it yourself. You spend all your time on it and you have no room for anything else.

EMAN: That wasn't his fault. I should first have asked him if he was fond of farming.

SUNMA: Oh, so he can choose? As if he shouldn't be thankful for being allowed to live.

EMAN: Sunma!

SUNMA: He does not like farming but he knows how to feast his dumb mouth on the fruits.

EMAN: But I want him to. I encourage him.

SUNMA: Well keep him. I don't want to see him any more.

EMAN: [*after some moments.*] But why? You cannot be telling all the truth. What has he done?

SUNMA: The sight of him fills me with revulsion.

EMAN: [*goes to her and holds her.*] What really is it? [SUNMA *avoids his eyes.*] It is almost as if you are forcing yourself to hate him. Why?

SUNMA: That is not true. Why should I?

EMAN: Then what is the secret? You've even played with him before.

SUNMA: I have always merely tolerated him. But I cannot any more. Suddenly my disgust won't take him any more. Perhaps . . . perhaps it is the new year. Yes, yes, it must be the new year.

EMAN: I don't believe that.

SUNMA: It must be. I am a woman, and these things matter. I don't want a mis-shape near me. Surely for one day in the year, I may demand some wholesomeness.

EMAN: I do not understand you.

> [SUNMA *is silent.*]

It was cruel of you. And to Ifada who is helpless and alone. We are the only friends he has.

SUNMA: No, just you. I have told you, with me it has always been only an act of kindness. And now I haven't any pity left for him.

EMAN: No. He is not a wholesome being.

> [*He turns back to looking through the window.*]

SUNMA: [*half-pleading.*] Ifada can rouse your pity. And yet if anything, I need more kindness from you. Every time my weakness betrays me, you close your mind against me . . . Eman . . . Eman . . .

> [A GIRL *comes in view, dragging an effigy by a rope attached to one of its legs. She stands for a while gazing at* EMAN. IFADA, *who has crept back shyly to his accustomed position, becomes somewhat excited when he sees the effigy. The* GIRL *is unsmiling. She possesses in fact, a kind of inscrutability which does not make her hard but is unsettling.*]

GIRL: Is the teacher in?

EMAN: [*smiling.*] No.

GIRL: Where is he gone?

EMAN: I really don't know. Shall I ask?

GIRL: Yes, do.

EMAN: [*turning slightly.*] Sunma, a girl outside wants to know . . .

> [SUNMA *turns away, goes into the inside room.*]

EMAN: Oh. [*Returns to the* GIRL, *but his slight gaiety is lost.*] There is no one at home who can tell me.

GIRL: Why are you not in?

EMAN: I don't really know. Maybe I went somewhere.

GIRL: All right. I will wait until you get back.

> [*She pulls the effigy to her, sits down.*]

EMAN: [*slowly regaining his amusement.*] So you are all ready for the new year.

GIRL: [*without turning around.*] I am not going to the festival.

EMAN: Then why have you got that?

GIRL: Do you mean my carrier? I am unwell you know. My mother says it will take away my sickness with the old year.

EMAN: Won't you share the carrier with your playmates?

GIRL: Oh, no. Don't you know I play alone? The other children won't come near me. Their mothers would beat them.

EMAN: But I have never seen you here. Why don't you come to the clinic?

GIRL: My mother said No.

> [*Gets up, begins to move off.*]

EMAN: You are not going away?

GIRL: I must not stay talking to you. If my mother caught me . . .

EMAN: All right, tell me what you want before you go.

GIRL: [*stops. For some moments she remains silent.*] I must have some clothes for my carrier.

EMAN: Is that all? You wait a moment.

> [SUNMA *comes out as he takes down a buba from the wall. She goes to the window and glares almost with hatred at the girl. The girl retreats hastily, still impassive.*]

By the way Sunma, do you know who that girl is?

SUNMA: I hope you don't really mean to give her that.

EMAN: Why not? I hardly ever use it.

SUNMA: Just the same don't give it to her. She is not a child. She is as evil as the rest of them.

EMAN: What has got into you today?

SUNMA: All right, all right. Do what you wish.

> [*she withdraws. Baffled,* EMAN *returns to the window.*]

EMAN: Here . . . will this do? Come and look at it.

GIRL: Throw it.

EMAN: What is the matter? I am not going to eat you.

GIRL: No one lets me come near them.

EMAN: But I am not afraid of catching your disease.

GIRL: Throw it.

> [EMAN *shrugs and tosses the buba. She takes it without a word and slips it on the effigy, completely absorbed in the task.* EMAN *watches for a while, then joins* SUNMA *in the inner room.*]

GIRL: [*after a long, cool survey of* IFADA.] You have a head like a spider's egg, and your mouth dribbles like a roof. But there is no one else. Would you like to play?

> [IFADA *nods eagerly, quite excited.*]

GIRL: You will have to get a stick.

> [IFADA *rushes around, finds a big stick and whirls it aloft, bearing down on the carrier.*]

GIRL: Wait. I don't want you to spoil it. If it gets torn I shall drive you away. Now, let me see how you are going to beat it.

> [IFADA *hits it gently.*]

GIRL: You may hit harder than that. As long as there is something left to hang at the end.

> [*She appraises him up and down.*]

You are not very tall . . . will you be able to hang it from a tree?

> [IFADA *nods, grinning happily.*]

GIRL: You will hang it up and I will set fire to it. [*Then, with surprising venom.*] But just because you are helping me, don't think it is going to cure you. I am the one who will get well at midnight, do you understand? It is my carrier and it is for me alone.

> [*She pulls at the rope to make sure that it is well attached to the leg.*]

Well don't stand there drooling. Let's go.

> [*She begins to walk off, dragging the effigy in the dust.* IFADA *remains where he is for some moments, seemingly puzzled. Then his face breaks into a large grin and he leaps after the procession, belabouring the effigy with all his strength. The stage remains empty for some moments. Then the horn of a lorry is sounded and* SUNMA *rushes out. The hooting continues for some time with a rhythmic pattern.* EMAN *comes out.*]

EMAN: I am going to the village . . . I shan't be back before nightfall.

SUNMA: [*blankly.*] Yes.

EMAN: [*hesitates.*] Well what do you want me to do?

SUNMA: The lorry was hooting just now.

EMAN: I didn't hear it.

SUNMA: It will leave in a few minutes. And you did promise we could go away.

EMAN: I promised nothing. Will you go home by yourself or shall I come back for you?

SUNMA: You don't even want me here?

EMAN: But you have to go home haven't you?

SUNMA: I had hoped we would watch the new year together—in some other place.

EMAN: Why do you continue to distress yourself?

SUNMA: Because you will not listen to me. Why do you continue to stay where nobody wants you?

EMAN: That is not true.

SUNMA: It is. You are wasting your life on people who really want you out of their way.

EMAN: You don't know what you are saying.

SUNMA: You think they love you? Do you think they care at all for what you—or I—do for them?

EMAN: *Them?* These are your own people. Sometimes you talk as if you were a stranger too.

SUNMA: I wonder if I really sprang from here. I know they are evil and I am not. From, the oldest to the smallest child, they are nourished in evil and unwholesomeness in which I have no part.

EMAN: You knew this when you returned?

SUNMA: You reproach me for trying at all?

EMAN: I reproach you with nothing? But you must leave me out of your plans. I can have no part in them.

SUNMA: [*nearly pleading.*] Once I could have run away. I would have gone and never looked back.

EMAN: I cannot listen when you talk like that.

SUNMA: I swear to you, I do not mind what happens afterwards. But you must help me tear myself away from here. I can no longer do it myself . . . It is only a little thing. And we have worked so hard this past year . . . surely we can go away for a week . . . even a few days would be enough.

EMAN: I have told you Sunma . . .

SUNMA: [*desperately.*] Two days Eman. Only two days.

EMAN: [*distressed.*] But I tell you I have no wish to go.

SUNMA: [*suddenly angry.*] Are you so afraid then?

EMAN: Me? Afraid of what?

SUNMA: You think you will not want to come back.

EMAN: [*pitying.*] You cannot dare me that way.

SUNMA: Then why won't you leave here, even for an hour? If you are so sure that your life is settled here, why are you afraid to do this thing for me? What is so wrong that you will not go into the next town for a day or two?

EMAN: I don't want to. I do not have to persuade you, or myself about anything. I simply have no desire to go away.

SUNMA: [*his quiet confidence appears to incense her.*] You are afraid. You accuse me of losing my sense of mission, but you are afraid to put yours to the test.

EMAN: You are wrong Sunma. I have no sense of mission. But I have found peace here and I am content with that.

SUNMA: I haven't. For a while I thought that too, but I found there could be no peace in the midst of so much cruelty. Eman, tonight at least, the last night of the old year . . .

EMAN: No Sunma. I find this too distressing; you should go home now.

SUNMA: It is the time for making changes in one's life Eman. Let's breathe in the new year away from here.

EMAN: You are hurting yourself.

SUNMA: Tonight. Only tonight. We will come back tomorrow as early as you like. But let us go away for this one night. Don't let another year break on me in this place . . . you don't know how important it is to me, but I will tell you, I will tell you on the way . . . but we must not be here today, Eman, do this one thing for me.

EMAN: [*sadly.*] I cannot.

SUNMA: [*suddenly calm.*] I was a fool to think it would be otherwise. The whole village may use you as they will but for me there is nothing. Sometimes I think you believe that doing anything for me makes you unfaithful to some part of your life. If it was a woman then I pity her for what she must have suffered.

[EMAN *winces and hardens slowly.* SUNMA *notices nothing.*]

Keeping faith with so much is slowly making you inhuman.

[*Seeing the change in* EMAN.] Eman. Eman. What is it?

[*As she goes towards him,* EMAN *goes into the house.*]

SUNMA: [*apprehensive, follows him.*] What did I say? Eman. Forgive me, forgive me please.

[EMAN *remains facing into the slow darkness of the room.* SUNMA, *distressed, cannot decide what to do.*]

I swear I didn't know . . . I would not have said it for all the world.

[*a lorry is heard taking off somewhere nearby. The sound comes up and slowly fades away into the distance.* SUNMA *starts visibly, goes slowly to the window.*]

SUNMA: [*as the sound dies off, to herself.*] What happens now?

EMAN: [*joining her at the window.*] What did you say?

SUNMA: Nothing.

EMAN: Was that not the lorry going off?

SUNMA: It was.

EMAN: I am sorry I couldn't help you.

[SUNMA, *about to speak, changes her mind.*]

EMAN: I think you ought to go home now.

SUNMA: No, don't send me away. It's the least you can do for me. Let me stay here until all the noise is over.

EMAN: But are you not needed at home? You have a part in the festival.

SUNMA: I have renounced it; I am Jaguna's eldest daughter only in name.

EMAN: Renouncing one's self is not so easy—surely you know that.

SUNMA: I don't want to talk about it. Will you at least let us be together tonight?

EMAN: But . . .

SUNMA: Unless you are afraid my father will accuse you of harbouring me.

EMAN: All right, we will go out together.

SUNMA: Go out? I want us to stay here?

EMAN: When there is so much going on outside?

SUNMA: Some day you will wish that you went away when I tried to make you.

EMAN: Are we going back to that?

SUNMA: No. I promise you I will not recall it again. But you must know that it was also for your sake that I tried to get us away.

EMAN: For me? How?

SUNMA: By yourself you can do nothing here. Have you not noticed how tightly we shut out strangers? Even if you lived here for a lifetime, you would remain a stranger.

EMAN: Perhaps that is what I like. There is peace in being a stranger.

SUNMA: For a while perhaps. But they would reject you in the end. I tell you it is only I who stand between you and contempt. And because of this you have earned their hatred. I don't know why I say this now, except that somehow, I feel that it no longer matters. It is only I who have stood between you and much humiliation.

EMAN: Think carefully before you say any more. I am incapable of feeling indebted to you. This will make no difference at all.

SUNMA: I ask for nothing. But you must know it all the same. It is true I hadn't the strength to go by myself. And I must confess this now, if you had come with me, I would have done everything to keep you from returning.

EMAN: I know that.

SUNMA: You see, I bare myself to you. For days I had thought it over, this was to be a new beginning for us. And I placed my fate wholly in your hands. Now the thought will not leave me, I have a feeling which will not be shaken off, that in some way, you have tonight totally destroyed my life.

EMAN: You are depressed, you don't know what you are saying.

SUNMA: Don't think I am accusing you. I say all this only because I cannot help it.

EMAN: We must not remain shut up here. Let us go and be part of the living.

SUNMA: No leave me alone.

EMAN: Surely you don't want to stay indoors when the whole town is alive with rejoicing.

SUNMA: Rejoicing! Is that what it seems to you? No, let us remain here. Whatever happens I must not go out until all this is over.

[*There is silence. It has grown much darker.*]

EMAN: I shall light the lamp.

SUNMA: [*eager to do something.*] No, let me do it.

[*She goes into the inner room.* EMAN *paces the room, stops by a shelf and toys with the seed in an 'ayo' board, takes down the whole board and places it on a table, playing by himself. The* GIRL *is now seen coming back, still dragging her 'carrier'.* IFADA *brings up the rear as before. As she comes round the corner of the house two men emerge from the shadows. A sack is thrown over* IFADA *'s head, the rope is pulled tight rendering him instantly helpless. The* GIRL *has reached the front of the house before she turns round at the sound of the scuffle. She is in time to see* IFADA *thrown over the shoulders and borne away. Her face betraying no emotion at all, the* GIRL *backs slowly away, turns and flees, leaving the 'carrier' behind.* SUNMA *enters, carrying two kerosene lamps. She hangs one up from the wall.*]

EMAN: One is enough.

SUNMA: I want to leave one outside.

[*She goes out, hangs the lamp from a nail just above the door. As she turns she sees the effigy and gasps.* EMAN *rushes out.*]

EMAN: What is it? Oh, is that what frightened you?

SUNMA: I thought . . . I didn't really see it properly.

[EMAN *goes towards the object, stoops to pick it up.*]

EMAN: It must belong to that sick girl.

SUNMA: Don't touch it.

EMAN: Let's keep it for her.

SUNMA: Leave it alone. Don't touch it Eman.

EMAN: [*shrugs and goes back.*] You are very nervous.

SUNMA: Let's go in.

EMAN: Wait. [*He detains her by the door, under the lamp.*] I know there is something more than you've told me. What are you afraid of tonight?

SUNMA: I was only scared by that thing. There is nothing else.

EMAN: I am not blind Sunma. It is true I would not run away when you wanted me to, but that doesn't mean I do not feel things. What does tonight really mean that it makes you so helpless?

SUNMA: It is only a mood. And your indifference to me . . . let's go in.

[EMAN *moves aside and she enters; he remains there for a moment and then follows. She fiddles with the lamp, looks vaguely round the room, then goes and shuts the door, bolting it. When she turns, it is to meet* EMAN *'s eyes, questioning.*]

SUNMA: There is a cold wind coming in.

[EMAN *keeps his gaze on her.*]

SUNMA: It was getting cold.

[*She moves guiltily to the table and stands by the 'ayo' board, rearranging the seed.* EMAN *remains where he is a few moments, then brings a stool and sits opposite her. She sits down also and they begin to play in silence.*]

SUNMA: What brought you here at all, Eman? And what makes you stay?

[*There is another silence.*]

SUNMA: I am not trying to share your life. I know you too well by now. But at least we have worked together since you came. Is there nothing at all I deserve to know?

EMAN: Let me continue a stranger—especially to you. Those who have much to give fulfil themselves only in total loneliness.

SUNMA: Then there is no love in what you do.

EMAN: There is. Love comes to me more easily with strangers.

SUNMA: That is unnatural.

EMAN: Not for me. I know I find consummation only when I have spent myself for a total stranger.

SUNMA: It seems unnatural to me. But then I am a woman. I have a woman's longings and weaknesses. And the ties of blood are very strong in me.

EMAN: [*smiling.*] You think I have cut loose from all these—ties of blood.

SUNMA: Sometimes you are so inhuman.

EMAN: I don't know what that means. But I am very much my father's son.

[*They play in silence. Suddenly* EMAN *pauses listening.*]

EMAN: Did you hear that?

SUNMA: [*quickly.*] I heard nothing . . . it's your turn.

EMAN: Perhaps some of the mummers are coming this way.

[EMAN *about to play, leaps up suddenly.*]

SUNMA: What is it? Don't you want to play any more?

[EMAN *moves to the door.*]

SUNMA: No. Don't go out Eman.

EMAN: If it's the dancers I want to ask them to stay. At least we won't have to miss everything.

SUNMA: No, no. Don't open the door. Let us keep out everyone tonight.

[*A terrified and disordered figure bursts suddenly around the corner, past the window and begins hammering at the door. It is* IFADA. *Desperate with terror, he pounds madly at the door, dumb-moaning all the while.*]

EMAN: Isn't that Ifada?

SUNMA: They are only fooling about. Don't pay any attention.

EMAN: [*looks round the window.*] That is Ifada. [*Begins to unbolt the door.*]

SUNMA: [*pulling at his hands.*] It is only a trick they are playing on you. Don't take any notice Eman.

EMAN: What are you saying? The boy is out of his senses with fear.

SUNMA: No, no. Don't interfere Eman. For God's sake don't interfere.

EMAN: Do you know something of this then?

SUNMA: You are a stranger here Eman. Just leave us alone and go your own way. There is nothing you can do.

EMAN: [*he tries to push her out of the way but she clings fiercely to him.*] Have you gone mad? I tell you the boy must come in.

SUNMA: Why won't you listen to me Eman? I tell you it's none of your business. For your own sake do as I say.

[EMAN *pushes her off, unbolts the door.* IFADA *rushes in, clasps* EMAN *round the knees, dumb-moaning against his legs.*]

EMAN: [*manages to re-bolt the door.*] What is it Ifada? What is the matter?

[*Shouts and voices are heard coming nearer the house.*]

SUNMA: Before it's too late, let him go. For once Eman, believe what I tell you. Don't harbour him or you will regret it all your life.

[EMAN *tries to calm* IFADA *who becomes more and more abject as the outside voices get nearer.*]

EMAN: What have they done to him? At least tell me that. What is going on Sunma?

SUNMA: [*with sudden venom.*] Monster! Could you not take yourself somewhere else?

EMAN: Stop talking like that.

SUNMA: He could have run into the bush couldn't he? Toad! Why must he follow us with his own disasters!

VOICES OUTSIDE: It's here . . . Round the back . . . Spread, spread . . . this way . . . no, head him off . . . use the bush path and head him off . . . get some more lights . . .
> [EMAN *listens. Lifts* IFADA *bodily and carries him into the inner room. Returns at once, shutting the door behind him.*]

SUNMA: [*slumps into a chair, resigned.*] You always follow your own way.

JAGUNA: [*comes round the corner followed by* OROGE *and three men, one bearing a torch.*] I knew he would come here.

OROGE: I hope our friend won't make trouble.

JAGUNA: He had better not. You, recall all the men and tell them to surround the house.

OROGE: But he may not be in the house after all.

JAGUNA: I know he is here . . . [*to the men.*] . . . go on, do as I say.
> [*He bangs on the door.*]
> Teacher, open your door . . . you two stay by the door. If I need you I will call you.
> [EMAN *opens the door.*]

JAGUNA: [*speaks as he enters.*] We know he is here.

EMAN: Who?

JAGUNA: Don't let us waste time. We are grown men, teacher. You understand me and I understand you. But we must take back the boy.

EMAN: This is my house.

JAGUNA: Daughter, you'd better tell your friend. I don't think he quite knows our ways. Tell him why he must give up the boy.

SUNMA: Father, I . . .

JAGUNA: Are you going to tell him or aren't you?

SUNMA: Father, I beg you, leave us alone tonight . . .

JAGUNA: I thought you might be a hindrance. Go home then if you will not use your sense.

SUNMA: But there are other ways . . .

JAGUNA: [*turning to the men.*] See that she gets home. I no longer trust her. If she gives trouble carry her. And see that the women stay with her until this is all over.
> [Sunma *departs, accompanied by one of the men.*]

JAGUNA: Now teacher . . .

OROGE: [*restrains him.*] You see, Mister Eman, it is like this. Right now, nobody knows that Ifada has taken refuge here. No one except us and our men—and they know how to keep their mouths shut. We don't want to have to burn down the house you see, but if the word gets around, we would have no choice.

JAGUNA: In fact, it may be too late already. A carrier should end up in the bush, not in a house. Anyone who doesn't guard his door when the carrier goes by has himself to blame. A contaminated house should be burnt down.

OROGE: But we are willing to let it pass. Only, you must bring him out quickly.

EMAN: All right. But at least you will let me ask you something.

JAGUNA: What is there to ask? Don't you understand what we have told you?

EMAN: Yes. But why did you pick on a helpless boy. Obviously he is not willing.

JAGUNA: What is the man talking about? Ifada is a godsend. Does he have to be willing?

EMAN: In my home we believe that a man should be willing.

OROGE: Mister Eman, I don't think you quite understand. This is not a simple matter at all. I don't know what you do, but here, it is not a cheap task for anybody. No one in his senses would do such a job. Why do you think we give refuge to idiots like him? We don't know where he came from. One morning, he is simply there, just like that. From nowhere at all. You see, there is purpose in that.

JAGUNA: We only waste time.

OROGE: Jaguna, be patient. After all, the man has been with us for some time now and deserves to know. The evil of the old year is no light thing to load on any man's head.

EMAN: I know something about that.

OROGE: You do? [*Turns to* JAGUNA *who snorts impatiently.*] You see I told you so didn't I? From the moment you came I saw you were one of the knowing ones.

JAGUNA: Then let him behave like a man and give back the boy.

EMAN: It is you who are not behaving like men.

JAGUNA: [*advances aggressively.*] That is a quick mouth you have . . .

OROGE: Patience Jaguna . . . if you want the new year to cushion the land there must be no deeds of anger. What did you mean my friend?

EMAN: It is a simple thing. A village which cannot produce its own carrier contains no men.

JAGUNA: Enough. Let there be no more talk or this business will be ruined by some rashness. You . . . come inside. Bring the boy out, he must be in the room there.

EMAN: Wait.

> [*The men hesitate.*]

JAGUNA: [*hitting the nearer one and propelling him forward.*] Go on. Have you changed masters now that you listen to what he says?

OROGE: [*sadly.*] I am sorry you would not understand Mister Eman. But you ought to know that no carrier may return to the village. If he does, the people will stone him to death. It has happened before. Surely it is too much to ask a man to give up his own soil.

EMAN: I know others who have done more.

> [IFADA *is brought out, abjectly dumb-moaning.*]

EMAN: You can see him with your own eyes. Does it really have meaning to use one as unwilling as that.

OROGE: [*smiling.*] He shall be willing. Not only willing but actually joyous. I am the one who prepares them all, and I have seen worse. This one escaped before I began to prepare him for the event. But you will see him later tonight, the most joyous creature in the festival. Then perhaps you will understand.

EMAN: Then it is only a deceit. Do you believe the spirit of a new year is so easily fooled?

JAGUNA: Take him out. [*The men carry out* IFADA.] You see, it is so easy to talk. You say there are no men in this village because they cannot provide a willing carrier. And yet I heard Oroge tell you we only use strangers. There is only one other stranger in the village, but I have not heard him offer himself [*spits*]. It is so easy to talk is it not?

> [*He turns his back on him. They go off, taking* IFADA *with them, limp and silent. The only sign of life is that he strains his neck to keep his eyes on* EMAN *till the very moment that he disappears from sight.* EMAN *remains where they left him, staring after the group.*]
>
> [*A blackout lasting no more than a minute. The lights come up slowly and* IFADA *is seen returning to the house. He stops at the window and looks in. Seeing no one, he bangs on the sill. Appears surprised that there is no response. He slithers down on his favourite spot, then sees the effigy still lying where the* GIRL *had dropped it in her flight. After some hesitation, he goes towards it, begins to strip it of the clothing. Just then the* GIRL *comes in.*]

GIRL: Hey, Leave that alone. You know it's mine.

> [IFADA *Pauses, then speeds up his action.*]

GIRL: I said it is mine. Leave it where you found it.

> [*She rushes at him and begins to struggle for possession of the carrier.*]

GIRL: Thief! Thief! Let it go, it is mine. Let it go. You animal, just because I let you play with it. Idiot! Idiot!

> [*The struggle becomes quite violent. The* GIRL *is hanging onto the effigy and* IFADA *lifts her with it, flinging her all about. The* GIRL *hangs on grimly.*]

GIRL: You are spoiling it . . . why don't you get your own? Thief! Let it go you thief!

[SUNMA *comes in walking very fast, throwing apprehensive glances over her shoulder. Seeing the two children, she becomes immediately angry. Advances on them.*]

SUNMA: So you've made this place your playground. Get away you untrained pigs. Get out of here.

[IFADA *flees at once, the* GIRL *retreats also, retaining possession of the 'carrier'.* SUNMA *goes to the door. She has her hand on the door when the significance of* IFADA's *presence strikes her for the first time. She stands rooted to the spot, then turns slowly around.*]

SUNMA: Ifada! What are you doing here?

[IFADA *is bewildered.* SUNMA *turns suddenly and rushes into the house, flying into the inner room and out again.*]

Eman! Eman! Eman!

[*She rushes outside.*]

Where did he go? Where did they take him?

[IFADA *distressed, points.* SUNMA *seizes him by the arm, drags him off.*]

Take me there at once. God help you if we are too late. You loathsome thing, if you let him suffer . . .

[*Her voice fades into other shouts, running footsteps, banged tins, bells, dogs, etc., rising in volume.*]

[*It is a narrow passageway between two mud-houses. At the far end one man after another is seen running across the entry, the noise dying off gradually. About half-way down the passage,* EMAN *is crouching against the wall, tense with apprehension. As the noise dies off, he seems to relax, but the alert hunted look is still in his eyes, which are ringed in a reddish colour. The rest of his body has been whitened with a floury substance. He is naked down to the waist, wears a baggy pair of trousers, calf-length, and around both feet are bangles.*]

EMAN: I will simply stay here till dawn. I have done enough. [*A window is thrown open and a* WOMAN *empties some slop from a pail. With a startled cry* EMAN *leaps aside to avoid it and the* WOMAN *puts out her head.*]

WOMAN: Oh, my head. What have I done? Forgive me neighbour . . . Eh, it's the carrier!

[*Very rapidly she clears her throat and spits on him, flings the pail at him and runs off, shouting.*]

He's here. The carrier is hiding in the passage. Quickly, I have found the carrier!

[*The cry is taken up and* EMAN *flees down the passage. Shortly afterwards his pursuers come pouring down the passage in full cry. After the last of them come* JAGUNA *and* OROGE.]

OROGE: Wait, wait. I cannot go so fast.

JAGUNA: We will rest a little then. We can do nothing anyway.

OROGE: If only he had let me prepare him.

JAGUNA: They are the ones who break first, these fools who think they were born to carry suffering like a hat. What are we to do now?

OROGE: When they catch him I must prepare him.

JAGUNA: He? It will be impossible now. There can be no joy left in that one.

OROGE: Still, it took him by surprise. He was not expecting what he met.

JAGUNA: Why then did he refuse to listen? Did he think he was coming to sit down to a feast. He had not even gone through one compound before he bolted. Did he think he was taken round the people to be blessed? A woman, that is all he is.

OROGE: No, no. He took the beating well enough. I think he is the kind who would let himself be beaten from night till dawn and not utter a sound. He would let himself be stoned until he dropped dead.

JAGUNA: Then what made him run like a coward?

OROGE: I don't know. I really don't know. It is a night of curses Jaguna. It is not many unprepared minds will remain unhinged under the load.

JAGUNA: We must find him. It is a poor beginning for a year when our own curses remain hovering over our homes because the carrier refused to take them.

[*They go. The scene changes.* EMAN *is crouching beside some shrubs, torn and bleeding.*]

EMAN: They are even guarding my house . . . as if I would go there, but I need water . . . they could at least grant me that . . . I can be thirsty too . . . [*he pricks his ears.*] . . . there must be a stream near by . . . [*as he looks round him, his eyes widen at a scene he encounters. An* OLD MAN, *short and vigorous looking is seated on a stool. He is also wearing calf-length baggy trousers, white. On his head, a white cap. An* ATTENDANT *is engaged in rubbing his body with oil. Round his eyes, two white rings have already been marked.*]

OLD MAN: Have they prepared the boat?

ATTENDANT: They are making the last sacrifice.

OLD MAN: Good. Did you send for my son?

ATTENDANT: He's on his way.

OLD MAN: I have never met the carrying of the boat with such a heavy heart. I hope nothing comes of it.

ATTENDANT: The gods will not desert us on that account.

OLD MAN: A man should be at his strongest when he takes the boat my friend. To be weighed down inside and out is not a wise thing. I hope when the moment comes I shall have found my strength.

[*Enter* EMAN, *a wrapper round his waist and a 'danski' (a brief Yoruba attire.) over it.*]

OLD MAN: I meant to wait until after my journey to the river, but my mind is so burdened with my own grief and yours I could not delay it. You know I must have all my strength. But I sit here, feeling it all eaten slowly away by my unspoken grief. It helps to say it out. It even helps to cry sometimes.

[*He signals to the* ATTENDANT *to leave them.*]

Come nearer . . . we will never meet again son. Not on this side of the flesh. What I do not know is whether you will return to take my place.

EMAN: I will never come back.

OLD MAN: Do you know what you are saying? Ours is a strong breed my son. It is only a strong breed that can take this boat to the river year after year and wax stronger on it. I have taken down each year's evils for over twenty years. I hoped you would follow me.

EMAN: My life here died with Omae.

OLD MAN: Omae died giving birth to your child and you think the world is ended. Eman, my pain did not begin when Omae died. Since you sent her to stay with me son, I lived with the burden of knowing that this child would die bearing your son.

EMAN: Father . . .

OLD MAN: Don't you know it was the same with you? And me? No woman survives the bearing of the strong ones. Son, it is not the mouth of the boaster that says he belongs to the strong breed. It is the tongue that is red with pain and black with sorrow. Twelve years you were away my son, and for those twelve years I knew the love of an old man for his daughter and the pain of a man helplessly awaiting his loss.

EMAN: I wish I had stayed away. I wish I never came back to meet her.

OLD MAN: It had to be. But you know now what slowly ate away my strength. I awaited your return with love and fear. Forgive me then if I say that your grief is light. It will pass. This grief may drive you now from home. But you must return.

EMAN: You do not understand. It is not grief alone.

OLD MAN: What is it then? Tell me, I can still learn.

EMAN: I was away twelve years. I changed much in that time.

OLD MAN: I am listening.

EMAN: I am unfitted for your work, father. I wish to say no more. But I am totally unfitted for your call.

OLD MAN: It is only time you need son. Stay longer and you will answer the urge of your blood.

EMAN: That I stayed at all was because of Omae. I did not expect to find her waiting. I would have taken her away, but hard as you claim to be, it would have killed you. And I was a tired man. I needed peace. Because Omae was peace, I stayed. Now nothing holds me here.

OLD MAN: Other men would rot and die doing this task year after year. It is strong medicine which only we can take. Our blood is strong like no other. Anything you do in life must be less than this, son.

EMAN: That is not true father.

OLD MAN: I tell you it is true. Your own blood will betray you son, because you cannot hold it back. If you make it do less than this, it will rush to your head and burst it open. I say what I know my son.

EMAN: There are other tasks in life father. This one is not for me. There are even greater things you know nothing of.

OLD MAN: I am very sad. You only go to give others what rightly belongs to us. You will use your strength among thieves. They are thieves because they take what is ours, they have no claim of blood to it. They will even lack the knowledge to use it wisely. Truth is my companion at this moment my son. I know everything I say will surely bring the sadness of truth.

EMAN: I am going father.

OLD MAN: Call my attendant. And be with me in your strength for this last journey. A-ah, did you hear that? It came out without my knowing it; this is indeed my last journey. But I am not afraid.

[EMAN *goes out. A few moments later, the* ATTENDANT *enters.*]

ATTENDANT: The boat is ready.

OLD MAN: So am I.

[*He sits perfectly still for several moments. Drumming begins somewhere in the distance, and the* OLD MAN *sways his head almost imperceptibly. Two men come in bearing a miniature boat, containing an indefinable mound. They rush it in and set it briskly down near the* OLD MAN, *and stand well back. The* OLD MAN *gets up slowly, the* ATTENDANT *watching him keenly. He signs to the men, who lift the boat quickly onto the* OLD MAN's *head. As soon as it touches his head, he holds it down with both hands and runs off, the men give him a start, then follow at a trot.*

As the last man disappears OROGE *limps in and comes face to face with* EMAN— *as carrier—who is now seen still standing beside the shrubs, staring into the scene he has just witnessed.* OROGE, *struck by the look on* EMAN's *face, looks anxiously behind him to see what has engaged* EMAN's *attention.* EMAN *notices him then, and the pair stare at each other.* JAGUNA *enters, sees him and shouts,* Here he is, *rushes at* EMAN *who is whipped back to the immediate and flees,* JAGUNA *in pursuit. Three or four others enter and follow them.* OROGE *remains where he is, thoughtful.*]

JAGUNA: [*re-enters.*] They have closed in on him now, we'll get him this time.

OROGE: It is nearly midnight.

JAGUNA: You were standing there looking at him as if he was some strange spirit. Why didn't you shout?

OROGE: You shouted didn't you? Did that catch him?

JAGUNA: Don't worry. We have him now. But things have taken a bad turn. It is no longer enough to drive him past every house. There is too much contamination about already.

OROGE: [*not listening.*] He saw something. Why may I not know what it was?

JAGUNA: What are you talking about?

OROGE: Hm. What is it?

JAGUNA: I said there is too much harm done already. The year will demand more from this carrier than we thought.

OROGE: What do you mean?

JAGUNA: Do we have to talk with the full mouth?

OROGE: S-sh . . . look!

[JAGUNA *turns just in time to see* SUNMA *fly at him, clawing at his face like a crazed tigress.*]

SUNMA: Murderer! What are you doing to him. Murderer! Murderer!

[JAGUNA *finds himself struggling really hard to keep off his daughter, he succeeds in pushing her off and striking her so hard on the face that she falls to her knees. He moves on her to hit her again.*]

OROGE: [*comes between.*] Think what you are doing Jaguna, she is your daughter.

JAGUNA: My daughter! Does this one look like my daughter? Let me cripple the harlot for life.

OROGE: That is a wicked thought Jaguna.

JAGUNA: Don't come between me and her.

OROGE: Nothing in anger—do you forget what tonight is?

JAGUNA: Can you blame me for forgetting?

[*Draws his hand across his cheek—it is covered with blood.*]

OROGE: This is an unhappy night for us all. I fear what is to come of it.

JAGUNA: Let's go. I cannot restrain myself in this creature's presence. My own daughter . . . and for a stranger . . .

[*They go off,* IFADA, *who came in with* SUNMA *and had stood apart, horror-stricken, comes shyly forward. He helps* SUNMA *up. They go off, he holding* SUNMA *bent and sobbing.*]

[*Enter* EMAN—*as carrier. He is physically present in the bounds of this next scene, a side of a round thatched hut. A young girl, about fourteen runs in, stops beside the hut. She looks carefully to see that she is not observed, puts her mouth to a little hole in the wall.*]

OMAE: Eman . . . Eman . . .

[EMAN—*as carrier—responds, as he does throughout the scene, but they are unaware of him.*]

EMAN: [*from inside.*] Who is it?

OMAE: It is me, Omae.

EMAN: How dare you come here!

[*Two hands appear at the hole and, pushing outwards, create a much larger hole through which* EMAN *puts out his head. It is* EMAN *as a boy, the same age as the girl.*]

Go away at once. Are you trying to get me in trouble!

OMAE: What is the matter?

EMAN: You. Go away.

OMAE: But I came to see you.

EMAN: Are you deaf? I say I don't want to see you. Now go before my tutor catches you.

OMAE: All right. Come out.

EMAN: Do what!

OMAE: Come out.

EMAN: You must be mad.

OMAE: [*sits on the ground.*] All right, if you don't come out I shall simply stay here until your tutor arrives.

EMAN: [*about to explode, thinks better of it and the head disappears. A moment later he emerges from behind the hut.*] What sort of evil has got into you?

OMAE: None. I just wanted to see you.

EMAN: [*his mimicry is nearly hysterical.*] None. I just wanted to see you. Do you think this place is the stream where you can go and molest innocent people?

OMAE: [*coyly.*] Aren't you glad to see me?

EMAN: I am not.

OMAE: Why?

EMAN: Why? Do you really ask me why? Because you are a woman and a most troublesome woman. Don't you know anything about this at all. We are not meant to see any woman. So go away before more harm is done.

OMAE: [*flirtatious.*] What is so secret about it anyway? What do they teach you.

EMAN: Nothing any woman can understand.

OMAE: Ha ha. You think we don't know eh? You've all come to be circumcised.

EMAN: Shut up. You don't know anything.

OMAE: Just think, all this time you haven't been circumcised, and you dared make eyes at us women.

EMAN: Thank you—woman. Now go.

OMAE: Do they give you enough to eat?

EMAN: [*testily.*] No. We are so hungry that when silly girls like you turn up, we eat them.

OMAE: [*feigning tears.*] Oh, oh, oh, he's abusing me. He's abusing me.

EMAN: [*alarmed.*] Don't try that here. Go quickly if you are going to cry.

OMAE: All right, I won't cry.

EMAN: Cry or no cry, go away and leave me alone. What do you think will happen if my tutor turns up now.

OMAE: He won't.

EMAN: [*mimicking.*] He won't. I suppose you are his wife and he tells you where he goes. In fact this is just the time he comes round to our huts. He could be at the next hut this very moment.

OMAE: Ha-ha. You're lying. I left him by the stream, pinching the girls' bottoms. Is that the sort of thing he teaches you?

EMAN: Don't say anything against him or I shall beat you. Isn't it you loose girls who tease him, wiggling your bottoms under his nose?

OMAE: [*going tearful again.*] A-ah, so I am one of those girls eh?

EMAN: Now don't you start accusing me of things I didn't say.

OMAE: But you said it. You said it.

EMAN: I didn't. Look Omae, someone will hear you and I'll be in disgrace. Why don't you go before anything happens.

OMAE: It's all right. My friends have promised to hold your old rascal tutor till I get back.

EMAN: Then you go back right now. I have work to do. [*Going in.*]

OMAE: [*runs after and tries to hold him.* EMAN *leaps back, genuinely scared.*] What is the matter? I was not going to bite you.

EMAN: Do you know what you nearly did? You almost touched me!

OMAE: Well?

EMAN: Well! Isn't it enough that you let me set my eyes on you? Must you now totally pollute me with your touch? Don't you understand anything?

OMAE: Oh, that.

EMAN: [*nearly screaming.*] It is not "oh that." Do you think this is only a joke or a little visit like spending the night with your grandmother? This is an important period of my life. Look, these huts, we built them with our own hands. Every boy builds his own. We learn things, do you understand? And we spend much time just thinking. At least, I do. It is the first time I have had nothing to do except think. Don't you see, I am becoming a man. For the first time, I understand that I have a life to fulfil. Has that thought ever worried you?

OMAE: You are frightening me.

EMAN: There. That is all you can say. And what use will that be when a man finds himself alone—like that? [*Points to the hut.*] A man must go on his own, go where no one can help him, and test his strength. Because he may find himself one day sitting alone in a wall round as that. In there, my mind could hold no other thought. I may never have such moments again to myself. Don't dare come to steal any more of it.

OMAE: [*this time genuinely tearful.*] Oh, I know you hate me. You only want to drive me away.

EMAN: [*impatiently.*] Yes, yes, I know I hate you—but go.

OMAE: [*going, all tears. Wipes her eyes, suddenly all mischief.*] Eman.

EMAN: What now?

OMAE: I only want to ask one thing . . . do you promise to tell me?

EMAN: Well, what is it?

OMAE: [*gleefully.*] Does it hurt?

[*She turns instantly and flees, landing straight into the arms of the returning tutor.*]

TUTOR: Te-he-he . . . what have we here? What little mouse leaps straight into the beak of the wise old owl eh?

[OMAE *struggles to free herself, flies to the opposite side, grimacing with distaste.*]

TUTOR: I suppose you merely came to pick some fruits eh? You did not sneak here to see any of my children.

OMAE: Yes, I came to steal your fruits.

TUTOR: Te-he-he . . . I thought so. And that dutiful son of mine over there. He saw you and came to chase you off my fruit trees didn't he? Te-he-he . . . I'm sure he did, isn't that so my young Eman?

EMAN: I was talking to her.

TUTOR: Indeed you were. Now be good enough to go into your hut until I decide your punishment. [EMAN *withdraws.*] Te-he-he . . . now my little daughter, you need not be afraid of me.

OMAE: [*spiritedly.*] I am not.

TUTOR: Good. Very good. We ought to be friendly. [*His voice becomes leering.*] Now this is nothing to worry you my daughter . . . a very small thing indeed. Although of course if I were to let it slip that your young Eman had broken a strong taboo, it might go hard on him you know. I am sure you would not like that to happen, would you?

OMAE: No.

TUTOR: Good. You are sensible my girl. Can you wash clothes?

OMAE: Yes.

TUTOR: Good. If you will come with me now to my hut, I shall give you some clothes to wash, and then we will forget all about this matter eh? Well, come on.

OMAE: I shall wait here. You go and bring the clothes.

TUTOR: Eh? What is that? Now now, don't make me angry. You should know better than to talk back to your elders. Come now.

[*He takes her by the arm, and tries to drag her off.*]

OMAE: No no, I won't come to your hut. Leave me. Leave me alone you shameless old man.

TUTOR: If you don't come I shall disgrace the whole family of Eman, and yours too.

[EMAN *re-enters with a small bundle.*]

EMAN: Leave her alone. Let us go Omae.

TUTOR: And where do you think you are going?

EMAN: Home.

TUTOR: Te-he-he . . . As easy as that eh? You think you can leave here at any time you please? Get right back inside that hut!

[EMAN *takes* OMAE *by the arm and begins to walk off.*]

TUTOR: Come back at once.

[*He goes after him and raises his stick.* EMAN *catches it, wrenches it from him and throws its away.*]

OMAE: [*hopping delightedly.*] Kill him. Beat him to death.

TUTOR: Help! Help! He is killing me! Help!

[*Alarmed,* EMAN *clamps his hand over his mouth.*]

EMAN: Old tutor, I don't mean you any harm, but you mustn't try to harm me either. [*he removes his hand.*]

TUTOR: You think you can get away with your crime. My report shall reach the elders before you ever get into town.

EMAN: You are afraid of what I will say about you? Don't worry. Only if you try to shame me, then will I speak. I am not going back to the village anyway. Just tell them I have gone, no more. If you say one word more then I shall hear of it the same day and I shall come back.

TUTOR: You are telling me what to do? But don't think to come back here even ten years from now. And don't send your children.

[*Goes off with threatening gestures.*]

EMAN: I won't come back.

OMAE: Smoked vulture! But Eman, he says you cannot return next year. What will you do?

EMAN: It is a small thing one can do in the big towns.

OMAE: I thought you were going to beat him that time. Why didn't you crackle his dirty hide?

EMAN: Listen carefully Omae . . . I am going on a journey.

OMAE: Come on. Tell me about it on the way.

EMAN: No, I go that way. I cannot return to the village.

OMAE: Because of that wretched man? Anyway you will first talk to your father.

EMAN: Go and see him for me. Tell him I have gone away for some time. I think he will know.

OMAE: But Eman . . .

EMAN: I haven't finished. You will go and live with him till I get back. I have spoken to him about you. Look after him!

OMAE: But what is this journey? When will you come back?

EMAN: I don't know. But this is a good moment to go. Nothing ties me down.

OMAE: But Eman, you want to leave me.

EMAN: Don't forget all I said. I don't know how long I will be. Stay in my father's house as long as you remember me. When you become tired of waiting, you must do as you please. You understand? You must do as you please.

OMAE: I cannot understand anything Eman. I don't know where you are going or why. Suppose you never came back! Don't go, Eman. Don't leave me by myself.

EMAN: I must go. Now let me see you on your way.

OMAE: I shall come with you.

EMAN: Come with me! And who will look after you? Me? You will only be in my way, you know that! You will hold me back and I shall desert you in a strange place. Go home and do as I say. Take care of my father and let him take care of you.

[*He starts going but* OMAE *clings to him.*]

OMAE: But Eman, stay the night at least. You will only lose your way. Your father Eman, what will he say? I won't remember what you said . . . come back to the village . . . I cannot return alone Eman . . . come with me as far as the crossroads.

[*His face set,* EMAN *strides off and* OMAE *loses balance as he increases his pace. Falling, she quickly wraps her arms around his ankle, but* EMAN *continues unchecked, dragging her along.*]

OMAE: Don't go Eman . . . Eman, don't leave me, don't leave me . . . don't leave your Omae . . . don't go Eman . . . don't leave your Omae . . .

[EMAN—*as carrier—makes a nervous move as if he intends to go after the vanished pair. He stops but continues to stare at the point where he last saw them. There is stillness for a while. Then the* GIRL *enters from the same place and remains looking at* EMAN. *Startled,* EMAN *looks apprehensively round him. The* GIRL *goes nearer but keeps beyond arm's length.*]

GIRL: Are you the carrier?

EMAN: Yes. I am Eman.

GIRL: Why are you hiding?

EMAN: I really came for a drink of water . . . er . . . is there anyone in front of the house?

GIRL: No.

EMAN: But there might be people in the house. Did you hear voices?

GIRL: There is no one here.

EMAN: Good. Thank you. [*He is about to go, stops suddenly.*] Er . . . would you . . . you will find a cup on the table. Could you bring me the water out here? The water-pot is in a corner. [*The* GIRL *goes. She enters the house, then, watching* EMAN *carefully, slips out and runs off.*]

EMAN: [*sitting.*] Perhaps they have all gone home. It will be good to rest. [*He hears voices and listens hard.*] Too late. [*Moves cautiously nearer the house.*] Quickly girl, I can hear people coming. Hurry up. [*Looks through the window.*] Where are you? Where is she? [*The truth dawns on him suddenly and he moves off, sadly.*]

[*Enter* JAGUNA *and* OROGE, *led by the* GIRL.]

GIRL: [*pointing.*]: He was there.

JAGUNA: Ay, he's gone now. He is a sly one is your friend. But it won't save him for ever.

OROGE: What was he doing when you saw him?

GIRL: He asked me for a drink of water.

JAGUNA, OROGE: Ah! [*They look at each other.*]

OROGE: We should have thought of that.

JAGUNA: He is surely finished now. If only we had thought of it earlier.

OROGE: It is not too late. There is still an hour before midnight.

JAGUNA: We must call back all the men. Now we need only wait for him—in the right place.

OROGE: Everyone must be told. We don't want anyone heading him off again.

JAGUNA: And it works so well. This is surely the help of the gods themselves Oroge. Don't you know at once what is on the path to the stream?

OROGE: The sacred trees.

JAGUNA: I tell you it is the very hand of the gods. Let us go.

[*An overgrown part of the village.* EMAN *wanders in, aimlessly, seemingly uncaring of discovery. Beyond him, an area lights up, revealing a group of people clustered round a spot, all the heads are bowed. One figure stands away and separate from them. Even as* EMAN *looks, the group breaks up and the people disperse, coming down and past him. Only three people are left, a man (*EMAN*) whose back is turned, the village* PRIEST *and the isolated one. They stand on opposite sides of the grave, the man on the mound of earth. The* PRIEST *walks round to the man's side and lays a hand on his shoulder.]*

PRIEST: Come.

EMAN: I will. Give me a few moments here alone.

PRIEST: Be comforted.

> *[They fall silent.]*

EMAN: I was gone twelve years but she waited. She whom I thought had too much of the laughing child in her. Twelve years I was a pilgrim, seeking the vain shrine of secret strength. And all the time, strange knowledge, this silent strength of my child-woman.

PRIEST: We all saw it. It was a lesson to us; we did not know that such goodness could be found among us.

EMAN: Then why? Why the wasted years if she had to perish giving birth to my child? *[They are both silent.]* I do not really know for what great meaning I searched. When I returned, I could not be certain I had found it. Until I reached my home and I found her a full-grown woman, still a child at heart. When I grew to believe it, I thought this, after all, is what I sought. It was here all the time. And I threw away my new-gained knowledge. I buried the part of me that was formed in strange places. I made a home in my birthplace.

PRIEST: That was as it should be.

EMAN: Any truth of that was killed in the cruelty of her brief happiness.

PRIEST: *[looks up and sees the figure standing away from them, the child in his arms. He is totally still.]* Your father—he is over there.

EMAN: I knew he would come. Has he my son with him?

PRIEST: Yes.

EMAN: He will let no one take the child. Go and comfort him priest. He loved Omae like a daughter, and you all know how well she looked after him. You see how strong we really are. In his heart of hearts the old man's love really awaited a daughter. Go and comfort him. His grief is more than mine.

> *[The* PRIEST *goes. The* OLD MAN *has stood well away from the burial group. His face is hard and his gaze unswerving from the grave. The* PRIEST *goes to him, pauses, but sees that he can make no dent in the man's grief. Bowed, he goes on his way.]*
>
> *[*EMAN, *as carrier, walking towards the graveside, the other* EMAN *having gone. His feet sink into the mound and he breaks slowly on to his knees, scooping up the sand in his hands and pouring it on his head. The scene blacks out slowly.]*
>
> *[Enter* JAGUNA *and* OROGE.*]*

OROGE: We have only a little time.

JAGUNA: He will come. All the wells are guarded. There is only the stream left him. The animal must come to drink.

OROGE: You are sure it will not fail—the trap I mean.

JAGUNA: When Jaguna sets the trap, even elephants pay homage—their trunks downwards and one leg up in the sky. When the carrier steps on the fallen twigs, it is up in the sacred trees with him.

OROGE: I shall breathe again when this long night is over.

> *[They go out.]*

[*Enter* EMAN—*as carrier—from the same direction as the last two entered. In front of him is still a figure, the* OLD MAN *as he was, carrying the dwarf boat.*]

EMAN: [*joyfully.*] Father.

[*The figure does not turn round.*]

EMAN: It is your son. Eman. [*He moves nearer.*] Don't you want to look at me? It is I, Eman. [*He moves nearer still.*]

OLD MAN: You are coming too close. Don't you know what I carry on my head?

EMAN: But father, I am your son.

OLD MAN: Then go back. We cannot give the two of us.

EMAN: Tell me first where you are going.

OLD MAN: Do you ask that? Where else but to the river?

EMAN: [*visibly relieved.*] I only wanted to be sure. My throat is burning. I have been looking for the stream all night.

OLD MAN: It is the other way.

EMAN: But you said . . .

OLD MAN: I take the longer way, you know how I must do this. It is quicker if you take the other way. Go now.

EMAN: No, I will only get lost again. I shall go with you.

OLD MAN: Go back my son. Go back.

EMAN: Why? Won't you even look at me?

OLD MAN: Listen to your father. Go back.

EMAN: But father!

[*He makes to hold him. Instantly the* OLD MAN *breaks into a rapid trot.* EMAN *hesitates, then follows, his strength nearly gone.*]

EMAN: Wait father. I am coming with you . . . wait . . . wait for me father . . .

[*There is a sound of twigs breaking, of a sudden trembling in the branches. Then silence.*]

[*The front of* EMAN'*s house. The effigy is hanging from the sheaves. Enter* SUNMA, *still supported by* IFADA, *she stands transfixed as she sees the hanging figure.* IFADA *appears to go mad, rushes at the object and tears it down.* SUNMA, *her last bit of will gone, crumbles against the wall. Some distance away from them, partly hidden, stands the* GIRL, *impassively watching.* IFADA *hugs the effigy to him, stands above.* SUNMA. *The* GIRL *remains where she is, observing.*

Almost at once, the villagers begin to return, subdued and guilty. They walk across the front, skirting the house as widely as they can. No word is exchanged. JAGUNA, *who is leading, sees* SUNMA *as soon as he comes in view. He stops at once, retreating slightly.*]

OROGE: [*almost whispering.*] What is it?

JAGUNA: The viper.

[OROGE *looks cautiously at the woman.*]

OROGE: I don't think she will even see you.

JAGUNA: Are you sure? I am in no frame of mind for another meeting with her.

OROGE: Let's go home.

JAGUNA: I am sick to the heart of the cowardice I have seen tonight.

OROGE: That is the nature of men.

JAGUNA: Then it is a sorry world to live in. We did it for them. It was all for their own common good. What did it benefit me whether the man lived or died. But did you see them? One and all they looked up at the man and words died in their throats.

OROGE: It was no common sight.

JAGUNA: Women could not have behaved so shamefully. One by one they crept off like sick dogs. Not one could raise a curse.

OROGE: It was not only him they fled. Do you see how unattended we are?

JAGUNA: There are those who will pay for this night's work!

OROGE: Ay, let us go home.

> [*They go off.* SUNMA, IFADA *and the* GIRL *remain as they are, the light fading slowly on them.*]

THE END

Credits